MORTGAGE PAYMENTS
Interest Compounded Semi Annually

prepared especially for

Peter Heiler Ltd.
70 Bloor Street East
Oshawa, Ontario
L1H 3M2

Tel. (905)436-2525
Fax. (905)723-6677

by

Computofacts
209 Sheppard Avenue East
Willowdale, Ontario, M2N 5W2
Canada

Publication No. 452

Great care has been taken in the
preparation of these tables although there is
no warranty of complete accuracy.

Printed and bound in Canada

Do you need an interest rate not available in this book?

Then get Computofacts Canadian Mortgage Interest Rate Software UPC 7-74948-00-1.

You will be able to prepare payment tables for *any* interest rate.

In addition to monthly payments, you can print out weekly, biweekly or semimonthly payments, all formatted just like in this book.

The disk includes an amortization schedule program so you can produce a schedule showing the interest, principal and balance for each payment.

A program is included to calculate interest rate buy-downs, mortgage discounts, premiums or yields.

Computofacts Canadian Mortgage Interest Rate Software has all the programs you need to check your mortgage.

Available at selected retailers or from Computofacts, 209 Sheppard Ave. East, Willowdale, Ontario M2N 5W2. Tel. (416)222-4361

Range of Tables

Blended Monthly Payments

Rates: 3% to 11% by ¼%
11% to 21% by 1%

Amortizations: 1 year to 26 years by 1 year
29, 30, 35, 40, 45 and 50 years

Amounts: $100 to $1,000 by $100 (also
$25 and $50)
$1,000 to $10,000 by $1,000
$10,000 to $400,000 by $10,000

*Note: All interest rates in this book are compounded
semi annually.*

BLENDED MONTHLY PAYMENTS
AMORTIZATION IN YEARS

Amount	1	2	3	4	5	6	7	8
25	2.12	1.08	.73	.56	.45	.38	.34	.30
50	4.24	2.15	1.46	1.11	.90	.76	.67	.59
100	8.47	4.30	2.91	2.22	1.80	1.52	1.33	1.18
200	16.94	8.60	5.82	4.43	3.60	3.04	2.65	2.35
300	25.41	12.90	8.73	6.64	5.39	4.56	3.97	3.52
400	33.88	17.19	11.63	8.86	7.19	6.08	5.29	4.69
500	42.35	21.49	14.54	11.07	8.99	7.60	6.61	5.87
600	50.82	25.79	17.45	13.28	10.78	9.12	7.93	7.04
700	59.28	30.09	20.36	15.49	12.58	10.63	9.25	8.21
800	67.75	34.38	23.26	17.71	14.37	12.15	10.57	9.38
900	76.22	38.68	26.17	19.92	16.17	13.67	11.89	10.55
1000	84.69	42.98	29.08	22.13	17.97	15.19	13.21	11.73
2000	169.38	85.95	58.15	44.26	35.93	30.38	26.41	23.45
3000	254.06	128.92	87.22	66.38	53.89	45.56	39.62	35.17
4000	338.75	171.90	116.30	88.51	71.85	60.75	52.82	46.89
5000	423.43	214.87	145.37	110.64	89.81	75.93	66.03	58.61
6000	508.12	257.84	174.44	132.76	107.77	91.12	79.23	70.33
7000	592.80	300.82	203.52	154.89	125.73	106.30	92.44	82.05
8000	677.49	343.79	232.59	177.01	143.69	121.49	105.64	93.77
9000	762.17	386.76	261.66	199.14	161.65	136.67	118.85	105.50
10000	846.86	429.73	290.74	221.27	179.61	151.86	132.05	117.22
20000	1693.71	859.46	581.47	442.53	359.21	303.71	264.10	234.43
30000	2540.56	1289.19	872.20	663.79	538.82	455.57	396.15	351.64
40000	3387.41	1718.92	1162.93	885.05	718.42	607.42	528.20	468.85
50000	4234.27	2148.65	1453.66	1106.31	898.03	759.27	660.25	586.06
60000	5081.12	2578.38	1744.39	1327.57	1077.63	911.13	792.30	703.27
70000	5927.97	3008.11	2035.12	1548.83	1257.24	1062.98	924.35	820.48
80000	6774.82	3437.84	2325.85	1770.09	1436.84	1214.83	1056.40	937.70
90000	7621.68	3867.57	2616.58	1991.36	1616.44	1366.69	1188.45	1054.91
100000	8468.53	4297.30	2907.31	2212.62	1796.05	1518.54	1320.50	1172.12
110000	9315.38	4727.03	3198.04	2433.88	1975.65	1670.40	1452.55	1289.33
120000	10162.23	5156.76	3488.77	2655.14	2155.26	1822.25	1584.60	1406.54
130000	11009.09	5586.49	3779.50	2876.40	2334.86	1974.10	1716.65	1523.75
140000	11855.94	6016.22	4070.23	3097.66	2514.47	2125.96	1848.69	1640.96
150000	12702.79	6445.95	4360.96	3318.92	2694.07	2277.81	1980.74	1758.18
160000	13549.64	6875.68	4651.69	3540.18	2873.67	2429.66	2112.79	1875.39
170000	14396.50	7305.41	4942.42	3761.44	3053.28	2581.52	2244.84	1992.60
180000	15243.35	7735.14	5233.15	3982.71	3232.88	2733.37	2376.89	2109.81
190000	16090.20	8164.87	5523.88	4203.97	3412.49	2885.22	2508.94	2227.02
200000	16937.05	8594.60	5814.61	4425.23	3592.09	3037.08	2640.99	2344.23
210000	17783.90	9024.33	6105.34	4646.49	3771.70	3188.93	2773.04	2461.44
220000	18630.76	9454.06	6396.07	4867.75	3951.30	3340.79	2905.09	2578.65
230000	19477.61	9883.79	6686.80	5089.01	4130.91	3492.64	3037.14	2695.87
240000	20324.46	10313.52	6977.53	5310.27	4310.51	3644.49	3169.19	2813.08
250000	21171.31	10743.25	7268.26	5531.53	4490.11	3796.35	3301.24	2930.29
260000	22018.17	11172.98	7558.99	5752.80	4669.72	3948.20	3433.29	3047.50
270000	22865.02	11602.71	7849.72	5974.06	4849.32	4100.05	3565.34	3164.71
280000	23711.87	12032.44	8140.45	6195.32	5028.93	4251.91	3697.38	3281.92
290000	24558.72	12462.17	8431.18	6416.58	5208.53	4403.76	3829.43	3399.13
300000	25405.58	12891.90	8721.91	6637.84	5388.14	4555.61	3961.48	3516.35
310000	26252.43	13321.63	9012.64	6859.10	5567.74	4707.47	4093.53	3633.56
320000	27099.28	13751.36	9303.37	7080.36	5747.34	4859.32	4225.58	3750.77
330000	27946.13	14181.09	9594.10	7301.62	5926.95	5011.18	4357.63	3867.98
340000	28792.99	14610.82	9884.83	7522.88	6106.55	5163.03	4489.68	3985.19
350000	29639.84	15040.55	10175.56	7744.15	6286.16	5314.88	4621.73	4102.40
360000	30486.69	15470.28	10466.29	7965.41	6465.76	5466.74	4753.78	4219.61
370000	31333.54	15900.01	10757.02	8186.67	6645.37	5618.59	4885.83	4336.82
380000	32180.39	16329.74	11047.75	8407.93	6824.97	5770.44	5017.88	4454.04
390000	33027.25	16759.47	11338.48	8629.19	7004.57	5922.30	5149.93	4571.25
400000	33874.10	17189.20	11629.21	8850.45	7184.18	6074.15	5281.98	4688.46

BLENDED MONTHLY PAYMENTS
AMORTIZATION IN YEARS

Amount	9	10	11	12	13	14	15	16
25	.27	.25	.23	.21	.20	.19	.18	.17
50	.53	.49	.45	.42	.39	.37	.35	.33
100	1.06	.97	.89	.83	.78	.73	.69	.66
200	2.12	1.93	1.78	1.66	1.55	1.46	1.38	1.32
300	3.18	2.90	2.67	2.49	2.33	2.19	2.07	1.97
400	4.23	3.86	3.56	3.31	3.10	2.92	2.76	2.63
500	5.29	4.83	4.45	4.14	3.88	3.65	3.45	3.28
600	6.35	5.79	5.34	4.97	4.65	4.38	4.14	3.94
700	7.40	6.76	6.23	5.79	5.42	5.11	4.83	4.59
800	8.46	7.72	7.12	6.62	6.20	5.84	5.52	5.25
900	9.52	8.69	8.01	7.45	6.97	6.56	6.21	5.90
1000	10.57	9.65	8.90	8.27	7.75	7.29	6.90	6.56
2000	21.14	19.30	17.80	16.54	15.49	14.58	13.80	13.12
3000	31.71	28.95	26.69	24.81	23.23	21.87	20.70	19.67
4000	42.28	38.60	35.59	33.08	30.97	29.16	27.59	26.23
5000	52.85	48.24	44.48	41.35	38.71	36.45	34.49	32.78
6000	63.42	57.89	53.38	49.62	46.45	43.73	41.39	39.34
7000	73.98	67.54	62.27	57.89	54.19	51.02	48.28	45.89
8000	84.55	77.19	71.17	66.16	61.93	58.31	55.18	52.45
9000	95.12	86.83	80.06	74.43	69.67	65.60	62.08	59.00
10000	105.69	96.48	88.96	82.70	77.41	72.89	68.97	65.56
20000	211.37	192.96	177.91	165.39	154.81	145.77	137.94	131.11
30000	317.06	289.43	266.86	248.08	232.22	218.65	206.91	196.66
40000	422.74	385.91	355.81	330.77	309.62	291.53	275.88	262.22
50000	528.43	482.38	444.76	413.46	387.03	364.41	344.85	327.77
60000	634.11	578.86	533.71	496.15	464.43	437.29	413.82	393.32
70000	739.80	675.33	622.66	578.85	541.83	510.17	482.79	458.88
80000	845.48	771.81	711.61	661.54	619.24	583.05	551.76	524.43
90000	951.16	868.28	800.57	744.23	696.64	655.93	620.72	589.98
100000	1056.85	964.76	889.52	826.92	774.05	728.81	689.69	655.54
110000	1162.53	1061.23	978.47	909.61	851.45	801.70	758.66	721.09
120000	1268.22	1157.71	1067.42	992.30	928.86	874.58	827.63	786.64
130000	1373.90	1254.18	1156.37	1074.99	1006.26	947.46	896.60	852.20
140000	1479.59	1350.66	1245.32	1157.69	1083.66	1020.34	965.57	917.75
150000	1585.27	1447.13	1334.27	1240.38	1161.07	1093.22	1034.54	983.30
160000	1690.95	1543.61	1423.22	1323.07	1238.47	1166.10	1103.51	1048.86
170000	1796.64	1640.08	1512.18	1405.76	1315.88	1238.98	1172.48	1114.41
180000	1902.32	1736.56	1601.13	1488.45	1393.28	1311.86	1241.44	1179.96
190000	2008.01	1833.03	1690.08	1571.14	1470.69	1384.74	1310.41	1245.52
200000	2113.69	1929.51	1779.03	1653.84	1548.09	1457.62	1379.38	1311.07
210000	2219.38	2025.98	1867.98	1736.53	1625.49	1530.50	1448.35	1376.62
220000	2325.06	2122.46	1956.93	1819.22	1702.90	1603.39	1517.32	1442.18
230000	2430.75	2218.93	2045.88	1901.91	1780.30	1676.27	1586.29	1507.73
240000	2536.43	2315.41	2134.83	1984.60	1857.71	1749.15	1655.26	1573.28
250000	2642.11	2411.88	2223.78	2067.29	1935.11	1822.03	1724.23	1638.84
260000	2747.80	2508.36	2312.74	2149.98	2012.51	1894.91	1793.19	1704.39
270000	2853.48	2604.83	2401.69	2232.68	2089.92	1967.79	1862.16	1769.94
280000	2959.17	2701.31	2490.64	2315.37	2167.32	2040.67	1931.13	1835.50
290000	3064.85	2797.78	2579.59	2398.06	2244.73	2113.55	2000.10	1901.05
300000	3170.54	2894.26	2668.54	2480.75	2322.13	2186.43	2069.07	1966.60
310000	3276.22	2990.73	2757.49	2563.44	2399.54	2259.31	2138.04	2032.16
320000	3381.90	3087.21	2846.44	2646.13	2476.94	2332.20	2207.01	2097.71
330000	3487.59	3183.68	2935.39	2728.82	2554.34	2405.08	2275.98	2163.26
340000	3593.27	3280.16	3024.35	2811.52	2631.75	2477.96	2344.95	2228.82
350000	3698.96	3376.63	3113.30	2894.21	2709.15	2550.84	2413.91	2294.37
360000	3804.64	3473.11	3202.25	2976.90	2786.56	2623.72	2482.88	2359.92
370000	3910.33	3569.58	3291.20	3059.59	2863.96	2696.60	2551.85	2425.48
380000	4016.01	3666.06	3380.15	3142.28	2941.37	2769.48	2620.82	2491.03
390000	4121.69	3762.53	3469.10	3224.97	3018.77	2842.36	2689.79	2556.58
400000	4227.38	3859.01	3558.05	3307.67	3096.17	2915.24	2758.76	2622.14

BLENDED MONTHLY PAYMENTS

AMORTIZATION IN YEARS

3%

Amount	17	18	19	20	21	22	23	24
25	.16	.15	.15	.14	.14	.13	.13	.13
50	.32	.30	.29	.28	.27	.26	.26	.25
100	.63	.60	.58	.56	.54	.52	.51	.49
200	1.26	1.20	1.16	1.11	1.07	1.04	1.01	.98
300	1.88	1.80	1.73	1.67	1.61	1.56	1.51	1.46
400	2.51	2.40	2.31	2.22	2.14	2.07	2.01	1.95
500	3.13	3.00	2.88	2.77	2.68	2.59	2.51	2.44
600	3.76	3.60	3.46	3.33	3.21	3.11	3.01	2.92
700	4.38	4.20	4.03	3.88	3.75	3.62	3.51	3.41
800	5.01	4.80	4.61	4.43	4.28	4.14	4.01	3.90
900	5.63	5.39	5.18	4.99	4.81	4.66	4.51	4.38
1000	6.26	5.99	5.76	5.54	5.35	5.17	5.02	4.87
2000	12.51	11.98	11.51	11.08	10.69	10.34	10.03	9.74
3000	18.77	17.97	17.26	16.62	16.04	15.51	15.04	14.60
4000	25.02	23.96	23.01	22.15	21.38	20.68	20.05	19.47
5000	31.28	29.95	28.76	27.69	26.73	25.85	25.06	24.33
6000	37.53	35.93	34.51	33.23	32.07	31.02	30.07	29.20
7000	43.79	41.92	40.26	38.76	37.41	36.19	35.08	34.06
8000	50.04	47.91	46.01	44.30	42.76	41.36	40.09	38.93
9000	56.30	53.90	51.76	49.84	48.10	46.53	45.10	43.79
10000	62.55	59.89	57.51	55.37	53.45	51.70	50.11	48.66
20000	125.10	119.77	115.01	110.74	106.89	103.40	100.22	97.32
30000	187.65	179.65	172.51	166.11	160.33	155.09	150.32	145.97
40000	250.19	239.53	230.01	221.47	213.77	206.79	200.43	194.63
50000	312.74	299.41	287.51	276.84	267.21	258.48	250.54	243.28
60000	375.29	359.29	345.02	332.21	320.65	310.18	300.64	291.94
70000	437.83	419.17	402.52	387.57	374.09	361.87	350.75	340.59
80000	500.38	479.05	460.02	442.94	427.53	413.57	400.86	389.25
90000	562.93	538.93	517.52	498.31	480.97	465.26	450.96	437.90
100000	625.47	598.81	575.02	553.67	534.41	516.96	501.07	486.56
110000	688.02	658.69	632.53	609.04	587.85	568.65	551.18	535.21
120000	750.57	718.57	690.03	664.41	641.29	620.35	601.28	583.87
130000	813.11	778.46	747.53	719.77	694.73	672.04	651.39	632.52
140000	875.66	838.34	805.03	775.14	748.18	723.74	701.50	681.18
150000	938.21	898.22	862.53	830.51	801.62	775.43	751.60	729.83
160000	1000.75	958.10	920.04	885.87	855.06	827.13	801.71	778.49
170000	1063.30	1017.98	977.54	941.24	908.50	878.82	851.82	827.14
180000	1125.85	1077.86	1035.04	996.61	961.94	930.52	901.92	875.80
190000	1188.39	1137.74	1092.54	1051.97	1015.38	982.21	952.03	924.45
200000	1250.94	1197.62	1150.04	1107.34	1068.82	1033.91	1002.13	973.11
210000	1313.49	1257.50	1207.54	1162.71	1122.26	1085.60	1052.24	1021.76
220000	1376.03	1317.38	1265.05	1218.07	1175.70	1137.30	1102.35	1070.42
230000	1438.58	1377.26	1322.55	1273.44	1229.14	1188.99	1152.45	1119.07
240000	1501.13	1437.14	1380.05	1328.81	1282.58	1240.69	1202.56	1167.73
250000	1563.67	1497.03	1437.55	1384.17	1336.02	1292.38	1252.67	1216.38
260000	1626.22	1556.91	1495.05	1439.54	1389.46	1344.08	1302.77	1265.04
270000	1688.77	1616.79	1552.56	1494.91	1442.90	1395.77	1352.88	1313.69
280000	1751.31	1676.67	1610.06	1550.28	1496.35	1447.47	1402.99	1362.35
290000	1813.86	1736.55	1667.56	1605.64	1549.79	1499.16	1453.09	1411.00
300000	1876.41	1796.43	1725.06	1661.01	1603.23	1550.86	1503.20	1459.66
310000	1938.95	1856.31	1782.56	1716.38	1656.67	1602.55	1553.31	1508.31
320000	2001.50	1916.19	1840.07	1771.74	1710.11	1654.25	1603.41	1556.97
330000	2064.05	1976.07	1897.57	1827.11	1763.55	1705.94	1653.52	1605.62
340000	2126.59	2035.95	1955.07	1882.48	1816.99	1757.64	1703.63	1654.28
350000	2189.14	2095.83	2012.57	1937.84	1870.43	1809.33	1753.73	1702.93
360000	2251.69	2155.71	2070.07	1993.21	1923.87	1861.03	1803.84	1751.59
370000	2314.23	2215.60	2127.57	2048.58	1977.31	1912.73	1853.94	1800.24
380000	2376.78	2275.48	2185.08	2103.94	2030.75	1964.42	1904.05	1848.90
390000	2439.33	2335.36	2242.58	2159.31	2084.19	2016.12	1954.16	1897.55
400000	2501.87	2395.24	2300.08	2214.68	2137.63	2067.81	2004.26	1946.21

7

3% BLENDED MONTHLY PAYMENTS
AMORTIZATION IN YEARS

Amount	25	26	29	30	35	40	45	50
25	.12	.12	.11	.11	.10	.09	.09	.09
50	.24	.24	.22	.22	.20	.18	.17	.17
100	.48	.47	.43	.43	.39	.36	.34	.33
200	.95	.93	.86	.85	.77	.72	.68	.65
300	1.42	1.39	1.29	1.27	1.16	1.08	1.01	.97
400	1.90	1.85	1.72	1.69	1.54	1.43	1.35	1.29
500	2.37	2.31	2.15	2.11	1.92	1.79	1.69	1.61
600	2.84	2.77	2.58	2.53	2.31	2.15	2.02	1.93
700	3.32	3.23	3.01	2.95	2.69	2.50	2.36	2.25
800	3.79	3.69	3.44	3.37	3.08	2.86	2.70	2.57
900	4.26	4.15	3.87	3.79	3.46	3.22	3.03	2.89
1000	4.74	4.62	4.30	4.21	3.84	3.57	3.37	3.21
2000	9.47	9.23	8.60	8.42	7.68	7.14	6.74	6.42
3000	14.20	13.84	12.89	12.62	11.52	10.71	10.10	9.63
4000	18.93	18.45	17.19	16.83	15.36	14.28	13.47	12.84
5000	23.67	23.06	21.48	21.04	19.20	17.85	16.83	16.05
6000	28.40	27.67	25.78	25.24	23.03	21.42	20.20	19.26
7000	33.13	32.28	30.08	29.45	26.87	24.99	23.57	22.46
8000	37.86	36.89	34.37	33.65	30.71	28.56	26.93	25.67
9000	42.60	41.50	38.67	37.86	34.55	32.13	30.30	28.88
10000	47.33	46.11	42.96	42.07	38.39	35.70	33.66	32.09
20000	94.65	92.21	85.92	84.13	76.77	71.39	67.32	64.17
30000	141.98	138.31	128.88	126.19	115.15	107.08	100.98	96.26
40000	189.30	184.41	171.84	168.25	153.53	142.77	134.64	128.34
50000	236.63	230.51	214.80	210.31	191.91	178.46	168.30	160.43
60000	283.95	276.61	257.76	252.37	230.29	214.15	201.96	192.51
70000	331.28	322.71	300.72	294.43	268.67	249.85	235.62	224.60
80000	378.60	368.81	343.68	336.49	307.06	285.54	269.28	256.68
90000	425.93	414.91	386.64	378.55	345.44	321.23	302.93	288.76
100000	473.25	461.01	429.60	420.61	383.82	356.92	336.59	320.85
110000	520.58	507.11	472.56	462.67	422.20	392.61	370.25	352.93
120000	567.90	553.21	515.52	504.73	460.58	428.30	403.91	385.02
130000	615.22	599.32	558.48	546.79	498.96	463.99	437.57	417.10
140000	662.55	645.42	601.44	588.85	537.34	499.69	471.23	449.19
150000	709.87	691.52	644.40	630.91	575.73	535.38	504.89	481.27
160000	757.20	737.62	687.36	672.97	614.11	571.07	538.55	513.35
170000	804.52	783.72	730.32	715.03	652.49	606.76	572.20	545.44
180000	851.85	829.82	773.28	757.09	690.87	642.45	605.86	577.52
190000	899.17	875.92	816.24	799.15	729.25	678.14	639.52	609.61
200000	946.50	922.02	859.20	841.21	767.63	713.83	673.18	641.69
210000	993.82	968.12	902.16	883.27	806.01	749.53	706.84	673.78
220000	1041.15	1014.22	945.12	925.33	844.40	785.22	740.50	705.86
230000	1088.47	1060.32	988.08	967.39	882.78	820.91	774.16	737.94
240000	1135.79	1106.42	1031.04	1009.45	921.16	856.60	807.82	770.03
250000	1183.12	1152.53	1074.00	1051.51	959.54	892.29	841.47	802.11
260000	1230.44	1198.63	1116.96	1093.57	997.92	927.98	875.13	834.20
270000	1277.77	1244.73	1159.92	1135.63	1036.30	963.67	908.79	866.28
280000	1325.09	1290.83	1202.88	1177.69	1074.68	999.37	942.45	898.37
290000	1372.42	1336.93	1245.84	1219.75	1113.07	1035.06	976.11	930.45
300000	1419.74	1383.03	1288.80	1261.81	1151.45	1070.75	1009.77	962.54
310000	1467.07	1429.13	1331.76	1303.87	1189.83	1106.44	1043.43	994.62
320000	1514.39	1475.23	1374.72	1345.93	1228.21	1142.13	1077.09	1026.70
330000	1561.72	1521.33	1417.68	1387.99	1266.59	1177.82	1110.75	1058.79
340000	1609.04	1567.43	1460.64	1430.05	1304.97	1213.51	1144.40	1090.87
350000	1656.36	1613.53	1503.60	1472.11	1343.35	1249.21	1178.06	1122.96
360000	1703.69	1659.63	1546.56	1514.17	1381.74	1284.90	1211.72	1155.04
370000	1751.01	1705.74	1589.52	1556.23	1420.12	1320.59	1245.38	1187.13
380000	1798.34	1751.84	1632.48	1598.30	1458.50	1356.28	1279.04	1219.21
390000	1845.66	1797.94	1675.44	1640.36	1496.88	1391.97	1312.70	1251.29
400000	1892.99	1844.04	1718.40	1682.42	1535.26	1427.66	1346.36	1283.38

8

BLENDED MONTHLY PAYMENTS 3¼%
AMORTIZATION IN YEARS

Amount	1	2	3	4	5	6	7	8
25	2.12	1.08	.73	.56	.46	.39	.34	.30
50	4.24	2.16	1.46	1.12	.91	.77	.67	.60
100	8.48	4.31	2.92	2.23	1.81	1.53	1.34	1.19
200	16.96	8.62	5.84	4.45	3.62	3.06	2.67	2.37
300	25.44	12.93	8.76	6.68	5.43	4.59	4.00	3.56
400	33.92	17.24	11.68	8.90	7.23	6.12	5.33	4.74
500	42.40	21.55	14.60	11.12	9.04	7.65	6.66	5.92
600	50.88	25.85	17.51	13.35	10.85	9.18	7.99	7.11
700	59.36	30.16	20.43	15.57	12.65	10.71	9.33	8.29
800	67.84	34.47	23.35	17.79	14.46	12.24	10.66	9.47
900	76.32	38.78	26.27	20.02	16.27	13.77	11.99	10.66
1000	84.80	43.09	29.19	22.24	18.08	15.30	13.32	11.84
2000	169.60	86.17	58.37	44.48	36.15	30.60	26.64	23.67
3000	254.40	129.25	87.55	66.71	54.22	45.89	39.95	35.51
4000	339.20	172.33	116.73	88.95	72.29	61.19	53.27	47.34
5000	423.99	215.42	145.91	111.18	90.36	76.48	66.59	59.17
6000	508.79	258.50	175.10	133.42	108.43	91.78	79.90	71.01
7000	593.59	301.58	204.28	155.65	126.50	107.08	93.22	82.84
8000	678.39	344.66	233.46	177.89	144.57	122.37	106.54	94.67
9000	763.18	387.75	262.64	200.12	162.64	137.67	119.85	106.51
10000	847.98	430.83	291.82	222.36	180.71	152.96	133.17	118.34
20000	1695.96	861.65	583.64	444.71	361.41	305.92	266.33	236.68
30000	2543.94	1292.47	875.46	667.06	542.11	458.88	399.50	355.01
40000	3391.91	1723.29	1167.28	889.42	722.82	611.84	532.66	473.35
50000	4239.89	2154.12	1459.10	1111.77	903.52	764.80	665.83	591.68
60000	5087.87	2584.94	1750.92	1334.12	1084.22	917.76	798.99	710.02
70000	5935.84	3015.76	2042.74	1556.48	1264.92	1070.72	932.15	828.35
80000	6783.82	3446.58	2334.56	1778.83	1445.63	1223.68	1065.32	946.69
90000	7631.80	3877.41	2626.38	2001.18	1626.33	1376.64	1198.48	1065.02
100000	8479.77	4308.23	2918.19	2223.54	1807.03	1529.60	1331.65	1183.36
110000	9327.75	4739.05	3210.01	2445.89	1987.74	1682.56	1464.81	1301.69
120000	10175.73	5169.87	3501.83	2668.24	2168.44	1835.52	1597.97	1420.03
130000	11023.70	5600.69	3793.65	2890.60	2349.14	1988.48	1731.14	1538.36
140000	11871.68	6031.52	4085.47	3112.95	2529.84	2141.44	1864.30	1656.70
150000	12719.66	6462.34	4377.29	3335.30	2710.55	2294.40	1997.47	1775.03
160000	13567.64	6893.16	4669.11	3557.66	2891.25	2447.36	2130.63	1893.37
170000	14415.61	7323.98	4960.93	3780.01	3071.95	2600.32	2263.79	2011.70
180000	15263.59	7754.81	5252.75	4002.36	3252.66	2753.28	2396.96	2130.04
190000	16111.57	8185.63	5544.56	4224.72	3433.36	2906.24	2530.12	2248.37
200000	16959.54	8616.45	5836.38	4447.07	3614.06	3059.20	2663.29	2366.71
210000	17807.52	9047.27	6128.20	4669.42	3794.76	3212.16	2796.45	2485.04
220000	18655.50	9478.10	6420.02	4891.78	3975.47	3365.12	2929.61	2603.38
230000	19503.47	9908.92	6711.84	5114.13	4156.17	3518.08	3062.78	2721.71
240000	20351.45	10339.74	7003.66	5336.48	4336.87	3671.04	3195.94	2840.05
250000	21199.43	10770.56	7295.48	5558.84	4517.58	3824.00	3329.11	2958.38
260000	22047.40	11201.38	7587.30	5781.19	4698.28	3976.96	3462.27	3076.72
270000	22895.38	11632.21	7879.12	6003.54	4878.98	4129.92	3595.43	3195.05
280000	23743.36	12063.03	8170.93	6225.90	5059.68	4282.88	3728.60	3313.39
290000	24591.33	12493.85	8462.75	6448.25	5240.39	4435.84	3861.76	3431.72
300000	25439.31	12924.67	8754.57	6670.60	5421.09	4588.80	3994.93	3550.06
310000	26287.29	13355.50	9046.39	6892.96	5601.79	4741.76	4128.09	3668.39
320000	27135.27	13786.32	9338.21	7115.31	5782.50	4894.72	4261.25	3786.73
330000	27983.24	14217.14	9630.03	7337.66	5963.20	5047.68	4394.42	3905.06
340000	28831.22	14647.96	9921.85	7560.02	6143.90	5200.64	4527.58	4023.40
350000	29679.20	15078.78	10213.67	7782.37	6324.60	5353.60	4660.75	4141.73
360000	30527.17	15509.61	10505.49	8004.72	6505.31	5506.56	4793.91	4260.07
370000	31375.15	15940.43	10797.30	8227.08	6686.01	5659.52	4927.07	4378.41
380000	32223.13	16371.25	11089.12	8449.43	6866.71	5812.48	5060.24	4496.74
390000	33071.10	16802.07	11380.94	8671.78	7047.42	5965.44	5193.40	4615.08
400000	33919.08	17232.90	11672.76	8894.14	7228.12	6118.40	5326.57	4733.41

9

3¼% BLENDED MONTHLY PAYMENTS
AMORTIZATION IN YEARS

Amount	9	10	11	12	13	14	15	16
25	.27	.25	.23	.21	.20	.19	.18	.17
50	.54	.49	.46	.42	.40	.38	.36	.34
100	1.07	.98	.91	.84	.79	.75	.71	.67
200	2.14	1.96	1.81	1.68	1.58	1.49	1.41	1.34
300	3.21	2.93	2.71	2.52	2.36	2.23	2.11	2.01
400	4.28	3.91	3.61	3.36	3.15	2.97	2.81	2.68
500	5.35	4.89	4.51	4.20	3.93	3.71	3.51	3.34
600	6.41	5.86	5.41	5.04	4.72	4.45	4.21	4.01
700	7.48	6.84	6.31	5.87	5.51	5.19	4.92	4.68
800	8.55	7.81	7.21	6.71	6.29	5.93	5.62	5.35
900	9.62	8.79	8.11	7.55	7.08	6.67	6.32	6.01
1000	10.69	9.77	9.02	8.39	7.86	7.41	7.02	6.68
2000	21.37	19.53	18.03	16.78	15.72	14.82	14.04	13.36
3000	32.05	29.29	27.04	25.16	23.58	22.22	21.05	20.03
4000	42.73	39.05	36.05	33.55	31.44	29.63	28.07	26.71
5000	53.41	48.81	45.06	41.93	39.29	37.04	35.09	33.38
6000	64.10	58.58	54.07	50.32	47.15	44.44	42.10	40.06
7000	74.78	68.34	63.08	58.70	55.01	51.85	49.12	46.73
8000	85.46	78.10	72.09	67.09	62.87	59.26	56.13	53.41
9000	96.14	87.86	81.10	75.47	70.72	66.66	63.15	60.08
10000	106.82	97.62	90.11	83.86	78.58	74.07	70.17	66.76
20000	213.64	195.24	180.21	167.71	157.16	148.13	140.33	133.52
30000	320.46	292.86	270.32	251.57	235.73	222.19	210.49	200.27
40000	427.28	390.48	360.42	335.42	314.31	296.26	280.65	267.03
50000	534.09	488.09	450.52	419.27	392.89	370.32	350.81	333.78
60000	640.91	585.71	540.63	503.13	471.46	444.38	420.97	400.54
70000	747.73	683.33	630.73	586.98	550.04	518.45	491.13	467.29
80000	854.55	780.95	720.83	670.84	628.62	592.51	561.29	534.05
90000	961.36	878.56	810.94	754.69	707.19	666.57	631.45	600.80
100000	1068.18	976.18	901.04	838.54	785.77	740.64	701.62	667.56
110000	1175.00	1073.80	991.15	922.40	864.35	814.70	771.78	734.32
120000	1281.82	1171.42	1081.25	1006.25	942.92	888.76	841.94	801.07
130000	1388.63	1269.04	1171.35	1090.10	1021.50	962.83	912.10	867.83
140000	1495.45	1366.65	1261.46	1173.96	1100.08	1036.89	982.26	934.58
150000	1602.27	1464.27	1351.56	1257.81	1178.65	1110.95	1052.42	1001.34
160000	1709.09	1561.89	1441.66	1341.67	1257.23	1185.01	1122.58	1068.09
170000	1815.90	1659.51	1531.77	1425.52	1335.80	1259.08	1192.74	1134.85
180000	1922.72	1757.12	1621.87	1509.37	1414.38	1333.14	1262.90	1201.60
190000	2029.54	1854.74	1711.97	1593.23	1492.96	1407.20	1333.06	1268.36
200000	2136.36	1952.36	1802.08	1677.08	1571.53	1481.27	1403.23	1335.12
210000	2243.17	2049.98	1892.18	1760.94	1650.11	1555.33	1473.39	1401.87
220000	2349.99	2147.60	1982.29	1844.79	1728.69	1629.39	1543.55	1468.63
230000	2456.81	2245.21	2072.39	1928.64	1807.26	1703.46	1613.71	1535.38
240000	2563.63	2342.83	2162.49	2012.50	1885.84	1777.52	1683.87	1602.14
250000	2670.44	2440.45	2252.60	2096.35	1964.42	1851.58	1754.03	1668.89
260000	2777.26	2538.07	2342.70	2180.20	2042.99	1925.65	1824.19	1735.65
270000	2884.08	2635.68	2432.80	2264.06	2121.57	1999.71	1894.35	1802.40
280000	2990.90	2733.30	2522.91	2347.91	2200.15	2073.77	1964.51	1869.16
290000	3097.71	2830.92	2613.01	2431.77	2278.72	2147.84	2034.67	1935.91
300000	3204.53	2928.54	2703.11	2515.62	2357.30	2221.90	2104.84	2002.67
310000	3311.35	3026.15	2793.22	2599.47	2435.87	2295.96	2175.00	2069.43
320000	3418.17	3123.77	2883.32	2683.33	2514.45	2370.02	2245.16	2136.18
330000	3524.98	3221.39	2973.43	2767.18	2593.03	2444.09	2315.32	2202.94
340000	3631.80	3319.01	3063.53	2851.03	2671.60	2518.15	2385.48	2269.69
350000	3738.62	3416.63	3153.63	2934.89	2750.18	2592.21	2455.64	2336.45
360000	3845.44	3514.24	3243.74	3018.74	2828.76	2666.28	2525.80	2403.20
370000	3952.25	3611.86	3333.84	3102.60	2907.33	2740.34	2595.96	2469.96
380000	4059.07	3709.48	3423.94	3186.45	2985.91	2814.40	2666.12	2536.71
390000	4165.89	3807.10	3514.05	3270.30	3064.49	2888.47	2736.28	2603.47
400000	4272.71	3904.71	3604.15	3354.16	3143.06	2962.53	2806.45	2670.23

BLENDED MONTHLY PAYMENTS $3\frac{1}{4}\%$

AMORTIZATION IN YEARS

Amount	17	18	19	20	21	22	23	24
25	.16	.16	.15	.15	.14	.14	.13	.13
50	.32	.31	.30	.29	.28	.27	.26	.25
100	.64	.62	.59	.57	.55	.53	.52	.50
200	1.28	1.23	1.18	1.14	1.10	1.06	1.03	1.00
300	1.92	1.84	1.77	1.70	1.65	1.59	1.55	1.50
400	2.56	2.45	2.35	2.27	2.19	2.12	2.06	2.00
500	3.19	3.06	2.94	2.84	2.74	2.65	2.57	2.50
600	3.83	3.67	3.53	3.40	3.29	3.18	3.09	3.00
700	4.47	4.28	4.12	3.97	3.83	3.71	3.60	3.50
800	5.11	4.89	4.70	4.53	4.38	4.24	4.12	4.00
900	5.74	5.50	5.29	5.10	4.93	4.77	4.63	4.50
1000	6.38	6.12	5.88	5.67	5.47	5.30	5.14	5.00
2000	12.76	12.23	11.75	11.33	10.94	10.60	10.28	9.99
3000	19.13	18.34	17.63	16.99	16.41	15.89	15.42	14.99
4000	25.51	24.45	23.50	22.65	21.88	21.19	20.56	19.98
5000	31.88	30.56	29.37	28.31	27.35	26.48	25.69	24.97
6000	38.26	36.67	35.25	33.97	32.82	31.78	30.83	29.97
7000	44.64	42.78	41.12	39.63	38.29	37.08	35.97	34.96
8000	51.01	48.89	46.99	45.29	43.76	42.37	41.11	39.95
9000	57.39	55.00	52.87	50.95	49.23	47.67	46.25	44.95
10000	63.76	61.11	58.74	56.61	54.70	52.96	51.38	49.94
20000	127.52	122.21	117.47	113.22	109.39	105.92	102.76	99.88
30000	191.28	183.31	176.21	169.83	164.08	158.88	154.14	149.82
40000	255.04	244.42	234.94	226.44	218.78	211.83	205.52	199.75
50000	318.80	305.52	293.68	283.05	273.47	264.79	256.90	249.69
60000	382.56	366.62	352.41	339.66	328.16	317.75	308.28	299.63
70000	446.32	427.73	411.14	396.27	382.86	370.71	359.66	349.57
80000	510.08	488.83	469.88	452.88	437.55	423.66	411.03	399.50
90000	573.84	549.93	528.61	509.49	492.24	476.62	462.41	449.44
100000	637.59	611.04	587.35	566.10	546.94	529.58	513.79	499.38
110000	701.35	672.14	646.08	622.71	601.63	582.54	565.17	549.32
120000	765.11	733.24	704.82	679.31	656.32	635.49	616.55	599.25
130000	828.87	794.35	763.55	735.92	711.01	688.45	667.93	649.19
140000	892.63	855.45	822.28	792.53	765.71	741.41	719.31	699.13
150000	956.39	916.55	881.02	849.14	820.40	794.37	770.69	749.06
160000	1020.15	977.65	939.75	905.75	875.09	847.32	822.06	799.00
170000	1083.91	1038.76	998.49	962.36	929.79	900.28	873.44	848.94
180000	1147.67	1099.86	1057.22	1018.97	984.48	953.24	924.82	898.88
190000	1211.42	1160.96	1115.95	1075.58	1039.17	1006.20	976.20	948.81
200000	1275.18	1222.07	1174.69	1132.19	1093.87	1059.15	1027.58	998.75
210000	1338.94	1283.17	1233.42	1188.80	1148.56	1112.11	1078.96	1048.69
220000	1402.70	1344.27	1292.16	1245.41	1203.25	1165.07	1130.34	1098.63
230000	1466.46	1405.38	1350.89	1302.01	1257.94	1218.03	1181.72	1148.56
240000	1530.22	1466.48	1409.63	1358.62	1312.64	1270.98	1233.09	1198.50
250000	1593.98	1527.58	1468.36	1415.23	1367.33	1323.94	1284.47	1248.44
260000	1657.74	1588.69	1527.09	1471.84	1422.02	1376.90	1335.85	1298.37
270000	1721.50	1649.79	1585.83	1528.45	1476.72	1429.86	1387.23	1348.31
280000	1785.26	1710.89	1644.56	1585.06	1531.41	1482.81	1438.61	1398.25
290000	1849.01	1771.99	1703.30	1641.67	1586.10	1535.77	1489.99	1448.19
300000	1912.77	1833.10	1762.03	1698.28	1640.80	1588.73	1541.37	1498.12
310000	1976.53	1894.20	1820.76	1754.89	1695.49	1641.69	1592.75	1548.06
320000	2040.29	1955.30	1879.50	1811.50	1750.18	1694.64	1644.12	1598.00
330000	2104.05	2016.41	1938.23	1868.11	1804.88	1747.60	1695.50	1647.94
340000	2167.81	2077.51	1996.97	1924.71	1859.57	1800.56	1746.88	1697.87
350000	2231.57	2138.61	2055.70	1981.32	1914.26	1853.52	1798.26	1747.81
360000	2295.33	2199.72	2114.44	2037.93	1968.95	1906.47	1849.64	1797.75
370000	2359.09	2260.82	2173.17	2094.54	2023.65	1959.43	1901.02	1847.68
380000	2422.84	2321.92	2231.90	2151.15	2078.34	2012.39	1952.40	1897.62
390000	2486.60	2383.03	2290.64	2207.76	2133.03	2065.34	2003.78	1947.56
400000	2550.36	2444.13	2349.37	2264.37	2187.73	2118.30	2055.15	1997.50

11

3¼% BLENDED MONTHLY PAYMENTS
AMORTIZATION IN YEARS

Amount	25	26	29	30	35	40	45	50
25	.13	.12	.12	.11	.10	.10	.09	.09
50	.25	.24	.23	.22	.20	.19	.18	.17
100	.49	.48	.45	.44	.40	.38	.36	.34
200	.98	.95	.89	.87	.80	.75	.71	.68
300	1.46	1.43	1.33	1.31	1.20	1.12	1.06	1.01
400	1.95	1.90	1.78	1.74	1.60	1.49	1.41	1.35
500	2.44	2.38	2.22	2.18	1.99	1.86	1.76	1.69
600	2.92	2.85	2.66	2.61	2.39	2.23	2.11	2.02
700	3.41	3.32	3.11	3.04	2.79	2.60	2.46	2.36
800	3.89	3.80	3.55	3.48	3.19	2.98	2.82	2.69
900	4.38	4.27	3.99	3.91	3.58	3.35	3.17	3.03
1000	4.87	4.75	4.43	4.35	3.98	3.72	3.52	3.37
2000	9.73	9.49	8.86	8.69	7.96	7.43	7.03	6.73
3000	14.59	14.23	13.29	13.03	11.94	11.14	10.55	10.09
4000	19.45	18.97	17.72	17.37	15.91	14.86	14.06	13.45
5000	24.31	23.71	22.15	21.71	19.89	18.57	17.57	16.81
6000	29.17	28.45	26.58	26.05	23.87	22.28	21.09	20.17
7000	34.04	33.19	31.01	30.39	27.84	25.99	24.60	23.53
8000	38.90	37.93	35.44	34.73	31.82	29.71	28.12	26.89
9000	43.76	42.67	39.87	39.07	35.80	33.42	31.63	30.25
10000	48.62	47.41	44.30	43.41	39.77	37.13	35.14	33.61
20000	97.24	94.81	88.59	86.81	79.54	74.26	70.28	67.22
30000	145.85	142.21	132.88	130.21	119.31	111.38	105.42	100.82
40000	194.47	189.62	177.17	173.61	159.08	148.51	140.56	134.43
50000	243.09	237.02	221.46	217.01	198.85	185.64	175.69	168.04
60000	291.70	284.42	265.75	260.41	238.62	222.76	210.83	201.64
70000	340.32	331.82	310.04	303.81	278.39	259.89	245.97	235.25
80000	388.94	379.23	354.33	347.21	318.16	297.01	281.11	268.85
90000	437.55	426.63	398.63	390.62	357.93	334.14	316.25	302.46
100000	486.17	474.03	442.92	434.02	397.70	371.27	351.38	336.07
110000	534.79	521.43	487.21	477.42	437.47	408.39	386.52	369.67
120000	583.40	568.84	531.50	520.82	477.24	445.52	421.66	403.28
130000	632.02	616.24	575.79	564.22	517.01	482.64	456.80	436.89
140000	680.64	663.64	620.08	607.62	556.78	519.77	491.94	470.49
150000	729.25	711.05	664.37	651.02	596.55	556.90	527.07	504.10
160000	777.87	758.45	708.66	694.42	636.32	594.02	562.21	537.70
170000	826.49	805.85	752.95	737.82	676.09	631.15	597.35	571.31
180000	875.10	853.25	797.25	781.23	715.86	668.27	632.49	604.92
190000	923.72	900.66	841.54	824.63	755.63	705.40	667.63	638.52
200000	972.34	948.06	885.83	868.03	795.40	742.53	702.76	672.13
210000	1020.95	995.46	930.12	911.43	835.17	779.65	737.90	705.74
220000	1069.57	1042.86	974.41	954.83	874.94	816.78	773.04	739.34
230000	1118.19	1090.27	1018.70	998.23	914.71	853.90	808.18	772.95
240000	1166.80	1137.67	1062.99	1041.63	954.48	891.03	843.32	806.55
250000	1215.42	1185.07	1107.28	1085.03	994.25	928.16	878.45	840.16
260000	1264.04	1232.48	1151.58	1128.43	1034.02	965.28	913.59	873.77
270000	1312.65	1279.88	1195.87	1171.84	1073.79	1002.41	948.73	907.37
280000	1361.27	1327.28	1240.16	1215.24	1113.56	1039.54	983.87	940.98
290000	1409.89	1374.68	1284.45	1258.64	1153.33	1076.66	1019.01	974.59
300000	1458.50	1422.09	1328.74	1302.04	1193.10	1113.79	1054.14	1008.19
310000	1507.12	1469.49	1373.03	1345.44	1232.87	1150.91	1089.28	1041.80
320000	1555.74	1516.89	1417.32	1388.84	1272.64	1188.04	1124.42	1075.40
330000	1604.35	1564.29	1461.61	1432.24	1312.41	1225.17	1159.56	1109.01
340000	1652.97	1611.70	1505.90	1475.64	1352.18	1262.29	1194.69	1142.62
350000	1701.59	1659.10	1550.20	1519.04	1391.95	1299.42	1229.83	1176.22
360000	1750.20	1706.50	1594.49	1562.45	1431.72	1336.54	1264.97	1209.83
370000	1798.82	1753.91	1638.78	1605.85	1471.49	1373.67	1300.11	1243.43
380000	1847.44	1801.31	1683.07	1649.25	1511.26	1410.80	1335.25	1277.04
390000	1896.05	1848.71	1727.36	1692.65	1551.03	1447.92	1370.38	1310.65
400000	1944.67	1896.11	1771.65	1736.05	1590.80	1485.05	1405.52	1344.25

BLENDED MONTHLY PAYMENTS $3\frac{1}{2}\%$

AMORTIZATION IN YEARS

Amount	1	2	3	4	5	6	7	8
25	2.13	1.08	.74	.56	.46	.39	.34	.30
50	4.25	2.16	1.47	1.12	.91	.78	.68	.60
100	8.50	4.32	2.93	2.24	1.82	1.55	1.35	1.20
200	16.99	8.64	5.86	4.47	3.64	3.09	2.69	2.39
300	25.48	12.96	8.79	6.71	5.46	4.63	4.03	3.59
400	33.97	17.28	11.72	8.94	7.28	6.17	5.38	4.78
500	42.46	21.60	14.65	11.18	9.10	7.71	6.72	5.98
600	50.95	25.92	17.58	13.41	10.91	9.25	8.06	7.17
700	59.44	30.24	20.51	15.65	12.73	10.79	9.40	8.37
800	67.93	34.56	23.44	17.88	14.55	12.33	10.75	9.56
900	76.42	38.88	26.37	20.12	16.37	13.87	12.09	10.76
1000	84.92	43.20	29.30	22.35	18.19	15.41	13.43	11.95
2000	169.83	86.39	58.59	44.69	36.37	30.82	26.86	23.90
3000	254.74	129.58	87.88	67.04	54.55	46.23	40.29	35.84
4000	339.65	172.77	117.17	89.38	72.73	61.63	53.72	47.79
5000	424.56	215.96	146.46	111.73	90.91	77.04	67.15	59.74
6000	509.47	259.15	175.75	134.07	109.09	92.45	80.58	71.68
7000	594.38	302.35	205.04	156.42	127.27	107.85	94.00	83.63
8000	679.29	345.54	234.33	178.76	145.45	123.26	107.43	95.58
9000	764.20	388.73	263.62	201.11	163.63	138.67	120.86	107.52
10000	849.11	431.92	292.91	223.45	181.81	154.07	134.29	119.47
20000	1698.21	863.84	585.82	446.90	363.61	308.14	268.57	238.93
30000	2547.31	1295.75	878.73	670.35	545.42	462.21	402.86	358.40
40000	3396.41	1727.67	1171.64	893.80	727.22	616.28	537.14	477.86
50000	4245.51	2159.58	1464.55	1117.24	909.03	770.35	671.42	597.33
60000	5094.61	2591.50	1757.46	1340.69	1090.83	924.42	805.71	716.79
70000	5943.71	3023.41	2050.37	1564.14	1272.64	1078.49	939.99	836.26
80000	6792.81	3455.33	2343.28	1787.59	1454.44	1232.56	1074.27	955.72
90000	7641.91	3887.24	2636.19	2011.03	1636.24	1386.63	1208.56	1075.19
100000	8491.02	4319.16	2929.10	2234.48	1818.05	1540.70	1342.84	1194.65
110000	9340.12	4751.07	3222.00	2457.93	1999.85	1694.77	1477.12	1314.11
120000	10189.22	5182.99	3514.91	2681.38	2181.66	1848.84	1611.41	1433.58
130000	11038.32	5614.90	3807.82	2904.83	2363.46	2002.91	1745.69	1553.04
140000	11887.42	6046.82	4100.73	3128.27	2545.27	2156.98	1879.97	1672.51
150000	12736.52	6478.73	4393.64	3351.72	2727.07	2311.05	2014.26	1791.97
160000	13585.62	6910.65	4686.55	3575.17	2908.88	2465.12	2148.54	1911.44
170000	14434.72	7342.56	4979.46	3798.62	3090.68	2619.19	2282.82	2030.90
180000	15283.82	7774.48	5272.37	4022.06	3272.48	2773.26	2417.11	2150.37
190000	16132.93	8206.39	5565.28	4245.51	3454.29	2927.33	2551.39	2269.83
200000	16982.03	8638.31	5858.19	4468.96	3636.09	3081.40	2685.68	2389.29
210000	17831.13	9070.22	6151.09	4692.41	3817.90	3235.47	2819.96	2508.76
220000	18680.23	9502.14	6444.00	4915.86	3999.70	3389.54	2954.24	2628.22
230000	19529.33	9934.05	6736.91	5139.30	4181.51	3543.61	3088.53	2747.69
240000	20378.43	10365.97	7029.82	5362.75	4363.31	3697.68	3222.81	2867.15
250000	21227.53	10797.88	7322.73	5586.20	4545.11	3851.75	3357.09	2986.62
260000	22076.63	11229.80	7615.64	5809.65	4726.92	4005.82	3491.38	3106.08
270000	22925.73	11661.72	7908.55	6033.09	4908.72	4159.89	3625.66	3225.55
280000	23774.84	12093.63	8201.46	6256.54	5090.53	4313.96	3759.94	3345.01
290000	24623.94	12525.55	8494.37	6479.99	5272.33	4468.03	3894.23	3464.47
300000	25473.04	12957.46	8787.28	6703.44	5454.14	4622.10	4028.51	3583.94
310000	26322.14	13389.38	9080.18	6926.88	5635.94	4776.17	4162.79	3703.40
320000	27171.24	13821.29	9373.09	7150.33	5817.75	4930.24	4297.08	3822.87
330000	28020.34	14253.21	9666.00	7373.78	5999.55	5084.31	4431.36	3942.33
340000	28869.44	14685.12	9958.91	7597.23	6181.35	5238.38	4565.64	4061.80
350000	29718.54	15117.04	10251.82	7820.68	6363.16	5392.45	4699.93	4181.26
360000	30567.64	15548.95	10544.73	8044.12	6544.96	5546.52	4834.21	4300.73
370000	31416.75	15980.87	10837.64	8267.57	6726.77	5700.59	4968.50	4420.19
380000	32265.85	16412.78	11130.55	8491.02	6908.57	5854.66	5102.78	4539.65
390000	33114.95	16844.70	11423.46	8714.47	7090.38	6008.73	5237.06	4659.12
400000	33964.05	17276.61	11716.37	8937.91	7272.18	6162.80	5371.35	4778.58

3½% BLENDED MONTHLY PAYMENTS
AMORTIZATION IN YEARS

Amount	9	10	11	12	13	14	15	16
25	.27	.25	.23	.22	.20	.19	.18	.17
50	.54	.50	.46	.43	.40	.38	.36	.34
100	1.08	.99	.92	.86	.80	.76	.72	.68
200	2.16	1.98	1.83	1.71	1.60	1.51	1.43	1.36
300	3.24	2.97	2.74	2.56	2.40	2.26	2.15	2.04
400	4.32	3.96	3.66	3.41	3.20	3.02	2.86	2.72
500	5.40	4.94	4.57	4.26	3.99	3.77	3.57	3.40
600	6.48	5.93	5.48	5.11	4.79	4.52	4.29	4.08
700	7.56	6.92	6.39	5.96	5.59	5.27	5.00	4.76
800	8.64	7.91	7.31	6.81	6.39	6.03	5.71	5.44
900	9.72	8.89	8.22	7.66	7.18	6.78	6.43	6.12
1000	10.80	9.88	9.13	8.51	7.98	7.53	7.14	6.80
2000	21.60	19.76	18.26	17.01	15.96	15.06	14.28	13.60
3000	32.39	29.64	27.38	25.51	23.93	22.58	21.41	20.40
4000	43.19	39.51	36.51	34.01	31.91	30.11	28.55	27.19
5000	53.98	49.39	45.64	42.52	39.88	37.63	35.69	33.99
6000	64.78	59.27	54.76	51.02	47.86	45.16	42.82	40.79
7000	75.57	69.14	63.89	59.52	55.84	52.68	49.96	47.58
8000	86.37	79.02	73.02	68.02	63.81	60.21	57.10	54.38
9000	97.17	88.90	82.14	76.53	71.79	67.74	64.23	61.18
10000	107.96	98.77	91.27	85.03	79.76	75.26	71.37	67.97
20000	215.92	197.54	182.53	170.05	159.52	150.52	142.73	135.94
30000	323.88	296.31	273.80	255.08	239.28	225.77	214.10	203.91
40000	431.83	395.08	365.06	340.10	319.04	301.03	285.46	271.88
50000	539.79	493.84	456.33	425.13	398.80	376.28	356.83	339.85
60000	647.75	592.61	547.59	510.15	478.55	451.54	428.19	407.82
70000	755.70	691.38	638.85	595.18	558.31	526.79	499.56	475.79
80000	863.66	790.15	730.12	680.20	638.07	602.05	570.92	543.76
90000	971.62	888.91	821.38	765.23	717.83	677.31	642.28	611.73
100000	1079.58	987.68	912.65	850.25	797.59	752.56	713.65	679.70
110000	1187.53	1086.45	1003.91	935.28	877.35	827.82	785.01	747.67
120000	1295.49	1185.22	1095.17	1020.30	957.10	903.07	856.38	815.64
130000	1403.45	1283.98	1186.44	1105.33	1036.86	978.33	927.74	883.61
140000	1511.40	1382.75	1277.70	1190.35	1116.62	1053.58	999.11	951.58
150000	1619.36	1481.52	1368.97	1275.38	1196.38	1128.84	1070.47	1019.55
160000	1727.32	1580.29	1460.23	1360.40	1276.14	1204.10	1141.83	1087.52
170000	1835.27	1679.05	1551.49	1445.43	1355.89	1279.35	1213.20	1155.49
180000	1943.23	1777.82	1642.76	1530.45	1435.65	1354.61	1284.56	1223.46
190000	2051.19	1876.59	1734.02	1615.48	1515.41	1429.86	1355.93	1291.43
200000	2159.15	1975.36	1825.29	1700.50	1595.17	1505.12	1427.29	1359.40
210000	2267.10	2074.13	1916.55	1785.53	1674.93	1580.37	1498.66	1427.37
220000	2375.06	2172.89	2007.81	1870.55	1754.69	1655.63	1570.02	1495.34
230000	2483.02	2271.66	2099.08	1955.58	1834.44	1730.88	1641.38	1563.31
240000	2590.97	2370.43	2190.34	2040.60	1914.20	1806.14	1712.75	1631.28
250000	2698.93	2469.20	2281.61	2125.63	1993.96	1881.40	1784.11	1699.24
260000	2806.89	2567.96	2372.87	2210.65	2073.72	1956.65	1855.48	1767.21
270000	2914.84	2666.73	2464.14	2295.68	2153.48	2031.91	1926.84	1835.18
280000	3022.80	2765.50	2555.40	2380.70	2233.23	2107.16	1998.21	1903.15
290000	3130.76	2864.27	2646.66	2465.73	2312.99	2182.42	2069.57	1971.12
300000	3238.72	2963.03	2737.93	2550.75	2392.75	2257.67	2140.93	2039.09
310000	3346.67	3061.80	2829.19	2635.78	2472.51	2332.93	2212.30	2107.06
320000	3454.63	3160.57	2920.46	2720.80	2552.27	2408.19	2283.66	2175.03
330000	3562.59	3259.34	3011.72	2805.83	2632.03	2483.44	2355.03	2243.00
340000	3670.54	3358.10	3102.98	2890.85	2711.78	2558.70	2426.39	2310.97
350000	3778.50	3456.87	3194.25	2975.88	2791.54	2633.95	2497.76	2378.94
360000	3886.46	3555.64	3285.51	3060.90	2871.30	2709.21	2569.12	2446.91
370000	3994.41	3654.41	3376.78	3145.93	2951.06	2784.46	2640.48	2514.88
380000	4102.37	3753.17	3468.04	3230.95	3030.82	2859.72	2711.85	2582.85
390000	4210.33	3851.94	3559.30	3315.97	3110.57	2934.97	2783.21	2650.82
400000	4318.29	3950.71	3650.57	3401.00	3190.33	3010.23	2854.58	2718.79

14

BLENDED MONTHLY PAYMENTS   3½%
AMORTIZATION IN YEARS

Amount	17	18	19	20	21	22	23	24
25	.17	.16	.15	.15	.14	.14	.14	.13
50	.33	.32	.30	.29	.28	.28	.27	.26
100	.65	.63	.60	.58	.56	.55	.53	.52
200	1.30	1.25	1.20	1.16	1.12	1.09	1.06	1.03
300	1.95	1.88	1.80	1.74	1.68	1.63	1.59	1.54
400	2.60	2.50	2.40	2.32	2.24	2.17	2.11	2.05
500	3.25	3.12	3.00	2.90	2.80	2.72	2.64	2.57
600	3.90	3.75	3.60	3.48	3.36	3.26	3.17	3.08
700	4.55	4.37	4.20	4.06	3.92	3.80	3.69	3.59
800	5.20	4.99	4.80	4.63	4.48	4.34	4.22	4.10
900	5.85	5.62	5.40	5.21	5.04	4.89	4.75	4.62
1000	6.50	6.24	6.00	5.79	5.60	5.43	5.27	5.13
2000	13.00	12.47	12.00	11.58	11.20	10.85	10.54	10.25
3000	19.50	18.71	18.00	17.36	16.79	16.28	15.81	15.38
4000	26.00	24.94	24.00	23.15	22.39	21.70	21.07	20.50
5000	32.50	31.17	30.00	28.94	27.99	27.12	26.34	25.62
6000	39.00	37.41	35.99	34.72	33.58	32.55	31.61	30.75
7000	45.49	43.64	41.99	40.51	39.18	37.97	36.87	35.87
8000	51.99	49.88	47.99	46.30	44.77	43.39	42.14	40.99
9000	58.49	56.11	53.99	52.08	50.37	48.82	47.41	46.12
10000	64.99	62.34	59.99	57.87	55.97	54.24	52.67	51.24
20000	129.97	124.68	119.97	115.74	111.93	108.48	105.34	102.48
30000	194.96	187.02	179.95	173.60	167.89	162.71	158.01	153.72
40000	259.94	249.36	239.93	231.47	223.85	216.95	210.68	204.95
50000	324.92	311.70	299.91	289.34	279.81	271.19	263.34	256.19
60000	389.91	374.04	359.89	347.20	335.77	325.42	316.01	307.43
70000	454.89	436.38	419.87	405.07	391.73	379.66	368.68	358.67
80000	519.88	498.72	479.85	462.94	447.69	433.89	421.35	409.90
90000	584.86	561.05	539.83	520.80	503.65	488.13	474.02	461.14
100000	649.84	623.39	599.81	578.67	559.61	542.37	526.68	512.38
110000	714.83	685.73	659.79	636.53	615.58	596.60	579.35	563.61
120000	779.81	748.07	719.77	694.40	671.54	650.84	632.02	614.85
130000	844.79	810.41	779.75	752.27	727.50	705.07	684.69	666.09
140000	909.78	872.75	839.73	810.13	783.46	759.31	737.36	717.33
150000	974.76	935.09	899.71	868.00	839.42	813.55	790.02	768.56
160000	1039.75	997.43	959.69	925.87	895.38	867.78	842.69	819.80
170000	1104.73	1059.76	1019.68	983.73	951.34	922.02	895.36	871.04
180000	1169.71	1122.10	1079.66	1041.60	1007.30	976.25	948.03	922.27
190000	1234.70	1184.44	1139.64	1099.46	1063.26	1030.49	1000.70	973.51
200000	1299.68	1246.78	1199.62	1157.33	1119.22	1084.73	1053.36	1024.75
210000	1364.66	1309.12	1259.60	1215.20	1175.18	1138.96	1106.03	1075.99
220000	1429.65	1371.46	1319.58	1273.06	1231.15	1193.20	1158.70	1127.22
230000	1494.63	1433.80	1379.56	1330.93	1287.11	1247.43	1211.37	1178.46
240000	1559.62	1496.14	1439.54	1388.80	1343.07	1301.67	1264.04	1229.70
250000	1624.60	1558.47	1499.52	1446.66	1399.03	1355.91	1316.70	1280.93
260000	1689.58	1620.81	1559.50	1504.53	1454.99	1410.14	1369.37	1332.17
270000	1754.57	1683.15	1619.48	1562.40	1510.95	1464.38	1422.04	1383.41
280000	1819.55	1745.49	1679.46	1620.26	1566.91	1518.61	1474.71	1434.65
290000	1884.54	1807.83	1739.44	1678.13	1622.87	1572.85	1527.38	1485.88
300000	1949.52	1870.17	1799.42	1735.99	1678.83	1627.09	1580.04	1537.12
310000	2014.50	1932.51	1859.40	1793.86	1734.79	1681.32	1632.71	1588.36
320000	2079.49	1994.85	1919.38	1851.73	1790.76	1735.56	1685.38	1639.59
330000	2144.47	2057.18	1979.37	1909.59	1846.72	1789.79	1738.05	1690.83
340000	2209.45	2119.52	2039.35	1967.46	1902.68	1844.03	1790.72	1742.07
350000	2274.44	2181.86	2099.33	2025.33	1958.64	1898.27	1843.38	1793.31
360000	2339.42	2244.20	2159.31	2083.19	2014.60	1952.50	1896.05	1844.54
370000	2404.41	2306.54	2219.29	2141.06	2070.56	2006.74	1948.72	1895.78
380000	2469.39	2368.88	2279.27	2198.92	2126.52	2060.97	2001.39	1947.02
390000	2534.37	2431.22	2339.25	2256.79	2182.48	2115.21	2054.06	1998.25
400000	2599.36	2493.56	2399.23	2314.66	2238.44	2169.45	2106.72	2049.49

3½% BLENDED MONTHLY PAYMENTS
AMORTIZATION IN YEARS

Amount	25	26	29	30	35	40	45	50
25	.13	.13	.12	.12	.11	.10	.10	.09
50	.25	.25	.23	.23	.21	.20	.19	.18
100	.50	.49	.46	.45	.42	.39	.37	.36
200	1.00	.98	.92	.90	.83	.78	.74	.71
300	1.50	1.47	1.37	1.35	1.24	1.16	1.10	1.06
400	2.00	1.95	1.83	1.80	1.65	1.55	1.47	1.41
500	2.50	2.44	2.29	2.24	2.06	1.93	1.84	1.76
600	3.00	2.93	2.74	2.69	2.48	2.32	2.20	2.11
700	3.50	3.42	3.20	3.14	2.89	2.71	2.57	2.47
800	4.00	3.90	3.66	3.59	3.30	3.09	2.94	2.82
900	4.50	4.39	4.11	4.03	3.71	3.48	3.30	3.17
1000	5.00	4.88	4.57	4.48	4.12	3.86	3.67	3.52
2000	9.99	9.75	9.13	8.96	8.24	7.72	7.33	7.04
3000	14.98	14.62	13.70	13.43	12.36	11.58	11.00	10.55
4000	19.98	19.49	18.26	17.91	16.48	15.44	14.66	14.07
5000	24.97	24.37	22.83	22.39	20.60	19.30	18.33	17.58
6000	29.96	29.24	27.39	26.86	24.71	23.16	21.99	21.10
7000	34.95	34.11	31.96	31.34	28.83	27.02	25.66	24.62
8000	39.95	38.98	36.52	35.82	32.95	30.88	29.32	28.13
9000	44.94	43.86	41.08	40.29	37.07	34.73	32.99	31.65
10000	49.93	48.73	45.65	44.77	41.19	38.59	36.65	35.16
20000	99.86	97.45	91.29	89.53	82.37	77.18	73.30	70.32
30000	149.79	146.18	136.94	134.30	123.55	115.77	109.94	105.48
40000	199.71	194.90	182.58	179.06	164.74	154.36	146.59	140.64
50000	249.64	243.62	228.22	223.82	205.92	192.94	183.24	175.80
60000	299.57	292.35	273.87	268.59	247.10	231.53	219.88	210.96
70000	349.49	341.07	319.51	313.35	288.29	270.12	256.53	246.12
80000	399.42	389.79	365.15	358.11	329.47	308.71	293.18	281.28
90000	449.35	438.52	410.80	402.88	370.65	347.30	329.82	316.44
100000	499.28	487.24	456.44	447.64	411.83	385.88	366.47	351.60
110000	549.20	535.97	502.08	492.40	453.02	424.47	403.11	386.76
120000	599.13	584.69	547.73	537.17	494.20	463.06	439.76	421.92
130000	649.06	633.41	593.37	581.93	535.38	501.65	476.41	457.07
140000	698.98	682.14	639.01	626.70	576.57	540.23	513.05	492.23
150000	748.91	730.86	684.66	671.46	617.75	578.82	549.70	527.39
160000	798.84	779.58	730.30	716.22	658.93	617.41	586.35	562.55
170000	848.76	828.31	775.94	760.99	700.11	656.00	622.99	597.71
180000	898.69	877.03	821.59	805.75	741.30	694.59	659.64	632.87
190000	948.62	925.75	867.23	850.51	782.48	733.17	696.29	668.03
200000	998.55	974.48	912.87	895.28	823.66	771.76	732.93	703.19
210000	1048.47	1023.20	958.52	940.04	864.85	810.35	769.58	738.35
220000	1098.40	1071.93	1004.16	984.80	906.03	848.94	806.22	773.51
230000	1148.33	1120.65	1049.80	1029.57	947.21	887.52	842.87	808.67
240000	1198.25	1169.37	1095.45	1074.33	988.39	926.11	879.52	843.83
250000	1248.18	1218.10	1141.09	1119.10	1029.58	964.70	916.16	878.98
260000	1298.11	1266.82	1186.73	1163.86	1070.76	1003.29	952.81	914.14
270000	1348.03	1315.54	1232.38	1208.62	1111.94	1041.88	989.46	949.30
280000	1397.96	1364.27	1278.02	1253.39	1153.13	1080.46	1026.10	984.46
290000	1447.89	1412.99	1323.66	1298.15	1194.31	1119.05	1062.75	1019.62
300000	1497.82	1461.72	1369.31	1342.91	1235.49	1157.64	1099.40	1054.78
310000	1547.74	1510.44	1414.95	1387.68	1276.67	1196.23	1136.04	1089.94
320000	1597.67	1559.16	1460.59	1432.44	1317.86	1234.81	1172.69	1125.10
330000	1647.60	1607.89	1506.24	1477.20	1359.04	1273.40	1209.33	1160.26
340000	1697.52	1656.61	1551.88	1521.97	1400.22	1311.99	1245.98	1195.42
350000	1747.45	1705.33	1597.52	1566.73	1441.41	1350.58	1282.63	1230.58
360000	1797.38	1754.06	1643.17	1611.50	1482.59	1389.17	1319.27	1265.74
370000	1847.31	1802.78	1688.81	1656.26	1523.77	1427.75	1355.92	1300.89
380000	1897.23	1851.50	1734.45	1701.02	1564.95	1466.34	1392.57	1336.05
390000	1947.16	1900.23	1780.10	1745.79	1606.14	1504.93	1429.21	1371.21
400000	1997.09	1948.95	1825.74	1790.55	1647.32	1543.52	1465.86	1406.37

Amount	1	2	3	4	5	6	7	8
25	2.13	1.09	.74	.57	.46	.39	.34	.31
50	4.26	2.17	1.48	1.13	.92	.78	.68	.61
100	8.51	4.34	2.95	2.25	1.83	1.56	1.36	1.21
200	17.01	8.67	5.89	4.50	3.66	3.11	2.71	2.42
300	25.51	13.00	8.83	6.74	5.49	4.66	4.07	3.62
400	34.01	17.33	11.77	8.99	7.32	6.21	5.42	4.83
500	42.52	21.66	14.71	11.23	9.15	7.76	6.78	6.03
600	51.02	25.99	17.65	13.48	10.98	9.32	8.13	7.24
700	59.52	30.32	20.59	15.72	12.81	10.87	9.48	8.45
800	68.02	34.65	23.53	17.97	14.64	12.42	10.84	9.65
900	76.53	38.98	26.47	20.21	16.47	13.97	12.19	10.86
1000	85.03	43.31	29.41	22.46	18.30	15.52	13.55	12.06
2000	170.05	86.61	58.81	44.91	36.59	31.04	27.09	24.12
3000	255.07	129.91	88.21	67.37	54.88	46.56	40.63	36.18
4000	340.10	173.21	117.61	89.82	73.17	62.08	54.17	48.24
5000	425.12	216.51	147.01	112.28	91.46	77.60	67.71	60.30
6000	510.14	259.81	176.41	134.73	109.75	93.12	81.25	72.36
7000	595.16	303.11	205.81	157.19	128.04	108.63	94.79	84.42
8000	680.19	346.41	235.21	179.64	146.33	124.15	108.33	96.48
9000	765.21	389.71	264.61	202.09	164.62	139.67	121.87	108.54
10000	850.23	433.01	294.01	224.55	182.91	155.19	135.41	120.60
20000	1700.46	866.02	588.01	449.09	365.82	310.37	270.82	241.20
30000	2550.68	1299.03	882.01	673.64	548.73	465.56	406.23	361.80
40000	3400.91	1732.04	1176.01	898.18	731.64	620.74	541.64	482.40
50000	4251.13	2165.05	1470.01	1122.73	914.55	775.92	677.04	603.00
60000	5101.36	2598.06	1764.01	1347.27	1097.46	931.11	812.45	723.60
70000	5951.58	3031.07	2058.01	1571.82	1280.37	1086.29	947.86	844.20
80000	6801.81	3464.07	2352.01	1796.36	1463.28	1241.48	1083.27	964.80
90000	7652.03	3897.08	2646.01	2020.90	1646.19	1396.66	1218.67	1085.40
100000	8502.26	4330.09	2940.01	2245.45	1829.09	1551.84	1354.08	1206.00
110000	9352.48	4763.10	3234.01	2469.99	2012.00	1707.03	1489.49	1326.60
120000	10202.71	5196.11	3528.01	2694.54	2194.91	1862.21	1624.90	1447.20
130000	11052.93	5629.12	3822.01	2919.08	2377.82	2017.40	1760.30	1567.80
140000	11903.16	6062.13	4116.01	3143.63	2560.73	2172.58	1895.71	1688.40
150000	12753.38	6495.13	4410.01	3368.17	2743.64	2327.76	2031.12	1808.99
160000	13603.61	6928.14	4704.01	3592.71	2926.55	2482.95	2166.53	1929.59
170000	14453.83	7361.15	4998.01	3817.26	3109.46	2638.13	2301.94	2050.19
180000	15304.06	7794.16	5292.01	4041.80	3292.37	2793.32	2437.34	2170.79
190000	16154.28	8227.17	5586.01	4266.35	3475.28	2948.50	2572.75	2291.39
200000	17004.51	8660.18	5880.01	4490.89	3658.18	3103.68	2708.16	2411.99
210000	17854.73	9093.19	6174.02	4715.44	3841.09	3258.87	2843.57	2532.59
220000	18704.96	9526.20	6468.02	4939.98	4024.00	3414.05	2978.97	2653.19
230000	19555.18	9959.20	6762.02	5164.53	4206.91	3569.24	3114.38	2773.79
240000	20405.41	10392.21	7056.02	5389.07	4389.82	3724.42	3249.79	2894.39
250000	21255.63	10825.22	7350.02	5613.61	4572.73	3879.60	3385.20	3014.99
260000	22105.86	11258.23	7644.02	5838.16	4755.64	4034.79	3520.60	3135.59
270000	22956.08	11691.24	7938.02	6062.70	4938.55	4189.97	3656.01	3256.19
280000	23806.31	12124.25	8232.02	6287.25	5121.46	4345.16	3791.42	3376.79
290000	24656.53	12557.26	8526.02	6511.79	5304.37	4500.34	3926.83	3497.38
300000	25506.76	12990.26	8820.02	6736.34	5487.27	4655.52	4062.24	3617.98
310000	26356.98	13423.27	9114.02	6960.88	5670.18	4810.71	4197.64	3738.58
320000	27207.21	13856.28	9408.02	7185.42	5853.09	4965.89	4333.05	3859.18
330000	28057.43	14289.29	9702.02	7409.97	6036.00	5121.08	4468.46	3979.78
340000	28907.66	14722.30	9996.02	7634.51	6218.91	5276.26	4603.87	4100.38
350000	29757.88	15155.31	10290.02	7859.06	6401.82	5431.44	4739.27	4220.98
360000	30608.11	15588.32	10584.02	8083.60	6584.73	5586.63	4874.68	4341.58
370000	31458.33	16021.32	10878.02	8308.15	6767.64	5741.81	5010.09	4462.18
380000	32308.56	16454.33	11172.02	8532.69	6950.55	5897.00	5145.50	4582.78
390000	33158.78	16887.34	11466.02	8757.24	7133.46	6052.18	5280.90	4703.38
400000	34009.01	17320.35	11760.02	8981.78	7316.36	6207.36	5416.31	4823.98

3¾% BLENDED MONTHLY PAYMENTS
AMORTIZATION IN YEARS

Amount	9	10	11	12	13	14	15	16
25	.28	.25	.24	.22	.21	.20	.19	.18
50	.55	.50	.47	.44	.41	.39	.37	.35
100	1.10	1.00	.93	.87	.81	.77	.73	.70
200	2.19	2.00	1.85	1.73	1.62	1.53	1.46	1.39
300	3.28	3.00	2.78	2.59	2.43	2.30	2.18	2.08
400	4.37	4.00	3.70	3.45	3.24	3.06	2.91	2.77
500	5.46	5.00	4.63	4.32	4.05	3.83	3.63	3.46
600	6.55	6.00	5.55	5.18	4.86	4.59	4.36	4.16
700	7.64	7.00	6.48	6.04	5.67	5.36	5.09	4.85
800	8.73	8.00	7.40	6.90	6.48	6.12	5.81	5.54
900	9.82	9.00	8.32	7.76	7.29	6.89	6.54	6.23
1000	10.92	10.00	9.25	8.63	8.10	7.65	7.26	6.92
2000	21.83	19.99	18.49	17.25	16.19	15.30	14.52	13.84
3000	32.74	29.98	27.73	25.87	24.29	22.94	21.78	20.76
4000	43.65	39.97	36.98	34.49	32.38	30.59	29.04	27.68
5000	54.56	49.97	46.22	43.11	40.48	38.23	36.29	34.60
6000	65.47	59.96	55.46	51.73	48.57	45.88	43.55	41.52
7000	76.38	69.95	64.71	60.35	56.67	53.53	50.81	48.44
8000	87.29	79.94	73.95	68.97	64.76	61.17	58.07	55.36
9000	98.20	89.94	83.19	77.59	72.86	68.82	65.33	62.28
10000	109.11	99.93	92.44	86.21	80.95	76.46	72.58	69.20
20000	218.21	199.85	184.87	172.41	161.90	152.92	145.16	138.40
30000	327.31	299.78	277.30	258.62	242.85	229.38	217.74	207.59
40000	436.42	399.70	369.73	344.82	323.80	305.84	290.32	276.79
50000	545.52	499.63	462.17	431.03	404.75	382.30	362.90	345.98
60000	654.62	599.55	554.60	517.23	485.70	458.76	435.48	415.18
70000	763.72	699.48	647.03	603.44	566.65	535.21	508.06	484.37
80000	872.83	799.40	739.46	689.64	647.60	611.67	580.63	553.57
90000	981.93	899.33	831.90	775.85	728.55	688.13	653.21	622.76
100000	1091.03	999.25	924.33	862.05	809.50	764.59	725.79	691.96
110000	1200.14	1099.18	1016.76	948.26	890.45	841.05	798.37	761.16
120000	1309.24	1199.10	1109.19	1034.46	971.40	917.51	870.95	830.35
130000	1418.34	1299.03	1201.63	1120.67	1052.35	993.96	943.53	899.55
140000	1527.44	1398.95	1294.06	1206.87	1133.30	1070.42	1016.11	968.74
150000	1636.55	1498.87	1386.49	1293.07	1214.25	1146.88	1088.68	1037.94
160000	1745.65	1598.80	1478.92	1379.28	1295.20	1223.34	1161.26	1107.13
170000	1854.75	1698.72	1571.36	1465.48	1376.15	1299.80	1233.84	1176.33
180000	1963.86	1798.65	1663.79	1551.69	1457.10	1376.26	1306.42	1245.52
190000	2072.96	1898.57	1756.22	1637.89	1538.04	1452.71	1379.00	1314.72
200000	2182.06	1998.50	1848.65	1724.10	1618.99	1529.17	1451.58	1383.91
210000	2291.16	2098.42	1941.09	1810.30	1699.94	1605.63	1524.16	1453.11
220000	2400.27	2198.35	2033.52	1896.51	1780.89	1682.09	1596.73	1522.31
230000	2509.37	2298.27	2125.95	1982.71	1861.84	1758.55	1669.31	1591.50
240000	2618.47	2398.20	2218.38	2068.92	1942.79	1835.01	1741.89	1660.70
250000	2727.58	2498.12	2310.82	2155.12	2023.74	1911.47	1814.47	1729.89
260000	2836.68	2598.05	2403.25	2241.33	2104.69	1987.92	1887.05	1799.09
270000	2945.78	2697.97	2495.68	2327.53	2185.64	2064.38	1959.63	1868.28
280000	3054.88	2797.89	2588.11	2413.73	2266.59	2140.84	2032.21	1937.48
290000	3163.99	2897.82	2680.54	2499.94	2347.54	2217.30	2104.79	2006.67
300000	3273.09	2997.74	2772.98	2586.14	2428.49	2293.76	2177.36	2075.87
310000	3382.19	3097.67	2865.41	2672.35	2509.44	2370.22	2249.94	2145.06
320000	3491.30	3197.59	2957.84	2758.55	2590.39	2446.67	2322.52	2214.26
330000	3600.40	3297.52	3050.27	2844.76	2671.34	2523.13	2395.10	2283.46
340000	3709.50	3397.44	3142.71	2930.96	2752.29	2599.59	2467.68	2352.65
350000	3818.60	3497.37	3235.14	3017.17	2833.24	2676.05	2540.26	2421.85
360000	3927.71	3597.29	3327.57	3103.37	2914.19	2752.51	2612.84	2491.04
370000	4036.81	3697.22	3420.00	3189.58	2995.13	2828.97	2685.41	2560.24
380000	4145.91	3797.14	3512.44	3275.78	3076.08	2905.42	2757.99	2629.43
390000	4255.02	3897.07	3604.87	3361.99	3157.03	2981.88	2830.57	2698.63
400000	4364.12	3996.99	3697.30	3448.19	3237.98	3058.34	2903.15	2767.82

18

BLENDED MONTHLY PAYMENTS $3\frac{3}{4}\%$

AMORTIZATION IN YEARS

Amount	17	18	19	20	21	22	23	24
25	.17	.16	.16	.15	.15	.14	.14	.14
50	.34	.32	.31	.30	.29	.28	.27	.27
100	.67	.64	.62	.60	.58	.56	.54	.53
200	1.33	1.28	1.23	1.19	1.15	1.12	1.08	1.06
300	1.99	1.91	1.84	1.78	1.72	1.67	1.62	1.58
400	2.65	2.55	2.45	2.37	2.29	2.23	2.16	2.11
500	3.32	3.18	3.07	2.96	2.87	2.78	2.70	2.63
600	3.98	3.82	3.68	3.55	3.44	3.34	3.24	3.16
700	4.64	4.46	4.29	4.14	4.01	3.89	3.78	3.68
800	5.30	5.09	4.90	4.74	4.58	4.45	4.32	4.21
900	5.96	5.73	5.52	5.33	5.16	5.00	4.86	4.73
1000	6.63	6.36	6.13	5.92	5.73	5.56	5.40	5.26
2000	13.25	12.72	12.25	11.83	11.45	11.11	10.80	10.52
3000	19.87	19.08	18.38	17.75	17.18	16.66	16.20	15.77
4000	26.49	25.44	24.50	23.66	22.90	22.22	21.59	21.03
5000	33.12	31.80	30.63	29.57	28.63	27.77	26.99	26.28
6000	39.74	38.16	36.75	35.49	34.35	33.32	32.39	31.54
7000	46.36	44.52	42.87	41.40	40.08	38.88	37.79	36.79
8000	52.98	50.88	49.00	47.32	45.80	44.43	43.18	42.05
9000	59.60	57.23	55.12	53.23	51.52	49.98	48.58	47.30
10000	66.23	63.59	61.25	59.14	57.25	55.54	53.98	52.56
20000	132.45	127.18	122.49	118.28	114.49	111.07	107.95	105.11
30000	198.67	190.77	183.73	177.42	171.74	166.60	161.93	157.67
40000	264.89	254.36	244.97	236.56	228.98	222.13	215.90	210.22
50000	331.11	317.94	306.21	295.70	286.23	277.66	269.88	262.78
60000	397.33	381.53	367.45	354.83	343.47	333.19	323.85	315.33
70000	463.55	445.12	428.69	413.97	400.71	388.72	377.82	367.89
80000	529.77	508.71	489.93	473.11	457.96	444.25	431.80	420.44
90000	596.00	572.29	551.17	532.25	515.20	499.78	485.77	473.00
100000	662.22	635.88	612.42	591.39	572.45	555.31	539.75	525.55
110000	728.44	699.47	673.66	650.53	629.69	610.84	593.72	578.10
120000	794.66	763.06	734.90	709.66	686.94	666.37	647.69	630.66
130000	860.88	826.64	796.14	768.80	744.18	721.90	701.67	683.21
140000	927.10	890.23	857.38	827.94	801.42	777.44	755.64	735.77
150000	993.32	953.82	918.62	887.08	858.67	832.97	809.62	788.32
160000	1059.54	1017.41	979.86	946.22	915.91	888.50	863.59	840.88
170000	1125.77	1081.00	1041.10	1005.35	973.16	944.03	917.56	893.43
180000	1191.99	1144.58	1102.34	1064.49	1030.40	999.56	971.54	945.99
190000	1258.21	1208.17	1163.58	1123.63	1087.65	1055.09	1025.51	998.54
200000	1324.43	1271.76	1224.83	1182.77	1144.89	1110.62	1079.49	1051.09
210000	1390.65	1335.35	1286.07	1241.91	1202.13	1166.15	1133.46	1103.65
220000	1456.87	1398.93	1347.31	1301.05	1259.38	1221.68	1187.43	1156.20
230000	1523.09	1462.52	1408.55	1360.18	1316.62	1277.21	1241.41	1208.76
240000	1589.31	1526.11	1469.79	1419.32	1373.87	1332.74	1295.38	1261.31
250000	1655.54	1589.70	1531.03	1478.46	1431.11	1388.27	1349.36	1313.87
260000	1721.76	1653.28	1592.27	1537.60	1488.36	1443.80	1403.33	1366.42
270000	1787.98	1716.87	1653.51	1596.74	1545.60	1499.34	1457.30	1418.98
280000	1854.20	1780.46	1714.75	1655.87	1602.84	1554.87	1511.28	1471.53
290000	1920.42	1844.05	1776.00	1715.01	1660.09	1610.40	1565.25	1524.09
300000	1986.64	1907.64	1837.24	1774.15	1717.33	1665.93	1619.23	1576.64
310000	2052.86	1971.22	1898.48	1833.29	1774.58	1721.46	1673.20	1629.19
320000	2119.08	2034.81	1959.72	1892.43	1831.82	1776.99	1727.17	1681.75
330000	2185.30	2098.40	2020.96	1951.57	1889.07	1832.52	1781.15	1734.30
340000	2251.53	2161.99	2082.20	2010.70	1946.31	1888.05	1835.12	1786.86
350000	2317.75	2225.57	2143.44	2069.84	2003.55	1943.58	1889.10	1839.41
360000	2383.97	2289.16	2204.68	2128.98	2060.80	1999.11	1943.07	1891.97
370000	2450.19	2352.75	2265.92	2188.12	2118.04	2054.64	1997.04	1944.52
380000	2516.41	2416.34	2327.16	2247.26	2175.29	2110.17	2051.02	1997.08
390000	2582.63	2479.92	2388.41	2306.39	2232.53	2165.70	2104.99	2049.63
400000	2648.85	2543.51	2449.65	2365.53	2289.78	2221.23	2158.97	2102.18

19

3¾% BLENDED MONTHLY PAYMENTS
AMORTIZATION IN YEARS

Amount	25	26	29	30	35	40	45	50
25	.13	.13	.12	.12	.11	.11	.10	.10
50	.26	.26	.24	.24	.22	.21	.20	.19
100	.52	.51	.48	.47	.43	.41	.39	.37
200	1.03	1.01	.95	.93	.86	.81	.77	.74
300	1.54	1.51	1.42	1.39	1.28	1.21	1.15	1.11
400	2.06	2.01	1.89	1.85	1.71	1.61	1.53	1.47
500	2.57	2.51	2.36	2.31	2.14	2.01	1.91	1.84
600	3.08	3.01	2.83	2.77	2.56	2.41	2.30	2.21
700	3.59	3.51	3.30	3.24	2.99	2.81	2.68	2.58
800	4.11	4.01	3.77	3.70	3.41	3.21	3.06	2.94
900	4.62	4.51	4.24	4.16	3.84	3.61	3.44	3.31
1000	5.13	5.01	4.71	4.62	4.27	4.01	3.82	3.68
2000	10.26	10.02	9.41	9.23	8.53	8.02	7.64	7.35
3000	15.38	15.02	14.11	13.85	12.79	12.03	11.46	11.03
4000	20.51	20.03	18.81	18.46	17.05	16.04	15.28	14.70
5000	25.63	25.04	23.51	23.08	21.31	20.04	19.10	18.38
6000	30.76	30.04	28.21	27.69	25.58	24.05	22.91	22.05
7000	35.88	35.05	32.92	32.31	29.84	28.06	26.73	25.72
8000	41.01	40.06	37.62	36.92	34.10	32.07	30.55	29.40
9000	46.14	45.06	42.32	41.54	38.36	36.07	34.37	33.07
10000	51.26	50.07	47.02	46.15	42.62	40.08	38.19	36.75
20000	102.52	100.13	94.04	92.30	85.24	80.16	76.37	73.49
30000	153.77	150.20	141.05	138.45	127.86	120.23	114.55	110.23
40000	205.03	200.26	188.07	184.59	170.48	160.31	152.74	146.97
50000	256.28	250.32	235.09	230.74	213.10	200.38	190.92	183.71
60000	307.54	300.39	282.10	276.89	255.72	240.46	229.10	220.46
70000	358.79	350.45	329.12	323.04	298.34	280.54	267.29	257.20
80000	410.05	400.51	376.13	369.18	340.96	320.61	305.47	293.94
90000	461.31	450.58	423.15	415.33	383.58	360.69	343.65	330.68
100000	512.56	500.64	470.17	461.48	426.20	400.76	381.83	367.42
110000	563.82	550.70	517.18	507.63	468.82	440.84	420.02	404.17
120000	615.07	600.77	564.20	553.77	511.44	480.91	458.20	440.91
130000	666.33	650.83	611.22	599.92	554.06	520.99	496.38	477.65
140000	717.58	700.89	658.23	646.07	596.68	561.07	534.57	514.39
150000	768.84	750.96	705.25	692.22	639.30	601.14	572.75	551.13
160000	820.09	801.02	752.26	738.36	681.92	641.22	610.93	587.87
170000	871.35	851.08	799.28	784.51	724.54	681.30	649.12	624.62
180000	922.61	901.15	846.30	830.66	767.16	721.37	687.30	661.36
190000	973.86	951.21	893.31	876.80	809.78	761.45	725.48	698.10
200000	1025.12	1001.27	940.33	922.95	852.40	801.52	763.66	734.84
210000	1076.37	1051.34	987.34	969.10	895.02	841.60	801.85	771.58
220000	1127.63	1101.40	1034.36	1015.25	937.64	881.67	840.03	808.33
230000	1178.88	1151.46	1081.38	1061.39	980.26	921.75	878.21	845.07
240000	1230.14	1201.53	1128.39	1107.54	1022.88	961.82	916.40	881.81
250000	1281.39	1251.59	1175.41	1153.69	1065.50	1001.90	954.58	918.55
260000	1332.65	1301.65	1222.43	1199.84	1108.12	1041.98	992.76	955.29
270000	1383.91	1351.72	1269.44	1245.98	1150.74	1082.05	1030.95	992.03
280000	1435.16	1401.78	1316.46	1292.13	1193.36	1122.13	1069.13	1028.78
290000	1486.42	1451.84	1363.47	1338.28	1235.98	1162.20	1107.31	1065.52
300000	1537.67	1501.91	1410.49	1384.43	1278.60	1202.28	1145.49	1102.26
310000	1588.93	1551.97	1457.51	1430.57	1321.22	1242.35	1183.68	1139.00
320000	1640.18	1602.03	1504.52	1476.72	1363.84	1282.43	1221.86	1175.74
330000	1691.44	1652.10	1551.54	1522.87	1406.46	1322.51	1260.04	1212.49
340000	1742.70	1702.16	1598.56	1569.01	1449.08	1362.58	1298.23	1249.23
350000	1793.95	1752.22	1645.57	1615.16	1491.70	1402.66	1336.41	1285.97
360000	1845.21	1802.29	1692.59	1661.31	1534.32	1442.73	1374.59	1322.71
370000	1896.46	1852.35	1739.60	1707.46	1576.94	1482.81	1412.78	1359.45
380000	1947.72	1902.41	1786.62	1753.60	1619.56	1522.89	1450.96	1396.19
390000	1998.97	1952.48	1833.64	1799.75	1662.18	1562.96	1489.14	1432.94
400000	2050.23	2002.54	1880.65	1845.90	1704.80	1603.04	1527.32	1469.68

BLENDED MONTHLY PAYMENTS

AMORTIZATION IN YEARS

4%

Amount	1	2	3	4	5	6	7	8
25	2.13	1.09	.74	.57	.47	.40	.35	.31
50	4.26	2.18	1.48	1.13	.93	.79	.69	.61
100	8.52	4.35	2.96	2.26	1.85	1.57	1.37	1.22
200	17.03	8.69	5.91	4.52	3.69	3.13	2.74	2.44
300	25.55	13.03	8.86	6.77	5.53	4.69	4.10	3.66
400	34.06	17.37	11.81	9.03	7.37	6.26	5.47	4.87
500	42.57	21.71	14.76	11.29	9.21	7.82	6.83	6.09
600	51.09	26.05	17.71	13.54	11.05	9.38	8.20	7.31
700	59.60	30.39	20.66	15.80	12.89	10.95	9.56	8.53
800	68.11	34.73	23.61	18.06	14.73	12.51	10.93	9.74
900	76.63	39.07	26.56	20.31	16.57	14.07	12.29	10.96
1000	85.14	43.42	29.51	22.57	18.41	15.64	13.66	12.18
2000	170.27	86.83	59.02	45.13	36.81	31.27	27.31	24.35
3000	255.41	130.24	88.53	67.70	55.21	46.90	40.97	36.53
4000	340.54	173.65	118.04	90.26	73.61	62.53	54.62	48.70
5000	425.68	217.06	147.55	112.83	92.01	78.16	68.27	60.87
6000	510.81	260.47	177.06	135.39	110.41	93.79	81.93	73.05
7000	595.95	303.88	206.57	157.96	128.82	109.42	95.58	85.22
8000	681.08	347.29	236.08	180.52	147.22	125.05	109.23	97.40
9000	766.22	390.70	265.59	203.08	165.62	140.68	122.89	109.57
10000	851.35	434.11	295.10	225.65	184.02	156.31	136.54	121.74
20000	1702.70	868.21	590.19	451.29	368.04	312.61	273.08	243.48
30000	2554.05	1302.31	885.29	676.93	552.05	468.91	409.61	365.22
40000	3405.40	1736.42	1180.38	902.58	736.07	625.21	546.15	486.96
50000	4256.75	2170.52	1475.47	1128.22	920.09	781.51	682.69	608.70
60000	5108.10	2604.62	1770.57	1353.86	1104.10	937.82	819.22	730.44
70000	5959.45	3038.72	2065.66	1579.51	1288.12	1094.12	955.76	852.18
80000	6810.79	3472.83	2360.75	1805.15	1472.14	1250.42	1092.30	973.92
90000	7662.14	3906.93	2655.85	2030.79	1656.15	1406.72	1228.83	1095.66
100000	8513.49	4341.03	2950.94	2256.44	1840.17	1563.02	1365.37	1217.40
110000	9364.84	4775.13	3246.03	2482.08	2024.19	1719.33	1501.91	1339.14
120000	10216.19	5209.24	3541.13	2707.72	2208.20	1875.63	1638.44	1460.88
130000	11067.54	5643.34	3836.22	2933.37	2392.22	2031.93	1774.98	1582.62
140000	11918.89	6077.44	4131.31	3159.01	2576.24	2188.23	1911.52	1704.36
150000	12770.23	6511.54	4426.41	3384.65	2760.25	2344.53	2048.05	1826.10
160000	13621.58	6945.65	4721.50	3610.30	2944.27	2500.83	2184.59	1947.84
170000	14472.93	7379.75	5016.59	3835.94	3128.29	2657.14	2321.13	2069.58
180000	15324.28	7813.85	5311.69	4061.58	3312.30	2813.44	2457.66	2191.32
190000	16175.63	8247.96	5606.78	4287.23	3496.32	2969.74	2594.20	2313.06
200000	17026.98	8682.06	5901.87	4512.87	3680.34	3126.04	2730.74	2434.80
210000	17878.33	9116.16	6196.97	4738.51	3864.35	3282.34	2867.27	2556.54
220000	18729.67	9550.26	6492.06	4964.16	4048.37	3438.65	3003.81	2678.28
230000	19581.02	9984.37	6787.15	5189.80	4232.39	3594.95	3140.35	2800.02
240000	20432.37	10418.47	7082.25	5415.44	4416.40	3751.25	3276.88	2921.76
250000	21283.72	10852.57	7377.34	5641.09	4600.42	3907.55	3413.42	3043.50
260000	22135.07	11286.67	7672.43	5866.73	4784.44	4063.85	3549.95	3165.24
270000	22986.42	11720.78	7967.53	6092.37	4968.45	4220.15	3686.49	3286.97
280000	23837.77	12154.88	8262.62	6318.01	5152.47	4376.46	3823.03	3408.71
290000	24689.11	12588.98	8557.71	6543.66	5336.49	4532.76	3959.56	3530.45
300000	25540.46	13023.08	8852.81	6769.30	5520.50	4689.06	4096.10	3652.19
310000	26391.81	13457.19	9147.90	6994.94	5704.52	4845.36	4232.64	3773.93
320000	27243.16	13891.29	9442.99	7220.59	5888.54	5001.66	4369.17	3895.67
330000	28094.51	14325.39	9738.09	7446.23	6072.55	5157.97	4505.71	4017.41
340000	28945.86	14759.50	10033.18	7671.87	6256.57	5314.27	4642.25	4139.15
350000	29797.21	15193.60	10328.27	7897.52	6440.59	5470.57	4778.78	4260.89
360000	30648.55	15627.70	10623.37	8123.16	6624.60	5626.87	4915.32	4382.63
370000	31499.90	16061.80	10918.46	8348.80	6808.62	5783.17	5051.86	4504.37
380000	32351.25	16495.91	11213.55	8574.45	6992.64	5939.47	5188.39	4626.11
390000	33202.60	16930.01	11508.65	8800.09	7176.65	6095.78	5324.93	4747.85
400000	34053.95	17364.11	11803.74	9025.73	7360.67	6252.08	5461.47	4869.59

21

4% BLENDED MONTHLY PAYMENTS
AMORTIZATION IN YEARS

Amount	9	10	11	12	13	14	15	16
25	.28	.26	.24	.22	.21	.20	.19	.18
50	.56	.51	.47	.44	.42	.39	.37	.36
100	1.11	1.02	.94	.88	.83	.78	.74	.71
200	2.21	2.03	1.88	1.75	1.65	1.56	1.48	1.41
300	3.31	3.04	2.81	2.63	2.47	2.34	2.22	2.12
400	4.42	4.05	3.75	3.50	3.29	3.11	2.96	2.82
500	5.52	5.06	4.69	4.37	4.11	3.89	3.70	3.53
600	6.62	6.07	5.62	5.25	4.93	4.67	4.43	4.23
700	7.72	7.08	6.56	6.12	5.76	5.44	5.17	4.94
800	8.83	8.09	7.49	7.00	6.58	6.22	5.91	5.64
900	9.93	9.10	8.43	7.87	7.40	7.00	6.65	6.34
1000	11.03	10.11	9.37	8.74	8.22	7.77	7.39	7.05
2000	22.06	20.22	18.73	17.48	16.44	15.54	14.77	14.09
3000	33.08	30.33	28.09	26.22	24.65	23.31	22.15	21.13
4000	44.11	40.44	37.45	34.96	32.87	31.07	29.53	28.18
5000	55.13	50.55	46.81	43.70	41.08	38.84	36.91	35.22
6000	66.16	60.66	56.17	52.44	49.30	46.61	44.29	42.26
7000	77.18	70.77	65.53	61.18	57.51	54.37	51.67	49.31
8000	88.21	80.88	74.89	69.92	65.73	62.14	59.05	56.35
9000	99.23	90.98	84.25	78.66	73.94	69.91	66.43	63.39
10000	110.26	101.09	93.61	87.40	82.16	77.68	73.81	70.44
20000	220.51	202.18	187.22	174.79	164.31	155.35	147.61	140.87
30000	330.77	303.27	280.83	262.18	246.46	233.02	221.42	211.30
40000	441.02	404.36	374.44	349.58	328.61	310.69	295.22	281.74
50000	551.28	505.45	468.05	436.97	410.76	388.36	369.02	352.17
60000	661.53	606.54	561.66	524.36	492.91	466.03	442.83	422.60
70000	771.79	707.63	655.27	611.76	575.06	543.70	516.63	493.04
80000	882.04	808.71	748.87	699.15	657.21	621.38	590.44	563.47
90000	992.30	909.80	842.48	786.54	739.36	699.05	664.24	633.90
100000	1102.55	1010.89	936.09	873.94	821.51	776.72	738.04	704.33
110000	1212.81	1111.98	1029.70	961.33	903.66	854.39	811.85	774.77
120000	1323.06	1213.07	1123.31	1048.72	985.81	932.06	885.65	845.20
130000	1433.32	1314.16	1216.92	1136.11	1067.96	1009.73	959.46	915.63
140000	1543.57	1415.25	1310.53	1223.51	1150.11	1087.40	1033.26	986.07
150000	1653.83	1516.34	1404.13	1310.90	1232.26	1165.08	1107.06	1056.50
160000	1764.08	1617.42	1497.74	1398.29	1314.41	1242.75	1180.87	1126.93
170000	1874.34	1718.51	1591.35	1485.69	1396.56	1320.42	1254.67	1197.37
180000	1984.59	1819.60	1684.96	1573.08	1478.71	1398.09	1328.47	1267.80
190000	2094.85	1920.69	1778.57	1660.47	1560.86	1475.76	1402.28	1338.23
200000	2205.10	2021.78	1872.18	1747.87	1643.01	1553.43	1476.08	1408.66
210000	2315.36	2122.87	1965.79	1835.26	1725.16	1631.10	1549.89	1479.10
220000	2425.61	2223.96	2059.39	1922.65	1807.31	1708.77	1623.69	1549.53
230000	2535.87	2325.05	2153.00	2010.04	1889.46	1786.45	1697.49	1619.96
240000	2646.12	2426.13	2246.61	2097.44	1971.61	1864.12	1771.30	1690.40
250000	2756.38	2527.22	2340.22	2184.83	2053.76	1941.79	1845.10	1760.83
260000	2866.63	2628.31	2433.83	2272.22	2135.91	2019.46	1918.91	1831.26
270000	2976.89	2729.40	2527.44	2359.62	2218.06	2097.13	1992.71	1901.70
280000	3087.14	2830.49	2621.05	2447.01	2300.21	2174.80	2066.51	1972.13
290000	3197.40	2931.58	2714.65	2534.40	2382.36	2252.47	2140.32	2042.56
300000	3307.65	3032.67	2808.26	2621.80	2464.51	2330.15	2214.12	2112.99
310000	3417.91	3133.75	2901.87	2709.19	2546.66	2407.82	2287.93	2183.43
320000	3528.16	3234.84	2995.48	2796.58	2628.81	2485.49	2361.73	2253.86
330000	3638.42	3335.93	3089.09	2883.97	2710.96	2563.16	2435.53	2324.29
340000	3748.67	3437.02	3182.70	2971.37	2793.11	2640.83	2509.34	2394.73
350000	3858.93	3538.11	3276.31	3058.76	2875.26	2718.50	2583.14	2465.16
360000	3969.18	3639.20	3369.91	3146.15	2957.41	2796.17	2656.94	2535.59
370000	4079.44	3740.29	3463.52	3233.55	3039.56	2873.84	2730.75	2606.03
380000	4189.69	3841.38	3557.13	3320.94	3121.71	2951.52	2804.55	2676.46
390000	4299.95	3942.46	3650.74	3408.33	3203.86	3029.19	2878.36	2746.89
400000	4410.20	4043.55	3744.35	3495.73	3286.01	3106.86	2952.16	2817.32

22

BLENDED MONTHLY PAYMENTS
AMORTIZATION IN YEARS

4%

Amount	17	18	19	20	21	22	23	24
25	.17	.17	.16	.16	.15	.15	.14	.14
50	.34	.33	.32	.31	.30	.29	.28	.27
100	.68	.65	.63	.61	.59	.57	.56	.54
200	1.35	1.30	1.26	1.21	1.18	1.14	1.11	1.08
300	2.03	1.95	1.88	1.82	1.76	1.71	1.66	1.62
400	2.70	2.60	2.51	2.42	2.35	2.28	2.22	2.16
500	3.38	3.25	3.13	3.03	2.93	2.85	2.77	2.70
600	4.05	3.90	3.76	3.63	3.52	3.42	3.32	3.24
700	4.73	4.54	4.38	4.23	4.10	3.98	3.88	3.78
800	5.40	5.19	5.01	4.84	4.69	4.55	4.43	4.32
900	6.08	5.84	5.63	5.44	5.27	5.12	4.98	4.86
1000	6.75	6.49	6.26	6.05	5.86	5.69	5.53	5.39
2000	13.50	12.97	12.51	12.09	11.71	11.37	11.06	10.78
3000	20.25	19.46	18.76	18.13	17.57	17.06	16.59	16.17
4000	26.99	25.94	25.01	24.17	23.42	22.74	22.12	21.56
5000	33.74	32.43	31.26	30.22	29.28	28.43	27.65	26.95
6000	40.49	38.91	37.51	36.26	35.13	34.11	33.18	32.34
7000	47.23	45.40	43.77	42.30	40.98	39.79	38.71	37.73
8000	53.98	51.88	50.02	48.34	46.84	45.48	44.24	43.12
9000	60.73	58.37	56.27	54.39	52.69	51.16	49.77	48.51
10000	67.48	64.85	62.52	60.43	58.55	56.85	55.30	53.89
20000	134.95	129.70	125.04	120.85	117.09	113.69	110.60	107.78
30000	202.42	194.55	187.55	181.28	175.63	170.53	165.89	161.67
40000	269.89	259.40	250.07	241.70	234.18	227.37	221.19	215.56
50000	337.36	324.25	312.58	302.13	292.72	284.21	276.49	269.45
60000	404.83	389.10	375.10	362.55	351.26	341.05	331.78	323.34
70000	472.30	453.95	437.61	422.98	409.80	397.89	387.08	377.23
80000	539.77	518.80	500.13	483.40	468.35	454.74	442.38	431.12
90000	607.24	583.65	562.64	543.83	526.89	511.58	497.67	485.01
100000	674.72	648.50	625.16	604.25	585.43	568.42	552.97	538.90
110000	742.19	713.35	687.67	664.68	643.98	625.26	608.27	592.78
120000	809.66	778.20	750.19	725.10	702.52	682.10	663.56	646.67
130000	877.13	843.05	812.70	785.53	761.06	738.94	718.86	700.56
140000	944.60	907.90	875.22	845.95	819.60	795.78	774.16	754.45
150000	1012.07	972.75	937.73	906.37	878.15	852.63	829.45	808.34
160000	1079.54	1037.60	1000.25	966.80	936.69	909.47	884.75	862.23
170000	1147.01	1102.45	1062.77	1027.22	995.23	966.31	940.05	916.12
180000	1214.48	1167.30	1125.28	1087.65	1053.78	1023.15	995.34	970.01
190000	1281.95	1232.15	1187.80	1148.07	1112.32	1079.99	1050.64	1023.90
200000	1349.43	1297.00	1250.31	1208.50	1170.86	1136.83	1105.94	1077.79
210000	1416.90	1361.85	1312.83	1268.92	1229.40	1193.67	1161.23	1131.67
220000	1484.37	1426.70	1375.34	1329.35	1287.95	1250.52	1216.53	1185.56
230000	1551.84	1491.55	1437.86	1389.77	1346.49	1307.36	1271.83	1239.45
240000	1619.31	1556.40	1500.37	1450.20	1405.03	1364.20	1327.12	1293.34
250000	1686.78	1621.25	1562.89	1510.62	1463.58	1421.04	1382.42	1347.23
260000	1754.25	1686.10	1625.40	1571.05	1522.12	1477.88	1437.72	1401.12
270000	1821.72	1750.95	1687.92	1631.47	1580.66	1534.72	1493.01	1455.01
280000	1889.19	1815.80	1750.43	1691.90	1639.20	1591.56	1548.31	1508.90
290000	1956.66	1880.65	1812.95	1752.32	1697.75	1648.40	1603.61	1562.79
300000	2024.14	1945.50	1875.46	1812.74	1756.29	1705.25	1658.90	1616.68
310000	2091.61	2010.35	1937.98	1873.17	1814.83	1762.09	1714.20	1670.57
320000	2159.08	2075.20	2000.50	1933.59	1873.38	1818.93	1769.50	1724.45
330000	2226.55	2140.05	2063.01	1994.02	1931.92	1875.77	1824.79	1778.34
340000	2294.02	2204.90	2125.53	2054.44	1990.46	1932.61	1880.09	1832.23
350000	2361.49	2269.75	2188.04	2114.87	2049.00	1989.45	1935.39	1886.12
360000	2428.96	2334.60	2250.56	2175.29	2107.55	2046.29	1990.68	1940.01
370000	2496.43	2399.45	2313.07	2235.72	2166.09	2103.14	2045.98	1993.90
380000	2563.90	2464.30	2375.59	2296.14	2224.63	2159.98	2101.28	2047.79
390000	2631.38	2529.15	2438.10	2356.57	2283.18	2216.82	2156.57	2101.68
400000	2698.85	2594.00	2500.62	2416.99	2341.72	2273.66	2211.87	2155.57

4% BLENDED MONTHLY PAYMENTS
AMORTIZATION IN YEARS

Amount	25	26	29	30	35	40	45	50
25	.14	.13	.13	.12	.12	.11	.10	.10
50	.27	.26	.25	.24	.23	.21	.20	.20
100	.53	.52	.49	.48	.45	.42	.40	.39
200	1.06	1.03	.97	.96	.89	.84	.80	.77
300	1.58	1.55	1.46	1.43	1.33	1.25	1.20	1.16
400	2.11	2.06	1.94	1.91	1.77	1.67	1.59	1.54
500	2.64	2.58	2.43	2.38	2.21	2.08	1.99	1.92
600	3.16	3.09	2.91	2.86	2.65	2.50	2.39	2.31
700	3.69	3.60	3.39	3.33	3.09	2.92	2.79	2.69
800	4.21	4.12	3.88	3.81	3.53	3.33	3.18	3.07
900	4.74	4.63	4.36	4.28	3.97	3.75	3.58	3.46
1000	5.27	5.15	4.85	4.76	4.41	4.16	3.98	3.84
2000	10.53	10.29	9.69	9.52	8.82	8.32	7.95	7.68
3000	15.79	15.43	14.53	14.27	13.23	12.48	11.93	11.51
4000	21.05	20.57	19.37	19.03	17.64	16.64	15.90	15.35
5000	26.31	25.72	24.21	23.78	22.05	20.80	19.88	19.18
6000	31.57	30.86	29.05	28.54	26.45	24.96	23.85	23.02
7000	36.83	36.00	33.89	33.29	30.86	29.12	27.83	26.85
8000	42.09	41.14	38.73	38.05	35.27	33.28	31.80	30.69
9000	47.35	46.28	43.57	42.80	39.68	37.44	35.78	34.52
10000	52.61	51.43	48.41	47.56	44.09	41.59	39.75	38.36
20000	105.21	102.85	96.82	95.11	88.17	83.18	79.50	76.71
30000	157.81	154.27	145.23	142.66	132.25	124.77	119.25	115.06
40000	210.41	205.69	193.64	190.21	176.33	166.36	158.99	153.42
50000	263.02	257.11	242.05	237.76	220.41	207.95	198.74	191.77
60000	315.62	308.53	290.46	285.32	264.49	249.54	238.49	230.12
70000	368.22	359.96	338.87	332.87	308.57	291.13	278.23	268.48
80000	420.82	411.38	387.28	380.42	352.65	332.72	317.98	306.83
90000	473.42	462.80	435.69	427.97	396.73	374.31	357.73	345.18
100000	526.03	514.22	484.10	475.52	440.81	415.90	397.47	383.53
110000	578.63	565.64	532.51	523.08	484.89	457.49	437.22	421.89
120000	631.23	617.06	580.92	570.63	528.97	499.08	476.97	460.24
130000	683.83	668.49	629.33	618.18	573.05	540.67	516.71	498.59
140000	736.43	719.91	677.73	665.73	617.13	582.25	556.46	536.95
150000	789.04	771.33	726.14	713.28	661.21	623.84	596.21	575.30
160000	841.64	822.75	774.55	760.83	705.29	665.43	635.95	613.65
170000	894.24	874.17	822.96	808.39	749.37	707.02	675.70	652.00
180000	946.84	925.59	871.37	855.94	793.45	748.61	715.45	690.36
190000	999.44	977.02	919.78	903.49	837.53	790.20	755.19	728.71
200000	1052.05	1028.44	968.19	951.04	881.61	831.79	794.94	767.06
210000	1104.65	1079.86	1016.60	998.59	925.69	873.38	834.69	805.42
220000	1157.25	1131.28	1065.01	1046.15	969.77	914.97	874.43	843.77
230000	1209.85	1182.70	1113.42	1093.70	1013.85	956.56	914.18	882.12
240000	1262.45	1234.12	1161.83	1141.25	1057.93	998.15	953.93	920.47
250000	1315.06	1285.55	1210.24	1188.80	1102.01	1039.74	993.67	958.83
260000	1367.66	1336.97	1258.65	1236.35	1146.09	1081.33	1033.42	997.18
270000	1420.26	1388.39	1307.06	1283.91	1190.17	1122.92	1073.17	1035.53
280000	1472.86	1439.81	1355.46	1331.46	1234.25	1164.50	1112.91	1073.89
290000	1525.46	1491.23	1403.87	1379.01	1278.33	1206.09	1152.66	1112.24
300000	1578.07	1542.65	1452.28	1426.56	1322.41	1247.68	1192.41	1150.59
310000	1630.67	1594.07	1500.69	1474.11	1366.49	1289.27	1232.15	1188.94
320000	1683.27	1645.50	1549.10	1521.66	1410.57	1330.86	1271.90	1227.30
330000	1735.87	1696.92	1597.51	1569.22	1454.65	1372.45	1311.65	1265.65
340000	1788.47	1748.34	1645.92	1616.77	1498.73	1414.04	1351.39	1304.00
350000	1841.08	1799.76	1694.33	1664.32	1542.81	1455.63	1391.14	1342.36
360000	1893.68	1851.18	1742.74	1711.87	1586.89	1497.22	1430.89	1380.71
370000	1946.28	1902.60	1791.15	1759.42	1630.97	1538.81	1470.63	1419.06
380000	1998.88	1954.03	1839.56	1806.98	1675.05	1580.40	1510.38	1457.41
390000	2051.48	2005.45	1887.97	1854.53	1719.13	1621.99	1550.13	1495.77
400000	2104.09	2056.87	1936.38	1902.08	1763.21	1663.58	1589.87	1534.12

BLENDED MONTHLY PAYMENTS 4¼%

AMORTIZATION IN YEARS

Amount	1	2	3	4	5	6	7	8
25	2.14	1.09	.75	.57	.47	.40	.35	.31
50	4.27	2.18	1.49	1.14	.93	.79	.69	.62
100	8.53	4.36	2.97	2.27	1.86	1.58	1.38	1.23
200	17.05	8.71	5.93	4.54	3.71	3.15	2.76	2.46
300	25.58	13.06	8.89	6.81	5.56	4.73	4.14	3.69
400	34.10	17.41	11.85	9.07	7.41	6.30	5.51	4.92
500	42.63	21.76	14.81	11.34	9.26	7.88	6.89	6.15
600	51.15	26.12	17.78	13.61	11.11	9.45	8.27	7.38
700	59.68	30.47	20.74	15.88	12.96	11.02	9.64	8.61
800	68.20	34.82	23.70	18.14	14.82	12.60	11.02	9.84
900	76.73	39.17	26.66	20.41	16.67	14.17	12.40	11.06
1000	85.25	43.52	29.62	22.68	18.52	15.75	13.77	12.29
2000	170.50	87.04	59.24	45.35	37.03	31.49	27.54	24.58
3000	255.75	130.56	88.86	68.03	55.54	47.23	41.31	36.87
4000	340.99	174.08	118.48	90.70	74.06	62.97	55.07	49.16
5000	426.24	217.60	148.10	113.38	92.57	78.72	68.84	61.45
6000	511.49	261.12	177.72	136.05	111.08	94.46	82.61	73.74
7000	596.74	304.64	207.34	158.73	129.59	110.20	96.37	86.02
8000	681.98	348.16	236.96	181.40	148.11	125.94	110.14	98.31
9000	767.23	391.68	266.57	204.07	166.62	141.69	123.91	110.60
10000	852.48	435.20	296.19	226.75	185.13	157.43	137.68	122.89
20000	1704.95	870.40	592.38	453.49	370.26	314.85	275.35	245.78
30000	2557.42	1305.60	888.57	680.24	555.39	472.28	413.02	368.66
40000	3409.89	1740.79	1184.76	906.98	740.51	629.70	550.69	491.55
50000	4262.36	2175.99	1480.94	1133.73	925.64	787.12	688.36	614.43
60000	5114.84	2611.19	1777.13	1360.47	1110.77	944.55	826.03	737.32
70000	5967.31	3046.39	2073.32	1587.21	1295.90	1101.97	963.70	860.20
80000	6819.78	3481.58	2369.51	1813.96	1481.02	1259.39	1101.37	983.09
90000	7672.25	3916.78	2665.69	2040.70	1666.15	1416.82	1239.04	1105.97
100000	8524.72	4351.98	2961.88	2267.45	1851.28	1574.24	1376.71	1228.86
110000	9377.20	4787.17	3258.07	2494.19	2036.41	1731.66	1514.38	1351.74
120000	10229.67	5222.37	3554.26	2720.94	2221.53	1889.09	1652.05	1474.63
130000	11082.14	5657.57	3850.44	2947.68	2406.66	2046.51	1789.72	1597.51
140000	11934.61	6092.77	4146.63	3174.42	2591.79	2203.93	1927.39	1720.40
150000	12787.08	6527.96	4442.82	3401.17	2776.91	2361.36	2065.06	1843.29
160000	13639.55	6963.16	4739.01	3627.91	2962.04	2518.78	2202.73	1966.17
170000	14492.03	7398.36	5035.19	3854.66	3147.17	2676.20	2340.40	2089.06
180000	15344.50	7833.56	5331.38	4081.40	3332.30	2833.63	2478.07	2211.94
190000	16196.97	8268.75	5627.57	4308.15	3517.42	2991.05	2615.74	2334.83
200000	17049.44	8703.95	5923.76	4534.89	3702.55	3148.48	2753.41	2457.71
210000	17901.91	9139.15	6219.95	4761.63	3887.68	3305.90	2891.08	2580.60
220000	18754.39	9574.34	6516.13	4988.38	4072.81	3463.32	3028.75	2703.48
230000	19606.86	10009.54	6812.32	5215.12	4257.93	3620.75	3166.42	2826.37
240000	20459.33	10444.74	7108.51	5441.87	4443.06	3778.17	3304.09	2949.25
250000	21311.80	10879.94	7404.70	5668.61	4628.19	3935.59	3441.76	3072.14
260000	22164.27	11315.13	7700.88	5895.36	4813.32	4093.02	3579.43	3195.02
270000	23016.75	11750.33	7997.07	6122.10	4998.44	4250.44	3717.10	3317.91
280000	23869.22	12185.53	8293.26	6348.84	5183.57	4407.86	3854.77	3440.80
290000	24721.69	12620.72	8589.45	6575.59	5368.70	4565.29	3992.44	3563.68
300000	25574.16	13055.92	8885.63	6802.33	5553.82	4722.71	4130.11	3686.57
310000	26426.63	13491.12	9181.82	7029.08	5738.95	4880.13	4267.78	3809.45
320000	27279.10	13926.32	9478.01	7255.82	5924.08	5037.56	4405.45	3932.34
330000	28131.58	14361.51	9774.20	7482.57	6109.21	5194.98	4543.12	4055.22
340000	28984.05	14796.71	10070.38	7709.31	6294.33	5352.40	4680.79	4178.11
350000	29836.52	15231.91	10366.57	7936.05	6479.46	5509.83	4818.46	4300.99
360000	30688.99	15667.11	10662.76	8162.80	6664.59	5667.25	4956.13	4423.88
370000	31541.46	16102.30	10958.95	8389.54	6849.72	5824.68	5093.80	4546.76
380000	32393.94	16537.50	11255.14	8616.29	7034.84	5982.10	5231.47	4669.65
390000	33246.41	16972.70	11551.32	8843.03	7219.97	6139.52	5369.14	4792.53
400000	34098.88	17407.89	11847.51	9069.78	7405.10	6296.95	5506.81	4915.42

25

4¼% BLENDED MONTHLY PAYMENTS
AMORTIZATION IN YEARS

Amount	9	10	11	12	13	14	15	16
25	.28	.26	.24	.23	.21	.20	.19	.18
50	.56	.52	.48	.45	.42	.40	.38	.36
100	1.12	1.03	.95	.89	.84	.79	.76	.72
200	2.23	2.05	1.90	1.78	1.67	1.58	1.51	1.44
300	3.35	3.07	2.85	2.66	2.51	2.37	2.26	2.16
400	4.46	4.10	3.80	3.55	3.34	3.16	3.01	2.87
500	5.58	5.12	4.74	4.43	4.17	3.95	3.76	3.59
600	6.69	6.14	5.69	5.32	5.01	4.74	4.51	4.31
700	7.80	7.16	6.64	6.21	5.84	5.53	5.26	5.02
800	8.92	8.19	7.59	7.09	6.67	6.32	6.01	5.74
900	10.03	9.21	8.54	7.98	7.51	7.11	6.76	6.46
1000	11.15	10.23	9.48	8.86	8.34	7.89	7.51	7.17
2000	22.29	20.46	18.96	17.72	16.68	15.78	15.01	14.34
3000	33.43	30.68	28.44	26.58	25.01	23.67	22.52	21.51
4000	44.57	40.91	37.92	35.44	33.35	31.56	30.02	28.68
5000	55.71	51.13	47.40	44.30	41.69	39.45	37.52	35.85
6000	66.85	61.36	56.88	53.16	50.02	47.34	45.03	43.01
7000	77.99	71.59	66.36	62.02	58.36	55.23	52.53	50.18
8000	89.14	81.81	75.84	70.88	66.69	63.12	60.04	57.35
9000	100.28	92.04	85.32	79.74	75.03	71.01	67.54	64.52
10000	111.42	102.26	94.80	88.60	83.37	78.90	75.04	71.69
20000	222.83	204.52	189.59	177.19	166.73	157.79	150.08	143.37
30000	334.24	306.78	284.38	265.78	250.09	236.69	225.12	215.05
40000	445.66	409.04	379.18	354.37	333.45	315.58	300.16	286.73
50000	557.07	511.30	473.97	442.96	416.81	394.48	375.20	358.42
60000	668.48	613.56	568.76	531.55	500.17	473.37	450.24	430.10
70000	779.90	715.82	663.55	620.14	583.53	552.27	525.28	501.78
80000	891.31	818.08	758.35	708.73	666.89	631.16	600.32	573.46
90000	1002.72	920.34	853.14	797.32	750.25	710.05	675.36	645.14
100000	1114.14	1022.60	947.93	885.91	833.61	788.95	750.40	716.83
110000	1225.55	1124.86	1042.72	974.50	916.97	867.84	825.44	788.51
120000	1336.96	1227.12	1137.52	1063.09	1000.33	946.74	900.48	860.19
130000	1448.38	1329.38	1232.31	1151.68	1083.69	1025.63	975.52	931.87
140000	1559.79	1431.64	1327.10	1240.27	1167.05	1104.53	1050.56	1003.55
150000	1671.20	1533.90	1421.89	1328.86	1250.41	1183.42	1125.60	1075.24
160000	1782.62	1636.16	1516.69	1417.45	1333.77	1262.32	1200.64	1146.92
170000	1894.03	1738.42	1611.48	1506.04	1417.13	1341.21	1275.68	1218.60
180000	2005.44	1840.68	1706.27	1594.63	1500.49	1420.10	1350.72	1290.28
190000	2116.86	1942.94	1801.06	1683.22	1583.85	1499.00	1425.76	1361.97
200000	2228.27	2045.20	1895.86	1771.81	1667.21	1577.89	1500.80	1433.65
210000	2339.68	2147.46	1990.65	1860.40	1750.57	1656.79	1575.84	1505.33
220000	2451.10	2249.72	2085.44	1948.99	1833.93	1735.68	1650.88	1577.01
230000	2562.51	2351.98	2180.23	2037.58	1917.29	1814.58	1725.92	1648.69
240000	2673.92	2454.24	2275.03	2126.17	2000.65	1893.47	1800.96	1720.38
250000	2785.34	2556.50	2369.82	2214.76	2084.01	1972.36	1876.00	1792.06
260000	2896.75	2658.76	2464.61	2303.35	2167.37	2051.26	1951.04	1863.74
270000	3008.16	2761.02	2559.41	2391.94	2250.73	2130.15	2026.08	1935.42
280000	3119.58	2863.28	2654.20	2480.53	2334.09	2209.05	2101.12	2007.10
290000	3230.99	2965.54	2748.99	2569.12	2417.45	2287.94	2176.16	2078.79
300000	3342.40	3067.80	2843.78	2657.71	2500.81	2366.84	2251.20	2150.47
310000	3453.82	3170.06	2938.58	2746.30	2584.17	2445.73	2326.24	2222.15
320000	3565.23	3272.32	3033.37	2834.89	2667.53	2524.63	2401.28	2293.83
330000	3676.64	3374.58	3128.16	2923.48	2750.89	2603.52	2476.32	2365.51
340000	3788.06	3476.84	3222.95	3012.07	2834.25	2682.41	2551.36	2437.20
350000	3899.47	3579.10	3317.75	3100.66	2917.61	2761.31	2626.40	2508.88
360000	4010.88	3681.36	3412.54	3189.25	3000.97	2840.20	2701.44	2580.56
370000	4122.30	3783.62	3507.33	3277.84	3084.33	2919.10	2776.48	2652.24
380000	4233.71	3885.88	3602.12	3366.43	3167.69	2997.99	2851.52	2723.93
390000	4345.12	3988.14	3696.92	3455.02	3251.05	3076.89	2926.56	2795.61
400000	4456.54	4090.40	3791.71	3543.61	3334.41	3155.78	3001.60	2867.29

BLENDED MONTHLY PAYMENTS 4¼%
AMORTIZATION IN YEARS

Amount	17	18	19	20	21	22	23	24
25	.18	.17	.16	.16	.15	.15	.15	.14
50	.35	.34	.32	.31	.30	.30	.29	.28
100	.69	.67	.64	.62	.60	.59	.57	.56
200	1.38	1.33	1.28	1.24	1.20	1.17	1.14	1.11
300	2.07	1.99	1.92	1.86	1.80	1.75	1.70	1.66
400	2.75	2.65	2.56	2.47	2.40	2.33	2.27	2.21
500	3.44	3.31	3.20	3.09	3.00	2.91	2.84	2.77
600	4.13	3.97	3.83	3.71	3.60	3.50	3.40	3.32
700	4.82	4.63	4.47	4.33	4.19	4.08	3.97	3.87
800	5.50	5.29	5.11	4.94	4.79	4.66	4.54	4.42
900	6.19	5.96	5.75	5.56	5.39	5.24	5.10	4.98
1000	6.88	6.62	6.39	6.18	5.99	5.82	5.67	5.53
2000	13.75	13.23	12.77	12.35	11.98	11.64	11.33	11.05
3000	20.62	19.84	19.15	18.52	17.96	17.46	17.00	16.58
4000	27.50	26.45	25.53	24.70	23.95	23.27	22.66	22.10
5000	34.37	33.07	31.91	30.87	29.93	29.09	28.32	27.63
6000	41.24	39.68	38.29	37.04	35.92	34.91	33.99	33.15
7000	48.12	46.29	44.67	43.21	41.90	40.72	39.65	38.67
8000	54.99	52.90	51.05	49.39	47.89	46.54	45.31	44.20
9000	61.86	59.52	57.43	55.56	53.88	52.36	50.98	49.72
10000	68.74	66.13	63.81	61.73	59.86	58.17	56.64	55.25
20000	137.47	132.25	127.61	123.46	119.72	116.34	113.28	110.49
30000	206.20	198.38	191.41	185.18	179.57	174.51	169.91	165.73
40000	274.94	264.50	255.22	246.91	239.43	232.68	226.55	220.97
50000	343.67	330.63	319.02	308.63	299.29	290.84	283.18	276.21
60000	412.40	396.75	382.82	370.36	359.14	349.01	339.82	331.45
70000	481.14	462.88	446.63	432.08	419.00	407.18	396.45	386.69
80000	549.87	529.00	510.43	493.81	478.86	465.35	453.09	441.93
90000	618.60	595.13	574.23	555.53	538.71	523.51	509.73	497.17
100000	687.34	661.25	638.04	617.26	598.57	581.68	566.36	552.41
110000	756.07	727.38	701.84	678.99	658.43	639.85	623.00	607.65
120000	824.80	793.50	765.64	740.71	718.28	698.02	679.63	662.89
130000	893.54	859.63	829.45	802.44	778.14	756.19	736.27	718.13
140000	962.27	925.75	893.25	864.16	838.00	814.35	792.90	773.37
150000	1031.00	991.88	957.05	925.89	897.85	872.52	849.54	828.61
160000	1099.74	1058.00	1020.86	987.61	957.71	930.69	906.18	883.85
170000	1168.47	1124.13	1084.66	1049.34	1017.56	988.86	962.81	939.09
180000	1237.20	1190.25	1148.46	1111.06	1077.42	1047.02	1019.45	994.34
190000	1305.93	1256.38	1212.27	1172.79	1137.28	1105.19	1076.08	1049.58
200000	1374.67	1322.50	1276.07	1234.51	1197.13	1163.36	1132.72	1104.82
210000	1443.40	1388.63	1339.87	1296.24	1256.99	1221.53	1189.35	1160.06
220000	1512.13	1454.75	1403.68	1357.97	1316.85	1279.69	1245.99	1215.30
230000	1580.87	1520.88	1467.48	1419.69	1376.70	1337.86	1302.62	1270.54
240000	1649.60	1587.00	1531.28	1481.42	1436.56	1396.03	1359.26	1325.78
250000	1718.33	1653.13	1595.09	1543.14	1496.42	1454.20	1415.90	1381.02
260000	1787.07	1719.25	1658.89	1604.87	1556.27	1512.37	1472.53	1436.26
270000	1855.80	1785.38	1722.69	1666.59	1616.13	1570.53	1529.17	1491.50
280000	1924.53	1851.50	1786.50	1728.32	1675.99	1628.70	1585.80	1546.74
290000	1993.27	1917.62	1850.30	1790.04	1735.84	1686.87	1642.44	1601.98
300000	2062.00	1983.75	1914.10	1851.77	1795.70	1745.04	1699.07	1657.22
310000	2130.73	2049.87	1977.91	1913.49	1855.56	1803.20	1755.71	1712.46
320000	2199.47	2116.00	2041.71	1975.22	1915.41	1861.37	1812.35	1767.70
330000	2268.20	2182.12	2105.51	2036.95	1975.27	1919.54	1868.98	1822.94
340000	2336.93	2248.25	2169.32	2098.67	2035.12	1977.71	1925.62	1878.18
350000	2405.66	2314.37	2233.12	2160.40	2094.98	2035.87	1982.25	1933.43
360000	2474.40	2380.50	2296.92	2222.12	2154.84	2094.04	2038.89	1988.67
370000	2543.13	2446.62	2360.73	2283.85	2214.69	2152.21	2095.52	2043.91
380000	2611.86	2512.75	2424.53	2345.57	2274.55	2210.38	2152.16	2099.15
390000	2680.60	2578.87	2488.33	2407.30	2334.41	2268.55	2208.79	2154.39
400000	2749.33	2645.00	2552.14	2469.02	2394.26	2326.71	2265.43	2209.63

4¼% BLENDED MONTHLY PAYMENTS
AMORTIZATION IN YEARS

Amount	25	26	29	30	35	40	45	50
25	.14	.14	.13	.13	.12	.11	.11	.10
50	.27	.27	.25	.25	.23	.22	.21	.20
100	.54	.53	.50	.49	.46	.44	.42	.40
200	1.08	1.06	1.00	.98	.92	.87	.83	.80
300	1.62	1.59	1.50	1.47	1.37	1.30	1.25	1.20
400	2.16	2.12	2.00	1.96	1.83	1.73	1.66	1.60
500	2.70	2.64	2.50	2.45	2.28	2.16	2.07	2.00
600	3.24	3.17	2.99	2.94	2.74	2.59	2.49	2.40
700	3.78	3.70	3.49	3.43	3.19	3.02	2.90	2.80
800	4.32	4.23	3.99	3.92	3.65	3.46	3.31	3.20
900	4.86	4.76	4.49	4.41	4.11	3.89	3.73	3.60
1000	5.40	5.28	4.99	4.90	4.56	4.32	4.14	4.00
2000	10.80	10.56	9.97	9.80	9.12	8.63	8.27	8.00
3000	16.19	15.84	14.95	14.70	13.67	12.94	12.41	12.00
4000	21.59	21.12	19.93	19.60	18.23	17.26	16.54	16.00
5000	26.99	26.40	24.92	24.49	22.79	21.57	20.67	20.00
6000	32.38	31.68	29.90	29.39	27.34	25.88	24.81	24.00
7000	37.78	36.96	34.88	34.29	31.90	30.19	28.94	28.00
8000	43.18	42.24	39.86	39.19	36.46	34.51	33.07	32.00
9000	48.57	47.52	44.84	44.08	41.01	38.82	37.21	36.00
10000	53.97	52.80	49.83	48.98	45.57	43.13	41.34	40.00
20000	107.94	105.60	99.65	97.96	91.13	86.26	82.68	79.99
30000	161.90	158.40	149.47	146.94	136.69	129.39	124.01	119.98
40000	215.87	211.20	199.29	195.91	182.26	172.51	165.35	159.97
50000	269.84	263.99	249.12	244.89	227.82	215.64	206.69	199.96
60000	323.80	316.79	298.94	293.87	273.38	258.77	248.02	239.95
70000	377.77	369.59	348.76	342.84	318.95	301.90	289.36	279.94
80000	431.73	422.39	398.58	391.82	364.51	345.02	330.70	319.93
90000	485.70	475.19	448.40	440.80	410.07	388.15	372.03	359.92
100000	539.67	527.98	498.23	489.77	455.64	431.28	413.37	399.91
110000	593.63	580.78	548.05	538.75	501.20	474.41	454.71	439.90
120000	647.60	633.58	597.87	587.73	546.76	517.53	496.04	479.90
130000	701.56	686.38	647.69	636.70	592.33	560.66	537.38	519.89
140000	755.53	739.18	697.52	685.68	637.89	603.79	578.72	559.88
150000	809.50	791.97	747.34	734.66	683.45	646.91	620.05	599.87
160000	863.46	844.77	797.16	783.63	729.02	690.04	661.39	639.86
170000	917.43	897.57	846.98	832.61	774.58	733.17	702.73	679.85
180000	971.39	950.37	896.80	881.59	820.14	776.30	744.06	719.84
190000	1025.36	1003.17	946.63	930.56	865.71	819.42	785.40	759.83
200000	1079.33	1055.96	996.45	979.54	911.27	862.55	826.74	799.82
210000	1133.29	1108.76	1046.27	1028.52	956.83	905.68	868.07	839.81
220000	1187.26	1161.56	1096.09	1077.49	1002.39	948.81	909.41	879.80
230000	1241.22	1214.36	1145.92	1126.47	1047.96	991.93	950.74	919.79
240000	1295.19	1267.16	1195.74	1175.45	1093.52	1035.06	992.08	959.79
250000	1349.16	1319.95	1245.56	1224.42	1139.08	1078.19	1033.42	999.78
260000	1403.12	1372.75	1295.38	1273.40	1184.65	1121.32	1074.75	1039.77
270000	1457.09	1425.55	1345.20	1322.38	1230.21	1164.44	1116.09	1079.76
280000	1511.05	1478.35	1395.03	1371.35	1275.77	1207.57	1157.43	1119.75
290000	1565.02	1531.15	1444.85	1420.33	1321.34	1250.70	1198.76	1159.74
300000	1618.99	1583.94	1494.67	1469.31	1366.90	1293.82	1240.10	1199.73
310000	1672.95	1636.74	1544.49	1518.28	1412.46	1336.95	1281.44	1239.72
320000	1726.92	1689.54	1594.31	1567.26	1458.03	1380.08	1322.77	1279.71
330000	1780.88	1742.34	1644.14	1616.24	1503.59	1423.21	1364.11	1319.70
340000	1834.85	1795.14	1693.96	1665.21	1549.15	1466.33	1405.45	1359.69
350000	1888.82	1847.93	1743.78	1714.19	1594.72	1509.46	1446.78	1399.68
360000	1942.78	1900.73	1793.60	1763.17	1640.28	1552.59	1488.12	1439.68
370000	1996.75	1953.53	1843.43	1812.14	1685.84	1595.72	1529.46	1479.67
380000	2050.71	2006.33	1893.25	1861.12	1731.41	1638.84	1570.79	1519.66
390000	2104.68	2059.13	1943.07	1910.10	1776.97	1681.97	1612.13	1559.65
400000	2158.65	2111.92	1992.89	1959.08	1822.53	1725.10	1653.47	1599.64

BLENDED MONTHLY PAYMENTS 4½%
AMORTIZATION IN YEARS

Amount	1	2	3	4	5	6	7	8
25	2.14	1.10	.75	.57	.47	.40	.35	.32
50	4.27	2.19	1.49	1.14	.94	.80	.70	.63
100	8.54	4.37	2.98	2.28	1.87	1.59	1.39	1.25
200	17.08	8.73	5.95	4.56	3.73	3.18	2.78	2.49
300	25.61	13.09	8.92	6.84	5.59	4.76	4.17	3.73
400	34.15	17.46	11.90	9.12	7.45	6.35	5.56	4.97
500	42.68	21.82	14.87	11.40	9.32	7.93	6.95	6.21
600	51.22	26.18	17.84	13.68	11.18	9.52	8.33	7.45
700	59.76	30.55	20.81	15.95	13.04	11.10	9.72	8.69
800	68.29	34.91	23.79	18.23	14.90	12.69	11.11	9.93
900	76.83	39.27	26.76	20.51	16.77	14.27	12.50	11.17
1000	85.36	43.63	29.73	22.79	18.63	15.86	13.89	12.41
2000	170.72	87.26	59.46	45.57	37.25	31.71	27.77	24.81
3000	256.08	130.89	89.19	68.36	55.88	47.57	41.65	37.22
4000	341.44	174.52	118.92	91.14	74.50	63.42	55.53	49.62
5000	426.80	218.15	148.65	113.93	93.13	79.28	69.41	62.02
6000	512.16	261.78	178.37	136.71	111.75	95.13	83.29	74.43
7000	597.52	305.41	208.10	159.50	130.37	110.99	97.17	86.83
8000	682.88	349.04	237.83	182.28	149.00	126.84	111.05	99.23
9000	768.24	392.67	267.56	205.07	167.62	142.70	124.93	111.64
10000	853.60	436.30	297.29	227.85	186.25	158.55	138.81	124.04
20000	1707.19	872.59	594.57	455.70	372.49	317.10	277.62	248.08
30000	2560.79	1308.88	891.85	683.55	558.73	475.65	416.43	372.11
40000	3414.38	1745.17	1189.14	911.40	744.97	634.20	555.24	496.15
50000	4267.98	2181.47	1486.42	1139.24	931.21	792.75	694.05	620.19
60000	5121.57	2617.76	1783.70	1367.09	1117.45	951.30	832.85	744.22
70000	5975.17	3054.05	2080.99	1594.94	1303.69	1109.85	971.66	868.26
80000	6828.76	3490.34	2378.27	1822.79	1489.93	1268.40	1110.47	992.30
90000	7682.36	3926.64	2675.55	2050.63	1676.17	1426.95	1249.28	1116.33
100000	8535.95	4362.93	2972.84	2278.48	1862.42	1585.50	1388.09	1240.37
110000	9389.55	4799.22	3270.12	2506.33	2048.66	1744.04	1526.89	1364.41
120000	10243.14	5235.51	3567.40	2734.18	2234.90	1902.59	1665.70	1488.44
130000	11096.74	5671.81	3864.69	2962.02	2421.14	2061.14	1804.51	1612.48
140000	11950.33	6108.10	4161.97	3189.87	2607.38	2219.69	1943.32	1736.52
150000	12803.93	6544.39	4459.25	3417.72	2793.62	2378.24	2082.13	1860.55
160000	13657.52	6980.68	4756.54	3645.57	2979.86	2536.79	2220.94	1984.59
170000	14511.12	7416.97	5053.82	3873.41	3166.10	2695.34	2359.74	2108.63
180000	15364.71	7853.27	5351.10	4101.26	3352.34	2853.89	2498.55	2232.66
190000	16218.31	8289.56	5648.39	4329.11	3538.58	3012.44	2637.36	2356.70
200000	17071.90	8725.85	5945.67	4556.96	3724.83	3170.99	2776.17	2480.74
210000	17925.50	9162.14	6242.95	4784.80	3911.07	3329.53	2914.98	2604.77
220000	18779.09	9598.44	6540.24	5012.65	4097.31	3488.08	3053.78	2728.81
230000	19632.69	10034.73	6837.52	5240.50	4283.55	3646.63	3192.59	2852.85
240000	20486.28	10471.02	7134.80	5468.35	4469.79	3805.18	3331.40	2976.88
250000	21339.87	10907.31	7432.09	5696.19	4656.03	3963.73	3470.21	3100.92
260000	22193.47	11343.61	7729.37	5924.04	4842.27	4122.28	3609.02	3224.96
270000	23047.06	11779.90	8026.65	6151.89	5028.51	4280.83	3747.82	3348.99
280000	23900.66	12216.19	8323.94	6379.74	5214.75	4439.38	3886.63	3473.03
290000	24754.25	12652.48	8621.22	6607.58	5400.99	4597.93	4025.44	3597.07
300000	25607.85	13088.78	8918.50	6835.43	5587.24	4756.48	4164.25	3721.10
310000	26461.44	13525.07	9215.79	7063.28	5773.48	4915.03	4303.06	3845.14
320000	27315.04	13961.36	9513.07	7291.13	5959.72	5073.57	4441.87	3969.18
330000	28168.63	14397.65	9810.35	7518.97	6145.96	5232.12	4580.67	4093.21
340000	29022.23	14833.94	10107.64	7746.82	6332.20	5390.67	4719.48	4217.25
350000	29875.82	15270.24	10404.92	7974.67	6518.44	5549.22	4858.29	4341.29
360000	30729.42	15706.53	10702.20	8202.52	6704.68	5707.77	4997.10	4465.32
370000	31583.01	16142.82	10999.49	8430.36	6890.92	5866.32	5135.91	4589.36
380000	32436.61	16579.11	11296.77	8658.21	7077.16	6024.87	5274.71	4713.39
390000	33290.20	17015.41	11594.05	8886.06	7263.40	6183.42	5413.52	4837.43
400000	34143.80	17451.70	11891.34	9113.91	7449.65	6341.97	5552.33	4961.47

4½% BLENDED MONTHLY PAYMENTS
AMORTIZATION IN YEARS

Amount	9	10	11	12	13	14	15	16
25	.29	.26	.24	.23	.22	.21	.20	.19
50	.57	.52	.48	.45	.43	.41	.39	.37
100	1.13	1.04	.96	.90	.85	.81	.77	.73
200	2.26	2.07	1.92	1.80	1.70	1.61	1.53	1.46
300	3.38	3.11	2.88	2.70	2.54	2.41	2.29	2.19
400	4.51	4.14	3.84	3.60	3.39	3.21	3.06	2.92
500	5.63	5.18	4.80	4.49	4.23	4.01	3.82	3.65
600	6.76	6.21	5.76	5.39	5.08	4.81	4.58	4.38
700	7.89	7.25	6.72	6.29	5.93	5.61	5.35	5.11
800	9.01	8.28	7.68	7.19	6.77	6.42	6.11	5.84
900	10.14	9.31	8.64	8.09	7.62	7.22	6.87	6.57
1000	11.26	10.35	9.60	8.98	8.46	8.02	7.63	7.30
2000	22.52	20.69	19.20	17.96	16.92	16.03	15.26	14.59
3000	33.78	31.04	28.80	26.94	25.38	24.04	22.89	21.89
4000	45.04	41.38	38.40	35.92	33.84	32.06	30.52	29.18
5000	56.29	51.72	48.00	44.90	42.29	40.07	38.15	36.48
6000	67.55	62.07	57.60	53.88	50.75	48.08	45.78	43.77
7000	78.81	72.41	67.19	62.86	59.21	56.09	53.41	51.06
8000	90.07	82.76	76.79	71.84	67.67	64.11	61.03	58.36
9000	101.33	93.10	86.39	80.82	76.13	72.12	68.66	65.65
10000	112.58	103.44	95.99	89.80	84.58	80.13	76.29	72.95
20000	225.16	206.88	191.97	179.60	169.16	160.26	152.58	145.89
30000	337.74	310.32	287.96	269.39	253.74	240.39	228.87	218.83
40000	450.32	413.76	383.94	359.19	338.32	320.51	305.15	291.78
50000	562.89	517.19	479.93	448.98	422.90	400.64	381.44	364.72
60000	675.47	620.63	575.91	538.78	507.48	480.77	457.73	437.66
70000	788.05	724.07	671.90	628.57	592.06	560.90	534.01	510.60
80000	900.63	827.51	767.88	718.37	676.64	641.02	610.30	583.55
90000	1013.21	930.95	863.86	808.16	761.22	721.15	686.59	656.49
100000	1125.78	1034.38	959.85	897.96	845.80	801.28	762.87	729.43
110000	1238.36	1137.82	1055.83	987.76	930.38	881.41	839.16	802.37
120000	1350.94	1241.26	1151.82	1077.55	1014.96	961.53	915.45	875.32
130000	1463.52	1344.70	1247.80	1167.35	1099.54	1041.66	991.73	948.26
140000	1576.09	1448.14	1343.79	1257.14	1184.12	1121.79	1068.02	1021.20
150000	1688.67	1551.57	1439.77	1346.94	1268.70	1201.92	1144.31	1094.15
160000	1801.25	1655.01	1535.76	1436.73	1353.28	1282.04	1220.59	1167.09
170000	1913.83	1758.45	1631.74	1526.53	1437.85	1362.17	1296.88	1240.03
180000	2026.41	1861.89	1727.72	1616.32	1522.43	1442.30	1373.17	1312.97
190000	2138.98	1965.33	1823.71	1706.12	1607.01	1522.43	1449.45	1385.92
200000	2251.56	2068.76	1919.69	1795.92	1691.59	1602.55	1525.74	1458.86
210000	2364.14	2172.20	2015.68	1885.71	1776.17	1682.68	1602.03	1531.80
220000	2476.72	2275.64	2111.66	1975.51	1860.75	1762.81	1678.31	1604.74
230000	2589.29	2379.08	2207.65	2065.30	1945.33	1842.94	1754.60	1677.69
240000	2701.87	2482.51	2303.63	2155.10	2029.91	1923.06	1830.89	1750.63
250000	2814.45	2585.95	2399.61	2244.89	2114.49	2003.19	1907.18	1823.57
260000	2927.03	2689.39	2495.60	2334.69	2199.07	2083.32	1983.46	1896.52
270000	3039.61	2792.83	2591.58	2424.48	2283.65	2163.45	2059.75	1969.46
280000	3152.18	2896.27	2687.57	2514.28	2368.23	2243.57	2136.04	2042.40
290000	3264.76	2999.70	2783.55	2604.08	2452.81	2323.70	2212.32	2115.34
300000	3377.34	3103.14	2879.54	2693.87	2537.39	2403.83	2288.61	2188.29
310000	3489.92	3206.58	2975.52	2783.67	2621.97	2483.96	2364.90	2261.23
320000	3602.49	3310.02	3071.51	2873.46	2706.55	2564.08	2441.18	2334.17
330000	3715.07	3413.46	3167.49	2963.26	2791.13	2644.21	2517.47	2407.11
340000	3827.65	3516.89	3263.47	3053.05	2875.70	2724.34	2593.76	2480.06
350000	3940.23	3620.33	3359.46	3142.85	2960.28	2804.47	2670.04	2553.00
360000	4052.81	3723.77	3455.44	3232.64	3044.86	2884.59	2746.33	2625.94
370000	4165.38	3827.21	3551.43	3322.44	3129.44	2964.72	2822.62	2698.89
380000	4277.96	3930.65	3647.41	3412.23	3214.02	3044.85	2898.90	2771.83
390000	4390.54	4034.08	3743.40	3502.03	3298.60	3124.98	2975.19	2844.77
400000	4503.12	4137.52	3839.38	3591.83	3383.18	3205.10	3051.48	2917.71

BLENDED MONTHLY PAYMENTS 4½%
AMORTIZATION IN YEARS

Amount	17	18	19	20	21	22	23	24
25	.18	.17	.17	.16	.16	.15	.15	.15
50	.36	.34	.33	.32	.31	.30	.29	.29
100	.71	.68	.66	.64	.62	.60	.58	.57
200	1.41	1.35	1.31	1.27	1.23	1.20	1.16	1.14
300	2.11	2.03	1.96	1.90	1.84	1.79	1.74	1.70
400	2.81	2.70	2.61	2.53	2.45	2.39	2.32	2.27
500	3.51	3.38	3.26	3.16	3.06	2.98	2.90	2.84
600	4.21	4.05	3.91	3.79	3.68	3.58	3.48	3.40
700	4.91	4.72	4.56	4.42	4.29	4.17	4.06	3.97
800	5.61	5.40	5.21	5.05	4.90	4.77	4.64	4.53
900	6.31	6.07	5.86	5.68	5.51	5.36	5.22	5.10
1000	7.01	6.75	6.52	6.31	6.12	5.96	5.80	5.67
2000	14.01	13.49	13.03	12.61	12.24	11.91	11.60	11.33
3000	21.01	20.23	19.54	18.92	18.36	17.86	17.40	16.99
4000	28.01	26.97	26.05	25.22	24.48	23.81	23.20	22.65
5000	35.01	33.71	32.56	31.53	30.60	29.76	29.00	28.31
6000	42.01	40.45	39.07	37.83	36.72	35.71	34.80	33.97
7000	49.01	47.19	45.58	44.13	42.83	41.66	40.60	39.63
8000	56.01	53.94	52.09	50.44	48.95	47.61	46.40	45.29
9000	63.01	60.68	58.60	56.74	55.07	53.56	52.20	50.95
10000	70.01	67.42	65.11	63.05	61.19	59.51	58.00	56.61
20000	140.02	134.83	130.21	126.09	122.37	119.02	115.99	113.22
30000	210.03	202.24	195.32	189.13	183.56	178.53	173.98	169.83
40000	280.03	269.66	260.42	252.17	244.74	238.04	231.97	226.44
50000	350.04	337.07	325.53	315.21	305.93	297.55	289.96	283.05
60000	420.05	404.48	390.63	378.25	367.11	357.06	347.95	339.66
70000	490.06	471.89	455.74	441.29	428.30	416.57	405.94	396.27
80000	560.06	539.31	520.84	504.33	489.48	476.08	463.93	452.88
90000	630.07	606.72	585.95	567.37	550.67	535.59	521.92	509.48
100000	700.08	674.13	651.05	630.41	611.85	595.10	579.91	566.09
110000	770.09	741.55	716.16	693.45	673.04	654.61	637.90	622.70
120000	840.09	808.96	781.26	756.49	734.22	714.12	695.89	679.31
130000	910.10	876.37	846.37	819.53	795.41	773.63	753.88	735.92
140000	980.11	943.78	911.47	882.57	856.59	833.14	811.87	792.53
150000	1050.12	1011.20	976.58	945.61	917.78	892.65	869.87	849.14
160000	1120.12	1078.61	1041.68	1008.65	978.96	952.16	927.86	905.75
170000	1190.13	1146.02	1106.79	1071.69	1040.15	1011.67	985.85	962.35
180000	1260.14	1213.43	1171.89	1134.73	1101.33	1071.18	1043.84	1018.96
190000	1330.15	1280.85	1237.00	1197.77	1162.52	1130.69	1101.83	1075.57
200000	1400.15	1348.26	1302.10	1260.82	1223.70	1190.20	1159.82	1132.18
210000	1470.16	1415.67	1367.21	1323.86	1284.89	1249.71	1217.81	1188.79
220000	1540.17	1483.09	1432.31	1386.90	1346.07	1309.21	1275.80	1245.40
230000	1610.18	1550.50	1497.42	1449.94	1407.26	1368.72	1333.79	1302.01
240000	1680.18	1617.91	1562.52	1512.98	1468.44	1428.23	1391.78	1358.62
250000	1750.19	1685.32	1627.63	1576.02	1529.63	1487.74	1449.77	1415.23
260000	1820.20	1752.74	1692.73	1639.06	1590.81	1547.25	1507.76	1471.83
270000	1890.21	1820.15	1757.84	1702.10	1652.00	1606.76	1565.75	1528.44
280000	1960.21	1887.56	1822.94	1765.14	1713.18	1666.27	1623.74	1585.05
290000	2030.22	1954.98	1888.04	1828.18	1774.37	1725.78	1681.74	1641.66
300000	2100.23	2022.39	1953.15	1891.22	1835.55	1785.29	1739.73	1698.27
310000	2170.24	2089.80	2018.25	1954.26	1896.74	1844.80	1797.72	1754.88
320000	2240.24	2157.21	2083.36	2017.30	1957.92	1904.31	1855.71	1811.49
330000	2310.25	2224.63	2148.46	2080.34	2019.11	1963.82	1913.70	1868.10
340000	2380.26	2292.04	2213.57	2143.38	2080.29	2023.33	1971.69	1924.70
350000	2450.27	2359.45	2278.67	2206.42	2141.48	2082.84	2029.68	1981.31
360000	2520.27	2426.86	2343.78	2269.46	2202.66	2142.35	2087.67	2037.92
370000	2590.28	2494.28	2408.88	2332.50	2263.85	2201.86	2145.66	2094.53
380000	2660.29	2561.69	2473.99	2395.54	2325.03	2261.37	2203.65	2151.14
390000	2730.29	2629.10	2539.09	2458.59	2386.22	2320.88	2261.64	2207.75
400000	2800.30	2696.52	2604.20	2521.63	2447.40	2380.39	2319.63	2264.36

31

4½% BLENDED MONTHLY PAYMENTS
AMORTIZATION IN YEARS

Amount	25	26	29	30	35	40	45	50
25	.14	.14	.13	.13	.12	.12	.11	.11
50	.28	.28	.26	.26	.24	.23	.22	.21
100	.56	.55	.52	.51	.48	.45	.43	.42
200	1.11	1.09	1.03	1.01	.95	.90	.86	.84
300	1.67	1.63	1.54	1.52	1.42	1.35	1.29	1.25
400	2.22	2.17	2.06	2.02	1.89	1.79	1.72	1.67
500	2.77	2.71	2.57	2.53	2.36	2.24	2.15	2.09
600	3.33	3.26	3.08	3.03	2.83	2.69	2.58	2.50
700	3.88	3.80	3.59	3.53	3.30	3.13	3.01	2.92
800	4.43	4.34	4.11	4.04	3.77	3.58	3.44	3.34
900	4.99	4.88	4.62	4.54	4.24	4.03	3.87	3.75
1000	5.54	5.42	5.13	5.05	4.71	4.47	4.30	4.17
2000	11.07	10.84	10.26	10.09	9.42	8.94	8.60	8.34
3000	16.61	16.26	15.38	15.13	14.13	13.41	12.89	12.50
4000	22.14	21.68	20.51	20.17	18.83	17.88	17.19	16.67
5000	27.68	27.10	25.63	25.22	23.54	22.35	21.48	20.83
6000	33.21	32.52	30.76	30.26	28.25	26.82	25.78	25.00
7000	38.75	37.94	35.88	35.30	32.95	31.29	30.07	29.16
8000	44.28	43.36	41.01	40.34	37.66	35.76	34.37	33.33
9000	49.82	48.78	46.13	45.38	42.37	40.23	38.66	37.49
10000	55.35	54.20	51.26	50.43	47.07	44.69	42.96	41.66
20000	110.70	108.39	102.51	100.85	94.14	89.38	85.91	83.31
30000	166.05	162.58	153.77	151.27	141.21	134.07	128.86	124.97
40000	221.39	216.77	205.02	201.69	188.28	178.76	171.81	166.62
50000	276.74	270.97	256.28	252.11	235.35	223.45	214.76	208.28
60000	332.09	325.16	307.53	302.53	282.41	268.14	257.71	249.93
70000	387.44	379.35	358.79	352.96	329.48	312.83	300.66	291.59
80000	442.78	433.54	410.04	403.38	376.55	357.52	343.61	333.24
90000	498.13	487.73	461.30	453.80	423.62	402.21	386.57	374.89
100000	553.48	541.93	512.55	504.22	470.69	446.90	429.52	416.55
110000	608.83	596.12	563.80	554.64	517.76	491.59	472.47	458.20
120000	664.17	650.31	615.06	605.06	564.82	536.27	515.42	499.86
130000	719.52	704.50	666.31	655.49	611.89	580.96	558.37	541.51
140000	774.87	758.70	717.57	705.91	658.96	625.65	601.32	583.17
150000	830.21	812.89	768.82	756.33	706.03	670.34	644.27	624.82
160000	885.56	867.08	820.08	806.75	753.10	715.03	687.22	666.48
170000	940.91	921.27	871.33	857.17	800.17	759.72	730.17	708.13
180000	996.26	975.46	922.59	907.59	847.23	804.41	773.13	749.78
190000	1051.60	1029.66	973.84	958.01	894.30	849.10	816.08	791.44
200000	1106.95	1083.85	1025.10	1008.44	941.37	893.79	859.03	833.09
210000	1162.30	1138.04	1076.35	1058.86	988.44	938.48	901.98	874.75
220000	1217.65	1192.23	1127.60	1109.28	1035.51	983.17	944.93	916.40
230000	1272.99	1246.43	1178.86	1159.70	1082.58	1027.85	987.88	958.06
240000	1328.34	1300.62	1230.11	1210.12	1129.64	1072.54	1030.83	999.71
250000	1383.69	1354.81	1281.37	1260.54	1176.71	1117.23	1073.78	1041.37
260000	1439.03	1409.00	1332.62	1310.97	1223.78	1161.92	1116.74	1083.02
270000	1494.38	1463.19	1383.88	1361.39	1270.85	1206.61	1159.69	1124.67
280000	1549.73	1517.39	1435.13	1411.81	1317.92	1251.30	1202.64	1166.33
290000	1605.08	1571.58	1486.39	1462.23	1364.98	1295.99	1245.59	1207.98
300000	1660.42	1625.77	1537.64	1512.65	1412.05	1340.68	1288.54	1249.64
310000	1715.77	1679.96	1588.89	1563.07	1459.12	1385.37	1331.49	1291.29
320000	1771.12	1734.16	1640.15	1613.49	1506.19	1430.06	1374.44	1332.95
330000	1826.47	1788.35	1691.40	1663.92	1553.26	1474.75	1417.39	1374.60
340000	1881.81	1842.54	1742.66	1714.34	1600.33	1519.44	1460.34	1416.25
350000	1937.16	1896.73	1793.91	1764.76	1647.39	1564.12	1503.30	1457.91
360000	1992.51	1950.92	1845.17	1815.18	1694.46	1608.81	1546.25	1499.56
370000	2047.85	2005.12	1896.42	1865.60	1741.53	1653.50	1589.20	1541.22
380000	2103.20	2059.31	1947.68	1916.02	1788.60	1698.19	1632.15	1582.87
390000	2158.55	2113.50	1998.93	1966.45	1835.67	1742.88	1675.10	1624.53
400000	2213.90	2167.69	2050.19	2016.87	1882.74	1787.57	1718.05	1666.18

BLENDED MONTHLY PAYMENTS 4¾%
AMORTIZATION IN YEARS

Amount	1	2	3	4	5	6	7	8
25	2.14	1.10	.75	.58	.47	.40	.35	.32
50	4.28	2.19	1.50	1.15	.94	.80	.70	.63
100	8.55	4.38	2.99	2.29	1.88	1.60	1.40	1.26
200	17.10	8.75	5.97	4.58	3.75	3.20	2.80	2.51
300	25.65	13.13	8.96	6.87	5.63	4.80	4.20	3.76
400	34.19	17.50	11.94	9.16	7.50	6.39	5.60	5.01
500	42.74	21.87	14.92	11.45	9.37	7.99	7.00	6.26
600	51.29	26.25	17.91	13.74	11.25	9.59	8.40	7.52
700	59.84	30.62	20.89	16.03	13.12	11.18	9.80	8.77
800	68.38	35.00	23.88	18.32	14.99	12.78	11.20	10.02
900	76.93	39.37	26.86	20.61	16.87	14.38	12.60	11.27
1000	85.48	43.74	29.84	22.90	18.74	15.97	14.00	12.52
2000	170.95	87.48	59.68	45.80	37.48	31.94	28.00	25.04
3000	256.42	131.22	89.52	68.69	56.21	47.91	41.99	37.56
4000	341.89	174.96	119.36	91.59	74.95	63.88	55.99	50.08
5000	427.36	218.70	149.20	114.48	93.68	79.84	69.98	62.60
6000	512.84	262.44	179.03	137.38	112.42	95.81	83.98	75.12
7000	598.31	306.18	208.87	160.27	131.16	111.78	97.97	87.64
8000	683.78	349.92	238.71	183.17	149.89	127.75	111.97	100.16
9000	769.25	393.65	268.55	206.06	168.63	143.72	125.96	112.68
10000	854.72	437.39	298.39	228.96	187.36	159.68	139.96	125.20
20000	1709.44	874.78	596.77	457.91	374.72	319.36	279.91	250.39
30000	2564.16	1312.17	895.15	686.86	562.08	479.04	419.86	375.58
40000	3418.87	1749.56	1193.53	915.82	749.44	638.72	559.81	500.78
50000	4273.59	2186.94	1491.91	1144.77	936.79	798.40	699.76	625.97
60000	5128.31	2624.33	1790.29	1373.72	1124.15	958.08	839.71	751.16
70000	5983.03	3061.72	2088.67	1602.68	1311.51	1117.75	979.66	876.36
80000	6837.74	3499.11	2387.05	1831.63	1498.87	1277.43	1119.61	1001.55
90000	7692.46	3936.50	2685.43	2060.58	1686.22	1437.11	1259.56	1126.74
100000	8547.18	4373.88	2983.81	2289.53	1873.58	1596.79	1399.51	1251.94
110000	9401.90	4811.27	3282.19	2518.49	2060.94	1756.47	1539.46	1377.13
120000	10256.61	5248.66	3580.57	2747.44	2248.30	1916.15	1679.42	1502.32
130000	11111.33	5686.05	3878.95	2976.39	2435.66	2075.82	1819.37	1627.52
140000	11966.05	6123.44	4177.33	3205.35	2623.01	2235.50	1959.32	1752.71
150000	12820.77	6560.82	4475.71	3434.30	2810.37	2395.18	2099.27	1877.90
160000	13675.48	6998.21	4774.09	3663.25	2997.73	2554.86	2239.22	2003.10
170000	14530.20	7435.60	5072.47	3892.21	3185.09	2714.54	2379.17	2128.29
180000	15384.92	7872.99	5370.85	4121.16	3372.44	2874.22	2519.12	2253.48
190000	16239.64	8310.38	5669.23	4350.11	3559.80	3033.89	2659.07	2378.67
200000	17094.35	8747.76	5967.61	4579.06	3747.16	3193.57	2799.02	2503.87
210000	17949.07	9185.15	6265.99	4808.02	3934.52	3353.25	2938.97	2629.06
220000	18803.79	9622.54	6564.37	5036.97	4121.87	3512.93	3078.92	2754.25
230000	19658.51	10059.93	6862.75	5265.92	4309.23	3672.61	3218.87	2879.45
240000	20513.22	10497.32	7161.13	5494.88	4496.59	3832.29	3358.83	3004.64
250000	21367.94	10934.70	7459.51	5723.83	4683.95	3991.96	3498.78	3129.83
260000	22222.66	11372.09	7757.89	5952.78	4871.31	4151.64	3638.73	3255.03
270000	23077.38	11809.48	8056.27	6181.74	5058.66	4311.32	3778.68	3380.22
280000	23932.09	12246.87	8354.65	6410.69	5246.02	4471.00	3918.63	3505.41
290000	24786.81	12684.26	8653.03	6639.64	5433.38	4630.68	4058.58	3630.61
300000	25641.53	13121.64	8951.41	6868.59	5620.74	4790.36	4198.53	3755.80
310000	26496.25	13559.03	9249.79	7097.55	5808.09	4950.03	4338.48	3880.99
320000	27350.96	13996.42	9548.17	7326.50	5995.45	5109.71	4478.43	4006.19
330000	28205.68	14433.81	9846.56	7555.45	6182.81	5269.39	4618.38	4131.38
340000	29060.40	14871.20	10144.94	7784.41	6370.17	5429.07	4758.33	4256.57
350000	29915.12	15308.58	10443.32	8013.36	6557.52	5588.75	4898.28	4381.77
360000	30769.83	15745.97	10741.70	8242.31	6744.88	5748.43	5038.24	4506.96
370000	31624.55	16183.36	11040.08	8471.27	6932.24	5908.10	5178.19	4632.15
380000	32479.27	16620.75	11338.46	8700.22	7119.60	6067.78	5318.14	4757.34
390000	33333.98	17058.14	11636.84	8929.17	7306.96	6227.46	5458.09	4882.54
400000	34188.70	17495.52	11935.22	9153.12	7494.31	6387.14	5598.04	5007.73

4¾% BLENDED MONTHLY PAYMENTS
AMORTIZATION IN YEARS

Amount	9	10	11	12	13	14	15	16
25	.29	.27	.25	.23	.22	.21	.20	.19
50	.57	.53	.49	.46	.43	.41	.39	.38
100	1.14	1.05	.98	.92	.86	.82	.78	.75
200	2.28	2.10	1.95	1.83	1.72	1.63	1.56	1.49
300	3.42	3.14	2.92	2.74	2.58	2.45	2.33	2.23
400	4.55	4.19	3.89	3.65	3.44	3.26	3.11	2.97
500	5.69	5.24	4.86	4.56	4.30	4.07	3.88	3.72
600	6.83	6.28	5.84	5.47	5.15	4.89	4.66	4.46
700	7.97	7.33	6.81	6.38	6.01	5.70	5.43	5.20
800	9.10	8.37	7.78	7.29	6.87	6.51	6.21	5.94
900	10.24	9.42	8.75	8.20	7.73	7.33	6.98	6.68
1000	11.38	10.47	9.72	9.11	8.59	8.14	7.76	7.43
2000	22.75	20.93	19.44	18.21	17.17	16.28	15.51	14.85
3000	34.13	31.39	29.16	27.31	25.75	24.42	23.27	22.27
4000	45.50	41.85	38.88	36.41	34.33	32.55	31.02	29.69
5000	56.88	52.32	48.60	45.51	42.91	40.69	38.78	37.11
6000	68.25	62.78	58.32	54.61	51.49	48.83	46.53	44.53
7000	79.63	73.24	68.03	63.71	60.07	56.96	54.29	51.96
8000	91.00	83.70	77.75	72.81	68.65	65.10	62.04	59.38
9000	102.38	94.17	87.47	81.91	77.23	73.24	69.79	66.80
10000	113.75	104.63	97.19	91.01	85.81	81.38	77.55	74.22
20000	227.50	209.25	194.37	182.02	171.62	162.75	155.09	148.43
30000	341.25	313.87	291.56	273.03	257.43	244.12	232.64	222.65
40000	455.00	418.50	388.74	364.04	343.24	325.49	310.18	296.86
50000	568.75	523.12	485.92	455.05	429.04	406.86	387.73	371.08
60000	682.50	627.74	583.11	546.06	514.85	488.23	465.27	445.29
70000	796.24	732.37	680.29	637.07	600.66	569.60	542.82	519.51
80000	909.99	836.99	777.48	728.08	686.47	650.97	620.36	593.72
90000	1023.74	941.61	874.66	819.09	772.28	732.34	697.90	667.94
100000	1137.49	1046.23	971.84	910.10	858.08	813.71	775.45	742.15
110000	1251.24	1150.86	1069.03	1001.11	943.89	895.08	852.99	816.37
120000	1364.99	1255.48	1166.21	1092.12	1029.70	976.45	930.54	890.58
130000	1478.74	1360.10	1263.40	1183.13	1115.51	1057.82	1008.08	964.80
140000	1592.48	1464.73	1360.58	1274.14	1201.32	1139.19	1085.63	1039.01
150000	1706.23	1569.35	1457.76	1365.15	1287.12	1220.56	1163.17	1113.22
160000	1819.98	1673.97	1554.95	1456.16	1372.93	1301.93	1240.71	1187.44
170000	1933.73	1778.60	1652.13	1547.17	1458.74	1383.30	1318.26	1261.65
180000	2047.48	1883.22	1749.31	1638.18	1544.55	1464.67	1395.80	1335.87
190000	2161.23	1987.84	1846.50	1729.19	1630.36	1546.04	1473.35	1410.08
200000	2274.98	2092.46	1943.68	1820.20	1716.16	1627.41	1550.89	1484.30
210000	2388.72	2197.09	2040.87	1911.20	1801.97	1708.79	1628.44	1558.51
220000	2502.47	2301.71	2138.05	2002.21	1887.78	1790.16	1705.98	1632.73
230000	2616.22	2406.33	2235.23	2093.22	1973.59	1871.53	1783.52	1706.94
240000	2729.97	2510.96	2332.42	2184.23	2059.39	1952.90	1861.07	1781.16
250000	2843.72	2615.58	2429.60	2275.24	2145.20	2034.27	1938.61	1855.37
260000	2957.47	2720.20	2526.79	2366.25	2231.01	2115.64	2016.16	1929.59
270000	3071.22	2824.83	2623.97	2457.26	2316.82	2197.01	2093.70	2003.80
280000	3184.96	2929.45	2721.15	2548.27	2402.63	2278.38	2171.25	2078.02
290000	3298.71	3034.07	2818.34	2639.28	2488.43	2359.75	2248.79	2152.23
300000	3412.46	3138.69	2915.52	2730.29	2574.24	2441.12	2326.33	2226.44
310000	3526.21	3243.32	3012.71	2821.30	2660.05	2522.49	2403.88	2300.66
320000	3639.96	3347.94	3109.89	2912.31	2745.86	2603.86	2481.42	2374.87
330000	3753.71	3452.56	3207.07	3003.32	2831.67	2685.23	2558.97	2449.09
340000	3867.46	3557.19	3304.26	3094.33	2917.47	2766.60	2636.51	2523.30
350000	3981.20	3661.81	3401.44	3185.34	3003.28	2847.97	2714.06	2597.52
360000	4094.95	3766.43	3498.62	3276.35	3089.09	2929.34	2791.60	2671.73
370000	4208.70	3871.05	3595.81	3367.36	3174.90	3010.71	2869.14	2745.95
380000	4322.45	3975.68	3692.99	3458.37	3260.71	3092.08	2946.69	2820.16
390000	4436.20	4080.30	3790.18	3549.38	3346.51	3173.45	3024.23	2894.38
400000	4549.95	4184.92	3887.36	3640.39	3432.32	3254.82	3101.78	2968.59

34

BLENDED MONTHLY PAYMENTS 4¾%
AMORTIZATION IN YEARS

Amount	17	18	19	20	21	22	23	24
25	.18	.18	.17	.17	.16	.16	.15	.15
50	.36	.35	.34	.33	.32	.31	.30	.29
100	.72	.69	.67	.65	.63	.61	.60	.58
200	1.43	1.38	1.33	1.29	1.26	1.22	1.19	1.16
300	2.14	2.07	2.00	1.94	1.88	1.83	1.79	1.74
400	2.86	2.75	2.66	2.58	2.51	2.44	2.38	2.32
500	3.57	3.44	3.33	3.22	3.13	3.05	2.97	2.90
600	4.28	4.13	3.99	3.87	3.76	3.66	3.57	3.48
700	5.00	4.81	4.65	4.51	4.38	4.27	4.16	4.06
800	5.71	5.50	5.32	5.15	5.01	4.87	4.75	4.64
900	6.42	6.19	5.98	5.80	5.63	5.48	5.35	5.22
1000	7.13	6.88	6.65	6.44	6.26	6.09	5.94	5.80
2000	14.26	13.75	13.29	12.88	12.51	12.18	11.88	11.60
3000	21.39	20.62	19.93	19.32	18.76	18.26	17.81	17.40
4000	28.52	27.49	26.57	25.75	25.02	24.35	23.75	23.20
5000	35.65	34.36	33.21	32.19	31.27	30.44	29.69	29.00
6000	42.78	41.23	39.86	38.63	37.52	36.52	35.62	34.80
7000	49.91	48.10	46.50	45.06	43.77	42.61	41.56	40.60
8000	57.04	54.98	53.14	51.50	50.03	48.70	47.49	46.40
9000	64.17	61.85	59.78	57.94	56.28	54.78	53.43	52.20
10000	71.30	68.72	66.42	64.37	62.53	60.87	59.37	58.00
20000	142.59	137.43	132.84	128.74	125.06	121.74	118.73	115.99
30000	213.89	206.15	199.26	193.11	187.59	182.60	178.09	173.99
40000	285.18	274.86	265.68	257.48	250.12	243.47	237.45	231.98
50000	356.47	343.57	332.10	321.85	312.65	304.34	296.81	289.97
60000	427.77	412.29	398.52	386.22	375.17	365.20	356.17	347.97
70000	499.06	481.00	464.94	450.59	437.70	426.07	415.54	405.96
80000	570.36	549.71	531.36	514.96	500.23	486.94	474.90	463.95
90000	641.65	618.43	597.78	579.33	562.76	547.80	534.26	521.95
100000	712.94	687.14	664.20	643.70	625.29	608.67	593.62	579.94
110000	784.24	755.85	730.62	708.07	687.81	669.54	652.98	637.93
120000	855.53	824.57	797.04	772.44	750.34	730.40	712.34	695.93
130000	926.82	893.28	863.46	836.81	812.87	791.27	771.71	753.92
140000	998.12	961.99	929.88	901.18	875.40	852.14	831.07	811.91
150000	1069.41	1030.71	996.30	965.55	937.93	913.00	890.43	869.91
160000	1140.71	1099.42	1062.72	1029.92	1000.45	973.87	949.79	927.90
170000	1212.00	1168.13	1129.14	1094.29	1062.98	1034.74	1009.15	985.89
180000	1283.29	1236.85	1195.56	1158.66	1125.51	1095.60	1068.51	1043.89
190000	1354.59	1305.56	1261.98	1223.03	1188.04	1156.47	1127.88	1101.88
200000	1425.88	1374.27	1328.40	1287.40	1250.57	1217.34	1187.24	1159.87
210000	1497.17	1442.99	1394.82	1351.77	1313.09	1278.20	1246.60	1217.87
220000	1568.47	1511.70	1461.24	1416.14	1375.62	1339.07	1305.96	1275.86
230000	1639.76	1580.41	1527.66	1480.51	1438.15	1399.94	1365.32	1333.85
240000	1711.06	1649.13	1594.08	1544.88	1500.68	1460.80	1424.68	1391.85
250000	1782.35	1717.84	1660.50	1609.24	1563.21	1521.67	1484.05	1449.84
260000	1853.64	1786.55	1726.92	1673.61	1625.73	1582.54	1543.41	1507.83
270000	1924.94	1855.27	1793.34	1737.98	1688.26	1643.40	1602.77	1565.83
280000	1996.23	1923.98	1859.76	1802.35	1750.79	1704.27	1662.13	1623.82
290000	2067.52	1992.69	1926.18	1866.72	1813.32	1765.14	1721.49	1681.82
300000	2138.82	2061.41	1992.60	1931.09	1875.85	1826.00	1780.85	1739.81
310000	2210.11	2130.12	2059.02	1995.46	1938.38	1886.87	1840.22	1797.80
320000	2281.41	2198.83	2125.44	2059.83	2000.90	1947.74	1899.58	1855.80
330000	2352.70	2267.55	2191.86	2124.20	2063.43	2008.60	1958.94	1913.79
340000	2423.99	2336.26	2258.28	2188.57	2125.96	2069.47	2018.30	1971.78
350000	2495.29	2404.98	2324.70	2252.94	2188.49	2130.34	2077.66	2029.78
360000	2566.58	2473.69	2391.12	2317.31	2251.02	2191.20	2137.02	2087.77
370000	2637.87	2542.40	2457.54	2381.68	2313.54	2252.07	2196.39	2145.76
380000	2709.17	2611.12	2523.96	2446.05	2376.07	2312.94	2255.75	2203.76
390000	2780.46	2679.83	2590.37	2510.42	2438.60	2373.80	2315.11	2261.75
400000	2851.76	2748.54	2656.79	2574.79	2501.13	2434.67	2374.47	2319.74

4¾% BLENDED MONTHLY PAYMENTS
AMORTIZATION IN YEARS

Amount	25	26	29	30	35	40	45	50
25	.15	.14	.14	.13	.13	.12	.12	.11
50	.29	.28	.27	.26	.25	.24	.23	.22
100	.57	.56	.53	.52	.49	.47	.45	.44
200	1.14	1.12	1.06	1.04	.98	.93	.90	.87
300	1.71	1.67	1.59	1.56	1.46	1.39	1.34	1.31
400	2.27	2.23	2.11	2.08	1.95	1.86	1.79	1.74
500	2.84	2.79	2.64	2.60	2.43	2.32	2.23	2.17
600	3.41	3.34	3.17	3.12	2.92	2.78	2.68	2.61
700	3.98	3.90	3.69	3.64	3.41	3.24	3.13	3.04
800	4.54	4.45	4.22	4.16	3.89	3.71	3.57	3.47
900	5.11	5.01	4.75	4.67	4.38	4.17	4.02	3.91
1000	5.68	5.57	5.28	5.19	4.86	4.63	4.46	4.34
2000	11.35	11.13	10.55	10.38	9.72	9.26	8.92	8.67
3000	17.03	16.69	15.82	15.57	14.58	13.89	13.38	13.01
4000	22.70	22.25	21.09	20.76	19.44	18.51	17.84	17.34
5000	28.38	27.81	26.36	25.95	24.30	23.14	22.30	21.68
6000	34.05	33.37	31.63	31.14	29.16	27.77	26.76	26.01
7000	39.73	38.93	36.90	36.33	34.02	32.40	31.22	30.34
8000	45.40	44.49	42.17	41.51	38.88	37.02	35.68	34.68
9000	51.08	50.05	47.44	46.70	43.74	41.65	40.14	39.01
10000	56.75	55.61	52.71	51.89	48.60	46.28	44.59	43.35
20000	113.50	111.21	105.42	103.78	97.19	92.55	89.18	86.69
30000	170.24	166.82	158.12	155.66	145.79	138.83	133.77	130.03
40000	226.99	222.42	210.83	207.55	194.38	185.10	178.36	173.37
50000	283.73	278.02	263.53	259.43	242.98	231.37	222.95	216.72
60000	340.48	333.63	316.24	311.32	291.57	277.65	267.54	260.06
70000	397.22	389.23	368.95	363.21	340.17	323.92	312.13	303.40
80000	453.97	444.84	421.65	415.09	388.76	370.20	356.72	346.74
90000	510.72	500.44	474.36	466.98	437.36	416.47	401.31	390.08
100000	567.46	556.04	527.06	518.86	485.95	462.74	445.90	433.43
110000	624.21	611.65	579.77	570.75	534.55	509.02	490.49	476.77
120000	680.95	667.25	632.48	622.63	583.14	555.29	535.08	520.11
130000	737.70	722.86	685.18	674.52	631.74	601.56	579.67	563.45
140000	794.44	778.46	737.89	726.41	680.33	647.84	624.26	606.80
150000	851.19	834.06	790.59	778.29	728.93	694.11	668.85	650.14
160000	907.93	889.67	843.30	830.18	777.52	740.39	713.44	693.48
170000	964.68	945.27	896.00	882.06	826.12	786.66	758.03	736.82
180000	1021.43	1000.88	948.71	933.95	874.71	832.93	802.62	780.16
190000	1078.17	1056.48	1001.42	985.84	923.31	879.21	847.21	823.51
200000	1134.92	1112.08	1054.12	1037.72	971.90	925.48	891.80	866.85
210000	1191.66	1167.69	1106.83	1089.61	1020.50	971.75	936.39	910.19
220000	1248.41	1223.29	1159.53	1141.49	1069.09	1018.03	980.98	953.53
230000	1305.15	1278.90	1212.24	1193.38	1117.69	1064.30	1025.57	996.87
240000	1361.90	1334.50	1264.95	1245.26	1166.28	1110.58	1070.16	1040.22
250000	1418.64	1390.10	1317.65	1297.15	1214.87	1156.85	1114.75	1083.56
260000	1475.39	1445.71	1370.36	1349.04	1263.47	1203.12	1159.33	1126.90
270000	1532.14	1501.31	1423.06	1400.92	1312.06	1249.40	1203.92	1170.24
280000	1588.88	1556.92	1475.77	1452.81	1360.66	1295.67	1248.51	1213.59
290000	1645.63	1612.52	1528.47	1504.69	1409.25	1341.94	1293.10	1256.93
300000	1702.37	1668.12	1581.18	1556.58	1457.85	1388.22	1337.69	1300.27
310000	1759.12	1723.73	1633.89	1608.47	1506.44	1434.49	1382.28	1343.61
320000	1815.86	1779.33	1686.59	1660.35	1555.04	1480.77	1426.87	1386.95
330000	1872.61	1834.94	1739.30	1712.24	1603.63	1527.04	1471.46	1430.30
340000	1929.35	1890.54	1792.00	1764.12	1652.23	1573.31	1516.05	1473.64
350000	1986.10	1946.14	1844.71	1816.01	1700.82	1619.59	1560.64	1516.98
360000	2042.85	2001.75	1897.42	1867.89	1749.42	1665.86	1605.23	1560.32
370000	2099.59	2057.35	1950.12	1919.78	1798.01	1712.13	1649.82	1603.67
380000	2156.34	2112.95	2002.83	1971.67	1846.61	1758.41	1694.41	1647.01
390000	2213.08	2168.56	2055.53	2023.55	1895.20	1804.68	1739.00	1690.35
400000	2269.83	2224.16	2108.24	2075.44	1943.80	1850.96	1783.59	1733.69

BLENDED MONTHLY PAYMENTS

AMORTIZATION IN YEARS

5%

Amount	1	2	3	4	5	6	7	8
25	2.14	1.10	.75	.58	.48	.41	.36	.32
50	4.28	2.20	1.50	1.16	.95	.81	.71	.64
100	8.56	4.39	3.00	2.31	1.89	1.61	1.42	1.27
200	17.12	8.77	5.99	4.61	3.77	3.22	2.83	2.53
300	25.68	13.16	8.99	6.91	5.66	4.83	4.24	3.80
400	34.24	17.54	11.98	9.21	7.54	6.44	5.65	5.06
500	42.80	21.93	14.98	11.51	9.43	8.05	7.06	6.32
600	51.36	26.31	17.97	13.81	11.31	9.65	8.47	7.59
700	59.91	30.70	20.97	16.11	13.20	11.26	9.88	8.85
800	68.47	35.08	23.96	18.41	15.08	12.87	11.29	10.11
900	77.03	39.47	26.96	20.71	16.97	14.48	12.70	11.38
1000	85.59	43.85	29.95	23.01	18.85	16.09	14.11	12.64
2000	171.17	87.70	59.90	46.02	37.70	32.17	28.22	25.28
3000	256.76	131.55	89.85	69.02	56.55	48.25	42.33	37.91
4000	342.34	175.40	119.80	92.03	75.40	64.33	56.44	50.55
5000	427.92	219.25	149.74	115.04	94.24	80.41	70.55	63.18
6000	513.51	263.10	179.69	138.04	113.09	96.49	84.66	75.82
7000	599.09	306.94	209.64	161.05	131.94	112.57	98.77	88.45
8000	684.68	350.79	239.59	184.05	150.79	128.65	112.88	101.09
9000	770.26	394.64	269.54	207.06	169.63	144.74	126.99	113.72
10000	855.84	438.49	299.48	230.07	188.48	160.82	141.10	126.36
20000	1711.68	876.97	598.96	460.13	376.96	321.63	282.20	252.72
30000	2567.52	1315.46	898.44	690.19	565.44	482.44	423.30	379.07
40000	3423.36	1753.94	1197.92	920.25	753.91	643.25	564.40	505.43
50000	4279.20	2192.43	1497.40	1150.31	942.39	804.06	705.50	631.78
60000	5135.04	2630.91	1796.88	1380.37	1130.87	964.87	846.59	758.14
70000	5990.88	3069.39	2096.36	1610.43	1319.35	1125.69	987.69	884.49
80000	6846.72	3507.88	2395.83	1840.49	1507.82	1286.50	1128.79	1010.85
90000	7702.56	3946.36	2695.31	2070.55	1696.30	1447.31	1269.89	1137.20
100000	8558.40	4384.85	2994.79	2300.61	1884.78	1608.12	1410.99	1263.56
110000	9414.24	4823.33	3294.27	2530.67	2073.26	1768.93	1552.08	1389.91
120000	10270.08	5261.82	3593.75	2760.73	2261.73	1929.74	1693.18	1516.27
130000	11125.92	5700.30	3893.23	2990.79	2450.21	2090.55	1834.28	1642.62
140000	11981.76	6138.78	4192.71	3220.85	2638.69	2251.37	1975.38	1768.98
150000	12837.60	6577.27	4492.19	3450.91	2827.17	2412.18	2116.48	1895.33
160000	13693.44	7015.75	4791.66	3680.97	3015.64	2572.99	2257.58	2021.69
170000	14549.28	7454.24	5091.14	3911.04	3204.12	2733.80	2398.67	2148.04
180000	15405.12	7892.72	5390.62	4141.10	3392.60	2894.61	2539.77	2274.40
190000	16260.96	8331.20	5690.10	4371.16	3581.08	3055.42	2680.87	2400.75
200000	17116.80	8769.69	5989.58	4601.22	3769.55	3216.23	2821.97	2527.11
210000	17972.64	9208.17	6289.06	4831.28	3958.03	3377.05	2963.07	2653.46
220000	18828.48	9646.66	6588.54	5061.34	4146.51	3537.86	3104.16	2779.82
230000	19684.32	10085.14	6888.01	5291.40	4334.99	3698.67	3245.26	2906.17
240000	20540.16	10523.63	7187.49	5521.46	4523.46	3859.48	3386.36	3032.53
250000	21396.00	10962.11	7486.97	5751.52	4711.94	4020.29	3527.46	3158.88
260000	22251.84	11400.59	7786.45	5981.58	4900.42	4181.10	3668.56	3285.24
270000	23107.68	11839.08	8085.93	6211.64	5088.89	4341.91	3809.66	3411.59
280000	23963.52	12277.56	8385.41	6441.70	5277.37	4502.73	3950.75	3537.95
290000	24819.36	12716.05	8684.89	6671.76	5465.85	4663.54	4091.85	3664.30
300000	25675.20	13154.53	8984.37	6901.82	5654.33	4824.35	4232.95	3790.66
310000	26531.04	13593.01	9283.84	7131.88	5842.80	4985.16	4374.05	3917.01
320000	27386.88	14031.50	9583.32	7361.94	6031.28	5145.97	4515.15	4043.37
330000	28242.72	14469.98	9882.80	7592.01	6219.76	5306.78	4656.24	4169.72
340000	29098.56	14908.47	10182.28	7822.07	6408.24	5467.59	4797.34	4296.08
350000	29954.40	15346.95	10481.76	8052.13	6596.71	5628.41	4938.44	4422.43
360000	30810.24	15785.44	10781.24	8282.19	6785.19	5789.22	5079.54	4548.79
370000	31666.08	16223.92	11080.72	8512.25	6973.67	5950.03	5220.64	4675.14
380000	32521.92	16662.40	11380.20	8742.31	7162.15	6110.84	5361.74	4801.50
390000	33377.75	17100.89	11679.67	8972.37	7350.62	6271.65	5502.83	4927.85
400000	34233.59	17539.37	11979.15	9202.43	7539.10	6432.46	5643.93	5054.21

5% BLENDED MONTHLY PAYMENTS
AMORTIZATION IN YEARS

Amount	9	10	11	12	13	14	15	16
25	.29	.27	.25	.24	.22	.21	.20	.19
50	.58	.53	.50	.47	.44	.42	.40	.38
100	1.15	1.06	.99	.93	.88	.83	.79	.76
200	2.30	2.12	1.97	1.85	1.75	1.66	1.58	1.51
300	3.45	3.18	2.96	2.77	2.62	2.48	2.37	2.27
400	4.60	4.24	3.94	3.69	3.49	3.31	3.16	3.02
500	5.75	5.30	4.92	4.62	4.36	4.14	3.95	3.78
600	6.90	6.35	5.91	5.54	5.23	4.96	4.73	4.53
700	8.05	7.41	6.89	6.46	6.10	5.79	5.52	5.29
800	9.20	8.47	7.88	7.38	6.97	6.61	6.31	6.04
900	10.35	9.53	8.86	8.31	7.84	7.44	7.10	6.80
1000	11.50	10.59	9.84	9.23	8.71	8.27	7.89	7.55
2000	22.99	21.17	19.68	18.45	17.41	16.53	15.77	15.10
3000	34.48	31.75	29.52	27.67	26.12	24.79	23.65	22.65
4000	45.98	42.33	39.36	36.90	34.82	33.05	31.53	30.20
5000	57.47	52.91	49.20	46.12	43.53	41.32	39.41	37.75
6000	68.96	63.49	59.04	55.34	52.23	49.58	47.29	45.30
7000	80.45	74.08	68.88	64.57	60.94	57.84	55.17	52.85
8000	91.95	84.66	78.72	73.79	69.64	66.10	63.05	60.40
9000	103.44	95.24	88.56	83.01	78.35	74.37	70.94	67.95
10000	114.93	105.82	98.40	92.24	87.05	82.63	78.82	75.50
20000	229.86	211.63	196.79	184.47	174.10	165.25	157.63	151.00
30000	344.78	317.45	295.18	276.70	261.14	247.88	236.44	226.50
40000	459.71	423.26	393.57	368.93	348.19	330.50	315.25	302.00
50000	574.63	529.08	491.96	461.16	435.23	413.12	394.07	377.49
60000	689.56	634.89	590.35	553.40	522.28	495.75	472.88	452.99
70000	804.48	740.71	688.74	645.63	609.32	578.37	551.69	528.49
80000	919.41	846.52	787.13	737.86	696.37	660.99	630.50	603.99
90000	1034.33	952.34	885.52	830.09	783.41	743.62	709.32	679.49
100000	1149.26	1058.15	983.92	922.32	870.46	826.24	788.13	754.98
110000	1264.18	1163.97	1082.31	1014.56	957.51	908.86	866.94	830.48
120000	1379.11	1269.78	1180.70	1106.79	1044.55	991.49	945.75	905.98
130000	1494.04	1375.60	1279.09	1199.02	1131.60	1074.11	1024.57	981.48
140000	1608.96	1481.41	1377.48	1291.25	1218.64	1156.73	1103.38	1056.98
150000	1723.89	1587.23	1475.87	1383.48	1305.69	1239.36	1182.19	1132.47
160000	1838.81	1693.04	1574.26	1475.72	1392.73	1321.98	1261.00	1207.97
170000	1953.74	1798.86	1672.65	1567.95	1479.78	1404.60	1339.82	1283.47
180000	2068.66	1904.67	1771.04	1660.18	1566.82	1487.23	1418.63	1358.97
190000	2183.59	2010.49	1869.43	1752.41	1653.87	1569.85	1497.44	1434.46
200000	2298.51	2116.30	1967.83	1844.64	1740.92	1652.47	1576.25	1509.96
210000	2413.44	2222.12	2066.22	1936.87	1827.96	1735.10	1655.06	1585.46
220000	2528.36	2327.93	2164.61	2029.11	1915.01	1817.72	1733.88	1660.96
230000	2643.29	2433.75	2263.00	2121.34	2002.05	1900.34	1812.69	1736.46
240000	2758.21	2539.56	2361.39	2213.57	2089.10	1982.97	1891.50	1811.95
250000	2873.14	2645.38	2459.78	2305.80	2176.14	2065.59	1970.31	1887.45
260000	2988.07	2751.19	2558.17	2398.03	2263.19	2148.21	2049.13	1962.95
270000	3102.99	2857.01	2656.56	2490.27	2350.23	2230.84	2127.94	2038.45
280000	3217.92	2962.82	2754.95	2582.50	2437.28	2313.46	2206.75	2113.95
290000	3332.84	3068.64	2853.34	2674.73	2524.33	2396.08	2285.56	2189.44
300000	3447.77	3174.45	2951.74	2766.96	2611.37	2478.71	2364.38	2264.94
310000	3562.69	3280.27	3050.13	2859.19	2698.42	2561.33	2443.19	2340.44
320000	3677.62	3386.08	3148.52	2951.43	2785.46	2643.95	2522.00	2415.94
330000	3792.54	3491.90	3246.91	3043.66	2872.51	2726.58	2600.81	2491.43
340000	3907.47	3597.71	3345.30	3135.89	2959.55	2809.20	2679.63	2566.93
350000	4022.39	3703.53	3443.69	3228.12	3046.60	2891.82	2758.44	2642.43
360000	4137.32	3809.34	3542.08	3320.35	3133.64	2974.45	2837.25	2717.93
370000	4252.25	3915.16	3640.47	3412.59	3220.69	3057.07	2916.06	2793.43
380000	4367.17	4020.97	3738.86	3504.82	3307.74	3139.69	2994.88	2868.92
390000	4482.10	4126.79	3837.25	3597.05	3394.78	3222.32	3073.69	2944.42
400000	4597.02	4232.60	3935.65	3689.28	3481.83	3304.94	3152.50	3019.92

BLENDED MONTHLY PAYMENTS 5%
AMORTIZATION IN YEARS

Amount	17	18	19	20	21	22	23	24
25	.19	.18	.17	.17	.16	.16	.16	.15
50	.37	.36	.34	.33	.32	.32	.31	.30
100	.73	.71	.68	.66	.64	.63	.61	.60
200	1.46	1.41	1.36	1.32	1.28	1.25	1.22	1.19
300	2.18	2.11	2.04	1.98	1.92	1.87	1.83	1.79
400	2.91	2.81	2.71	2.63	2.56	2.49	2.43	2.38
500	3.63	3.51	3.39	3.29	3.20	3.12	3.04	2.97
600	4.36	4.21	4.07	3.95	3.84	3.74	3.65	3.57
700	5.09	4.91	4.75	4.60	4.48	4.36	4.26	4.16
800	5.81	5.61	5.42	5.26	5.12	4.98	4.86	4.76
900	6.54	6.31	6.10	5.92	5.75	5.61	5.47	5.35
1000	7.26	7.01	6.78	6.58	6.39	6.23	6.08	5.94
2000	14.52	14.01	13.55	13.15	12.78	12.45	12.15	11.88
3000	21.78	21.01	20.33	19.72	19.17	18.68	18.23	17.82
4000	29.04	28.02	27.10	26.29	25.56	24.90	24.30	23.76
5000	36.30	35.02	33.88	32.86	31.95	31.12	30.38	29.70
6000	43.56	42.02	40.65	39.43	38.34	37.35	36.45	35.64
7000	50.82	49.02	47.43	46.00	44.72	43.57	42.53	41.58
8000	58.08	56.03	54.20	52.58	51.11	49.80	48.60	47.52
9000	65.34	63.03	60.98	59.15	57.50	56.02	54.68	53.46
10000	72.60	70.03	67.75	65.72	63.89	62.24	60.75	59.40
20000	145.19	140.06	135.50	131.43	127.78	124.48	121.50	118.79
30000	217.78	210.09	203.25	197.14	191.66	186.72	182.25	178.19
40000	290.37	280.11	271.00	262.86	255.55	248.96	243.00	237.58
50000	362.97	350.14	338.74	328.57	319.43	311.20	303.75	296.98
60000	435.56	420.17	406.49	394.28	383.32	373.44	364.49	356.37
70000	508.15	490.19	474.24	459.99	447.20	435.68	425.24	415.76
80000	580.74	560.22	541.99	525.71	511.09	497.91	485.99	475.16
90000	653.33	630.25	609.74	591.42	574.98	560.15	546.74	534.55
100000	725.93	700.27	677.48	657.13	638.86	622.39	607.49	593.95
110000	798.52	770.30	745.23	722.84	702.75	684.63	668.23	653.34
120000	871.11	840.33	812.98	788.56	766.63	746.87	728.98	712.74
130000	943.70	910.35	880.73	854.27	830.52	809.11	789.73	772.13
140000	1016.29	980.38	948.48	919.98	894.40	871.35	850.48	831.52
150000	1088.89	1050.41	1016.22	985.69	958.29	933.59	911.23	890.92
160000	1161.48	1120.43	1083.97	1051.41	1022.18	995.82	971.98	950.31
170000	1234.07	1190.46	1151.72	1117.12	1086.06	1058.06	1032.72	1009.71
180000	1306.66	1260.49	1219.47	1182.83	1149.95	1120.30	1093.47	1069.10
190000	1379.25	1330.51	1287.21	1248.54	1213.83	1182.54	1154.22	1128.50
200000	1451.85	1400.54	1354.96	1314.26	1277.72	1244.78	1214.97	1187.89
210000	1524.44	1470.57	1422.71	1379.97	1341.60	1307.02	1275.72	1247.28
220000	1597.03	1540.59	1490.46	1445.68	1405.49	1369.26	1336.46	1306.68
230000	1669.62	1610.62	1558.21	1511.39	1469.37	1431.50	1397.21	1366.07
240000	1742.21	1680.65	1625.95	1577.11	1533.26	1493.73	1457.96	1425.47
250000	1814.81	1750.67	1693.70	1642.82	1597.15	1555.97	1518.71	1484.86
260000	1887.40	1820.70	1761.45	1708.53	1661.03	1618.21	1579.46	1544.26
270000	1959.99	1890.73	1829.20	1774.24	1724.92	1680.45	1640.21	1603.65
280000	2032.58	1960.75	1896.95	1839.96	1788.80	1742.69	1700.95	1663.04
290000	2105.17	2030.78	1964.69	1905.67	1852.69	1804.93	1761.70	1722.44
300000	2177.77	2100.81	2032.44	1971.38	1916.57	1867.17	1822.45	1781.83
310000	2250.36	2170.83	2100.19	2037.09	1980.46	1929.41	1883.20	1841.23
320000	2322.95	2240.86	2167.94	2102.81	2044.35	1991.64	1943.95	1900.62
330000	2395.54	2310.89	2235.68	2168.52	2108.23	2053.88	2004.69	1960.02
340000	2468.13	2380.91	2303.43	2234.23	2172.12	2116.12	2065.44	2019.41
350000	2540.73	2450.94	2371.18	2299.94	2236.00	2178.36	2126.19	2078.80
360000	2613.32	2520.97	2438.93	2365.66	2299.89	2240.60	2186.94	2138.20
370000	2685.91	2590.99	2506.68	2431.37	2363.77	2302.84	2247.69	2197.59
380000	2758.50	2661.02	2574.42	2497.08	2427.66	2365.08	2308.44	2256.99
390000	2831.09	2731.05	2642.17	2562.79	2491.55	2427.32	2369.18	2316.38
400000	2903.69	2801.07	2709.92	2628.51	2555.43	2489.55	2429.93	2375.78

5% BLENDED MONTHLY PAYMENTS
AMORTIZATION IN YEARS

Amount	25	26	29	30	35	40	45	50
25	.15	.15	.14	.14	.13	.12	.12	.12
50	.30	.29	.28	.27	.26	.24	.24	.23
100	.59	.58	.55	.54	.51	.48	.47	.46
200	1.17	1.15	1.09	1.07	1.01	.96	.93	.91
300	1.75	1.72	1.63	1.61	1.51	1.44	1.39	1.36
400	2.33	2.29	2.17	2.14	2.01	1.92	1.86	1.81
500	2.91	2.86	2.71	2.67	2.51	2.40	2.32	2.26
600	3.49	3.43	3.26	3.21	3.01	2.88	2.78	2.71
700	4.08	4.00	3.80	3.74	3.51	3.36	3.24	3.16
800	4.66	4.57	4.34	4.27	4.02	3.84	3.71	3.61
900	5.24	5.14	4.88	4.81	4.52	4.31	4.17	4.06
1000	5.82	5.71	5.42	5.34	5.02	4.79	4.63	4.51
2000	11.64	11.41	10.84	10.68	10.03	9.58	9.26	9.02
3000	17.45	17.11	16.26	16.02	15.05	14.37	13.88	13.52
4000	23.27	22.82	21.68	21.35	20.06	19.16	18.51	18.03
5000	29.09	28.52	27.09	26.69	25.08	23.95	23.13	22.53
6000	34.90	34.22	32.51	32.03	30.09	28.73	27.76	27.04
7000	40.72	39.93	37.93	37.36	35.10	33.52	32.38	31.54
8000	46.53	45.63	43.35	42.70	40.12	38.31	37.01	36.05
9000	52.35	51.33	48.76	48.04	45.13	43.10	41.63	40.55
10000	58.17	57.04	54.18	53.37	50.15	47.89	46.26	45.06
20000	116.33	114.07	108.36	106.74	100.29	95.77	92.51	90.11
30000	174.49	171.10	162.53	160.11	150.43	143.65	138.76	135.16
40000	232.65	228.14	216.71	213.48	200.57	191.53	185.01	180.22
50000	290.81	285.17	270.88	266.85	250.72	239.41	231.26	225.27
60000	348.97	342.20	325.06	320.22	300.86	287.29	277.51	270.32
70000	407.13	399.24	379.24	373.59	351.00	335.17	323.76	315.37
80000	465.29	456.27	433.41	426.96	401.14	383.05	370.01	360.43
90000	523.45	513.30	487.59	480.33	451.28	430.93	416.26	405.48
100000	581.61	570.33	541.76	533.70	501.43	478.81	462.51	450.53
110000	639.77	627.37	595.94	587.06	551.57	526.69	508.76	495.59
120000	697.93	684.40	650.11	640.43	601.71	574.57	555.01	540.64
130000	756.09	741.43	704.29	693.80	651.85	622.45	601.26	585.69
140000	814.25	798.47	758.47	747.17	701.99	670.33	647.51	630.74
150000	872.41	855.50	812.64	800.54	752.14	718.21	693.77	675.80
160000	930.57	912.53	866.82	853.91	802.28	766.09	740.02	720.85
170000	988.73	969.56	920.99	907.28	852.42	813.97	786.27	765.90
180000	1046.89	1026.60	975.17	960.65	902.56	861.85	832.52	810.95
190000	1105.05	1083.63	1029.34	1014.02	952.70	909.73	878.77	856.01
200000	1163.21	1140.66	1083.52	1067.39	1002.85	957.61	925.02	901.06
210000	1221.38	1197.70	1137.70	1120.76	1052.99	1005.49	971.27	946.11
220000	1279.54	1254.73	1191.87	1174.12	1103.13	1053.37	1017.52	991.17
230000	1337.70	1311.76	1246.05	1227.49	1153.27	1101.25	1063.77	1036.22
240000	1395.86	1368.79	1300.22	1280.86	1203.41	1149.13	1110.02	1081.27
250000	1454.02	1425.83	1354.40	1334.23	1253.56	1197.01	1156.27	1126.32
260000	1512.18	1482.86	1408.58	1387.60	1303.70	1244.89	1202.52	1171.38
270000	1570.34	1539.89	1462.75	1440.97	1353.84	1292.78	1248.77	1216.43
280000	1628.50	1596.93	1516.93	1494.34	1403.98	1340.66	1295.02	1261.48
290000	1686.66	1653.96	1571.10	1547.71	1454.12	1388.54	1341.27	1306.53
300000	1744.82	1710.99	1625.28	1601.08	1504.27	1436.42	1387.53	1351.59
310000	1802.98	1768.02	1679.45	1654.45	1554.41	1484.30	1433.78	1396.64
320000	1861.14	1825.06	1733.63	1707.82	1604.55	1532.18	1480.03	1441.69
330000	1919.30	1882.09	1787.81	1761.18	1654.69	1580.06	1526.28	1486.75
340000	1977.46	1939.12	1841.98	1814.55	1704.83	1627.94	1572.53	1531.80
350000	2035.62	1996.16	1896.16	1867.92	1754.98	1675.82	1618.78	1576.85
360000	2093.78	2053.19	1950.33	1921.29	1805.12	1723.70	1665.03	1621.90
370000	2151.94	2110.22	2004.51	1974.66	1855.26	1771.58	1711.28	1666.96
380000	2210.10	2167.25	2058.68	2028.03	1905.40	1819.46	1757.53	1712.01
390000	2268.26	2224.29	2112.86	2081.40	1955.55	1867.34	1803.78	1757.06
400000	2326.42	2281.32	2167.04	2134.77	2005.69	1915.22	1850.03	1802.12

40

BLENDED MONTHLY PAYMENTS 5¼%
AMORTIZATION IN YEARS

Amount	1	2	3	4	5	6	7	8
25	2.15	1.10	.76	.58	.48	.41	.36	.32
50	4.29	2.20	1.51	1.16	.95	.81	.72	.64
100	8.57	4.40	3.01	2.32	1.90	1.62	1.43	1.28
200	17.14	8.80	6.02	4.63	3.80	3.24	2.85	2.56
300	25.71	13.19	9.02	6.94	5.69	4.86	4.27	3.83
400	34.28	17.59	12.03	9.25	7.59	6.48	5.70	5.11
500	42.85	21.98	15.03	11.56	9.49	8.10	7.12	6.38
600	51.42	26.38	18.04	13.88	11.38	9.72	8.54	7.66
700	59.99	30.78	21.05	16.19	13.28	11.34	9.96	8.93
800	68.56	35.17	24.05	18.50	15.17	12.96	11.39	10.21
900	77.13	39.57	27.06	20.81	17.07	14.58	12.81	11.48
1000	85.70	43.96	30.06	23.12	18.97	16.20	14.23	12.76
2000	171.40	87.92	60.12	46.24	37.93	32.39	28.46	25.51
3000	257.09	131.88	90.18	69.36	56.89	48.59	42.68	38.26
4000	342.79	175.84	120.24	92.47	75.85	64.78	56.91	51.01
5000	428.49	219.80	150.29	115.59	94.81	80.98	71.13	63.77
6000	514.18	263.75	180.35	138.71	113.77	97.17	85.36	76.52
7000	599.88	307.71	210.41	161.82	132.73	113.37	99.58	89.27
8000	685.57	351.67	240.47	184.94	151.69	129.56	113.81	102.02
9000	771.27	395.63	270.53	208.06	170.65	145.76	128.03	114.78
10000	856.97	439.59	300.58	231.18	189.61	161.95	142.26	127.53
20000	1713.93	879.17	601.16	462.35	379.21	323.90	284.51	255.05
30000	2570.89	1318.75	901.74	693.52	568.81	485.85	426.76	382.57
40000	3427.85	1758.33	1202.32	924.69	758.41	647.80	569.01	510.09
50000	4284.81	2197.91	1502.90	1155.86	948.01	809.75	711.26	637.62
60000	5141.78	2637.49	1803.48	1387.03	1137.61	971.70	853.51	765.14
70000	5998.74	3077.07	2104.05	1618.20	1327.21	1133.64	995.76	892.66
80000	6855.70	3516.65	2404.63	1849.37	1516.81	1295.59	1138.01	1020.18
90000	7712.66	3956.23	2705.21	2080.54	1706.41	1457.54	1280.26	1147.71
100000	8569.62	4395.81	3005.79	2311.71	1896.01	1619.49	1422.51	1275.23
110000	9426.58	4835.40	3306.37	2542.88	2085.61	1781.44	1564.76	1402.75
120000	10283.55	5274.98	3606.95	2774.05	2275.21	1943.39	1707.01	1530.27
130000	11140.51	5714.56	3907.52	3005.22	2464.81	2105.33	1849.26	1657.80
140000	11997.47	6154.14	4208.10	3236.39	2654.41	2267.28	1991.51	1785.32
150000	12854.43	6593.72	4508.68	3467.56	2844.01	2429.23	2133.76	1912.84
160000	13711.39	7033.30	4809.26	3698.73	3033.61	2591.18	2276.01	2040.36
170000	14568.35	7472.88	5109.84	3929.90	3223.21	2753.13	2418.26	2167.89
180000	15425.32	7912.46	5410.42	4161.07	3412.81	2915.08	2560.51	2295.41
190000	16282.28	8352.04	5711.00	4392.24	3602.41	3077.02	2702.76	2422.93
200000	17139.24	8791.62	6011.57	4623.41	3792.01	3238.97	2845.01	2550.45
210000	17996.20	9231.20	6312.15	4854.58	3981.61	3400.92	2987.26	2677.98
220000	18853.16	9670.79	6612.73	5085.75	4171.21	3562.87	3129.51	2805.50
230000	19710.12	10110.37	6913.31	5316.92	4360.81	3724.82	3271.76	2933.02
240000	20567.09	10549.95	7213.89	5548.10	4550.41	3886.77	3414.01	3060.54
250000	21424.05	10989.53	7514.47	5779.27	4740.01	4048.71	3556.26	3188.06
260000	22281.01	11429.11	7815.04	6010.44	4929.61	4210.66	3698.51	3315.59
270000	23137.97	11868.69	8115.62	6241.61	5119.21	4372.61	3840.76	3443.11
280000	23994.93	12308.27	8416.20	6472.78	5308.81	4534.56	3983.01	3570.63
290000	24851.90	12747.85	8716.78	6703.95	5498.41	4696.51	4125.26	3698.15
300000	25708.86	13187.43	9017.36	6935.12	5688.01	4858.46	4267.51	3825.68
310000	26565.82	13627.01	9317.94	7166.29	5877.61	5020.40	4409.76	3953.20
320000	27422.78	14066.59	9618.51	7397.46	6067.21	5182.35	4552.01	4080.72
330000	28279.74	14506.18	9919.09	7628.63	6256.81	5344.30	4694.26	4208.24
340000	29136.70	14945.76	10219.67	7859.80	6446.41	5506.25	4836.51	4335.77
350000	29993.67	15385.34	10520.25	8090.97	6636.01	5668.20	4978.76	4463.29
360000	30850.63	15824.92	10820.83	8322.14	6825.61	5830.15	5121.01	4590.81
370000	31707.59	16264.50	11121.41	8553.31	7015.21	5992.09	5263.26	4718.33
380000	32564.55	16704.08	11421.99	8784.48	7204.81	6154.04	5405.51	4845.86
390000	33421.51	17143.66	11722.56	9015.65	7394.41	6315.99	5547.76	4973.38
400000	34278.47	17583.24	12023.14	9246.82	7584.01	6477.94	5690.01	5100.90

41

5¼% BLENDED MONTHLY PAYMENTS
AMORTIZATION IN YEARS

Amount	9	10	11	12	13	14	15	16
25	.30	.27	.25	.24	.23	.21	.21	.20
50	.59	.54	.50	.47	.45	.42	.41	.39
100	1.17	1.08	1.00	.94	.89	.84	.81	.77
200	2.33	2.15	2.00	1.87	1.77	1.68	1.61	1.54
300	3.49	3.22	2.99	2.81	2.65	2.52	2.41	2.31
400	4.65	4.29	3.99	3.74	3.54	3.36	3.21	3.08
500	5.81	5.36	4.99	4.68	4.42	4.20	4.01	3.84
600	6.97	6.43	5.98	5.61	5.30	5.04	4.81	4.61
700	8.13	7.50	6.98	6.55	6.19	5.88	5.61	5.38
800	9.29	8.57	7.97	7.48	7.07	6.72	6.41	6.15
900	10.45	9.64	8.97	8.42	7.95	7.55	7.21	6.92
1000	11.62	10.71	9.97	9.35	8.83	8.39	8.01	7.68
2000	23.23	21.41	19.93	18.70	17.66	16.78	16.02	15.36
3000	34.84	32.11	29.89	28.04	26.49	25.17	24.03	23.04
4000	46.45	42.81	39.85	37.39	35.32	33.56	32.04	30.72
5000	58.06	53.51	49.81	46.74	44.15	41.95	40.05	38.40
6000	69.67	64.21	59.77	56.08	52.98	50.34	48.06	46.08
7000	81.28	74.91	69.73	65.43	61.81	58.73	56.07	53.76
8000	92.89	85.62	79.69	74.78	70.64	67.11	64.08	61.44
9000	104.50	96.32	89.65	84.12	79.47	75.50	72.09	69.12
10000	116.11	107.02	99.61	93.47	88.30	83.89	80.10	76.80
20000	232.22	214.03	199.22	186.93	176.59	167.78	160.19	153.59
30000	348.33	321.05	298.82	280.39	264.88	251.66	240.28	230.38
40000	464.44	428.06	398.43	373.86	353.17	335.55	320.37	307.17
50000	580.55	535.07	498.03	467.32	441.47	419.44	400.46	383.97
60000	696.66	642.09	597.64	560.78	529.76	503.32	480.55	460.76
70000	812.76	749.10	697.25	654.24	618.05	587.21	560.64	537.55
80000	928.87	856.12	796.85	747.71	706.34	671.09	640.73	614.34
90000	1044.98	963.13	896.46	841.17	794.64	754.98	720.82	691.13
100000	1161.09	1070.14	996.06	934.63	882.93	838.87	800.91	767.93
110000	1277.20	1177.16	1095.67	1028.09	971.22	922.75	881.01	844.72
120000	1393.31	1284.17	1195.27	1121.56	1059.51	1006.64	961.10	921.51
130000	1509.41	1391.18	1294.88	1215.02	1147.80	1090.52	1041.19	998.30
140000	1625.52	1498.20	1394.49	1308.48	1236.10	1174.41	1121.28	1075.10
150000	1741.63	1605.21	1494.09	1401.94	1324.39	1258.30	1201.37	1151.89
160000	1857.74	1712.23	1593.70	1495.41	1412.68	1342.18	1281.46	1228.68
170000	1973.85	1819.24	1693.30	1588.87	1500.97	1426.07	1361.55	1305.47
180000	2089.96	1926.25	1792.91	1682.33	1589.27	1509.95	1441.64	1382.26
190000	2206.06	2033.27	1892.52	1775.80	1677.56	1593.84	1521.73	1459.06
200000	2322.17	2140.28	1992.12	1869.26	1765.85	1677.73	1601.82	1535.85
210000	2438.28	2247.29	2091.73	1962.72	1854.14	1761.61	1681.91	1612.64
220000	2554.39	2354.31	2191.33	2056.18	1942.43	1845.50	1762.01	1689.43
230000	2670.50	2461.32	2290.94	2149.65	2030.73	1929.38	1842.10	1766.23
240000	2786.61	2568.34	2390.54	2243.11	2119.02	2013.27	1922.19	1843.02
250000	2902.71	2675.35	2490.15	2336.57	2207.31	2097.16	2002.28	1919.81
260000	3018.82	2782.36	2589.76	2430.03	2295.60	2181.04	2082.37	1996.60
270000	3134.93	2889.38	2689.36	2523.50	2383.90	2264.93	2162.46	2073.39
280000	3251.04	2996.39	2788.97	2616.96	2472.19	2348.81	2242.55	2150.19
290000	3367.15	3103.40	2888.57	2710.42	2560.48	2432.70	2322.64	2226.98
300000	3483.26	3210.42	2988.18	2803.88	2648.77	2516.59	2402.73	2303.77
310000	3599.36	3317.43	3087.78	2897.35	2737.06	2600.47	2482.82	2380.56
320000	3715.47	3424.45	3187.39	2990.81	2825.36	2684.36	2562.91	2457.36
330000	3831.58	3531.46	3287.00	3084.27	2913.65	2768.24	2643.01	2534.15
340000	3947.69	3638.47	3386.60	3177.73	3001.94	2852.13	2723.10	2610.94
350000	4063.80	3745.49	3486.21	3271.20	3090.23	2936.02	2803.19	2687.73
360000	4179.91	3852.50	3585.81	3364.66	3178.53	3019.90	2883.28	2764.52
370000	4296.02	3959.51	3685.42	3458.12	3266.82	3103.79	2963.37	2841.32
380000	4412.12	4066.53	3785.03	3551.59	3355.11	3187.67	3043.46	2918.11
390000	4528.23	4173.54	3884.63	3645.05	3443.40	3271.56	3123.55	2994.90
400000	4644.34	4280.56	3984.24	3738.51	3531.69	3355.45	3203.64	3071.69

BLENDED MONTHLY PAYMENTS 5¼%
AMORTIZATION IN YEARS

Amount	17	18	19	20	21	22	23	24
25	.19	.18	.18	.17	.17	.16	.16	.16
50	.37	.36	.35	.34	.33	.32	.32	.31
100	.74	.72	.70	.68	.66	.64	.63	.61
200	1.48	1.43	1.39	1.35	1.31	1.28	1.25	1.22
300	2.22	2.15	2.08	2.02	1.96	1.91	1.87	1.83
400	2.96	2.86	2.77	2.69	2.62	2.55	2.49	2.44
500	3.70	3.57	3.46	3.36	3.27	3.19	3.11	3.05
600	4.44	4.29	4.15	4.03	3.92	3.82	3.73	3.65
700	5.18	5.00	4.84	4.70	4.57	4.46	4.36	4.26
800	5.92	5.71	5.53	5.37	5.23	5.10	4.98	4.87
900	6.66	6.43	6.22	6.04	5.88	5.73	5.60	5.48
1000	7.40	7.14	6.91	6.71	6.53	6.37	6.22	6.09
2000	14.79	14.28	13.82	13.42	13.06	12.73	12.44	12.17
3000	22.18	21.41	20.73	20.13	19.58	19.09	18.65	18.25
4000	29.57	28.55	27.64	26.83	26.11	25.46	24.87	24.33
5000	36.96	35.68	34.55	33.54	32.63	31.82	31.08	30.41
6000	44.35	42.82	41.46	40.25	39.16	38.18	37.30	36.49
7000	51.74	49.95	48.37	46.95	45.69	44.54	43.51	42.57
8000	59.13	57.09	55.28	53.66	52.21	50.91	49.73	48.65
9000	66.52	64.22	62.19	60.37	58.74	57.27	55.94	54.73
10000	73.91	71.36	69.09	67.07	65.26	63.63	62.16	60.82
20000	147.81	142.71	138.18	134.14	130.52	127.26	124.31	121.63
30000	221.71	214.06	207.27	201.21	195.78	190.88	186.46	182.44
40000	295.61	285.41	276.36	268.28	261.03	254.51	248.61	243.25
50000	369.52	356.77	345.45	335.35	326.29	318.13	310.76	304.06
60000	443.42	428.12	414.54	402.42	391.55	381.76	372.91	364.87
70000	517.32	499.47	483.63	469.49	456.81	445.38	435.06	425.68
80000	591.22	570.82	552.72	536.56	522.06	509.01	497.21	486.49
90000	665.12	642.18	621.81	603.63	587.32	572.64	559.36	547.30
100000	739.03	713.53	690.90	670.70	652.58	636.26	621.51	608.11
110000	812.93	784.88	759.98	737.76	717.84	699.89	683.66	668.93
120000	886.83	856.23	829.07	804.83	783.09	763.51	745.81	729.74
130000	960.73	927.59	898.16	871.90	848.35	827.14	807.96	790.55
140000	1034.63	998.94	967.25	938.97	913.61	890.76	870.11	851.36
150000	1108.54	1070.29	1036.34	1006.04	978.87	954.39	932.26	912.17
160000	1182.44	1141.64	1105.43	1073.11	1044.12	1018.02	994.41	972.98
170000	1256.34	1213.00	1174.52	1140.18	1109.38	1081.64	1056.56	1033.79
180000	1330.24	1284.35	1243.61	1207.25	1174.64	1145.27	1118.71	1094.60
190000	1404.15	1355.70	1312.70	1274.32	1239.90	1208.89	1180.86	1155.41
200000	1478.05	1427.05	1381.79	1341.39	1305.15	1272.52	1243.01	1216.22
210000	1551.95	1498.40	1450.88	1408.46	1370.41	1336.14	1305.16	1277.03
220000	1625.85	1569.76	1519.96	1475.52	1435.67	1399.77	1367.31	1337.85
230000	1699.75	1641.11	1589.05	1542.59	1500.93	1463.40	1429.46	1398.66
240000	1773.66	1712.46	1658.14	1609.66	1566.18	1527.02	1491.61	1459.47
250000	1847.56	1783.81	1727.23	1676.73	1631.44	1590.65	1553.76	1520.28
260000	1921.46	1855.17	1796.32	1743.80	1696.70	1654.27	1615.91	1581.09
270000	1995.36	1926.52	1865.41	1810.87	1761.96	1717.90	1678.06	1641.90
280000	2069.26	1997.87	1934.50	1877.94	1827.21	1781.52	1740.21	1702.71
290000	2143.17	2069.22	2003.59	1945.01	1892.47	1845.15	1802.36	1763.52
300000	2217.07	2140.58	2072.68	2012.08	1957.73	1908.78	1864.51	1824.33
310000	2290.97	2211.93	2141.77	2079.15	2022.99	1972.40	1926.66	1885.14
320000	2364.87	2283.28	2210.86	2146.22	2088.24	2036.03	1988.81	1945.96
330000	2438.77	2354.63	2279.94	2213.28	2153.50	2099.65	2050.96	2006.77
340000	2512.68	2425.99	2349.03	2280.35	2218.76	2163.28	2113.11	2067.58
350000	2586.58	2497.34	2418.12	2347.42	2284.02	2226.90	2175.26	2128.39
360000	2660.48	2568.69	2487.21	2414.49	2349.27	2290.53	2237.41	2189.20
370000	2734.38	2640.04	2556.30	2481.56	2414.53	2354.15	2299.56	2250.01
380000	2808.29	2711.40	2625.39	2548.63	2479.79	2417.78	2361.71	2310.82
390000	2882.19	2782.75	2694.48	2615.70	2545.05	2481.41	2423.86	2371.63
400000	2956.09	2854.10	2763.57	2682.77	2610.30	2545.03	2486.01	2432.44

5¼% BLENDED MONTHLY PAYMENTS
AMORTIZATION IN YEARS

Amount	25	26	29	30	35	40	45	50
25	.15	.15	.14	.14	.13	.13	.12	.12
50	.30	.30	.28	.28	.26	.25	.24	.24
100	.60	.59	.56	.55	.52	.50	.48	.47
200	1.20	1.17	1.12	1.10	1.04	1.00	.96	.94
300	1.79	1.76	1.67	1.65	1.56	1.49	1.44	1.41
400	2.39	2.34	2.23	2.20	2.07	1.99	1.92	1.88
500	2.98	2.93	2.79	2.75	2.59	2.48	2.40	2.34
600	3.58	3.51	3.34	3.30	3.11	2.98	2.88	2.81
700	4.18	4.10	3.90	3.85	3.62	3.47	3.36	3.28
800	4.77	4.68	4.46	4.39	4.14	3.97	3.84	3.75
900	5.37	5.27	5.01	4.94	4.66	4.46	4.32	4.22
1000	5.96	5.85	5.57	5.49	5.18	4.96	4.80	4.68
2000	11.92	11.70	11.14	10.98	10.35	9.91	9.59	9.36
3000	17.88	17.55	16.70	16.47	15.52	14.86	14.38	14.04
4000	23.84	23.40	22.27	21.95	20.69	19.81	19.18	18.72
5000	29.80	29.24	27.84	27.44	25.86	24.76	23.97	23.40
6000	35.76	35.09	33.40	32.93	31.03	29.71	28.76	28.08
7000	41.72	40.94	38.97	38.41	36.20	34.66	33.56	32.75
8000	47.68	46.79	44.54	43.90	41.37	39.61	38.35	37.43
9000	53.64	52.64	50.10	49.39	46.54	44.56	43.14	42.11
10000	59.60	58.48	55.67	54.88	51.71	49.51	47.94	46.79
20000	119.19	116.96	111.33	109.75	103.42	99.02	95.87	93.57
30000	178.78	175.44	167.00	164.62	155.13	148.53	143.80	140.36
40000	238.37	233.92	222.66	219.49	206.84	198.04	191.74	187.14
50000	297.96	292.40	278.32	274.36	258.55	247.55	239.67	233.93
60000	357.56	350.88	333.99	329.23	310.26	297.05	287.60	280.71
70000	417.15	409.36	389.65	384.10	361.97	346.56	335.54	327.50
80000	476.74	467.83	445.32	438.97	413.68	396.07	383.47	374.28
90000	536.33	526.31	500.98	493.84	465.39	445.58	431.40	421.07
100000	595.92	584.79	556.64	548.71	517.10	495.09	479.34	467.85
110000	655.51	643.27	612.31	603.58	568.81	544.59	527.27	514.64
120000	715.11	701.75	667.97	658.45	620.52	594.10	575.20	561.42
130000	774.70	760.23	723.63	713.33	672.23	643.61	623.14	608.21
140000	834.29	818.71	779.30	768.20	723.94	693.12	671.07	654.99
150000	893.88	877.18	834.96	823.07	775.65	742.63	719.00	701.78
160000	953.47	935.66	890.63	877.94	827.36	792.13	766.94	748.56
170000	1013.07	994.14	946.29	932.81	879.06	841.64	814.87	795.35
180000	1072.66	1052.62	1001.95	987.68	930.77	891.15	862.80	842.13
190000	1132.25	1111.10	1057.62	1042.55	982.48	940.66	910.74	888.92
200000	1191.84	1169.58	1113.28	1097.42	1034.19	990.17	958.67	935.70
210000	1251.43	1228.06	1168.95	1152.29	1085.90	1039.67	1006.60	982.49
220000	1311.02	1286.53	1224.61	1207.16	1137.61	1089.18	1054.54	1029.27
230000	1370.62	1345.01	1280.27	1262.03	1189.32	1138.69	1102.47	1076.06
240000	1430.21	1403.49	1335.94	1316.90	1241.03	1188.20	1150.40	1122.84
250000	1489.80	1461.97	1391.60	1371.78	1292.74	1237.71	1198.34	1169.63
260000	1549.39	1520.45	1447.26	1426.65	1344.45	1287.22	1246.27	1216.41
270000	1608.98	1578.93	1502.93	1481.52	1396.16	1336.72	1294.20	1263.20
280000	1668.58	1637.41	1558.59	1536.39	1447.87	1386.23	1342.14	1309.98
290000	1728.17	1695.89	1614.26	1591.26	1499.58	1435.74	1390.07	1356.77
300000	1787.76	1754.36	1669.92	1646.13	1551.29	1485.25	1438.00	1403.55
310000	1847.35	1812.84	1725.58	1701.00	1603.00	1534.76	1485.94	1450.33
320000	1906.94	1871.32	1781.25	1755.87	1654.71	1584.26	1533.87	1497.12
330000	1966.53	1929.80	1836.91	1810.74	1706.42	1633.77	1581.80	1543.90
340000	2026.13	1988.28	1892.58	1865.61	1758.12	1683.28	1629.74	1590.69
350000	2085.72	2046.76	1948.24	1920.48	1809.83	1732.79	1677.67	1637.47
360000	2145.31	2105.24	2003.90	1975.35	1861.54	1782.30	1725.60	1684.26
370000	2204.90	2163.71	2059.57	2030.23	1913.25	1831.80	1773.54	1731.04
380000	2264.49	2222.19	2115.23	2085.10	1964.96	1881.31	1821.47	1777.83
390000	2324.09	2280.67	2170.89	2139.97	2016.67	1930.82	1869.40	1824.61
400000	2383.68	2339.15	2226.56	2194.84	2068.38	1980.33	1917.34	1871.40

44

BLENDED MONTHLY PAYMENTS $5\frac{1}{2}\%$

AMORTIZATION IN YEARS

Amount	1	2	3	4	5	6	7	8
25	2.15	1.11	.76	.59	.48	.41	.36	.33
50	4.30	2.21	1.51	1.17	.96	.82	.72	.65
100	8.59	4.41	3.02	2.33	1.91	1.64	1.44	1.29
200	17.17	8.82	6.04	4.65	3.82	3.27	2.87	2.58
300	25.75	13.23	9.06	6.97	5.73	4.90	4.31	3.87
400	34.33	17.63	12.07	9.30	7.63	6.53	5.74	5.15
500	42.91	22.04	15.09	11.62	9.54	8.16	7.18	6.44
600	51.49	26.45	18.11	13.94	11.45	9.79	8.61	7.73
700	60.07	30.85	21.12	16.26	13.36	11.42	10.04	9.01
800	68.65	35.26	24.14	18.59	15.26	13.05	11.48	10.30
900	77.23	39.67	27.16	20.91	17.17	14.68	12.91	11.59
1000	85.81	44.07	30.17	23.23	19.08	16.31	14.35	12.87
2000	171.62	88.14	60.34	46.46	38.15	32.62	28.69	25.74
3000	257.43	132.21	90.51	69.69	57.22	48.93	43.03	38.61
4000	343.24	176.28	120.68	92.92	76.30	65.24	57.37	51.48
5000	429.05	220.34	150.84	116.15	95.37	81.55	71.71	64.35
6000	514.86	264.41	181.01	139.37	114.44	97.86	86.05	77.22
7000	600.66	308.48	211.18	162.60	133.51	114.17	100.39	90.09
8000	686.47	352.55	241.35	185.83	152.59	130.48	114.73	102.96
9000	772.28	396.62	271.52	209.06	171.66	146.79	129.07	115.83
10000	858.09	440.68	301.68	232.29	190.73	163.09	143.41	128.70
20000	1716.17	881.36	603.36	464.57	381.46	326.18	286.82	257.39
30000	2574.26	1322.04	905.04	696.85	572.18	489.27	430.22	386.09
40000	3432.34	1762.72	1206.72	929.13	762.91	652.36	573.63	514.78
50000	4290.42	2203.40	1508.40	1161.42	953.63	815.45	717.04	643.48
60000	5148.51	2644.07	1810.08	1393.70	1144.36	978.54	860.44	772.17
70000	6006.59	3084.75	2111.76	1625.98	1335.08	1141.63	1003.85	900.87
80000	6864.67	3525.43	2413.44	1858.26	1525.81	1304.72	1147.26	1029.56
90000	7722.76	3966.11	2715.12	2090.55	1716.54	1467.81	1290.66	1158.26
100000	8580.84	4406.79	3016.80	2322.83	1907.26	1630.89	1434.07	1286.95
110000	9438.92	4847.46	3318.48	2555.11	2097.99	1793.98	1577.48	1415.65
120000	10297.01	5288.14	3620.16	2787.39	2288.71	1957.07	1720.88	1544.34
130000	11155.09	5728.82	3921.84	3019.68	2479.44	2120.16	1864.29	1673.04
140000	12013.17	6169.50	4223.52	3251.96	2670.16	2283.25	2007.69	1801.73
150000	12871.26	6610.18	4525.20	3484.24	2860.89	2446.34	2151.10	1930.43
160000	13729.34	7050.86	4826.88	3716.52	3051.62	2609.43	2294.51	2059.12
170000	14587.42	7491.53	5128.56	3948.81	3242.34	2772.52	2437.91	2187.82
180000	15445.51	7932.21	5430.24	4181.09	3433.07	2935.61	2581.32	2316.51
190000	16303.59	8372.89	5731.92	4413.37	3623.79	3098.70	2724.73	2445.21
200000	17161.67	8813.57	6033.60	4645.65	3814.52	3261.78	2868.13	2573.90
210000	18019.76	9254.25	6335.28	4877.94	4005.24	3424.87	3011.54	2702.60
220000	18877.84	9694.92	6636.95	5110.22	4195.97	3587.96	3154.95	2831.29
230000	19735.92	10135.60	6938.63	5342.50	4386.70	3751.05	3298.35	2959.99
240000	20594.01	10576.28	7240.31	5574.78	4577.42	3914.14	3441.76	3088.68
250000	21452.09	11016.96	7541.99	5807.06	4768.15	4077.23	3585.17	3217.38
260000	22310.17	11457.64	7843.67	6039.35	4958.87	4240.32	3728.57	3346.07
270000	23168.26	11898.32	8145.35	6271.63	5149.60	4403.41	3871.98	3474.77
280000	24026.34	12338.99	8447.03	6503.91	5340.32	4566.50	4015.38	3603.46
290000	24884.42	12779.67	8748.71	6736.19	5531.05	4729.59	4158.79	3732.16
300000	25742.51	13220.35	9050.39	6968.48	5721.77	4892.67	4302.20	3860.85
310000	26600.59	13661.03	9352.07	7200.76	5912.50	5055.76	4445.60	3989.55
320000	27458.67	14101.71	9653.75	7433.04	6103.23	5218.85	4589.01	4118.24
330000	28316.76	14542.38	9955.43	7665.32	6293.95	5381.94	4732.42	4246.94
340000	29174.84	14983.06	10257.11	7897.61	6484.68	5545.03	4875.82	4375.63
350000	30032.92	15423.74	10558.79	8129.89	6675.40	5708.12	5019.23	4504.33
360000	30891.01	15864.42	10860.47	8362.17	6866.13	5871.21	5162.64	4633.02
370000	31749.09	16305.10	11162.15	8594.45	7056.85	6034.30	5306.04	4761.72
380000	32607.17	16745.78	11463.83	8826.74	7247.58	6197.39	5449.45	4890.41
390000	33465.26	17186.45	11765.51	9059.02	7438.31	6360.48	5592.86	5019.11
400000	34323.34	17627.13	12067.19	9291.30	7629.03	6523.56	5736.26	5147.80

45

5½% BLENDED MONTHLY PAYMENTS
AMORTIZATION IN YEARS

Amount	9	10	11	12	13	14	15	16
25	.30	.28	.26	.24	.23	.22	.21	.20
50	.59	.55	.51	.48	.45	.43	.41	.40
100	1.18	1.09	1.01	.95	.90	.86	.82	.79
200	2.35	2.17	2.02	1.90	1.80	1.71	1.63	1.57
300	3.52	3.25	3.03	2.85	2.69	2.56	2.45	2.35
400	4.70	4.33	4.04	3.79	3.59	3.41	3.26	3.13
500	5.87	5.42	5.05	4.74	4.48	4.26	4.07	3.91
600	7.04	6.50	6.05	5.69	5.38	5.11	4.89	4.69
700	8.22	7.58	7.06	6.63	6.27	5.97	5.70	5.47
800	9.39	8.66	8.07	7.58	7.17	6.82	6.52	6.25
900	10.56	9.74	9.08	8.53	8.06	7.67	7.33	7.03
1000	11.73	10.83	10.09	9.48	8.96	8.52	8.14	7.81
2000	23.46	21.65	20.17	18.95	17.91	17.04	16.28	15.62
3000	35.19	32.47	30.25	28.42	26.87	25.55	24.42	23.43
4000	46.92	43.29	40.34	37.89	35.82	34.07	32.56	31.24
5000	58.65	54.11	50.42	47.36	44.78	42.58	40.69	39.05
6000	70.38	64.94	60.50	56.83	53.73	51.10	48.83	46.86
7000	82.11	75.76	70.58	66.30	62.69	59.62	56.97	54.67
8000	93.84	86.58	80.67	75.77	71.64	68.13	65.11	62.48
9000	105.57	97.40	90.75	85.24	80.60	76.65	73.25	70.29
10000	117.30	108.22	100.83	94.71	89.55	85.16	81.38	78.10
20000	234.60	216.44	201.66	189.41	179.10	170.32	162.76	156.20
30000	351.90	324.66	302.49	284.11	268.65	255.48	244.14	234.30
40000	469.19	432.88	403.32	378.81	358.20	340.64	325.52	312.40
50000	586.49	541.10	504.15	473.51	447.74	425.80	406.90	390.49
60000	703.79	649.32	604.97	568.21	537.29	510.96	488.28	468.59
70000	821.09	757.54	705.80	662.92	626.84	596.11	569.66	546.69
80000	938.38	865.76	806.63	757.62	716.39	681.27	651.04	624.79
90000	1055.68	973.98	907.46	852.32	805.94	766.43	732.42	702.88
100000	1172.98	1082.20	1008.29	947.02	895.48	851.59	813.80	780.98
110000	1290.28	1190.42	1109.11	1041.72	985.03	936.75	895.18	859.08
120000	1407.57	1298.64	1209.94	1136.42	1074.58	1021.91	976.56	937.18
130000	1524.87	1406.86	1310.77	1231.13	1164.13	1107.06	1057.94	1015.27
140000	1642.17	1515.08	1411.60	1325.83	1253.68	1192.22	1139.32	1093.37
150000	1759.47	1623.30	1512.43	1420.53	1343.22	1277.38	1220.70	1171.47
160000	1876.76	1731.52	1613.25	1515.23	1432.77	1362.54	1302.08	1249.57
170000	1994.06	1839.73	1714.08	1609.93	1522.32	1447.70	1383.46	1327.66
180000	2111.36	1947.95	1814.91	1704.63	1611.87	1532.86	1464.84	1405.76
190000	2228.66	2056.17	1915.74	1799.34	1701.42	1618.01	1546.22	1483.86
200000	2345.95	2164.39	2016.57	1894.04	1790.96	1703.17	1627.60	1561.96
210000	2463.25	2272.61	2117.40	1988.74	1880.51	1788.33	1708.98	1640.05
220000	2580.55	2380.83	2218.22	2083.44	1970.06	1873.49	1790.36	1718.15
230000	2697.85	2489.05	2319.05	2178.14	2059.61	1958.65	1871.74	1796.25
240000	2815.14	2597.27	2419.88	2272.84	2149.16	2043.81	1953.12	1874.35
250000	2932.44	2705.49	2520.71	2367.55	2238.70	2128.96	2034.50	1952.44
260000	3049.74	2813.71	2621.54	2462.25	2328.25	2214.12	2115.88	2030.54
270000	3167.04	2921.93	2722.36	2556.95	2417.80	2299.28	2197.26	2108.64
280000	3284.33	3030.15	2823.19	2651.65	2507.35	2384.44	2278.64	2186.74
290000	3401.63	3138.37	2924.02	2746.35	2596.90	2469.60	2360.02	2264.83
300000	3518.93	3246.59	3024.85	2841.05	2686.44	2554.76	2441.40	2342.93
310000	3636.23	3354.81	3125.68	2935.76	2775.99	2639.91	2522.78	2421.03
320000	3753.52	3463.03	3226.50	3030.46	2865.54	2725.07	2604.16	2499.13
330000	3870.82	3571.25	3327.33	3125.16	2955.09	2810.23	2685.54	2577.22
340000	3988.12	3679.46	3428.16	3219.86	3044.64	2895.39	2766.92	2655.32
350000	4105.42	3787.68	3528.99	3314.56	3134.18	2980.55	2848.30	2733.42
360000	4222.71	3895.90	3629.82	3409.26	3223.73	3065.71	2929.68	2811.52
370000	4340.01	4004.12	3730.65	3503.97	3313.28	3150.86	3011.06	2889.62
380000	4457.31	4112.34	3831.47	3598.67	3402.83	3236.02	3092.44	2967.71
390000	4574.60	4220.56	3932.30	3693.37	3492.37	3321.18	3173.82	3045.81
400000	4691.90	4328.78	4033.13	3788.07	3581.92	3406.34	3255.20	3123.91

BLENDED MONTHLY PAYMENTS 5½%
AMORTIZATION IN YEARS

Amount	17	18	19	20	21	22	23	24
25	.19	.19	.18	.18	.17	.17	.16	.16
50	.38	.37	.36	.35	.34	.33	.32	.32
100	.76	.73	.71	.69	.67	.66	.64	.63
200	1.51	1.46	1.41	1.37	1.34	1.31	1.28	1.25
300	2.26	2.19	2.12	2.06	2.00	1.96	1.91	1.87
400	3.01	2.91	2.82	2.74	2.67	2.61	2.55	2.49
500	3.77	3.64	3.53	3.43	3.34	3.26	3.18	3.12
600	4.52	4.37	4.23	4.11	4.00	3.91	3.82	3.74
700	5.27	5.09	4.94	4.80	4.67	4.56	4.45	4.36
800	6.02	5.82	5.64	5.48	5.34	5.21	5.09	4.98
900	6.78	6.55	6.34	6.16	6.00	5.86	5.73	5.61
1000	7.53	7.27	7.05	6.85	6.67	6.51	6.36	6.23
2000	15.05	14.54	14.09	13.69	13.33	13.01	12.72	12.45
3000	22.57	21.81	21.14	20.54	20.00	19.51	19.08	18.68
4000	30.09	29.08	28.18	27.38	26.66	26.02	25.43	24.90
5000	37.62	36.35	35.23	34.22	33.33	32.52	31.79	31.13
6000	45.14	43.62	42.27	41.07	39.99	39.02	38.15	37.35
7000	52.66	50.89	49.32	47.91	46.66	45.52	44.50	43.58
8000	60.18	58.16	56.36	54.76	53.32	52.03	50.86	49.80
9000	67.71	65.43	63.40	61.60	59.98	58.53	57.22	56.02
10000	75.23	72.70	70.45	68.44	66.65	65.03	63.57	62.25
20000	150.45	145.39	140.89	136.88	133.29	130.06	127.14	124.49
30000	225.68	218.08	211.33	205.32	199.93	195.09	190.71	186.73
40000	300.90	290.77	281.78	273.76	266.58	260.11	254.27	248.98
50000	376.12	363.46	352.22	342.20	333.22	325.14	317.84	311.22
60000	451.35	436.15	422.66	410.64	399.86	390.17	381.41	373.46
70000	526.57	508.84	493.11	479.08	466.51	455.20	444.97	435.71
80000	601.80	581.53	563.55	547.52	533.15	520.22	508.54	497.95
90000	677.02	654.22	633.99	615.96	599.79	585.25	572.11	560.19
100000	752.24	726.91	704.44	684.40	666.44	650.28	635.68	622.44
110000	827.47	799.60	774.88	752.84	733.08	715.30	699.24	684.68
120000	902.69	872.29	845.32	821.27	799.72	780.33	762.81	746.92
130000	977.92	944.98	915.77	889.71	866.37	845.36	826.38	809.17
140000	1053.14	1017.67	986.21	958.15	933.01	910.39	889.94	871.41
150000	1128.36	1090.36	1056.65	1026.59	999.65	975.41	953.51	933.65
160000	1203.59	1163.05	1127.10	1095.03	1066.30	1040.44	1017.08	995.90
170000	1278.81	1235.74	1197.54	1163.47	1132.94	1105.47	1080.64	1058.14
180000	1354.03	1308.43	1267.98	1231.91	1199.58	1170.49	1144.21	1120.38
190000	1429.26	1381.12	1338.43	1300.35	1266.23	1235.52	1207.78	1182.63
200000	1504.48	1453.81	1408.87	1368.79	1332.87	1300.55	1271.35	1244.87
210000	1579.71	1526.50	1479.31	1437.23	1399.51	1365.58	1334.91	1307.11
220000	1654.93	1599.19	1549.75	1505.67	1466.16	1430.60	1398.48	1369.36
230000	1730.15	1671.88	1620.20	1574.10	1532.80	1495.63	1462.05	1431.60
240000	1805.38	1744.57	1690.64	1642.54	1599.44	1560.66	1525.61	1493.84
250000	1880.60	1817.26	1761.08	1710.98	1666.09	1625.68	1589.18	1556.08
260000	1955.83	1889.95	1831.53	1779.42	1732.73	1690.71	1652.75	1618.33
270000	2031.05	1962.64	1901.97	1847.86	1799.37	1755.74	1716.31	1680.57
280000	2106.27	2035.33	1972.41	1916.30	1866.02	1820.77	1779.88	1742.81
290000	2181.50	2108.03	2042.86	1984.74	1932.66	1885.79	1843.45	1805.06
300000	2256.72	2180.72	2113.30	2053.18	1999.30	1950.82	1907.02	1867.30
310000	2331.94	2253.41	2183.74	2121.62	2065.95	2015.85	1970.58	1929.54
320000	2407.17	2326.10	2254.19	2190.06	2132.59	2080.87	2034.15	1991.79
330000	2482.39	2398.79	2324.63	2258.50	2199.23	2145.90	2097.72	2054.03
340000	2557.62	2471.48	2395.07	2326.94	2265.88	2210.93	2161.28	2116.27
350000	2632.84	2544.17	2465.52	2395.37	2332.52	2275.96	2224.85	2178.52
360000	2708.06	2616.86	2535.96	2463.81	2399.16	2340.98	2288.42	2240.76
370000	2783.29	2689.55	2606.40	2532.25	2465.81	2406.01	2351.98	2303.00
380000	2858.51	2762.24	2676.85	2600.69	2532.45	2471.04	2415.55	2365.25
390000	2933.74	2834.93	2747.29	2669.13	2599.09	2536.06	2479.12	2427.49
400000	3008.96	2907.62	2817.73	2737.57	2665.74	2601.09	2542.69	2489.73

47

5½% BLENDED MONTHLY PAYMENTS
AMORTIZATION IN YEARS

Amount	25	26	29	30	35	40	45	50
25	.16	.15	.15	.15	.14	.13	.13	.13
50	.31	.30	.29	.29	.27	.26	.25	.25
100	.62	.60	.58	.57	.54	.52	.50	.49
200	1.23	1.20	1.15	1.13	1.07	1.03	1.00	.98
300	1.84	1.80	1.72	1.70	1.60	1.54	1.49	1.46
400	2.45	2.40	2.29	2.26	2.14	2.05	1.99	1.95
500	3.06	3.00	2.86	2.82	2.67	2.56	2.49	2.43
600	3.67	3.60	3.44	3.39	3.20	3.07	2.98	2.92
700	4.28	4.20	4.01	3.95	3.74	3.59	3.48	3.40
800	4.89	4.80	4.58	4.52	4.27	4.10	3.98	3.89
900	5.50	5.40	5.15	5.08	4.80	4.61	4.47	4.37
1000	6.11	6.00	5.72	5.64	5.33	5.12	4.97	4.86
2000	12.21	11.99	11.44	11.28	10.66	10.24	9.93	9.71
3000	18.32	17.99	17.16	16.92	15.99	15.35	14.90	14.57
4000	24.42	23.98	22.87	22.56	21.32	20.47	19.86	19.42
5000	30.52	29.98	28.59	28.20	26.65	25.58	24.82	24.27
6000	36.63	35.97	34.31	33.84	31.98	30.70	29.79	29.13
7000	42.73	41.96	40.02	39.48	37.31	35.81	34.75	33.98
8000	48.84	47.96	45.74	45.12	42.64	40.93	39.71	38.83
9000	54.94	53.95	51.46	50.76	47.97	46.05	44.68	43.69
10000	61.04	59.95	57.17	56.40	53.30	51.16	49.64	48.54
20000	122.08	119.89	114.34	112.79	106.60	102.32	99.28	97.08
30000	183.12	179.83	171.51	169.18	159.89	153.47	148.91	145.62
40000	244.16	239.77	228.68	225.57	213.19	204.63	198.55	194.15
50000	305.20	299.71	285.85	281.96	266.49	255.78	248.19	242.69
60000	366.24	359.65	343.02	338.35	319.78	306.94	297.82	291.23
70000	427.28	419.59	400.19	394.74	373.08	358.10	347.46	339.76
80000	488.32	479.53	457.36	451.13	426.37	409.25	397.10	388.30
90000	549.36	539.47	514.53	507.52	479.67	460.41	446.73	436.84
100000	610.40	599.41	571.70	563.91	532.97	511.56	496.37	485.38
110000	671.44	659.35	628.87	620.30	586.26	562.72	546.00	533.91
120000	732.47	719.30	686.04	676.69	639.56	613.88	595.64	582.45
130000	793.51	779.24	743.21	733.08	692.86	665.03	645.28	630.99
140000	854.55	839.18	800.38	789.47	746.15	716.19	694.91	679.52
150000	915.59	899.12	857.55	845.86	799.45	767.34	744.55	728.06
160000	976.63	959.06	914.72	902.26	852.74	818.50	794.19	776.60
170000	1037.67	1019.00	971.89	958.65	906.04	869.66	843.82	825.14
180000	1098.71	1078.94	1029.06	1015.04	959.34	920.81	893.46	873.67
190000	1159.75	1138.88	1086.23	1071.43	1012.63	971.97	943.10	922.21
200000	1220.79	1198.82	1143.40	1127.82	1065.93	1023.12	992.73	970.75
210000	1281.83	1258.76	1200.57	1184.21	1119.22	1074.28	1042.37	1019.28
220000	1342.87	1318.70	1257.74	1240.60	1172.52	1125.44	1092.00	1067.82
230000	1403.91	1378.65	1314.90	1296.99	1225.82	1176.59	1141.64	1116.36
240000	1464.94	1438.59	1372.07	1353.38	1279.11	1227.75	1191.28	1164.89
250000	1525.98	1498.53	1429.24	1409.77	1332.41	1278.90	1240.91	1213.43
260000	1587.02	1558.47	1486.41	1466.16	1385.71	1330.06	1290.55	1261.97
270000	1648.06	1618.41	1543.58	1522.55	1439.00	1381.22	1340.19	1310.51
280000	1709.10	1678.35	1600.75	1578.94	1492.30	1432.37	1389.82	1359.04
290000	1770.14	1738.29	1657.92	1635.33	1545.59	1483.53	1439.46	1407.58
300000	1831.18	1798.23	1715.09	1691.72	1598.89	1534.68	1489.09	1456.12
310000	1892.22	1858.17	1772.26	1748.11	1652.19	1585.84	1538.73	1504.65
320000	1953.26	1918.11	1829.43	1804.51	1705.48	1637.00	1588.37	1553.19
330000	2014.30	1978.05	1886.60	1860.90	1758.78	1688.15	1638.00	1601.73
340000	2075.34	2037.99	1943.77	1917.29	1812.07	1739.31	1687.64	1650.27
350000	2136.38	2097.94	2000.94	1973.68	1865.37	1790.46	1737.28	1698.80
360000	2197.41	2157.88	2058.11	2030.07	1918.67	1841.62	1786.91	1747.34
370000	2258.45	2217.82	2115.28	2086.46	1971.96	1892.78	1836.55	1795.88
380000	2319.49	2277.76	2172.45	2142.85	2025.26	1943.93	1886.19	1844.41
390000	2380.53	2337.70	2229.62	2199.24	2078.56	1995.09	1935.82	1892.95
400000	2441.57	2397.64	2286.79	2255.63	2131.85	2046.24	1985.46	1941.49

BLENDED MONTHLY PAYMENTS
AMORTIZATION IN YEARS

5¾%

Amount	1	2	3	4	5	6	7	8
25	2.15	1.11	.76	.59	.48	.42	.37	.33
50	4.30	2.21	1.52	1.17	.96	.83	.73	.65
100	8.60	4.42	3.03	2.34	1.92	1.65	1.45	1.30
200	17.19	8.84	6.06	4.67	3.84	3.29	2.90	2.60
300	25.78	13.26	9.09	7.01	5.76	4.93	4.34	3.90
400	34.37	17.68	12.12	9.34	7.68	6.57	5.79	5.20
500	42.97	22.09	15.14	11.67	9.60	8.22	7.23	6.50
600	51.56	26.51	18.17	14.01	11.52	9.86	8.68	7.80
700	60.15	30.93	21.20	16.34	13.43	11.50	10.12	9.10
800	68.74	35.35	24.23	18.68	15.35	13.14	11.57	10.39
900	77.33	39.76	27.26	21.01	17.27	14.79	13.02	11.69
1000	85.93	44.18	30.28	23.34	19.19	16.43	14.46	12.99
2000	171.85	88.36	60.56	46.68	38.38	32.85	28.92	25.98
3000	257.77	132.54	90.84	70.02	57.56	49.28	43.38	38.97
4000	343.69	176.72	121.12	93.36	76.75	65.70	57.83	51.95
5000	429.61	220.89	151.40	116.70	95.93	82.12	72.29	64.94
6000	515.53	265.07	181.67	140.04	115.12	98.55	86.75	77.93
7000	601.45	309.25	211.95	163.38	134.30	114.97	101.20	90.92
8000	687.37	353.43	242.23	186.72	153.49	131.39	115.66	103.90
9000	773.29	397.60	272.51	210.06	172.67	147.82	130.12	116.89
10000	859.21	441.78	302.79	233.40	191.86	164.24	144.57	129.88
20000	1718.41	883.56	605.57	466.80	383.71	328.47	289.14	259.75
30000	2577.62	1325.33	908.35	700.19	575.57	492.71	433.71	389.62
40000	3436.82	1767.11	1211.13	933.59	767.42	656.94	578.27	519.50
50000	4296.03	2208.88	1513.91	1166.99	959.28	821.17	722.84	649.37
60000	5155.23	2650.66	1816.70	1400.38	1151.13	985.41	867.41	779.24
70000	6014.44	3092.44	2119.48	1633.78	1342.98	1149.64	1011.98	909.11
80000	6873.64	3534.21	2422.26	1867.18	1534.84	1313.87	1156.54	1038.99
90000	7732.85	3975.99	2725.04	2100.57	1726.69	1478.11	1301.11	1168.86
100000	8592.05	4417.76	3027.82	2333.97	1918.55	1642.34	1445.68	1298.73
110000	9451.26	4859.54	3330.61	2567.37	2110.40	1806.57	1590.25	1428.61
120000	10310.46	5301.32	3633.39	2800.76	2302.26	1970.81	1734.81	1558.48
130000	11169.67	5743.09	3936.17	3034.16	2494.11	2135.04	1879.38	1688.35
140000	12028.87	6184.87	4238.95	3267.56	2685.96	2299.27	2023.95	1818.22
150000	12888.08	6626.64	4541.73	3500.95	2877.82	2463.51	2168.51	1948.10
160000	13747.28	7068.42	4844.52	3734.35	3069.67	2627.74	2313.08	2077.97
170000	14606.49	7510.20	5147.30	3967.75	3261.53	2791.97	2457.65	2207.84
180000	15465.69	7951.97	5450.08	4201.14	3453.38	2956.21	2602.22	2337.72
190000	16324.90	8393.75	5752.86	4434.54	3645.24	3120.44	2746.78	2467.59
200000	17184.10	8835.52	6055.64	4667.93	3837.09	3284.67	2891.35	2597.46
210000	18043.31	9277.30	6358.43	4901.33	4028.94	3448.91	3035.92	2727.33
220000	18902.51	9719.08	6661.21	5134.73	4220.80	3613.14	3180.49	2857.21
230000	19761.71	10160.85	6963.99	5368.12	4412.65	3777.37	3325.05	2987.08
240000	20620.92	10602.63	7266.77	5601.52	4604.51	3941.61	3469.62	3116.95
250000	21480.12	11044.40	7569.55	5834.92	4796.36	4105.84	3614.19	3246.83
260000	22339.33	11486.18	7872.34	6068.31	4988.21	4270.07	3758.76	3376.70
270000	23198.53	11927.96	8175.12	6301.71	5180.07	4434.31	3903.32	3506.57
280000	24057.74	12369.73	8477.90	6535.11	5371.92	4598.54	4047.89	3636.44
290000	24916.94	12811.51	8780.68	6768.50	5563.78	4762.77	4192.46	3766.32
300000	25776.15	13253.28	9083.46	7001.90	5755.63	4927.01	4337.02	3896.19
310000	26635.35	13695.06	9386.25	7235.30	5947.49	5091.24	4481.59	4026.06
320000	27494.56	14136.84	9689.03	7468.69	6139.34	5255.47	4626.16	4155.94
330000	28353.76	14578.61	9991.81	7702.09	6331.19	5419.71	4770.73	4285.81
340000	29212.97	15020.39	10294.59	7935.49	6523.05	5583.94	4915.29	4415.68
350000	30072.17	15462.16	10597.37	8168.88	6714.90	5748.17	5059.86	4545.55
360000	30931.38	15903.94	10900.16	8402.28	6906.76	5912.41	5204.43	4675.43
370000	31790.58	16345.72	11202.94	8635.68	7098.61	6076.64	5349.00	4805.30
380000	32649.79	16787.49	11505.72	8869.07	7290.47	6240.87	5493.56	4935.17
390000	33508.99	17229.27	11808.50	9102.47	7482.32	6405.11	5638.13	5065.05
400000	34368.20	17671.04	12111.28	9335.86	7674.17	6569.34	5782.70	5194.92

5¾% BLENDED MONTHLY PAYMENTS
AMORTIZATION IN YEARS

Amount	9	10	11	12	13	14	15	16
25	.30	.28	.26	.24	.23	.22	.21	.20
50	.60	.55	.52	.48	.46	.44	.42	.40
100	1.19	1.10	1.03	.96	.91	.87	.83	.80
200	2.37	2.19	2.05	1.92	1.82	1.73	1.66	1.59
300	3.56	3.29	3.07	2.88	2.73	2.60	2.49	2.39
400	4.74	4.38	4.09	3.84	3.64	3.46	3.31	3.18
500	5.93	5.48	5.11	4.80	4.55	4.33	4.14	3.98
600	7.11	6.57	6.13	5.76	5.45	5.19	4.97	4.77
700	8.30	7.67	7.15	6.72	6.36	6.06	5.79	5.56
800	9.48	8.76	8.17	7.68	7.27	6.92	6.62	6.36
900	10.67	9.85	9.19	8.64	8.18	7.78	7.45	7.15
1000	11.85	10.95	10.21	9.60	9.09	8.65	8.27	7.95
2000	23.70	21.89	20.42	19.19	18.17	17.29	16.54	15.89
3000	35.55	32.83	30.62	28.79	27.25	25.94	24.81	23.83
4000	47.40	43.78	40.83	38.38	36.33	34.58	33.08	31.77
5000	59.25	54.72	51.03	47.98	45.41	43.23	41.34	39.71
6000	71.10	65.66	61.24	57.57	54.49	51.87	49.61	47.65
7000	82.95	76.61	71.45	67.17	63.57	60.51	57.88	55.59
8000	94.80	87.55	81.65	76.76	72.66	69.16	66.15	63.54
9000	106.65	98.49	91.86	86.36	81.74	77.80	74.42	71.48
10000	118.50	109.44	102.06	95.95	90.82	86.45	82.68	79.42
20000	236.99	218.87	204.12	191.90	181.63	172.89	165.36	158.83
30000	355.48	328.30	306.18	287.85	272.44	259.33	248.04	238.25
40000	473.98	437.73	408.24	383.80	363.26	345.77	330.72	317.66
50000	592.47	547.16	510.29	479.75	454.07	432.21	413.40	397.07
60000	710.96	656.60	612.35	575.70	544.88	518.65	496.08	476.49
70000	829.45	766.03	714.41	671.65	635.69	605.09	578.76	555.90
80000	947.95	875.46	816.47	767.60	726.51	691.53	661.44	635.32
90000	1066.44	984.89	918.53	863.55	817.32	777.97	744.12	714.73
100000	1184.93	1094.32	1020.58	959.49	908.13	864.41	826.79	794.14
110000	1303.42	1203.76	1122.64	1055.44	998.94	950.85	909.47	873.56
120000	1421.92	1313.19	1224.70	1151.39	1089.76	1037.29	992.15	952.97
130000	1540.41	1422.62	1326.76	1247.34	1180.57	1123.73	1074.83	1032.38
140000	1658.90	1532.05	1428.82	1343.29	1271.38	1210.17	1157.51	1111.80
150000	1777.39	1641.48	1530.87	1439.24	1362.19	1296.61	1240.19	1191.21
160000	1895.89	1750.91	1632.93	1535.19	1453.01	1383.05	1322.87	1270.63
170000	2014.38	1860.35	1734.99	1631.14	1543.82	1469.49	1405.55	1350.04
180000	2132.87	1969.78	1837.05	1727.09	1634.63	1555.93	1488.23	1429.45
190000	2251.36	2079.21	1939.11	1823.03	1725.44	1642.37	1570.91	1508.87
200000	2369.86	2188.64	2041.16	1918.98	1816.26	1728.81	1653.58	1588.28
210000	2488.35	2298.07	2143.22	2014.93	1907.07	1815.25	1736.26	1667.70
220000	2606.84	2407.51	2245.28	2110.88	1997.88	1901.69	1818.94	1747.11
230000	2725.33	2516.94	2347.34	2206.83	2088.69	1988.13	1901.62	1826.52
240000	2843.83	2626.37	2449.40	2302.78	2179.51	2074.57	1984.30	1905.94
250000	2962.32	2735.80	2551.45	2398.73	2270.32	2161.01	2066.98	1985.35
260000	3080.81	2845.23	2653.51	2494.68	2361.13	2247.45	2149.66	2064.76
270000	3199.30	2954.66	2755.57	2590.63	2451.94	2333.89	2232.34	2144.18
280000	3317.80	3064.10	2857.63	2686.57	2542.76	2420.33	2315.02	2223.59
290000	3436.29	3173.53	2959.69	2782.52	2633.57	2506.77	2397.70	2303.01
300000	3554.78	3282.96	3061.74	2878.47	2724.38	2593.21	2480.37	2382.42
310000	3673.27	3392.39	3163.80	2974.42	2815.19	2679.65	2563.05	2461.83
320000	3791.77	3501.82	3265.86	3070.37	2906.01	2766.09	2645.73	2541.25
330000	3910.26	3611.26	3367.92	3166.32	2996.82	2852.53	2728.41	2620.66
340000	4028.75	3720.69	3469.98	3262.27	3087.63	2938.97	2811.09	2700.08
350000	4147.24	3830.12	3572.03	3358.22	3178.44	3025.41	2893.77	2779.49
360000	4265.74	3939.55	3674.09	3454.17	3269.26	3111.85	2976.45	2858.90
370000	4384.23	4048.98	3776.15	3550.11	3360.07	3198.30	3059.13	2938.32
380000	4502.72	4158.41	3878.21	3646.06	3450.88	3284.74	3141.81	3017.73
390000	4621.21	4267.85	3980.26	3742.01	3541.70	3371.18	3224.48	3097.14
400000	4739.71	4377.28	4082.32	3837.96	3632.51	3457.62	3307.16	3176.56

BLENDED MONTHLY PAYMENTS 5¾%
AMORTIZATION IN YEARS

Amount	17	18	19	20	21	22	23	24
25	.20	.19	.18	.18	.18	.17	.17	.16
50	.39	.38	.36	.35	.35	.34	.33	.32
100	.77	.75	.72	.70	.69	.67	.65	.64
200	1.54	1.49	1.44	1.40	1.37	1.33	1.30	1.28
300	2.30	2.23	2.16	2.10	2.05	2.00	1.95	1.92
400	3.07	2.97	2.88	2.80	2.73	2.66	2.60	2.55
500	3.83	3.71	3.60	3.50	3.41	3.33	3.25	3.19
600	4.60	4.45	4.31	4.19	4.09	3.99	3.90	3.83
700	5.36	5.19	5.03	4.89	4.77	4.66	4.55	4.46
800	6.13	5.93	5.75	5.59	5.45	5.32	5.20	5.10
900	6.90	6.67	6.47	6.29	6.13	5.98	5.85	5.74
1000	7.66	7.41	7.19	6.99	6.81	6.65	6.50	6.37
2000	15.32	14.81	14.37	13.97	13.61	13.29	13.00	12.74
3000	22.97	22.22	21.55	20.95	20.42	19.94	19.50	19.11
4000	30.63	29.62	28.73	27.93	27.22	26.58	26.00	25.48
5000	38.28	37.03	35.91	34.92	34.03	33.23	32.50	31.85
6000	45.94	44.43	43.09	41.90	40.83	39.87	39.00	38.22
7000	53.59	51.83	50.27	48.88	47.64	46.52	45.50	44.59
8000	61.25	59.24	57.45	55.86	54.44	53.16	52.00	50.96
9000	68.91	66.64	64.63	62.85	61.24	59.80	58.50	57.33
10000	76.56	74.05	71.81	69.83	68.05	66.45	65.00	63.70
20000	153.12	148.09	143.62	139.65	136.09	132.89	130.00	127.39
30000	229.68	222.13	215.43	209.47	204.13	199.33	195.00	191.08
40000	306.23	296.17	287.24	279.29	272.18	265.78	260.00	254.77
50000	382.79	370.21	359.05	349.12	340.22	332.22	325.00	318.46
60000	459.35	444.25	430.86	418.94	408.26	398.66	390.00	382.15
70000	535.90	518.29	502.67	488.76	476.31	465.11	455.00	445.84
80000	612.46	592.33	574.48	558.58	544.35	531.55	520.00	509.53
90000	689.02	666.37	646.29	628.41	612.39	597.99	584.99	573.22
100000	765.58	740.41	718.10	698.23	680.43	664.43	649.99	636.91
110000	842.13	814.45	789.91	768.05	748.48	730.88	714.99	700.60
120000	918.69	888.49	861.72	837.87	816.52	797.32	779.99	764.29
130000	995.25	962.53	933.53	907.70	884.56	863.76	844.99	827.98
140000	1071.80	1036.57	1005.34	977.52	952.61	930.21	909.99	891.68
150000	1148.36	1110.61	1077.15	1047.34	1020.65	996.65	974.99	955.37
160000	1224.92	1184.65	1148.96	1117.16	1088.69	1063.09	1039.99	1019.06
170000	1301.48	1258.69	1220.77	1186.99	1156.74	1129.54	1104.98	1082.75
180000	1378.03	1332.73	1292.58	1256.81	1224.78	1195.98	1169.98	1146.44
190000	1454.59	1406.77	1364.39	1326.63	1292.82	1262.42	1234.98	1210.13
200000	1531.15	1480.81	1436.20	1396.45	1360.86	1328.86	1299.98	1273.82
210000	1607.70	1554.85	1508.01	1466.28	1428.91	1395.31	1364.98	1337.51
220000	1684.26	1628.90	1579.82	1536.10	1496.95	1461.75	1429.98	1401.20
230000	1760.82	1702.94	1651.63	1605.92	1564.99	1528.19	1494.98	1464.89
240000	1837.38	1776.98	1723.44	1675.74	1633.04	1594.64	1559.98	1528.58
250000	1913.93	1851.02	1795.25	1745.57	1701.08	1661.08	1624.97	1592.27
260000	1990.49	1925.06	1867.06	1815.39	1769.12	1727.52	1689.97	1655.96
270000	2067.05	1999.10	1938.87	1885.21	1837.17	1793.97	1754.97	1719.65
280000	2143.60	2073.14	2010.68	1955.03	1905.21	1860.41	1819.97	1783.35
290000	2220.16	2147.18	2082.49	2024.86	1973.25	1926.85	1884.97	1847.04
300000	2296.72	2221.22	2154.30	2094.68	2041.29	1993.29	1949.97	1910.73
310000	2373.28	2295.26	2226.11	2164.50	2109.34	2059.74	2014.97	1974.42
320000	2449.83	2369.30	2297.92	2234.32	2177.38	2126.18	2079.97	2038.11
330000	2526.39	2443.34	2369.73	2304.15	2245.42	2192.62	2144.97	2101.80
340000	2602.95	2517.38	2441.54	2373.97	2313.47	2259.07	2209.96	2165.49
350000	2679.50	2591.42	2513.35	2443.79	2381.51	2325.51	2274.96	2229.18
360000	2756.06	2665.46	2585.16	2513.61	2449.55	2391.95	2339.96	2292.87
370000	2832.62	2739.50	2656.97	2583.44	2517.60	2458.40	2404.96	2356.56
380000	2909.18	2813.54	2728.78	2653.26	2585.64	2524.84	2469.96	2420.25
390000	2985.73	2887.58	2800.59	2723.08	2653.68	2591.28	2534.96	2483.94
400000	3062.29	2961.62	2872.40	2792.90	2721.72	2657.72	2599.96	2547.63

51

5¾% BLENDED MONTHLY PAYMENTS
AMORTIZATION IN YEARS

Amount	25	26	29	30	35	40	45	50
25	.16	.16	.15	.15	.14	.14	.13	.13
50	.32	.31	.30	.29	.28	.27	.26	.26
100	.63	.62	.59	.58	.55	.53	.52	.51
200	1.26	1.23	1.18	1.16	1.10	1.06	1.03	1.01
300	1.88	1.85	1.77	1.74	1.65	1.59	1.55	1.51
400	2.51	2.46	2.35	2.32	2.20	2.12	2.06	2.02
500	3.13	3.08	2.94	2.90	2.75	2.65	2.57	2.52
600	3.76	3.69	3.53	3.48	3.30	3.17	3.09	3.02
700	4.38	4.30	4.11	4.06	3.85	3.70	3.60	3.53
800	5.01	4.92	4.70	4.64	4.40	4.23	4.11	4.03
900	5.63	5.53	5.29	5.22	4.95	4.76	4.63	4.53
1000	6.26	6.15	5.87	5.80	5.50	5.29	5.14	5.04
2000	12.51	12.29	11.74	11.59	10.99	10.57	10.28	10.07
3000	18.76	18.43	17.61	17.38	16.48	15.85	15.41	15.10
4000	25.01	24.57	23.48	23.18	21.97	21.13	20.55	20.13
5000	31.26	30.71	29.35	28.97	27.46	26.42	25.68	25.16
6000	37.51	36.86	35.22	34.76	32.95	31.70	30.82	30.19
7000	43.76	43.00	41.09	40.55	38.44	36.98	35.96	35.22
8000	50.01	49.14	46.96	46.35	43.93	42.26	41.09	40.25
9000	56.26	55.28	52.83	52.14	49.42	47.55	46.23	45.28
10000	62.51	61.42	58.70	57.93	54.91	52.83	51.36	50.31
20000	125.01	122.84	117.39	115.86	109.81	105.65	102.72	100.62
30000	187.51	184.26	176.08	173.79	164.71	158.47	154.08	150.93
40000	250.01	245.68	234.78	231.72	219.61	211.30	205.44	201.24
50000	312.52	307.10	293.47	289.64	274.51	264.12	256.80	251.55
60000	375.02	368.52	352.16	347.57	329.41	316.94	308.16	301.85
70000	437.52	429.94	410.85	405.50	384.32	369.77	359.52	352.16
80000	500.02	491.36	469.55	463.43	439.22	422.59	410.87	402.47
90000	562.52	552.78	528.24	521.36	494.12	475.41	462.23	452.78
100000	625.03	614.20	586.93	579.28	549.02	528.24	513.59	503.09
110000	687.53	675.62	645.62	637.21	603.92	581.06	564.95	553.40
120000	750.03	737.04	704.32	695.14	658.82	633.88	616.31	603.70
130000	812.53	798.46	763.01	753.07	713.73	686.71	667.67	654.01
140000	875.04	859.87	821.70	811.00	768.63	739.53	719.03	704.32
150000	937.54	921.29	880.39	868.92	823.53	792.35	770.39	754.63
160000	1000.04	982.71	939.09	926.85	878.43	845.18	821.74	804.94
170000	1062.54	1044.13	997.78	984.78	933.33	898.00	873.10	855.24
180000	1125.04	1105.55	1056.47	1042.71	988.23	950.82	924.46	905.55
190000	1187.55	1166.97	1115.16	1100.64	1043.14	1003.65	975.82	955.86
200000	1250.05	1228.39	1173.86	1158.56	1098.04	1056.47	1027.18	1006.17
210000	1312.55	1289.81	1232.55	1216.49	1152.94	1109.29	1078.54	1056.48
220000	1375.05	1351.23	1291.24	1274.42	1207.84	1162.11	1129.90	1106.79
230000	1437.56	1412.65	1349.93	1332.35	1262.74	1214.94	1181.26	1157.09
240000	1500.06	1474.07	1408.63	1390.28	1317.64	1267.76	1232.61	1207.40
250000	1562.56	1535.49	1467.32	1448.20	1372.55	1320.58	1283.97	1257.71
260000	1625.06	1596.91	1526.01	1506.13	1427.45	1373.41	1335.33	1308.02
270000	1687.56	1658.32	1584.70	1564.06	1482.35	1426.23	1386.69	1358.33
280000	1750.07	1719.74	1643.40	1621.99	1537.25	1479.05	1438.05	1408.63
290000	1812.57	1781.16	1702.09	1679.92	1592.15	1531.88	1489.41	1458.94
300000	1875.07	1842.58	1760.78	1737.84	1647.05	1584.70	1540.77	1509.25
310000	1937.57	1904.00	1819.47	1795.77	1701.96	1637.52	1592.12	1559.56
320000	2000.08	1965.42	1878.17	1853.70	1756.86	1690.35	1643.48	1609.87
330000	2062.58	2026.84	1936.86	1911.63	1811.76	1743.17	1694.84	1660.18
340000	2125.08	2088.26	1995.55	1969.56	1866.66	1795.99	1746.20	1710.48
350000	2187.58	2149.68	2054.24	2027.48	1921.56	1848.82	1797.56	1760.79
360000	2250.08	2211.10	2112.94	2085.41	1976.46	1901.64	1848.92	1811.10
370000	2312.59	2272.52	2171.63	2143.34	2031.37	1954.46	1900.28	1861.41
380000	2375.09	2333.94	2230.32	2201.27	2086.27	2007.29	1951.64	1911.72
390000	2437.59	2395.36	2289.01	2259.20	2141.17	2060.11	2002.99	1962.03
400000	2500.09	2456.78	2347.71	2317.12	2196.07	2112.93	2054.35	2012.33

52

BLENDED MONTHLY PAYMENTS 6%

AMORTIZATION IN YEARS

Amount	1	2	3	4	5	6	7	8
25	2.16	1.11	.76	.59	.49	.42	.37	.33
50	4.31	2.22	1.52	1.18	.97	.83	.73	.66
100	8.61	4.43	3.04	2.35	1.93	1.66	1.46	1.32
200	17.21	8.86	6.08	4.70	3.86	3.31	2.92	2.63
300	25.81	13.29	9.12	7.04	5.79	4.97	4.38	3.94
400	34.42	17.72	12.16	9.39	7.72	6.62	5.83	5.25
500	43.02	22.15	15.20	11.73	9.65	8.27	7.29	6.56
600	51.62	26.58	18.24	14.08	11.58	9.93	8.75	7.87
700	60.23	31.01	21.28	16.42	13.51	11.58	10.21	9.18
800	68.83	35.43	24.32	18.77	15.44	13.24	11.66	10.49
900	77.43	39.86	27.35	21.11	17.37	14.89	13.12	11.80
1000	86.04	44.29	30.39	23.46	19.30	16.54	14.58	13.11
2000	172.07	88.58	60.78	46.91	38.60	33.08	29.15	26.22
3000	258.10	132.87	91.17	70.36	57.90	49.62	43.72	39.32
4000	344.14	177.15	121.56	93.81	77.20	66.16	58.30	52.43
5000	430.17	221.44	151.95	117.26	96.50	82.70	72.87	65.53
6000	516.20	265.73	182.34	140.71	115.80	99.23	87.44	78.64
7000	602.23	310.02	212.73	164.16	135.10	115.77	102.02	91.74
8000	688.27	354.30	243.11	187.62	154.39	132.31	116.59	104.85
9000	774.30	398.59	273.50	211.07	173.69	148.85	131.16	117.96
10000	860.33	442.88	303.89	234.52	192.99	165.39	145.74	131.06
20000	1720.66	885.75	607.78	469.03	385.98	330.77	291.47	262.12
30000	2580.98	1328.63	911.66	703.54	578.96	496.15	437.20	393.17
40000	3441.31	1771.50	1215.55	938.06	771.95	661.53	582.94	524.23
50000	4301.63	2214.38	1519.43	1172.57	964.93	826.91	728.67	655.28
60000	5161.96	2657.25	1823.32	1407.08	1157.92	992.29	874.40	786.34
70000	6022.29	3100.13	2127.21	1641.59	1350.91	1157.67	1020.13	917.40
80000	6882.61	3543.00	2431.09	1876.11	1543.89	1323.06	1165.87	1048.45
90000	7742.94	3985.87	2734.98	2110.62	1736.88	1488.44	1311.60	1179.51
100000	8603.26	4428.75	3038.86	2345.13	1929.86	1653.82	1457.33	1310.56
110000	9463.59	4871.62	3342.75	2579.65	2122.85	1819.20	1603.06	1441.62
120000	10323.91	5314.50	3646.63	2814.16	2315.83	1984.58	1748.80	1572.68
130000	11184.24	5757.37	3950.52	3048.67	2508.82	2149.96	1894.53	1703.73
140000	12044.57	6200.25	4254.41	3283.18	2701.81	2315.34	2040.26	1834.79
150000	12904.89	6643.12	4558.29	3517.70	2894.79	2480.73	2186.00	1965.84
160000	13765.22	7085.99	4862.18	3752.21	3087.78	2646.11	2331.73	2096.90
170000	14625.54	7528.87	5166.06	3986.72	3280.76	2811.49	2477.46	2227.96
180000	15485.87	7971.74	5469.95	4221.23	3473.75	2976.87	2623.19	2359.01
190000	16346.20	8414.62	5773.83	4455.75	3666.73	3142.25	2768.93	2490.07
200000	17206.52	8857.49	6077.72	4690.26	3859.72	3307.63	2914.66	2621.12
210000	18066.85	9300.37	6381.61	4924.77	4052.71	3473.01	3060.39	2752.18
220000	18927.17	9743.24	6685.49	5159.29	4245.69	3638.40	3206.12	2883.24
230000	19787.50	10186.11	6989.38	5393.80	4438.68	3803.78	3351.86	3014.29
240000	20647.82	10628.99	7293.26	5628.31	4631.66	3969.16	3497.59	3145.35
250000	21508.15	11071.86	7597.15	5862.82	4824.65	4134.54	3643.32	3276.40
260000	22368.48	11514.74	7901.03	6097.34	5017.63	4299.92	3789.06	3407.46
270000	23228.80	11957.61	8204.92	6331.85	5210.62	4465.30	3934.79	3538.52
280000	24089.13	12400.49	8508.81	6566.36	5403.61	4630.68	4080.52	3669.57
290000	24949.45	12843.36	8812.69	6800.87	5596.59	4796.07	4226.25	3800.63
300000	25809.78	13286.23	9116.58	7035.39	5789.58	4961.45	4371.99	3931.68
310000	26670.10	13729.11	9420.46	7269.90	5982.56	5126.83	4517.72	4062.74
320000	27530.43	14171.98	9724.35	7504.41	6175.55	5292.21	4663.45	4193.80
330000	28390.76	14614.86	10028.24	7738.93	6368.53	5457.59	4809.18	4324.85
340000	29251.08	15057.73	10332.12	7973.44	6561.52	5622.97	4954.92	4455.91
350000	30111.41	15500.61	10636.01	8207.95	6754.51	5788.35	5100.65	4586.96
360000	30971.73	15943.48	10939.89	8442.46	6947.49	5953.74	5246.38	4718.02
370000	31832.06	16386.35	11243.78	8676.98	7140.48	6119.12	5392.12	4849.08
380000	32692.39	16829.23	11547.66	8911.49	7333.46	6284.50	5537.85	4980.13
390000	33552.71	17272.10	11851.55	9146.00	7526.45	6449.88	5683.58	5111.19
400000	34413.04	17714.98	12155.44	9380.52	7719.43	6615.26	5829.31	5242.24

53

6% BLENDED MONTHLY PAYMENTS
AMORTIZATION IN YEARS

Amount	9	10	11	12	13	14	15	16
25	.30	.28	.26	.25	.24	.22	.21	.21
50	.60	.56	.52	.49	.47	.44	.42	.41
100	1.20	1.11	1.04	.98	.93	.88	.84	.81
200	2.40	2.22	2.07	1.95	1.85	1.76	1.68	1.62
300	3.60	3.32	3.10	2.92	2.77	2.64	2.52	2.43
400	4.79	4.43	4.14	3.89	3.69	3.51	3.36	3.23
500	5.99	5.54	5.17	4.87	4.61	4.39	4.20	4.04
600	7.19	6.64	6.20	5.84	5.53	5.27	5.04	4.85
700	8.38	7.75	7.24	6.81	6.45	6.15	5.88	5.66
800	9.58	8.86	8.27	7.78	7.37	7.02	6.72	6.46
900	10.78	9.96	9.30	8.75	8.29	7.90	7.56	7.27
1000	11.97	11.07	10.33	9.73	9.21	8.78	8.40	8.08
2000	23.94	22.14	20.66	19.45	18.42	17.55	16.80	16.15
3000	35.91	33.20	30.99	29.17	27.63	26.32	25.20	24.23
4000	47.88	44.27	41.32	38.89	36.84	35.10	33.60	32.30
5000	59.85	55.33	51.65	48.61	46.05	43.87	42.00	40.38
6000	71.82	66.40	61.98	58.33	55.26	52.64	50.40	48.45
7000	83.79	77.46	72.31	68.05	64.47	61.42	58.80	56.52
8000	95.76	88.53	82.64	77.77	73.67	70.19	67.20	64.60
9000	107.73	99.59	92.97	87.49	82.88	78.96	75.59	72.67
10000	119.70	110.66	103.30	97.21	92.09	87.74	83.99	80.75
20000	239.39	221.31	206.60	194.41	184.18	175.47	167.98	161.49
30000	359.09	331.96	309.89	291.62	276.26	263.20	251.97	242.23
40000	478.78	442.61	413.19	388.82	368.35	350.93	335.96	322.97
50000	598.47	553.26	516.48	486.03	460.44	438.66	419.95	403.71
60000	718.17	663.91	619.78	583.23	552.52	526.40	503.93	484.45
70000	837.86	774.56	723.07	680.44	644.61	614.13	587.92	565.19
80000	957.55	885.21	826.37	777.64	736.69	701.86	671.91	645.93
90000	1077.25	995.86	929.66	874.84	828.78	789.59	755.90	726.67
100000	1196.94	1106.51	1032.96	972.05	920.87	877.32	839.89	807.41
110000	1316.63	1217.17	1136.25	1069.25	1012.95	965.05	923.88	888.15
120000	1436.33	1327.82	1239.55	1166.46	1105.04	1052.79	1007.86	968.90
130000	1556.02	1438.47	1342.84	1263.66	1197.12	1140.52	1091.85	1049.64
140000	1675.72	1549.12	1446.14	1360.87	1289.21	1228.25	1175.84	1130.38
150000	1795.41	1659.77	1549.43	1458.07	1381.30	1315.98	1259.83	1211.12
160000	1915.10	1770.42	1652.73	1555.27	1473.38	1403.71	1343.82	1291.86
170000	2034.80	1881.07	1756.02	1652.48	1565.47	1491.44	1427.81	1372.60
180000	2154.49	1991.72	1859.32	1749.68	1657.55	1579.18	1511.79	1453.34
190000	2274.18	2102.37	1962.61	1846.89	1749.64	1666.91	1595.78	1534.08
200000	2393.88	2213.02	2065.91	1944.09	1841.73	1754.64	1679.77	1614.82
210000	2513.57	2323.68	2169.20	2041.30	1933.81	1842.37	1763.76	1695.56
220000	2633.26	2434.33	2272.50	2138.50	2025.90	1930.10	1847.75	1776.30
230000	2752.96	2544.98	2375.80	2235.70	2117.98	2017.83	1931.74	1857.05
240000	2872.65	2655.63	2479.09	2332.91	2210.07	2105.57	2015.72	1937.79
250000	2992.34	2766.28	2582.39	2430.11	2302.16	2193.30	2099.71	2018.53
260000	3112.04	2876.93	2685.68	2527.32	2394.24	2281.03	2183.70	2099.27
270000	3231.73	2987.58	2788.98	2624.52	2486.33	2368.76	2267.69	2180.01
280000	3351.43	3098.23	2892.27	2721.73	2578.41	2456.49	2351.68	2260.75
290000	3471.12	3208.88	2995.57	2818.93	2670.50	2544.22	2435.67	2341.49
300000	3590.81	3319.53	3098.86	2916.13	2762.59	2631.96	2519.65	2422.23
310000	3710.51	3430.19	3202.16	3013.34	2854.67	2719.69	2603.64	2502.97
320000	3830.20	3540.84	3305.45	3110.54	2946.76	2807.42	2687.63	2583.71
330000	3949.89	3651.49	3408.75	3207.75	3038.84	2895.15	2771.62	2664.45
340000	4069.59	3762.14	3512.04	3304.95	3130.93	2982.88	2855.61	2745.20
350000	4189.28	3872.79	3615.34	3402.16	3223.02	3070.61	2939.59	2825.94
360000	4308.97	3983.44	3718.63	3499.36	3315.10	3158.35	3023.58	2906.68
370000	4428.67	4094.09	3821.93	3596.56	3407.19	3246.08	3107.57	2987.42
380000	4548.36	4204.74	3925.22	3693.77	3499.27	3333.81	3191.56	3068.16
390000	4668.05	4315.39	4028.52	3790.97	3591.36	3421.54	3275.55	3148.90
400000	4787.75	4426.04	4131.81	3888.18	3683.45	3509.27	3359.54	3229.64

BLENDED MONTHLY PAYMENTS
AMORTIZATION IN YEARS
6%

Amount	17	18	19	20	21	22	23	24
25	.20	.19	.19	.18	.18	.17	.17	.17
50	.39	.38	.37	.36	.35	.34	.34	.33
100	.78	.76	.74	.72	.70	.68	.67	.66
200	1.56	1.51	1.47	1.43	1.39	1.36	1.33	1.31
300	2.34	2.27	2.20	2.14	2.09	2.04	2.00	1.96
400	3.12	3.02	2.93	2.85	2.78	2.72	2.66	2.61
500	3.90	3.78	3.66	3.57	3.48	3.40	3.33	3.26
600	4.68	4.53	4.40	4.28	4.17	4.08	3.99	3.91
700	5.46	5.28	5.13	4.99	4.87	4.76	4.66	4.57
800	6.24	6.04	5.86	5.70	5.56	5.43	5.32	5.22
900	7.02	6.79	6.59	6.41	6.26	6.11	5.99	5.87
1000	7.80	7.55	7.32	7.13	6.95	6.79	6.65	6.52
2000	15.59	15.09	14.64	14.25	13.90	13.58	13.29	13.04
3000	23.38	22.63	21.96	21.37	20.84	20.37	19.94	19.55
4000	31.17	30.17	29.28	28.49	27.79	27.15	26.58	26.07
5000	38.96	37.71	36.60	35.61	34.73	33.94	33.23	32.58
6000	46.75	45.25	43.92	42.74	41.68	40.73	39.87	39.10
7000	54.54	52.79	51.24	49.86	48.62	47.52	46.52	45.61
8000	62.33	60.33	58.56	56.98	55.57	54.30	53.16	52.13
9000	70.12	67.87	65.88	64.10	62.52	61.09	59.81	58.64
10000	77.91	75.41	73.19	71.22	69.46	67.88	66.45	65.16
20000	155.81	150.81	146.38	142.44	138.92	135.75	132.90	130.31
30000	233.71	226.21	219.57	213.66	208.37	203.62	199.34	195.46
40000	311.61	301.62	292.76	284.88	277.83	271.50	265.79	260.62
50000	389.51	377.02	365.95	356.10	347.29	339.37	332.23	325.77
60000	467.42	452.42	439.14	427.32	416.74	407.24	398.68	390.92
70000	545.32	527.82	512.33	498.54	486.20	475.12	465.12	456.08
80000	623.22	603.23	585.52	569.76	555.65	542.99	531.57	521.23
90000	701.12	678.63	658.71	640.97	625.11	610.86	598.01	586.38
100000	779.02	754.03	731.90	712.19	694.57	678.73	664.46	651.54
110000	856.92	829.43	805.09	783.41	764.02	746.61	730.90	716.69
120000	934.83	904.84	878.28	854.63	833.48	814.48	797.35	781.84
130000	1012.73	980.24	951.47	925.85	902.94	882.35	863.79	847.00
140000	1090.63	1055.64	1024.66	997.07	972.39	950.23	930.24	912.15
150000	1168.53	1131.04	1097.84	1068.29	1041.85	1018.10	996.68	977.30
160000	1246.43	1206.45	1171.03	1139.51	1111.30	1085.97	1063.13	1042.46
170000	1324.33	1281.85	1244.22	1210.73	1180.76	1153.84	1129.57	1107.61
180000	1402.24	1357.25	1317.41	1281.94	1250.22	1221.72	1196.02	1172.76
190000	1480.14	1432.65	1390.60	1353.16	1319.67	1289.59	1262.46	1237.92
200000	1558.04	1508.06	1463.79	1424.38	1389.13	1357.46	1328.91	1303.07
210000	1635.94	1583.46	1536.98	1495.60	1458.59	1425.34	1395.35	1368.22
220000	1713.84	1658.86	1610.17	1566.82	1528.04	1493.21	1461.80	1433.38
230000	1791.75	1734.26	1683.36	1638.04	1597.50	1561.08	1528.24	1498.53
240000	1869.65	1809.67	1756.55	1709.26	1666.95	1628.95	1594.69	1563.68
250000	1947.55	1885.07	1829.74	1780.48	1736.41	1696.83	1661.13	1628.84
260000	2025.45	1960.47	1902.93	1851.69	1805.87	1764.70	1727.58	1693.99
270000	2103.35	2035.87	1976.12	1922.91	1875.32	1832.57	1794.02	1759.14
280000	2181.25	2111.28	2049.31	1994.13	1944.78	1900.45	1860.47	1824.30
290000	2259.16	2186.68	2122.49	2065.35	2014.24	1968.32	1926.91	1889.45
300000	2337.06	2262.08	2195.68	2136.57	2083.69	2036.19	1993.36	1954.60
310000	2414.96	2337.48	2268.87	2207.79	2153.15	2104.06	2059.80	2019.75
320000	2492.86	2412.89	2342.06	2279.01	2222.60	2171.94	2126.25	2084.91
330000	2570.76	2488.29	2415.25	2350.23	2292.06	2239.81	2192.69	2150.06
340000	2648.66	2563.69	2488.44	2421.45	2361.52	2307.68	2259.14	2215.21
350000	2726.57	2639.09	2561.63	2492.66	2430.97	2375.56	2325.58	2280.37
360000	2804.47	2714.50	2634.82	2563.88	2500.43	2443.43	2392.03	2345.52
370000	2882.37	2789.90	2708.01	2635.10	2569.89	2511.30	2458.47	2410.67
380000	2960.27	2865.30	2781.20	2706.32	2639.34	2579.17	2524.92	2475.83
390000	3038.17	2940.70	2854.39	2777.54	2708.80	2647.05	2591.36	2540.98
400000	3116.08	3016.11	2927.58	2848.76	2778.25	2714.92	2657.81	2606.13

55

6% BLENDED MONTHLY PAYMENTS
AMORTIZATION IN YEARS

Amount	25	26	29	30	35	40	45	50
25	.16	.16	.16	.15	.15	.14	.14	.14
50	.32	.32	.31	.30	.29	.28	.27	.27
100	.64	.63	.61	.60	.57	.55	.54	.53
200	1.28	1.26	1.21	1.19	1.14	1.10	1.07	1.05
300	1.92	1.89	1.81	1.79	1.70	1.64	1.60	1.57
400	2.56	2.52	2.41	2.38	2.27	2.19	2.13	2.09
500	3.20	3.15	3.02	2.98	2.83	2.73	2.66	2.61
600	3.84	3.78	3.62	3.57	3.40	3.28	3.19	3.13
700	4.48	4.41	4.22	4.17	3.96	3.82	3.72	3.65
800	5.12	5.04	4.82	4.76	4.53	4.37	4.25	4.17
900	5.76	5.67	5.43	5.36	5.09	4.91	4.78	4.69
1000	6.40	6.30	6.03	5.95	5.66	5.46	5.31	5.21
2000	12.80	12.59	12.05	11.90	11.31	10.91	10.62	10.42
3000	19.20	18.88	18.07	17.85	16.96	16.36	15.93	15.63
4000	25.60	25.17	24.10	23.80	22.62	21.81	21.24	20.84
5000	32.00	31.46	30.12	29.75	28.27	27.26	26.55	26.05
6000	38.39	37.75	36.14	35.69	33.92	32.71	31.86	31.26
7000	44.79	44.04	42.17	41.64	39.57	38.16	37.17	36.47
8000	51.19	50.34	48.19	47.59	45.23	43.61	42.48	41.68
9000	57.59	56.63	54.21	53.54	50.88	49.06	47.79	46.89
10000	63.99	62.92	60.24	59.49	56.53	54.51	53.10	52.10
20000	127.97	125.83	120.47	118.97	113.06	109.02	106.20	104.20
30000	191.95	188.75	180.70	178.45	169.58	163.53	159.30	156.30
40000	255.93	251.66	240.93	237.93	226.11	218.04	212.40	208.39
50000	319.91	314.57	301.17	297.42	282.63	272.55	265.50	260.49
60000	383.89	377.49	361.40	356.90	339.16	327.06	318.60	312.59
70000	447.87	440.40	421.63	416.38	395.68	381.57	371.70	364.68
80000	511.85	503.31	481.86	475.86	452.21	436.08	424.80	416.78
90000	575.83	566.23	542.10	535.35	508.73	490.58	477.90	468.88
100000	639.81	629.14	602.33	594.83	565.26	545.09	531.00	520.97
110000	703.79	692.05	662.56	654.31	621.78	599.60	584.10	573.07
120000	767.77	754.97	722.79	713.79	678.31	654.11	637.20	625.17
130000	831.75	817.88	783.02	773.28	734.83	708.62	690.30	677.27
140000	895.73	880.79	843.26	832.76	791.36	763.13	743.40	729.36
150000	959.71	943.71	903.49	892.24	847.88	817.64	796.50	781.46
160000	1023.70	1006.62	963.72	951.72	904.41	872.15	849.59	833.56
170000	1087.68	1069.53	1023.95	1011.20	960.93	926.65	902.69	885.65
180000	1151.66	1132.45	1084.19	1070.69	1017.46	981.16	955.79	937.75
190000	1215.64	1195.36	1144.42	1130.17	1073.98	1035.67	1008.89	989.85
200000	1279.62	1258.27	1204.65	1189.65	1130.51	1090.18	1061.99	1041.94
210000	1343.60	1321.19	1264.88	1249.13	1187.03	1144.69	1115.09	1094.04
220000	1407.58	1384.10	1325.11	1308.62	1243.56	1199.20	1168.19	1146.14
230000	1471.56	1447.01	1385.35	1368.10	1300.08	1253.71	1221.29	1198.24
240000	1535.54	1509.93	1445.58	1427.58	1356.61	1308.22	1274.39	1250.33
250000	1599.52	1572.84	1505.81	1487.06	1413.14	1362.72	1327.49	1302.43
260000	1663.50	1635.75	1566.04	1546.55	1469.66	1417.23	1380.59	1354.53
270000	1727.48	1698.67	1626.28	1606.03	1526.19	1471.74	1433.69	1406.62
280000	1791.46	1761.58	1686.51	1665.51	1582.71	1526.25	1486.79	1458.72
290000	1855.44	1824.49	1746.74	1724.99	1639.24	1580.76	1539.89	1510.82
300000	1919.42	1887.41	1806.97	1784.48	1695.76	1635.27	1592.99	1562.91
310000	1983.41	1950.32	1867.20	1843.96	1752.29	1689.78	1646.08	1615.01
320000	2047.39	2013.23	1927.44	1903.44	1808.81	1744.29	1699.18	1667.11
330000	2111.37	2076.15	1987.67	1962.92	1865.34	1798.80	1752.28	1719.21
340000	2175.35	2139.06	2047.90	2022.40	1921.86	1853.30	1805.38	1771.30
350000	2239.33	2201.97	2108.13	2081.89	1978.39	1907.81	1858.48	1823.40
360000	2303.31	2264.89	2168.37	2141.37	2034.91	1962.32	1911.58	1875.50
370000	2367.29	2327.80	2228.60	2200.85	2091.44	2016.83	1964.68	1927.59
380000	2431.27	2390.71	2288.83	2260.33	2147.96	2071.34	2017.78	1979.69
390000	2495.25	2453.63	2349.06	2319.82	2204.49	2125.85	2070.88	2031.79
400000	2559.23	2516.54	2409.29	2379.30	2261.01	2180.36	2123.98	2083.88

AMORTIZATION IN YEARS

Amount	1	2	3	4	5	6	7	8
25	2.16	1.11	.77	.59	.49	.42	.37	.34
50	4.31	2.22	1.53	1.18	.98	.84	.74	.67
100	8.62	4.44	3.05	2.36	1.95	1.67	1.47	1.33
200	17.23	8.88	6.10	4.72	3.89	3.34	2.94	2.65
300	25.85	13.32	9.15	7.07	5.83	5.00	4.41	3.97
400	34.46	17.76	12.20	9.43	7.77	6.67	5.88	5.29
500	43.08	22.20	15.25	11.79	9.71	8.33	7.35	6.62
600	51.69	26.64	18.30	14.14	11.65	10.00	8.82	7.94
700	60.31	31.08	21.35	16.50	13.59	11.66	10.29	9.26
800	68.92	35.52	24.40	18.86	15.53	13.33	11.76	10.58
900	77.54	39.96	27.45	21.21	17.48	14.99	13.23	11.91
1000	86.15	44.40	30.50	23.57	19.42	16.66	14.70	13.23
2000	172.29	88.80	61.00	47.13	38.83	33.31	29.39	26.45
3000	258.44	133.20	91.50	70.69	58.24	49.96	44.08	39.68
4000	344.58	177.59	122.00	94.26	77.65	66.62	58.77	52.90
5000	430.73	221.99	152.50	117.82	97.07	83.27	73.46	66.13
6000	516.87	266.39	183.00	141.38	116.48	99.92	88.15	79.35
7000	603.02	310.79	213.50	164.95	135.89	116.58	102.84	92.58
8000	689.16	355.18	244.00	188.51	155.30	133.23	117.53	105.80
9000	775.31	399.58	274.50	212.07	174.71	149.88	132.22	119.02
10000	861.45	443.98	305.00	235.64	194.13	166.54	146.91	132.25
20000	1722.90	887.95	609.99	471.27	388.25	333.07	293.81	264.49
30000	2584.34	1331.92	914.98	706.90	582.37	499.60	440.71	396.74
40000	3445.79	1775.90	1219.97	942.53	776.49	666.14	587.62	528.98
50000	4307.24	2219.87	1524.96	1178.16	970.61	832.67	734.52	661.23
60000	5168.68	2663.84	1829.95	1413.79	1164.73	999.20	881.42	793.47
70000	6030.13	3107.82	2134.94	1649.42	1358.85	1165.74	1028.32	925.72
80000	6891.58	3551.79	2439.93	1885.05	1552.97	1332.27	1175.23	1057.96
90000	7753.02	3995.76	2744.92	2120.69	1747.09	1498.80	1322.13	1190.20
100000	8614.47	4439.74	3049.91	2356.32	1941.21	1665.34	1469.03	1322.45
110000	9475.92	4883.71	3354.90	2591.95	2135.33	1831.87	1615.93	1454.69
120000	10337.36	5327.68	3659.90	2827.58	2329.45	1998.40	1762.84	1586.94
130000	11198.81	5771.66	3964.89	3063.21	2523.57	2164.94	1909.74	1719.18
140000	12060.26	6215.63	4269.88	3298.84	2717.69	2331.47	2056.64	1851.43
150000	12921.70	6659.60	4574.87	3534.47	2911.81	2498.00	2203.54	1983.67
160000	13783.15	7103.58	4879.86	3770.10	3105.93	2664.54	2350.45	2115.91
170000	14644.60	7547.55	5184.85	4005.73	3300.05	2831.07	2497.35	2248.16
180000	15506.04	7991.52	5489.84	4241.37	3494.17	2997.60	2644.25	2380.40
190000	16367.49	8435.49	5794.83	4477.00	3688.29	3164.14	2791.15	2512.65
200000	17228.94	8879.47	6099.82	4712.63	3882.41	3330.67	2938.06	2644.89
210000	18090.38	9323.44	6404.81	4948.26	4076.53	3497.20	3084.96	2777.14
220000	18951.83	9767.41	6709.80	5183.89	4270.65	3663.74	3231.86	2909.38
230000	19813.27	10211.39	7014.80	5419.52	4464.77	3830.27	3378.76	3041.62
240000	20674.72	10655.36	7319.79	5655.15	4658.89	3996.80	3525.67	3173.87
250000	21536.17	11099.33	7624.78	5890.78	4853.01	4163.33	3672.57	3306.11
260000	22397.61	11543.31	7929.77	6126.41	5047.13	4329.87	3819.47	3438.36
270000	23259.06	11987.28	8234.76	6362.05	5241.25	4496.40	3966.37	3570.60
280000	24120.51	12431.25	8539.75	6597.68	5435.37	4662.93	4113.28	3702.85
290000	24981.95	12875.23	8844.74	6833.31	5629.49	4829.47	4260.18	3835.09
300000	25843.40	13319.20	9149.73	7068.94	5823.61	4996.00	4407.08	3967.33
310000	26704.85	13763.17	9454.72	7304.57	6017.73	5162.53	4553.98	4099.58
320000	27566.29	14207.15	9759.71	7540.20	6211.85	5329.07	4700.89	4231.82
330000	28427.74	14651.12	10064.70	7775.83	6405.97	5495.60	4847.79	4364.07
340000	29289.19	15095.09	10369.69	8011.46	6600.09	5662.13	4994.69	4496.31
350000	30150.63	15539.07	10674.69	8247.09	6794.21	5828.67	5141.59	4628.56
360000	31012.08	15983.04	10979.68	8482.73	6988.33	5995.20	5288.50	4760.80
370000	31873.53	16427.01	11284.67	8718.36	7182.45	6161.73	5435.40	4893.04
380000	32734.97	16870.98	11589.66	8953.99	7376.57	6328.27	5582.30	5025.29
390000	33596.42	17314.96	11894.65	9189.62	7570.69	6494.80	5729.20	5157.53
400000	34457.87	17758.93	12199.64	9425.25	7764.81	6661.33	5876.11	5289.78

AMORTIZATION IN YEARS

Amount	9	10	11	12	13	14	15	16
25	.31	.28	.27	.25	.24	.23	.22	.21
50	.61	.56	.53	.50	.47	.45	.43	.42
100	1.21	1.12	1.05	.99	.94	.90	.86	.83
200	2.42	2.24	2.10	1.97	1.87	1.79	1.71	1.65
300	3.63	3.36	3.14	2.96	2.81	2.68	2.56	2.47
400	4.84	4.48	4.19	3.94	3.74	3.57	3.42	3.29
500	6.05	5.60	5.23	4.93	4.67	4.46	4.27	4.11
600	7.26	6.72	6.28	5.91	5.61	5.35	5.12	4.93
700	8.47	7.84	7.32	6.90	6.54	6.24	5.98	5.75
800	9.68	8.96	8.37	7.88	7.47	7.13	6.83	6.57
900	10.89	10.07	9.41	8.87	8.41	8.02	7.68	7.39
1000	12.10	11.19	10.46	9.85	9.34	8.91	8.54	8.21
2000	24.19	22.38	20.91	19.70	18.68	17.81	17.07	16.42
3000	36.28	33.57	31.37	29.55	28.02	26.71	25.60	24.63
4000	48.37	44.76	41.82	39.39	37.35	35.62	34.13	32.84
5000	60.47	55.94	52.27	49.24	46.69	44.52	42.66	41.04
6000	72.55	67.13	62.73	59.09	56.03	53.42	51.19	49.25
7000	84.64	78.32	73.18	68.93	65.36	62.33	59.72	57.46
8000	96.73	89.51	83.64	78.78	74.70	71.23	68.25	65.67
9000	108.82	100.69	94.09	88.63	84.04	80.13	76.78	73.88
10000	120.91	111.88	104.54	98.47	93.37	89.04	85.31	82.08
20000	241.81	223.76	209.08	196.94	186.74	178.07	170.62	164.16
30000	362.71	335.64	313.62	295.41	280.11	267.10	255.93	246.24
40000	483.61	447.51	418.16	393.88	373.48	356.14	341.24	328.32
50000	604.51	559.39	522.70	492.34	466.85	445.17	426.54	410.40
60000	725.41	671.27	627.24	590.81	560.21	534.20	511.85	492.48
70000	846.31	783.14	731.78	689.28	653.58	623.23	597.16	574.56
80000	967.21	895.02	836.32	787.75	746.95	712.27	682.47	656.63
90000	1088.11	1006.90	940.86	886.21	840.32	801.30	767.77	738.71
100000	1209.01	1118.77	1045.40	984.68	933.69	890.33	853.08	820.79
110000	1329.91	1230.65	1149.94	1083.15	1027.06	979.36	938.39	902.87
120000	1450.81	1342.53	1254.48	1181.62	1120.42	1068.40	1023.70	984.95
130000	1571.71	1454.40	1359.02	1280.09	1213.79	1157.43	1109.00	1067.03
140000	1692.61	1566.28	1463.56	1378.55	1307.16	1246.46	1194.31	1149.11
150000	1813.51	1678.16	1568.10	1477.02	1400.53	1335.49	1279.62	1231.18
160000	1934.41	1790.03	1672.64	1575.49	1493.90	1424.53	1364.93	1313.26
170000	2055.32	1901.91	1777.18	1673.96	1587.27	1513.56	1450.23	1395.34
180000	2176.22	2013.79	1881.72	1772.42	1680.63	1602.59	1535.54	1477.42
190000	2297.12	2125.66	1986.26	1870.89	1774.00	1691.62	1620.85	1559.50
200000	2418.02	2237.54	2090.80	1969.36	1867.37	1780.66	1706.16	1641.58
210000	2538.92	2349.42	2195.34	2067.83	1960.74	1869.69	1791.47	1723.66
220000	2659.82	2461.30	2299.88	2166.30	2054.11	1958.72	1876.77	1805.73
230000	2780.72	2573.17	2404.42	2264.76	2147.47	2047.75	1962.08	1887.81
240000	2901.62	2685.05	2508.96	2363.23	2240.84	2136.79	2047.39	1969.89
250000	3022.52	2796.93	2613.50	2461.70	2334.21	2225.82	2132.70	2051.97
260000	3143.42	2908.80	2718.04	2560.17	2427.58	2314.85	2218.00	2134.05
270000	3264.32	3020.68	2822.58	2658.63	2520.95	2403.88	2303.31	2216.13
280000	3385.22	3132.56	2927.12	2757.10	2614.32	2492.92	2388.62	2298.21
290000	3506.12	3244.43	3031.66	2855.57	2707.68	2581.95	2473.93	2380.29
300000	3627.02	3356.31	3136.20	2954.04	2801.05	2670.98	2559.23	2462.36
310000	3747.92	3468.19	3240.74	3052.51	2894.42	2760.01	2644.54	2544.44
320000	3868.82	3580.06	3345.28	3150.97	2987.79	2849.05	2729.85	2626.52
330000	3989.73	3691.94	3449.82	3249.44	3081.16	2938.08	2815.16	2708.60
340000	4110.63	3803.82	3554.36	3347.91	3174.53	3027.11	2900.46	2790.68
350000	4231.53	3915.69	3658.90	3446.38	3267.89	3116.14	2985.77	2872.76
360000	4352.43	4027.57	3763.44	3544.84	3361.26	3205.18	3071.08	2954.84
370000	4473.33	4139.45	3867.98	3643.31	3454.63	3294.21	3156.39	3036.91
380000	4594.23	4251.32	3972.52	3741.78	3548.00	3383.24	3241.70	3118.99
390000	4715.13	4363.20	4077.06	3840.25	3641.37	3472.28	3327.00	3201.07
400000	4836.03	4475.08	4181.60	3938.72	3734.73	3561.31	3412.31	3283.15

Amount	17	18	19	20	21	22	23	24
25	.20	.20	.19	.19	.18	.18	.17	.17
50	.40	.39	.38	.37	.36	.35	.34	.34
100	.80	.77	.75	.73	.71	.70	.68	.67
200	1.59	1.54	1.50	1.46	1.42	1.39	1.36	1.34
300	2.38	2.31	2.24	2.18	2.13	2.08	2.04	2.00
400	3.18	3.08	2.99	2.91	2.84	2.78	2.72	2.67
500	3.97	3.84	3.73	3.64	3.55	3.47	3.40	3.34
600	4.76	4.61	4.48	4.36	4.26	4.16	4.08	4.00
700	5.55	5.38	5.23	5.09	4.97	4.86	4.76	4.67
800	6.35	6.15	5.97	5.82	5.68	5.55	5.44	5.34
900	7.14	6.91	6.72	6.54	6.38	6.24	6.12	6.00
1000	7.93	7.68	7.46	7.27	7.09	6.94	6.80	6.67
2000	15.86	15.36	14.92	14.53	14.18	13.87	13.59	13.33
3000	23.78	23.04	22.38	21.79	21.27	20.80	20.38	19.99
4000	31.71	30.72	29.84	29.06	28.36	27.73	27.17	26.66
5000	39.63	38.39	37.30	36.32	35.45	34.66	33.96	33.32
6000	47.56	46.07	44.75	43.58	42.53	41.59	40.75	39.98
7000	55.49	53.75	52.21	50.84	49.62	48.53	47.54	46.65
8000	63.41	61.43	59.67	58.11	56.71	55.46	54.33	53.31
9000	71.34	69.10	67.13	65.37	63.80	62.39	61.12	59.97
10000	79.26	76.78	74.59	72.63	70.89	69.32	67.91	66.64
20000	158.52	153.56	149.17	145.26	141.77	138.64	135.82	133.27
30000	237.78	230.33	223.75	217.89	212.65	207.95	203.72	199.90
40000	317.04	307.11	298.33	290.52	283.54	277.27	271.63	266.53
50000	396.29	383.89	372.91	363.15	354.42	346.59	339.53	333.16
60000	475.55	460.66	447.49	435.77	425.30	415.90	407.44	399.79
70000	554.81	537.44	522.07	508.40	496.18	485.22	475.34	466.42
80000	634.07	614.22	596.65	581.03	567.07	554.54	543.25	533.05
90000	713.32	690.99	671.23	653.66	637.95	623.85	611.16	599.68
100000	792.58	767.77	745.81	726.29	708.83	693.17	679.06	666.31
110000	871.84	844.55	820.40	798.91	779.72	762.49	746.97	732.94
120000	951.10	921.32	894.98	871.54	850.60	831.80	814.87	799.57
130000	1030.35	998.10	969.56	944.17	921.48	901.12	882.78	866.20
140000	1109.61	1074.88	1044.14	1016.80	992.36	970.44	950.68	932.83
150000	1188.87	1151.65	1118.72	1089.43	1063.25	1039.75	1018.59	999.46
160000	1268.13	1228.43	1193.30	1162.05	1134.13	1109.07	1086.50	1066.09
170000	1347.39	1305.20	1267.88	1234.68	1205.01	1178.39	1154.40	1132.72
180000	1426.64	1381.98	1342.46	1307.31	1275.90	1247.70	1222.31	1199.35
190000	1505.90	1458.76	1417.04	1379.94	1346.78	1317.02	1290.21	1265.98
200000	1585.16	1535.53	1491.62	1452.57	1417.66	1386.34	1358.12	1332.61
210000	1664.42	1612.31	1566.21	1525.20	1488.54	1455.65	1426.02	1399.24
220000	1743.67	1689.09	1640.79	1597.82	1559.43	1524.97	1493.93	1465.87
230000	1822.93	1765.86	1715.37	1670.45	1630.31	1594.29	1561.84	1532.50
240000	1902.19	1842.64	1789.95	1743.08	1701.19	1663.60	1629.74	1599.13
250000	1981.45	1919.42	1864.53	1815.71	1772.08	1732.92	1697.65	1665.76
260000	2060.70	1996.19	1939.11	1888.34	1842.96	1802.24	1765.55	1732.40
270000	2139.96	2072.97	2013.69	1960.96	1913.84	1871.55	1833.46	1799.03
280000	2219.22	2149.75	2088.27	2033.59	1984.72	1940.87	1901.36	1865.66
290000	2298.48	2226.52	2162.85	2106.22	2055.61	2010.19	1969.27	1932.29
300000	2377.74	2303.30	2237.43	2178.85	2126.49	2079.50	2037.18	1998.92
310000	2456.99	2380.07	2312.02	2251.48	2197.37	2148.82	2105.08	2065.55
320000	2536.25	2456.85	2386.60	2324.10	2268.26	2218.14	2172.99	2132.18
330000	2615.51	2533.63	2461.18	2396.73	2339.14	2287.45	2240.89	2198.81
340000	2694.77	2610.40	2535.76	2469.36	2410.02	2356.77	2308.80	2265.44
350000	2774.02	2687.18	2610.34	2541.99	2480.90	2426.09	2376.70	2332.07
360000	2853.28	2763.96	2684.92	2614.62	2551.79	2495.40	2444.61	2398.70
370000	2932.54	2840.73	2759.50	2687.25	2622.67	2564.72	2512.52	2465.33
380000	3011.80	2917.51	2834.08	2759.87	2693.55	2634.04	2580.42	2531.96
390000	3091.05	2994.29	2908.66	2832.50	2764.44	2703.35	2648.33	2598.59
400000	3170.31	3071.06	2983.24	2905.13	2835.32	2772.67	2716.23	2665.22

6¼% BLENDED MONTHLY PAYMENTS
AMORTIZATION IN YEARS

Amount	25	26	29	30	35	40	45	50
25	.17	.17	.16	.16	.15	.15	.14	.14
50	.33	.33	.31	.31	.30	.29	.28	.27
100	.66	.65	.62	.62	.59	.57	.55	.54
200	1.31	1.29	1.24	1.23	1.17	1.13	1.10	1.08
300	1.97	1.94	1.86	1.84	1.75	1.69	1.65	1.62
400	2.62	2.58	2.48	2.45	2.33	2.25	2.20	2.16
500	3.28	3.23	3.09	3.06	2.91	2.82	2.75	2.70
600	3.93	3.87	3.71	3.67	3.49	3.38	3.30	3.24
700	4.59	4.51	4.33	4.28	4.08	3.94	3.85	3.78
800	5.24	5.16	4.95	4.89	4.66	4.50	4.39	4.32
900	5.90	5.80	5.57	5.50	5.24	5.06	4.94	4.86
1000	6.55	6.45	6.18	6.11	5.82	5.63	5.49	5.40
2000	13.10	12.89	12.36	12.22	11.64	11.25	10.98	10.79
3000	19.65	19.33	18.54	18.32	17.45	16.87	16.46	16.18
4000	26.19	25.77	24.72	24.43	23.27	22.49	21.95	21.57
5000	32.74	32.22	30.90	30.53	29.09	28.11	27.43	26.96
6000	39.29	38.66	37.08	36.64	34.90	33.73	32.92	32.35
7000	45.84	45.10	43.26	42.74	40.72	39.35	38.41	37.74
8000	52.38	51.54	49.44	48.85	46.54	44.97	43.89	43.13
9000	58.93	57.99	55.61	54.95	52.35	50.60	49.38	48.52
10000	65.48	64.43	61.79	61.06	58.17	56.22	54.86	53.91
20000	130.95	128.85	123.58	122.11	116.34	112.43	109.72	107.81
30000	196.43	193.27	185.37	183.16	174.50	168.64	164.58	161.71
40000	261.90	257.70	247.16	244.22	232.67	224.85	219.43	215.61
50000	327.38	322.12	308.95	305.27	290.84	281.06	274.29	269.52
60000	392.85	386.54	370.73	366.32	349.00	337.28	329.15	323.42
70000	458.32	450.97	432.52	427.38	407.17	393.49	384.01	377.32
80000	523.80	515.39	494.31	488.43	465.33	449.70	438.86	431.22
90000	589.27	579.81	556.10	549.48	523.50	505.91	493.72	485.12
100000	654.75	644.23	617.89	610.54	581.67	562.12	548.58	539.03
110000	720.22	708.66	679.68	671.59	639.83	618.34	603.43	592.93
120000	785.69	773.08	741.46	732.64	698.00	674.55	658.29	646.83
130000	851.17	837.50	803.25	793.70	756.16	730.76	713.15	700.73
140000	916.64	901.93	865.04	854.75	814.33	786.97	768.01	754.64
150000	982.12	966.35	926.83	915.80	872.50	843.18	822.86	808.54
160000	1047.59	1030.77	988.62	976.86	930.66	899.40	877.72	862.44
170000	1113.07	1095.20	1050.41	1037.91	988.83	955.61	932.58	916.34
180000	1178.54	1159.62	1112.19	1098.96	1046.99	1011.82	987.43	970.24
190000	1244.01	1224.04	1173.98	1160.02	1105.16	1068.03	1042.29	1024.15
200000	1309.49	1288.46	1235.77	1221.07	1163.33	1124.24	1097.15	1078.05
210000	1374.96	1352.89	1297.56	1282.12	1221.49	1180.46	1152.01	1131.95
220000	1440.44	1417.31	1359.35	1343.18	1279.66	1236.67	1206.86	1185.85
230000	1505.91	1481.73	1421.13	1404.23	1337.83	1292.88	1261.72	1239.75
240000	1571.38	1546.16	1482.92	1465.28	1395.99	1349.09	1316.58	1293.66
250000	1636.86	1610.58	1544.71	1526.34	1454.16	1405.30	1371.43	1347.56
260000	1702.33	1675.00	1606.50	1587.39	1512.32	1461.52	1426.29	1401.46
270000	1767.81	1739.43	1668.29	1648.44	1570.49	1517.73	1481.15	1455.36
280000	1833.28	1803.85	1730.08	1709.50	1628.66	1573.94	1536.01	1509.27
290000	1898.76	1868.27	1791.86	1770.55	1686.82	1630.15	1590.86	1563.17
300000	1964.23	1932.69	1853.65	1831.60	1744.99	1686.36	1645.72	1617.07
310000	2029.70	1997.12	1915.44	1892.66	1803.15	1742.58	1700.58	1670.97
320000	2095.18	2061.54	1977.23	1953.71	1861.32	1798.79	1755.44	1724.87
330000	2160.65	2125.96	2039.02	2014.76	1919.49	1855.00	1810.29	1778.78
340000	2226.13	2190.39	2100.81	2075.82	1977.65	1911.21	1865.15	1832.68
350000	2291.60	2254.81	2162.59	2136.87	2035.82	1967.42	1920.01	1886.58
360000	2357.07	2319.23	2224.38	2197.92	2093.98	2023.64	1974.86	1940.48
370000	2422.55	2383.65	2286.17	2258.98	2152.15	2079.85	2029.72	1994.39
380000	2488.02	2448.08	2347.96	2320.03	2210.32	2136.06	2084.58	2048.29
390000	2553.50	2512.50	2409.75	2381.08	2268.48	2192.27	2139.44	2102.19
400000	2618.97	2576.92	2471.54	2442.14	2326.65	2248.48	2194.29	2156.09

BLENDED MONTHLY PAYMENTS

AMORTIZATION IN YEARS

6½%

Amount	1	2	3	4	5	6	7	8
25	2.16	1.12	.77	.60	.49	.42	.38	.34
50	4.32	2.23	1.54	1.19	.98	.84	.75	.67
100	8.63	4.46	3.07	2.37	1.96	1.68	1.49	1.34
200	17.26	8.91	6.13	4.74	3.91	3.36	2.97	2.67
300	25.88	13.36	9.19	7.11	5.86	5.04	4.45	4.01
400	34.51	17.81	12.25	9.48	7.82	6.71	5.93	5.34
500	43.13	22.26	15.31	11.84	9.77	8.39	7.41	6.68
600	51.76	26.71	18.37	14.21	11.72	10.07	8.89	8.01
700	60.38	31.16	21.43	16.58	13.67	11.74	10.37	9.35
800	69.01	35.61	24.49	18.95	15.63	13.42	11.85	10.68
900	77.64	40.06	27.55	21.31	17.58	15.10	13.33	12.01
1000	86.26	44.51	30.61	23.68	19.53	16.77	14.81	13.35
2000	172.52	89.02	61.22	47.36	39.06	33.54	29.62	26.69
3000	258.78	133.53	91.83	71.03	58.58	50.31	44.43	40.04
4000	345.03	178.03	122.44	94.71	78.11	67.08	59.24	53.38
5000	431.29	222.54	153.05	118.38	97.63	83.85	74.04	66.72
6000	517.55	267.05	183.66	142.06	117.16	100.62	88.85	80.07
7000	603.80	311.56	214.27	165.73	136.69	117.39	103.66	93.41
8000	690.06	356.06	244.88	189.41	156.21	134.16	118.47	106.76
9000	776.32	400.57	275.49	213.08	175.74	150.92	133.27	120.10
10000	862.57	445.08	306.10	236.76	195.26	167.69	148.08	133.44
20000	1725.14	890.15	612.20	473.51	390.52	335.38	296.16	266.88
30000	2587.71	1335.22	918.30	710.26	585.78	503.07	444.24	400.32
40000	3450.27	1780.30	1224.39	947.01	781.03	670.76	592.31	533.76
50000	4312.84	2225.37	1530.49	1183.76	976.29	838.45	740.39	667.19
60000	5175.41	2670.44	1836.59	1420.51	1171.55	1006.14	888.47	800.63
70000	6037.97	3115.51	2142.69	1657.27	1366.81	1173.83	1036.54	934.07
80000	6900.54	3560.59	2448.78	1894.02	1562.06	1341.51	1184.62	1067.51
90000	7763.11	4005.66	2754.88	2130.77	1757.32	1509.20	1332.70	1200.95
100000	8625.67	4450.73	3060.98	2367.52	1952.58	1676.89	1480.77	1334.38
110000	9488.24	4895.80	3367.08	2604.27	2147.84	1844.58	1628.85	1467.82
120000	10350.81	5340.88	3673.17	2841.02	2343.09	2012.27	1776.93	1601.26
130000	11213.37	5785.95	3979.27	3077.78	2538.35	2179.96	1925.00	1734.70
140000	12075.94	6231.02	4285.37	3314.53	2733.61	2347.65	2073.08	1868.13
150000	12938.51	6676.09	4591.46	3551.28	2928.87	2515.33	2221.16	2001.57
160000	13801.08	7121.17	4897.56	3788.03	3124.12	2683.02	2369.23	2135.01
170000	14663.64	7566.24	5203.66	4024.78	3319.38	2850.71	2517.31	2268.45
180000	15526.21	8011.31	5509.76	4261.53	3514.64	3018.40	2665.39	2401.89
190000	16388.78	8456.38	5815.85	4498.29	3709.90	3186.09	2813.47	2535.32
200000	17251.34	8901.46	6121.95	4735.04	3905.15	3353.78	2961.54	2668.76
210000	18113.91	9346.53	6428.05	4971.79	4100.41	3521.47	3109.62	2802.20
220000	18976.48	9791.60	6734.15	5208.54	4295.67	3689.16	3257.70	2935.64
230000	19839.04	10236.67	7040.24	5445.29	4490.93	3856.84	3405.77	3069.07
240000	20701.61	10681.75	7346.34	5682.04	4686.18	4024.53	3553.85	3202.51
250000	21564.18	11126.82	7652.44	5918.80	4881.44	4192.22	3701.93	3335.95
260000	22426.74	11571.89	7958.54	6155.55	5076.70	4359.91	3850.00	3469.39
270000	23289.31	12016.96	8264.63	6392.30	5271.96	4527.60	3998.08	3602.83
280000	24151.88	12462.04	8570.73	6629.05	5467.21	4695.29	4146.16	3736.26
290000	25014.45	12907.11	8876.83	6865.80	5662.47	4862.98	4294.23	3869.70
300000	25877.01	13352.18	9182.92	7102.55	5857.73	5030.66	4442.31	4003.14
310000	26739.58	13797.25	9489.02	7339.31	6052.99	5198.35	4590.39	4136.58
320000	27602.15	14242.33	9795.12	7576.06	6248.24	5366.04	4738.46	4270.02
330000	28464.71	14687.40	10101.22	7812.81	6443.50	5533.73	4886.54	4403.45
340000	29327.28	15132.47	10407.31	8049.56	6638.76	5701.42	5034.62	4536.89
350000	30189.85	15577.54	10713.41	8286.31	6834.02	5869.11	5182.69	4670.33
360000	31052.41	16022.62	11019.51	8523.06	7029.27	6036.80	5330.77	4803.77
370000	31914.98	16467.69	11325.61	8759.82	7224.53	6204.49	5478.85	4937.20
380000	32777.55	16912.76	11631.70	8996.57	7419.79	6372.17	5626.93	5070.64
390000	33640.11	17357.83	11937.80	9233.32	7615.05	6539.86	5775.00	5204.08
400000	34502.68	17802.91	12243.90	9470.07	7810.30	6707.55	5923.08	5337.52

61

6½% BLENDED MONTHLY PAYMENTS
AMORTIZATION IN YEARS

Amount	9	10	11	12	13	14	15	16
25	.31	.29	.27	.25	.24	.23	.22	.21
50	.62	.57	.53	.50	.48	.46	.44	.42
100	1.23	1.14	1.06	1.00	.95	.91	.87	.84
200	2.45	2.27	2.12	2.00	1.90	1.81	1.74	1.67
300	3.67	3.40	3.18	3.00	2.84	2.72	2.60	2.51
400	4.89	4.53	4.24	3.99	3.79	3.62	3.47	3.34
500	6.11	5.66	5.29	4.99	4.74	4.52	4.34	4.18
600	7.33	6.79	6.35	5.99	5.68	5.43	5.20	5.01
700	8.55	7.92	7.41	6.99	6.63	6.33	6.07	5.84
800	9.77	9.05	8.47	7.98	7.58	7.23	6.94	6.68
900	11.00	10.18	9.53	8.98	8.52	8.14	7.80	7.51
1000	12.22	11.32	10.58	9.98	9.47	9.04	8.67	8.35
2000	24.43	22.63	21.16	19.95	18.94	18.07	17.33	16.69
3000	36.64	33.94	31.74	29.93	28.40	27.11	26.00	25.03
4000	48.85	45.25	42.32	39.90	37.87	36.14	34.66	33.38
5000	61.06	56.56	52.90	49.87	47.33	45.18	43.32	41.72
6000	73.27	67.87	63.48	59.85	56.80	54.21	51.99	50.06
7000	85.48	79.18	74.06	69.82	66.27	63.24	60.65	58.40
8000	97.70	90.49	84.64	79.80	75.73	72.28	69.31	66.75
9000	109.91	101.80	95.22	89.77	85.20	81.31	77.98	75.09
10000	122.12	113.11	105.80	99.74	94.66	90.35	86.64	83.43
20000	244.23	226.22	211.59	199.48	189.32	180.69	173.28	166.86
30000	366.35	339.33	317.38	299.22	283.98	271.03	259.92	250.29
40000	488.46	452.44	423.17	398.96	378.64	361.38	346.55	333.71
50000	610.57	565.55	528.96	498.70	473.30	451.72	433.19	417.14
60000	732.69	678.66	634.76	598.44	567.96	542.06	519.83	500.57
70000	854.80	791.77	740.55	698.18	662.62	632.40	606.46	583.99
80000	976.91	904.88	846.34	797.92	757.28	722.75	693.10	667.42
90000	1099.03	1017.99	952.13	897.66	851.94	813.09	779.74	750.85
100000	1221.14	1131.10	1057.92	997.40	946.60	903.43	866.37	834.27
110000	1343.25	1244.21	1163.72	1097.14	1041.26	993.78	953.01	917.70
120000	1465.37	1357.32	1269.51	1196.88	1135.91	1084.12	1039.65	1001.13
130000	1587.48	1470.43	1375.30	1296.62	1230.57	1174.46	1126.29	1084.55
140000	1709.60	1583.54	1481.09	1396.35	1325.23	1264.80	1212.92	1167.98
150000	1831.71	1696.64	1586.88	1496.09	1419.89	1355.15	1299.56	1251.41
160000	1953.82	1809.75	1692.68	1595.83	1514.55	1445.49	1386.20	1334.84
170000	2075.94	1922.86	1798.47	1695.57	1609.21	1535.83	1472.84	1418.26
180000	2198.05	2035.97	1904.26	1795.31	1703.87	1626.17	1559.47	1501.69
190000	2320.16	2149.08	2010.05	1895.05	1798.53	1716.52	1646.11	1585.12
200000	2442.28	2262.19	2115.84	1994.79	1893.19	1806.86	1732.74	1668.54
210000	2564.39	2375.30	2221.64	2094.53	1987.85	1897.20	1819.38	1751.97
220000	2686.50	2488.41	2327.43	2194.27	2082.51	1987.55	1906.02	1835.40
230000	2808.62	2601.52	2433.22	2294.01	2177.17	2077.89	1992.65	1918.82
240000	2930.73	2714.63	2539.01	2393.75	2271.82	2168.23	2079.29	2002.25
250000	3052.84	2827.74	2644.80	2493.49	2366.48	2258.57	2165.93	2085.68
260000	3174.96	2940.85	2750.59	2593.23	2461.14	2348.92	2252.57	2169.10
270000	3297.07	3053.96	2856.39	2692.97	2555.80	2439.26	2339.20	2252.53
280000	3419.19	3167.07	2962.18	2792.70	2650.46	2529.60	2425.84	2335.96
290000	3541.30	3280.17	3067.97	2892.44	2745.12	2619.94	2512.48	2419.38
300000	3663.41	3393.28	3173.76	2992.18	2839.78	2710.29	2599.11	2502.81
310000	3785.53	3506.39	3279.55	3091.92	2934.44	2800.63	2685.75	2586.24
320000	3907.64	3619.50	3385.35	3191.66	3029.10	2890.97	2772.39	2669.67
330000	4029.75	3732.61	3491.14	3291.40	3123.76	2981.32	2859.02	2753.09
340000	4151.87	3845.72	3596.93	3391.14	3218.42	3071.66	2945.66	2836.52
350000	4273.98	3958.83	3702.72	3490.88	3313.08	3162.00	3032.30	2919.95
360000	4396.09	4071.94	3808.51	3590.62	3407.73	3252.34	3118.94	3003.37
370000	4518.21	4185.05	3914.31	3690.36	3502.39	3342.69	3205.57	3086.80
380000	4640.32	4298.16	4020.10	3790.10	3597.05	3433.03	3292.21	3170.23
390000	4762.43	4411.27	4125.89	3889.84	3691.71	3523.37	3378.85	3253.65
400000	4884.55	4524.38	4231.68	3989.58	3786.37	3613.71	3465.48	3337.08

BLENDED MONTHLY PAYMENTS

6½%

AMORTIZATION IN YEARS

Amount	17	18	19	20	21	22	23	24
25	.21	.20	.19	.19	.19	.18	.18	.18
50	.41	.40	.38	.38	.37	.36	.35	.35
100	.81	.79	.76	.75	.73	.71	.70	.69
200	1.62	1.57	1.52	1.49	1.45	1.42	1.39	1.37
300	2.42	2.35	2.28	2.23	2.17	2.13	2.09	2.05
400	3.23	3.13	3.04	2.97	2.90	2.84	2.78	2.73
500	4.04	3.91	3.80	3.71	3.62	3.54	3.47	3.41
600	4.84	4.69	4.56	4.45	4.34	4.25	4.17	4.09
700	5.65	5.48	5.32	5.19	5.07	4.96	4.86	4.77
800	6.45	6.26	6.08	5.93	5.79	5.67	5.56	5.45
900	7.26	7.04	6.84	6.67	6.51	6.37	6.25	6.14
1000	8.07	7.82	7.60	7.41	7.24	7.08	6.94	6.82
2000	16.13	15.64	15.20	14.82	14.47	14.16	13.88	13.63
3000	24.19	23.45	22.80	22.22	21.70	21.24	20.82	20.44
4000	32.25	31.27	30.40	29.63	28.93	28.31	27.76	27.25
5000	40.32	39.09	38.00	37.03	36.17	35.39	34.70	34.07
6000	48.38	46.90	45.60	44.44	43.40	42.47	41.63	40.88
7000	56.44	54.72	53.19	51.84	50.63	49.55	48.57	47.69
8000	64.50	62.53	60.79	59.25	57.86	56.62	55.51	54.50
9000	72.57	70.35	68.39	66.65	65.10	63.70	62.45	61.31
10000	80.63	78.17	75.99	74.06	72.33	70.78	69.39	68.13
20000	161.25	156.33	151.97	148.11	144.65	141.55	138.77	136.25
30000	241.88	234.49	227.96	222.16	216.97	212.33	208.15	204.37
40000	322.50	312.65	303.94	296.21	289.30	283.10	277.53	272.49
50000	403.13	390.81	379.93	370.26	361.62	353.87	346.91	340.61
60000	483.75	468.98	455.91	444.31	433.94	424.65	416.29	408.74
70000	564.38	547.14	531.90	518.36	506.26	495.42	485.67	476.86
80000	645.00	625.30	607.88	592.41	578.59	566.20	555.05	544.98
90000	725.63	703.46	683.87	666.46	650.91	636.97	624.43	613.10
100000	806.25	781.62	759.85	740.51	723.23	707.74	693.81	681.22
110000	886.88	859.79	835.84	814.56	795.55	778.52	763.19	749.35
120000	967.50	937.95	911.82	888.61	867.88	849.29	832.57	817.47
130000	1048.13	1016.11	987.81	962.66	940.20	920.07	901.95	885.59
140000	1128.75	1094.27	1063.79	1036.71	1012.52	990.84	971.33	953.71
150000	1209.38	1172.43	1139.78	1110.76	1084.84	1061.61	1040.71	1021.83
160000	1290.00	1250.60	1215.76	1184.81	1157.17	1132.39	1110.09	1089.96
170000	1370.62	1328.76	1291.75	1258.86	1229.49	1203.16	1179.47	1158.08
180000	1451.25	1406.92	1367.73	1332.91	1301.81	1273.93	1248.85	1226.20
190000	1531.87	1485.08	1443.72	1406.96	1374.13	1344.71	1318.23	1294.32
200000	1612.50	1563.24	1519.70	1481.01	1446.46	1415.48	1387.61	1362.44
210000	1693.12	1641.41	1595.69	1555.06	1518.78	1486.26	1456.99	1430.57
220000	1773.75	1719.57	1671.67	1629.11	1591.10	1557.03	1526.37	1498.69
230000	1854.37	1797.73	1747.66	1703.16	1663.42	1627.80	1595.75	1566.81
240000	1935.00	1875.89	1823.64	1777.21	1735.75	1698.58	1665.13	1634.93
250000	2015.62	1954.05	1899.63	1851.26	1808.07	1769.35	1734.51	1703.05
260000	2096.25	2032.22	1975.61	1925.31	1880.39	1840.13	1803.89	1771.18
270000	2176.87	2110.38	2051.60	1999.36	1952.72	1910.90	1873.27	1839.30
280000	2257.50	2188.54	2127.58	2073.41	2025.04	1981.67	1942.65	1907.42
290000	2338.12	2266.70	2203.57	2147.46	2097.36	2052.45	2012.03	1975.54
300000	2418.75	2344.86	2279.55	2221.51	2169.68	2123.22	2081.41	2043.66
310000	2499.37	2423.03	2355.54	2295.56	2242.01	2194.00	2150.79	2111.78
320000	2579.99	2501.19	2431.52	2369.61	2314.33	2264.77	2220.17	2179.91
330000	2660.62	2579.35	2507.50	2443.66	2386.65	2335.54	2289.55	2248.03
340000	2741.24	2657.51	2583.49	2517.71	2458.97	2406.32	2358.93	2316.15
350000	2821.87	2735.67	2659.47	2591.76	2531.30	2477.09	2428.31	2384.27
360000	2902.49	2813.84	2735.46	2665.81	2603.62	2547.86	2497.69	2452.39
370000	2983.12	2892.00	2811.44	2739.86	2675.94	2618.64	2567.07	2520.52
380000	3063.74	2970.16	2887.43	2813.91	2748.26	2689.41	2636.45	2588.64
390000	3144.37	3048.32	2963.41	2887.96	2820.59	2760.19	2705.83	2656.76
400000	3224.99	3126.48	3039.40	2962.01	2892.91	2830.96	2775.21	2724.88

63

6½% BLENDED MONTHLY PAYMENTS
AMORTIZATION IN YEARS

Amount	25	26	29	30	35	40	45	50
25	.17	.17	.16	.16	.15	.15	.15	.14
50	.34	.33	.32	.32	.30	.29	.29	.28
100	.67	.66	.64	.63	.60	.58	.57	.56
200	1.34	1.32	1.27	1.26	1.20	1.16	1.14	1.12
300	2.01	1.98	1.91	1.88	1.80	1.74	1.70	1.68
400	2.68	2.64	2.54	2.51	2.40	2.32	2.27	2.23
500	3.35	3.30	3.17	3.14	3.00	2.90	2.84	2.79
600	4.02	3.96	3.81	3.76	3.59	3.48	3.40	3.35
700	4.69	4.62	4.44	4.39	4.19	4.06	3.97	3.91
800	5.36	5.28	5.07	5.02	4.79	4.64	4.54	4.46
900	6.03	5.94	5.71	5.64	5.39	5.22	5.10	5.02
1000	6.70	6.60	6.34	6.27	5.99	5.80	5.67	5.58
2000	13.40	13.19	12.68	12.53	11.97	11.59	11.33	11.15
3000	20.10	19.79	19.01	18.80	17.95	17.38	16.99	16.72
4000	26.80	26.38	25.35	25.06	23.93	23.18	22.66	22.29
5000	33.50	32.98	31.69	31.33	29.92	28.97	28.32	27.87
6000	40.19	39.57	38.02	37.59	35.90	34.76	33.98	33.44
7000	46.89	46.17	44.36	43.85	41.88	40.56	39.65	39.01
8000	53.59	52.76	50.69	50.12	47.86	46.35	45.31	44.58
9000	60.29	59.36	57.03	56.38	53.85	52.14	50.97	50.16
10000	66.99	65.95	63.37	62.65	59.83	57.94	56.64	55.73
20000	133.97	131.90	126.73	125.29	119.65	115.87	113.27	111.45
30000	200.95	197.85	190.09	187.93	179.48	173.80	169.90	167.17
40000	267.93	263.80	253.45	250.57	239.30	231.73	226.53	222.90
50000	334.92	329.74	316.81	313.21	299.12	289.66	283.16	278.62
60000	401.90	395.69	380.17	375.85	358.95	347.60	339.79	334.34
70000	468.88	461.64	443.53	438.49	418.77	405.53	396.42	390.06
80000	535.86	527.59	506.89	501.13	478.59	463.46	453.05	445.79
90000	602.85	593.53	570.25	563.77	538.42	521.39	509.69	501.51
100000	669.83	659.48	633.61	626.41	598.24	579.32	566.32	557.23
110000	736.81	725.43	696.97	689.05	658.07	637.26	622.95	612.95
120000	803.79	791.38	760.33	751.69	717.89	695.19	679.58	668.68
130000	870.78	857.32	823.69	814.33	777.71	753.12	736.21	724.40
140000	937.76	923.27	887.05	876.97	837.54	811.05	792.84	780.12
150000	1004.74	989.22	950.41	939.61	897.36	868.98	849.47	835.84
160000	1071.72	1055.17	1013.77	1002.25	957.18	926.92	906.10	891.57
170000	1138.71	1121.11	1077.13	1064.89	1017.01	984.85	962.74	947.29
180000	1205.69	1187.06	1140.49	1127.53	1076.83	1042.78	1019.37	1003.01
190000	1272.67	1253.01	1203.85	1190.17	1136.66	1100.71	1076.00	1058.74
200000	1339.65	1318.96	1267.21	1252.81	1196.48	1158.64	1132.63	1114.46
210000	1406.63	1384.90	1330.57	1315.45	1256.30	1216.57	1189.26	1170.18
220000	1473.62	1450.85	1393.93	1378.09	1316.13	1274.51	1245.89	1225.90
230000	1540.60	1516.80	1457.29	1440.73	1375.95	1332.44	1302.52	1281.63
240000	1607.58	1582.75	1520.65	1503.37	1435.77	1390.37	1359.15	1337.35
250000	1674.56	1648.69	1584.01	1566.01	1495.60	1448.30	1415.79	1393.07
260000	1741.55	1714.64	1647.37	1628.65	1555.42	1506.23	1472.42	1448.79
270000	1808.53	1780.59	1710.73	1691.29	1615.25	1564.17	1529.05	1504.52
280000	1875.51	1846.54	1774.09	1753.93	1675.07	1622.10	1585.68	1560.24
290000	1942.49	1912.48	1837.45	1816.57	1734.89	1680.03	1642.31	1615.96
300000	2009.48	1978.43	1900.81	1879.21	1794.72	1737.96	1698.94	1671.68
310000	2076.46	2044.38	1964.17	1941.85	1854.54	1795.89	1755.57	1727.41
320000	2143.44	2110.33	2027.53	2004.49	1914.36	1853.83	1812.20	1783.13
330000	2210.42	2176.27	2090.89	2067.13	1974.19	1911.76	1868.84	1838.85
340000	2277.41	2242.22	2154.25	2129.77	2034.01	1969.69	1925.47	1894.57
350000	2344.39	2308.17	2217.61	2192.41	2093.83	2027.62	1982.10	1950.30
360000	2411.37	2374.12	2280.97	2255.05	2153.66	2085.55	2038.73	2006.02
370000	2478.35	2440.06	2344.33	2317.69	2213.48	2143.48	2095.36	2061.74
380000	2545.34	2506.01	2407.69	2380.33	2273.31	2201.42	2151.99	2117.47
390000	2612.32	2571.96	2471.05	2442.97	2333.13	2259.35	2208.62	2173.19
400000	2679.30	2637.91	2534.41	2505.61	2392.95	2317.28	2265.25	2228.91

BLENDED MONTHLY PAYMENTS 6¾%
AMORTIZATION IN YEARS

Amount	1	2	3	4	5	6	7	8
25	2.16	1.12	.77	.60	.50	.43	.38	.34
50	4.32	2.24	1.54	1.19	.99	.85	.75	.68
100	8.64	4.47	3.08	2.38	1.97	1.69	1.50	1.35
200	17.28	8.93	6.15	4.76	3.93	3.38	2.99	2.70
300	25.92	13.39	9.22	7.14	5.90	5.07	4.48	4.04
400	34.55	17.85	12.29	9.52	7.86	6.76	5.98	5.39
500	43.19	22.31	15.37	11.90	9.82	8.45	7.47	6.74
600	51.83	26.78	18.44	14.28	11.79	10.14	8.96	8.08
700	60.46	31.24	21.51	16.66	13.75	11.82	10.45	9.43
800	69.10	35.70	24.58	19.03	15.72	13.51	11.95	10.78
900	77.74	40.16	27.65	21.41	17.68	15.20	13.44	12.12
1000	86.37	44.62	30.73	23.79	19.64	16.89	14.93	13.47
2000	172.74	89.24	61.45	47.58	39.28	33.77	29.86	26.93
3000	259.11	133.86	92.17	71.37	58.92	50.66	44.78	40.40
4000	345.48	178.47	122.89	95.15	78.56	67.54	59.71	53.86
5000	431.85	223.09	153.61	118.94	98.20	84.43	74.63	67.32
6000	518.22	267.71	184.33	142.73	117.84	101.31	89.56	80.79
7000	604.59	312.33	215.05	166.52	137.48	118.20	104.48	94.25
8000	690.95	356.94	245.77	190.30	157.12	135.08	119.41	107.71
9000	777.32	401.56	276.49	214.09	176.76	151.97	134.34	121.18
10000	863.69	446.18	307.21	237.88	196.40	168.85	149.26	134.64
20000	1727.38	892.35	614.42	475.75	392.80	337.70	298.52	269.28
30000	2591.07	1338.52	921.62	713.63	589.20	506.55	447.77	403.91
40000	3454.75	1784.69	1228.83	951.50	785.60	675.40	597.03	538.55
50000	4318.44	2230.87	1536.03	1189.38	981.99	844.24	746.28	673.19
60000	5182.13	2677.04	1843.24	1427.25	1178.39	1013.09	895.54	807.82
70000	6045.81	3123.21	2150.44	1665.12	1374.79	1181.94	1044.79	942.46
80000	6909.50	3569.38	2457.65	1903.00	1571.19	1350.79	1194.05	1077.10
90000	7773.19	4015.56	2764.85	2140.87	1767.58	1519.63	1343.31	1211.73
100000	8636.87	4461.73	3072.06	2378.75	1963.98	1688.48	1492.56	1346.37
110000	9500.56	4907.90	3379.26	2616.62	2160.38	1857.33	1641.82	1481.01
120000	10364.25	5354.07	3686.47	2854.50	2356.78	2026.18	1791.07	1615.64
130000	11227.94	5800.25	3993.67	3092.37	2553.17	2195.03	1940.33	1750.28
140000	12091.62	6246.42	4300.88	3330.24	2749.57	2363.87	2089.58	1884.92
150000	12955.31	6692.59	4608.08	3568.12	2945.97	2532.72	2238.84	2019.55
160000	13819.00	7138.76	4915.29	3805.99	3142.37	2701.57	2388.09	2154.19
170000	14682.68	7584.94	5222.49	4043.87	3338.77	2870.42	2537.35	2288.83
180000	15546.37	8031.11	5529.70	4281.74	3535.16	3039.26	2686.61	2423.46
190000	16410.06	8477.28	5836.90	4519.62	3731.56	3208.11	2835.86	2558.10
200000	17273.74	8923.45	6144.11	4757.49	3927.96	3376.96	2985.12	2692.73
210000	18137.43	9369.63	6451.31	4995.36	4124.36	3545.81	3134.37	2827.37
220000	19001.12	9815.80	6758.52	5233.24	4320.75	3714.66	3283.63	2962.01
230000	19864.81	10261.97	7065.72	5471.11	4517.15	3883.50	3432.88	3096.64
240000	20728.49	10708.14	7372.93	5708.99	4713.55	4052.35	3582.14	3231.28
250000	21592.18	11154.32	7680.13	5946.86	4909.95	4221.20	3731.39	3365.92
260000	22455.87	11600.49	7987.34	6184.74	5106.34	4390.05	3880.65	3500.55
270000	23319.55	12046.66	8294.54	6422.61	5302.74	4558.89	4029.91	3635.19
280000	24183.24	12492.83	8601.75	6660.48	5499.14	4727.74	4179.16	3769.83
290000	25046.93	12939.00	8908.95	6898.36	5695.54	4896.59	4328.42	3904.46
300000	25910.61	13385.18	9216.16	7136.23	5891.93	5065.44	4477.67	4039.10
310000	26774.30	13831.35	9523.36	7374.11	6088.33	5234.29	4626.93	4173.74
320000	27637.99	14277.52	9830.57	7611.98	6284.73	5403.13	4776.18	4308.37
330000	28501.68	14723.69	10137.77	7849.86	6481.13	5571.98	4925.44	4443.01
340000	29365.36	15169.87	10444.98	8087.73	6677.53	5740.83	5074.69	4577.65
350000	30229.05	15616.04	10752.18	8325.60	6873.92	5909.68	5223.95	4712.28
360000	31092.74	16062.21	11059.39	8563.48	7070.32	6078.52	5373.21	4846.92
370000	31956.42	16508.38	11366.59	8801.35	7266.72	6247.37	5522.46	4981.56
380000	32820.11	16954.56	11673.80	9039.23	7463.12	6416.22	5671.72	5116.19
390000	33683.80	17400.73	11981.00	9277.10	7659.51	6585.07	5820.97	5250.83
400000	34547.48	17846.90	12288.21	9514.98	7855.91	6753.92	5970.23	5385.46

6¾% BLENDED MONTHLY PAYMENTS
AMORTIZATION IN YEARS

Amount	9	10	11	12	13	14	15	16
25	.31	.29	.27	.26	.24	.23	.22	.22
50	.62	.58	.54	.51	.48	.46	.44	.43
100	1.24	1.15	1.08	1.02	.96	.92	.88	.85
200	2.47	2.29	2.15	2.03	1.92	1.84	1.76	1.70
300	3.70	3.44	3.22	3.04	2.88	2.75	2.64	2.55
400	4.94	4.58	4.29	4.05	3.84	3.67	3.52	3.40
500	6.17	5.72	5.36	5.06	4.80	4.59	4.40	4.24
600	7.40	6.87	6.43	6.07	5.76	5.50	5.28	5.09
700	8.64	8.01	7.50	7.08	6.72	6.42	6.16	5.94
800	9.87	9.15	8.57	8.09	7.68	7.34	7.04	6.79
900	11.10	10.30	9.64	9.10	8.64	8.25	7.92	7.64
1000	12.34	11.44	10.71	10.11	9.60	9.17	8.80	8.48
2000	24.67	22.87	21.42	20.21	19.20	18.34	17.60	16.96
3000	37.00	34.31	32.12	30.31	28.79	27.50	26.40	25.44
4000	49.34	45.74	42.83	40.41	38.39	36.67	35.20	33.92
5000	61.67	57.18	53.53	50.51	47.98	45.84	43.99	42.40
6000	74.00	68.61	64.24	60.62	57.58	55.00	52.79	50.88
7000	86.34	80.05	74.94	70.72	67.18	64.17	61.59	59.35
8000	98.67	91.48	85.65	80.82	76.77	73.33	70.39	67.83
9000	111.00	102.92	96.35	90.92	86.37	82.50	79.18	76.31
10000	123.34	114.35	107.06	101.02	95.96	91.67	87.98	84.79
20000	246.67	228.70	214.11	202.04	191.92	183.33	175.96	169.58
30000	370.00	343.05	321.16	303.06	287.88	274.99	263.93	254.36
40000	493.33	457.40	428.21	404.08	383.84	366.65	351.91	339.15
50000	616.67	571.75	535.26	505.10	479.80	458.32	439.89	423.93
60000	740.00	686.10	642.31	606.12	575.76	549.98	527.86	508.72
70000	863.33	800.44	749.36	707.14	671.72	641.64	615.84	593.50
80000	986.66	914.79	856.41	808.15	767.67	733.30	703.81	678.29
90000	1110.00	1029.14	963.47	909.17	863.63	824.96	791.79	763.07
100000	1233.33	1143.49	1070.52	1010.19	959.59	916.63	879.77	847.86
110000	1356.66	1257.84	1177.57	1111.21	1055.55	1008.29	967.74	932.65
120000	1479.99	1372.19	1284.62	1212.23	1151.51	1099.95	1055.72	1017.43
130000	1603.33	1486.53	1391.67	1313.25	1247.47	1191.61	1143.69	1102.22
140000	1726.66	1600.88	1498.72	1414.27	1343.43	1283.28	1231.67	1187.00
150000	1849.99	1715.23	1605.77	1515.29	1439.38	1374.94	1319.65	1271.79
160000	1973.32	1829.58	1712.82	1616.30	1535.34	1466.60	1407.62	1356.57
170000	2096.66	1943.93	1819.88	1717.32	1631.30	1558.26	1495.60	1441.36
180000	2219.99	2058.28	1926.93	1818.34	1727.26	1649.92	1583.57	1526.14
190000	2343.32	2172.62	2033.98	1919.36	1823.22	1741.59	1671.55	1610.93
200000	2466.65	2286.97	2141.03	2020.38	1919.18	1833.25	1759.53	1695.72
210000	2589.99	2401.32	2248.08	2121.40	2015.14	1924.91	1847.50	1780.50
220000	2713.32	2515.67	2355.13	2222.42	2111.10	2016.57	1935.48	1865.29
230000	2836.65	2630.02	2462.18	2323.44	2207.05	2108.23	2023.45	1950.07
240000	2959.98	2744.37	2569.23	2424.45	2303.01	2199.90	2111.43	2034.86
250000	3083.32	2858.71	2676.29	2525.47	2398.97	2291.56	2199.41	2119.64
260000	3206.65	2973.06	2783.34	2626.49	2494.93	2383.22	2287.38	2204.43
270000	3329.98	3087.41	2890.39	2727.51	2590.89	2474.88	2375.36	2289.21
280000	3453.31	3201.76	2997.44	2828.53	2686.85	2566.55	2463.34	2374.00
290000	3576.65	3316.11	3104.49	2929.55	2782.81	2658.21	2551.31	2458.79
300000	3699.98	3430.46	3211.54	3030.57	2878.76	2749.87	2639.29	2543.57
310000	3823.31	3544.80	3318.59	3131.59	2974.72	2841.53	2727.26	2628.36
320000	3946.64	3659.15	3425.64	3232.60	3070.68	2933.19	2815.24	2713.14
330000	4069.97	3773.50	3532.69	3333.62	3166.64	3024.86	2903.22	2797.93
340000	4193.31	3887.85	3639.75	3434.64	3262.60	3116.52	2991.19	2882.71
350000	4316.64	4002.20	3746.80	3535.66	3358.56	3208.18	3079.17	2967.50
360000	4439.97	4116.55	3853.85	3636.68	3454.52	3299.84	3167.14	3052.28
370000	4563.30	4230.90	3960.90	3737.70	3550.48	3391.50	3255.12	3137.07
380000	4686.64	4345.24	4067.95	3838.72	3646.43	3483.17	3343.10	3221.86
390000	4809.97	4459.59	4175.00	3939.74	3742.39	3574.83	3431.07	3306.64
400000	4933.30	4573.94	4282.05	4040.75	3838.35	3666.49	3519.05	3391.43

BLENDED MONTHLY PAYMENTS 6¾%
AMORTIZATION IN YEARS

Amount	17	18	19	20	21	22	23	24
25	.21	.20	.20	.19	.19	.19	.18	.18
50	.42	.40	.39	.38	.37	.37	.36	.35
100	.83	.80	.78	.76	.74	.73	.71	.70
200	1.65	1.60	1.55	1.51	1.48	1.45	1.42	1.40
300	2.47	2.39	2.33	2.27	2.22	2.17	2.13	2.09
400	3.29	3.19	3.10	3.02	2.96	2.89	2.84	2.79
500	4.11	3.98	3.88	3.78	3.69	3.62	3.55	3.49
600	4.93	4.78	4.65	4.53	4.43	4.34	4.26	4.18
700	5.75	5.57	5.42	5.29	5.17	5.06	4.97	4.88
800	6.57	6.37	6.20	6.04	5.91	5.78	5.67	5.58
900	7.39	7.17	6.97	6.80	6.64	6.51	6.38	6.27
1000	8.21	7.96	7.75	7.55	7.38	7.23	7.09	6.97
2000	16.41	15.92	15.49	15.10	14.76	14.45	14.18	13.93
3000	24.61	23.87	23.23	22.65	22.14	21.68	21.27	20.89
4000	32.81	31.83	30.97	30.20	29.52	28.90	28.35	27.86
5000	41.01	39.78	38.71	37.75	36.89	36.13	35.44	34.82
6000	49.21	47.74	46.45	45.30	44.27	43.35	42.53	41.78
7000	57.41	55.70	54.19	52.84	51.65	50.58	49.61	48.74
8000	65.61	63.65	61.93	60.39	59.03	57.80	56.70	55.71
9000	73.81	71.61	69.67	67.94	66.40	65.03	63.79	62.67
10000	82.01	79.56	77.41	75.49	73.78	72.25	70.87	69.63
20000	164.01	159.12	154.81	150.97	147.56	144.49	141.74	139.26
30000	246.01	238.68	232.21	226.46	221.33	216.74	212.61	208.89
40000	328.02	318.24	309.61	301.94	295.11	288.98	283.48	278.52
50000	410.02	397.80	387.01	377.43	368.88	361.23	354.35	348.14
60000	492.02	477.36	464.41	452.91	442.66	433.47	425.22	417.77
70000	574.02	556.92	541.81	528.40	516.43	505.72	496.08	487.40
80000	656.03	636.48	619.21	603.88	590.21	577.96	566.95	557.03
90000	738.03	716.04	696.61	679.36	663.98	650.21	637.82	626.65
100000	820.03	795.60	774.01	754.85	737.76	722.45	708.69	696.28
110000	902.03	875.15	851.41	830.33	811.53	794.69	779.56	765.91
120000	984.04	954.71	928.81	905.82	885.31	866.94	850.43	835.54
130000	1066.04	1034.27	1006.21	981.30	959.08	939.18	921.30	905.16
140000	1148.04	1113.83	1083.61	1056.79	1032.86	1011.43	992.16	974.79
150000	1230.04	1193.39	1161.02	1132.27	1106.63	1083.67	1063.03	1044.42
160000	1312.05	1272.95	1238.42	1207.76	1180.41	1155.92	1133.90	1114.05
170000	1394.05	1352.51	1315.82	1283.24	1254.18	1228.16	1204.77	1183.67
180000	1476.05	1432.07	1393.22	1358.72	1327.96	1300.41	1275.64	1253.30
190000	1558.06	1511.63	1470.62	1434.21	1401.73	1372.65	1346.51	1322.93
200000	1640.06	1591.19	1548.02	1509.69	1475.51	1444.89	1417.37	1392.56
210000	1722.06	1670.74	1625.42	1585.18	1549.29	1517.14	1488.24	1462.18
220000	1804.06	1750.30	1702.82	1660.66	1623.06	1589.38	1559.11	1531.81
230000	1886.07	1829.86	1780.22	1736.15	1696.84	1661.63	1629.98	1601.44
240000	1968.07	1909.42	1857.62	1811.63	1770.61	1733.87	1700.85	1671.07
250000	2050.07	1988.98	1935.02	1887.12	1844.39	1806.12	1771.72	1740.69
260000	2132.07	2068.54	2012.42	1962.60	1918.16	1878.36	1842.59	1810.32
270000	2214.08	2148.10	2089.82	2038.08	1991.94	1950.61	1913.45	1879.95
280000	2296.08	2227.66	2167.22	2113.57	2065.71	2022.85	1984.32	1949.58
290000	2378.08	2307.22	2244.63	2189.05	2139.49	2095.09	2055.19	2019.20
300000	2460.08	2386.78	2322.03	2264.54	2213.26	2167.34	2126.06	2088.83
310000	2542.09	2466.34	2399.43	2340.02	2287.04	2239.58	2196.93	2158.46
320000	2624.09	2545.89	2476.83	2415.51	2360.81	2311.83	2267.80	2228.09
330000	2706.09	2625.45	2554.23	2490.99	2434.59	2384.07	2338.66	2297.71
340000	2788.10	2705.01	2631.63	2566.48	2508.36	2456.32	2409.53	2367.34
350000	2870.10	2784.57	2709.03	2641.96	2582.14	2528.56	2480.40	2436.97
360000	2952.10	2864.13	2786.43	2717.44	2655.91	2600.81	2551.27	2506.60
370000	3034.10	2943.69	2863.83	2792.93	2729.69	2673.05	2622.14	2576.22
380000	3116.11	3023.25	2941.23	2868.41	2803.46	2745.30	2693.01	2645.85
390000	3198.11	3102.81	3018.63	2943.90	2877.24	2817.54	2763.88	2715.48
400000	3280.11	3182.37	3096.03	3019.38	2951.01	2889.78	2834.74	2785.11

6¾% BLENDED MONTHLY PAYMENTS
AMORTIZATION IN YEARS

Amount	25	26	29	30	35	40	45	50
25	.18	.17	.17	.17	.16	.15	.15	.15
50	.35	.34	.33	.33	.31	.30	.30	.29
100	.69	.68	.65	.65	.62	.60	.59	.58
200	1.38	1.35	1.30	1.29	1.23	1.20	1.17	1.16
300	2.06	2.03	1.95	1.93	1.85	1.80	1.76	1.73
400	2.75	2.70	2.60	2.57	2.46	2.39	2.34	2.31
500	3.43	3.38	3.25	3.22	3.08	2.99	2.93	2.88
600	4.12	4.05	3.90	3.86	3.69	3.59	3.51	3.46
700	4.80	4.73	4.55	4.50	4.31	4.18	4.09	4.03
800	5.49	5.40	5.20	5.14	4.92	4.78	4.68	4.61
900	6.17	6.08	5.85	5.79	5.54	5.38	5.26	5.19
1000	6.86	6.75	6.50	6.43	6.15	5.97	5.85	5.76
2000	13.71	13.50	12.99	12.85	12.30	11.94	11.69	11.52
3000	20.56	20.25	19.49	19.28	18.45	17.91	17.53	17.27
4000	27.41	27.00	25.98	25.70	24.60	23.87	23.37	23.03
5000	34.26	33.75	32.48	32.13	30.75	29.84	29.22	28.78
6000	41.11	40.50	38.97	38.55	36.90	35.81	35.06	34.54
7000	47.96	47.25	45.47	44.97	43.05	41.77	40.90	40.30
8000	54.81	53.99	51.96	51.40	49.20	47.74	46.74	46.05
9000	61.66	60.74	58.46	57.82	55.35	53.71	52.58	51.81
10000	68.51	67.49	64.95	64.25	61.50	59.67	58.43	57.56
20000	137.01	134.98	129.90	128.49	123.00	119.34	116.85	115.12
30000	205.52	202.47	194.85	192.73	184.50	179.01	175.27	172.68
40000	274.02	269.95	259.79	256.98	245.99	238.68	233.69	230.23
50000	342.53	337.44	324.74	321.22	307.49	298.34	292.11	287.79
60000	411.03	404.93	389.69	385.46	368.99	358.01	350.53	345.35
70000	479.54	472.41	454.64	449.70	430.49	417.68	408.95	402.91
80000	548.04	539.90	519.58	513.95	491.98	477.35	467.37	460.46
90000	616.55	607.39	584.53	578.19	553.48	537.01	525.79	518.02
100000	685.05	674.87	649.48	642.43	614.98	596.68	584.21	575.58
110000	753.56	742.36	714.43	706.68	676.48	656.35	642.63	633.13
120000	822.06	809.85	779.37	770.92	737.97	716.02	701.05	690.69
130000	890.57	877.33	844.32	835.16	799.47	775.68	759.47	748.25
140000	959.07	944.82	909.27	899.40	860.97	835.35	817.89	805.81
150000	1027.58	1012.31	974.22	963.65	922.46	895.02	876.31	863.36
160000	1096.08	1079.79	1039.16	1027.89	983.96	954.69	934.73	920.92
170000	1164.59	1147.28	1104.11	1092.13	1045.46	1014.36	993.15	978.48
180000	1233.09	1214.77	1169.06	1156.37	1106.96	1074.02	1051.57	1036.04
190000	1301.60	1282.25	1234.00	1220.62	1168.45	1133.69	1109.99	1093.59
200000	1370.10	1349.74	1298.95	1284.86	1229.95	1193.36	1168.41	1151.15
210000	1438.61	1417.23	1363.90	1349.10	1291.45	1253.03	1226.84	1208.71
220000	1507.11	1484.72	1428.85	1413.35	1352.95	1312.69	1285.26	1266.26
230000	1575.62	1552.20	1493.79	1477.59	1414.44	1372.36	1343.68	1323.82
240000	1644.12	1619.69	1558.74	1541.83	1475.94	1432.03	1402.10	1381.38
250000	1712.63	1687.18	1623.69	1606.07	1537.44	1491.70	1460.52	1438.94
260000	1781.13	1754.66	1688.64	1670.32	1598.94	1551.36	1518.94	1496.49
270000	1849.64	1822.15	1753.58	1734.56	1660.43	1611.03	1577.36	1554.05
280000	1918.14	1889.64	1818.53	1798.80	1721.93	1670.70	1635.78	1611.61
290000	1986.65	1957.12	1883.48	1863.05	1783.43	1730.37	1694.20	1669.16
300000	2055.15	2024.61	1948.43	1927.29	1844.92	1790.03	1752.62	1726.72
310000	2123.66	2092.10	2013.37	1991.53	1906.42	1849.70	1811.04	1784.28
320000	2192.16	2159.58	2078.32	2055.77	1967.92	1909.37	1869.46	1841.84
330000	2260.67	2227.07	2143.27	2120.02	2029.42	1969.04	1927.88	1899.39
340000	2329.17	2294.56	2208.21	2184.26	2090.91	2028.71	1986.30	1956.95
350000	2397.68	2362.04	2273.16	2248.50	2152.41	2088.37	2044.72	2014.51
360000	2466.18	2429.53	2338.11	2312.74	2213.91	2148.04	2103.14	2072.07
370000	2534.69	2497.02	2403.06	2376.99	2275.41	2207.71	2161.56	2129.62
380000	2603.19	2564.50	2468.00	2441.23	2336.90	2267.38	2219.98	2187.18
390000	2671.70	2631.99	2532.95	2505.47	2398.40	2327.04	2278.40	2244.74
400000	2740.20	2699.48	2597.90	2569.72	2459.90	2386.71	2336.82	2302.29

BLENDED MONTHLY PAYMENTS 7%
AMORTIZATION IN YEARS

Amount	1	2	3	4	5	6	7	8
25	2.17	1.12	.78	.60	.50	.43	.38	.34
50	4.33	2.24	1.55	1.20	.99	.86	.76	.68
100	8.65	4.48	3.09	2.39	1.98	1.71	1.51	1.36
200	17.30	8.95	6.17	4.78	3.96	3.41	3.01	2.72
300	25.95	13.42	9.25	7.17	5.93	5.11	4.52	4.08
400	34.60	17.90	12.34	9.56	7.91	6.81	6.02	5.44
500	43.25	22.37	15.42	11.95	9.88	8.51	7.53	6.80
600	51.89	26.84	18.50	14.34	11.86	10.21	9.03	8.16
700	60.54	31.31	21.59	16.73	13.83	11.91	10.54	9.51
800	69.19	35.79	24.67	19.12	15.81	13.61	12.04	10.87
900	77.84	40.26	27.75	21.51	17.78	15.31	13.54	12.23
1000	86.49	44.73	30.84	23.90	19.76	17.01	15.05	13.59
2000	172.97	89.46	61.67	47.80	39.51	34.01	30.09	27.17
3000	259.45	134.19	92.50	71.70	59.27	51.01	45.14	40.76
4000	345.93	178.91	123.33	95.60	79.02	68.01	60.18	54.34
5000	432.41	223.64	154.16	119.50	98.78	85.01	75.22	67.93
6000	518.89	268.37	184.99	143.40	118.53	102.01	90.27	81.51
7000	605.37	313.10	215.82	167.30	138.28	119.01	105.31	95.09
8000	691.85	357.82	246.66	191.20	158.04	136.01	120.36	108.68
9000	778.33	402.55	277.49	215.10	177.79	153.01	135.40	122.26
10000	864.81	447.28	308.32	239.00	197.55	170.02	150.44	135.85
20000	1729.62	894.55	616.63	478.00	395.09	340.03	300.88	271.69
30000	2594.43	1341.82	924.95	717.00	592.63	510.04	451.32	407.53
40000	3459.23	1789.10	1233.26	956.00	790.17	680.05	601.76	543.37
50000	4324.04	2236.37	1541.58	1195.00	987.71	850.06	752.20	679.21
60000	5188.85	2683.64	1849.89	1434.00	1185.25	1020.07	902.64	815.05
70000	6053.65	3130.91	2158.20	1673.00	1382.79	1190.08	1053.08	950.89
80000	6918.46	3578.19	2466.52	1912.00	1580.33	1360.09	1203.51	1086.73
90000	7783.27	4025.46	2774.83	2151.00	1777.87	1530.10	1353.95	1222.57
100000	8648.07	4472.73	3083.15	2389.00	1975.41	1700.11	1504.39	1358.41
110000	9512.88	4920.01	3391.46	2628.99	2172.95	1870.12	1654.83	1494.25
120000	10377.69	5367.28	3699.78	2867.99	2370.49	2040.13	1805.27	1630.09
130000	11242.49	5814.55	4008.09	3106.99	2568.03	2210.14	1955.71	1765.93
140000	12107.30	6261.82	4316.40	3345.99	2765.58	2380.15	2106.15	1901.77
150000	12972.11	6709.10	4624.72	3584.99	2963.12	2550.16	2256.58	2037.61
160000	13836.91	7156.37	4933.03	3823.99	3160.66	2720.17	2407.02	2173.45
170000	14701.72	7603.64	5241.35	4062.99	3358.20	2890.18	2557.46	2309.29
180000	15566.53	8050.92	5549.66	4301.99	3555.74	3060.19	2707.90	2445.13
190000	16431.33	8498.19	5857.97	4540.99	3753.28	3230.20	2858.34	2580.97
200000	17296.14	8945.46	6166.29	4779.98	3950.82	3400.22	3008.78	2716.81
210000	18160.95	9392.73	6474.60	5018.98	4148.36	3570.23	3159.22	2852.65
220000	19025.75	9840.01	6782.92	5257.98	4345.90	3740.24	3309.66	2988.49
230000	19890.56	10287.28	7091.23	5496.98	4543.44	3910.25	3460.09	3124.33
240000	20755.37	10734.55	7399.55	5735.98	4740.98	4080.26	3610.53	3260.17
250000	21620.17	11181.83	7707.86	5974.98	4938.52	4250.27	3760.97	3396.01
260000	22484.98	11629.10	8016.17	6213.98	5136.06	4420.28	3911.41	3531.85
270000	23349.79	12076.37	8324.49	6452.98	5333.61	4590.29	4061.85	3667.69
280000	24214.59	12523.64	8632.80	6691.98	5531.15	4760.30	4212.29	3803.53
290000	25079.40	12970.92	8941.12	6930.98	5728.69	4930.31	4362.73	3939.37
300000	25944.21	13418.19	9249.43	7169.97	5926.23	5100.32	4513.16	4075.21
310000	26809.01	13865.46	9557.74	7408.97	6123.77	5270.33	4663.60	4211.05
320000	27673.82	14312.73	9866.06	7647.97	6321.31	5440.34	4814.04	4346.89
330000	28538.63	14760.01	10174.37	7886.97	6518.85	5610.35	4964.48	4482.73
340000	29403.43	15207.28	10482.69	8125.97	6716.39	5780.36	5114.92	4618.58
350000	30268.24	15654.55	10791.00	8364.97	6913.93	5950.37	5265.36	4754.42
360000	31133.05	16101.83	11099.32	8603.97	7111.47	6120.38	5415.80	4890.26
370000	31997.85	16549.10	11407.63	8842.97	7309.01	6290.39	5566.24	5026.10
380000	32862.66	16996.37	11715.94	9081.97	7506.55	6460.40	5716.67	5161.94
390000	33727.47	17443.64	12024.26	9320.97	7704.09	6630.42	5867.11	5297.78
400000	34592.27	17890.92	12332.57	9559.96	7901.63	6800.43	6017.55	5433.62

7% BLENDED MONTHLY PAYMENTS
AMORTIZATION IN YEARS

Amount	9	10	11	12	13	14	15	16
25	.32	.29	.28	.26	.25	.24	.23	.22
50	.63	.58	.55	.52	.49	.47	.45	.44
100	1.25	1.16	1.09	1.03	.98	.93	.90	.87
200	2.50	2.32	2.17	2.05	1.95	1.86	1.79	1.73
300	3.74	3.47	3.25	3.07	2.92	2.79	2.68	2.59
400	4.99	4.63	4.34	4.10	3.90	3.72	3.58	3.45
500	6.23	5.78	5.42	5.12	4.87	4.65	4.47	4.31
600	7.48	6.94	6.50	6.14	5.84	5.58	5.36	5.17
700	8.72	8.10	7.59	7.17	6.81	6.51	6.26	6.04
800	9.97	9.25	8.67	8.19	7.79	7.44	7.15	6.90
900	11.22	10.41	9.75	9.21	8.76	8.37	8.04	7.76
1000	12.46	11.56	10.84	10.24	9.73	9.30	8.94	8.62
2000	24.92	23.12	21.67	20.47	19.46	18.60	17.87	17.24
3000	37.37	34.68	32.50	30.70	29.19	27.90	26.80	25.85
4000	49.83	46.24	43.33	40.93	38.91	37.20	35.73	34.47
5000	62.28	57.80	54.16	51.16	48.64	46.50	44.67	43.08
6000	74.74	69.36	65.00	61.39	58.37	55.80	53.60	51.70
7000	87.19	80.92	75.83	71.62	68.09	65.10	62.53	60.31
8000	99.65	92.48	86.66	81.85	77.82	74.40	71.46	68.93
9000	112.11	104.04	97.49	92.08	87.55	83.70	80.40	77.54
10000	124.56	115.60	108.32	102.31	97.27	93.00	89.33	86.16
20000	249.12	231.19	216.64	204.62	194.54	185.99	178.65	172.31
30000	373.68	346.79	324.96	306.92	291.81	278.98	267.98	258.47
40000	498.23	462.38	433.28	409.23	389.07	371.97	357.30	344.62
50000	622.79	577.97	541.59	511.54	486.34	464.96	446.63	430.78
60000	747.35	693.57	649.91	613.84	583.61	557.95	535.95	516.93
70000	871.90	809.16	758.23	716.15	680.87	650.94	625.28	603.09
80000	996.46	924.76	866.55	818.45	778.14	743.93	714.60	689.24
90000	1121.02	1040.35	974.86	920.76	875.41	836.92	803.93	775.40
100000	1245.58	1155.94	1083.18	1023.07	972.67	929.91	893.25	861.55
110000	1370.13	1271.54	1191.50	1125.37	1069.94	1022.90	982.58	947.70
120000	1494.69	1387.13	1299.82	1227.68	1167.21	1115.89	1071.90	1033.86
130000	1619.25	1502.73	1408.14	1329.98	1264.47	1208.88	1161.23	1120.01
140000	1743.80	1618.32	1516.45	1432.29	1361.74	1301.87	1250.55	1206.17
150000	1868.36	1733.91	1624.77	1534.60	1459.01	1394.87	1339.88	1292.32
160000	1992.92	1849.51	1733.09	1636.90	1556.27	1487.86	1429.20	1378.48
170000	2117.48	1965.10	1841.41	1739.21	1653.54	1580.85	1518.53	1464.63
180000	2242.03	2080.70	1949.72	1841.51	1750.81	1673.84	1607.85	1550.79
190000	2366.59	2196.29	2058.04	1943.82	1848.07	1766.83	1697.18	1636.94
200000	2491.15	2311.88	2166.36	2046.13	1945.34	1859.82	1786.50	1723.09
210000	2615.70	2427.48	2274.68	2148.43	2042.61	1952.81	1875.83	1809.25
220000	2740.26	2543.07	2382.99	2250.74	2139.87	2045.80	1965.15	1895.40
230000	2864.82	2658.67	2491.31	2353.04	2237.14	2138.79	2054.48	1981.56
240000	2989.38	2774.26	2599.63	2455.35	2334.41	2231.78	2143.80	2067.71
250000	3113.93	2889.85	2707.95	2557.66	2431.67	2324.77	2233.13	2153.87
260000	3238.49	3005.45	2816.27	2659.96	2528.94	2417.76	2322.45	2240.02
270000	3363.05	3121.04	2924.58	2762.27	2626.21	2510.75	2411.78	2326.18
280000	3487.60	3236.64	3032.90	2864.57	2723.47	2603.74	2501.10	2412.33
290000	3612.16	3352.23	3141.22	2966.88	2820.74	2696.74	2590.43	2498.49
300000	3736.72	3467.82	3249.54	3069.19	2918.01	2789.73	2679.75	2584.64
310000	3861.27	3583.42	3357.85	3171.49	3015.27	2882.72	2769.08	2670.79
320000	3985.83	3699.01	3466.17	3273.80	3112.54	2975.71	2858.40	2756.95
330000	4110.39	3814.61	3574.49	3376.11	3209.81	3068.70	2947.73	2843.10
340000	4234.95	3930.20	3682.81	3478.41	3307.07	3161.69	3037.05	2929.26
350000	4359.50	4045.79	3791.13	3580.72	3404.34	3254.68	3126.38	3015.41
360000	4484.06	4161.39	3899.44	3683.02	3501.61	3347.67	3215.70	3101.57
370000	4608.62	4276.98	4007.76	3785.33	3598.87	3440.66	3305.03	3187.72
380000	4733.17	4392.58	4116.08	3887.64	3696.14	3533.65	3394.35	3273.88
390000	4857.73	4508.17	4224.40	3989.94	3793.41	3626.64	3483.68	3360.03
400000	4982.29	4623.76	4332.71	4092.25	3890.67	3719.63	3573.00	3446.18

70

BLENDED MONTHLY PAYMENTS

AMORTIZATION IN YEARS

7%

Amount	17	18	19	20	21	22	23	24
25	.21	.21	.20	.20	.19	.19	.19	.18
50	.42	.41	.40	.39	.38	.37	.37	.36
100	.84	.81	.79	.77	.76	.74	.73	.72
200	1.67	1.62	1.58	1.54	1.51	1.48	1.45	1.43
300	2.51	2.43	2.37	2.31	2.26	2.22	2.18	2.14
400	3.34	3.24	3.16	3.08	3.01	2.95	2.90	2.85
500	4.17	4.05	3.95	3.85	3.77	3.69	3.62	3.56
600	5.01	4.86	4.73	4.62	4.52	4.43	4.35	4.27
700	5.84	5.67	5.52	5.39	5.27	5.17	5.07	4.99
800	6.68	6.48	6.31	6.16	6.02	5.90	5.79	5.70
900	7.51	7.29	7.10	6.93	6.78	6.64	6.52	6.41
1000	8.34	8.10	7.89	7.70	7.53	7.38	7.24	7.12
2000	16.68	16.20	15.77	15.39	15.05	14.75	14.48	14.23
3000	25.02	24.30	23.65	23.08	22.58	22.12	21.72	21.35
4000	33.36	32.39	31.54	30.78	30.10	29.50	28.95	28.46
5000	41.70	40.49	39.42	38.47	37.63	36.87	36.19	35.58
6000	50.04	48.59	47.30	46.16	45.15	44.24	43.43	42.69
7000	58.38	56.68	55.18	53.86	52.67	51.61	50.66	49.81
8000	66.72	64.78	63.07	61.55	60.20	58.99	57.90	56.92
9000	75.06	72.88	70.95	69.24	67.72	66.36	65.14	64.04
10000	83.40	80.97	78.83	76.94	75.25	73.73	72.38	71.15
20000	166.79	161.94	157.66	153.87	150.49	147.46	144.75	142.30
30000	250.18	242.91	236.49	230.80	225.73	221.19	217.12	213.45
40000	333.57	323.87	315.32	307.73	300.97	294.92	289.49	284.59
50000	416.96	404.84	394.15	384.66	376.21	368.65	361.86	355.74
60000	500.35	485.81	472.98	461.59	451.45	442.37	434.23	426.89
70000	583.75	566.78	551.80	538.52	526.69	516.10	506.60	498.03
80000	667.14	647.74	630.63	615.45	601.93	589.83	578.97	569.18
90000	750.53	728.71	709.46	692.38	677.17	663.56	651.34	640.33
100000	833.92	809.68	788.29	769.32	752.41	737.29	723.71	711.47
110000	917.31	890.65	867.12	846.25	827.65	811.01	796.08	782.62
120000	1000.70	971.61	945.95	923.18	902.89	884.74	868.45	853.77
130000	1084.09	1052.58	1024.77	1000.11	978.13	958.47	940.82	924.91
140000	1167.49	1133.55	1103.60	1077.04	1053.37	1032.20	1013.19	996.06
150000	1250.88	1214.52	1182.43	1153.97	1128.61	1105.93	1085.56	1067.21
160000	1334.27	1295.48	1261.26	1230.90	1203.85	1179.66	1157.93	1138.35
170000	1417.66	1376.45	1340.09	1307.83	1279.09	1253.38	1230.30	1209.50
180000	1501.05	1457.42	1418.92	1384.76	1354.33	1327.11	1302.67	1280.65
190000	1584.44	1538.39	1497.74	1461.70	1429.58	1400.84	1375.04	1351.79
200000	1667.83	1619.35	1576.57	1538.63	1504.82	1474.57	1447.41	1422.94
210000	1751.23	1700.32	1655.40	1615.56	1580.06	1548.30	1519.78	1494.09
220000	1834.62	1781.29	1734.23	1692.49	1655.30	1622.02	1592.15	1565.23
230000	1918.01	1862.26	1813.06	1769.42	1730.54	1695.75	1664.52	1636.38
240000	2001.40	1943.22	1891.89	1846.35	1805.78	1769.48	1736.89	1707.53
250000	2084.79	2024.19	1970.71	1923.28	1881.02	1843.21	1809.26	1778.68
260000	2168.18	2105.16	2049.54	2000.21	1956.26	1916.94	1881.63	1849.82
270000	2251.57	2186.12	2128.37	2077.14	2031.50	1990.66	1954.00	1920.97
280000	2334.97	2267.09	2207.20	2154.07	2106.74	2064.39	2026.37	1992.12
290000	2418.36	2348.06	2286.03	2231.01	2181.98	2138.12	2098.74	2063.26
300000	2501.75	2429.03	2364.86	2307.94	2257.22	2211.85	2171.11	2134.41
310000	2585.14	2509.99	2443.68	2384.87	2332.46	2285.58	2243.48	2205.56
320000	2668.53	2590.96	2522.51	2461.80	2407.70	2359.31	2315.85	2276.70
330000	2751.92	2671.93	2601.34	2538.73	2482.94	2433.03	2388.22	2347.85
340000	2835.31	2752.90	2680.17	2615.66	2558.18	2506.76	2460.59	2419.00
350000	2918.71	2833.86	2759.00	2692.59	2633.42	2580.49	2532.96	2490.14
360000	3002.10	2914.83	2837.83	2769.52	2708.66	2654.22	2605.33	2561.29
370000	3085.49	2995.80	2916.65	2846.45	2783.91	2727.95	2677.70	2632.44
380000	3168.88	3076.77	2995.48	2923.39	2859.15	2801.67	2750.07	2703.58
390000	3252.27	3157.73	3074.31	3000.32	2934.39	2875.40	2822.44	2774.73
400000	3335.66	3238.70	3153.14	3077.25	3009.63	2949.13	2894.81	2845.88

71

Amount	25	26	29	30	35	40	45	50
25	.18	.18	.17	.17	.16	.16	.16	.15
50	.36	.35	.34	.33	.32	.31	.31	.30
100	.71	.70	.67	.66	.64	.62	.61	.60
200	1.41	1.39	1.34	1.32	1.27	1.23	1.21	1.19
300	2.11	2.08	2.00	1.98	1.90	1.85	1.81	1.79
400	2.81	2.77	2.67	2.64	2.53	2.46	2.41	2.38
500	3.51	3.46	3.33	3.30	3.16	3.08	3.02	2.98
600	4.21	4.15	4.00	3.96	3.80	3.69	3.62	3.57
700	4.91	4.84	4.66	4.62	4.43	4.30	4.22	4.16
800	5.61	5.53	5.33	5.27	5.06	4.92	4.82	4.76
900	6.31	6.22	5.99	5.93	5.69	5.53	5.43	5.35
1000	7.01	6.91	6.66	6.59	6.32	6.15	6.03	5.95
2000	14.01	13.81	13.31	13.18	12.64	12.29	12.05	11.89
3000	21.02	20.72	19.97	19.76	18.96	18.43	18.07	17.83
4000	28.02	27.62	26.62	26.35	25.28	24.57	24.09	23.77
5000	35.03	34.53	33.28	32.94	31.60	30.71	30.12	29.71
6000	42.03	41.43	39.93	39.52	37.92	36.86	36.14	35.65
7000	49.03	48.33	46.59	46.11	44.24	43.00	42.16	41.59
8000	56.04	55.24	53.24	52.69	50.55	49.14	48.18	47.53
9000	63.04	62.14	59.90	59.28	56.87	55.28	54.21	53.47
10000	70.05	69.05	66.55	65.87	63.19	61.42	60.23	59.41
20000	140.09	138.09	133.10	131.73	126.38	122.84	120.45	118.81
30000	210.13	207.13	199.65	197.59	189.56	184.26	180.68	178.22
40000	280.17	276.17	266.20	263.45	252.75	245.68	240.90	237.62
50000	350.21	345.21	332.75	329.31	315.94	307.10	301.12	297.03
60000	420.25	414.25	399.30	395.17	379.12	368.52	361.35	356.43
70000	490.30	483.29	465.85	461.03	442.31	429.93	421.57	415.84
80000	560.34	552.33	532.40	526.89	505.50	491.35	481.80	475.24
90000	630.38	621.37	598.95	592.75	568.68	552.77	542.02	534.65
100000	700.42	690.41	665.50	658.61	631.87	614.19	602.24	594.05
110000	770.46	759.45	732.05	724.47	695.05	675.61	662.47	653.46
120000	840.50	828.49	798.60	790.33	758.24	737.03	722.69	712.86
130000	910.55	897.53	865.15	856.19	821.43	798.44	782.92	772.27
140000	980.59	966.57	931.70	922.05	884.61	859.86	843.14	831.67
150000	1050.63	1035.61	998.25	987.91	947.80	921.28	903.36	891.08
160000	1120.67	1104.65	1064.80	1053.77	1010.99	982.70	963.59	950.48
170000	1190.71	1173.69	1131.35	1119.63	1074.17	1044.12	1023.81	1009.89
180000	1260.75	1242.73	1197.90	1185.49	1137.36	1105.54	1084.04	1069.29
190000	1330.79	1311.77	1264.44	1251.35	1200.54	1166.96	1144.26	1128.70
200000	1400.84	1380.81	1330.99	1317.21	1263.73	1228.37	1204.48	1188.10
210000	1470.88	1449.85	1397.54	1383.07	1326.92	1289.79	1264.71	1247.51
220000	1540.92	1518.89	1464.09	1448.93	1390.10	1351.21	1324.93	1306.91
230000	1610.96	1587.93	1530.64	1514.79	1453.29	1412.63	1385.16	1366.32
240000	1681.00	1656.97	1597.19	1580.65	1516.48	1474.05	1445.38	1425.72
250000	1751.04	1726.01	1663.74	1646.51	1579.66	1535.47	1505.60	1485.13
260000	1821.09	1795.05	1730.29	1712.37	1642.85	1596.88	1565.83	1544.53
270000	1891.13	1864.10	1796.84	1778.23	1706.03	1658.30	1626.05	1603.94
280000	1961.17	1933.14	1863.39	1844.09	1769.22	1719.72	1686.28	1663.34
290000	2031.21	2002.18	1929.94	1909.95	1832.41	1781.14	1746.50	1722.75
300000	2101.25	2071.22	1996.49	1975.81	1895.59	1842.56	1806.72	1782.15
310000	2171.29	2140.26	2063.04	2041.68	1958.78	1903.98	1866.95	1841.56
320000	2241.34	2209.30	2129.59	2107.54	2021.97	1965.40	1927.17	1900.96
330000	2311.38	2278.34	2196.14	2173.40	2085.15	2026.81	1987.40	1960.37
340000	2381.42	2347.38	2262.69	2239.26	2148.34	2088.23	2047.62	2019.77
350000	2451.46	2416.42	2329.24	2305.12	2211.52	2149.65	2107.84	2079.18
360000	2521.50	2485.46	2395.79	2370.98	2274.71	2211.07	2168.07	2138.58
370000	2591.54	2554.50	2462.34	2436.84	2337.90	2272.49	2228.29	2197.99
380000	2661.58	2623.54	2528.88	2502.70	2401.08	2333.91	2288.52	2257.39
390000	2731.63	2692.58	2595.43	2568.56	2464.27	2395.32	2348.74	2316.80
400000	2801.67	2761.62	2661.98	2634.42	2527.46	2456.74	2408.96	2376.20

BLENDED MONTHLY PAYMENTS 7¼%
AMORTIZATION IN YEARS

Amount	1	2	3	4	5	6	7	8
25	2.17	1.13	.78	.61	.50	.43	.38	.35
50	4.33	2.25	1.55	1.21	1.00	.86	.76	.69
100	8.66	4.49	3.10	2.41	1.99	1.72	1.52	1.38
200	17.32	8.97	6.19	4.81	3.98	3.43	3.04	2.75
300	25.98	13.46	9.29	7.21	5.97	5.14	4.55	4.12
400	34.64	17.94	12.38	9.61	7.95	6.85	6.07	5.49
500	43.30	22.42	15.48	12.01	9.94	8.56	7.59	6.86
600	51.96	26.91	18.57	14.41	11.93	10.28	9.10	8.23
700	60.62	31.39	21.66	16.81	13.91	11.99	10.62	9.60
800	69.28	35.87	24.76	19.22	15.90	13.70	12.14	10.97
900	77.94	40.36	27.85	21.62	17.89	15.41	13.65	12.34
1000	86.60	44.84	30.95	24.02	19.87	17.12	15.17	13.71
2000	173.19	89.68	61.89	48.03	39.74	34.24	30.33	27.41
3000	259.78	134.52	92.83	72.04	59.61	51.36	45.49	41.12
4000	346.38	179.35	123.77	96.06	79.48	68.48	60.66	54.82
5000	432.97	224.19	154.72	120.07	99.35	85.59	75.82	68.53
6000	519.56	269.03	185.66	144.08	119.22	102.71	90.98	82.23
7000	606.15	313.87	216.60	168.09	139.09	119.83	106.14	95.94
8000	692.75	358.70	247.54	192.11	158.95	136.95	121.31	109.64
9000	779.34	403.54	278.49	216.12	178.82	154.06	136.47	123.35
10000	865.93	448.38	309.43	240.13	198.69	171.18	151.63	137.05
20000	1731.86	896.75	618.85	480.26	397.38	342.36	303.26	274.10
30000	2597.78	1345.13	928.28	720.38	596.07	513.54	454.88	411.15
40000	3463.71	1793.50	1237.70	960.51	794.75	684.71	606.51	548.20
50000	4329.64	2241.87	1547.13	1200.63	993.44	855.89	758.14	685.25
60000	5195.56	2690.25	1856.55	1440.76	1192.13	1027.07	909.76	822.30
70000	6061.49	3138.62	2165.98	1680.89	1390.81	1198.24	1061.39	959.35
80000	6927.41	3586.99	2475.40	1921.01	1589.50	1369.42	1213.01	1096.40
90000	7793.34	4035.37	2784.83	2161.14	1788.19	1540.60	1364.64	1233.45
100000	8659.27	4483.74	3094.25	2401.26	1986.87	1711.77	1516.27	1370.50
110000	9525.19	4932.12	3403.68	2641.39	2185.56	1882.95	1667.89	1507.55
120000	10391.12	5380.49	3713.10	2881.51	2384.25	2054.13	1819.52	1644.60
130000	11257.05	5828.86	4022.52	3121.64	2582.93	2225.30	1971.14	1781.64
140000	12122.97	6277.24	4331.95	3361.77	2781.62	2396.48	2122.77	1918.69
150000	12988.90	6725.61	4641.37	3601.89	2980.31	2567.66	2274.40	2055.74
160000	13854.82	7173.98	4950.80	3842.02	3178.99	2738.84	2426.02	2192.79
170000	14720.75	7622.36	5260.22	4082.14	3377.68	2910.01	2577.65	2329.84
180000	15586.68	8070.73	5569.65	4322.27	3576.37	3081.19	2729.28	2466.89
190000	16452.60	8519.11	5879.07	4562.40	3775.05	3252.37	2880.90	2603.94
200000	17318.53	8967.48	6188.50	4802.52	3973.74	3423.54	3032.53	2740.99
210000	18184.45	9415.85	6497.92	5042.65	4172.43	3594.72	3184.15	2878.04
220000	19050.38	9864.23	6807.35	5282.77	4371.11	3765.90	3335.78	3015.09
230000	19916.31	10312.60	7116.77	5522.90	4569.80	3937.07	3487.41	3152.14
240000	20782.23	10760.97	7426.19	5763.02	4768.49	4108.25	3639.03	3289.19
250000	21648.16	11209.35	7735.62	6003.15	4967.17	4279.43	3790.66	3426.23
260000	22514.09	11657.72	8045.04	6243.28	5165.86	4450.60	3942.28	3563.28
270000	23380.01	12106.10	8354.47	6483.40	5364.55	4621.78	4093.91	3700.33
280000	24245.94	12554.47	8663.89	6723.53	5563.23	4792.96	4245.54	3837.38
290000	25111.86	13002.84	8973.32	6963.65	5761.92	4964.13	4397.16	3974.43
300000	25977.79	13451.22	9282.74	7203.78	5960.61	5135.31	4548.79	4111.48
310000	26843.72	13899.59	9592.17	7443.90	6159.29	5306.49	4700.41	4248.53
320000	27709.64	14347.96	9901.59	7684.03	6357.98	5477.67	4852.04	4385.58
330000	28575.57	14796.34	10211.02	7924.16	6556.67	5648.84	5003.67	4522.63
340000	29441.50	15244.71	10520.44	8164.28	6755.35	5820.02	5155.29	4659.68
350000	30307.42	15693.09	10829.86	8404.41	6954.04	5991.20	5306.92	4796.73
360000	31173.35	16141.46	11139.29	8644.53	7152.73	6162.37	5458.55	4933.78
370000	32039.27	16589.83	11448.71	8884.66	7351.41	6333.55	5610.17	5070.83
380000	32905.20	17038.21	11758.14	9124.79	7550.10	6504.73	5761.80	5207.87
390000	33771.13	17486.58	12067.56	9364.91	7748.79	6675.90	5913.42	5344.92
400000	34637.05	17934.95	12376.99	9605.04	7947.47	6847.08	6065.05	5481.97

7¼% BLENDED MONTHLY PAYMENTS
AMORTIZATION IN YEARS

Amount	9	10	11	12	13	14	15	16
25	.32	.30	.28	.26	.25	.24	.23	.22
50	.63	.59	.55	.52	.50	.48	.46	.44
100	1.26	1.17	1.10	1.04	.99	.95	.91	.88
200	2.52	2.34	2.20	2.08	1.98	1.89	1.82	1.76
300	3.78	3.51	3.29	3.11	2.96	2.83	2.73	2.63
400	5.04	4.68	4.39	4.15	3.95	3.78	3.63	3.51
500	6.29	5.85	5.48	5.19	4.93	4.72	4.54	4.38
600	7.55	7.02	6.58	6.22	5.92	5.66	5.45	5.26
700	8.81	8.18	7.68	7.26	6.91	6.61	6.35	6.13
800	10.07	9.35	8.77	8.29	7.89	7.55	7.26	7.01
900	11.33	10.52	9.87	9.33	8.88	8.49	8.17	7.88
1000	12.58	11.69	10.96	10.37	9.86	9.44	9.07	8.76
2000	25.16	23.37	21.92	20.73	19.72	18.87	18.14	17.51
3000	37.74	35.06	32.88	31.09	29.58	28.30	27.21	26.27
4000	50.32	46.74	43.84	41.45	39.44	37.74	36.28	35.02
5000	62.90	58.43	54.80	51.81	49.30	47.17	45.35	43.77
6000	75.48	70.11	65.76	62.17	59.15	56.60	54.42	52.53
7000	88.06	81.80	76.72	72.53	69.01	66.03	63.48	61.28
8000	100.64	93.48	87.68	82.89	78.87	75.47	72.55	70.03
9000	113.21	105.17	98.64	93.25	88.73	84.90	81.62	78.79
10000	125.79	116.85	109.60	103.61	98.59	94.33	90.69	87.54
20000	251.58	233.70	219.19	207.21	197.17	188.66	181.37	175.07
30000	377.37	350.54	328.78	310.81	295.75	282.99	272.06	262.61
40000	503.16	467.39	438.37	414.41	394.34	377.32	362.74	350.14
50000	628.94	584.24	547.96	518.01	492.92	471.65	453.42	437.67
60000	754.73	701.08	657.55	621.61	591.50	565.97	544.11	525.21
70000	880.52	817.93	767.14	725.21	690.09	660.30	634.79	612.74
80000	1006.31	934.77	876.74	828.81	788.67	754.63	725.47	700.27
90000	1132.09	1051.62	986.33	932.42	887.25	848.96	816.16	787.81
100000	1257.88	1168.47	1095.92	1036.02	985.84	943.29	906.84	875.34
110000	1383.67	1285.31	1205.51	1139.62	1084.42	1037.62	997.52	962.87
120000	1509.46	1402.16	1315.10	1243.22	1183.00	1131.94	1088.21	1050.41
130000	1635.24	1519.00	1424.69	1346.82	1281.59	1226.27	1178.89	1137.94
140000	1761.03	1635.85	1534.28	1450.42	1380.17	1320.60	1269.57	1225.48
150000	1886.82	1752.70	1643.88	1554.02	1478.75	1414.93	1360.26	1313.01
160000	2012.61	1869.54	1753.47	1657.62	1577.34	1509.26	1450.94	1400.54
170000	2138.39	1986.39	1863.06	1761.23	1675.92	1603.59	1541.62	1488.08
180000	2264.18	2103.23	1972.65	1864.83	1774.50	1697.91	1632.31	1575.61
190000	2389.97	2220.08	2082.24	1968.43	1873.08	1792.24	1722.99	1663.14
200000	2515.76	2336.93	2191.83	2072.03	1971.67	1886.57	1813.67	1750.68
210000	2641.54	2453.77	2301.42	2175.63	2070.25	1980.90	1904.36	1838.21
220000	2767.33	2570.62	2411.02	2279.23	2168.83	2075.23	1995.04	1925.74
230000	2893.12	2687.47	2520.61	2382.83	2267.42	2169.56	2085.72	2013.28
240000	3018.91	2804.31	2630.20	2486.43	2366.00	2263.88	2176.41	2100.81
250000	3144.69	2921.16	2739.79	2590.04	2464.58	2358.21	2267.09	2188.34
260000	3270.48	3038.00	2849.38	2693.64	2563.17	2452.54	2357.77	2275.88
270000	3396.27	3154.85	2958.97	2797.24	2661.75	2546.87	2448.46	2363.41
280000	3522.06	3271.70	3068.56	2900.84	2760.33	2641.20	2539.14	2450.95
290000	3647.84	3388.54	3178.16	3004.44	2858.92	2735.52	2629.82	2538.48
300000	3773.63	3505.39	3287.75	3108.04	2957.50	2829.85	2720.51	2626.01
310000	3899.42	3622.23	3397.34	3211.64	3056.08	2924.18	2811.19	2713.55
320000	4025.21	3739.08	3506.93	3315.24	3154.67	3018.51	2901.87	2801.08
330000	4151.00	3855.93	3616.52	3418.85	3253.25	3112.84	2992.56	2888.61
340000	4276.78	3972.77	3726.11	3522.45	3351.83	3207.17	3083.24	2976.15
350000	4402.57	4089.62	3835.70	3626.05	3450.41	3301.49	3173.92	3063.68
360000	4528.36	4206.46	3945.30	3729.65	3549.00	3395.82	3264.61	3151.21
370000	4654.15	4323.31	4054.89	3833.25	3647.58	3490.15	3355.29	3238.75
380000	4779.93	4440.16	4164.48	3936.85	3746.16	3584.48	3445.97	3326.28
390000	4905.72	4557.00	4274.07	4040.45	3844.75	3678.81	3536.66	3413.82
400000	5031.51	4673.85	4383.66	4144.05	3943.33	3773.14	3627.34	3501.35

74

BLENDED MONTHLY PAYMENTS 7¼%
AMORTIZATION IN YEARS

Amount	17	18	19	20	21	22	23	24
25	.22	.21	.21	.20	.20	.19	.19	.19
50	.43	.42	.41	.40	.39	.38	.37	.37
100	.85	.83	.81	.79	.77	.76	.74	.73
200	1.70	1.65	1.61	1.57	1.54	1.51	1.48	1.46
300	2.55	2.48	2.41	2.36	2.31	2.26	2.22	2.19
400	3.40	3.30	3.22	3.14	3.07	3.01	2.96	2.91
500	4.24	4.12	4.02	3.92	3.84	3.77	3.70	3.64
600	5.09	4.95	4.82	4.71	4.61	4.52	4.44	4.37
700	5.94	5.77	5.62	5.49	5.38	5.27	5.18	5.09
800	6.79	6.60	6.43	6.28	6.14	6.02	5.92	5.82
900	7.64	7.42	7.23	7.06	6.91	6.78	6.65	6.55
1000	8.48	8.24	8.03	7.84	7.68	7.53	7.39	7.27
2000	16.96	16.48	16.06	15.68	15.35	15.05	14.78	14.54
3000	25.44	24.72	24.09	23.52	23.02	22.57	22.17	21.81
4000	33.92	32.96	32.11	31.36	30.69	30.09	29.56	29.08
5000	42.40	41.20	40.14	39.20	38.36	37.62	36.95	36.34
6000	50.88	49.44	48.17	47.04	46.04	45.14	44.34	43.61
7000	59.36	57.68	56.19	54.88	53.71	52.66	51.72	50.88
8000	67.84	65.91	64.22	62.72	61.38	60.18	59.11	58.15
9000	76.32	74.15	72.25	70.56	69.05	67.71	66.50	65.42
10000	84.80	82.39	80.27	78.39	76.72	75.23	73.89	72.68
20000	169.59	164.78	160.54	156.78	153.44	150.45	147.77	145.36
30000	254.38	247.17	240.81	235.17	230.16	225.68	221.66	218.04
40000	339.17	329.55	321.08	313.56	306.88	300.90	295.54	290.72
50000	423.96	411.94	401.34	391.95	383.60	376.13	369.43	363.40
60000	508.75	494.33	481.61	470.34	460.31	451.35	443.31	436.08
70000	593.54	576.71	561.88	548.73	537.03	526.58	517.20	508.76
80000	678.33	659.10	642.15	627.12	613.75	601.80	591.08	581.44
90000	763.12	741.49	722.41	705.51	690.47	677.03	664.97	654.12
100000	847.91	823.87	802.68	783.90	767.19	752.25	738.85	726.80
110000	932.70	906.26	882.95	862.29	843.91	827.48	812.74	799.48
120000	1017.50	988.65	963.22	940.68	920.62	902.70	886.62	872.16
130000	1102.29	1071.03	1043.48	1019.07	997.34	977.92	960.51	944.84
140000	1187.08	1153.42	1123.75	1097.46	1074.06	1053.15	1034.39	1017.52
150000	1271.87	1235.81	1204.02	1175.85	1150.78	1128.37	1108.28	1090.20
160000	1356.66	1318.20	1284.29	1254.24	1227.50	1203.60	1182.16	1162.88
170000	1441.45	1400.58	1364.55	1332.63	1304.22	1278.82	1256.05	1235.56
180000	1526.24	1482.97	1444.82	1411.02	1380.93	1354.05	1329.93	1308.24
190000	1611.03	1565.36	1525.09	1489.41	1457.65	1429.27	1403.82	1380.92
200000	1695.82	1647.74	1605.36	1567.80	1534.37	1504.50	1477.70	1453.60
210000	1780.61	1730.13	1685.62	1646.19	1611.09	1579.72	1551.59	1526.28
220000	1865.40	1812.52	1765.89	1724.58	1687.81	1654.95	1625.47	1598.95
230000	1950.20	1894.90	1846.16	1802.97	1764.53	1730.17	1699.36	1671.63
240000	2034.99	1977.29	1926.43	1881.36	1841.24	1805.39	1773.24	1744.31
250000	2119.78	2059.68	2006.70	1959.75	1917.96	1880.62	1847.13	1816.99
260000	2204.57	2142.06	2086.96	2038.14	1994.68	1955.84	1921.01	1889.67
270000	2289.36	2224.45	2167.23	2116.53	2071.40	2031.07	1994.90	1962.35
280000	2374.15	2306.84	2247.50	2194.92	2148.12	2106.29	2068.78	2035.03
290000	2458.94	2389.23	2327.77	2273.31	2224.83	2181.52	2142.67	2107.71
300000	2543.73	2471.61	2408.03	2351.70	2301.55	2256.74	2216.55	2180.39
310000	2628.52	2554.00	2488.30	2430.09	2378.27	2331.97	2290.44	2253.07
320000	2713.31	2636.39	2568.57	2508.48	2454.99	2407.19	2364.32	2325.75
330000	2798.10	2718.77	2648.84	2586.87	2531.71	2482.42	2438.21	2398.43
340000	2882.90	2801.16	2729.10	2665.26	2608.43	2557.64	2512.09	2471.11
350000	2967.69	2883.55	2809.37	2743.65	2685.14	2632.86	2585.98	2543.79
360000	3052.48	2965.93	2889.64	2822.04	2761.86	2708.09	2659.86	2616.47
370000	3137.27	3048.32	2969.91	2900.42	2838.58	2783.31	2733.75	2689.15
380000	3222.06	3130.71	3050.17	2978.81	2915.30	2858.54	2807.63	2761.83
390000	3306.85	3213.09	3130.44	3057.20	2992.02	2933.76	2881.52	2834.51
400000	3391.64	3295.48	3210.71	3135.59	3068.74	3008.99	2955.40	2907.19

7¼% BLENDED MONTHLY PAYMENTS
AMORTIZATION IN YEARS

Amount	25	26	29	30	35	40	45	50
25	.18	.18	.18	.17	.17	.16	.16	.16
50	.36	.36	.35	.34	.33	.32	.32	.31
100	.72	.71	.69	.68	.65	.64	.63	.62
200	1.44	1.42	1.37	1.35	1.30	1.27	1.25	1.23
300	2.15	2.12	2.05	2.03	1.95	1.90	1.87	1.84
400	2.87	2.83	2.73	2.70	2.60	2.53	2.49	2.46
500	3.58	3.54	3.41	3.38	3.25	3.16	3.11	3.07
600	4.30	4.24	4.09	4.05	3.90	3.80	3.73	3.68
700	5.02	4.95	4.78	4.73	4.55	4.43	4.35	4.29
800	5.73	5.65	5.46	5.40	5.20	5.06	4.97	4.91
900	6.45	6.36	6.14	6.08	5.85	5.69	5.59	5.52
1000	7.16	7.07	6.82	6.75	6.49	6.32	6.21	6.13
2000	14.32	14.13	13.64	13.50	12.98	12.64	12.41	12.26
3000	21.48	21.19	20.45	20.25	19.47	18.96	18.62	18.38
4000	28.64	28.25	27.27	27.00	25.96	25.28	24.82	24.51
5000	35.80	35.31	34.09	33.75	32.45	31.60	31.03	30.64
6000	42.96	42.37	40.90	40.50	38.94	37.92	37.23	36.76
7000	50.12	49.43	47.72	47.25	45.43	44.23	43.43	42.89
8000	57.28	56.49	54.54	54.00	51.92	50.55	49.64	49.02
9000	64.44	63.55	61.35	60.75	58.41	56.87	55.84	55.14
10000	71.60	70.61	68.17	67.50	64.89	63.19	62.05	61.27
20000	143.19	141.22	136.34	134.99	129.78	126.37	124.09	122.53
30000	214.78	211.83	204.50	202.48	194.67	189.56	186.13	183.80
40000	286.37	282.44	272.67	269.97	259.56	252.74	248.17	245.06
50000	357.96	353.04	340.84	337.47	324.45	315.92	310.21	306.33
60000	429.56	423.65	409.00	404.96	389.34	379.11	372.25	367.59
70000	501.15	494.26	477.17	472.45	454.23	442.29	434.29	428.86
80000	572.74	564.87	545.33	539.94	519.12	505.47	496.33	490.12
90000	644.33	635.48	613.50	607.44	584.01	568.66	558.37	551.39
100000	715.92	706.08	681.67	674.93	648.90	631.84	620.41	612.65
110000	787.52	776.69	749.83	742.42	713.79	695.02	682.45	673.92
120000	859.11	847.30	818.00	809.91	778.68	758.21	744.49	735.18
130000	930.70	917.91	886.16	877.41	843.57	821.39	806.53	796.45
140000	1002.29	988.51	954.33	944.90	908.46	884.57	868.58	857.71
150000	1073.88	1059.12	1022.50	1012.39	973.35	947.76	930.62	918.97
160000	1145.47	1129.73	1090.66	1079.88	1038.24	1010.94	992.66	980.24
170000	1217.07	1200.34	1158.83	1147.38	1103.13	1074.12	1054.70	1041.50
180000	1288.66	1270.95	1226.99	1214.87	1168.02	1137.31	1116.74	1102.77
190000	1360.25	1341.55	1295.16	1282.36	1232.91	1200.49	1178.78	1164.03
200000	1431.84	1412.16	1363.33	1349.85	1297.80	1263.67	1240.82	1225.30
210000	1503.43	1482.77	1431.49	1417.35	1362.69	1326.86	1302.86	1286.56
220000	1575.03	1553.38	1499.66	1484.84	1427.58	1390.04	1364.90	1347.83
230000	1646.62	1623.99	1567.82	1552.33	1492.47	1453.23	1426.94	1409.09
240000	1718.21	1694.59	1635.99	1619.82	1557.36	1516.41	1488.98	1470.36
250000	1789.80	1765.20	1704.16	1687.32	1622.25	1579.59	1551.02	1531.62
260000	1861.39	1835.81	1772.32	1754.81	1687.14	1642.78	1613.06	1592.89
270000	1932.99	1906.42	1840.49	1822.30	1752.03	1705.96	1675.11	1654.15
280000	2004.58	1977.02	1908.65	1889.79	1816.92	1769.14	1737.15	1715.42
290000	2076.17	2047.63	1976.82	1957.29	1881.81	1832.33	1799.19	1776.68
300000	2147.76	2118.24	2044.99	2024.78	1946.70	1895.51	1861.23	1837.94
310000	2219.35	2188.85	2113.15	2092.27	2011.59	1958.69	1923.27	1899.21
320000	2290.94	2259.46	2181.32	2159.76	2076.48	2021.88	1985.31	1960.47
330000	2362.54	2330.06	2249.48	2227.26	2141.37	2085.06	2047.35	2021.74
340000	2434.13	2400.67	2317.65	2294.75	2206.26	2148.24	2109.39	2083.00
350000	2505.72	2471.28	2385.82	2362.24	2271.15	2211.43	2171.43	2144.27
360000	2577.31	2541.89	2453.98	2429.73	2336.04	2274.61	2233.47	2205.53
370000	2648.90	2612.49	2522.15	2497.23	2400.93	2337.79	2295.51	2266.80
380000	2720.50	2683.10	2590.31	2564.72	2465.82	2400.98	2357.55	2328.06
390000	2792.09	2753.71	2658.48	2632.21	2530.71	2464.16	2419.59	2389.33
400000	2863.68	2824.32	2726.65	2699.70	2595.60	2527.34	2481.63	2450.59

76

BLENDED MONTHLY PAYMENTS 7½%

AMORTIZATION IN YEARS

Amount	1	2	3	4	5	6	7	8
25	2.17	1.13	.78	.61	.50	.44	.39	.35
50	4.34	2.25	1.56	1.21	1.00	.87	.77	.70
100	8.68	4.50	3.11	2.42	2.00	1.73	1.53	1.39
200	17.35	8.99	6.22	4.83	4.00	3.45	3.06	2.77
300	26.02	13.49	9.32	7.24	6.00	5.18	4.59	4.15
400	34.69	17.98	12.43	9.66	8.00	6.90	6.12	5.54
500	43.36	22.48	15.53	12.07	10.00	8.62	7.65	6.92
600	52.03	26.97	18.64	14.48	12.00	10.35	9.17	8.30
700	60.70	31.47	21.74	16.89	13.99	12.07	10.70	9.68
800	69.37	35.96	24.85	19.31	15.99	13.79	12.23	11.07
900	78.04	40.46	27.95	21.72	17.99	15.52	13.76	12.45
1000	86.71	44.95	31.06	24.13	19.99	17.24	15.29	13.83
2000	173.41	89.90	62.11	48.26	39.97	34.47	30.57	27.66
3000	260.12	134.85	93.17	72.38	59.96	51.71	45.85	41.48
4000	346.82	179.80	124.22	96.51	79.94	68.94	61.13	55.31
5000	433.53	224.74	155.27	120.63	99.92	86.18	76.41	69.14
6000	520.23	269.69	186.33	144.76	119.91	103.41	91.70	82.96
7000	606.94	314.64	217.38	168.88	139.89	120.65	106.98	96.79
8000	693.64	359.59	248.43	193.01	159.87	137.88	122.26	110.62
9000	780.35	404.53	279.49	217.13	179.86	155.12	137.54	124.44
10000	867.05	449.48	310.54	241.26	199.84	172.35	152.82	138.27
20000	1734.10	898.96	621.08	482.51	399.68	344.70	305.64	276.53
30000	2601.14	1348.43	931.61	723.77	599.51	517.05	458.46	414.79
40000	3468.19	1797.91	1242.15	965.02	799.35	689.39	611.28	553.06
50000	4335.23	2247.38	1552.69	1206.28	999.18	861.74	764.09	691.32
60000	5202.28	2696.86	1863.22	1447.53	1199.02	1034.09	916.91	829.58
70000	6069.32	3146.33	2173.76	1688.79	1398.85	1206.43	1069.73	967.85
80000	6936.37	3595.81	2484.30	1930.04	1598.69	1378.78	1222.55	1106.11
90000	7803.41	4045.28	2794.83	2171.30	1798.52	1551.13	1375.37	1244.37
100000	8670.46	4494.76	3105.37	2412.55	1998.36	1723.47	1528.18	1382.64
110000	9537.50	4944.23	3415.90	2653.81	2198.20	1895.82	1681.00	1520.90
120000	10404.55	5393.71	3726.44	2895.06	2398.03	2068.17	1833.82	1659.16
130000	11271.59	5843.18	4036.98	3136.32	2597.87	2240.51	1986.64	1797.43
140000	12138.64	6292.66	4347.51	3377.57	2797.70	2412.86	2139.46	1935.69
150000	13005.68	6742.13	4658.05	3618.83	2997.54	2585.21	2292.27	2073.95
160000	13872.73	7191.61	4968.59	3860.08	3197.37	2757.55	2445.09	2212.22
170000	14739.78	7641.08	5279.12	4101.33	3397.21	2929.90	2597.91	2350.48
180000	15606.82	8090.56	5589.66	4342.59	3597.04	3102.25	2750.73	2488.74
190000	16473.87	8540.03	5900.19	4583.84	3796.88	3274.60	2903.55	2627.00
200000	17340.91	8989.51	6210.73	4825.10	3996.71	3446.94	3056.36	2765.27
210000	18207.96	9438.98	6521.27	5066.35	4196.55	3619.29	3209.18	2903.53
220000	19075.00	9888.46	6831.80	5307.61	4396.39	3791.64	3362.00	3041.79
230000	19942.05	10337.93	7142.34	5548.86	4596.22	3963.98	3514.82	3180.06
240000	20809.09	10787.41	7452.88	5790.12	4796.06	4136.33	3667.64	3318.32
250000	21676.14	11236.88	7763.41	6031.37	4995.89	4308.68	3820.45	3456.58
260000	22543.18	11686.36	8073.95	6272.63	5195.73	4481.02	3973.27	3594.85
270000	23410.23	12135.83	8384.48	6513.88	5395.56	4653.37	4126.09	3733.11
280000	24277.27	12585.31	8695.02	6755.14	5595.40	4825.72	4278.91	3871.37
290000	25144.32	13034.78	9005.56	6996.39	5795.23	4998.06	4431.72	4009.64
300000	26011.36	13484.26	9316.09	7237.65	5995.07	5170.41	4584.54	4147.90
310000	26878.41	13933.73	9626.63	7478.90	6194.91	5342.76	4737.36	4286.16
320000	27745.45	14383.21	9937.17	7720.16	6394.74	5515.10	4890.18	4424.43
330000	28612.50	14832.68	10247.70	7961.41	6594.58	5687.45	5043.00	4562.69
340000	29479.55	15282.16	10558.24	8202.66	6794.41	5859.80	5195.81	4700.95
350000	30346.59	15731.63	10868.77	8443.92	6994.25	6032.15	5348.63	4839.22
360000	31213.64	16181.11	11179.31	8685.17	7194.08	6204.49	5501.45	4977.48
370000	32080.68	16630.59	11489.85	8926.43	7393.92	6376.84	5654.27	5115.74
380000	32947.73	17080.06	11800.38	9167.68	7593.75	6549.19	5807.09	5254.00
390000	33814.77	17529.54	12110.92	9408.94	7793.59	6721.53	5959.90	5392.27
400000	34681.82	17979.01	12421.46	9650.19	7993.42	6893.88	6112.72	5530.53

7½% BLENDED MONTHLY PAYMENTS
AMORTIZATION IN YEARS

Amount	9	10	11	12	13	14	15	16
25	.32	.30	.28	.27	.25	.24	.24	.23
50	.64	.60	.56	.53	.50	.48	.47	.45
100	1.28	1.19	1.11	1.05	1.00	.96	.93	.89
200	2.55	2.37	2.22	2.10	2.00	1.92	1.85	1.78
300	3.82	3.55	3.33	3.15	3.00	2.88	2.77	2.67
400	5.09	4.73	4.44	4.20	4.00	3.83	3.69	3.56
500	6.36	5.91	5.55	5.25	5.00	4.79	4.61	4.45
600	7.63	7.09	6.66	6.30	6.00	5.75	5.53	5.34
700	8.90	8.27	7.77	7.35	7.00	6.70	6.45	6.23
800	10.17	9.45	8.87	8.40	8.00	7.66	7.37	7.12
900	11.44	10.63	9.98	9.45	9.00	8.62	8.29	8.01
1000	12.71	11.82	11.09	10.50	10.00	9.57	9.21	8.90
2000	25.41	23.63	22.18	20.99	19.99	19.14	18.42	17.79
3000	38.11	35.44	33.27	31.48	29.98	28.71	27.62	26.68
4000	50.81	47.25	44.35	41.97	39.97	38.27	36.83	35.57
5000	63.52	59.06	55.44	52.46	49.96	47.84	46.03	44.47
6000	76.22	70.87	66.53	62.95	59.95	57.41	55.24	53.36
7000	88.92	82.68	77.62	73.44	69.94	66.98	64.44	62.25
8000	101.62	94.49	88.70	83.93	79.93	76.54	73.65	71.14
9000	114.33	106.30	99.79	94.42	89.92	86.11	82.85	80.04
10000	127.03	118.11	110.88	104.91	99.91	95.68	92.06	88.93
20000	254.05	236.21	221.75	209.81	199.82	191.35	184.11	177.85
30000	381.08	354.32	332.62	314.72	299.73	287.03	276.16	266.77
40000	508.10	472.42	443.49	419.62	399.64	382.70	368.21	355.70
50000	635.12	590.53	554.37	524.53	499.54	478.38	460.26	444.62
60000	762.15	708.63	665.24	629.43	599.45	574.05	552.31	533.54
70000	889.17	826.74	776.11	734.33	699.36	669.73	644.36	622.46
80000	1016.20	944.84	886.98	839.24	799.27	765.40	736.42	711.39
90000	1143.22	1062.95	997.85	944.14	899.18	861.08	828.47	800.31
100000	1270.24	1181.05	1108.73	1049.05	999.08	956.75	920.52	889.23
110000	1397.27	1299.16	1219.60	1153.95	1098.99	1052.43	1012.57	978.15
120000	1524.29	1417.26	1330.47	1258.85	1198.90	1148.10	1104.62	1067.08
130000	1651.31	1535.37	1441.34	1363.76	1298.81	1243.78	1196.67	1156.00
140000	1778.34	1653.47	1552.22	1468.66	1398.72	1339.45	1288.72	1244.92
150000	1905.36	1771.57	1663.09	1573.57	1498.62	1435.13	1380.78	1333.85
160000	2032.39	1889.68	1773.96	1678.47	1598.53	1530.80	1472.83	1422.77
170000	2159.41	2007.78	1884.83	1783.37	1698.44	1626.48	1564.88	1511.69
180000	2286.43	2125.89	1995.70	1888.28	1798.35	1722.15	1656.93	1600.61
190000	2413.46	2243.99	2106.58	1993.18	1898.26	1817.83	1748.98	1689.54
200000	2540.48	2362.10	2217.45	2098.09	1998.16	1913.50	1841.03	1778.46
210000	2667.51	2480.20	2328.32	2202.99	2098.07	2009.18	1933.08	1867.38
220000	2794.53	2598.31	2439.19	2307.90	2197.98	2104.85	2025.14	1956.30
230000	2921.55	2716.41	2550.07	2412.80	2297.89	2200.53	2117.19	2045.23
240000	3048.58	2834.52	2660.94	2517.70	2397.80	2296.20	2209.24	2134.15
250000	3175.60	2952.62	2771.81	2622.61	2497.70	2391.87	2301.29	2223.07
260000	3302.62	3070.73	2882.68	2727.51	2597.61	2487.55	2393.34	2312.00
270000	3429.65	3188.83	2993.55	2832.42	2697.52	2583.22	2485.39	2400.92
280000	3556.67	3306.94	3104.43	2937.32	2797.43	2678.90	2577.44	2489.84
290000	3683.70	3425.04	3215.30	3042.22	2897.34	2774.57	2669.49	2578.76
300000	3810.72	3543.14	3326.17	3147.13	2997.25	2870.25	2761.55	2667.69
310000	3937.74	3661.25	3437.04	3252.03	3097.15	2965.92	2853.60	2756.61
320000	4064.77	3779.35	3547.92	3356.94	3197.06	3061.60	2945.65	2845.53
330000	4191.79	3897.46	3658.79	3461.84	3296.97	3157.27	3037.70	2934.45
340000	4318.82	4015.56	3769.66	3566.74	3396.88	3252.95	3129.75	3023.38
350000	4445.84	4133.67	3880.53	3671.65	3496.78	3348.62	3221.80	3112.30
360000	4572.86	4251.77	3991.40	3776.55	3596.69	3444.30	3313.85	3201.22
370000	4699.89	4369.88	4102.28	3881.46	3696.60	3539.97	3405.91	3290.15
380000	4826.91	4487.98	4213.15	3986.36	3796.51	3635.65	3497.96	3379.07
390000	4953.93	4606.09	4324.02	4091.27	3896.42	3731.32	3590.01	3467.99
400000	5080.96	4724.19	4434.89	4196.17	3996.32	3827.00	3682.06	3556.91

Amount	17	18	19	20	21	22	23	24
25	.22	.21	.21	.20	.20	.20	.19	.19
50	.44	.42	.41	.40	.40	.39	.38	.38
100	.87	.84	.82	.80	.79	.77	.76	.75
200	1.73	1.68	1.64	1.60	1.57	1.54	1.51	1.49
300	2.59	2.52	2.46	2.40	2.35	2.31	2.27	2.23
400	3.45	3.36	3.27	3.20	3.13	3.07	3.02	2.97
500	4.32	4.20	4.09	4.00	3.92	3.84	3.78	3.72
600	5.18	5.03	4.91	4.80	4.70	4.61	4.53	4.46
700	6.04	5.87	5.73	5.60	5.48	5.38	5.28	5.20
800	6.90	6.71	6.54	6.39	6.26	6.14	6.04	5.94
900	7.76	7.55	7.36	7.19	7.04	6.91	6.79	6.69
1000	8.63	8.39	8.18	7.99	7.83	7.68	7.55	7.43
2000	17.25	16.77	16.35	15.98	15.65	15.35	15.09	14.85
3000	25.87	25.15	24.52	23.96	23.47	23.03	22.63	22.27
4000	34.49	33.53	32.69	31.95	31.29	30.70	30.17	29.70
5000	43.11	41.91	40.86	39.94	39.11	38.37	37.71	37.12
6000	51.73	50.30	49.04	47.92	46.93	46.05	45.25	44.54
7000	60.35	58.68	57.21	55.91	54.75	53.72	52.79	51.96
8000	68.97	67.06	65.38	63.89	62.57	61.39	60.33	59.39
9000	77.59	75.44	73.55	71.88	70.39	69.07	67.88	66.81
10000	86.21	83.82	81.72	79.87	78.21	76.74	75.42	74.23
20000	172.41	167.64	163.44	159.73	156.42	153.47	150.83	148.46
30000	258.61	251.46	245.16	239.59	234.63	230.21	226.24	222.68
40000	344.81	335.27	326.88	319.45	312.84	306.94	301.65	296.91
50000	431.01	419.09	408.60	399.31	391.05	383.67	377.07	371.13
60000	517.21	502.91	490.31	479.17	469.25	460.41	452.48	445.36
70000	603.41	586.73	572.03	559.03	547.46	537.14	527.89	519.58
80000	689.61	670.54	653.75	638.89	625.67	613.87	603.30	593.81
90000	775.81	754.36	735.47	718.75	703.88	690.61	678.72	668.03
100000	862.01	838.18	817.19	798.61	782.09	767.34	754.13	742.26
110000	948.21	922.00	898.91	878.47	860.30	844.07	829.54	816.48
120000	1034.42	1005.81	980.62	958.33	938.50	920.81	904.95	890.71
130000	1120.62	1089.63	1062.34	1038.19	1016.71	997.54	980.37	964.93
140000	1206.82	1173.45	1144.06	1118.05	1094.92	1074.27	1055.78	1039.16
150000	1293.02	1257.27	1225.78	1197.91	1173.13	1151.01	1131.19	1113.39
160000	1379.22	1341.08	1307.50	1277.77	1251.34	1227.74	1206.60	1187.61
170000	1465.42	1424.90	1389.22	1357.63	1329.54	1304.47	1282.02	1261.84
180000	1551.62	1508.72	1470.93	1437.49	1407.75	1381.21	1357.43	1336.06
190000	1637.82	1592.54	1552.65	1517.35	1485.96	1457.94	1432.84	1410.29
200000	1724.02	1676.35	1634.37	1597.21	1564.17	1534.68	1508.25	1484.51
210000	1810.22	1760.17	1716.09	1677.07	1642.38	1611.41	1583.67	1558.74
220000	1896.42	1843.99	1797.81	1756.93	1720.59	1688.14	1659.08	1632.96
230000	1982.62	1927.81	1879.53	1836.79	1798.79	1764.88	1734.49	1707.19
240000	2068.83	2011.62	1961.24	1916.65	1877.00	1841.61	1809.90	1781.41
250000	2155.03	2095.44	2042.96	1996.51	1955.21	1918.34	1885.32	1855.64
260000	2241.23	2179.26	2124.68	2076.37	2033.42	1995.08	1960.73	1929.86
270000	2327.43	2263.07	2206.40	2156.23	2111.63	2071.81	2036.14	2004.09
280000	2413.63	2346.89	2288.12	2236.09	2189.83	2148.54	2111.55	2078.31
290000	2499.83	2430.71	2369.83	2315.95	2268.04	2225.28	2186.97	2152.54
300000	2586.03	2514.53	2451.55	2395.81	2346.25	2302.01	2262.38	2226.77
310000	2672.23	2598.34	2533.27	2475.67	2424.46	2378.74	2337.79	2300.99
320000	2758.43	2682.16	2614.99	2555.53	2502.67	2455.48	2413.20	2375.22
330000	2844.63	2765.98	2696.71	2635.39	2580.88	2532.21	2488.62	2449.44
340000	2930.83	2849.80	2778.43	2715.25	2659.08	2608.94	2564.03	2523.67
350000	3017.04	2933.61	2860.14	2795.11	2737.29	2685.68	2639.44	2597.89
360000	3103.24	3017.43	2941.86	2874.97	2815.50	2762.41	2714.85	2672.12
370000	3189.44	3101.25	3023.58	2954.83	2893.71	2839.15	2790.27	2746.34
380000	3275.64	3185.07	3105.30	3034.69	2971.92	2915.88	2865.68	2820.57
390000	3361.84	3268.88	3187.02	3114.55	3050.12	2992.61	2941.09	2894.79
400000	3448.04	3352.70	3268.74	3194.41	3128.33	3069.35	3016.50	2969.02

7½% BLENDED MONTHLY PAYMENTS
AMORTIZATION IN YEARS

Amount	25	26	29	30	35	40	45	50
25	.19	.19	.18	.18	.17	.17	.16	.16
50	.37	.37	.35	.35	.34	.33	.32	.32
100	.74	.73	.70	.70	.67	.65	.64	.64
200	1.47	1.45	1.40	1.39	1.34	1.30	1.28	1.27
300	2.20	2.17	2.10	2.08	2.00	1.95	1.92	1.90
400	2.93	2.89	2.80	2.77	2.67	2.60	2.56	2.53
500	3.66	3.61	3.49	3.46	3.34	3.25	3.20	3.16
600	4.39	4.34	4.19	4.15	4.00	3.90	3.84	3.79
700	5.13	5.06	4.89	4.84	4.67	4.55	4.48	4.42
800	5.86	5.78	5.59	5.54	5.33	5.20	5.11	5.06
900	6.59	6.50	6.29	6.23	6.00	5.85	5.75	5.69
1000	7.32	7.22	6.98	6.92	6.67	6.50	6.39	6.32
2000	14.64	14.44	13.96	13.83	13.33	13.00	12.78	12.63
3000	21.95	21.66	20.94	20.75	19.99	19.49	19.17	18.95
4000	29.27	28.88	27.92	27.66	26.65	25.99	25.55	25.26
5000	36.58	36.10	34.90	34.57	33.31	32.49	31.94	31.57
6000	43.90	43.32	41.88	41.49	39.97	38.98	38.33	37.89
7000	51.21	50.54	48.86	48.40	46.63	45.48	44.71	44.20
8000	58.53	57.76	55.84	55.32	53.29	51.97	51.10	50.51
9000	65.84	64.97	62.82	62.23	59.95	58.47	57.49	56.83
10000	73.16	72.19	69.80	69.14	66.61	64.97	63.87	63.14
20000	146.32	144.38	139.60	138.28	133.22	129.93	127.74	126.28
30000	219.47	216.57	209.39	207.42	199.83	194.89	191.61	189.41
40000	292.63	288.76	279.19	276.56	266.44	259.85	255.48	252.55
50000	365.78	360.95	348.99	345.70	333.04	324.81	319.35	315.68
60000	438.94	433.14	418.78	414.84	399.65	389.78	383.22	378.82
70000	512.09	505.33	488.58	483.98	466.26	454.74	447.09	441.95
80000	585.25	577.52	558.38	553.11	532.87	519.70	510.96	505.09
90000	658.40	649.70	628.17	622.25	599.47	584.66	574.83	568.22
100000	731.56	721.89	697.97	691.39	666.08	649.62	638.70	631.36
110000	804.72	794.08	767.77	760.53	732.69	714.59	702.57	694.50
120000	877.87	866.27	837.56	829.67	799.30	779.55	766.44	757.63
130000	951.03	938.46	907.36	898.81	865.90	844.51	830.31	820.77
140000	1024.18	1010.65	977.16	967.95	932.51	909.47	894.18	883.90
150000	1097.34	1082.84	1046.95	1037.08	999.12	974.43	958.05	947.04
160000	1170.49	1155.03	1116.75	1106.22	1065.73	1039.40	1021.92	1010.17
170000	1243.65	1227.22	1186.55	1175.36	1132.33	1104.36	1085.79	1073.31
180000	1316.80	1299.40	1256.34	1244.50	1198.94	1169.32	1149.66	1136.44
190000	1389.96	1371.59	1326.14	1313.64	1265.55	1234.28	1213.53	1199.58
200000	1463.11	1443.78	1395.94	1382.78	1332.16	1299.24	1277.40	1262.71
210000	1536.27	1515.97	1465.73	1451.92	1398.77	1364.21	1341.27	1325.85
220000	1609.43	1588.16	1535.53	1521.05	1465.37	1429.17	1405.14	1388.99
230000	1682.58	1660.35	1605.33	1590.19	1531.98	1494.13	1469.01	1452.12
240000	1755.74	1732.54	1675.12	1659.33	1598.59	1559.09	1532.88	1515.26
250000	1828.89	1804.73	1744.92	1728.47	1665.20	1624.05	1596.75	1578.39
260000	1902.05	1876.91	1814.72	1797.61	1731.80	1689.02	1660.62	1641.53
270000	1975.20	1949.10	1884.51	1866.75	1798.41	1753.98	1724.49	1704.66
280000	2048.36	2021.29	1954.31	1935.89	1865.02	1818.94	1788.36	1767.80
290000	2121.51	2093.48	2024.11	2005.02	1931.63	1883.90	1852.23	1830.93
300000	2194.67	2165.67	2093.90	2074.16	1998.23	1948.86	1916.10	1894.07
310000	2267.83	2237.86	2163.70	2143.30	2064.84	2013.83	1979.97	1957.20
320000	2340.98	2310.05	2233.50	2212.44	2131.45	2078.79	2043.84	2020.34
330000	2414.14	2382.24	2303.29	2281.58	2198.06	2143.75	2107.71	2083.48
340000	2487.29	2454.43	2373.09	2350.72	2264.66	2208.71	2171.58	2146.61
350000	2560.45	2526.61	2442.88	2419.86	2331.27	2273.67	2235.45	2209.75
360000	2633.60	2598.80	2512.68	2488.99	2397.88	2338.64	2299.32	2272.88
370000	2706.76	2670.99	2582.48	2558.13	2464.49	2403.60	2363.19	2336.02
380000	2779.91	2743.18	2652.27	2627.27	2531.10	2468.56	2427.06	2399.15
390000	2853.07	2815.37	2722.07	2696.41	2597.70	2533.52	2490.93	2462.29
400000	2926.22	2887.56	2791.87	2765.55	2664.31	2598.48	2554.80	2525.42

BLENDED MONTHLY PAYMENTS 7¾%
AMORTIZATION IN YEARS

Amount	1	2	3	4	5	6	7	8
25	2.18	1.13	.78	.61	.51	.44	.39	.35
50	4.35	2.26	1.56	1.22	1.01	.87	.78	.70
100	8.69	4.51	3.12	2.43	2.01	1.74	1.55	1.40
200	17.37	9.02	6.24	4.85	4.02	3.48	3.09	2.79
300	26.05	13.52	9.35	7.28	6.03	5.21	4.63	4.19
400	34.73	18.03	12.47	9.70	8.04	6.95	6.17	5.58
500	43.41	22.53	15.59	12.12	10.05	8.68	7.71	6.98
600	52.09	27.04	18.70	14.55	12.06	10.42	9.25	8.37
700	60.78	31.55	21.82	16.97	14.07	12.15	10.79	9.77
800	69.46	36.05	24.94	19.40	16.08	13.89	12.33	11.16
900	78.14	40.56	28.05	21.82	18.09	15.62	13.87	12.56
1000	86.82	45.06	31.17	24.24	20.10	17.36	15.41	13.95
2000	173.64	90.12	62.33	48.48	40.20	34.71	30.81	27.90
3000	260.45	135.18	93.50	72.72	60.30	52.06	46.21	41.85
4000	347.27	180.24	124.66	96.96	80.40	69.41	61.61	55.80
5000	434.09	225.29	155.83	121.20	100.50	86.77	77.01	69.75
6000	520.90	270.35	186.99	145.44	120.60	104.12	92.41	83.69
7000	607.72	315.41	218.16	169.67	140.70	121.47	107.81	97.64
8000	694.54	360.47	249.32	193.91	160.79	138.82	123.22	111.59
9000	781.35	405.52	280.49	218.15	180.89	156.17	138.62	125.54
10000	868.17	450.58	311.65	242.39	200.99	173.53	154.02	139.49
20000	1736.33	901.16	623.30	484.78	401.98	347.05	308.03	278.97
30000	2604.50	1351.74	934.95	727.16	602.97	520.57	462.05	418.45
40000	3472.66	1802.31	1246.60	969.55	803.95	694.09	616.06	557.93
50000	4340.83	2252.89	1558.25	1211.93	1004.94	867.61	770.08	697.42
60000	5208.99	2703.47	1869.90	1454.32	1205.93	1041.13	924.09	836.90
70000	6077.15	3154.04	2181.55	1696.70	1406.91	1214.65	1078.10	976.38
80000	6945.32	3604.62	2493.20	1939.09	1607.90	1388.17	1232.12	1115.86
90000	7813.48	4055.20	2804.85	2181.48	1808.89	1561.69	1386.13	1255.34
100000	8681.65	4505.78	3116.50	2423.86	2009.88	1735.21	1540.15	1394.83
110000	9549.81	4956.35	3428.15	2666.25	2210.86	1908.73	1694.16	1534.31
120000	10417.97	5406.93	3739.80	2908.63	2411.85	2082.25	1848.17	1673.79
130000	11286.14	5857.51	4051.45	3151.02	2612.84	2255.77	2002.19	1813.27
140000	12154.30	6308.08	4363.09	3393.40	2813.82	2429.29	2156.20	1952.75
150000	13022.47	6758.66	4674.74	3635.79	3014.81	2602.81	2310.22	2092.24
160000	13890.63	7209.24	4986.39	3878.18	3215.80	2776.33	2464.23	2231.72
170000	14758.79	7659.82	5298.04	4120.56	3416.79	2949.85	2618.24	2371.20
180000	15626.96	8110.39	5609.69	4362.95	3617.77	3123.37	2772.26	2510.68
190000	16495.12	8560.97	5921.34	4605.33	3818.76	3296.89	2926.27	2650.17
200000	17363.29	9011.55	6232.99	4847.72	4019.75	3470.41	3080.29	2789.65
210000	18231.45	9462.12	6544.64	5090.10	4220.73	3643.93	3234.30	2929.13
220000	19099.62	9912.70	6856.29	5332.49	4421.72	3817.45	3388.31	3068.61
230000	19967.78	10363.28	7167.94	5574.88	4622.71	3990.97	3542.33	3208.09
240000	20835.94	10813.85	7479.59	5817.26	4823.70	4164.49	3696.34	3347.58
250000	21704.11	11264.43	7791.24	6059.65	5024.68	4338.02	3850.36	3487.06
260000	22572.27	11715.01	8102.89	6302.03	5225.67	4511.54	4004.37	3626.54
270000	23440.44	12165.59	8414.53	6544.42	5426.66	4685.06	4158.38	3766.02
280000	24308.60	12616.16	8726.18	6786.80	5627.64	4858.58	4312.40	3905.50
290000	25176.76	13066.74	9037.83	7029.19	5828.63	5032.10	4466.41	4044.99
300000	26044.93	13517.32	9349.48	7271.57	6029.62	5205.62	4620.43	4184.47
310000	26913.09	13967.89	9661.13	7513.96	6230.61	5379.14	4774.44	4323.95
320000	27781.26	14418.47	9972.78	7756.35	6431.59	5552.66	4928.45	4463.43
330000	28649.42	14869.05	10284.43	7998.73	6632.58	5726.18	5082.47	4602.92
340000	29517.58	15319.63	10596.08	8241.12	6833.57	5899.70	5236.48	4742.40
350000	30385.75	15770.20	10907.73	8483.50	7034.55	6073.22	5390.50	4881.88
360000	31253.91	16220.78	11219.38	8725.89	7235.54	6246.74	5544.51	5021.36
370000	32122.08	16671.36	11531.03	8968.27	7436.53	6420.26	5698.52	5160.84
380000	32990.24	17121.93	11842.68	9210.66	7637.52	6593.78	5852.54	5300.33
390000	33858.40	17572.51	12154.33	9453.05	7838.50	6767.30	6006.55	5439.81
400000	34726.57	18023.09	12465.98	9695.43	8039.49	6940.82	6160.57	5579.29

7¾% BLENDED MONTHLY PAYMENTS
AMORTIZATION IN YEARS

Amount	9	10	11	12	13	14	15	16
25	.33	.30	.29	.27	.26	.25	.24	.23
50	.65	.60	.57	.54	.51	.49	.47	.46
100	1.29	1.20	1.13	1.07	1.02	.98	.94	.91
200	2.57	2.39	2.25	2.13	2.03	1.95	1.87	1.81
300	3.85	3.59	3.37	3.19	3.04	2.92	2.81	2.71
400	5.14	4.78	4.49	4.25	4.05	3.89	3.74	3.62
500	6.42	5.97	5.61	5.32	5.07	4.86	4.68	4.52
600	7.70	7.17	6.73	6.38	6.08	5.83	5.61	5.42
700	8.98	8.36	7.86	7.44	7.09	6.80	6.55	6.33
800	10.27	9.55	8.98	8.50	8.10	7.77	7.48	7.23
900	11.55	10.75	10.10	9.56	9.12	8.74	8.41	8.13
1000	12.83	11.94	11.22	10.63	10.13	9.71	9.35	9.04
2000	25.66	23.88	22.44	21.25	20.25	19.41	18.69	18.07
3000	38.48	35.82	33.65	31.87	30.38	29.11	28.03	27.10
4000	51.31	47.75	44.87	42.49	40.50	38.82	37.38	36.13
5000	64.14	59.69	56.09	53.11	50.63	48.52	46.72	45.17
6000	76.96	71.63	67.30	63.73	60.75	58.22	56.06	54.20
7000	89.79	83.56	78.52	74.36	70.87	67.93	65.41	63.23
8000	102.62	95.50	89.73	84.98	81.00	77.63	74.75	72.26
9000	115.44	107.44	100.95	95.60	91.12	87.33	84.09	81.29
10000	128.27	119.37	112.17	106.22	101.25	97.04	93.43	90.33
20000	256.54	238.74	224.33	212.43	202.49	194.07	186.86	180.65
30000	384.80	358.11	336.49	318.65	303.73	291.10	280.29	270.97
40000	513.07	477.48	448.65	424.86	404.97	388.13	373.72	361.29
50000	641.33	596.85	560.81	531.08	506.21	485.16	467.15	451.61
60000	769.60	716.22	672.97	637.29	607.45	582.19	560.58	541.94
70000	897.87	835.59	785.13	743.51	708.69	679.22	654.01	632.26
80000	1026.13	954.96	897.29	849.72	809.93	776.25	747.43	722.58
90000	1154.40	1074.33	1009.45	955.94	911.17	873.28	840.86	812.90
100000	1282.66	1193.70	1121.61	1062.15	1012.42	970.31	934.29	903.22
110000	1410.93	1313.07	1233.77	1168.37	1113.66	1067.34	1027.72	993.54
120000	1539.19	1432.44	1345.93	1274.58	1214.90	1164.37	1121.15	1083.87
130000	1667.46	1551.81	1458.09	1380.80	1316.14	1261.40	1214.58	1174.19
140000	1795.73	1671.18	1570.25	1487.01	1417.38	1358.43	1308.01	1264.51
150000	1923.99	1790.55	1682.41	1593.23	1518.62	1455.46	1401.44	1354.83
160000	2052.26	1909.92	1794.57	1699.44	1619.86	1552.49	1494.86	1445.15
170000	2180.52	2029.29	1906.73	1805.65	1721.10	1649.52	1588.29	1535.47
180000	2308.79	2148.66	2018.89	1911.87	1822.34	1746.55	1681.72	1625.80
190000	2437.06	2268.03	2131.05	2018.08	1923.58	1843.58	1775.15	1716.12
200000	2565.32	2387.40	2243.21	2124.30	2024.83	1940.61	1868.58	1806.44
210000	2693.59	2506.77	2355.37	2230.51	2126.07	2037.64	1962.01	1896.76
220000	2821.85	2626.14	2467.53	2336.73	2227.31	2134.67	2055.44	1987.08
230000	2950.12	2745.51	2579.69	2442.94	2328.55	2231.70	2148.87	2077.40
240000	3078.38	2864.88	2691.85	2549.16	2429.79	2328.73	2242.29	2167.73
250000	3206.65	2984.25	2804.01	2655.37	2531.03	2425.76	2335.72	2258.05
260000	3334.92	3103.61	2916.17	2761.59	2632.27	2522.79	2429.15	2348.37
270000	3463.18	3222.98	3028.33	2867.80	2733.51	2619.82	2522.58	2438.69
280000	3591.45	3342.35	3140.49	2974.02	2834.75	2716.85	2616.01	2529.01
290000	3719.71	3461.72	3252.65	3080.23	2936.00	2813.88	2709.44	2619.33
300000	3847.98	3581.09	3364.81	3186.45	3037.24	2910.91	2802.87	2709.66
310000	3976.24	3700.46	3476.97	3292.66	3138.48	3007.94	2896.29	2799.98
320000	4104.51	3819.83	3589.13	3398.87	3239.72	3104.97	2989.72	2890.30
330000	4232.78	3939.20	3701.29	3505.09	3340.96	3202.00	3083.15	2980.62
340000	4361.04	4058.57	3813.45	3611.30	3442.20	3299.03	3176.58	3070.94
350000	4489.31	4177.94	3925.61	3717.52	3543.44	3396.06	3270.01	3161.26
360000	4617.57	4297.31	4037.77	3823.73	3644.68	3493.09	3363.44	3251.59
370000	4745.84	4416.68	4149.93	3929.95	3745.92	3590.12	3456.87	3341.91
380000	4874.11	4536.05	4262.09	4036.16	3847.16	3687.15	3550.30	3432.23
390000	5002.37	4655.42	4374.25	4142.38	3948.41	3784.18	3643.72	3522.55
400000	5130.64	4774.79	4486.41	4248.59	4049.65	3881.21	3737.15	3612.87

BLENDED MONTHLY PAYMENTS

AMORTIZATION IN YEARS

7¾%

Amount	17	18	19	20	21	22	23	24
25	.22	.22	.21	.21	.20	.20	.20	.19
50	.44	.43	.42	.41	.40	.40	.39	.38
100	.88	.86	.84	.82	.80	.79	.77	.76
200	1.76	1.71	1.67	1.63	1.60	1.57	1.54	1.52
300	2.63	2.56	2.50	2.45	2.40	2.35	2.31	2.28
400	3.51	3.42	3.33	3.26	3.19	3.14	3.08	3.04
500	4.39	4.27	4.16	4.07	3.99	3.92	3.85	3.79
600	5.26	5.12	5.00	4.89	4.79	4.70	4.62	4.55
700	6.14	5.97	5.83	5.70	5.58	5.48	5.39	5.31
800	7.01	6.83	6.66	6.51	6.38	6.27	6.16	6.07
900	7.89	7.68	7.49	7.33	7.18	7.05	6.93	6.83
1000	8.77	8.53	8.32	8.14	7.98	7.83	7.70	7.58
2000	17.53	17.06	16.64	16.27	15.95	15.66	15.40	15.16
3000	26.29	25.58	24.96	24.41	23.92	23.48	23.09	22.74
4000	35.05	34.11	33.28	32.54	31.89	31.31	30.79	30.32
5000	43.82	42.63	41.60	40.68	39.86	39.13	38.48	37.90
6000	52.58	51.16	49.91	48.81	47.83	46.96	46.18	45.48
7000	61.34	59.69	58.23	56.94	55.80	54.78	53.87	53.05
8000	70.10	68.21	66.55	65.08	63.77	62.61	61.57	60.63
9000	78.86	76.74	74.87	73.21	71.74	70.43	69.26	68.21
10000	87.63	85.26	83.19	81.35	79.72	78.26	76.96	75.79
20000	175.25	170.52	166.37	162.69	159.43	156.51	153.91	151.57
30000	262.87	255.78	249.55	244.03	239.14	234.77	230.86	227.36
40000	350.49	341.04	332.73	325.37	318.85	313.02	307.82	303.14
50000	438.11	426.30	415.91	406.72	398.56	391.28	384.77	378.92
60000	525.73	511.56	499.09	488.06	478.27	469.53	461.72	454.71
70000	613.35	596.82	582.27	569.40	557.98	547.79	538.67	530.49
80000	700.97	682.07	665.45	650.74	637.69	626.04	615.63	606.28
90000	788.60	767.33	748.63	732.09	717.40	704.30	692.58	682.06
100000	876.22	852.59	831.81	813.43	797.11	782.55	769.53	757.84
110000	963.84	937.85	914.99	894.77	876.82	860.81	846.48	833.63
120000	1051.46	1023.11	998.17	976.11	956.53	939.06	923.44	909.41
130000	1139.08	1108.37	1081.35	1057.45	1036.24	1017.32	1000.39	985.20
140000	1226.70	1193.63	1164.53	1138.80	1115.95	1095.57	1077.34	1060.98
150000	1314.32	1278.89	1247.71	1220.14	1195.66	1173.83	1154.29	1136.76
160000	1401.94	1364.14	1330.89	1301.48	1275.37	1252.08	1231.25	1212.55
170000	1489.57	1449.40	1414.07	1382.82	1355.08	1330.34	1308.20	1288.33
180000	1577.19	1534.66	1497.25	1464.17	1434.79	1408.59	1385.15	1364.12
190000	1664.81	1619.92	1580.43	1545.51	1514.50	1486.84	1462.10	1439.90
200000	1752.43	1705.18	1663.61	1626.85	1594.21	1565.10	1539.06	1515.68
210000	1840.05	1790.44	1746.79	1708.19	1673.92	1643.35	1616.01	1591.47
220000	1927.67	1875.70	1829.97	1789.54	1753.63	1721.61	1692.96	1667.25
230000	2015.29	1960.96	1913.15	1870.88	1833.34	1799.86	1769.92	1743.04
240000	2102.91	2046.21	1996.33	1952.22	1913.05	1878.12	1846.87	1818.82
250000	2190.53	2131.47	2079.51	2033.56	1992.76	1956.37	1923.82	1894.60
260000	2278.16	2216.73	2162.69	2114.90	2072.47	2034.63	2000.77	1970.39
270000	2365.78	2301.99	2245.87	2196.25	2152.18	2112.88	2077.73	2046.17
280000	2453.40	2387.25	2329.05	2277.59	2231.89	2191.14	2154.68	2121.96
290000	2541.02	2472.51	2412.23	2358.93	2311.60	2269.39	2231.63	2197.74
300000	2628.64	2557.77	2495.41	2440.27	2391.31	2347.65	2308.58	2273.52
310000	2716.26	2643.02	2578.59	2521.62	2471.02	2425.90	2385.54	2349.31
320000	2803.88	2728.28	2661.77	2602.96	2550.73	2504.16	2462.49	2425.09
330000	2891.50	2813.54	2744.95	2684.30	2630.44	2582.41	2539.44	2500.88
340000	2979.13	2898.80	2828.13	2765.64	2710.15	2660.67	2616.39	2576.66
350000	3066.75	2984.06	2911.31	2846.99	2789.86	2738.92	2693.35	2652.44
360000	3154.37	3069.32	2994.49	2928.33	2869.57	2817.18	2770.30	2728.23
370000	3241.99	3154.58	3077.67	3009.67	2949.28	2895.43	2847.25	2804.01
380000	3329.61	3239.84	3160.85	3091.01	3028.99	2973.68	2924.20	2879.80
390000	3417.23	3325.09	3244.03	3172.35	3108.70	3051.94	3001.16	2955.58
400000	3504.85	3410.35	3327.21	3253.70	3188.41	3130.19	3078.11	3031.36

7¾% BLENDED MONTHLY PAYMENTS
AMORTIZATION IN YEARS

Amount	25	26	29	30	35	40	45	50
25	.19	.19	.18	.18	.18	.17	.17	.17
50	.38	.37	.36	.36	.35	.34	.33	.33
100	.75	.74	.72	.71	.69	.67	.66	.66
200	1.50	1.48	1.43	1.42	1.37	1.34	1.32	1.31
300	2.25	2.22	2.15	2.13	2.06	2.01	1.98	1.96
400	2.99	2.96	2.86	2.84	2.74	2.68	2.63	2.61
500	3.74	3.69	3.58	3.54	3.42	3.34	3.29	3.26
600	4.49	4.43	4.29	4.25	4.11	4.01	3.95	3.91
700	5.24	5.17	5.01	4.96	4.79	4.68	4.60	4.56
800	5.98	5.91	5.72	5.67	5.47	5.35	5.26	5.21
900	6.73	6.65	6.43	6.38	6.16	6.01	5.92	5.86
1000	7.48	7.38	7.15	7.08	6.84	6.68	6.58	6.51
2000	14.95	14.76	14.29	14.16	13.67	13.36	13.15	13.01
3000	22.42	22.14	21.44	21.24	20.51	20.03	19.72	19.51
4000	29.90	29.52	28.58	28.32	27.34	26.71	26.29	26.01
5000	37.37	36.90	35.73	35.40	34.17	33.38	32.86	32.51
6000	44.84	44.27	42.87	42.48	41.01	40.06	39.43	39.01
7000	52.32	51.65	50.01	49.56	47.84	46.73	46.00	45.52
8000	59.79	59.03	57.16	56.64	54.68	53.41	52.57	52.02
9000	67.26	66.41	64.30	63.72	61.51	60.08	59.14	58.52
10000	74.74	73.79	71.45	70.80	68.34	66.76	65.72	65.02
20000	149.47	147.57	142.89	141.60	136.68	133.51	131.43	130.04
30000	224.20	221.35	214.33	212.40	205.02	200.26	197.14	195.05
40000	298.93	295.14	285.77	283.20	273.36	267.02	262.85	260.07
50000	373.67	368.92	357.21	354.00	341.70	333.77	328.56	325.09
60000	448.40	442.70	428.65	424.79	410.04	400.52	394.27	390.10
70000	523.13	516.49	500.09	495.59	478.38	467.28	459.98	455.12
80000	597.86	590.27	571.53	566.39	546.71	534.03	525.69	520.14
90000	672.59	664.05	642.97	637.19	615.05	600.78	591.40	585.15
100000	747.33	737.84	714.41	707.99	683.39	667.54	657.11	650.17
110000	822.06	811.62	785.85	778.79	751.73	734.29	722.82	715.19
120000	896.79	885.40	857.29	849.58	820.07	801.04	788.53	780.20
130000	971.52	959.18	928.73	920.38	888.41	867.80	854.24	845.22
140000	1046.25	1032.97	1000.17	991.18	956.75	934.55	919.95	910.24
150000	1120.99	1106.75	1071.61	1061.98	1025.09	1001.30	985.67	975.25
160000	1195.72	1180.53	1143.05	1132.78	1093.42	1068.06	1051.38	1040.27
170000	1270.45	1254.32	1214.50	1203.58	1161.76	1134.81	1117.09	1105.28
180000	1345.18	1328.10	1285.94	1274.37	1230.10	1201.56	1182.80	1170.30
190000	1419.91	1401.88	1357.38	1345.17	1298.44	1268.31	1248.51	1235.32
200000	1494.65	1475.67	1428.82	1415.97	1366.78	1335.07	1314.22	1300.33
210000	1569.38	1549.45	1500.26	1486.77	1435.12	1401.82	1379.93	1365.35
220000	1644.11	1623.23	1571.70	1557.57	1503.46	1468.57	1445.64	1430.37
230000	1718.84	1697.01	1643.14	1628.37	1571.80	1535.33	1511.35	1495.38
240000	1793.58	1770.80	1714.58	1699.16	1640.13	1602.08	1577.06	1560.40
250000	1868.31	1844.58	1786.02	1769.96	1708.47	1668.83	1642.77	1625.42
260000	1943.04	1918.36	1857.46	1840.76	1776.81	1735.59	1708.48	1690.43
270000	2017.77	1992.15	1928.90	1911.56	1845.15	1802.34	1774.19	1755.45
280000	2092.50	2065.93	2000.34	1982.36	1913.49	1869.09	1839.90	1820.47
290000	2167.24	2139.71	2071.78	2053.16	1981.83	1935.85	1905.61	1885.48
300000	2241.97	2213.50	2143.22	2123.95	2050.17	2002.60	1971.33	1950.50
310000	2316.70	2287.28	2214.66	2194.75	2118.51	2069.35	2037.04	2015.52
320000	2391.43	2361.06	2286.10	2265.55	2186.84	2136.11	2102.75	2080.53
330000	2466.16	2434.84	2357.54	2336.35	2255.18	2202.86	2168.46	2145.55
340000	2540.90	2508.63	2428.99	2407.15	2323.52	2269.61	2234.17	2210.56
350000	2615.63	2582.41	2500.43	2477.95	2391.86	2336.36	2299.88	2275.58
360000	2690.36	2656.19	2571.87	2548.74	2460.20	2403.12	2365.59	2340.60
370000	2765.09	2729.98	2643.31	2619.54	2528.54	2469.87	2431.30	2405.61
380000	2839.82	2803.76	2714.75	2690.34	2596.88	2536.62	2497.01	2470.63
390000	2914.56	2877.54	2786.19	2761.14	2665.22	2603.38	2562.72	2535.65
400000	2989.29	2951.33	2857.63	2831.94	2733.55	2670.13	2628.43	2600.66

84

Amount	1	2	3	4	5	6	7	8
25	2.18	1.13	.79	.61	.51	.44	.39	.36
50	4.35	2.26	1.57	1.22	1.02	.88	.78	.71
100	8.70	4.52	3.13	2.44	2.03	1.75	1.56	1.41
200	17.39	9.04	6.26	4.88	4.05	3.50	3.11	2.82
300	26.08	13.56	9.39	7.31	6.07	5.25	4.66	4.23
400	34.78	18.07	12.52	9.75	8.09	6.99	6.21	5.63
500	43.47	22.59	15.64	12.18	10.11	8.74	7.77	7.04
600	52.16	27.11	18.77	14.62	12.13	10.49	9.32	8.45
700	60.85	31.62	21.90	17.05	14.15	12.23	10.87	9.85
800	69.55	36.14	25.03	19.49	16.18	13.98	12.42	11.26
900	78.24	40.66	28.15	21.92	18.20	15.73	13.97	12.67
1000	86.93	45.17	31.28	24.36	20.22	17.47	15.53	14.08
2000	173.86	90.34	62.56	48.71	40.43	34.94	31.05	28.15
3000	260.79	135.51	93.83	73.06	60.65	52.41	46.57	42.22
4000	347.72	180.68	125.11	97.41	80.86	69.88	62.09	56.29
5000	434.65	225.84	156.39	121.76	101.08	87.35	77.61	70.36
6000	521.57	271.01	187.66	146.12	121.29	104.82	93.13	84.43
7000	608.50	316.18	218.94	170.47	141.50	122.29	108.66	98.50
8000	695.43	361.35	250.22	194.82	161.72	139.76	124.18	112.57
9000	782.36	406.52	281.49	219.17	181.93	157.23	139.70	126.64
10000	869.29	451.68	312.77	243.52	202.15	174.70	155.22	140.71
20000	1738.57	903.36	625.53	487.04	404.29	349.40	310.43	281.42
30000	2607.85	1355.04	938.30	730.56	606.43	524.10	465.65	422.12
40000	3477.14	1806.72	1251.06	974.08	808.57	698.80	620.86	562.83
50000	4346.42	2258.40	1563.82	1217.60	1010.71	873.49	776.08	703.54
60000	5215.70	2710.08	1876.59	1461.12	1212.85	1048.19	931.29	844.24
70000	6084.98	3161.76	2189.35	1704.64	1415.00	1222.89	1086.51	984.95
80000	6954.27	3613.44	2502.11	1948.15	1617.14	1397.59	1241.72	1125.65
90000	7823.55	4065.12	2814.88	2191.67	1819.28	1572.28	1396.93	1266.36
100000	8692.83	4516.80	3127.64	2435.19	2021.42	1746.98	1552.15	1407.07
110000	9562.11	4968.48	3440.40	2678.71	2223.56	1921.68	1707.36	1547.77
120000	10431.40	5420.16	3753.17	2922.23	2425.70	2096.38	1862.58	1688.48
130000	11300.68	5871.84	4065.93	3165.75	2627.85	2271.07	2017.79	1829.18
140000	12169.96	6323.52	4378.69	3409.27	2829.99	2445.77	2173.01	1969.89
150000	13039.24	6775.20	4691.46	3652.79	3032.13	2620.47	2328.22	2110.60
160000	13908.53	7226.88	5004.22	3896.30	3234.27	2795.17	2483.44	2251.30
170000	14777.81	7678.56	5316.99	4139.82	3436.41	2969.86	2638.65	2392.01
180000	15647.09	8130.24	5629.75	4383.34	3638.55	3144.56	2793.86	2532.72
190000	16516.37	8581.92	5942.51	4626.86	3840.69	3319.26	2949.08	2673.42
200000	17385.66	9033.59	6255.28	4870.38	4042.84	3493.96	3104.29	2814.13
210000	18254.94	9485.27	6568.04	5113.90	4244.98	3668.65	3259.51	2954.83
220000	19124.22	9936.95	6880.80	5357.42	4447.12	3843.35	3414.72	3095.54
230000	19993.50	10388.63	7193.57	5600.93	4649.26	4018.05	3569.94	3236.25
240000	20862.79	10840.31	7506.33	5844.45	4851.40	4192.75	3725.15	3376.95
250000	21732.07	11291.99	7819.09	6087.97	5053.54	4367.44	3880.37	3517.66
260000	22601.35	11743.67	8131.86	6331.49	5255.69	4542.14	4035.58	3658.36
270000	23470.63	12195.35	8444.62	6575.01	5457.83	4716.84	4190.79	3799.07
280000	24339.92	12647.03	8757.38	6818.53	5659.97	4891.54	4346.01	3939.78
290000	25209.20	13098.71	9070.15	7062.05	5862.11	5066.23	4501.22	4080.48
300000	26078.48	13550.39	9382.91	7305.57	6064.25	5240.93	4656.44	4221.19
310000	26947.76	14002.07	9695.67	7549.08	6266.39	5415.63	4811.65	4361.89
320000	27817.05	14453.75	10008.44	7792.60	6468.54	5590.33	4966.87	4502.60
330000	28686.33	14905.43	10321.20	8036.12	6670.68	5765.02	5122.08	4643.31
340000	29555.61	15357.11	10633.97	8279.64	6872.82	5939.72	5277.30	4784.01
350000	30424.90	15808.79	10946.73	8523.16	7074.96	6114.42	5432.51	4924.72
360000	31294.18	16260.47	11259.49	8766.68	7277.10	6289.12	5587.72	5065.43
370000	32163.46	16712.15	11572.26	9010.20	7479.24	6463.81	5742.94	5206.13
380000	33032.74	17163.83	11885.02	9253.72	7681.38	6638.51	5898.15	5346.84
390000	33902.03	17615.51	12197.78	9497.23	7883.53	6813.21	6053.37	5487.54
400000	34771.31	18067.18	12510.55	9740.75	8085.67	6987.91	6208.58	5628 25

8% BLENDED MONTHLY PAYMENTS
AMORTIZATION IN YEARS

Amount	9	10	11	12	13	14	15	16
25	.33	.31	.29	.27	.26	.25	.24	.23
50	.65	.61	.57	.54	.52	.50	.48	.46
100	1.30	1.21	1.14	1.08	1.03	.99	.95	.92
200	2.60	2.42	2.27	2.16	2.06	1.97	1.90	1.84
300	3.89	3.62	3.41	3.23	3.08	2.96	2.85	2.76
400	5.19	4.83	4.54	4.31	4.11	3.94	3.80	3.67
500	6.48	6.04	5.68	5.38	5.13	4.92	4.75	4.59
600	7.78	7.24	6.81	6.46	6.16	5.91	5.69	5.51
700	9.07	8.45	7.95	7.53	7.19	6.89	6.64	6.43
800	10.37	9.66	9.08	8.61	8.21	7.88	7.59	7.34
900	11.66	10.86	10.22	9.68	9.24	8.86	8.54	8.26
1000	12.96	12.07	11.35	10.76	10.26	9.84	9.49	9.18
2000	25.91	24.13	22.70	21.51	20.52	19.68	18.97	18.35
3000	38.86	36.20	34.04	32.26	30.78	29.52	28.45	27.52
4000	51.81	48.26	45.39	43.02	41.04	39.36	37.93	36.70
5000	64.76	60.33	56.73	53.77	51.30	49.20	47.41	45.87
6000	77.71	72.39	68.08	64.52	61.55	59.04	56.89	55.04
7000	90.66	84.45	79.42	75.28	71.81	68.88	66.38	64.22
8000	103.62	96.52	90.77	86.03	82.07	78.72	75.86	73.39
9000	116.57	108.58	102.11	96.78	92.33	88.56	85.34	82.56
10000	129.52	120.65	113.46	107.54	102.59	98.40	94.82	91.74
20000	259.03	241.29	226.91	215.07	205.17	196.79	189.64	183.47
30000	388.55	361.93	340.37	322.60	307.75	295.19	284.45	275.20
40000	518.06	482.57	453.82	430.14	410.33	393.58	379.27	366.93
50000	647.57	603.21	567.28	537.67	512.92	491.98	474.08	458.66
60000	777.09	723.85	680.73	645.20	615.50	590.37	568.90	550.39
70000	906.60	844.49	794.19	752.73	718.08	688.76	663.71	642.12
80000	1036.11	965.13	907.64	860.27	820.66	787.16	758.53	733.85
90000	1165.63	1085.77	1021.10	967.80	923.25	885.55	853.34	825.58
100000	1295.14	1206.41	1134.55	1075.33	1025.83	983.95	948.16	917.31
110000	1424.65	1327.05	1248.01	1182.87	1128.41	1082.34	1042.97	1009.04
120000	1554.17	1447.70	1361.46	1290.40	1230.99	1180.74	1137.79	1100.77
130000	1683.68	1568.34	1474.92	1397.93	1333.57	1279.13	1232.60	1192.50
140000	1813.19	1688.98	1588.37	1505.46	1436.16	1377.52	1327.42	1284.23
150000	1942.71	1809.62	1701.83	1613.00	1538.74	1475.92	1422.23	1375.96
160000	2072.22	1930.26	1815.28	1720.53	1641.32	1574.31	1517.05	1467.69
170000	2201.73	2050.90	1928.74	1828.06	1743.90	1672.71	1611.87	1559.42
180000	2331.25	2171.54	2042.19	1935.60	1846.49	1771.10	1706.68	1651.15
190000	2460.76	2292.18	2155.65	2043.13	1949.07	1869.50	1801.50	1742.88
200000	2590.27	2412.82	2269.10	2150.66	2051.65	1967.89	1896.31	1834.61
210000	2719.79	2533.46	2382.56	2258.19	2154.23	2066.28	1991.13	1926.34
220000	2849.30	2654.10	2496.01	2365.73	2256.82	2164.68	2085.94	2018.08
230000	2978.81	2774.75	2609.47	2473.26	2359.40	2263.07	2180.76	2109.81
240000	3108.33	2895.39	2722.92	2580.79	2461.98	2361.47	2275.57	2201.54
250000	3237.84	3016.03	2836.38	2688.33	2564.56	2459.86	2370.39	2293.27
260000	3367.35	3136.67	2949.83	2795.86	2667.14	2558.25	2465.20	2385.00
270000	3496.87	3257.31	3063.29	2903.39	2769.73	2656.65	2560.02	2476.73
280000	3626.38	3377.95	3176.74	3010.92	2872.31	2755.04	2654.83	2568.46
290000	3755.90	3498.59	3290.20	3118.46	2974.89	2853.44	2749.65	2660.19
300000	3885.41	3619.23	3403.65	3225.99	3077.47	2951.83	2844.46	2751.92
310000	4014.92	3739.87	3517.11	3333.52	3180.06	3050.23	2939.28	2843.65
320000	4144.44	3860.51	3630.56	3441.06	3282.64	3148.62	3034.09	2935.38
330000	4273.95	3981.15	3744.02	3548.59	3385.22	3247.01	3128.91	3027.11
340000	4403.46	4101.80	3857.47	3656.12	3487.80	3345.41	3223.73	3118.84
350000	4532.98	4222.44	3970.93	3763.65	3590.39	3443.80	3318.54	3210.57
360000	4662.49	4343.08	4084.38	3871.19	3692.97	3542.20	3413.36	3302.30
370000	4792.00	4463.72	4197.83	3978.72	3795.55	3640.59	3508.17	3394.03
380000	4921.52	4584.36	4311.29	4086.25	3898.13	3738.99	3602.99	3485.76
390000	5051.03	4705.00	4424.74	4193.79	4000.71	3837.38	3697.80	3577.49
400000	5180.54	4825.64	4538.20	4301.32	4103.30	3935.77	3792.62	3669.22

86

BLENDED MONTHLY PAYMENTS

AMORTIZATION IN YEARS

8%

Amount	17	18	19	20	21	22	23	24
25	.23	.22	.22	.21	.21	.20	.20	.20
50	.45	.44	.43	.42	.41	.40	.40	.39
100	.90	.87	.85	.83	.82	.80	.79	.78
200	1.79	1.74	1.70	1.66	1.63	1.60	1.58	1.55
300	2.68	2.61	2.54	2.49	2.44	2.40	2.36	2.33
400	3.57	3.47	3.39	3.32	3.25	3.20	3.15	3.10
500	4.46	4.34	4.24	4.15	4.07	3.99	3.93	3.87
600	5.35	5.21	5.08	4.98	4.88	4.79	4.72	4.65
700	6.24	6.07	5.93	5.80	5.69	5.59	5.50	5.42
800	7.13	6.94	6.78	6.63	6.50	6.39	6.29	6.19
900	8.02	7.81	7.62	7.46	7.32	7.19	7.07	6.97
1000	8.91	8.68	8.47	8.29	8.13	7.98	7.86	7.74
2000	17.82	17.35	16.94	16.57	16.25	15.96	15.71	15.48
3000	26.72	26.02	25.40	24.86	24.37	23.94	23.56	23.21
4000	35.63	34.69	33.87	33.14	32.49	31.92	31.41	30.95
5000	44.53	43.36	42.33	41.42	40.62	39.90	39.26	38.68
6000	53.44	52.03	50.80	49.71	48.74	47.88	47.11	46.42
7000	62.34	60.70	59.26	57.99	56.86	55.86	54.96	54.15
8000	71.25	69.37	67.73	66.27	64.98	63.84	62.81	61.89
9000	80.15	78.04	76.19	74.56	73.11	71.81	70.66	69.62
10000	89.06	86.72	84.66	82.84	81.23	79.79	78.51	77.36
20000	178.11	173.43	169.31	165.68	162.45	159.58	157.01	154.71
30000	267.16	260.14	253.96	248.51	243.68	239.37	235.52	232.07
40000	356.21	346.85	338.62	331.35	324.90	319.16	314.02	309.42
50000	445.26	433.56	423.27	414.18	406.12	398.94	392.53	386.78
60000	534.32	520.27	507.92	497.02	487.35	478.73	471.03	464.13
70000	623.37	606.98	592.58	579.86	568.57	558.52	549.54	541.49
80000	712.42	693.69	677.23	662.69	649.79	638.31	628.04	618.84
90000	801.47	780.40	761.88	745.53	731.02	718.10	706.55	696.20
100000	890.52	867.11	846.54	828.36	812.24	797.88	785.05	773.55
110000	979.57	953.82	931.19	911.20	893.46	877.67	863.56	850.91
120000	1068.63	1040.53	1015.84	994.03	974.69	957.46	942.06	928.26
130000	1157.68	1127.24	1100.49	1076.87	1055.91	1037.25	1020.57	1005.62
140000	1246.73	1213.95	1185.15	1159.71	1137.14	1117.04	1099.07	1082.97
150000	1335.78	1300.66	1269.80	1242.54	1218.36	1196.82	1177.58	1160.33
160000	1424.83	1387.38	1354.45	1325.38	1299.58	1276.61	1256.08	1237.68
170000	1513.88	1474.09	1439.11	1408.21	1380.81	1356.40	1334.59	1315.04
180000	1602.94	1560.80	1523.76	1491.05	1462.03	1436.19	1413.09	1392.39
190000	1691.99	1647.51	1608.41	1573.88	1543.25	1515.98	1491.60	1469.75
200000	1781.04	1734.22	1693.07	1656.72	1624.48	1595.76	1570.10	1547.10
210000	1870.09	1820.93	1777.72	1739.56	1705.70	1675.55	1648.61	1624.46
220000	1959.14	1907.64	1862.37	1822.39	1786.92	1755.34	1727.11	1701.81
230000	2048.20	1994.35	1947.03	1905.23	1868.15	1835.13	1805.62	1779.17
240000	2137.25	2081.06	2031.68	1988.06	1949.37	1914.91	1884.12	1856.52
250000	2226.30	2167.77	2116.33	2070.90	2030.59	1994.70	1962.63	1933.88
260000	2315.35	2254.48	2200.98	2153.73	2111.82	2074.49	2041.13	2011.23
270000	2404.40	2341.19	2285.64	2236.57	2193.04	2154.28	2119.64	2088.59
280000	2493.45	2427.90	2370.29	2319.41	2274.27	2234.07	2198.14	2165.94
290000	2582.51	2514.61	2454.94	2402.24	2355.49	2313.85	2276.65	2243.30
300000	2671.56	2601.32	2539.60	2485.08	2436.71	2393.64	2355.15	2320.65
310000	2760.61	2688.03	2624.25	2567.91	2517.94	2473.43	2433.66	2398.01
320000	2849.66	2774.75	2708.90	2650.75	2599.16	2553.22	2512.16	2475.36
330000	2938.71	2861.46	2793.56	2733.58	2680.38	2633.01	2590.67	2552.72
340000	3027.76	2948.17	2878.21	2816.42	2761.61	2712.79	2669.17	2630.07
350000	3116.82	3034.88	2962.86	2899.26	2842.83	2792.58	2747.68	2707.43
360000	3205.87	3121.59	3047.52	2982.09	2924.05	2872.37	2826.18	2784.78
370000	3294.92	3208.30	3132.17	3064.93	3005.28	2952.16	2904.69	2862.14
380000	3383.97	3295.01	3216.82	3147.76	3086.50	3031.95	2983.19	2939.49
390000	3473.02	3381.72	3301.47	3230.60	3167.73	3111.73	3061.70	3016.85
400000	3562.07	3468.43	3386.13	3313.43	3248.95	3191.52	3140.20	3094.20

87

8% BLENDED MONTHLY PAYMENTS
AMORTIZATION IN YEARS

Amount	25	26	29	30	35	40	45	50
25	.20	.19	.19	.19	.18	.18	.17	.17
50	.39	.38	.37	.37	.36	.35	.34	.34
100	.77	.76	.74	.73	.71	.69	.68	.67
200	1.53	1.51	1.47	1.45	1.41	1.38	1.36	1.34
300	2.29	2.27	2.20	2.18	2.11	2.06	2.03	2.01
400	3.06	3.02	2.93	2.90	2.81	2.75	2.71	2.68
500	3.82	3.77	3.66	3.63	3.51	3.43	3.38	3.35
600	4.58	4.53	4.39	4.35	4.21	4.12	4.06	4.02
700	5.35	5.28	5.12	5.08	4.91	4.80	4.73	4.69
800	6.11	6.04	5.85	5.85	5.61	5.49	5.41	5.36
900	6.87	6.79	6.58	6.53	6.31	6.18	6.09	6.03
1000	7.64	7.54	7.31	7.25	7.01	6.86	6.76	6.70
2000	15.27	15.08	14.62	14.50	14.02	13.72	13.52	13.39
3000	22.90	22.62	21.93	21.75	21.03	20.57	20.27	20.08
4000	30.53	30.16	29.24	28.99	28.04	27.43	27.03	26.77
5000	38.17	37.70	36.55	36.24	35.05	34.28	33.79	33.46
6000	45.80	45.24	43.86	43.49	42.05	41.14	40.54	40.15
7000	53.43	52.78	51.17	50.73	49.06	47.99	47.30	46.84
8000	61.06	60.32	58.48	57.98	56.07	54.85	54.05	53.53
9000	68.69	67.86	65.79	65.23	63.08	61.71	60.81	60.22
10000	76.33	75.39	73.10	72.48	70.09	68.56	67.57	66.91
20000	152.65	150.78	146.20	144.95	140.17	137.12	135.13	133.82
30000	228.97	226.17	219.30	217.42	210.25	205.67	202.69	200.73
40000	305.29	301.56	292.40	289.89	280.34	274.23	270.25	267.63
50000	381.61	376.95	365.49	362.36	350.42	342.79	337.82	334.54
60000	457.93	452.34	438.59	434.83	420.50	411.34	405.38	401.45
70000	534.25	527.73	511.69	507.30	490.58	479.90	472.94	468.35
80000	610.58	603.12	584.79	579.77	560.67	548.45	540.50	535.26
90000	686.90	678.51	657.88	652.24	630.75	617.01	608.06	602.17
100000	763.22	753.90	730.98	724.72	700.83	685.57	675.63	669.07
110000	839.54	829.29	804.08	797.19	770.91	754.12	743.19	735.98
120000	915.86	904.68	877.18	869.66	841.00	822.68	810.75	802.89
130000	992.18	980.07	950.27	942.13	911.08	891.24	878.31	869.79
140000	1068.50	1055.46	1023.37	1014.60	981.16	959.79	945.87	936.70
150000	1144.83	1130.85	1096.47	1087.07	1051.24	1028.35	1013.44	1003.61
160000	1221.15	1206.24	1169.57	1159.54	1121.33	1096.90	1081.00	1070.51
170000	1297.47	1281.63	1242.67	1232.01	1191.41	1165.46	1148.56	1137.42
180000	1373.79	1357.02	1315.76	1304.48	1261.49	1234.02	1216.12	1204.33
190000	1450.11	1432.41	1388.86	1376.96	1331.58	1302.57	1283.69	1271.23
200000	1526.43	1507.80	1461.96	1449.43	1401.66	1371.13	1351.25	1338.14
210000	1602.75	1583.19	1535.06	1521.90	1471.74	1439.69	1418.81	1405.05
220000	1679.07	1658.58	1608.15	1594.37	1541.82	1508.24	1486.37	1471.95
230000	1755.40	1733.97	1681.25	1666.84	1611.91	1576.80	1553.93	1538.86
240000	1831.72	1809.36	1754.35	1739.31	1681.99	1645.35	1621.50	1605.77
250000	1908.04	1884.75	1827.45	1811.78	1752.07	1713.91	1689.06	1672.67
260000	1984.36	1960.14	1900.54	1884.25	1822.15	1782.47	1756.62	1739.58
270000	2060.68	2035.53	1973.64	1956.72	1892.24	1851.02	1824.18	1806.49
280000	2137.00	2110.92	2046.74	2029.20	1962.32	1919.58	1891.74	1873.39
290000	2213.32	2186.31	2119.84	2101.67	2032.40	1988.14	1959.31	1940.30
300000	2289.65	2261.70	2192.94	2174.14	2102.48	2056.69	2026.87	2007.21
310000	2365.97	2337.09	2266.03	2246.61	2172.57	2125.25	2094.43	2074.11
320000	2442.29	2412.48	2339.13	2319.08	2242.65	2193.80	2161.99	2141.02
330000	2518.61	2487.87	2412.23	2391.55	2312.73	2262.36	2229.56	2207.93
340000	2594.93	2563.26	2485.33	2464.02	2382.81	2330.92	2297.12	2274.83
350000	2671.25	2638.65	2558.42	2536.49	2452.90	2399.47	2364.68	2341.74
360000	2747.57	2714.04	2631.52	2608.96	2522.98	2468.03	2432.24	2408.65
370000	2823.89	2789.43	2704.62	2681.44	2593.06	2536.59	2499.80	2475.55
380000	2900.22	2864.82	2777.72	2753.91	2663.15	2605.14	2567.37	2542.46
390000	2976.54	2940.21	2850.81	2826.38	2733.23	2673.70	2634.93	2609.37
400000	3052.86	3015.60	2923.91	2898.85	2803.31	2742.25	2702.49	2676.27

88

BLENDED MONTHLY PAYMENTS   8¼%
AMORTIZATION IN YEARS

Amount	1	2	3	4	5	6	7	8
25	2.18	1.14	.79	.62	.51	.44	.40	.36
50	4.36	2.27	1.57	1.23	1.02	.88	.79	.71
100	8.71	4.53	3.14	2.45	2.04	1.76	1.57	1.42
200	17.41	9.06	6.28	4.90	4.07	3.52	3.13	2.84
300	26.12	13.59	9.42	7.34	6.10	5.28	4.70	4.26
400	34.82	18.12	12.56	9.79	8.14	7.04	6.26	5.68
500	43.53	22.64	15.70	12.24	10.17	8.80	7.83	7.10
600	52.23	27.17	18.84	14.68	12.20	10.56	9.39	8.52
700	60.93	31.70	21.98	17.13	14.24	12.32	10.95	9.94
800	69.64	36.23	25.12	19.58	16.27	14.08	12.52	11.36
900	78.34	40.76	28.25	22.02	18.30	15.83	14.08	12.78
1000	87.05	45.28	31.39	24.47	20.33	17.59	15.65	14.20
2000	174.09	90.56	62.78	48.94	40.66	35.18	31.29	28.39
3000	261.13	135.84	94.17	73.40	60.99	52.77	46.93	42.59
4000	348.17	181.12	125.56	97.87	81.32	70.36	62.57	56.78
5000	435.21	226.40	156.94	122.33	101.65	87.94	78.21	70.97
6000	522.25	271.67	188.33	146.80	121.98	105.53	93.86	85.17
7000	609.29	316.95	219.72	171.26	142.31	123.12	109.50	99.36
8000	696.33	362.23	251.11	195.73	162.64	140.71	125.14	113.55
9000	783.37	407.51	282.50	220.19	182.97	158.30	140.78	127.75
10000	870.41	452.79	313.88	244.66	203.30	175.88	156.42	141.94
20000	1740.81	905.57	627.76	489.31	406.60	351.76	312.84	283.88
30000	2611.21	1358.35	941.64	733.97	609.90	527.64	469.26	425.81
40000	3481.61	1811.13	1255.52	978.62	813.20	703.52	625.68	567.75
50000	4352.01	2263.92	1569.40	1223.27	1016.50	879.40	782.10	709.68
60000	5222.41	2716.70	1883.28	1467.93	1219.80	1055.27	938.52	851.62
70000	6092.81	3169.48	2197.16	1712.58	1423.10	1231.15	1094.94	993.55
80000	6963.01	3622.26	2511.04	1957.24	1626.40	1407.03	1251.36	1135.49
90000	7833.61	4075.05	2824.92	2201.89	1829.69	1582.91	1407.78	1277.42
100000	8704.01	4527.83	3138.80	2446.54	2032.99	1758.79	1564.20	1419.36
110000	9574.41	4980.61	3452.68	2691.20	2236.29	1934.67	1720.62	1561.29
120000	10444.81	5433.39	3766.55	2935.85	2439.59	2110.54	1877.03	1703.23
130000	11315.21	5886.18	4080.43	3180.50	2642.89	2286.42	2033.45	1845.16
140000	12185.62	6338.96	4394.31	3425.16	2846.19	2462.30	2189.87	1987.10
150000	13056.02	6791.74	4708.19	3669.81	3049.49	2638.18	2346.29	2129.03
160000	13926.42	7244.52	5022.07	3914.47	3252.79	2814.06	2502.71	2270.97
170000	14796.82	7697.31	5335.95	4159.12	3456.09	2989.93	2659.13	2412.90
180000	15667.22	8150.09	5649.83	4403.77	3659.38	3165.81	2815.55	2554.84
190000	16537.62	8602.87	5963.71	4648.43	3862.68	3341.69	2971.97	2696.77
200000	17408.02	9055.65	6277.59	4893.08	4065.98	3517.57	3128.39	2838.71
210000	18278.42	9508.44	6591.47	5137.73	4269.28	3693.45	3284.81	2980.64
220000	19148.82	9961.22	6905.35	5382.39	4472.58	3869.33	3441.23	3122.58
230000	20019.22	10414.00	7219.22	5627.04	4675.88	4045.20	3597.64	3264.51
240000	20889.62	10866.78	7533.10	5871.70	4879.18	4221.08	3754.06	3406.45
250000	21760.02	11319.57	7846.98	6116.35	5082.48	4396.96	3910.48	3548.38
260000	22630.42	11772.35	8160.86	6361.00	5285.77	4572.84	4066.90	3690.32
270000	23500.82	12225.13	8474.74	6605.66	5489.07	4748.72	4223.32	3832.25
280000	24371.23	12677.91	8788.62	6850.31	5692.37	4924.59	4379.74	3974.19
290000	25241.63	13130.70	9102.50	7094.96	5895.67	5100.47	4536.16	4116.12
300000	26112.03	13583.48	9416.38	7339.62	6098.97	5276.35	4692.58	4258.06
310000	26982.43	14036.26	9730.26	7584.27	6302.27	5452.23	4849.00	4399.99
320000	27852.83	14489.04	10044.14	7828.93	6505.57	5628.11	5005.42	4541.93
330000	28723.23	14941.82	10358.02	8073.58	6708.87	5803.99	5161.84	4683.86
340000	29593.63	15394.61	10671.89	8318.23	6912.17	5979.86	5318.25	4825.80
350000	30464.03	15847.39	10985.77	8562.89	7115.46	6155.74	5474.67	4967.73
360000	31334.43	16300.17	11299.65	8807.54	7318.76	6331.62	5631.09	5109.67
370000	32204.83	16752.95	11613.53	9052.19	7522.06	6507.50	5787.51	5251.60
380000	33075.23	17205.74	11927.41	9296.85	7725.36	6683.38	5943.93	5393.54
390000	33945.63	17658.52	12241.29	9541.50	7928.66	6859.25	6100.35	5535.47
400000	34816.03	18111.30	12555.17	9786.16	8131.96	7035.13	6256.77	5677.41

8¼% BLENDED MONTHLY PAYMENTS
AMORTIZATION IN YEARS

Amount	9	10	11	12	13	14	15	16
25	.33	.31	.29	.28	.26	.25	.25	.24
50	.66	.61	.58	.55	.52	.50	.49	.47
100	1.31	1.22	1.15	1.09	1.04	1.00	.97	.94
200	2.62	2.44	2.30	2.18	2.08	2.00	1.93	1.87
300	3.93	3.66	3.45	3.27	3.12	3.00	2.89	2.80
400	5.24	4.88	4.60	4.36	4.16	4.00	3.85	3.73
500	6.54	6.10	5.74	5.45	5.20	4.99	4.82	4.66
600	7.85	7.32	6.89	6.54	6.24	5.99	5.78	5.59
700	9.16	8.54	8.04	7.63	7.28	6.99	6.74	6.53
800	10.47	9.76	9.19	8.71	8.32	7.99	7.70	7.46
900	11.77	10.98	10.33	9.80	9.36	8.98	8.66	8.39
1000	13.08	12.20	11.48	10.89	10.40	9.98	9.63	9.32
2000	26.16	24.39	22.96	21.78	20.79	19.96	19.25	18.63
3000	39.24	36.58	34.43	32.66	31.18	29.94	28.87	27.95
4000	52.31	48.77	45.91	43.55	41.58	39.91	38.49	37.26
5000	65.39	60.96	57.38	54.43	51.97	49.89	48.11	46.58
6000	78.47	73.16	68.86	65.32	62.36	59.87	57.73	55.89
7000	91.54	85.35	80.33	76.21	72.76	69.84	67.35	65.21
8000	104.62	97.54	91.81	87.09	83.15	79.82	76.97	74.52
9000	117.70	109.73	103.29	97.98	93.54	89.80	86.59	83.84
10000	130.77	121.92	114.76	108.86	103.94	99.77	96.22	93.15
20000	261.54	243.84	229.52	217.72	207.87	199.54	192.43	186.30
30000	392.31	365.76	344.27	326.58	311.80	299.31	288.64	279.45
40000	523.07	487.68	459.03	435.44	415.73	399.07	384.85	372.60
50000	653.84	609.60	573.79	544.30	519.66	498.84	481.06	465.75
60000	784.61	731.52	688.54	653.16	623.59	598.61	577.27	558.90
70000	915.37	853.43	803.30	762.01	727.53	698.37	673.48	652.05
80000	1046.14	975.35	918.06	870.87	831.46	798.14	769.69	745.20
90000	1176.91	1097.27	1032.81	979.73	935.39	897.91	865.90	838.34
100000	1307.67	1219.19	1147.57	1088.59	1039.32	997.67	962.12	931.49
110000	1438.44	1341.11	1262.33	1197.45	1143.25	1097.44	1058.33	1024.64
120000	1569.21	1463.03	1377.08	1306.31	1247.18	1197.21	1154.54	1117.79
130000	1699.97	1584.95	1491.84	1415.17	1351.12	1296.98	1250.75	1210.94
140000	1830.74	1706.86	1606.60	1524.02	1455.05	1396.74	1346.96	1304.09
150000	1961.51	1828.78	1721.35	1632.88	1558.98	1496.51	1443.17	1397.24
160000	2092.27	1950.70	1836.11	1741.74	1662.91	1596.28	1539.38	1490.39
170000	2223.04	2072.62	1950.87	1850.60	1766.84	1696.04	1635.59	1583.54
180000	2353.81	2194.54	2065.62	1959.46	1870.77	1795.81	1731.80	1676.68
190000	2484.57	2316.46	2180.38	2068.32	1974.71	1895.58	1828.01	1769.83
200000	2615.34	2438.37	2295.14	2177.18	2078.64	1995.34	1924.23	1862.98
210000	2746.11	2560.29	2409.89	2286.03	2182.57	2095.11	2020.44	1956.13
220000	2876.87	2682.21	2524.65	2394.89	2286.50	2194.88	2116.65	2049.28
230000	3007.64	2804.13	2639.41	2503.75	2390.43	2294.64	2212.86	2142.43
240000	3138.41	2926.05	2754.16	2612.61	2494.36	2394.41	2309.07	2235.58
250000	3269.17	3047.97	2868.92	2721.47	2598.30	2494.18	2405.28	2328.73
260000	3399.94	3169.89	2983.68	2830.33	2702.23	2593.95	2501.49	2421.87
270000	3530.71	3291.80	3098.43	2939.19	2806.16	2693.71	2597.70	2515.02
280000	3661.47	3413.72	3213.19	3048.04	2910.09	2793.48	2693.91	2608.17
290000	3792.24	3535.64	3327.95	3156.90	3014.02	2893.25	2790.12	2701.32
300000	3923.01	3657.56	3442.70	3265.76	3117.95	2993.01	2886.34	2794.47
310000	4053.77	3779.48	3557.46	3374.62	3221.89	3092.78	2982.55	2887.62
320000	4184.54	3901.40	3672.22	3483.48	3325.82	3192.55	3078.76	2980.77
330000	4315.31	4023.32	3786.97	3592.34	3429.75	3292.31	3174.97	3073.92
340000	4446.07	4145.23	3901.73	3701.19	3533.68	3392.08	3271.18	3167.07
350000	4576.84	4267.15	4016.49	3810.05	3637.61	3491.85	3367.39	3260.21
360000	4707.61	4389.07	4131.24	3918.91	3741.54	3591.62	3463.60	3353.36
370000	4838.37	4510.99	4246.00	4027.77	3845.48	3691.38	3559.81	3446.51
380000	4969.14	4632.91	4360.76	4136.63	3949.41	3791.15	3656.02	3539.66
390000	5099.91	4754.83	4475.51	4245.49	4053.34	3890.92	3752.24	3632.81
400000	5230.67	4876.74	4590.27	4354.35	4157.27	3990.68	3848.45	3725.96

Amount	17	18	19	20	21	22	23	24
25	.23	.23	.22	.22	.21	.21	.21	.20
50	.46	.45	.44	.43	.42	.41	.41	.40
100	.91	.89	.87	.85	.83	.82	.81	.79
200	1.81	1.77	1.73	1.69	1.66	1.63	1.61	1.58
300	2.72	2.65	2.59	2.54	2.49	2.44	2.41	2.37
400	3.62	3.53	3.45	3.38	3.31	3.26	3.21	3.16
500	4.53	4.41	4.31	4.22	4.14	4.07	4.01	3.95
600	5.43	5.30	5.17	5.07	4.97	4.88	4.81	4.74
700	6.34	6.18	6.03	5.91	5.80	5.70	5.61	5.53
800	7.24	7.06	6.90	6.75	6.62	6.51	6.41	6.32
900	8.15	7.94	7.76	7.60	7.45	7.32	7.21	7.11
1000	9.05	8.82	8.62	8.44	8.28	8.14	8.01	7.90
2000	18.10	17.64	17.23	16.87	16.55	16.27	16.02	15.79
3000	27.15	26.46	25.85	25.31	24.83	24.40	24.03	23.69
4000	36.20	35.27	34.46	33.74	33.10	32.54	32.03	31.58
5000	45.25	44.09	43.07	42.18	41.38	40.67	40.04	39.47
6000	54.30	52.91	51.69	50.61	49.65	48.80	48.05	47.37
7000	63.35	61.73	60.30	59.04	57.93	56.94	56.05	55.26
8000	72.40	70.54	68.91	67.48	66.20	65.07	64.06	63.16
9000	81.45	79.36	77.53	75.91	74.48	73.20	72.07	71.05
10000	90.50	88.18	86.14	84.35	82.75	81.34	80.07	78.94
20000	180.99	176.35	172.28	168.69	165.50	162.67	160.14	157.88
30000	271.48	264.52	258.42	253.03	248.25	244.00	240.21	236.82
40000	361.97	352.70	344.55	337.37	331.00	325.34	320.28	315.76
50000	452.47	440.87	430.69	421.71	413.75	406.67	400.35	394.70
60000	542.96	529.04	516.83	506.05	496.50	488.00	480.42	473.63
70000	633.45	617.22	602.96	590.39	579.25	569.33	560.49	552.57
80000	723.94	705.39	689.10	674.73	661.99	650.67	640.56	631.51
90000	814.44	793.56	775.24	759.07	744.74	732.00	720.63	710.45
100000	904.93	881.74	861.37	843.41	827.49	813.33	800.70	789.39
110000	995.42	969.91	947.51	927.75	910.24	894.67	880.77	868.32
120000	1085.91	1058.08	1033.65	1012.09	992.99	976.00	960.84	947.26
130000	1176.41	1146.25	1119.78	1096.43	1075.74	1057.33	1040.91	1026.20
140000	1266.90	1234.43	1205.92	1180.77	1158.49	1138.66	1120.97	1105.14
150000	1357.39	1322.60	1292.06	1265.11	1241.23	1220.00	1201.04	1184.08
160000	1447.88	1410.77	1378.19	1349.45	1323.98	1301.33	1281.11	1263.02
170000	1538.37	1498.95	1464.33	1433.79	1406.73	1382.66	1361.18	1341.95
180000	1628.87	1587.12	1550.47	1518.13	1489.48	1464.00	1441.25	1420.89
190000	1719.36	1675.29	1636.60	1602.47	1572.23	1545.33	1521.32	1499.83
200000	1809.85	1763.47	1722.74	1686.81	1654.98	1626.66	1601.39	1578.77
210000	1900.34	1851.64	1808.88	1771.15	1737.73	1707.99	1681.46	1657.71
220000	1990.84	1939.81	1895.01	1855.49	1820.47	1789.33	1761.53	1736.64
230000	2081.33	2027.98	1981.15	1939.83	1903.22	1870.66	1841.60	1815.58
240000	2171.82	2116.16	2067.29	2024.17	1985.97	1951.99	1921.67	1894.52
250000	2262.31	2204.33	2153.43	2108.51	2068.72	2033.33	2001.74	1973.46
260000	2352.81	2292.50	2239.56	2192.85	2151.47	2114.66	2081.81	2052.40
270000	2443.30	2380.68	2325.70	2277.19	2234.22	2195.99	2161.88	2131.34
280000	2533.79	2468.85	2411.84	2361.54	2316.97	2277.32	2241.94	2210.27
290000	2624.28	2557.02	2497.97	2445.88	2399.71	2358.66	2322.01	2289.21
300000	2714.78	2645.20	2584.11	2530.22	2482.46	2439.99	2402.08	2368.15
310000	2805.27	2733.37	2670.25	2614.56	2565.21	2521.32	2482.15	2447.09
320000	2895.76	2821.54	2756.38	2698.90	2647.96	2602.66	2562.22	2526.03
330000	2986.25	2909.72	2842.52	2783.24	2730.71	2683.99	2642.29	2604.96
340000	3076.74	2997.89	2928.66	2867.58	2813.46	2765.32	2722.36	2683.90
350000	3167.24	3086.06	3014.79	2951.92	2896.21	2846.65	2802.43	2762.84
360000	3257.73	3174.23	3100.93	3036.26	2978.95	2927.99	2882.50	2841.78
370000	3348.22	3262.41	3187.07	3120.60	3061.70	3009.32	2962.57	2920.72
380000	3438.71	3350.58	3273.20	3204.94	3144.45	3090.65	3042.64	2999.66
390000	3529.21	3438.75	3359.34	3289.28	3227.20	3171.99	3122.71	3078.59
400000	3619.70	3526.93	3445.48	3373.62	3309.95	3253.32	3202.78	3157.53

8¼% BLENDED MONTHLY PAYMENTS
AMORTIZATION IN YEARS

Amount	25	26	29	30	35	40	45	50
25	.20	.20	.19	.19	.18	.18	.18	.18
50	.39	.39	.38	.38	.36	.36	.35	.35
100	.78	.78	.75	.75	.72	.71	.70	.69
200	1.56	1.55	1.50	1.49	1.44	1.41	1.39	1.38
300	2.34	2.32	2.25	2.23	2.16	2.12	2.09	2.07
400	3.12	3.09	3.00	2.97	2.88	2.82	2.78	2.76
500	3.90	3.86	3.74	3.71	3.60	3.52	3.48	3.45
600	4.68	4.63	4.49	4.45	4.32	4.23	4.17	4.13
700	5.46	5.40	5.24	5.20	5.03	4.93	4.86	4.82
800	6.24	6.17	5.99	5.94	5.75	5.63	5.56	5.51
900	7.02	6.94	6.73	6.68	6.47	6.34	6.25	6.20
1000	7.80	7.71	7.48	7.42	7.19	7.04	6.95	6.89
2000	15.59	15.41	14.96	14.84	14.37	14.08	13.89	13.77
3000	23.38	23.11	22.44	22.25	21.56	21.12	20.83	20.65
4000	31.17	30.81	29.91	29.67	28.74	28.15	27.77	27.53
5000	38.97	38.51	37.39	37.08	35.92	35.19	34.72	34.41
6000	46.76	46.21	44.87	44.50	43.11	42.23	41.66	41.29
7000	54.55	53.91	52.34	51.91	50.29	49.26	48.60	48.17
8000	62.34	61.61	59.82	59.33	57.48	56.30	55.54	55.05
9000	70.14	69.31	67.30	66.75	64.66	63.34	62.49	61.93
10000	77.93	77.01	74.77	74.16	71.84	70.38	69.43	68.81
20000	155.85	154.02	149.54	148.32	143.68	140.75	138.85	137.62
30000	233.77	231.03	224.31	222.47	215.52	211.12	208.28	206.42
40000	311.70	308.04	299.07	296.63	287.36	281.49	277.70	275.23
50000	389.62	385.05	373.84	370.79	359.20	351.86	347.12	344.03
60000	467.54	462.06	448.61	444.94	431.04	422.23	416.55	412.84
70000	545.47	539.07	523.38	519.10	502.88	492.60	485.97	481.64
80000	623.39	616.08	598.14	593.26	574.71	562.97	555.39	550.45
90000	701.31	693.09	672.91	667.41	646.55	633.34	624.82	619.25
100000	779.23	770.10	747.68	741.57	718.39	703.71	694.24	688.06
110000	857.16	847.11	822.45	815.73	790.23	774.08	763.66	756.86
120000	935.08	924.12	897.21	889.88	862.07	844.45	833.09	825.67
130000	1013.00	1001.13	971.98	964.04	933.91	914.82	902.51	894.48
140000	1090.93	1078.14	1046.75	1038.20	1005.75	985.19	971.93	963.28
150000	1168.85	1155.14	1121.52	1112.35	1077.59	1055.56	1041.36	1032.09
160000	1246.77	1232.15	1196.28	1186.51	1149.42	1125.93	1110.78	1100.89
170000	1324.69	1309.16	1271.05	1260.66	1221.26	1196.30	1180.21	1169.70
180000	1402.62	1386.17	1345.82	1334.82	1293.10	1266.68	1249.63	1238.50
190000	1480.54	1463.18	1420.58	1408.98	1364.94	1337.05	1319.05	1307.31
200000	1558.46	1540.19	1495.35	1483.13	1436.78	1407.42	1388.48	1376.11
210000	1636.39	1617.20	1570.12	1557.29	1508.62	1477.79	1457.90	1444.92
220000	1714.31	1694.21	1644.89	1631.45	1580.46	1548.16	1527.32	1513.72
230000	1792.23	1771.22	1719.65	1705.60	1652.29	1618.53	1596.75	1582.53
240000	1870.15	1848.23	1794.42	1779.76	1724.13	1688.90	1666.17	1651.34
250000	1948.08	1925.24	1869.19	1853.92	1795.97	1759.27	1735.59	1720.14
260000	2026.00	2002.25	1943.96	1928.07	1867.81	1829.64	1805.02	1788.95
270000	2103.92	2079.26	2018.72	2002.23	1939.65	1900.01	1874.44	1857.75
280000	2181.85	2156.27	2093.49	2076.39	2011.49	1970.38	1943.86	1926.56
290000	2259.77	2233.28	2168.26	2150.54	2083.33	2040.75	2013.29	1995.36
300000	2337.69	2310.28	2243.03	2224.70	2155.17	2111.12	2082.71	2064.17
310000	2415.61	2387.29	2317.79	2298.86	2227.00	2181.49	2152.13	2132.97
320000	2493.54	2464.30	2392.56	2373.01	2298.84	2251.86	2221.56	2201.78
330000	2571.46	2541.31	2467.33	2447.17	2370.68	2322.23	2290.98	2270.58
340000	2649.38	2618.32	2542.09	2521.32	2442.52	2392.60	2360.41	2339.39
350000	2727.31	2695.33	2616.86	2595.48	2514.36	2462.97	2429.83	2408.20
360000	2805.23	2772.34	2691.63	2669.64	2586.20	2533.35	2499.25	2477.00
370000	2883.15	2849.35	2766.40	2743.79	2658.04	2603.72	2568.68	2545.81
380000	2961.07	2926.36	2841.16	2817.95	2729.88	2674.09	2638.10	2614.61
390000	3039.00	3003.37	2915.93	2892.11	2801.71	2744.46	2707.52	2683.42
400000	3116.92	3080.38	2990.70	2966.26	2873.55	2814.83	2776.95	2752.22

92

BLENDED MONTHLY PAYMENTS 8½%
AMORTIZATION IN YEARS

Amount	1	2	3	4	5	6	7	8
25	2.18	1.14	.79	.62	.52	.45	.40	.36
50	4.36	2.27	1.58	1.23	1.03	.89	.79	.72
100	8.72	4.54	3.15	2.46	2.05	1.78	1.58	1.44
200	17.44	9.08	6.30	4.92	4.09	3.55	3.16	2.87
300	26.15	13.62	9.45	7.38	6.14	5.32	4.73	4.30
400	34.87	18.16	12.60	9.84	8.18	7.09	6.31	5.73
500	43.58	22.70	15.75	12.29	10.23	8.86	7.89	7.16
600	52.30	27.24	18.90	14.75	12.27	10.63	9.46	8.60
700	61.01	31.78	22.05	17.21	14.32	12.40	11.04	10.03
800	69.73	36.32	25.20	19.67	16.36	14.17	12.62	11.46
900	78.44	40.85	28.35	22.13	18.41	15.94	14.19	12.89
1000	87.16	45.39	31.50	24.58	20.45	17.71	15.77	14.32
2000	174.31	90.78	63.00	49.16	40.90	35.42	31.53	28.64
3000	261.46	136.17	94.50	73.74	61.34	53.12	47.29	42.96
4000	348.61	181.56	126.00	98.32	81.79	70.83	63.06	57.27
5000	435.76	226.95	157.50	122.90	102.23	88.54	78.82	71.59
6000	522.92	272.34	189.00	147.48	122.68	106.24	94.58	85.91
7000	610.07	317.73	220.50	172.06	143.13	123.95	110.34	100.22
8000	697.22	363.11	252.00	196.64	163.57	141.65	126.11	114.54
9000	784.37	408.50	283.50	221.22	184.02	159.36	141.87	128.86
10000	871.52	453.89	315.00	245.80	204.46	177.07	157.63	143.17
20000	1743.04	907.78	630.00	491.59	408.92	354.13	315.26	286.34
30000	2614.56	1361.66	944.99	737.38	613.38	531.19	472.89	429.51
40000	3486.08	1815.55	1259.99	983.17	817.84	708.25	630.52	572.68
50000	4357.60	2269.43	1574.98	1228.96	1022.30	885.32	788.15	715.85
60000	5229.12	2723.32	1889.98	1474.75	1226.76	1062.38	945.77	859.02
70000	6100.63	3177.21	2204.98	1720.54	1431.22	1239.44	1103.40	1002.19
80000	6972.15	3631.09	2519.97	1966.33	1635.68	1416.50	1261.03	1145.36
90000	7843.67	4084.98	2834.97	2212.12	1840.13	1593.57	1418.66	1288.53
100000	8715.19	4538.86	3149.96	2457.91	2044.59	1770.63	1576.29	1431.69
110000	9586.71	4992.75	3464.96	2703.70	2249.05	1947.69	1733.91	1574.86
120000	10458.23	5446.64	3779.96	2949.50	2453.51	2124.75	1891.54	1718.03
130000	11329.75	5900.52	4094.95	3195.29	2657.97	2301.82	2049.17	1861.20
140000	12201.26	6354.41	4409.95	3441.08	2862.43	2478.88	2206.80	2004.37
150000	13072.78	6808.29	4724.94	3686.87	3066.89	2655.94	2364.43	2147.54
160000	13944.30	7262.18	5039.94	3932.66	3271.35	2833.00	2522.05	2290.71
170000	14815.82	7716.06	5354.94	4178.45	3475.81	3010.07	2679.68	2433.88
180000	15687.34	8169.95	5669.93	4424.24	3680.26	3187.13	2837.31	2577.05
190000	16558.86	8623.84	5984.93	4670.03	3884.72	3364.19	2994.94	2720.21
200000	17430.38	9077.72	6299.92	4915.82	4089.18	3541.25	3152.57	2863.38
210000	18301.89	9531.61	6614.92	5161.61	4293.64	3718.32	3310.19	3006.55
220000	19173.41	9985.49	6929.92	5407.40	4498.10	3895.38	3467.82	3149.72
230000	20044.93	10439.38	7244.91	5653.20	4702.56	4072.44	3625.45	3292.89
240000	20916.45	10893.27	7559.91	5898.99	4907.02	4249.50	3783.08	3436.06
250000	21787.97	11347.15	7874.90	6144.78	5111.48	4426.56	3940.71	3579.23
260000	22659.49	11801.04	8189.90	6390.57	5315.94	4603.63	4098.33	3722.40
270000	23531.01	12254.92	8504.90	6636.36	5520.39	4780.69	4255.96	3865.57
280000	24402.52	12708.81	8819.89	6882.15	5724.85	4957.75	4413.59	4008.74
290000	25274.04	13162.69	9134.89	7127.94	5929.31	5134.81	4571.22	4151.90
300000	26145.56	13616.58	9449.88	7373.73	6133.77	5311.88	4728.85	4295.07
310000	27017.08	14070.47	9764.88	7619.52	6338.23	5488.94	4886.47	4438.24
320000	27888.60	14524.35	10079.87	7865.31	6542.69	5666.00	5044.10	4581.41
330000	28760.12	14978.24	10394.87	8111.10	6747.15	5843.06	5201.73	4724.58
340000	29631.64	15432.12	10709.87	8356.90	6951.61	6020.13	5359.36	4867.75
350000	30503.15	15886.01	11024.86	8602.69	7156.07	6197.19	5516.99	5010.92
360000	31374.67	16339.90	11339.86	8848.48	7360.52	6374.25	5674.61	5154.09
370000	32246.19	16793.78	11654.85	9094.27	7564.98	6551.31	5832.24	5297.26
380000	33117.71	17247.67	11969.85	9340.06	7769.44	6728.38	5989.87	5440.42
390000	33989.23	17701.55	12284.85	9585.85	7973.90	6905.44	6147.50	5583.59
400000	34860.75	18155.44	12599.84	9831.64	8178.36	7082.50	6305.13	5726.76

93

8½% BLENDED MONTHLY PAYMENTS
AMORTIZATION IN YEARS

Amount	9	10	11	12	13	14	15	16
25	.34	.31	.30	.28	.27	.26	.25	.24
50	.67	.62	.59	.56	.53	.51	.49	.48
100	1.33	1.24	1.17	1.11	1.06	1.02	.98	.95
200	2.65	2.47	2.33	2.21	2.11	2.03	1.96	1.90
300	3.97	3.70	3.49	3.31	3.16	3.04	2.93	2.84
400	5.29	4.93	4.65	4.41	4.22	4.05	3.91	3.79
500	6.61	6.17	5.81	5.51	5.27	5.06	4.89	4.73
600	7.93	7.40	6.97	6.62	6.32	6.07	5.86	5.68
700	9.25	8.63	8.13	7.72	7.38	7.09	6.84	6.63
800	10.57	9.86	9.29	8.82	8.43	8.10	7.81	7.57
900	11.89	11.09	10.45	9.92	9.48	9.11	8.79	8.52
1000	13.21	12.33	11.61	11.02	10.53	10.12	9.77	9.46
2000	26.41	24.65	23.22	22.04	21.06	20.23	19.53	18.92
3000	39.61	36.97	34.82	33.06	31.59	30.35	29.29	28.38
4000	52.82	49.29	46.43	44.08	42.12	40.46	39.05	37.84
5000	66.02	61.61	58.04	55.10	52.65	50.58	48.81	47.29
6000	79.22	73.93	69.64	66.12	63.18	60.69	58.57	56.75
7000	92.42	86.25	81.25	77.14	73.71	70.81	68.34	66.21
8000	105.63	98.57	92.86	88.16	84.24	80.92	78.10	75.67
9000	118.83	110.89	104.46	99.18	94.77	91.04	87.86	85.12
10000	132.03	123.21	116.07	110.20	105.29	101.15	97.62	94.58
20000	264.06	246.41	232.14	220.39	210.58	202.30	195.24	189.16
30000	396.08	369.61	348.20	330.58	315.87	303.45	292.85	283.74
40000	528.11	492.81	464.27	440.77	421.16	404.60	390.47	378.31
50000	660.13	616.02	580.33	550.96	526.45	505.75	488.08	472.89
60000	792.16	739.22	696.40	661.15	631.74	606.89	585.70	567.47
70000	924.18	862.42	812.46	771.35	737.03	708.04	683.32	662.04
80000	1056.21	985.62	928.53	881.54	842.32	809.19	780.93	756.62
90000	1188.24	1108.83	1044.59	991.73	947.61	910.34	878.55	851.20
100000	1320.26	1232.03	1160.66	1101.92	1052.90	1011.49	976.16	945.77
110000	1452.29	1355.23	1276.72	1212.11	1158.18	1112.64	1073.78	1040.35
120000	1584.31	1478.43	1392.79	1322.30	1263.47	1213.78	1171.39	1134.93
130000	1716.34	1601.64	1508.85	1432.50	1368.76	1314.93	1269.01	1229.50
140000	1848.36	1724.84	1624.92	1542.69	1474.05	1416.08	1366.63	1324.08
150000	1980.39	1848.04	1740.98	1652.88	1579.34	1517.23	1464.24	1418.66
160000	2112.42	1971.24	1857.05	1763.07	1684.63	1618.38	1561.86	1513.23
170000	2244.44	2094.44	1973.11	1873.26	1789.92	1719.52	1659.47	1607.81
180000	2376.47	2217.65	2089.18	1983.45	1895.21	1820.67	1757.09	1702.39
190000	2508.49	2340.85	2205.24	2093.65	2000.50	1921.82	1854.70	1796.96
200000	2640.52	2464.05	2321.31	2203.84	2105.79	2022.97	1952.32	1891.54
210000	2772.54	2587.25	2437.37	2314.03	2211.07	2124.12	2049.94	1986.12
220000	2904.57	2710.46	2553.44	2424.22	2316.36	2225.27	2147.55	2080.69
230000	3036.59	2833.66	2669.50	2534.41	2421.65	2326.41	2245.17	2175.27
240000	3168.62	2956.86	2785.57	2644.60	2526.94	2427.56	2342.78	2269.85
250000	3300.65	3080.06	2901.64	2754.80	2632.23	2528.71	2440.40	2364.42
260000	3432.67	3203.27	3017.70	2864.99	2737.52	2629.86	2538.02	2459.00
270000	3564.70	3326.47	3133.77	2975.18	2842.81	2731.01	2635.63	2553.58
280000	3696.72	3449.67	3249.83	3085.37	2948.10	2832.15	2733.25	2648.15
290000	3828.75	3572.87	3365.90	3195.56	3053.39	2933.30	2830.86	2742.73
300000	3960.77	3696.08	3481.96	3305.75	3158.68	3034.45	2928.48	2837.31
310000	4092.80	3819.28	3598.03	3415.95	3263.96	3135.60	3026.09	2931.88
320000	4224.83	3942.48	3714.09	3526.14	3369.25	3236.75	3123.71	3026.46
330000	4356.85	4065.68	3830.16	3636.33	3474.54	3337.90	3221.33	3121.04
340000	4488.88	4188.88	3946.22	3746.52	3579.83	3439.04	3318.94	3215.61
350000	4620.90	4312.09	4062.29	3856.71	3685.12	3540.19	3416.56	3310.19
360000	4752.93	4435.29	4178.35	3966.90	3790.41	3641.34	3514.17	3404.77
370000	4884.95	4558.49	4294.42	4077.10	3895.70	3742.49	3611.79	3499.34
380000	5016.98	4681.69	4410.48	4187.29	4000.99	3843.64	3709.40	3593.92
390000	5149.01	4804.90	4526.55	4297.48	4106.28	3944.78	3807.02	3688.50
400000	5281.03	4928.10	4642.61	4407.67	4211.57	4045.93	3904.64	3783.07

BLENDED MONTHLY PAYMENTS 8½%
AMORTIZATION IN YEARS

Amount	17	18	19	20	21	22	23	24
25	.23	.23	.22	.22	.22	.21	.21	.21
50	.46	.45	.44	.43	.43	.42	.41	.41
100	.92	.90	.88	.86	.85	.83	.82	.81
200	1.84	1.80	1.76	1.72	1.69	1.66	1.64	1.62
300	2.76	2.69	2.63	2.58	2.53	2.49	2.45	2.42
400	3.68	3.59	3.51	3.44	3.38	3.32	3.27	3.23
500	4.60	4.49	4.39	4.30	4.22	4.15	4.09	4.03
600	5.52	5.38	5.26	5.16	5.06	4.98	4.90	4.84
700	6.44	6.28	6.14	6.01	5.90	5.81	5.72	5.64
800	7.36	7.18	7.02	6.87	6.75	6.64	6.54	6.45
900	8.28	8.07	7.89	7.73	7.59	7.47	7.35	7.25
1000	9.20	8.97	8.77	8.59	8.43	8.29	8.17	8.06
2000	18.39	17.93	17.53	17.18	16.86	16.58	16.33	16.11
3000	27.59	26.90	26.29	25.76	25.29	24.87	24.50	24.16
4000	36.78	35.86	35.06	34.35	33.72	33.16	32.66	32.22
5000	45.98	44.83	43.82	42.93	42.15	41.45	40.83	40.27
6000	55.17	53.79	52.58	51.52	50.58	49.74	48.99	48.32
7000	64.36	62.76	61.35	60.10	59.00	58.03	57.16	56.38
8000	73.56	71.72	70.11	68.69	67.43	66.32	65.32	64.43
9000	82.75	80.69	78.87	77.28	75.86	74.61	73.49	72.48
10000	91.95	89.65	87.64	85.86	84.29	82.89	81.65	80.54
20000	183.89	179.30	175.27	171.72	168.57	165.78	163.30	161.07
30000	275.83	268.94	262.90	257.57	252.86	248.67	244.94	241.60
40000	367.78	358.59	350.53	343.43	337.14	331.56	326.59	322.14
50000	459.72	448.23	438.16	429.28	421.43	414.45	408.23	402.67
60000	551.66	537.88	525.79	515.14	505.71	497.34	489.88	483.20
70000	643.60	627.52	613.42	601.00	590.00	580.23	571.52	563.74
80000	735.55	717.17	701.05	686.85	674.28	663.12	653.17	644.27
90000	827.49	806.82	788.69	772.71	758.57	746.01	734.81	724.80
100000	919.43	896.46	876.32	858.56	842.85	828.90	816.46	805.34
110000	1011.38	986.11	963.95	944.42	927.14	911.79	898.10	885.87
120000	1103.32	1075.75	1051.58	1030.28	1011.42	994.68	979.75	966.40
130000	1195.26	1165.40	1139.21	1116.13	1095.71	1077.56	1061.39	1046.94
140000	1287.20	1255.04	1226.84	1201.99	1179.99	1160.45	1143.04	1127.47
150000	1379.15	1344.69	1314.47	1287.84	1264.28	1243.34	1224.68	1208.00
160000	1471.09	1434.34	1402.10	1373.70	1348.56	1326.23	1306.33	1288.54
170000	1563.03	1523.98	1489.74	1459.56	1432.85	1409.12	1387.97	1369.07
180000	1654.98	1613.63	1577.37	1545.41	1517.13	1492.01	1469.62	1449.60
190000	1746.92	1703.27	1665.00	1631.27	1601.42	1574.90	1551.26	1530.14
200000	1838.86	1792.92	1752.63	1717.12	1685.70	1657.79	1632.91	1610.67
210000	1930.80	1882.56	1840.26	1802.98	1769.99	1740.68	1714.55	1691.20
220000	2022.75	1972.21	1927.89	1888.84	1854.27	1823.57	1796.20	1771.73
230000	2114.69	2061.86	2015.52	1974.69	1938.56	1906.46	1877.85	1852.27
240000	2206.63	2151.50	2103.15	2060.55	2022.84	1989.35	1959.49	1932.80
250000	2298.58	2241.15	2190.78	2146.40	2107.13	2072.23	2041.14	2013.33
260000	2390.52	2330.79	2278.42	2232.26	2191.41	2155.12	2122.78	2093.87
270000	2482.46	2420.44	2366.05	2318.11	2275.70	2238.01	2204.43	2174.40
280000	2574.40	2510.08	2453.68	2403.97	2359.98	2320.90	2286.07	2254.93
290000	2666.35	2599.73	2541.31	2489.83	2444.27	2403.79	2367.72	2335.47
300000	2758.29	2689.38	2628.94	2575.68	2528.55	2486.68	2449.36	2416.00
310000	2850.23	2779.02	2716.57	2661.54	2612.83	2569.57	2531.01	2496.53
320000	2942.18	2868.67	2804.20	2747.39	2697.12	2652.46	2612.65	2577.07
330000	3034.12	2958.31	2891.83	2833.25	2781.40	2735.35	2694.30	2657.60
340000	3126.06	3047.96	2979.47	2919.11	2865.69	2818.24	2775.94	2738.13
350000	3218.00	3137.60	3067.10	3004.96	2949.97	2901.13	2857.59	2818.67
360000	3309.95	3227.25	3154.73	3090.82	3034.26	2984.02	2939.23	2899.20
370000	3401.89	3316.90	3242.36	3176.67	3118.54	3066.90	3020.88	2979.73
380000	3493.83	3406.54	3329.99	3262.53	3202.83	3149.79	3102.52	3060.27
390000	3585.78	3496.19	3417.62	3348.39	3287.11	3232.68	3184.17	3140.80
400000	3677.72	3585.83	3505.25	3434.24	3371.40	3315.57	3265.81	3221.33

8½% BLENDED MONTHLY PAYMENTS
AMORTIZATION IN YEARS

Amount	25	26	29	30	35	40	45	50
25	.20	.20	.20	.19	.19	.19	.18	.18
50	.40	.40	.39	.38	.37	.37	.36	.36
100	.80	.79	.77	.76	.74	.73	.72	.71
200	1.60	1.58	1.53	1.52	1.48	1.45	1.43	1.42
300	2.39	2.36	2.30	2.28	2.21	2.17	2.14	2.13
400	3.19	3.15	3.06	3.04	2.95	2.89	2.86	2.83
500	3.98	3.94	3.83	3.80	3.69	3.61	3.57	3.54
600	4.78	4.72	4.59	4.56	4.42	4.34	4.28	4.25
700	5.57	5.51	5.36	5.31	5.16	5.06	5.00	4.95
800	6.37	6.30	6.12	6.07	5.89	5.78	5.71	5.66
900	7.16	7.08	6.89	6.83	6.63	6.50	6.42	6.37
1000	7.96	7.87	7.65	7.59	7.37	7.22	7.13	7.08
2000	15.91	15.73	15.29	15.18	14.73	14.44	14.26	14.15
3000	23.87	23.60	22.94	22.76	22.09	21.66	21.39	21.22
4000	31.82	31.46	30.58	30.35	29.45	28.88	28.52	28.29
5000	39.77	39.33	38.23	37.93	36.81	36.10	35.65	35.36
6000	47.73	47.19	45.87	45.52	44.17	43.32	42.78	42.43
7000	55.68	55.05	53.52	53.10	51.53	50.54	49.91	49.50
8000	63.63	62.92	61.16	60.69	58.89	57.76	57.04	56.57
9000	71.59	70.78	68.81	68.27	66.25	64.98	64.17	63.65
10000	79.54	78.65	76.45	75.86	73.61	72.20	71.30	70.72
20000	159.08	157.29	152.90	151.71	147.22	144.40	142.59	141.43
30000	238.61	235.93	229.35	227.57	220.82	216.59	213.89	212.14
40000	318.15	314.57	305.80	303.42	294.43	288.79	285.18	282.85
50000	397.69	393.21	382.25	379.27	368.04	360.98	356.48	353.56
60000	477.22	471.85	458.70	455.13	441.64	433.18	427.77	424.28
70000	556.76	550.49	535.15	530.98	515.25	505.37	499.06	494.99
80000	636.30	629.13	611.60	606.84	588.86	577.57	570.36	565.70
90000	715.83	707.77	688.05	682.69	662.46	649.76	641.65	636.41
100000	795.37	786.41	764.50	758.54	736.07	721.96	712.95	707.12
110000	874.90	865.05	840.95	834.40	809.67	794.15	784.24	777.84
120000	954.44	943.69	917.39	910.25	883.28	866.35	855.53	848.55
130000	1033.98	1022.33	993.84	986.11	956.89	938.55	926.83	919.26
140000	1113.51	1100.97	1070.29	1061.96	1030.49	1010.74	998.12	989.97
150000	1193.05	1179.62	1146.74	1137.81	1104.10	1082.94	1069.42	1060.68
160000	1272.59	1258.26	1223.19	1213.67	1177.71	1155.13	1140.71	1131.39
170000	1352.12	1336.90	1299.64	1289.52	1251.31	1227.33	1212.00	1202.11
180000	1431.66	1415.54	1376.09	1365.38	1324.92	1299.52	1283.30	1272.82
190000	1511.20	1494.18	1452.54	1441.23	1398.52	1371.72	1354.59	1343.53
200000	1590.73	1572.82	1528.99	1517.08	1472.13	1443.91	1425.89	1414.24
210000	1670.27	1651.46	1605.44	1592.94	1545.74	1516.11	1497.18	1484.95
220000	1749.80	1730.10	1681.89	1668.79	1619.34	1588.30	1568.48	1555.67
230000	1829.34	1808.74	1758.33	1744.65	1692.95	1660.50	1639.77	1626.38
240000	1908.88	1887.38	1834.78	1820.50	1766.56	1732.69	1711.06	1697.09
250000	1988.41	1966.02	1911.23	1896.35	1840.16	1804.89	1782.36	1767.80
260000	2067.95	2044.66	1987.68	1972.21	1913.77	1877.09	1853.65	1838.51
270000	2147.49	2123.30	2064.13	2048.06	1987.38	1949.28	1924.95	1909.23
280000	2227.02	2201.94	2140.58	2123.91	2060.98	2021.48	1996.24	1979.94
290000	2306.56	2280.59	2217.03	2199.77	2134.59	2093.67	2067.53	2050.65
300000	2386.10	2359.23	2293.48	2275.62	2208.19	2165.87	2138.83	2121.36
310000	2465.63	2437.87	2369.93	2351.48	2281.80	2238.06	2210.12	2192.07
320000	2545.17	2516.51	2446.38	2427.33	2355.41	2310.26	2281.42	2262.78
330000	2624.70	2595.15	2522.83	2503.18	2429.01	2382.45	2352.71	2333.50
340000	2704.24	2673.79	2599.28	2579.04	2502.62	2454.65	2424.00	2404.21
350000	2783.78	2752.43	2675.72	2654.89	2576.23	2526.84	2495.30	2474.92
360000	2863.31	2831.07	2752.17	2730.75	2649.83	2599.04	2566.59	2545.63
370000	2942.85	2909.71	2828.62	2806.60	2723.44	2671.24	2637.89	2616.34
380000	3022.39	2988.35	2905.07	2882.45	2797.04	2743.43	2709.18	2687.06
390000	3101.92	3066.99	2981.52	2958.31	2870.65	2815.63	2780.47	2757.77
400000	3181.46	3145.63	3057.97	3034.16	2944.26	2887.82	2851.77	2828.48

BLENDED MONTHLY PAYMENTS 8¾%

AMORTIZATION IN YEARS

Amount	1	2	3	4	5	6	7	8
25	2.19	1.14	.80	.62	.52	.45	.40	.37
50	4.37	2.28	1.59	1.24	1.03	.90	.80	.73
100	8.73	4.55	3.17	2.47	2.06	1.79	1.59	1.45
200	17.46	9.10	6.33	4.94	4.12	3.57	3.18	2.89
300	26.18	13.65	9.49	7.41	6.17	5.35	4.77	4.34
400	34.91	18.20	12.65	9.88	8.23	7.14	6.36	5.78
500	43.64	22.75	15.81	12.35	10.29	8.92	7.95	7.23
600	52.36	27.30	18.97	14.82	12.34	10.70	9.54	8.67
700	61.09	31.85	22.13	17.29	14.40	12.48	11.12	10.11
800	69.82	36.40	25.29	19.76	16.45	14.27	12.71	11.56
900	78.54	40.95	28.46	22.23	18.51	16.05	14.30	13.00
1000	87.27	45.50	31.62	24.70	20.57	17.83	15.89	14.45
2000	174.53	91.00	63.23	49.39	41.13	35.66	31.77	28.89
3000	261.80	136.50	94.84	74.08	61.69	53.48	47.66	43.33
4000	349.06	182.00	126.45	98.78	82.25	71.31	63.54	57.77
5000	436.32	227.50	158.06	123.47	102.82	89.13	79.43	72.21
6000	523.59	273.00	189.67	148.16	123.38	106.96	95.31	86.65
7000	610.85	318.50	221.28	172.86	143.94	124.78	111.19	101.09
8000	698.11	364.00	252.90	197.55	164.50	142.61	127.08	115.53
9000	785.38	409.50	284.51	222.24	185.06	160.43	142.96	129.97
10000	872.64	454.99	316.12	246.94	205.63	178.26	158.85	144.41
20000	1745.28	909.98	632.23	493.87	411.25	356.51	317.69	288.82
30000	2617.91	1364.97	948.35	740.80	616.87	534.76	476.53	433.23
40000	3490.55	1819.96	1264.46	987.73	822.49	713.01	635.37	577.64
50000	4363.19	2274.95	1580.58	1234.66	1028.11	891.26	794.21	722.04
60000	5235.82	2729.94	1896.69	1481.59	1233.74	1069.51	953.05	866.45
70000	6108.46	3184.93	2212.80	1728.52	1439.36	1247.76	1111.89	1010.86
80000	6981.09	3639.92	2528.92	1975.45	1644.98	1426.01	1270.73	1155.27
90000	7853.73	4094.91	2845.03	2222.38	1850.60	1604.26	1429.58	1299.67
100000	8726.37	4549.90	3161.15	2469.31	2056.22	1782.51	1588.42	1444.08
110000	9599.00	5004.89	3477.26	2716.24	2261.84	1960.76	1747.26	1588.49
120000	10471.64	5459.88	3793.37	2963.17	2467.47	2139.01	1906.10	1732.90
130000	11344.27	5914.87	4109.49	3210.10	2673.09	2317.26	2064.94	1877.31
140000	12216.91	6369.86	4425.60	3457.03	2878.71	2495.51	2223.78	2021.71
150000	13089.55	6824.85	4741.72	3703.96	3084.33	2673.76	2382.62	2166.12
160000	13962.18	7279.84	5057.83	3950.89	3289.95	2852.01	2541.46	2310.53
170000	14834.82	7734.83	5373.94	4197.82	3495.57	3030.26	2700.30	2454.94
180000	15707.45	8189.82	5690.06	4444.75	3701.20	3208.51	2859.15	2599.34
190000	16580.09	8644.81	6006.17	4691.68	3906.82	3386.76	3017.99	2743.75
200000	17452.73	9099.80	6322.29	4938.61	4112.44	3565.01	3176.83	2888.16
210000	18325.36	9554.79	6638.40	5185.54	4318.06	3743.26	3335.67	3032.57
220000	19198.00	10009.78	6954.51	5432.47	4523.68	3921.51	3494.51	3176.97
230000	20070.63	10464.77	7270.63	5679.40	4729.30	4099.76	3653.35	3321.38
240000	20943.27	10919.76	7586.74	5926.33	4934.93	4278.01	3812.19	3465.79
250000	21815.91	11374.75	7902.86	6173.26	5140.55	4456.26	3971.03	3610.20
260000	22688.54	11829.74	8218.97	6420.19	5346.17	4634.51	4129.87	3754.61
270000	23561.18	12284.73	8535.08	6667.12	5551.79	4812.76	4288.72	3899.01
280000	24433.82	12739.72	8851.20	6914.05	5757.41	4991.01	4447.56	4043.42
290000	25306.45	13194.71	9167.31	7160.98	5963.03	5169.26	4606.40	4187.83
300000	26179.09	13649.70	9483.43	7407.91	6168.66	5347.51	4765.24	4332.24
310000	27051.72	14104.69	9799.54	7654.84	6374.28	5525.76	4924.08	4476.64
320000	27924.36	14559.68	10115.65	7901.77	6579.90	5704.01	5082.92	4621.05
330000	28797.00	15014.67	10431.77	8148.70	6785.52	5882.26	5241.76	4765.46
340000	29669.63	15469.66	10747.88	8395.63	6991.14	6060.51	5400.60	4909.87
350000	30542.27	15924.65	11064.00	8642.56	7196.76	6238.76	5559.44	5054.28
360000	31414.90	16379.64	11380.11	8889.49	7402.39	6417.01	5718.29	5198.68
370000	32287.54	16834.63	11696.22	9136.42	7608.01	6595.26	5877.13	5343.09
380000	33160.18	17289.62	12012.34	9383.35	7813.63	6773.51	6035.97	5487.50
390000	34032.81	17744.61	12328.45	9630.28	8019.25	6951.76	6194.81	5631.91
400000	34905.45	18199.60	12644.57	9877.21	8224.87	7130.01	6353.65	5776.31

8¾% BLENDED MONTHLY PAYMENTS
AMORTIZATION IN YEARS

Amount	9	10	11	12	13	14	15	16
25	.34	.32	.30	.28	.27	.26	.25	.25
50	.67	.63	.59	.56	.54	.52	.50	.49
100	1.34	1.25	1.18	1.12	1.07	1.03	1.00	.97
200	2.67	2.49	2.35	2.24	2.14	2.06	1.99	1.93
300	4.00	3.74	3.53	3.35	3.20	3.08	2.98	2.89
400	5.34	4.98	4.70	4.47	4.27	4.11	3.97	3.85
500	6.67	6.23	5.87	5.58	5.34	5.13	4.96	4.81
600	8.00	7.47	7.05	6.70	6.40	6.16	5.95	5.77
700	9.34	8.72	8.22	7.81	7.47	7.18	6.94	6.73
800	10.67	9.96	9.40	8.93	8.54	8.21	7.93	7.69
900	12.00	11.21	10.57	10.04	9.60	9.23	8.92	8.65
1000	13.33	12.45	11.74	11.16	10.67	10.26	9.91	9.61
2000	26.66	24.90	23.48	22.31	21.34	20.51	19.81	19.21
3000	39.99	37.35	35.22	33.46	32.00	30.77	29.71	28.81
4000	53.32	49.80	46.96	44.62	42.67	41.02	39.62	38.41
5000	66.65	62.25	58.70	55.77	53.33	51.27	49.52	48.01
6000	79.98	74.70	70.43	66.92	64.00	61.53	59.42	57.61
7000	93.31	87.15	82.17	78.08	74.66	71.78	69.33	67.21
8000	106.64	99.60	93.91	89.23	85.33	82.04	79.23	76.82
9000	119.97	112.05	105.65	100.38	95.99	92.29	89.13	86.42
10000	133.30	124.50	117.39	111.54	106.66	102.54	99.03	96.02
20000	266.59	248.99	234.77	223.07	213.31	205.08	198.06	192.03
30000	399.88	373.48	352.15	334.60	319.97	307.62	297.09	288.05
40000	533.17	497.97	469.53	446.13	426.62	410.16	396.12	384.06
50000	666.46	622.47	586.91	557.67	533.28	512.69	495.15	480.07
60000	799.75	746.96	704.29	669.20	639.93	615.23	594.18	576.09
70000	933.04	871.45	821.67	780.73	746.59	717.77	693.21	672.10
80000	1066.33	995.94	939.05	892.26	853.24	820.31	792.24	768.12
90000	1199.62	1120.44	1056.43	1003.79	959.89	922.85	891.27	864.13
100000	1332.91	1244.93	1173.81	1115.33	1066.55	1025.38	990.30	960.14
110000	1466.20	1369.42	1291.19	1226.86	1173.20	1127.92	1089.33	1056.16
120000	1599.49	1493.91	1408.57	1338.39	1279.86	1230.46	1188.36	1152.17
130000	1732.78	1618.41	1525.95	1449.92	1386.51	1333.00	1287.39	1248.19
140000	1866.07	1742.90	1643.33	1561.46	1493.17	1435.54	1386.42	1344.20
150000	1999.36	1867.39	1760.71	1672.99	1599.82	1538.07	1485.45	1440.21
160000	2132.65	1991.88	1878.10	1784.52	1706.47	1640.61	1584.48	1536.23
170000	2265.94	2116.38	1995.48	1896.05	1813.13	1743.15	1683.51	1632.24
180000	2399.23	2240.87	2112.86	2007.58	1919.78	1845.69	1782.54	1728.25
190000	2532.52	2365.36	2230.24	2119.12	2026.44	1948.22	1881.56	1824.27
200000	2665.81	2489.85	2347.62	2230.65	2133.09	2050.76	1980.59	1920.28
210000	2799.10	2614.34	2465.00	2342.18	2239.75	2153.30	2079.62	2016.30
220000	2932.39	2738.84	2582.38	2453.71	2346.40	2255.84	2178.65	2112.31
230000	3065.68	2863.33	2699.76	2565.25	2453.05	2358.38	2277.68	2208.32
240000	3198.97	2987.82	2817.14	2676.78	2559.71	2460.91	2376.71	2304.34
250000	3332.26	3112.31	2934.52	2788.31	2666.36	2563.45	2475.74	2400.35
260000	3465.55	3236.81	3051.90	2899.84	2773.02	2665.99	2574.77	2496.37
270000	3598.84	3361.30	3169.28	3011.37	2879.67	2768.53	2673.80	2592.38
280000	3732.13	3485.79	3286.66	3122.91	2986.33	2871.07	2772.83	2688.39
290000	3865.42	3610.28	3404.04	3234.44	3092.98	2973.60	2871.86	2784.41
300000	3998.71	3734.78	3521.42	3345.97	3199.63	3076.14	2970.89	2880.42
310000	4132.00	3859.27	3638.80	3457.50	3306.29	3178.68	3069.92	2976.43
320000	4265.29	3983.76	3756.19	3569.03	3412.94	3281.22	3168.95	3072.45
330000	4398.58	4108.25	3873.57	3680.57	3519.60	3383.76	3267.98	3168.46
340000	4531.87	4232.75	3990.95	3792.10	3626.25	3486.29	3367.01	3264.48
350000	4665.16	4357.24	4108.33	3903.63	3732.91	3588.83	3466.04	3360.49
360000	4798.45	4481.73	4225.71	4015.16	3839.56	3691.37	3565.07	3456.50
370000	4931.74	4606.22	4343.09	4126.70	3946.21	3793.91	3664.09	3552.52
380000	5065.03	4730.72	4460.47	4238.23	4052.87	3896.44	3763.12	3648.53
390000	5198.32	4855.21	4577.85	4349.76	4159.52	3998.98	3862.15	3744.55
400000	5331.61	4979.70	4695.23	4461.29	4266.18	4101.52	3961.18	3840.56

BLENDED MONTHLY PAYMENTS   8¾%
AMORTIZATION IN YEARS

Amount	17	18	19	20	21	22	23	24
25	.24	.23	.23	.22	.22	.22	.21	.21
50	.47	.46	.45	.44	.43	.43	.42	.42
100	.94	.92	.90	.88	.86	.85	.84	.83
200	1.87	1.83	1.79	1.75	1.72	1.69	1.67	1.65
300	2.81	2.74	2.68	2.63	2.58	2.54	2.50	2.47
400	3.74	3.65	3.57	3.50	3.44	3.38	3.33	3.29
500	4.68	4.56	4.46	4.37	4.30	4.23	4.17	4.11
600	5.61	5.47	5.35	5.25	5.15	5.07	5.00	4.93
700	6.54	6.38	6.24	6.12	6.01	5.92	5.83	5.75
800	7.48	7.30	7.14	7.00	6.87	6.76	6.66	6.58
900	8.41	8.21	8.03	7.87	7.73	7.61	7.50	7.40
1000	9.35	9.12	8.92	8.74	8.59	8.45	8.33	8.22
2000	18.69	18.23	17.83	17.48	17.17	16.90	16.65	16.43
3000	28.03	27.34	26.75	26.22	25.75	25.34	24.97	24.65
4000	37.37	36.46	35.66	34.96	34.34	33.79	33.30	32.86
5000	46.71	45.57	44.57	43.70	42.92	42.23	41.62	41.07
6000	56.05	54.68	53.49	52.43	51.50	50.68	49.94	49.29
7000	65.39	63.79	62.40	61.17	60.09	59.12	58.27	57.50
8000	74.73	72.91	71.31	69.91	68.67	67.57	66.59	65.72
9000	84.07	82.02	80.23	78.65	77.25	76.02	74.91	73.93
10000	93.41	91.13	89.14	87.39	85.84	84.46	83.24	82.14
20000	186.81	182.26	178.28	174.77	171.67	168.92	166.47	164.28
30000	280.21	273.39	267.41	262.15	257.50	253.38	249.70	246.42
40000	373.62	364.52	356.55	349.53	343.33	337.83	332.94	328.56
50000	467.02	455.65	445.68	436.92	429.17	422.29	416.17	410.70
60000	560.42	546.78	534.82	524.30	515.00	506.75	499.40	492.84
70000	653.83	637.90	623.96	611.68	600.83	591.20	582.63	574.98
80000	747.23	729.03	713.09	699.06	686.66	675.66	665.87	657.12
90000	840.63	820.16	802.23	786.44	772.49	760.12	749.10	739.26
100000	934.04	911.29	891.36	873.83	858.33	844.57	832.33	821.40
110000	1027.44	1002.42	980.50	961.21	944.16	929.03	915.56	903.54
120000	1120.84	1093.55	1069.64	1048.59	1029.99	1013.49	998.80	985.68
130000	1214.24	1184.68	1158.77	1135.97	1115.82	1097.94	1082.03	1067.82
140000	1307.65	1275.80	1247.91	1223.36	1201.65	1182.40	1165.26	1149.96
150000	1401.05	1366.93	1337.04	1310.74	1287.49	1266.86	1248.49	1232.10
160000	1494.45	1458.06	1426.18	1398.12	1373.32	1351.31	1331.73	1314.24
170000	1587.86	1549.19	1515.32	1485.50	1459.15	1435.77	1414.96	1396.38
180000	1681.26	1640.32	1604.45	1572.88	1544.98	1520.23	1498.19	1478.52
190000	1774.66	1731.45	1693.59	1660.27	1630.81	1604.68	1581.42	1560.66
200000	1868.07	1822.57	1782.72	1747.65	1716.65	1689.14	1664.66	1642.80
210000	1961.47	1913.70	1871.86	1835.03	1802.48	1773.60	1747.89	1724.94
220000	2054.87	2004.83	1961.00	1922.41	1888.31	1858.05	1831.12	1807.08
230000	2148.28	2095.96	2050.13	2009.80	1974.14	1942.51	1914.35	1889.22
240000	2241.68	2187.09	2139.27	2097.18	2059.97	2026.97	1997.59	1971.36
250000	2335.08	2278.22	2228.40	2184.56	2145.81	2111.42	2080.82	2053.50
260000	2428.48	2369.35	2317.54	2271.94	2231.64	2195.88	2164.05	2135.64
270000	2521.89	2460.47	2406.68	2359.32	2317.47	2280.34	2247.28	2217.78
280000	2615.29	2551.60	2495.81	2446.71	2403.30	2364.79	2330.52	2299.92
290000	2708.69	2642.73	2584.95	2534.09	2489.13	2449.25	2413.75	2382.05
300000	2802.10	2733.86	2674.08	2621.47	2574.97	2533.71	2496.98	2464.19
310000	2895.50	2824.99	2763.22	2708.85	2660.80	2618.16	2580.21	2546.33
320000	2988.90	2916.12	2852.36	2796.24	2746.63	2702.62	2663.45	2628.47
330000	3082.31	3007.24	2941.49	2883.62	2832.46	2787.08	2746.68	2710.61
340000	3175.71	3098.37	3030.63	2971.00	2918.29	2871.53	2829.91	2792.75
350000	3269.11	3189.50	3119.76	3058.38	3004.13	2955.99	2913.14	2874.89
360000	3362.52	3280.63	3208.90	3145.76	3089.96	3040.45	2996.38	2957.03
370000	3455.92	3371.76	3298.04	3233.15	3175.79	3124.90	3079.61	3039.17
380000	3549.32	3462.89	3387.17	3320.53	3261.62	3209.36	3162.84	3121.31
390000	3642.72	3554.02	3476.31	3407.91	3347.45	3293.82	3246.07	3203.45
400000	3736.13	3645.14	3565.44	3495.29	3433.29	3378.27	3329.31	3285.59

8¾% BLENDED MONTHLY PAYMENTS
AMORTIZATION IN YEARS

Amount	25	26	29	30	35	40	45	50
25	.21	.21	.20	.20	.19	.19	.19	.19
50	.41	.41	.40	.39	.38	.38	.37	.37
100	.82	.81	.79	.78	.76	.75	.74	.73
200	1.63	1.61	1.57	1.56	1.51	1.49	1.47	1.46
300	2.44	2.41	2.35	2.33	2.27	2.23	2.20	2.18
400	3.25	3.22	3.13	3.11	3.02	2.97	2.93	2.91
500	4.06	4.02	3.91	3.88	3.77	3.71	3.66	3.64
600	4.87	4.82	4.69	4.66	4.53	4.45	4.40	4.36
700	5.69	5.62	5.47	5.43	5.28	5.19	5.13	5.09
800	6.50	6.43	6.26	6.21	6.04	5.93	5.86	5.82
900	7.31	7.23	7.04	6.99	6.79	6.67	6.59	6.54
1000	8.12	8.03	7.82	7.76	7.54	7.41	7.32	7.27
2000	16.24	16.06	15.63	15.52	15.08	14.81	14.64	14.53
3000	24.35	24.09	23.45	23.27	22.62	22.21	21.96	21.79
4000	32.47	32.12	31.26	31.03	30.16	29.62	29.27	29.06
5000	40.59	40.15	39.08	38.79	37.70	37.02	36.59	36.32
6000	48.70	48.18	46.89	46.54	45.24	44.42	43.91	43.58
7000	56.82	56.20	54.70	54.30	52.77	51.83	51.23	50.84
8000	64.93	64.23	62.52	62.06	60.31	59.23	58.54	58.11
9000	73.05	72.26	70.33	69.81	67.85	66.63	65.86	65.37
10000	81.17	80.29	78.15	77.57	75.39	74.04	73.18	72.63
20000	162.33	160.57	156.29	155.13	150.77	148.07	146.35	145.26
30000	243.49	240.86	234.43	232.69	226.16	222.10	219.52	217.88
40000	324.65	321.14	312.58	310.26	301.54	296.13	292.70	290.51
50000	405.81	401.42	390.72	387.82	376.93	370.16	365.87	363.13
60000	486.97	481.71	468.86	465.38	452.31	444.19	439.04	435.76
70000	568.13	561.99	547.00	542.95	527.70	518.22	512.22	508.38
80000	649.30	642.28	625.15	620.51	603.08	592.25	585.39	581.01
90000	730.46	722.56	703.29	698.07	678.47	666.28	658.56	653.63
100000	811.62	802.84	781.43	775.64	753.85	740.31	731.74	726.26
110000	892.78	883.13	859.57	853.20	829.24	814.34	804.91	798.88
120000	973.94	963.41	937.72	930.76	904.62	888.37	878.08	871.51
130000	1055.10	1043.69	1015.86	1008.32	980.01	962.40	951.26	944.13
140000	1136.26	1123.98	1094.00	1085.89	1055.39	1036.43	1024.43	1016.76
150000	1217.43	1204.26	1172.14	1163.45	1130.78	1110.46	1097.60	1089.38
160000	1298.59	1284.55	1250.29	1241.01	1206.16	1184.49	1170.78	1162.01
170000	1379.75	1364.83	1328.43	1318.58	1281.55	1258.52	1243.95	1234.63
180000	1460.91	1445.11	1406.57	1396.14	1356.93	1332.55	1317.12	1307.26
190000	1542.07	1525.40	1484.71	1473.70	1432.32	1406.58	1390.29	1379.88
200000	1623.23	1605.68	1562.86	1551.27	1507.70	1480.61	1463.47	1452.51
210000	1704.39	1685.96	1641.00	1628.83	1583.09	1554.64	1536.64	1525.14
220000	1785.56	1766.25	1719.14	1706.39	1658.47	1628.67	1609.81	1597.76
230000	1866.72	1846.53	1797.28	1783.95	1733.86	1702.70	1682.99	1670.39
240000	1947.88	1926.82	1875.43	1861.52	1809.24	1776.73	1756.16	1743.01
250000	2029.04	2007.10	1953.57	1939.08	1884.63	1850.76	1829.33	1815.64
260000	2110.20	2087.38	2031.71	2016.64	1960.01	1924.79	1902.51	1888.26
270000	2191.36	2167.67	2109.85	2094.21	2035.40	1998.82	1975.68	1960.89
280000	2272.52	2247.95	2188.00	2171.77	2110.78	2072.85	2048.85	2033.51
290000	2353.69	2328.23	2266.14	2249.33	2186.17	2146.88	2122.03	2106.14
300000	2434.85	2408.52	2344.28	2326.90	2261.55	2220.91	2195.20	2178.76
310000	2516.01	2488.80	2422.43	2404.46	2336.94	2294.94	2268.37	2251.39
320000	2597.17	2569.09	2500.57	2482.02	2412.32	2368.97	2341.55	2324.01
330000	2678.33	2649.37	2578.71	2559.58	2487.71	2443.00	2414.72	2396.64
340000	2759.49	2729.65	2656.85	2637.15	2563.09	2517.03	2487.89	2469.26
350000	2840.65	2809.94	2735.00	2714.71	2638.48	2591.06	2561.06	2541.89
360000	2921.82	2890.22	2813.14	2792.27	2713.86	2665.09	2634.24	2614.51
370000	3002.98	2970.50	2891.28	2869.84	2789.25	2739.12	2707.41	2687.14
380000	3084.14	3050.79	2969.42	2947.40	2864.63	2813.15	2780.58	2759.76
390000	3165.30	3131.07	3047.57	3024.96	2940.02	2887.18	2853.76	2832.39
400000	3246.46	3211.36	3125.71	3102.53	3015.40	2961.21	2926.93	2905.01

BLENDED MONTHLY PAYMENTS

AMORTIZATION IN YEARS

9%

Amount	1	2	3	4	5	6	7	8
25	2.19	1.15	.80	.63	.52	.45	.41	.37
50	4.37	2.29	1.59	1.25	1.04	.90	.81	.73
100	8.74	4.57	3.18	2.49	2.07	1.80	1.61	1.46
200	17.48	9.13	6.35	4.97	4.14	3.59	3.21	2.92
300	26.22	13.69	9.52	7.45	6.21	5.39	4.81	4.37
400	34.96	18.25	12.69	9.93	8.28	7.18	6.41	5.83
500	43.69	22.81	15.87	12.41	10.34	8.98	8.01	7.29
600	52.43	27.37	19.04	14.89	12.41	10.77	9.61	8.74
700	61.17	31.93	22.21	17.37	14.48	12.57	11.21	10.20
800	69.91	36.49	25.38	19.85	16.55	14.36	12.81	11.66
900	78.64	41.05	28.56	22.33	18.62	16.15	14.41	13.11
1000	87.38	45.61	31.73	24.81	20.68	17.95	16.01	14.57
2000	174.76	91.22	63.45	49.62	41.36	35.89	32.02	29.14
3000	262.13	136.83	95.18	74.43	62.04	53.84	48.02	43.70
4000	349.51	182.44	126.90	99.23	82.72	71.78	64.03	58.27
5000	436.88	228.05	158.62	124.04	103.40	89.73	80.03	72.83
6000	524.26	273.66	190.35	148.85	124.08	107.67	96.04	87.40
7000	611.63	319.27	222.07	173.65	144.76	125.61	112.05	101.96
8000	699.01	364.88	253.79	198.46	165.43	143.56	128.05	116.53
9000	786.38	410.49	285.52	223.27	186.11	161.50	144.06	131.09
10000	873.76	456.10	317.24	248.08	206.79	179.45	160.06	145.66
20000	1747.51	912.19	634.47	496.15	413.58	358.89	320.12	291.31
30000	2621.26	1368.29	951.71	744.22	620.37	538.33	480.18	436.96
40000	3495.02	1824.38	1268.94	992.29	827.15	717.77	640.24	582.61
50000	4368.77	2280.48	1586.17	1240.36	1033.94	897.21	800.30	728.26
60000	5242.52	2736.57	1903.41	1488.43	1240.73	1076.65	960.36	873.91
70000	6116.28	3192.66	2220.64	1736.50	1447.52	1256.09	1120.41	1019.56
80000	6990.03	3648.76	2537.87	1984.57	1654.30	1435.54	1280.47	1165.22
90000	7863.78	4104.85	2855.11	2232.65	1861.09	1614.98	1440.53	1310.87
100000	8737.54	4560.95	3172.34	2480.72	2067.88	1794.42	1600.59	1456.52
110000	9611.29	5017.04	3489.57	2728.79	2274.67	1973.86	1760.65	1602.17
120000	10485.04	5473.14	3806.81	2976.86	2481.45	2153.30	1920.71	1747.82
130000	11358.80	5929.23	4124.04	3224.93	2688.24	2332.74	2080.76	1893.47
140000	12232.55	6385.32	4441.27	3473.00	2895.03	2512.18	2240.82	2039.12
150000	13106.30	6841.42	4758.51	3721.07	3101.81	2691.62	2400.88	2184.78
160000	13980.06	7297.51	5075.74	3969.14	3308.60	2871.07	2560.94	2330.43
170000	14853.81	7753.61	5392.97	4217.22	3515.39	3050.51	2721.00	2476.08
180000	15727.56	8209.70	5710.21	4465.29	3722.18	3229.95	2881.06	2621.73
190000	16601.32	8665.79	6027.44	4713.36	3928.96	3409.39	3041.12	2767.38
200000	17475.07	9121.89	6344.67	4961.43	4135.75	3588.83	3201.17	2913.03
210000	18348.82	9577.98	6661.91	5209.50	4342.54	3768.27	3361.23	3058.68
220000	19222.58	10034.08	6979.14	5457.57	4549.33	3947.71	3521.29	3204.33
230000	20096.33	10490.17	7296.37	5705.64	4756.11	4127.15	3681.35	3349.99
240000	20970.08	10946.27	7613.61	5953.71	4962.90	4306.60	3841.41	3495.64
250000	21843.84	11402.36	7930.84	6201.79	5169.69	4486.04	4001.47	3641.29
260000	22717.59	11858.45	8248.07	6449.86	5376.47	4665.48	4161.52	3786.94
270000	23591.34	12314.55	8565.31	6697.93	5583.26	4844.92	4321.58	3932.59
280000	24465.10	12770.64	8882.54	6946.00	5790.05	5024.36	4481.64	4078.24
290000	25338.85	13226.74	9199.77	7194.07	5996.84	5203.80	4641.70	4223.89
300000	26212.60	13682.83	9517.01	7442.14	6203.62	5383.24	4801.76	4369.55
310000	27086.36	14138.92	9834.24	7690.21	6410.41	5562.68	4961.82	4515.20
320000	27960.11	14595.02	10151.47	7938.28	6617.20	5742.13	5121.88	4660.85
330000	28833.86	15051.11	10468.71	8186.36	6823.99	5921.57	5281.93	4806.50
340000	29707.62	15507.21	10785.94	8434.43	7030.77	6101.01	5441.99	4952.15
350000	30581.37	15963.30	11103.17	8682.50	7237.56	6280.45	5602.05	5097.80
360000	31455.12	16419.40	11420.41	8930.57	7444.35	6459.89	5762.11	5243.45
370000	32328.88	16875.49	11737.64	9178.64	7651.13	6639.33	5922.17	5389.11
380000	33202.63	17331.58	12054.88	9426.71	7857.92	6818.77	6082.23	5534.76
390000	34076.38	17787.68	12372.11	9674.78	8064.71	6998.21	6242.28	5680.41
400000	34950.14	18243.77	12689.34	9922.85	8271.50	7177.66	6402.34	5826.06

9% BLENDED MONTHLY PAYMENTS
AMORTIZATION IN YEARS

Amount	9	10	11	12	13	14	15	16
25	.34	.32	.30	.29	.28	.26	.26	.25
50	.68	.63	.60	.57	.55	.52	.51	.49
100	1.35	1.26	1.19	1.13	1.09	1.04	1.01	.98
200	2.70	2.52	2.38	2.26	2.17	2.08	2.01	1.95
300	4.04	3.78	3.57	3.39	3.25	3.12	3.02	2.93
400	5.39	5.04	4.75	4.52	4.33	4.16	4.02	3.90
500	6.73	6.29	5.94	5.65	5.41	5.20	5.03	4.88
600	8.08	7.55	7.13	6.78	6.49	6.24	6.03	5.85
700	9.42	8.81	8.31	7.91	7.57	7.28	7.04	6.83
800	10.77	10.07	9.50	9.04	8.65	8.32	8.04	7.80
900	12.12	11.33	10.69	10.16	9.73	9.36	9.05	8.78
1000	13.46	12.58	11.88	11.29	10.81	10.40	10.05	9.75
2000	26.92	25.16	23.75	22.58	21.61	20.79	20.10	19.50
3000	40.37	37.74	35.62	33.87	32.41	31.19	30.14	29.24
4000	53.83	50.32	47.49	45.16	43.22	41.58	40.19	38.99
5000	67.29	62.90	59.36	56.44	54.02	51.97	50.23	48.74
6000	80.74	75.48	71.23	67.73	64.82	62.37	60.28	58.48
7000	94.20	88.06	83.10	79.02	75.62	72.76	70.32	68.23
8000	107.65	100.64	94.97	90.31	86.43	83.15	80.37	77.97
9000	121.11	113.21	106.84	101.60	97.23	93.55	90.41	87.72
10000	134.57	125.79	118.71	112.88	108.03	103.94	100.46	97.47
20000	269.13	251.58	237.41	225.76	216.06	207.88	200.91	194.93
30000	403.69	377.37	356.11	338.64	324.09	311.81	301.36	292.39
40000	538.25	503.16	474.82	451.52	432.11	415.75	401.81	389.85
50000	672.81	628.95	593.52	564.40	540.14	519.68	502.26	487.31
60000	807.37	754.74	712.22	677.28	648.17	623.62	602.72	584.77
70000	941.93	880.52	830.92	790.16	756.20	727.56	703.17	682.23
80000	1076.49	1006.31	949.63	903.04	864.22	831.49	803.62	779.69
90000	1211.05	1132.10	1068.33	1015.92	972.25	935.43	904.07	877.15
100000	1345.61	1257.89	1187.03	1128.80	1080.28	1039.36	1004.52	974.61
110000	1480.17	1383.68	1305.74	1241.68	1188.31	1143.30	1104.98	1072.07
120000	1614.73	1509.47	1424.44	1354.56	1296.33	1247.24	1205.43	1169.53
130000	1749.29	1635.26	1543.14	1467.44	1404.36	1351.17	1305.88	1266.99
140000	1883.85	1761.04	1661.84	1580.32	1512.39	1455.11	1406.33	1364.45
150000	2018.41	1886.83	1780.55	1693.20	1620.42	1559.04	1506.78	1461.91
160000	2152.97	2012.62	1899.25	1806.08	1728.44	1662.98	1607.24	1559.37
170000	2287.53	2138.41	2017.95	1918.96	1836.47	1766.92	1707.69	1656.83
180000	2422.09	2264.20	2136.66	2031.84	1944.50	1870.85	1808.14	1754.29
190000	2556.65	2389.99	2255.36	2144.72	2052.53	1974.79	1908.59	1851.75
200000	2691.21	2515.78	2374.06	2257.60	2160.55	2078.72	2009.04	1949.21
210000	2825.77	2641.56	2492.76	2370.48	2268.58	2182.66	2109.49	2046.67
220000	2960.33	2767.35	2611.47	2483.36	2376.61	2286.59	2209.95	2144.13
230000	3094.89	2893.14	2730.17	2596.24	2484.64	2390.53	2310.40	2241.59
240000	3229.45	3018.93	2848.87	2709.12	2592.66	2494.47	2410.85	2339.05
250000	3364.01	3144.72	2967.57	2822.00	2700.69	2598.40	2511.30	2436.51
260000	3498.57	3270.51	3086.28	2934.88	2808.72	2702.34	2611.75	2533.97
270000	3633.13	3396.30	3204.98	3047.76	2916.75	2806.27	2712.21	2631.43
280000	3767.69	3522.08	3323.68	3160.64	3024.77	2910.21	2812.66	2728.89
290000	3902.25	3647.87	3442.39	3273.52	3132.80	3014.15	2913.11	2826.35
300000	4036.81	3773.66	3561.09	3386.40	3240.83	3118.08	3013.56	2923.81
310000	4171.37	3899.45	3679.79	3499.28	3348.86	3222.02	3114.01	3021.27
320000	4305.93	4025.24	3798.49	3612.16	3456.88	3325.95	3214.47	3118.73
330000	4440.49	4151.03	3917.20	3725.04	3564.91	3429.89	3314.92	3216.19
340000	4575.05	4276.82	4035.90	3837.92	3672.94	3533.83	3415.37	3313.65
350000	4709.61	4402.60	4154.60	3950.80	3780.97	3637.76	3515.82	3411.11
360000	4844.17	4528.39	4273.31	4063.68	3888.99	3741.70	3616.27	3508.57
370000	4978.73	4654.18	4392.01	4176.56	3997.02	3845.63	3716.72	3606.03
380000	5113.29	4779.97	4510.71	4289.44	4105.05	3949.57	3817.18	3703.49
390000	5247.85	4905.76	4629.41	4402.32	4213.07	4053.50	3917.63	3800.95
400000	5382.41	5031.55	4748.12	4515.20	4321.10	4157.44	4018.08	3898.42

BLENDED MONTHLY PAYMENTS

AMORTIZATION IN YEARS

9%

Amount	17	18	19	20	21	22	23	24
25	.24	.24	.23	.23	.22	.22	.22	.21
50	.48	.47	.46	.45	.44	.44	.43	.42
100	.95	.93	.91	.89	.88	.87	.85	.84
200	1.90	1.86	1.82	1.78	1.75	1.73	1.70	1.68
300	2.85	2.78	2.72	2.67	2.63	2.59	2.55	2.52
400	3.80	3.71	3.63	3.56	3.50	3.45	3.40	3.36
500	4.75	4.64	4.54	4.45	4.37	4.31	4.25	4.19
600	5.70	5.56	5.44	5.34	5.25	5.17	5.09	5.03
700	6.65	6.49	6.35	6.23	6.12	6.03	5.94	5.87
800	7.59	7.41	7.26	7.12	7.00	6.89	6.79	6.71
900	8.54	8.34	8.16	8.01	7.87	7.75	7.64	7.54
1000	9.49	9.27	9.07	8.90	8.74	8.61	8.49	8.38
2000	18.98	18.53	18.14	17.79	17.48	17.21	16.97	16.76
3000	28.47	27.79	27.20	26.68	26.22	25.82	25.45	25.13
4000	37.95	37.05	36.27	35.57	34.96	34.42	33.94	33.51
5000	47.44	46.32	45.33	44.46	43.70	43.02	42.42	41.88
6000	56.93	55.58	54.40	53.36	52.44	51.63	50.90	50.26
7000	66.42	64.84	63.46	62.25	61.18	60.23	59.39	58.64
8000	75.90	74.10	72.53	71.14	69.92	68.83	67.87	67.01
9000	85.39	83.36	81.59	80.03	78.66	77.44	76.35	75.39
10000	94.88	92.63	90.66	88.92	87.39	86.04	84.84	83.76
20000	189.75	185.25	181.31	177.84	174.78	172.08	169.67	167.52
30000	284.62	277.87	271.96	266.76	262.17	258.11	254.50	251.28
40000	379.50	370.49	362.61	355.68	349.56	344.15	339.33	335.03
50000	474.37	463.11	453.26	444.60	436.95	430.18	424.16	418.79
60000	569.24	555.73	543.91	533.52	524.34	516.22	508.99	502.55
70000	664.12	648.35	634.56	622.44	611.73	602.25	593.82	586.31
80000	758.99	740.97	725.21	711.36	699.12	688.29	678.65	670.06
90000	853.86	833.60	815.86	800.28	786.51	774.32	763.48	753.82
100000	948.73	926.22	906.51	889.19	873.90	860.36	848.31	837.58
110000	1043.61	1018.84	997.17	978.11	961.29	946.39	933.14	921.34
120000	1138.48	1111.46	1087.82	1067.03	1048.68	1032.43	1017.98	1005.09
130000	1233.35	1204.08	1178.47	1155.95	1136.07	1118.46	1102.81	1088.85
140000	1328.23	1296.70	1269.12	1244.87	1223.46	1204.50	1187.64	1172.61
150000	1423.10	1389.32	1359.77	1333.79	1310.85	1290.53	1272.47	1256.36
160000	1517.97	1481.94	1450.42	1422.71	1398.24	1376.57	1357.30	1340.12
170000	1612.84	1574.57	1541.07	1511.63	1485.63	1462.60	1442.13	1423.88
180000	1707.72	1667.19	1631.72	1600.55	1573.02	1548.64	1526.96	1507.64
190000	1802.59	1759.81	1722.37	1689.47	1660.41	1634.67	1611.79	1591.39
200000	1897.46	1852.43	1813.02	1778.38	1747.80	1720.71	1696.62	1675.15
210000	1992.34	1945.05	1903.68	1867.30	1835.19	1806.74	1781.45	1758.91
220000	2087.21	2037.67	1994.33	1956.22	1922.58	1892.78	1866.28	1842.67
230000	2182.08	2130.29	2084.98	2045.14	2009.97	1978.81	1951.12	1926.42
240000	2276.95	2222.91	2175.63	2134.06	2097.36	2064.85	2035.95	2010.18
250000	2371.83	2315.53	2266.28	2222.98	2184.75	2150.88	2120.78	2093.94
260000	2466.70	2408.16	2356.93	2311.90	2272.14	2236.92	2205.61	2177.69
270000	2561.57	2500.78	2447.58	2400.82	2359.53	2322.95	2290.44	2261.45
280000	2656.45	2593.40	2538.23	2489.74	2446.92	2408.99	2375.27	2345.21
290000	2751.32	2686.02	2628.88	2578.65	2534.31	2495.02	2460.10	2428.97
300000	2846.19	2778.64	2719.53	2667.57	2621.70	2581.06	2544.93	2512.72
310000	2941.06	2871.26	2810.19	2756.49	2709.09	2667.09	2629.76	2596.48
320000	3035.94	2963.88	2900.84	2845.41	2796.48	2753.13	2714.59	2680.24
330000	3130.81	3056.50	2991.49	2934.33	2883.87	2839.17	2799.42	2764.00
340000	3225.68	3149.13	3082.14	3023.25	2971.26	2925.20	2884.26	2847.75
350000	3320.56	3241.75	3172.79	3112.17	3058.65	3011.24	2969.09	2931.51
360000	3415.43	3334.37	3263.44	3201.09	3146.04	3097.27	3053.92	3015.27
370000	3510.30	3426.99	3354.09	3290.01	3233.43	3183.31	3138.75	3099.02
380000	3605.17	3519.61	3444.74	3378.93	3320.82	3269.34	3223.58	3182.78
390000	3700.05	3612.23	3535.39	3467.84	3408.21	3355.38	3308.41	3266.54
400000	3794.92	3704.85	3626.04	3556.76	3495.60	3441.41	3393.24	3350.30

BLENDED MONTHLY PAYMENTS
AMORTIZATION IN YEARS

Amount	25	26	29	30	35	40	45	50
25	.21	.21	.20	.20	.20	.19	.19	.19
50	.42	.41	.40	.40	.39	.38	.38	.38
100	.83	.82	.80	.80	.78	.76	.76	.75
200	1.66	1.64	1.60	1.59	1.55	1.52	1.51	1.50
300	2.49	2.46	2.40	2.38	2.32	2.28	2.26	2.24
400	3.32	3.28	3.20	3.18	3.09	3.04	3.01	2.99
500	4.14	4.10	4.00	3.97	3.86	3.80	3.76	3.73
600	4.97	4.92	4.80	4.76	4.64	4.56	4.51	4.48
700	5.80	5.74	5.59	5.55	5.41	5.32	5.26	5.22
800	6.63	6.56	6.39	6.35	6.18	6.07	6.01	5.97
900	7.46	7.38	7.19	7.14	6.95	6.83	6.76	6.71
1000	8.28	8.20	7.99	7.93	7.72	7.59	7.51	7.46
2000	16.56	16.39	15.97	15.86	15.44	15.18	15.02	14.91
3000	24.84	24.59	23.96	23.79	23.16	22.77	22.52	22.37
4000	33.12	32.78	31.94	31.72	30.87	30.35	30.03	29.82
5000	41.40	40.97	39.93	39.65	38.59	37.94	37.53	37.28
6000	49.68	49.17	47.91	47.57	46.31	45.53	45.04	44.73
7000	57.96	57.36	55.90	55.50	54.03	53.12	52.55	52.19
8000	66.24	65.56	63.88	63.43	61.74	60.70	60.05	59.64
9000	74.52	73.75	71.87	71.36	69.46	68.29	67.56	67.10
10000	82.80	81.94	79.85	79.29	77.18	75.88	75.06	74.55
20000	165.60	163.88	159.70	158.57	154.35	151.75	150.12	149.09
30000	248.40	245.82	239.55	237.85	231.53	227.63	225.18	223.64
40000	331.20	327.76	319.39	317.14	308.70	303.50	300.24	298.18
50000	413.99	409.70	399.24	396.42	385.87	379.38	375.30	372.73
60000	496.79	491.63	479.09	475.70	463.05	455.25	450.36	447.27
70000	579.59	573.57	558.94	554.99	540.22	531.12	525.42	521.82
80000	662.39	655.51	638.78	634.27	617.40	607.00	600.48	596.36
90000	745.18	737.45	718.63	713.55	694.57	682.87	675.54	670.91
100000	827.98	819.39	798.48	792.84	771.74	758.75	750.60	745.45
110000	910.78	901.32	878.33	872.12	848.92	834.62	825.66	820.00
120000	993.58	983.26	958.17	951.40	926.09	910.49	900.72	894.54
130000	1076.38	1065.20	1038.02	1030.69	1003.27	986.37	975.78	969.09
140000	1159.17	1147.14	1117.87	1109.97	1080.44	1062.24	1050.84	1043.63
150000	1241.97	1229.08	1197.71	1189.25	1157.61	1138.12	1125.90	1118.18
160000	1324.77	1311.02	1277.56	1268.54	1234.79	1213.99	1200.96	1192.72
170000	1407.57	1392.95	1357.41	1347.82	1311.96	1289.86	1276.02	1267.27
180000	1490.36	1474.89	1437.26	1427.10	1389.14	1365.74	1351.08	1341.81
190000	1573.16	1556.83	1517.10	1506.39	1466.31	1441.61	1426.14	1416.36
200000	1655.96	1638.77	1596.95	1585.67	1543.48	1517.49	1501.20	1490.90
210000	1738.76	1720.71	1676.80	1664.95	1620.66	1593.36	1576.26	1565.45
220000	1821.56	1802.64	1756.65	1744.24	1697.83	1669.23	1651.32	1639.99
230000	1904.35	1884.58	1836.49	1823.52	1775.00	1745.11	1726.38	1714.54
240000	1987.15	1966.52	1916.34	1902.80	1852.18	1820.98	1801.44	1789.08
250000	2069.95	2048.46	1996.19	1982.09	1929.35	1896.86	1876.50	1863.63
260000	2152.75	2130.40	2076.03	2061.37	2006.53	1972.73	1951.56	1938.17
270000	2235.54	2212.33	2155.88	2140.65	2083.70	2048.60	2026.62	2012.72
280000	2318.34	2294.27	2235.73	2219.94	2160.87	2124.48	2101.68	2087.26
290000	2401.14	2376.21	2315.58	2299.22	2238.05	2200.35	2176.74	2161.81
300000	2483.94	2458.15	2395.42	2378.50	2315.22	2276.23	2251.80	2236.35
310000	2566.73	2540.09	2475.27	2457.79	2392.40	2352.10	2326.86	2310.90
320000	2649.53	2622.03	2555.12	2537.07	2469.57	2427.97	2401.92	2385.44
330000	2732.33	2703.96	2634.97	2616.35	2546.74	2503.85	2476.98	2459.99
340000	2815.13	2785.90	2714.81	2695.64	2623.92	2579.72	2552.04	2534.53
350000	2897.93	2867.84	2794.66	2774.92	2701.09	2655.60	2627.10	2609.08
360000	2980.72	2949.78	2874.51	2854.20	2778.27	2731.47	2702.16	2683.62
370000	3063.52	3031.72	2954.35	2933.49	2855.44	2807.34	2777.22	2758.17
380000	3146.32	3113.65	3034.20	3012.77	2932.61	2883.22	2852.28	2832.71
390000	3229.12	3195.59	3114.05	3092.05	3009.79	2959.09	2927.34	2907.26
400000	3311.91	3277.53	3193.90	3171.34	3086.96	3034.97	3002.40	2981.80

Amount	1	2	3	4	5	6	7	8
25	2.19	1.15	.80	.63	.52	.46	.41	.37
50	4.38	2.29	1.60	1.25	1.04	.91	.81	.74
100	8.75	4.58	3.19	2.50	2.08	1.81	1.62	1.47
200	17.50	9.15	6.37	4.99	4.16	3.62	3.23	2.94
300	26.25	13.72	9.56	7.48	6.24	5.42	4.84	4.41
400	35.00	18.29	12.74	9.97	8.32	7.23	6.46	5.88
500	43.75	22.86	15.92	12.47	10.40	9.04	8.07	7.35
600	52.50	27.44	19.11	14.96	12.48	10.84	9.68	8.82
700	61.25	32.01	22.29	17.45	14.56	12.65	11.29	10.29
800	69.99	36.58	25.47	19.94	16.64	14.46	12.91	11.76
900	78.74	41.15	28.66	22.43	18.72	16.26	14.52	13.23
1000	87.49	45.72	31.84	24.93	20.80	18.07	16.13	14.69
2000	174.98	91.44	63.68	49.85	41.60	36.13	32.26	29.38
3000	262.47	137.16	95.51	74.77	62.39	54.20	48.39	44.07
4000	349.95	182.88	127.35	99.69	83.19	72.26	64.52	58.76
5000	437.44	228.60	159.18	124.61	103.98	90.32	80.64	73.45
6000	524.93	274.32	191.02	149.53	124.78	108.39	96.77	88.14
7000	612.41	320.04	222.85	174.46	145.57	126.45	112.90	102.83
8000	699.90	365.76	254.69	199.38	166.37	144.51	129.03	117.52
9000	787.39	411.48	286.52	224.30	187.17	162.58	145.16	132.21
10000	874.88	457.20	318.36	249.22	207.96	180.64	161.28	146.90
20000	1749.75	914.40	636.71	498.43	415.92	361.28	322.56	293.80
30000	2624.62	1371.60	955.07	747.65	623.87	541.91	483.84	440.70
40000	3499.49	1828.80	1273.42	996.86	831.83	722.55	645.12	587.60
50000	4374.36	2286.00	1591.78	1246.08	1039.78	903.18	806.40	734.50
60000	5249.23	2743.20	1910.13	1495.29	1247.74	1083.82	967.68	881.40
70000	6124.10	3200.40	2228.48	1744.51	1455.69	1264.46	1128.96	1028.30
80000	6998.97	3657.60	2546.84	1993.72	1663.65	1445.09	1290.24	1175.20
90000	7873.84	4114.80	2865.19	2242.93	1871.61	1625.73	1451.52	1322.10
100000	8748.71	4572.00	3183.55	2492.15	2079.56	1806.36	1612.80	1469.00
110000	9623.58	5029.19	3501.90	2741.36	2287.52	1987.00	1774.08	1615.90
120000	10498.45	5486.39	3820.25	2990.58	2495.47	2167.64	1935.36	1762.80
130000	11373.32	5943.59	4138.61	3239.79	2703.43	2348.27	2096.64	1909.70
140000	12248.19	6400.79	4456.96	3489.01	2911.38	2528.91	2257.92	2056.60
150000	13123.06	6857.99	4775.32	3738.22	3119.34	2709.54	2419.20	2203.50
160000	13997.93	7315.19	5093.67	3987.44	3327.30	2890.18	2580.48	2350.40
170000	14872.80	7772.39	5412.02	4236.65	3535.25	3070.82	2741.76	2497.30
180000	15747.67	8229.59	5730.38	4485.86	3743.21	3251.45	2903.04	2644.20
190000	16622.54	8686.79	6048.73	4735.08	3951.16	3432.09	3064.32	2791.10
200000	17497.41	9143.99	6367.09	4984.29	4159.12	3612.72	3225.60	2938.00
210000	18372.28	9601.19	6685.44	5233.51	4367.07	3793.36	3386.88	3084.90
220000	19247.15	10058.38	7003.79	5482.72	4575.03	3973.99	3548.16	3231.80
230000	20122.02	10515.58	7322.15	5731.94	4782.98	4154.63	3709.44	3378.70
240000	20996.89	10972.78	7640.50	5981.15	4990.94	4335.27	3870.72	3525.60
250000	21871.76	11429.98	7958.86	6230.37	5198.90	4515.90	4032.00	3672.50
260000	22746.63	11887.18	8277.21	6479.58	5406.85	4696.54	4193.28	3819.40
270000	23621.50	12344.38	8595.56	6728.79	5614.81	4877.17	4354.56	3966.30
280000	24496.37	12801.58	8913.92	6978.01	5822.76	5057.81	4515.84	4113.20
290000	25371.24	13258.78	9232.27	7227.22	6030.72	5238.45	4677.12	4260.10
300000	26246.11	13715.98	9550.63	7476.44	6238.67	5419.08	4838.40	4407.00
310000	27120.98	14173.18	9868.98	7725.65	6446.63	5599.72	4999.68	4553.90
320000	27995.85	14630.38	10187.33	7974.87	6654.59	5780.35	5160.96	4700.80
330000	28870.72	15087.57	10505.69	8224.08	6862.54	5960.99	5322.24	4847.70
340000	29745.59	15544.77	10824.04	8473.30	7070.50	6141.63	5483.52	4994.60
350000	30620.46	16001.97	11142.40	8722.51	7278.45	6322.26	5644.80	5141.50
360000	31495.33	16459.17	11460.75	8971.72	7486.41	6502.90	5806.08	5288.40
370000	32370.20	16916.37	11779.11	9220.94	7694.36	6683.53	5967.36	5435.30
380000	33245.07	17373.57	12097.46	9470.15	7902.32	6864.17	6128.64	5582.20
390000	34119.94	17830.77	12415.81	9719.37	8110.27	7044.80	6289.92	5729.10
400000	34994.81	18287.97	12734.17	9968.58	8318.23	7225.44	6451.20	5876.00

9¼% BLENDED MONTHLY PAYMENTS
AMORTIZATION IN YEARS

Amount	9	10	11	12	13	14	15	16
25	.34	.32	.31	.29	.28	.27	.26	.25
50	.68	.64	.61	.58	.55	.53	.51	.50
100	1.36	1.28	1.21	1.15	1.10	1.06	1.02	.99
200	2.72	2.55	2.41	2.29	2.19	2.11	2.04	1.98
300	4.08	3.82	3.61	3.43	3.29	3.17	3.06	2.97
400	5.44	5.09	4.81	4.57	4.38	4.22	4.08	3.96
500	6.80	6.36	6.01	5.72	5.48	5.27	5.10	4.95
600	8.16	7.63	7.21	6.86	6.57	6.33	6.12	5.94
700	9.51	8.90	8.41	8.00	7.66	7.38	7.14	6.93
800	10.87	10.17	9.61	9.14	8.76	8.43	8.16	7.92
900	12.23	11.44	10.81	10.29	9.85	9.49	9.17	8.91
1000	13.59	12.71	12.01	11.43	10.95	10.54	10.19	9.90
2000	27.17	25.42	24.01	22.85	21.89	21.07	20.38	19.79
3000	40.76	38.13	36.01	34.28	32.83	31.61	30.57	29.68
4000	54.34	50.84	48.02	45.70	43.77	42.14	40.76	39.57
5000	67.92	63.55	60.02	57.12	54.71	52.68	50.95	49.46
6000	81.51	76.26	72.02	68.55	65.65	63.21	61.13	59.35
7000	95.09	88.97	84.03	79.97	76.59	73.74	71.32	69.25
8000	108.67	101.68	96.03	91.39	87.53	84.28	81.51	79.14
9000	122.26	114.39	108.03	102.82	98.47	94.81	91.70	89.03
10000	135.84	127.10	120.04	114.24	109.41	105.35	101.89	98.92
20000	271.68	254.19	240.07	228.48	218.82	210.69	203.77	197.84
30000	407.51	381.28	360.10	342.71	328.23	316.03	305.65	296.75
40000	543.35	508.37	480.13	456.95	437.64	421.37	407.54	395.67
50000	679.18	635.46	600.16	571.18	547.05	526.72	509.42	494.58
60000	815.02	762.55	720.19	685.42	656.45	632.06	611.30	593.50
70000	950.85	889.64	840.23	799.65	765.86	737.40	713.19	692.41
80000	1086.69	1016.73	960.26	913.89	875.27	842.74	815.07	791.33
90000	1222.52	1143.82	1080.29	1028.12	984.68	948.08	916.95	890.25
100000	1358.36	1270.91	1200.32	1142.36	1094.09	1053.43	1018.83	989.16
110000	1494.20	1398.00	1320.35	1256.59	1203.50	1158.77	1120.72	1088.08
120000	1630.03	1525.09	1440.38	1370.83	1312.90	1264.11	1222.60	1186.99
130000	1765.87	1652.19	1560.42	1485.06	1422.31	1369.45	1324.48	1285.91
140000	1901.70	1779.28	1680.45	1599.30	1531.72	1474.79	1426.37	1384.82
150000	2037.54	1906.37	1800.48	1713.53	1641.13	1580.14	1528.25	1483.74
160000	2173.37	2033.46	1920.51	1827.77	1750.54	1685.48	1630.13	1582.66
170000	2309.21	2160.55	2040.54	1942.00	1859.95	1790.82	1732.02	1681.57
180000	2445.04	2287.64	2160.57	2056.24	1969.35	1896.16	1833.90	1780.49
190000	2580.88	2414.73	2280.61	2170.47	2078.76	2001.51	1935.78	1879.40
200000	2716.72	2541.82	2400.64	2284.71	2188.17	2106.85	2037.66	1978.32
210000	2852.55	2668.91	2520.67	2398.94	2297.58	2212.19	2139.55	2077.23
220000	2988.39	2796.00	2640.70	2513.18	2406.99	2317.53	2241.43	2176.15
230000	3124.22	2923.09	2760.73	2627.41	2516.40	2422.87	2343.31	2275.07
240000	3260.06	3050.18	2880.76	2741.65	2625.80	2528.22	2445.20	2373.98
250000	3395.89	3177.28	3000.80	2855.88	2735.21	2633.56	2547.08	2472.90
260000	3531.73	3304.37	3120.83	2970.12	2844.62	2738.90	2648.96	2571.81
270000	3667.56	3431.46	3240.86	3084.35	2954.03	2844.24	2750.85	2670.73
280000	3803.40	3558.55	3360.89	3198.59	3063.44	2949.58	2852.73	2769.64
290000	3939.24	3685.64	3480.92	3312.82	3172.85	3054.93	2954.61	2868.56
300000	4075.07	3812.73	3600.95	3427.06	3282.25	3160.27	3056.49	2967.48
310000	4210.91	3939.82	3720.98	3541.29	3391.66	3265.61	3158.38	3066.39
320000	4346.74	4066.91	3841.02	3655.53	3501.07	3370.95	3260.26	3165.31
330000	4482.58	4194.00	3961.05	3769.76	3610.48	3476.29	3362.14	3264.22
340000	4618.41	4321.09	4081.08	3884.00	3719.89	3581.64	3464.03	3363.14
350000	4754.25	4448.18	4201.11	3998.23	3829.30	3686.98	3565.91	3462.05
360000	4890.08	4575.27	4321.14	4112.47	3938.70	3792.32	3667.79	3560.97
370000	5025.92	4702.37	4441.17	4226.70	4048.11	3897.66	3769.68	3659.89
380000	5161.76	4829.46	4561.21	4340.94	4157.52	4003.01	3871.56	3758.80
390000	5297.59	4956.55	4681.24	4455.17	4266.93	4108.35	3973.44	3857.72
400000	5433.43	5083.64	4801.27	4569.41	4376.34	4213.69	4075.32	3956.63

106

Amount	17	18	19	20	21	22	23	24
25	.25	.24	.24	.23	.23	.22	.22	.22
50	.49	.48	.47	.46	.45	.44	.44	.43
100	.97	.95	.93	.91	.89	.88	.87	.86
200	1.93	1.89	1.85	1.81	1.78	1.76	1.73	1.71
300	2.90	2.83	2.77	2.72	2.67	2.63	2.60	2.57
400	3.86	3.77	3.69	3.62	3.56	3.51	3.46	3.42
500	4.82	4.71	4.61	4.53	4.45	4.39	4.33	4.27
600	5.79	5.65	5.54	5.43	5.34	5.26	5.19	5.13
700	6.75	6.59	6.46	6.34	6.23	6.14	6.06	5.98
800	7.71	7.53	7.38	7.24	7.12	7.01	6.92	6.84
900	8.68	8.48	8.30	8.15	8.01	7.89	7.78	7.69
1000	9.64	9.42	9.22	9.05	8.90	8.77	8.65	8.54
2000	19.28	18.83	18.44	18.10	17.80	17.53	17.29	17.08
3000	28.91	28.24	27.66	27.14	26.69	26.29	25.94	25.62
4000	38.55	37.65	36.88	36.19	35.59	35.05	34.58	34.16
5000	48.18	47.07	46.09	45.24	44.48	43.82	43.23	42.70
6000	57.82	56.48	55.31	54.28	53.38	52.58	51.87	51.24
7000	67.45	65.89	64.53	63.33	62.28	61.34	60.51	59.78
8000	77.09	75.30	73.75	72.38	71.17	70.10	69.16	68.31
9000	86.72	84.72	82.96	81.42	80.07	78.87	77.80	76.85
10000	96.36	94.13	92.18	90.47	88.96	87.63	86.45	85.39
20000	192.71	188.25	184.36	180.94	177.92	175.25	172.89	170.78
30000	289.06	282.38	276.53	271.40	266.88	262.88	259.33	256.16
40000	385.41	376.50	368.71	361.87	355.84	350.50	345.77	341.55
50000	481.77	470.62	460.89	452.33	444.80	438.13	432.21	426.93
60000	578.12	564.75	553.06	542.80	533.75	525.75	518.65	512.32
70000	674.47	658.87	645.24	633.27	622.71	613.37	605.09	597.71
80000	770.82	752.99	737.41	723.73	711.67	701.00	691.53	683.09
90000	867.17	847.12	829.59	814.20	800.63	788.62	777.97	768.48
100000	963.53	941.24	921.77	904.66	889.59	876.25	864.41	853.86
110000	1059.88	1035.36	1013.94	995.13	978.55	963.87	950.85	939.25
120000	1156.23	1129.49	1106.12	1085.60	1067.50	1051.50	1037.29	1024.63
130000	1252.58	1223.61	1198.29	1176.06	1156.46	1139.12	1123.73	1110.02
140000	1348.93	1317.74	1290.47	1266.53	1245.42	1226.74	1210.17	1195.41
150000	1445.29	1411.86	1382.65	1356.99	1334.38	1314.37	1296.61	1280.79
160000	1541.64	1505.98	1474.82	1447.46	1423.34	1401.99	1383.05	1366.18
170000	1637.99	1600.11	1567.00	1537.93	1512.30	1489.62	1469.49	1451.56
180000	1734.34	1694.23	1659.17	1628.39	1601.25	1577.24	1555.93	1536.95
190000	1830.70	1788.35	1751.35	1718.86	1690.21	1664.87	1642.37	1622.34
200000	1927.05	1882.48	1843.53	1809.32	1779.17	1752.49	1728.81	1707.72
210000	2023.40	1976.60	1935.70	1899.79	1868.13	1840.11	1815.25	1793.11
220000	2119.75	2070.72	2027.88	1990.26	1957.09	1927.74	1901.69	1878.49
230000	2216.10	2164.85	2120.05	2080.72	2046.05	2015.36	1988.13	1963.88
240000	2312.46	2258.97	2212.23	2171.19	2135.00	2102.99	2074.57	2049.26
250000	2408.81	2353.10	2304.41	2261.65	2223.96	2190.61	2161.01	2134.65
260000	2505.16	2447.22	2396.58	2352.12	2312.92	2278.24	2247.45	2220.04
270000	2601.51	2541.34	2488.76	2442.59	2401.88	2365.86	2333.89	2305.42
280000	2697.86	2635.47	2580.93	2533.05	2490.84	2453.48	2420.33	2390.81
290000	2794.22	2729.59	2673.11	2623.52	2579.80	2541.11	2506.77	2476.19
300000	2890.57	2823.71	2765.29	2713.98	2668.75	2628.73	2593.21	2561.58
310000	2986.92	2917.84	2857.46	2804.45	2757.71	2716.36	2679.65	2646.96
320000	3083.27	3011.96	2949.64	2894.92	2846.67	2803.98	2766.09	2732.35
330000	3179.62	3106.08	3041.81	2985.38	2935.63	2891.60	2852.53	2817.74
340000	3275.98	3200.21	3133.99	3075.85	3024.59	2979.23	2938.97	2903.12
350000	3372.33	3294.33	3226.17	3166.31	3113.55	3066.85	3025.41	2988.51
360000	3468.68	3388.46	3318.34	3256.78	3202.50	3154.48	3111.85	3073.89
370000	3565.03	3482.58	3410.52	3347.25	3291.46	3242.10	3198.29	3159.28
380000	3661.39	3576.70	3502.69	3437.71	3380.42	3329.73	3284.73	3244.67
390000	3757.74	3670.83	3594.87	3528.18	3469.38	3417.35	3371.17	3330.05
400000	3854.09	3764.95	3687.05	3618.64	3558.34	3504.97	3457.61	3415.44

9¼% BLENDED MONTHLY PAYMENTS
AMORTIZATION IN YEARS

Amount	25	26	29	30	35	40	45	50
25	.22	.21	.21	.21	.20	.20	.20	.20
50	.43	.42	.41	.41	.40	.39	.39	.39
100	.85	.84	.82	.82	.79	.78	.77	.77
200	1.69	1.68	1.64	1.63	1.58	1.56	1.54	1.53
300	2.54	2.51	2.45	2.44	2.37	2.34	2.31	2.30
400	3.38	3.35	3.27	3.25	3.16	3.11	3.08	3.06
500	4.23	4.19	4.08	4.06	3.95	3.89	3.85	3.83
600	5.07	5.02	4.90	4.87	4.74	4.67	4.62	4.59
700	5.92	5.86	5.71	5.68	5.53	5.45	5.39	5.36
800	6.76	6.69	6.53	6.49	6.32	6.22	6.16	6.12
900	7.61	7.53	7.35	7.30	7.11	7.00	6.93	6.89
1000	8.45	8.37	8.16	8.11	7.90	7.78	7.70	7.65
2000	16.89	16.73	16.32	16.21	15.80	15.55	15.40	15.30
3000	25.34	25.09	24.47	24.31	23.70	23.32	23.09	22.95
4000	33.78	33.45	32.63	32.41	31.59	31.10	30.79	30.59
5000	42.23	41.81	40.79	40.51	39.49	38.87	38.48	38.24
6000	50.67	50.17	48.94	48.61	47.39	46.64	46.18	45.89
7000	59.12	58.53	57.10	56.71	55.29	54.41	53.87	53.53
8000	67.56	66.89	65.26	64.82	63.18	62.19	61.57	61.18
9000	76.01	75.25	73.41	72.92	71.08	69.96	69.26	68.83
10000	84.45	83.61	81.57	81.02	78.98	77.73	76.96	76.48
20000	168.89	167.21	163.13	162.03	157.95	155.46	153.91	152.95
30000	253.34	250.82	244.69	243.05	236.92	233.18	230.87	229.42
40000	337.78	334.42	326.26	324.06	315.90	310.91	307.82	305.89
50000	422.23	418.02	407.82	405.08	394.87	388.64	384.77	382.36
60000	506.67	501.63	489.38	486.09	473.84	466.36	461.73	458.83
70000	591.12	585.23	570.94	567.10	552.81	544.09	538.68	535.30
80000	675.56	668.83	652.51	648.12	631.79	621.82	615.64	611.77
90000	760.01	752.44	734.07	729.13	710.76	699.54	692.59	688.24
100000	844.45	836.04	815.63	810.15	789.73	777.27	769.54	764.71
110000	928.90	919.64	897.20	891.16	868.71	855.00	846.50	841.18
120000	1013.34	1003.25	978.76	972.18	947.68	932.72	923.45	917.65
130000	1097.79	1086.85	1060.32	1053.19	1026.65	1010.45	1000.41	994.12
140000	1182.03	1170.45	1141.88	1134.20	1105.62	1088.18	1077.36	1070.59
150000	1266.68	1254.06	1223.45	1215.22	1184.60	1165.90	1154.31	1147.06
160000	1351.12	1337.66	1305.01	1296.23	1263.57	1243.63	1231.27	1223.53
170000	1435.57	1421.26	1386.57	1377.25	1342.54	1321.36	1308.22	1300.00
180000	1520.01	1504.87	1468.14	1458.26	1421.51	1399.08	1385.17	1376.47
190000	1604.46	1588.47	1549.70	1539.27	1500.49	1476.81	1462.13	1452.94
200000	1688.90	1672.07	1631.26	1620.29	1579.46	1554.54	1539.08	1529.41
210000	1773.35	1755.68	1712.82	1701.30	1658.43	1632.26	1616.04	1605.88
220000	1857.79	1839.28	1794.39	1782.32	1737.41	1709.99	1692.99	1682.35
230000	1942.24	1922.88	1875.95	1863.33	1816.38	1787.72	1769.94	1758.82
240000	2026.68	2006.49	1957.51	1944.35	1895.35	1865.44	1846.90	1835.29
250000	2111.13	2090.09	2039.07	2025.36	1974.32	1943.17	1923.85	1911.76
260000	2195.57	2173.69	2120.64	2106.37	2053.30	2020.89	2000.81	1988.23
270000	2280.02	2257.30	2202.20	2187.39	2132.27	2098.62	2077.76	2064.70
280000	2364.46	2340.90	2283.76	2268.40	2211.24	2176.35	2154.71	2141.17
290000	2448.91	2424.50	2365.33	2349.42	2290.21	2254.07	2231.67	2217.64
300000	2533.35	2508.11	2446.89	2430.43	2369.19	2331.80	2308.62	2294.11
310000	2617.80	2591.71	2528.45	2511.45	2448.16	2409.53	2385.57	2370.58
320000	2702.24	2675.31	2610.01	2592.46	2527.13	2487.25	2462.53	2447.05
330000	2786.69	2758.92	2691.58	2673.47	2606.11	2564.98	2539.48	2523.52
340000	2871.13	2842.52	2773.14	2754.49	2685.08	2642.71	2616.44	2599.99
350000	2955.58	2926.12	2854.70	2835.50	2764.05	2720.43	2693.39	2676.46
360000	3040.02	3009.73	2936.27	2916.52	2843.02	2798.16	2770.34	2752.93
370000	3124.47	3093.33	3017.83	2997.53	2922.00	2875.89	2847.30	2829.40
380000	3208.91	3176.93	3099.39	3078.54	3000.97	2953.61	2924.25	2905.87
390000	3293.36	3260.54	3180.95	3159.56	3079.94	3031.34	3001.21	2982.34
400000	3377.80	3344.14	3262.52	3240.57	3158.92	3109.07	3078.16	3058.81

BLENDED MONTHLY PAYMENTS 9½%
AMORTIZATION IN YEARS

Amount	1	2	3	4	5	6	7	8
25	2.19	1.15	.80	.63	.53	.46	.41	.38
50	4.38	2.30	1.60	1.26	1.05	.91	.82	.75
100	8.76	4.59	3.20	2.51	2.10	1.82	1.63	1.49
200	17.52	9.17	6.39	5.01	4.19	3.64	3.26	2.97
300	26.28	13.75	9.59	7.52	6.28	5.46	4.88	4.45
400	35.04	18.34	12.78	10.02	8.37	7.28	6.51	5.93
500	43.80	22.92	15.98	12.52	10.46	9.10	8.13	7.41
600	52.56	27.50	19.17	15.03	12.55	10.92	9.76	8.89
700	61.32	32.09	22.37	17.53	14.64	12.73	11.38	10.38
800	70.08	36.67	25.56	20.03	16.74	14.55	13.01	11.86
900	78.84	41.25	28.76	22.54	18.83	16.37	14.63	13.34
1000	87.60	45.84	31.95	25.04	20.92	18.19	16.26	14.82
2000	175.20	91.67	63.90	50.08	41.83	36.37	32.51	29.64
3000	262.80	137.50	95.85	75.11	62.74	54.56	48.76	44.45
4000	350.40	183.33	127.80	100.15	83.66	72.74	65.01	59.27
5000	438.00	229.16	159.74	125.18	104.57	90.92	81.26	74.08
6000	525.60	274.99	191.69	150.22	125.48	109.11	97.51	88.90
7000	613.20	320.82	223.64	175.26	146.39	127.29	113.76	103.71
8000	700.79	366.65	255.59	200.29	167.31	145.47	130.01	118.53
9000	788.39	412.48	287.53	225.33	188.22	163.66	146.26	133.34
10000	875.99	458.31	319.48	250.36	209.13	181.84	162.51	148.16
20000	1751.98	916.61	638.96	500.72	418.26	363.67	325.02	296.31
30000	2627.97	1374.92	958.43	751.08	627.39	545.51	487.52	444.46
40000	3503.96	1833.22	1277.91	1001.44	836.51	727.34	650.03	592.62
50000	4379.94	2291.53	1597.38	1251.80	1045.64	909.17	812.53	740.77
60000	5255.93	2749.83	1916.86	1502.16	1254.77	1091.01	975.04	888.92
70000	6131.91	3208.14	2236.34	1752.52	1463.89	1272.84	1137.54	1037.08
80000	7007.90	3666.44	2555.81	2002.88	1673.02	1454.68	1300.05	1185.23
90000	7883.89	4124.74	2875.29	2253.24	1882.15	1636.51	1462.55	1333.38
100000	8759.87	4583.05	3194.76	2503.60	2091.27	1818.34	1625.06	1481.54
110000	9635.86	5041.35	3514.24	2753.96	2300.40	2000.18	1787.57	1629.69
120000	10511.85	5499.66	3833.72	3004.32	2509.53	2182.01	1950.07	1777.84
130000	11387.83	5957.96	4153.19	3254.68	2718.65	2363.85	2112.58	1926.00
140000	12263.82	6416.27	4472.67	3505.04	2927.78	2545.68	2275.08	2074.15
150000	13139.81	6874.57	4792.14	3755.40	3136.91	2727.51	2437.59	2222.30
160000	14015.79	7332.88	5111.62	4005.76	3346.03	2909.35	2600.09	2370.45
170000	14891.78	7791.18	5431.10	4256.12	3555.16	3091.18	2762.60	2518.61
180000	15767.77	8249.48	5750.57	4506.48	3764.29	3273.02	2925.10	2666.76
190000	16643.75	8707.79	6070.05	4756.84	3973.41	3454.85	3087.61	2814.91
200000	17519.74	9166.09	6389.52	5007.20	4182.54	3636.68	3250.12	2963.07
210000	18395.73	9624.40	6709.00	5257.56	4391.67	3818.52	3412.62	3111.22
220000	19271.71	10082.70	7028.48	5507.92	4600.79	4000.35	3575.13	3259.37
230000	20147.70	10541.01	7347.95	5758.28	4809.92	4182.19	3737.63	3407.53
240000	21023.69	10999.31	7667.43	6008.64	5019.05	4364.02	3900.14	3555.68
250000	21899.67	11457.62	7986.90	6259.00	5228.17	4545.85	4062.64	3703.83
260000	22775.66	11915.92	8306.38	6509.35	5437.30	4727.69	4225.15	3851.99
270000	23651.65	12374.22	8625.86	6759.71	5646.43	4909.52	4387.65	4000.14
280000	24527.63	12832.53	8945.33	7010.07	5855.55	5091.36	4550.16	4148.29
290000	25403.62	13290.83	9264.81	7260.43	6064.68	5273.19	4712.67	4296.45
300000	26279.61	13749.14	9584.28	7510.79	6273.81	5455.02	4875.17	4444.60
310000	27155.59	14207.44	9903.76	7761.15	6482.93	5636.86	5037.68	4592.75
320000	28031.58	14665.75	10223.24	8011.51	6692.06	5818.69	5200.18	4740.90
330000	28907.57	15124.05	10542.71	8261.87	6901.19	6000.53	5362.69	4889.06
340000	29783.55	15582.36	10862.19	8512.23	7110.31	6182.36	5525.19	5037.21
350000	30659.54	16040.66	11181.66	8762.59	7319.44	6364.19	5687.70	5185.36
360000	31535.53	16498.96	11501.14	9012.95	7528.57	6546.03	5850.20	5333.52
370000	32411.51	16957.27	11820.62	9263.31	7737.69	6727.86	6012.71	5481.67
380000	33287.50	17415.57	12140.09	9513.67	7946.82	6909.70	6175.21	5629.82
390000	34163.49	17873.88	12459.57	9764.03	8155.95	7091.53	6337.72	5777.98
400000	35039.47	18332.18	12779.04	10014.39	8365.07	7273.36	6500.23	5926.13

9½% BLENDED MONTHLY PAYMENTS
AMORTIZATION IN YEARS

Amount	9	10	11	12	13	14	15	16
25	.35	.33	.31	.29	.28	.27	.26	.26
50	.69	.65	.61	.58	.56	.54	.52	.51
100	1.38	1.29	1.22	1.16	1.11	1.07	1.04	1.01
200	2.75	2.57	2.43	2.32	2.22	2.14	2.07	2.01
300	4.12	3.86	3.65	3.47	3.33	3.21	3.10	3.02
400	5.49	5.14	4.86	4.63	4.44	4.28	4.14	4.02
500	6.86	6.42	6.07	5.78	5.54	5.34	5.17	5.02
600	8.23	7.71	7.29	6.94	6.65	6.41	6.20	6.03
700	9.60	8.99	8.50	8.10	7.76	7.48	7.24	7.03
800	10.97	10.28	9.71	9.25	8.87	8.55	8.27	8.04
900	12.35	11.56	10.93	10.41	9.98	9.61	9.30	9.04
1000	13.72	12.84	12.14	11.56	11.08	10.68	10.34	10.04
2000	27.43	25.68	24.28	23.12	22.16	21.36	20.67	20.08
3000	41.14	38.52	36.42	34.68	33.24	32.03	31.00	30.12
4000	54.85	51.36	48.55	46.24	44.32	42.71	41.33	40.16
5000	68.56	64.20	60.69	57.80	55.40	53.38	51.67	50.20
6000	82.27	77.04	72.83	69.36	66.48	64.06	62.00	60.23
7000	95.99	89.88	84.96	80.92	77.56	74.73	72.33	70.27
8000	109.70	102.72	97.10	92.48	88.64	85.41	82.66	80.31
9000	123.41	115.56	109.24	104.04	99.72	96.09	93.00	90.35
10000	137.12	128.40	121.37	115.60	110.80	106.76	103.33	100.39
20000	274.24	256.80	242.74	231.20	221.60	213.52	206.65	200.77
30000	411.35	385.20	364.11	346.80	332.40	320.27	309.97	301.15
40000	548.47	513.60	485.47	462.39	443.19	427.03	413.30	401.53
50000	685.59	642.00	606.84	577.99	553.99	533.79	516.62	501.91
60000	822.70	770.40	728.21	693.59	664.79	640.54	619.94	602.29
70000	959.82	898.80	849.57	809.19	775.58	747.30	723.26	702.67
80000	1096.94	1027.20	970.94	924.78	886.38	854.06	826.59	803.05
90000	1234.05	1155.60	1092.31	1040.38	997.18	960.81	929.91	903.43
100000	1371.17	1284.00	1213.68	1155.98	1107.97	1067.57	1033.23	1003.81
110000	1508.29	1412.40	1335.04	1271.57	1218.77	1174.33	1136.55	1104.19
120000	1645.40	1540.79	1456.41	1387.17	1329.57	1281.08	1239.88	1204.57
130000	1782.52	1669.19	1577.78	1502.77	1440.36	1387.84	1343.20	1304.95
140000	1919.64	1797.59	1699.14	1618.37	1551.16	1494.60	1446.52	1405.33
150000	2056.75	1925.99	1820.51	1733.96	1661.96	1601.35	1549.84	1505.71
160000	2193.87	2054.39	1941.88	1849.56	1772.75	1708.11	1653.17	1606.09
170000	2330.98	2182.79	2063.24	1965.16	1883.55	1814.86	1756.49	1706.47
180000	2468.10	2311.19	2184.61	2080.76	1994.35	1921.62	1859.81	1806.85
190000	2605.22	2439.59	2305.98	2196.35	2105.14	2028.38	1963.13	1907.23
200000	2742.33	2567.99	2427.35	2311.95	2215.94	2135.13	2066.46	2007.61
210000	2879.45	2696.39	2548.71	2427.55	2326.74	2241.89	2169.78	2107.99
220000	3016.57	2824.79	2670.08	2543.14	2437.53	2348.65	2273.10	2208.37
230000	3153.68	2953.19	2791.45	2658.74	2548.33	2455.40	2376.43	2308.75
240000	3290.80	3081.58	2912.81	2774.34	2659.13	2562.16	2479.75	2409.13
250000	3427.92	3209.98	3034.18	2889.94	2769.92	2668.92	2583.07	2509.51
260000	3565.03	3338.38	3155.55	3005.53	2880.72	2775.67	2686.39	2609.89
270000	3702.15	3466.78	3276.92	3121.13	2991.52	2882.43	2789.72	2710.27
280000	3839.27	3595.18	3398.28	3236.73	3102.32	2989.19	2893.04	2810.65
290000	3976.38	3723.58	3519.65	3352.32	3213.11	3095.94	2996.36	2911.03
300000	4113.50	3851.98	3641.02	3467.92	3323.91	3202.70	3099.68	3011.41
310000	4250.61	3980.38	3762.38	3583.52	3434.71	3309.45	3203.01	3111.79
320000	4387.73	4108.78	3883.75	3699.12	3545.50	3416.21	3306.33	3212.17
330000	4524.85	4237.18	4005.12	3814.71	3656.30	3522.97	3409.65	3312.55
340000	4661.96	4365.58	4126.48	3930.31	3767.10	3629.72	3512.97	3412.93
350000	4799.08	4493.97	4247.85	4045.91	3877.89	3736.48	3616.30	3513.31
360000	4936.20	4622.37	4369.22	4161.51	3988.69	3843.24	3719.62	3613.69
370000	5073.31	4750.77	4490.59	4277.10	4099.49	3949.99	3822.94	3714.07
380000	5210.43	4879.17	4611.95	4392.70	4210.28	4056.75	3926.26	3814.45
390000	5347.55	5007.57	4733.32	4508.30	4321.08	4163.51	4029.59	3914.83
400000	5484.66	5135.97	4854.69	4623.89	4431.88	4270.26	4132.91	4015.21

Amount	17	18	19	20	21	22	23	24
25	.25	.24	.24	.24	.23	.23	.23	.22
50	.49	.48	.47	.47	.46	.45	.45	.44
100	.98	.96	.94	.93	.91	.90	.89	.88
200	1.96	1.92	1.88	1.85	1.82	1.79	1.77	1.75
300	2.94	2.87	2.82	2.77	2.72	2.68	2.65	2.62
400	3.92	3.83	3.75	3.69	3.63	3.57	3.53	3.49
500	4.90	4.79	4.69	4.61	4.53	4.47	4.41	4.36
600	5.88	5.74	5.63	5.53	5.44	5.36	5.29	5.23
700	6.85	6.70	6.56	6.45	6.34	6.25	6.17	6.10
800	7.83	7.66	7.50	7.37	7.25	7.14	7.05	6.97
900	8.81	8.61	8.44	8.29	8.15	8.04	7.93	7.84
1000	9.79	9.57	9.38	9.21	9.06	8.93	8.81	8.71
2000	19.57	19.13	18.75	18.41	18.11	17.85	17.62	17.41
3000	29.36	28.70	28.12	27.61	27.17	26.77	26.42	26.11
4000	39.14	38.26	37.49	36.81	36.22	35.69	35.23	34.81
5000	48.93	47.82	46.86	46.02	45.27	44.62	44.03	43.52
6000	58.71	57.39	56.23	55.22	54.33	53.54	52.84	52.22
7000	68.49	66.95	65.60	64.42	63.38	62.46	61.65	60.92
8000	78.28	76.51	74.97	73.62	72.43	71.38	70.45	69.62
9000	88.06	86.08	84.34	82.83	81.49	80.31	79.26	78.33
10000	97.85	95.64	93.72	92.03	90.54	89.23	88.06	87.03
20000	195.69	191.28	187.43	184.05	181.08	178.45	176.12	174.05
30000	293.53	286.91	281.14	276.07	271.62	267.68	264.18	261.08
40000	391.37	382.55	374.85	368.10	362.15	356.90	352.24	348.10
50000	489.21	478.18	468.56	460.12	452.69	446.12	440.30	435.13
60000	587.05	573.82	562.27	552.14	543.23	535.35	528.36	522.15
70000	684.89	669.45	655.98	644.17	633.76	624.57	616.42	609.18
80000	782.73	765.09	749.69	736.19	724.30	713.79	704.48	696.20
90000	880.57	860.73	843.40	828.21	814.84	803.02	792.54	783.23
100000	978.41	956.36	937.11	920.24	905.37	892.24	880.60	870.25
110000	1076.25	1052.00	1030.83	1012.26	995.91	981.47	968.66	957.28
120000	1174.09	1147.63	1124.54	1104.28	1086.45	1070.69	1056.72	1044.30
130000	1271.93	1243.27	1218.25	1196.30	1176.98	1159.91	1144.78	1131.33
140000	1369.77	1338.90	1311.96	1288.33	1267.52	1249.14	1232.84	1218.35
150000	1467.61	1434.54	1405.67	1380.35	1358.06	1338.36	1320.90	1305.38
160000	1565.45	1530.18	1499.38	1472.37	1448.60	1427.58	1408.96	1392.40
170000	1663.30	1625.81	1593.09	1564.40	1539.13	1516.81	1497.02	1479.43
180000	1761.14	1721.45	1686.80	1656.42	1629.67	1606.03	1585.08	1566.45
190000	1858.98	1817.08	1780.51	1748.44	1720.21	1695.25	1673.14	1653.48
200000	1956.82	1912.72	1874.22	1840.47	1810.74	1784.48	1761.20	1740.50
210000	2054.66	2008.35	1967.93	1932.49	1901.28	1873.70	1849.26	1827.53
220000	2152.50	2103.99	2061.65	2024.51	1991.82	1962.93	1937.32	1914.55
230000	2250.34	2199.62	2155.36	2116.54	2082.35	2052.15	2025.38	2001.58
240000	2348.18	2295.26	2249.07	2208.56	2172.89	2141.37	2113.44	2088.60
250000	2446.02	2390.90	2342.78	2300.58	2263.43	2230.60	2201.49	2175.63
260000	2543.86	2486.53	2436.49	2392.60	2353.96	2319.82	2289.55	2262.65
270000	2641.70	2582.17	2530.20	2484.63	2444.50	2409.04	2377.61	2349.68
280000	2739.54	2677.80	2623.91	2576.65	2535.04	2498.27	2465.67	2436.70
290000	2837.38	2773.44	2717.62	2668.67	2625.58	2587.49	2553.73	2523.73
300000	2935.22	2869.07	2811.33	2760.70	2716.11	2676.72	2641.79	2610.75
310000	3033.06	2964.71	2905.04	2852.72	2806.65	2765.94	2729.85	2697.78
320000	3130.90	3060.35	2998.75	2944.74	2897.19	2855.16	2817.91	2784.80
330000	3228.75	3155.98	3092.47	3036.77	2987.72	2944.39	2905.97	2871.82
340000	3326.59	3251.62	3186.18	3128.79	3078.26	3033.61	2994.03	2958.85
350000	3424.43	3347.25	3279.89	3220.81	3168.80	3122.83	3082.09	3045.87
360000	3522.27	3442.89	3373.60	3312.83	3259.33	3212.06	3170.15	3132.90
370000	3620.11	3538.52	3467.31	3404.86	3349.87	3301.28	3258.21	3219.92
380000	3717.95	3634.16	3561.02	3496.88	3440.41	3390.50	3346.27	3306.95
390000	3815.79	3729.79	3654.73	3588.90	3530.94	3479.73	3434.33	3393.97
400000	3913.63	3825.43	3748.44	3680.93	3621.48	3568.95	3522.39	3481.00

111

9½% BLENDED MONTHLY PAYMENTS
AMORTIZATION IN YEARS

Amount	25	26	29	30	35	40	45	50
25	.22	.22	.21	.21	.21	.20	.20	.20
50	.44	.43	.42	.42	.41	.40	.40	.40
100	.87	.86	.84	.83	.81	.80	.79	.79
200	1.73	1.71	1.67	1.66	1.62	1.60	1.58	1.57
300	2.59	2.56	2.50	2.49	2.43	2.39	2.37	2.36
400	3.45	3.42	3.34	3.32	3.24	3.19	3.16	3.14
500	4.31	4.27	4.17	4.14	4.04	3.98	3.95	3.93
600	5.17	5.12	5.00	4.97	4.85	4.78	4.74	4.71
700	6.03	5.97	5.84	5.80	5.66	5.58	5.52	5.49
800	6.89	6.83	6.67	6.63	6.47	6.37	6.31	6.28
900	7.75	7.68	7.50	7.45	7.28	7.17	7.10	7.06
1000	8.62	8.53	8.33	8.28	8.08	7.96	7.89	7.85
2000	17.23	17.06	16.66	16.56	16.16	15.92	15.78	15.69
3000	25.84	25.59	24.99	24.83	24.24	23.88	23.66	23.53
4000	34.45	34.12	33.32	33.11	32.32	31.84	31.55	31.37
5000	43.06	42.64	41.65	41.38	40.40	39.80	39.43	39.21
6000	51.67	51.17	49.98	49.66	48.47	47.76	47.32	47.05
7000	60.28	59.70	58.31	57.93	56.55	55.72	55.20	54.89
8000	68.89	68.23	66.64	66.21	64.63	63.67	63.09	62.73
9000	77.50	76.76	74.96	74.48	72.71	71.63	70.97	70.57
10000	86.11	85.28	83.29	82.76	80.79	79.59	78.86	78.41
20000	172.21	170.56	166.58	165.52	161.57	159.18	157.71	156.81
30000	258.31	255.84	249.87	248.27	242.35	238.77	236.57	235.21
40000	344.42	341.12	333.16	331.03	323.13	318.35	315.42	313.61
50000	430.52	426.40	416.45	413.78	403.91	397.94	394.28	392.01
60000	516.62	511.68	499.74	496.54	484.69	477.53	473.13	470.41
70000	602.72	596.96	583.03	579.29	565.47	557.11	551.99	548.81
80000	688.83	682.24	666.31	662.05	646.25	636.70	630.84	627.21
90000	774.93	767.52	749.60	744.80	727.03	716.29	709.69	705.61
100000	861.03	852.80	832.89	827.56	807.81	795.88	788.55	784.01
110000	947.14	938.08	916.18	910.31	888.60	875.46	867.40	862.41
120000	1033.24	1023.36	999.47	993.07	969.38	955.05	946.26	940.81
130000	1119.34	1108.64	1082.76	1075.83	1050.16	1034.64	1025.11	1019.21
140000	1205.44	1193.91	1166.05	1158.58	1130.94	1114.22	1103.97	1097.61
150000	1291.55	1279.19	1249.34	1241.34	1211.72	1193.81	1182.82	1176.01
160000	1377.65	1364.47	1332.62	1324.09	1292.50	1273.40	1261.67	1254.41
170000	1463.75	1449.75	1415.91	1406.85	1373.28	1352.98	1340.53	1332.81
180000	1549.85	1535.03	1499.20	1489.60	1454.06	1432.57	1419.38	1411.21
190000	1635.96	1620.31	1582.49	1572.36	1534.84	1512.16	1498.24	1489.61
200000	1722.06	1705.59	1665.78	1655.11	1615.62	1591.75	1577.09	1568.02
210000	1808.16	1790.87	1749.07	1737.87	1696.40	1671.33	1655.95	1646.42
220000	1894.27	1876.15	1832.36	1820.62	1777.19	1750.92	1734.80	1724.82
230000	1980.37	1961.43	1915.64	1903.38	1857.97	1830.51	1813.65	1803.22
240000	2066.47	2046.71	1998.93	1986.13	1938.75	1910.09	1892.51	1881.62
250000	2152.57	2131.99	2082.22	2068.89	2019.53	1989.68	1971.36	1960.02
260000	2238.68	2217.27	2165.51	2151.65	2100.31	2069.27	2050.22	2038.42
270000	2324.78	2302.55	2248.80	2234.40	2181.09	2148.86	2129.07	2116.82
280000	2410.88	2387.82	2332.09	2317.16	2261.87	2228.44	2207.93	2195.22
290000	2496.99	2473.10	2415.38	2399.91	2342.65	2308.03	2286.78	2273.62
300000	2583.09	2558.38	2498.67	2482.67	2423.43	2387.62	2365.63	2352.02
310000	2669.19	2643.66	2581.95	2565.42	2504.21	2467.20	2444.49	2430.42
320000	2755.29	2728.94	2665.24	2648.18	2584.99	2546.79	2523.34	2508.82
330000	2841.40	2814.22	2748.53	2730.93	2665.78	2626.38	2602.20	2587.22
340000	2927.50	2899.50	2831.82	2813.69	2746.56	2705.96	2681.05	2665.62
350000	3013.60	2984.78	2915.11	2896.44	2827.34	2785.55	2759.91	2744.02
360000	3099.70	3070.06	2998.40	2979.20	2908.12	2865.14	2838.76	2822.42
370000	3185.81	3155.34	3081.69	3061.95	2988.90	2944.73	2917.62	2900.82
380000	3271.91	3240.62	3164.97	3144.71	3069.68	3024.31	2996.47	2979.22
390000	3358.01	3325.90	3248.26	3227.47	3150.46	3103.90	3075.32	3057.63
400000	3444.12	3411.18	3331.55	3310.22	3231.24	3183.49	3154.18	3136.03

BLENDED MONTHLY PAYMENTS
AMORTIZATION IN YEARS

9¾%

Amount	1	2	3	4	5	6	7	8
25	2.20	1.15	.81	.63	.53	.46	.41	.38
50	4.39	2.30	1.61	1.26	1.06	.92	.82	.75
100	8.78	4.60	3.21	2.52	2.11	1.84	1.64	1.50
200	17.55	9.19	6.42	5.04	4.21	3.67	3.28	2.99
300	26.32	13.79	9.62	7.55	6.31	5.50	4.92	4.49
400	35.09	18.38	12.83	10.07	8.42	7.33	6.55	5.98
500	43.86	22.98	16.03	12.58	10.52	9.16	8.19	7.48
600	52.63	27.57	19.24	15.10	12.62	10.99	9.83	8.97
700	61.40	32.16	22.45	17.61	14.73	12.82	11.47	10.46
800	70.17	36.76	25.65	20.13	16.83	14.65	13.10	11.96
900	78.94	41.35	28.86	22.64	18.93	16.48	14.74	13.45
1000	87.72	45.95	32.06	25.16	21.04	18.31	16.38	14.95
2000	175.43	91.89	64.12	50.31	42.07	36.61	32.75	29.89
3000	263.14	137.83	96.18	75.46	63.10	54.92	49.13	44.83
4000	350.85	183.77	128.24	100.61	84.13	73.22	65.50	59.77
5000	438.56	229.71	160.30	125.76	105.16	91.52	81.87	74.71
6000	526.27	275.65	192.36	150.91	126.19	109.83	98.25	89.65
7000	613.98	321.59	224.42	176.06	147.22	128.13	114.62	104.59
8000	701.69	367.53	256.48	201.21	168.25	146.43	130.99	119.53
9000	789.40	413.47	288.54	226.36	189.28	164.74	147.37	134.48
10000	877.11	459.42	320.60	251.51	210.31	183.04	163.74	149.42
20000	1754.21	918.83	641.20	503.02	420.61	366.08	327.48	298.83
30000	2631.31	1378.24	961.80	754.53	630.91	549.11	491.21	448.24
40000	3508.42	1837.65	1282.40	1006.03	841.21	732.15	654.95	597.65
50000	4385.52	2297.06	1603.00	1257.54	1051.51	915.18	818.68	747.06
60000	5262.62	2756.47	1923.60	1509.05	1261.81	1098.22	982.42	896.47
70000	6139.73	3215.88	2244.20	1760.55	1472.11	1281.25	1146.15	1045.88
80000	7016.83	3675.29	2564.80	2012.06	1682.41	1464.29	1309.89	1195.29
90000	7893.93	4134.70	2885.40	2263.57	1892.71	1647.32	1473.62	1344.71
100000	8771.03	4594.11	3206.00	2515.07	2103.01	1830.36	1637.36	1494.12
110000	9648.14	5053.52	3526.59	2766.58	2313.31	2013.40	1801.09	1643.53
120000	10525.24	5512.93	3847.19	3018.09	2523.61	2196.43	1964.83	1792.94
130000	11402.34	5972.34	4167.79	3269.59	2733.91	2379.47	2128.56	1942.35
140000	12279.45	6431.75	4488.39	3521.10	2944.21	2562.50	2292.30	2091.76
150000	13156.55	6891.16	4808.99	3772.61	3154.51	2745.54	2456.03	2241.17
160000	14033.65	7350.57	5129.59	4024.11	3364.81	2928.57	2619.77	2390.58
170000	14910.75	7809.98	5450.19	4275.62	3575.11	3111.61	2783.50	2539.99
180000	15787.86	8269.39	5770.79	4527.13	3785.41	3294.64	2947.24	2689.41
190000	16664.96	8728.80	6091.39	4778.63	3995.71	3477.68	3110.97	2838.82
200000	17542.06	9188.21	6411.99	5030.14	4206.01	3660.71	3274.71	2988.23
210000	18419.17	9647.62	6732.59	5281.65	4416.32	3843.75	3438.44	3137.64
220000	19296.27	10107.03	7053.18	5533.15	4626.62	4026.79	3602.18	3287.05
230000	20173.37	10566.44	7373.78	5784.66	4836.92	4209.82	3765.92	3436.46
240000	21050.47	11025.85	7694.38	6036.17	5047.22	4392.86	3929.65	3585.87
250000	21927.58	11485.26	8014.98	6287.67	5257.52	4575.89	4093.39	3735.28
260000	22804.68	11944.67	8335.58	6539.18	5467.82	4758.93	4257.12	3884.69
270000	23681.78	12404.08	8656.18	6790.69	5678.12	4941.96	4420.86	4034.11
280000	24558.89	12863.49	8976.78	7042.20	5888.42	5125.00	4584.59	4183.52
290000	25435.99	13322.90	9297.38	7293.70	6098.72	5308.03	4748.33	4332.93
300000	26313.09	13782.31	9617.98	7545.21	6309.02	5491.07	4912.06	4482.34
310000	27190.20	14241.72	9938.58	7796.72	6519.32	5674.11	5075.80	4631.75
320000	28067.30	14701.13	10259.18	8048.22	6729.62	5857.14	5239.53	4781.16
330000	28944.40	15160.55	10579.77	8299.73	6939.92	6040.18	5403.27	4930.57
340000	29821.50	15619.96	10900.37	8551.24	7150.22	6223.21	5567.00	5079.98
350000	30698.61	16079.37	11220.97	8802.74	7360.52	6406.25	5730.74	5229.40
360000	31575.71	16538.78	11541.57	9054.25	7570.82	6589.28	5894.47	5378.81
370000	32452.81	16998.19	11862.17	9305.76	7781.12	6772.32	6058.21	5528.22
380000	33329.92	17457.60	12182.77	9557.26	7991.42	6955.35	6221.94	5677.63
390000	34207.02	17917.01	12503.37	9808.77	8201.72	7138.39	6385.68	5827.04
400000	35084.12	18376.42	12823.97	10060.28	8412.02	7321.42	6549.41	5976.45

9¾% BLENDED MONTHLY PAYMENTS
AMORTIZATION IN YEARS

Amount	9	10	11	12	13	14	15	16
25	.35	.33	.31	.30	.29	.28	.27	.26
50	.70	.65	.62	.59	.57	.55	.53	.51
100	1.39	1.30	1.23	1.17	1.13	1.09	1.05	1.02
200	2.77	2.60	2.46	2.34	2.25	2.17	2.10	2.04
300	4.16	3.90	3.69	3.51	3.37	3.25	3.15	3.06
400	5.54	5.19	4.91	4.68	4.49	4.33	4.20	4.08
500	6.93	6.49	6.14	5.85	5.61	5.41	5.24	5.10
600	8.31	7.79	7.37	7.02	6.74	6.50	6.29	6.12
700	9.69	9.08	8.59	8.19	7.86	7.58	7.34	7.13
800	11.08	10.38	9.82	9.36	8.98	8.66	8.39	8.15
900	12.46	11.68	11.05	10.53	10.10	9.74	9.43	9.17
1000	13.85	12.98	12.28	11.70	11.22	10.82	10.48	10.19
2000	27.69	25.95	24.55	23.40	22.44	21.64	20.96	20.38
3000	41.53	38.92	36.82	35.09	33.66	32.46	31.44	30.56
4000	55.37	51.89	49.09	46.79	44.88	43.28	41.91	40.75
5000	69.21	64.86	61.36	58.49	56.10	54.09	52.39	50.93
6000	83.05	77.83	73.63	70.18	67.32	64.91	62.87	61.12
7000	96.89	90.80	85.90	81.88	78.54	75.73	73.34	71.30
8000	110.73	103.78	98.17	93.58	89.76	86.55	83.82	81.49
9000	124.57	116.75	110.44	105.27	100.98	97.37	94.30	91.67
10000	138.41	129.72	122.71	116.97	112.20	108.18	104.78	101.86
20000	276.81	259.43	245.42	233.94	224.39	216.36	209.55	203.71
30000	415.21	389.15	368.13	350.90	336.58	324.54	314.32	305.56
40000	553.62	518.86	490.84	467.87	448.78	432.72	419.09	407.42
50000	692.02	648.57	613.55	584.84	560.97	540.90	523.86	509.27
60000	830.42	778.29	736.26	701.80	673.16	649.08	628.63	611.12
70000	968.82	908.00	858.97	818.77	785.36	757.26	733.40	712.98
80000	1107.23	1037.71	981.68	935.74	897.55	865.44	838.17	814.83
90000	1245.63	1167.43	1104.39	1052.70	1009.74	973.61	942.94	916.68
100000	1384.03	1297.14	1227.10	1169.67	1121.93	1081.79	1047.71	1018.54
110000	1522.43	1426.85	1349.80	1286.64	1234.13	1189.97	1152.48	1120.39
120000	1660.84	1556.57	1472.51	1403.60	1346.32	1298.15	1257.25	1222.24
130000	1799.24	1686.28	1595.22	1520.57	1458.51	1406.33	1362.02	1324.10
140000	1937.64	1815.99	1717.93	1637.54	1570.71	1514.51	1466.79	1425.95
150000	2076.05	1945.71	1840.64	1754.50	1682.90	1622.69	1571.56	1527.80
160000	2214.45	2075.42	1963.35	1871.47	1795.09	1730.87	1676.34	1629.66
170000	2352.85	2205.13	2086.06	1988.44	1907.28	1839.04	1781.11	1731.51
180000	2491.25	2334.85	2208.77	2105.40	2019.48	1947.22	1885.88	1833.36
190000	2629.66	2464.56	2331.48	2222.37	2131.67	2055.40	1990.65	1935.22
200000	2768.06	2594.27	2454.19	2339.33	2243.86	2163.58	2095.42	2037.07
210000	2906.46	2723.99	2576.89	2456.30	2356.06	2271.76	2200.19	2138.92
220000	3044.86	2853.70	2699.60	2573.27	2468.25	2379.94	2304.96	2240.78
230000	3183.27	2983.41	2822.31	2690.23	2580.44	2488.12	2409.73	2342.63
240000	3321.67	3113.13	2945.02	2807.20	2692.63	2596.30	2514.50	2444.48
250000	3460.07	3242.84	3067.73	2924.17	2804.83	2704.47	2619.27	2546.34
260000	3598.48	3372.55	3190.44	3041.13	2917.02	2812.65	2724.04	2648.19
270000	3736.88	3502.27	3313.15	3158.10	3029.21	2920.83	2828.81	2750.04
280000	3875.28	3631.98	3435.86	3275.07	3141.41	3029.01	2933.58	2851.89
290000	4013.68	3761.69	3558.57	3392.03	3253.60	3137.19	3038.35	2953.75
300000	4152.09	3891.41	3681.28	3509.00	3365.79	3245.37	3143.12	3055.60
310000	4290.49	4021.12	3803.99	3625.97	3477.98	3353.55	3247.90	3157.45
320000	4428.89	4150.84	3926.69	3742.93	3590.18	3461.73	3352.67	3259.31
330000	4567.29	4280.55	4049.40	3859.90	3702.37	3569.90	3457.44	3361.16
340000	4705.70	4410.26	4172.11	3976.87	3814.56	3678.08	3562.21	3463.01
350000	4844.10	4539.98	4294.82	4093.83	3926.76	3786.26	3666.98	3564.87
360000	4982.50	4669.69	4417.53	4210.80	4038.95	3894.44	3771.75	3666.72
370000	5120.91	4799.40	4540.24	4327.77	4151.14	4002.62	3876.52	3768.57
380000	5259.31	4929.12	4662.95	4444.73	4263.33	4110.80	3981.29	3870.43
390000	5397.71	5058.83	4785.66	4561.70	4375.53	4218.98	4086.06	3972.28
400000	5536.11	5188.54	4908.37	4678.66	4487.72	4327.16	4190.83	4074.13

BLENDED MONTHLY PAYMENTS 9¾%

AMORTIZATION IN YEARS

Amount	17	18	19	20	21	22	23	24
25	.25	.25	.24	.24	.24	.23	.23	.23
50	.50	.49	.48	.47	.47	.46	.45	.45
100	1.00	.98	.96	.94	.93	.91	.90	.89
200	1.99	1.95	1.91	1.88	1.85	1.82	1.80	1.78
300	2.99	2.92	2.86	2.81	2.77	2.73	2.70	2.67
400	3.98	3.89	3.82	3.75	3.69	3.64	3.59	3.55
500	4.97	4.86	4.77	4.68	4.61	4.55	4.49	4.44
600	5.97	5.83	5.72	5.62	5.53	5.45	5.39	5.33
700	6.96	6.81	6.67	6.56	6.45	6.36	6.28	6.21
800	7.95	7.78	7.63	7.49	7.38	7.27	7.18	7.10
900	8.95	8.75	8.58	8.43	8.30	8.18	8.08	7.99
1000	9.94	9.72	9.53	9.36	9.22	9.09	8.97	8.87
2000	19.87	19.44	19.06	18.72	18.43	18.17	17.94	17.74
3000	29.81	29.15	28.58	28.08	27.64	27.25	26.91	26.61
4000	39.74	38.87	38.11	37.44	36.86	36.34	35.88	35.47
5000	49.67	48.58	47.63	46.80	46.07	45.42	44.85	44.34
6000	59.61	58.30	57.16	56.16	55.28	54.50	53.82	53.21
7000	69.54	68.01	66.68	65.52	64.49	63.59	62.79	62.08
8000	79.48	77.73	76.21	74.88	73.71	72.67	71.76	70.94
9000	89.41	87.45	85.73	84.24	82.92	81.75	80.73	79.81
10000	99.34	97.16	95.26	93.59	92.13	90.84	89.69	88.68
20000	198.68	194.32	190.52	187.18	184.26	181.67	179.38	177.35
30000	298.02	291.48	285.77	280.77	276.38	272.50	269.07	266.03
40000	397.36	388.63	381.03	374.36	368.51	363.34	358.76	354.70
50000	496.70	485.79	476.28	467.95	460.63	454.17	448.45	443.38
60000	596.03	582.95	571.54	561.54	552.76	545.00	538.14	532.05
70000	695.37	680.10	666.79	655.13	644.88	635.84	627.83	620.72
80000	794.71	777.26	762.05	748.72	737.01	726.67	717.52	709.40
90000	894.05	874.42	857.30	842.31	829.13	817.50	807.21	798.07
100000	993.39	971.58	952.56	935.90	921.26	908.34	896.90	886.75
110000	1092.73	1068.73	1047.81	1029.49	1013.39	999.17	986.59	975.42
120000	1192.06	1165.89	1143.07	1123.08	1105.51	1090.00	1076.28	1064.09
130000	1291.40	1263.05	1238.33	1216.67	1197.64	1180.84	1165.97	1152.77
140000	1390.74	1360.20	1333.58	1310.26	1289.76	1271.67	1255.66	1241.44
150000	1490.08	1457.36	1428.84	1403.85	1381.89	1362.50	1345.35	1330.12
160000	1589.42	1554.52	1524.09	1497.44	1474.01	1453.34	1435.03	1418.79
170000	1688.75	1651.67	1619.35	1591.03	1566.14	1544.17	1524.72	1507.46
180000	1788.09	1748.83	1714.60	1684.62	1658.26	1635.00	1614.41	1596.14
190000	1887.43	1845.99	1809.86	1778.21	1750.39	1725.84	1704.10	1684.81
200000	1986.77	1943.15	1905.11	1871.80	1842.51	1816.67	1793.79	1773.49
210000	2086.11	2040.30	2000.37	1965.39	1934.64	1907.50	1883.48	1862.16
220000	2185.45	2137.46	2095.62	2058.98	2026.77	1998.34	1973.17	1950.84
230000	2284.78	2234.62	2190.88	2152.57	2118.89	2089.17	2062.86	2039.51
240000	2384.12	2331.77	2286.13	2246.16	2211.02	2180.00	2152.55	2128.18
250000	2483.46	2428.93	2381.39	2339.75	2303.14	2270.84	2242.24	2216.86
260000	2582.80	2526.09	2476.65	2433.34	2395.27	2361.67	2331.93	2305.53
270000	2682.14	2623.24	2571.90	2526.93	2487.39	2452.50	2421.62	2394.21
280000	2781.47	2720.40	2667.16	2620.52	2579.52	2543.34	2511.31	2482.88
290000	2880.81	2817.56	2762.41	2714.11	2671.64	2634.17	2601.00	2571.55
300000	2980.15	2914.72	2857.67	2807.70	2763.77	2725.00	2690.69	2660.23
310000	3079.49	3011.87	2952.92	2901.29	2855.89	2815.83	2780.38	2748.90
320000	3178.83	3109.03	3048.18	2994.88	2948.02	2906.67	2870.06	2837.58
330000	3278.17	3206.19	3143.43	3088.47	3040.15	2997.50	2959.75	2926.25
340000	3377.50	3303.34	3238.69	3182.06	3132.27	3088.33	3049.44	3014.92
350000	3476.84	3400.50	3333.94	3275.65	3224.40	3179.17	3139.13	3103.60
360000	3576.18	3497.66	3429.20	3369.24	3316.52	3270.00	3228.82	3192.27
370000	3675.52	3594.81	3524.45	3462.83	3408.65	3360.83	3318.51	3280.95
380000	3774.86	3691.97	3619.71	3556.42	3500.77	3451.67	3408.20	3369.62
390000	3874.20	3789.13	3714.97	3650.01	3592.90	3542.50	3497.89	3458.30
400000	3973.53	3886.29	3810.22	3743.60	3685.02	3633.33	3587.58	3546.97

Amount	25	26	29	30	35	40	45	50
25	.22	.22	.22	.22	.21	.21	.21	.21
50	.44	.44	.43	.43	.42	.41	.41	.41
100	.88	.87	.86	.85	.83	.82	.81	.81
200	1.76	1.74	1.71	1.70	1.66	1.63	1.62	1.61
300	2.64	2.61	2.56	2.54	2.48	2.45	2.43	2.42
400	3.52	3.48	3.41	3.39	3.31	3.26	3.24	3.22
500	4.39	4.35	4.26	4.23	4.13	4.08	4.04	4.02
600	5.27	5.22	5.11	5.08	4.96	4.89	4.85	4.83
700	6.15	6.09	5.96	5.92	5.79	5.71	5.66	5.63
800	7.03	6.96	6.81	6.77	6.61	6.52	6.47	6.43
900	7.90	7.83	7.66	7.61	7.44	7.34	7.27	7.24
1000	8.78	8.70	8.51	8.46	8.26	8.15	8.08	8.04
2000	17.56	17.40	17.01	16.91	16.52	16.30	16.16	16.07
3000	26.34	26.09	25.51	25.36	24.78	24.44	24.23	24.11
4000	35.11	34.79	34.01	33.81	33.04	32.59	32.31	32.14
5000	43.89	43.49	42.52	42.26	41.30	40.73	40.39	40.17
6000	52.67	52.18	51.02	50.71	49.56	48.88	48.46	48.21
7000	61.44	60.88	59.52	59.16	57.82	57.02	56.54	56.24
8000	70.22	69.58	68.02	67.61	66.08	65.17	64.61	64.27
9000	79.00	78.27	76.53	76.06	74.34	73.31	72.69	72.31
10000	87.78	86.97	85.03	84.51	82.60	81.46	80.77	80.34
20000	175.55	173.94	170.05	169.02	165.20	162.91	161.53	160.68
30000	263.32	260.90	255.08	253.52	247.80	244.37	242.29	241.01
40000	351.09	347.87	340.10	338.03	330.40	325.82	323.05	321.35
50000	438.86	434.83	425.13	422.54	412.99	407.28	403.81	401.68
60000	526.63	521.80	510.15	507.04	495.59	488.73	484.57	482.02
70000	614.40	608.76	595.18	591.55	578.19	570.19	565.33	562.35
80000	702.17	695.73	680.20	676.06	660.79	651.64	646.09	642.69
90000	789.94	782.69	765.23	760.56	743.39	733.10	726.85	723.02
100000	877.71	869.66	850.25	845.07	825.98	814.55	807.61	803.36
110000	965.48	956.62	935.27	929.58	908.58	896.01	888.37	883.69
120000	1053.25	1043.59	1020.30	1014.08	991.18	977.46	969.13	964.03
130000	1141.03	1130.55	1105.32	1098.59	1073.78	1058.92	1049.89	1044.36
140000	1228.80	1217.52	1190.35	1183.09	1156.38	1140.37	1130.66	1124.70
150000	1316.57	1304.48	1275.37	1267.60	1238.97	1221.83	1211.42	1205.03
160000	1404.34	1391.45	1360.40	1352.11	1321.57	1303.28	1292.18	1285.37
170000	1492.11	1478.42	1445.42	1436.61	1404.17	1384.74	1372.94	1365.71
180000	1579.88	1565.38	1530.45	1521.12	1486.77	1466.19	1453.70	1446.04
190000	1667.65	1652.35	1615.47	1605.63	1569.36	1547.65	1534.46	1526.38
200000	1755.42	1739.31	1700.50	1690.13	1651.96	1629.10	1615.22	1606.71
210000	1843.19	1826.28	1785.52	1774.64	1734.56	1710.56	1695.98	1687.05
220000	1930.96	1913.24	1870.54	1859.15	1817.16	1792.01	1776.74	1767.38
230000	2018.73	2000.21	1955.57	1943.65	1899.76	1873.47	1857.50	1847.72
240000	2106.50	2087.17	2040.59	2028.16	1982.35	1954.92	1938.26	1928.05
250000	2194.27	2174.14	2125.62	2112.67	2064.95	2036.38	2019.02	2008.39
260000	2282.05	2261.10	2210.64	2197.17	2147.55	2117.83	2099.78	2088.72
270000	2369.82	2348.07	2295.67	2281.68	2230.15	2199.29	2180.54	2169.06
280000	2457.59	2435.03	2380.69	2366.18	2312.75	2280.74	2261.31	2249.39
290000	2545.36	2522.00	2465.72	2450.69	2395.34	2362.20	2342.07	2329.73
300000	2633.13	2608.96	2550.74	2535.20	2477.94	2443.65	2422.83	2410.06
310000	2720.90	2695.93	2635.76	2619.70	2560.54	2525.11	2503.59	2490.40
320000	2808.67	2782.90	2720.79	2704.21	2643.14	2606.56	2584.35	2570.74
330000	2896.44	2869.86	2805.81	2788.72	2725.74	2688.02	2665.11	2651.07
340000	2984.21	2956.83	2890.84	2873.22	2808.33	2769.47	2745.87	2731.41
350000	3071.98	3043.79	2975.86	2957.73	2890.93	2850.93	2826.63	2811.74
360000	3159.75	3130.76	3060.89	3042.24	2973.53	2932.38	2907.39	2892.08
370000	3247.52	3217.72	3145.91	3126.74	3056.13	3013.84	2988.15	2972.41
380000	3335.30	3304.69	3230.94	3211.25	3138.72	3095.29	3068.91	3052.75
390000	3423.07	3391.65	3315.96	3295.76	3221.32	3176.75	3149.67	3133.08
400000	3510.84	3478.62	3400.99	3380.26	3303.92	3258.20	3230.43	3213.42

BLENDED MONTHLY PAYMENTS

AMORTIZATION IN YEARS

10%

Amount	1	2	3	4	5	6	7	8
25	2.20	1.16	.81	.64	.53	.47	.42	.38
50	4.40	2.31	1.61	1.27	1.06	.93	.83	.76
100	8.79	4.61	3.22	2.53	2.12	1.85	1.65	1.51
200	17.57	9.22	6.44	5.06	4.23	3.69	3.30	3.02
300	26.35	13.82	9.66	7.58	6.35	5.53	4.95	4.53
400	35.13	18.43	12.87	10.11	8.46	7.37	6.60	6.03
500	43.92	23.03	16.09	12.64	10.58	9.22	8.25	7.54
600	52.70	27.64	19.31	15.16	12.69	11.06	9.90	9.05
700	61.48	32.24	22.53	17.69	14.81	12.90	11.55	10.55
800	70.26	36.85	25.74	20.22	16.92	14.74	13.20	12.06
900	79.04	41.45	28.96	22.74	19.04	16.59	14.85	13.57
1000	87.83	46.06	32.18	25.27	21.15	18.43	16.50	15.07
2000	175.65	92.11	64.35	50.54	42.30	36.85	33.00	30.14
3000	263.47	138.16	96.52	75.80	63.45	55.28	49.50	45.21
4000	351.29	184.21	128.69	101.07	84.60	73.70	65.99	60.27
5000	439.11	230.26	160.87	126.33	105.74	92.13	82.49	75.34
6000	526.94	276.31	193.04	151.60	126.89	110.55	98.99	90.41
7000	614.76	322.37	225.21	176.86	148.04	128.97	115.48	105.48
8000	702.58	368.42	257.38	202.13	169.19	147.40	131.98	120.54
9000	790.40	414.47	289.56	227.40	190.33	165.82	148.48	135.61
10000	878.22	460.52	321.73	252.66	211.48	184.25	164.97	150.68
20000	1756.44	921.04	643.45	505.32	422.96	368.49	329.94	301.35
30000	2634.66	1381.55	965.18	757.97	634.44	552.73	494.91	452.03
40000	3512.88	1842.07	1286.90	1010.63	845.91	736.97	659.88	602.70
50000	4391.10	2302.59	1608.62	1263.28	1057.39	921.21	824.85	753.37
60000	5269.32	2763.10	1930.35	1515.94	1268.87	1105.45	989.82	904.05
70000	6147.54	3223.62	2252.07	1768.60	1480.34	1289.69	1154.79	1054.72
80000	7025.76	3684.14	2573.79	2021.25	1691.82	1473.93	1319.76	1205.40
90000	7903.97	4144.65	2895.52	2273.91	1903.30	1658.17	1484.73	1356.07
100000	8782.19	4605.17	3217.24	2526.56	2114.77	1842.41	1649.70	1506.74
110000	9660.41	5065.69	3538.96	2779.22	2326.25	2026.65	1814.66	1657.42
120000	10538.63	5526.20	3860.69	3031.88	2537.73	2210.89	1979.63	1808.09
130000	11416.85	5986.72	4182.41	3284.53	2749.21	2395.13	2144.60	1958.77
140000	12295.07	6447.24	4504.13	3537.19	2960.68	2579.37	2309.57	2109.44
150000	13173.29	6907.75	4825.86	3789.84	3172.16	2763.61	2474.54	2260.11
160000	14051.51	7368.27	5147.58	4042.50	3383.64	2947.85	2639.51	2410.79
170000	14929.72	7828.79	5469.30	4295.16	3595.11	3132.09	2804.48	2561.46
180000	15807.94	8289.30	5791.03	4547.81	3806.59	3316.33	2969.45	2712.14
190000	16686.16	8749.82	6112.75	4800.47	4018.07	3500.57	3134.42	2862.81
200000	17564.38	9210.34	6434.47	5053.12	4229.54	3684.81	3299.39	3013.48
210000	18442.60	9670.85	6756.20	5305.78	4441.02	3869.05	3464.35	3164.16
220000	19320.82	10131.37	7077.92	5558.44	4652.50	4053.29	3629.32	3314.83
230000	20199.04	10591.89	7399.64	5811.09	4863.98	4237.53	3794.29	3465.51
240000	21077.26	11052.40	7721.37	6063.75	5075.45	4421.78	3959.26	3616.18
250000	21955.48	11512.92	8043.09	6316.40	5286.93	4606.02	4124.23	3766.85
260000	22833.69	11973.44	8364.81	6569.06	5498.41	4790.26	4289.20	3917.53
270000	23711.91	12433.95	8686.54	6821.72	5709.88	4974.50	4454.17	4068.20
280000	24590.13	12894.47	9008.26	7074.37	5921.36	5158.74	4619.14	4218.87
290000	25468.35	13354.99	9329.99	7327.03	6132.84	5342.98	4784.11	4369.55
300000	26346.57	13815.50	9651.71	7579.68	6344.31	5527.22	4949.08	4520.22
310000	27224.79	14276.02	9973.43	7832.34	6555.79	5711.46	5114.04	4670.90
320000	28103.01	14736.54	10295.16	8085.00	6767.27	5895.70	5279.01	4821.57
330000	28981.23	15197.05	10616.88	8337.65	6978.75	6079.94	5443.98	4972.24
340000	29859.44	15657.57	10938.60	8590.31	7190.22	6264.18	5608.95	5122.92
350000	30737.66	16118.09	11260.33	8842.96	7401.70	6448.42	5773.92	5273.59
360000	31615.88	16578.60	11582.05	9095.62	7613.18	6632.66	5938.89	5424.27
370000	32494.10	17039.12	11903.77	9348.28	7824.65	6816.90	6103.86	5574.94
380000	33372.32	17499.64	12225.50	9600.93	8036.13	7001.14	6268.83	5725.61
390000	34250.54	17960.15	12547.22	9853.59	8247.61	7185.38	6433.80	5876.29
400000	35128.76	18420.67	12868.94	10106.24	8459.08	7369.62	6598.77	6026.96

10% BLENDED MONTHLY PAYMENTS
AMORTIZATION IN YEARS

Amount	9	10	11	12	13	14	15	16
25	.35	.33	.32	.30	.29	.28	.27	.26
50	.70	.66	.63	.60	.57	.55	.54	.52
100	1.40	1.32	1.25	1.19	1.14	1.10	1.07	1.04
200	2.80	2.63	2.49	2.37	2.28	2.20	2.13	2.07
300	4.20	3.94	3.73	3.56	3.41	3.29	3.19	3.11
400	5.59	5.25	4.97	4.74	4.55	4.39	4.25	4.14
500	6.99	6.56	6.21	5.92	5.68	5.49	5.32	5.17
600	8.39	7.87	7.45	7.11	6.82	6.58	6.38	6.21
700	9.78	9.18	8.69	8.29	7.96	7.68	7.44	7.24
800	11.18	10.49	9.93	9.47	9.09	8.77	8.50	8.27
900	12.58	11.80	11.17	10.66	10.23	9.87	9.57	9.31
1000	13.97	13.11	12.41	11.84	11.36	10.97	10.63	10.34
2000	27.94	26.21	24.82	23.67	22.72	21.93	21.25	20.67
3000	41.91	39.32	37.22	35.51	34.08	32.89	31.87	31.01
4000	55.88	52.42	49.63	47.34	45.44	43.85	42.50	41.34
5000	69.85	65.52	62.03	59.18	56.80	54.81	53.12	51.67
6000	83.82	78.63	74.44	71.01	68.16	65.77	63.74	62.01
7000	97.79	91.73	86.85	82.84	79.52	76.73	74.36	72.34
8000	111.76	104.83	99.25	94.68	90.88	87.69	84.99	82.67
9000	125.73	117.94	111.66	106.51	102.24	98.65	95.61	93.01
10000	139.70	131.04	124.06	118.35	113.60	109.61	106.23	103.34
20000	279.39	262.07	248.12	236.69	227.20	219.22	212.46	206.67
30000	419.09	393.11	372.18	355.03	340.79	328.83	318.69	310.01
40000	558.78	524.14	496.24	473.38	454.39	438.44	424.91	413.34
50000	698.48	655.17	620.29	591.72	567.99	548.05	531.14	516.68
60000	838.17	786.21	744.35	710.06	681.58	657.66	637.37	620.01
70000	977.87	917.24	868.41	828.40	795.18	767.27	743.59	723.35
80000	1117.56	1048.27	992.47	946.75	908.78	876.88	849.82	826.68
90000	1257.25	1179.31	1116.52	1065.09	1022.37	986.49	956.05	930.02
100000	1396.95	1310.34	1240.58	1183.43	1135.97	1096.10	1062.27	1033.35
110000	1536.64	1441.38	1364.64	1301.78	1249.57	1205.70	1168.50	1136.69
120000	1676.34	1572.41	1488.70	1420.12	1363.16	1315.31	1274.73	1240.02
130000	1816.03	1703.44	1612.75	1538.46	1476.76	1424.92	1380.96	1343.36
140000	1955.73	1834.48	1736.81	1656.80	1590.35	1534.53	1487.18	1446.69
150000	2095.42	1965.51	1860.87	1775.15	1703.95	1644.14	1593.41	1550.03
160000	2235.11	2096.54	1984.93	1893.49	1817.55	1753.75	1699.64	1653.36
170000	2374.81	2227.58	2108.98	2011.83	1931.14	1863.36	1805.86	1756.70
180000	2514.50	2358.61	2233.04	2130.17	2044.74	1972.97	1912.09	1860.03
190000	2654.20	2489.64	2357.10	2248.52	2158.34	2082.58	2018.32	1963.37
200000	2793.89	2620.68	2481.16	2366.86	2271.93	2192.19	2124.54	2066.70
210000	2933.59	2751.71	2605.21	2485.20	2385.53	2301.79	2230.77	2170.04
220000	3073.28	2882.75	2729.27	2603.55	2499.13	2411.40	2337.00	2273.37
230000	3212.97	3013.78	2853.33	2721.89	2612.72	2521.01	2443.23	2376.71
240000	3352.67	3144.81	2977.39	2840.23	2726.32	2630.62	2549.45	2480.04
250000	3492.36	3275.85	3101.44	2958.57	2839.91	2740.23	2655.68	2583.38
260000	3632.06	3406.88	3225.50	3076.92	2953.51	2849.84	2761.91	2686.71
270000	3771.75	3537.91	3349.56	3195.26	3067.11	2959.45	2868.13	2790.05
280000	3911.45	3668.95	3473.62	3313.60	3180.70	3069.06	2974.36	2893.38
290000	4051.14	3799.98	3597.67	3431.94	3294.30	3178.67	3080.59	2996.72
300000	4190.84	3931.02	3721.73	3550.29	3407.90	3288.28	3186.81	3100.05
310000	4330.53	4062.05	3845.79	3668.63	3521.49	3397.88	3293.04	3203.39
320000	4470.22	4193.08	3969.85	3786.97	3635.09	3507.49	3399.27	3306.72
330000	4609.92	4324.12	4093.90	3905.32	3748.69	3617.10	3505.50	3410.06
340000	4749.61	4455.15	4217.96	4023.66	3862.28	3726.71	3611.72	3513.39
350000	4889.31	4586.18	4342.02	4142.00	3975.88	3836.32	3717.95	3616.73
360000	5029.00	4717.22	4466.08	4260.34	4089.48	3945.93	3824.18	3720.06
370000	5168.70	4848.25	4590.13	4378.69	4203.07	4055.54	3930.40	3823.40
380000	5308.39	4979.28	4714.19	4497.03	4316.67	4165.15	4036.63	3926.73
390000	5448.08	5110.32	4838.25	4615.37	4430.26	4274.76	4142.86	4030.07
400000	5587.78	5241.35	4962.31	4733.71	4543.86	4384.37	4249.08	4133.40

BLENDED MONTHLY PAYMENTS
AMORTIZATION IN YEARS
10%

Amount	17	18	19	20	21	22	23	24
25	.26	.25	.25	.24	.24	.24	.23	.23
50	.51	.50	.49	.48	.47	.47	.46	.46
100	1.01	.99	.97	.96	.94	.93	.92	.91
200	2.02	1.98	1.94	1.91	1.88	1.85	1.83	1.81
300	3.03	2.97	2.91	2.86	2.82	2.78	2.74	2.71
400	4.04	3.95	3.88	3.81	3.75	3.70	3.66	3.62
500	5.05	4.94	4.85	4.76	4.69	4.63	4.57	4.52
600	6.06	5.93	5.81	5.71	5.63	5.55	5.48	5.42
700	7.06	6.91	6.78	6.67	6.57	6.48	6.40	6.33
800	8.07	7.90	7.75	7.62	7.50	7.40	7.31	7.23
900	9.08	8.89	8.72	8.57	8.44	8.33	8.22	8.13
1000	10.09	9.87	9.69	9.52	9.38	9.25	9.14	9.04
2000	20.17	19.74	19.37	19.04	18.75	18.50	18.27	18.07
3000	30.26	29.61	29.05	28.55	28.12	27.74	27.40	27.10
4000	40.34	39.48	38.73	38.07	37.49	36.99	36.54	36.14
5000	50.43	49.35	48.41	47.59	46.87	46.23	45.67	45.17
6000	60.51	59.22	58.09	57.10	56.24	55.48	54.80	54.20
7000	70.60	69.09	67.77	66.62	65.61	64.72	63.94	63.24
8000	80.68	78.96	77.45	76.14	74.98	73.97	73.07	72.27
9000	90.77	88.82	87.13	85.65	84.36	83.21	82.20	81.30
10000	100.85	98.69	96.81	95.17	93.73	92.46	91.33	90.34
20000	201.69	197.38	193.62	190.34	187.45	184.91	182.66	180.67
30000	302.54	296.07	290.43	285.50	281.18	277.36	273.99	271.00
40000	403.38	394.76	387.24	380.67	374.90	369.82	365.32	361.34
50000	504.23	493.44	484.05	475.84	468.62	462.27	456.65	451.67
60000	605.07	592.13	580.86	571.00	562.35	554.72	547.98	542.00
70000	705.92	690.82	677.67	666.17	656.07	647.17	639.31	632.34
80000	806.76	789.51	774.48	761.34	749.80	739.63	730.64	722.67
90000	907.61	888.19	871.29	856.50	843.52	832.08	821.97	813.00
100000	1008.45	986.88	968.10	951.67	937.24	924.53	913.30	903.34
110000	1109.30	1085.57	1064.91	1046.84	1030.97	1016.98	1004.62	993.67
120000	1210.14	1184.26	1161.72	1142.00	1124.69	1109.44	1095.95	1084.00
130000	1310.99	1282.94	1258.53	1237.17	1218.41	1201.89	1187.28	1174.34
140000	1411.83	1381.63	1355.34	1332.34	1312.14	1294.34	1278.61	1264.67
150000	1512.68	1480.32	1452.14	1427.50	1405.86	1386.79	1369.94	1355.00
160000	1613.52	1579.01	1548.95	1522.67	1499.59	1479.25	1461.27	1445.34
170000	1714.37	1677.69	1645.76	1617.83	1593.31	1571.70	1552.60	1535.67
180000	1815.21	1776.38	1742.57	1713.00	1687.03	1664.15	1643.93	1626.00
190000	1916.06	1875.07	1839.38	1808.17	1780.76	1756.60	1735.26	1716.34
200000	2016.90	1973.76	1936.19	1903.33	1874.48	1849.06	1826.59	1806.67
210000	2117.74	2072.44	2033.00	1998.50	1968.20	1941.51	1917.91	1897.00
220000	2218.59	2171.13	2129.81	2093.67	2061.93	2033.96	2009.24	1987.34
230000	2319.43	2269.82	2226.62	2188.83	2155.65	2126.41	2100.57	2077.67
240000	2420.28	2368.51	2323.43	2284.00	2249.38	2218.87	2191.90	2168.00
250000	2521.12	2467.20	2420.24	2379.17	2343.10	2311.32	2283.23	2258.34
260000	2621.97	2565.88	2517.05	2474.33	2436.82	2403.77	2374.56	2348.67
270000	2722.81	2664.57	2613.86	2569.50	2530.55	2496.23	2465.89	2439.00
280000	2823.66	2763.26	2710.67	2664.67	2624.27	2588.68	2557.22	2529.34
290000	2924.50	2861.95	2807.48	2759.83	2718.00	2681.13	2648.55	2619.67
300000	3025.35	2960.63	2904.28	2855.00	2811.72	2773.58	2739.88	2710.00
310000	3126.19	3059.32	3001.09	2950.16	2905.44	2866.04	2831.21	2800.34
320000	3227.04	3158.01	3097.90	3045.33	2999.17	2958.49	2922.53	2890.67
330000	3327.88	3256.70	3194.71	3140.50	3092.89	3050.94	3013.86	2981.00
340000	3428.73	3355.38	3291.52	3235.66	3186.61	3143.39	3105.19	3071.34
350000	3529.57	3454.07	3388.33	3330.83	3280.34	3235.85	3196.52	3161.67
360000	3630.42	3552.76	3485.14	3426.00	3374.06	3328.30	3287.85	3252.00
370000	3731.26	3651.45	3581.95	3521.16	3467.79	3420.75	3379.18	3342.34
380000	3832.11	3750.13	3678.76	3616.33	3561.51	3513.20	3470.51	3432.67
390000	3932.95	3848.82	3775.57	3711.50	3655.23	3605.66	3561.84	3523.00
400000	4033.79	3947.51	3872.38	3806.66	3748.96	3698.11	3653.17	3613.34

119

10% BLENDED MONTHLY PAYMENTS
AMORTIZATION IN YEARS

Amount	25	26	29	30	35	40	45	50
25	.23	.23	.22	.22	.22	.21	.21	.21
50	.45	.45	.44	.44	.43	.42	.42	.42
100	.90	.89	.87	.87	.85	.84	.83	.83
200	1.79	1.78	1.74	1.73	1.69	1.67	1.66	1.65
300	2.69	2.66	2.61	2.59	2.54	2.50	2.49	2.47
400	3.58	3.55	3.48	3.46	3.38	3.34	3.31	3.30
500	4.48	4.44	4.34	4.32	4.23	4.17	4.14	4.12
600	5.37	5.32	5.21	5.18	5.07	5.00	4.97	4.94
700	6.27	6.21	6.08	6.04	5.91	5.84	5.79	5.76
800	7.16	7.10	6.95	6.91	6.76	6.67	6.62	6.59
900	8.06	7.98	7.81	7.77	7.60	7.50	7.45	7.41
1000	8.95	8.87	8.68	8.63	8.45	8.34	8.27	8.23
2000	17.89	17.74	17.36	17.26	16.89	16.67	16.54	16.46
3000	26.84	26.60	26.04	25.89	25.33	25.00	24.81	24.69
4000	35.78	35.47	34.71	34.51	33.77	33.34	33.07	32.91
5000	44.73	44.34	43.39	43.14	42.22	41.67	41.34	41.14
6000	53.67	53.20	52.07	51.77	50.66	50.00	49.61	49.37
7000	62.62	62.07	60.74	60.39	59.10	58.34	57.88	57.60
8000	71.56	70.93	69.42	69.02	67.54	66.67	66.14	65.82
9000	80.51	79.80	78.10	77.65	75.99	75.00	74.41	74.05
10000	89.45	88.67	86.77	86.27	84.43	83.33	82.68	82.28
20000	178.90	177.33	173.54	172.54	168.85	166.66	165.35	164.55
30000	268.35	265.99	260.31	258.81	253.27	249.99	248.02	246.83
40000	357.80	354.65	347.08	345.07	337.70	333.32	330.70	329.10
50000	447.25	443.31	433.85	431.34	422.12	416.65	413.37	411.38
60000	536.70	531.97	520.62	517.61	506.54	499.98	496.04	493.65
70000	626.15	620.63	607.39	603.87	590.97	583.31	578.71	575.92
80000	715.59	709.29	694.16	690.14	675.39	666.64	661.39	658.20
90000	805.04	797.96	780.93	776.41	759.81	749.97	744.06	740.47
100000	894.49	886.62	867.70	862.67	844.24	833.30	826.73	822.75
110000	983.94	975.28	954.47	948.94	928.66	916.63	909.40	905.02
120000	1073.39	1063.94	1041.24	1035.21	1013.08	999.96	992.08	987.29
130000	1162.84	1152.60	1128.01	1121.47	1097.51	1083.29	1074.75	1069.57
140000	1252.29	1241.26	1214.78	1207.74	1181.93	1166.62	1157.42	1151.84
150000	1341.74	1329.92	1301.55	1294.01	1266.35	1249.95	1240.09	1234.12
160000	1431.18	1418.58	1388.32	1380.27	1350.78	1333.28	1322.77	1316.39
170000	1520.63	1507.25	1475.09	1466.54	1435.20	1416.61	1405.44	1398.66
180000	1610.08	1595.91	1561.86	1552.81	1519.62	1499.94	1488.11	1480.94
190000	1699.53	1684.57	1648.63	1639.07	1604.04	1583.27	1570.78	1563.21
200000	1788.98	1773.23	1735.40	1725.34	1688.47	1666.60	1653.46	1645.49
210000	1878.43	1861.89	1822.17	1811.61	1772.89	1749.93	1736.13	1727.76
220000	1967.88	1950.55	1908.94	1897.87	1857.31	1833.26	1818.80	1810.04
230000	2057.33	2039.21	1995.71	1984.14	1941.74	1916.59	1901.47	1892.31
240000	2146.77	2127.87	2082.48	2070.41	2026.16	1999.92	1984.15	1974.58
250000	2236.22	2216.54	2169.25	2156.67	2110.58	2083.25	2066.82	2056.86
260000	2325.67	2305.20	2256.02	2242.94	2195.01	2166.58	2149.49	2139.13
270000	2415.12	2393.86	2342.79	2329.21	2279.43	2249.91	2232.16	2221.41
280000	2504.57	2482.52	2429.56	2415.48	2363.85	2333.24	2314.84	2303.68
290000	2594.02	2571.18	2516.33	2501.74	2448.28	2416.57	2397.51	2385.95
300000	2683.47	2659.84	2603.10	2588.01	2532.70	2499.90	2480.18	2468.23
310000	2772.92	2748.50	2689.87	2674.28	2617.12	2583.23	2562.85	2550.50
320000	2862.36	2837.16	2776.64	2760.54	2701.55	2666.56	2645.53	2632.78
330000	2951.81	2925.83	2863.41	2846.81	2785.97	2749.89	2728.20	2715.05
340000	3041.26	3014.49	2950.18	2933.08	2870.39	2833.22	2810.87	2797.32
350000	3130.71	3103.15	3036.95	3019.34	2954.81	2916.55	2893.54	2879.60
360000	3220.16	3191.81	3123.72	3105.61	3039.24	2999.88	2976.22	2961.87
370000	3309.61	3280.47	3210.49	3191.88	3123.66	3083.21	3058.89	3044.15
380000	3399.06	3369.13	3297.26	3278.14	3208.08	3166.54	3141.56	3126.42
390000	3488.51	3457.79	3384.03	3364.41	3292.51	3249.87	3224.23	3208.70
400000	3577.95	3546.45	3470.80	3450.68	3376.93	3333.20	3306.91	3290.97

BLENDED MONTHLY PAYMENTS 10¼%

AMORTIZATION IN YEARS

Amount	1	2	3	4	5	6	7	8
25	2.20	1.16	.81	.64	.54	.47	.42	.38
50	4.40	2.31	1.62	1.27	1.07	.93	.84	.76
100	8.80	4.62	3.23	2.54	2.13	1.86	1.67	1.52
200	17.59	9.24	6.46	5.08	4.26	3.71	3.33	3.04
300	26.39	13.85	9.69	7.62	6.38	5.57	4.99	4.56
400	35.18	18.47	12.92	10.16	8.51	7.42	6.65	6.08
500	43.97	23.09	16.15	12.70	10.64	9.28	8.32	7.60
600	52.77	27.70	19.38	15.23	12.76	11.13	9.98	9.12
700	61.56	32.32	22.60	17.77	14.89	12.99	11.64	10.64
800	70.35	36.93	25.83	20.31	17.02	14.84	13.30	12.16
900	79.15	41.55	29.06	22.85	19.14	16.70	14.96	13.68
1000	87.94	46.17	32.29	25.39	21.27	18.55	16.63	15.20
2000	175.87	92.33	64.57	50.77	42.54	37.09	33.25	30.39
3000	263.81	138.49	96.86	76.15	63.80	55.64	49.87	45.59
4000	351.74	184.65	129.14	101.53	85.07	74.18	66.49	60.78
5000	439.67	230.82	161.43	126.91	106.33	92.73	83.11	75.98
6000	527.61	276.98	193.71	152.29	127.60	111.27	99.73	91.17
7000	615.54	323.14	226.00	177.67	148.86	129.82	116.35	106.36
8000	703.47	369.30	258.28	203.05	170.13	148.36	132.97	121.56
9000	791.41	415.47	290.57	228.43	191.40	166.91	149.59	136.75
10000	879.34	461.63	322.85	253.81	212.66	185.45	166.21	151.95
20000	1758.67	923.25	645.70	507.62	425.32	370.90	332.42	303.89
30000	2638.01	1384.88	968.55	761.43	637.97	556.35	498.63	455.83
40000	3517.34	1846.50	1291.40	1015.23	850.63	741.80	664.83	607.77
50000	4396.68	2308.12	1614.25	1269.04	1063.29	927.25	831.04	759.71
60000	5276.01	2769.75	1937.10	1522.85	1275.94	1112.70	997.25	911.65
70000	6155.35	3231.37	2259.95	1776.65	1488.60	1298.15	1163.45	1063.59
80000	7034.68	3692.99	2582.80	2030.46	1701.25	1483.59	1329.66	1215.54
90000	7914.01	4154.62	2905.65	2284.27	1913.91	1669.04	1495.87	1367.48
100000	8793.35	4616.24	3228.50	2538.08	2126.57	1854.49	1662.07	1519.42
110000	9672.68	5077.86	3551.34	2791.88	2339.22	2039.94	1828.28	1671.36
120000	10552.02	5539.49	3874.19	3045.69	2551.88	2225.39	1994.49	1823.30
130000	11431.35	6001.11	4197.04	3299.50	2764.54	2410.84	2160.69	1975.24
140000	12310.69	6462.73	4519.89	3553.30	2977.19	2596.29	2326.90	2127.18
150000	13190.02	6924.36	4842.74	3807.11	3189.85	2781.74	2493.11	2279.13
160000	14069.36	7385.98	5165.59	4060.92	3402.50	2967.18	2659.32	2431.07
170000	14948.69	7847.60	5488.44	4314.73	3615.16	3152.63	2825.52	2583.01
180000	15828.02	8309.23	5811.29	4568.53	3827.82	3338.08	2991.73	2734.95
190000	16707.36	8770.85	6134.14	4822.34	4040.47	3523.53	3157.94	2886.89
200000	17586.69	9232.47	6456.99	5076.15	4253.13	3708.98	3324.14	3038.83
210000	18466.03	9694.10	6779.84	5329.95	4465.78	3894.43	3490.35	3190.77
220000	19345.36	10155.72	7102.68	5583.76	4678.44	4079.88	3656.56	3342.72
230000	20224.70	10617.34	7425.53	5837.57	4891.10	4265.33	3822.76	3494.66
240000	21104.03	11078.97	7748.38	6091.38	5103.75	4450.77	3988.97	3646.60
250000	21983.36	11540.59	8071.23	6345.18	5316.41	4636.22	4155.18	3798.54
260000	22862.70	12002.21	8394.08	6598.99	5529.07	4821.67	4321.38	3950.48
270000	23742.03	12463.84	8716.93	6852.80	5741.72	5007.12	4487.59	4102.42
280000	24621.37	12925.46	9039.78	7106.60	5954.38	5192.57	4653.80	4254.36
290000	25500.70	13387.09	9362.63	7360.41	6167.03	5378.02	4820.00	4406.31
300000	26380.04	13848.71	9685.48	7614.22	6379.69	5563.47	4986.21	4558.25
310000	27259.37	14310.33	10008.33	7868.02	6592.35	5748.92	5152.42	4710.19
320000	28138.71	14771.96	10331.18	8121.83	6805.00	5934.36	5318.63	4862.13
330000	29018.04	15233.58	10654.02	8375.64	7017.66	6119.81	5484.83	5014.07
340000	29897.37	15695.20	10976.87	8629.45	7230.31	6305.26	5651.04	5166.01
350000	30776.71	16156.83	11299.72	8883.25	7442.97	6490.71	5817.25	5317.95
360000	31656.04	16618.45	11622.57	9137.06	7655.63	6676.16	5983.45	5469.89
370000	32535.38	17080.07	11945.42	9390.87	7868.28	6861.61	6149.66	5621.84
380000	33414.71	17541.70	12268.27	9644.67	8080.94	7047.06	6315.87	5773.78
390000	34294.05	18003.32	12591.12	9898.48	8293.60	7232.51	6482.07	5925.72
400000	35173.38	18464.94	12913.97	10152.29	8506.25	7417.95	6648.28	6077.66

121

10¼%   BLENDED MONTHLY PAYMENTS
AMORTIZATION IN YEARS

Amount	9	10	11	12	13	14	15	16
25	.36	.34	.32	.30	.29	.28	.27	.27
50	.71	.67	.63	.60	.58	.56	.54	.53
100	1.41	1.33	1.26	1.20	1.16	1.12	1.08	1.05
200	2.82	2.65	2.51	2.40	2.31	2.23	2.16	2.10
300	4.23	3.98	3.77	3.60	3.46	3.34	3.24	3.15
400	5.64	5.30	5.02	4.79	4.61	4.45	4.31	4.20
500	7.05	6.62	6.28	5.99	5.76	5.56	5.39	5.25
600	8.46	7.95	7.53	7.19	6.91	6.67	6.47	6.29
700	9.87	9.27	8.78	8.39	8.06	7.78	7.54	7.34
800	11.28	10.59	10.04	9.58	9.21	8.89	8.62	8.39
900	12.69	11.92	11.29	10.78	10.36	10.00	9.70	9.44
1000	14.10	13.24	12.55	11.98	11.51	11.11	10.77	10.49
2000	28.20	26.48	25.09	23.95	23.01	22.21	21.54	20.97
3000	42.30	39.71	37.63	35.92	34.51	33.32	32.31	31.45
4000	56.40	52.95	50.17	47.90	46.01	44.42	43.08	41.94
5000	70.50	66.18	62.71	59.87	57.51	55.53	53.85	52.42
6000	84.60	79.42	75.25	71.84	69.01	66.63	64.62	62.90
7000	98.70	92.66	87.79	83.81	80.51	77.74	75.39	73.38
8000	112.80	105.89	100.33	95.79	92.01	88.84	86.16	83.87
9000	126.90	119.13	112.88	107.76	103.51	99.95	96.93	94.35
10000	141.00	132.36	125.42	119.73	115.01	111.05	107.70	104.83
20000	281.99	264.72	250.83	239.46	230.02	222.10	215.39	209.66
30000	422.98	397.08	376.24	359.18	345.03	333.15	323.08	314.48
40000	563.97	529.44	501.65	478.91	460.03	444.19	430.77	419.31
50000	704.96	661.80	627.07	598.63	575.04	555.24	538.46	524.13
60000	845.95	794.16	752.48	718.36	690.05	666.29	646.15	628.96
70000	986.94	926.52	877.89	838.09	805.06	777.33	753.85	733.78
80000	1127.94	1058.88	1003.30	957.81	920.06	888.38	861.54	838.61
90000	1268.93	1191.24	1128.72	1077.54	1035.07	999.43	969.23	943.43
100000	1409.92	1323.60	1254.13	1197.26	1150.08	1110.48	1076.92	1048.26
110000	1550.91	1455.96	1379.54	1316.99	1265.09	1221.52	1184.61	1153.08
120000	1691.90	1588.32	1504.95	1436.72	1380.09	1332.57	1292.30	1257.91
130000	1832.89	1720.68	1630.37	1556.44	1495.10	1443.62	1399.99	1362.73
140000	1973.88	1853.04	1755.78	1676.17	1610.11	1554.66	1507.69	1467.56
150000	2114.87	1985.40	1881.19	1795.89	1725.11	1665.71	1615.38	1572.38
160000	2255.87	2117.76	2006.60	1915.62	1840.12	1776.76	1723.07	1677.21
170000	2396.86	2250.12	2132.02	2035.35	1955.13	1887.80	1830.76	1782.03
180000	2537.85	2382.48	2257.43	2155.07	2070.14	1998.85	1938.45	1886.86
190000	2678.84	2514.84	2382.84	2274.80	2185.14	2109.90	2046.14	1991.68
200000	2819.83	2647.20	2508.25	2394.52	2300.15	2220.95	2153.83	2096.51
210000	2960.82	2779.56	2633.67	2514.25	2415.16	2331.99	2261.53	2201.34
220000	3101.81	2911.92	2759.08	2633.98	2530.17	2443.04	2369.22	2306.16
230000	3242.80	3044.28	2884.49	2753.70	2645.17	2554.09	2476.91	2410.99
240000	3383.80	3176.64	3009.90	2873.43	2760.18	2665.13	2584.60	2515.81
250000	3524.79	3309.00	3135.31	2993.15	2875.19	2776.18	2692.29	2620.64
260000	3665.78	3441.36	3260.73	3112.88	2990.19	2887.23	2799.98	2725.46
270000	3806.77	3573.72	3386.14	3232.60	3105.20	2998.28	2907.68	2830.29
280000	3947.76	3706.08	3511.55	3352.33	3220.21	3109.32	3015.37	2935.11
290000	4088.75	3838.44	3636.96	3472.06	3335.22	3220.37	3123.06	3039.94
300000	4229.74	3970.80	3762.38	3591.78	3450.22	3331.42	3230.75	3144.76
310000	4370.73	4103.16	3887.79	3711.51	3565.23	3442.46	3338.44	3249.59
320000	4511.73	4235.52	4013.20	3831.23	3680.24	3553.51	3446.13	3354.41
330000	4652.72	4367.88	4138.61	3950.96	3795.25	3664.56	3553.82	3459.24
340000	4793.71	4500.24	4264.03	4070.69	3910.25	3775.60	3661.52	3564.06
350000	4934.70	4632.60	4389.44	4190.41	4025.26	3886.65	3769.21	3668.89
360000	5075.69	4764.96	4514.85	4310.14	4140.27	3997.70	3876.90	3773.71
370000	5216.68	4897.32	4640.26	4429.86	4255.28	4108.75	3984.59	3878.54
380000	5357.67	5029.68	4765.68	4549.59	4370.28	4219.79	4092.28	3983.36
390000	5498.67	5162.04	4891.09	4669.32	4485.29	4330.84	4199.97	4088.19
400000	5639.66	5294.40	5016.50	4789.04	4600.30	4441.89	4307.66	4193.01

122

Amount	17	18	19	20	21	22	23	24
25	.26	.26	.25	.25	.24	.24	.24	.24
50	.52	.51	.50	.49	.48	.48	.47	.47
100	1.03	1.01	.99	.97	.96	.95	.93	.93
200	2.05	2.01	1.97	1.94	1.91	1.89	1.86	1.85
300	3.08	3.01	2.96	2.91	2.86	2.83	2.79	2.77
400	4.10	4.01	3.94	3.88	3.82	3.77	3.72	3.69
500	5.12	5.02	4.92	4.84	4.77	4.71	4.65	4.61
600	6.15	6.02	5.91	5.81	5.72	5.65	5.58	5.53
700	7.17	7.02	6.89	6.78	6.68	6.59	6.51	6.45
800	8.19	8.02	7.87	7.75	7.63	7.53	7.44	7.37
900	9.22	9.03	8.86	8.71	8.58	8.47	8.37	8.29
1000	10.24	10.03	9.84	9.68	9.54	9.41	9.30	9.21
2000	20.48	20.05	19.68	19.36	19.07	18.82	18.60	18.41
3000	30.71	30.07	29.52	29.03	28.60	28.23	27.90	27.61
4000	40.95	40.10	39.35	38.71	38.14	37.64	37.20	36.81
5000	51.19	50.12	49.19	48.38	47.67	47.05	46.49	46.01
6000	61.42	60.14	59.03	58.06	57.20	56.45	55.79	55.21
7000	71.66	70.16	68.87	67.73	66.74	65.86	65.09	64.41
8000	81.89	80.19	78.70	77.41	76.27	75.27	74.39	73.61
9000	92.13	90.21	88.54	87.08	85.80	84.68	83.69	82.81
10000	102.37	100.23	98.38	96.76	95.34	94.09	92.98	92.01
20000	204.73	200.46	196.75	193.51	190.67	188.17	185.96	184.01
30000	307.09	300.69	295.12	290.26	286.00	282.25	278.94	276.01
40000	409.45	400.91	393.49	387.01	381.33	376.33	371.92	368.01
50000	511.81	501.14	491.87	483.77	476.66	470.41	464.90	460.02
60000	614.17	601.37	590.24	580.52	571.99	564.49	557.87	552.02
70000	716.53	701.60	688.61	677.27	667.33	658.58	650.85	644.02
80000	818.89	801.82	786.98	774.02	762.66	752.66	743.83	736.02
90000	921.25	902.05	885.36	870.78	857.99	846.74	836.81	828.02
100000	1023.61	1002.28	983.73	967.53	953.32	940.82	929.79	920.03
110000	1125.97	1102.50	1082.10	1064.28	1048.65	1034.90	1022.77	1012.03
120000	1228.33	1202.73	1180.47	1161.03	1143.98	1128.98	1115.74	1104.03
130000	1330.69	1302.96	1278.85	1257.79	1239.32	1223.06	1208.72	1196.03
140000	1433.05	1403.19	1377.22	1354.54	1334.65	1317.15	1301.70	1288.03
150000	1535.41	1503.41	1475.59	1451.29	1429.98	1411.23	1394.68	1380.04
160000	1637.77	1603.64	1573.96	1548.04	1525.31	1505.31	1487.66	1472.04
170000	1740.13	1703.87	1672.34	1644.79	1620.64	1599.39	1580.64	1564.04
180000	1842.49	1804.09	1770.71	1741.55	1715.97	1693.47	1673.61	1656.04
190000	1944.85	1904.32	1869.08	1838.30	1811.31	1787.55	1766.59	1748.04
200000	2047.21	2004.55	1967.45	1935.05	1906.64	1881.64	1859.57	1840.05
210000	2149.57	2104.78	2065.83	2031.80	2001.97	1975.72	1952.55	1932.05
220000	2251.93	2205.00	2164.20	2128.56	2097.30	2069.80	2045.53	2024.05
230000	2354.29	2305.23	2262.57	2225.31	2192.63	2163.88	2138.51	2116.05
240000	2456.65	2405.46	2360.94	2322.06	2287.96	2257.96	2231.48	2208.05
250000	2559.01	2505.69	2459.32	2418.81	2383.30	2352.04	2324.46	2300.06
260000	2661.37	2605.91	2557.69	2515.57	2478.63	2446.12	2417.44	2392.06
270000	2763.73	2706.14	2656.06	2612.32	2573.96	2540.21	2510.42	2484.06
280000	2866.09	2806.37	2754.43	2709.07	2669.29	2634.29	2603.40	2576.06
290000	2968.45	2906.59	2852.81	2805.82	2764.62	2728.37	2696.38	2668.07
300000	3070.81	3006.82	2951.18	2902.57	2859.95	2822.45	2789.35	2760.07
310000	3173.17	3107.05	3049.55	2999.33	2955.28	2916.53	2882.33	2852.07
320000	3275.53	3207.28	3147.92	3096.08	3050.62	3010.61	2975.31	2944.07
330000	3377.89	3307.50	3246.30	3192.83	3145.95	3104.70	3068.29	3036.07
340000	3480.25	3407.73	3344.67	3289.58	3241.28	3198.78	3161.27	3128.08
350000	3582.61	3507.96	3443.04	3386.34	3336.61	3292.86	3254.25	3220.08
360000	3684.97	3608.18	3541.41	3483.09	3431.94	3386.94	3347.22	3312.08
370000	3787.33	3708.41	3639.79	3579.84	3527.27	3481.02	3440.20	3404.08
380000	3889.69	3808.64	3738.16	3676.59	3622.61	3575.10	3533.18	3496.08
390000	3992.05	3908.87	3836.53	3773.35	3717.94	3669.18	3626.16	3588.09
400000	4094.41	4009.09	3934.90	3870.10	3813.27	3763.27	3719.14	3680.09

10¼%   BLENDED MONTHLY PAYMENTS
AMORTIZATION IN YEARS

Amount	25	26	29	30	35	40	45	50
25	.23	.23	.23	.23	.22	.22	.22	.22
50	.46	.46	.45	.45	.44	.43	.43	.43
100	.92	.91	.89	.89	.87	.86	.85	.85
200	1.83	1.81	1.78	1.77	1.73	1.71	1.70	1.69
300	2.74	2.72	2.66	2.65	2.59	2.56	2.54	2.53
400	3.65	3.62	3.55	3.53	3.46	3.41	3.39	3.37
500	4.56	4.52	4.43	4.41	4.32	4.27	4.23	4.22
600	5.47	5.43	5.32	5.29	5.18	5.12	5.08	5.06
700	6.38	6.33	6.20	6.17	6.04	5.97	5.93	5.90
800	7.30	7.23	7.09	7.05	6.91	6.82	6.77	6.74
900	8.21	8.14	7.97	7.93	7.77	7.67	7.62	7.58
1000	9.12	9.04	8.86	8.81	8.63	8.53	8.46	8.43
2000	18.23	18.08	17.71	17.61	17.26	17.05	16.92	16.85
3000	27.35	27.11	26.56	26.42	25.88	25.57	25.38	25.27
4000	36.46	36.15	35.41	35.22	34.51	34.09	33.84	33.69
5000	45.57	45.19	44.27	44.02	43.13	42.61	42.30	42.11
6000	54.69	54.22	53.12	52.83	51.76	51.13	50.76	50.53
7000	63.80	63.26	61.97	61.63	60.38	59.65	59.22	58.96
8000	72.91	72.30	70.82	70.43	69.01	68.17	67.68	67.38
9000	82.03	81.33	79.68	79.24	77.64	76.69	76.14	75.80
10000	91.14	90.37	88.53	88.04	86.26	85.22	84.59	84.22
20000	182.28	180.74	177.05	176.08	172.52	170.43	169.18	168.44
30000	273.41	271.10	265.58	264.11	258.77	255.64	253.77	252.65
40000	364.55	361.47	354.10	352.15	345.03	340.85	338.36	336.87
50000	455.69	451.84	442.63	440.19	431.29	426.06	422.95	421.09
60000	546.82	542.20	531.15	528.22	517.54	511.27	507.54	505.30
70000	637.96	632.57	619.68	616.26	603.80	596.48	592.13	589.52
80000	729.09	722.94	708.20	704.29	690.05	681.69	676.72	673.74
90000	820.23	813.30	796.72	792.33	776.31	766.90	761.31	757.95
100000	911.37	903.67	885.25	880.37	862.57	852.11	845.90	842.17
110000	1002.50	994.04	973.77	968.40	948.82	937.33	930.49	926.39
120000	1093.64	1084.40	1062.30	1056.44	1035.08	1022.54	1015.08	1010.60
130000	1184.78	1174.77	1150.82	1144.47	1121.34	1107.75	1099.66	1094.82
140000	1275.91	1265.14	1239.35	1232.51	1207.59	1192.96	1184.25	1179.03
150000	1367.05	1355.50	1327.87	1320.55	1293.85	1278.17	1268.84	1263.25
160000	1458.18	1445.87	1416.39	1408.58	1380.10	1363.38	1353.43	1347.47
170000	1549.32	1536.24	1504.92	1496.62	1466.36	1448.59	1438.02	1431.68
180000	1640.46	1626.60	1593.44	1584.66	1552.62	1533.80	1522.61	1515.90
190000	1731.59	1716.97	1681.97	1672.69	1638.87	1619.01	1607.20	1600.12
200000	1822.73	1807.34	1770.49	1760.73	1725.13	1704.22	1691.79	1684.33
210000	1913.87	1897.70	1859.02	1848.76	1811.38	1789.44	1776.38	1768.55
220000	2005.00	1988.07	1947.54	1936.80	1897.64	1874.65	1860.97	1852.77
230000	2096.14	2078.44	2036.07	2024.84	1983.90	1959.86	1945.56	1936.98
240000	2187.27	2168.80	2124.59	2112.87	2070.15	2045.07	2030.15	2021.20
250000	2278.41	2259.17	2213.11	2200.91	2156.41	2130.28	2114.73	2105.41
260000	2369.55	2349.54	2301.64	2288.94	2242.67	2215.49	2199.32	2189.63
270000	2460.68	2439.90	2390.16	2376.98	2328.92	2300.70	2283.91	2273.85
280000	2551.82	2530.27	2478.69	2465.02	2415.18	2385.91	2368.50	2358.06
290000	2642.96	2620.64	2567.21	2553.05	2501.43	2471.12	2453.09	2442.28
300000	2734.09	2711.00	2655.74	2641.09	2587.69	2556.33	2537.68	2526.50
310000	2825.23	2801.37	2744.26	2729.13	2673.95	2641.55	2622.27	2610.71
320000	2916.36	2891.74	2832.78	2817.16	2760.20	2726.76	2706.86	2694.93
330000	3007.50	2982.10	2921.31	2905.20	2846.46	2811.97	2791.45	2779.15
340000	3098.64	3072.47	3009.83	2993.23	2932.71	2897.18	2876.04	2863.36
350000	3189.77	3162.84	3098.36	3081.27	3018.97	2982.39	2960.63	2947.58
360000	3280.91	3253.20	3186.88	3169.31	3105.23	3067.60	3045.22	3031.79
370000	3372.05	3343.57	3275.41	3257.34	3191.48	3152.81	3129.81	3116.01
380000	3463.18	3433.94	3363.93	3345.38	3277.74	3238.02	3214.39	3200.23
390000	3554.32	3524.30	3452.46	3433.41	3364.00	3323.23	3298.98	3284.44
400000	3645.45	3614.67	3540.98	3521.45	3450.25	3408.44	3383.57	3368.66

BLENDED MONTHLY PAYMENTS
AMORTIZATION IN YEARS
10½%

Amount	1	2	3	4	5	6	7	8
25	2.21	1.16	.81	.64	.54	.47	.42	.39
50	4.41	2.32	1.62	1.28	1.07	.94	.84	.77
100	8.81	4.63	3.24	2.55	2.14	1.87	1.68	1.54
200	17.61	9.26	6.48	5.10	4.28	3.74	3.35	3.07
300	26.42	13.89	9.72	7.65	6.42	5.60	5.03	4.60
400	35.22	18.51	12.96	10.20	8.56	7.47	6.70	6.13
500	44.03	23.14	16.20	12.75	10.70	9.34	8.38	7.67
600	52.83	27.77	19.44	15.30	12.84	11.20	10.05	9.20
700	61.64	32.40	22.68	17.85	14.97	13.07	11.73	10.73
800	70.44	37.02	25.92	20.40	17.11	14.94	13.40	12.26
900	79.25	41.65	29.16	22.95	19.25	16.80	15.08	13.79
1000	88.05	46.28	32.40	25.50	21.39	18.67	16.75	15.33
2000	176.09	92.55	64.80	51.00	42.77	37.34	33.49	30.65
3000	264.14	138.82	97.20	76.49	64.16	56.00	50.24	45.97
4000	352.18	185.10	129.60	101.99	85.54	74.67	66.98	61.29
5000	440.23	231.37	161.99	127.49	106.92	93.34	83.73	76.61
6000	528.27	277.64	194.39	152.98	128.31	112.00	100.47	91.93
7000	616.32	323.92	226.79	178.48	149.69	130.67	117.22	107.25
8000	704.36	370.19	259.19	203.97	171.08	149.33	133.96	122.58
9000	792.41	416.46	291.58	229.47	192.46	168.00	150.71	137.90
10000	880.45	462.74	323.98	254.97	213.84	186.67	167.45	153.22
20000	1760.90	925.47	647.96	509.93	427.68	373.33	334.90	306.43
30000	2641.35	1388.20	971.93	764.89	641.52	559.99	502.35	459.65
40000	3521.80	1850.93	1295.91	1019.85	855.36	746.65	669.80	612.86
50000	4402.25	2313.66	1619.88	1274.81	1069.20	933.31	837.25	766.07
60000	5282.70	2776.39	1943.86	1529.77	1283.03	1119.97	1004.70	919.29
70000	6163.15	3239.12	2267.84	1784.73	1496.87	1306.63	1172.15	1072.50
80000	7043.60	3701.85	2591.81	2039.69	1710.71	1493.29	1339.60	1225.71
90000	7924.05	4164.58	2915.79	2294.65	1924.55	1679.95	1507.04	1378.93
100000	8804.50	4627.31	3239.76	2549.61	2138.39	1866.61	1674.49	1532.14
110000	9684.95	5090.04	3563.74	2804.57	2352.22	2053.27	1841.94	1685.35
120000	10565.40	5552.77	3887.72	3059.53	2566.06	2239.93	2009.39	1838.57
130000	11445.85	6015.50	4211.69	3314.49	2779.90	2426.59	2176.84	1991.78
140000	12326.30	6478.24	4535.67	3569.45	2993.74	2613.25	2344.29	2144.99
150000	13206.75	6940.97	4859.64	3824.41	3207.58	2799.91	2511.74	2298.21
160000	14087.20	7403.70	5183.62	4079.37	3421.41	2986.57	2679.19	2451.42
170000	14967.65	7866.43	5507.60	4334.33	3635.25	3173.23	2846.63	2604.63
180000	15848.10	8329.16	5831.57	4589.29	3849.09	3359.89	3014.08	2757.85
190000	16728.55	8791.89	6155.55	4844.25	4062.93	3546.55	3181.53	2911.06
200000	17609.00	9254.62	6479.52	5099.21	4276.77	3733.21	3348.98	3064.28
210000	18489.45	9717.35	6803.50	5354.17	4490.60	3919.87	3516.43	3217.49
220000	19369.90	10180.08	7127.47	5609.13	4704.44	4106.53	3683.88	3370.70
230000	20250.35	10642.81	7451.45	5864.09	4918.28	4293.19	3851.33	3523.92
240000	21130.80	11105.54	7775.43	6119.05	5132.12	4479.85	4018.78	3677.13
250000	22011.25	11568.27	8099.40	6374.01	5345.96	4666.52	4186.22	3830.34
260000	22891.70	12031.00	8423.38	6628.97	5559.79	4853.18	4353.67	3983.56
270000	23772.15	12493.73	8747.35	6883.93	5773.63	5039.84	4521.12	4136.77
280000	24652.60	12956.47	9071.33	7138.89	5987.47	5226.50	4688.57	4289.98
290000	25533.04	13419.20	9395.31	7393.85	6201.31	5413.16	4856.02	4443.20
300000	26413.49	13881.93	9719.28	7648.81	6415.15	5599.82	5023.47	4596.41
310000	27293.94	14344.66	10043.26	7903.77	6628.98	5786.48	5190.92	4749.62
320000	28174.39	14807.39	10367.23	8158.73	6842.82	5973.14	5358.37	4902.84
330000	29054.84	15270.12	10691.21	8413.69	7056.66	6159.80	5525.81	5056.05
340000	29935.29	15732.85	11015.19	8668.65	7270.50	6346.46	5693.26	5209.26
350000	30815.74	16195.58	11339.16	8923.61	7484.34	6533.12	5860.71	5362.48
360000	31696.19	16658.31	11663.14	9178.57	7698.17	6719.78	6028.16	5515.69
370000	32576.64	17121.04	11987.11	9433.53	7912.01	6906.44	6195.61	5668.91
380000	33457.09	17583.77	12311.09	9688.49	8125.85	7093.10	6363.06	5822.12
390000	34337.54	18046.50	12635.07	9943.45	8339.69	7279.76	6530.51	5975.33
400000	35217.99	18509.23	12959.04	10198.41	8553.53	7466.42	6697.96	6128.55

10½% BLENDED MONTHLY PAYMENTS
AMORTIZATION IN YEARS

Amount	9	10	11	12	13	14	15	16
25	.36	.34	.32	.31	.30	.29	.28	.27
50	.72	.67	.64	.61	.59	.57	.55	.54
100	1.43	1.34	1.27	1.22	1.17	1.13	1.10	1.07
200	2.85	2.68	2.54	2.43	2.33	2.25	2.19	2.13
300	4.27	4.02	3.81	3.64	3.50	3.38	3.28	3.19
400	5.70	5.35	5.08	4.85	4.66	4.50	4.37	4.26
500	7.12	6.69	6.34	6.06	5.83	5.63	5.46	5.32
600	8.54	8.03	7.61	7.27	6.99	6.75	6.55	6.38
700	9.97	9.36	8.88	8.48	8.15	7.88	7.65	7.45
800	11.39	10.70	10.15	9.69	9.32	9.00	8.74	8.51
900	12.81	12.04	11.41	10.91	10.48	10.13	9.83	9.57
1000	14.23	13.37	12.68	12.12	11.65	11.25	10.92	10.64
2000	28.46	26.74	25.36	24.23	23.29	22.50	21.84	21.27
3000	42.69	40.11	38.04	36.34	34.93	33.75	32.75	31.90
4000	56.92	53.48	50.71	48.45	46.58	45.00	43.67	42.53
5000	71.15	66.85	63.39	60.56	58.22	56.25	54.59	53.17
6000	85.38	80.22	76.07	72.67	69.86	67.50	65.50	63.80
7000	99.61	93.59	88.75	84.79	81.50	78.75	76.42	74.43
8000	113.84	106.96	101.42	96.90	93.15	90.00	87.34	85.06
9000	128.07	120.33	114.10	109.01	104.79	101.25	98.25	95.70
10000	142.30	133.70	126.78	121.12	116.43	112.50	109.17	106.33
20000	284.59	267.39	253.55	242.24	232.86	224.99	218.33	212.65
30000	426.89	401.08	380.33	363.35	349.28	337.48	327.50	318.98
40000	569.18	534.77	507.10	484.47	465.71	449.98	436.66	425.30
50000	711.47	668.46	633.87	605.58	582.13	562.47	545.83	531.62
60000	853.77	802.16	760.65	726.70	698.56	674.96	654.99	637.95
70000	996.06	935.85	887.42	847.82	814.98	787.45	764.15	744.27
80000	1138.35	1069.54	1014.19	968.93	931.41	899.95	873.32	850.60
90000	1280.65	1203.23	1140.97	1090.05	1047.83	1012.44	982.48	956.92
100000	1422.94	1336.92	1267.74	1211.16	1164.26	1124.93	1091.65	1063.24
110000	1565.23	1470.61	1394.51	1332.28	1280.69	1237.43	1200.81	1169.57
120000	1707.53	1604.31	1521.29	1453.40	1397.11	1349.92	1309.97	1275.89
130000	1849.82	1738.00	1648.06	1574.51	1513.54	1462.41	1419.14	1382.22
140000	1992.11	1871.69	1774.84	1695.63	1629.96	1574.90	1528.30	1488.54
150000	2134.41	2005.38	1901.61	1816.74	1746.39	1687.40	1637.47	1594.86
160000	2276.70	2139.07	2028.38	1937.86	1862.81	1799.89	1746.63	1701.19
170000	2418.99	2272.76	2155.16	2058.98	1979.24	1912.38	1855.79	1807.51
180000	2561.29	2406.46	2281.93	2180.09	2095.66	2024.87	1964.96	1913.83
190000	2703.58	2540.15	2408.70	2301.21	2212.09	2137.37	2074.12	2020.16
200000	2845.87	2673.84	2535.48	2422.32	2328.51	2249.86	2183.29	2126.48
210000	2988.17	2807.53	2662.25	2543.44	2444.94	2362.35	2292.45	2232.81
220000	3130.46	2941.22	2789.02	2664.56	2561.37	2474.85	2401.61	2339.13
230000	3272.76	3074.91	2915.80	2785.67	2677.79	2587.34	2510.78	2445.45
240000	3415.05	3208.61	3042.57	2906.79	2794.22	2699.83	2619.94	2551.78
250000	3557.34	3342.30	3169.35	3027.90	2910.64	2812.32	2729.11	2658.10
260000	3699.64	3475.99	3296.12	3149.02	3027.07	2924.82	2838.27	2764.43
270000	3841.93	3609.68	3422.89	3270.14	3143.49	3037.31	2947.43	2870.75
280000	3984.22	3743.37	3549.67	3391.25	3259.92	3149.80	3056.60	2977.07
290000	4126.52	3877.07	3676.44	3512.37	3376.34	3262.30	3165.76	3083.40
300000	4268.81	4010.76	3803.21	3633.48	3492.77	3374.79	3274.93	3189.72
310000	4411.10	4144.45	3929.99	3754.60	3609.20	3487.28	3384.09	3296.04
320000	4553.40	4278.14	4056.76	3875.71	3725.62	3599.77	3493.25	3402.37
330000	4695.69	4411.83	4183.53	3996.83	3842.05	3712.27	3602.42	3508.69
340000	4837.98	4545.52	4310.31	4117.95	3958.47	3824.76	3711.58	3615.02
350000	4980.28	4679.22	4437.08	4239.06	4074.90	3937.25	3820.75	3721.34
360000	5122.57	4812.91	4563.86	4360.18	4191.32	4049.74	3929.91	3827.66
370000	5264.86	4946.60	4690.63	4481.29	4307.75	4162.24	4039.07	3933.99
380000	5407.16	5080.29	4817.40	4602.41	4424.17	4274.73	4148.24	4040.31
390000	5549.45	5213.98	4944.18	4723.53	4540.60	4387.22	4257.40	4146.64
400000	5691.74	5347.67	5070.95	4844.64	4657.02	4499.72	4366.57	4252.96

126

BLENDED MONTHLY PAYMENTS 10½%
AMORTIZATION IN YEARS

Amount	17	18	19	20	21	22	23	24
25	.26	.26	.25	.25	.25	.24	.24	.24
50	.52	.51	.50	.50	.49	.48	.48	.47
100	1.04	1.02	1.00	.99	.97	.96	.95	.94
200	2.08	2.04	2.00	1.97	1.94	1.92	1.90	1.88
300	3.12	3.06	3.00	2.96	2.91	2.88	2.84	2.82
400	4.16	4.08	4.00	3.94	3.88	3.83	3.79	3.75
500	5.20	5.09	5.00	4.92	4.85	4.79	4.74	4.69
600	6.24	6.11	6.00	5.91	5.82	5.75	5.68	5.63
700	7.28	7.13	7.00	6.89	6.79	6.71	6.63	6.56
800	8.32	8.15	8.00	7.87	7.76	7.66	7.58	7.50
900	9.35	9.16	9.00	8.86	8.73	8.62	8.52	8.44
1000	10.39	10.18	10.00	9.84	9.70	9.58	9.47	9.37
2000	20.78	20.36	19.99	19.67	19.39	19.15	18.93	18.74
3000	31.17	30.54	29.99	29.51	29.09	28.72	28.40	28.11
4000	41.56	40.72	39.98	39.34	38.78	38.29	37.86	37.48
5000	51.95	50.89	49.98	49.18	48.48	47.86	47.32	46.85
6000	62.34	61.07	59.97	59.01	58.17	57.44	56.79	56.21
7000	72.72	71.25	69.97	68.85	67.87	67.01	66.25	65.58
8000	83.11	81.43	79.96	78.68	77.56	76.58	75.71	74.95
9000	93.50	91.60	89.96	88.52	87.26	86.15	85.18	84.32
10000	103.89	101.78	99.95	98.35	96.95	95.72	94.64	93.69
20000	207.77	203.56	199.89	196.70	193.90	191.44	189.28	187.37
30000	311.66	305.33	299.84	295.05	290.85	287.16	283.92	281.05
40000	415.54	407.11	399.78	393.39	387.80	382.88	378.55	374.73
50000	519.42	508.88	499.73	491.74	484.75	478.60	473.19	468.41
60000	623.31	610.66	599.67	590.09	581.70	574.32	567.83	562.09
70000	727.19	712.43	699.62	688.44	678.65	670.04	662.46	655.77
80000	831.08	814.21	799.56	786.78	775.59	765.76	757.10	749.45
90000	934.96	915.99	899.51	885.13	872.54	861.48	851.74	843.13
100000	1038.84	1017.76	999.45	983.48	969.49	957.20	946.37	936.81
110000	1142.73	1119.54	1099.40	1081.83	1066.44	1052.92	1041.01	1030.49
120000	1246.61	1221.31	1199.34	1180.17	1163.39	1148.64	1135.65	1124.17
130000	1350.50	1323.09	1299.28	1278.52	1260.34	1244.36	1230.28	1217.85
140000	1454.38	1424.86	1399.23	1376.87	1357.29	1340.08	1324.92	1311.53
150000	1558.26	1526.64	1499.17	1475.22	1454.23	1435.80	1419.56	1405.21
160000	1662.15	1628.42	1599.12	1573.56	1551.18	1531.52	1514.20	1498.89
170000	1766.03	1730.19	1699.06	1671.91	1648.13	1627.24	1608.83	1592.57
180000	1869.92	1831.97	1799.01	1770.26	1745.08	1722.96	1703.47	1686.25
190000	1973.80	1933.74	1898.95	1868.60	1842.03	1818.68	1798.11	1779.93
200000	2077.68	2035.52	1998.90	1966.95	1938.98	1914.40	1892.74	1873.61
210000	2181.57	2137.29	2098.84	2065.30	2035.93	2010.12	1987.38	1967.29
220000	2285.45	2239.07	2198.79	2163.65	2132.88	2105.84	2082.02	2060.97
230000	2389.34	2340.85	2298.73	2261.99	2229.82	2201.56	2176.65	2154.65
240000	2493.22	2442.62	2398.68	2360.34	2326.77	2297.28	2271.29	2248.33
250000	2597.10	2544.40	2498.62	2458.69	2423.72	2393.00	2365.93	2342.01
260000	2700.99	2646.17	2598.56	2557.04	2520.67	2488.72	2460.56	2435.69
270000	2804.87	2747.95	2698.51	2655.38	2617.62	2584.44	2555.20	2529.37
280000	2908.76	2849.72	2798.45	2753.73	2714.57	2680.16	2649.84	2623.05
290000	3012.64	2951.50	2898.40	2852.08	2811.52	2775.88	2744.47	2716.73
300000	3116.52	3053.27	2998.34	2950.43	2908.46	2871.60	2839.11	2810.41
310000	3220.41	3155.05	3098.29	3048.77	3005.41	2967.32	2933.75	2904.09
320000	3324.29	3256.83	3198.23	3147.12	3102.36	3063.04	3028.39	2997.77
330000	3428.18	3358.60	3298.18	3245.47	3199.31	3158.76	3123.02	3091.45
340000	3532.06	3460.38	3398.12	3343.81	3296.26	3254.48	3217.66	3185.13
350000	3635.94	3562.15	3498.07	3442.16	3393.21	3350.20	3312.30	3278.81
360000	3739.83	3663.93	3598.01	3540.51	3490.16	3445.92	3406.93	3372.49
370000	3843.71	3765.70	3697.96	3638.86	3587.11	3541.64	3501.57	3466.17
380000	3947.60	3867.48	3797.90	3737.20	3684.05	3637.36	3596.21	3559.85
390000	4051.48	3969.26	3897.84	3835.55	3781.00	3733.08	3690.84	3653.53
400000	4155.36	4071.03	3997.79	3933.90	3877.95	3828.80	3785.48	3747.21

10½% BLENDED MONTHLY PAYMENTS
AMORTIZATION IN YEARS

Amount	25	26	29	30	35	40	45	50
25	.24	.24	.23	.23	.23	.22	.22	.22
50	.47	.47	.46	.45	.45	.44	.44	.44
100	.93	.93	.91	.90	.89	.88	.87	.87
200	1.86	1.85	1.81	1.80	1.77	1.75	1.74	1.73
300	2.79	2.77	2.71	2.70	2.65	2.62	2.60	2.59
400	3.72	3.69	3.62	3.60	3.53	3.49	3.47	3.45
500	4.65	4.61	4.52	4.50	4.41	4.36	4.33	4.31
600	5.57	5.53	5.42	5.39	5.29	5.23	5.20	5.17
700	6.50	6.45	6.33	6.29	6.17	6.10	6.06	6.04
800	7.43	7.37	7.23	7.19	7.05	6.97	6.93	6.90
900	8.36	8.29	8.13	8.09	7.93	7.84	7.79	7.76
1000	9.29	9.21	9.03	8.99	8.81	8.71	8.66	8.62
2000	18.57	18.42	18.06	17.97	17.62	17.42	17.31	17.24
3000	27.85	27.63	27.09	26.95	26.43	26.13	25.96	25.85
4000	37.14	36.84	36.12	35.93	35.24	34.84	34.61	34.47
5000	46.42	46.05	45.15	44.91	44.05	43.55	43.26	43.09
6000	55.70	55.25	54.18	53.89	52.86	52.26	51.91	51.70
7000	64.99	64.46	63.21	62.87	61.67	60.97	60.56	60.32
8000	74.27	73.67	72.24	71.86	70.48	69.68	69.21	68.93
9000	83.55	82.88	81.26	80.84	79.29	78.39	77.86	77.55
10000	92.84	92.09	90.29	89.82	88.10	87.10	86.52	86.17
20000	185.67	184.17	180.58	179.63	176.20	174.20	173.03	172.33
30000	278.50	276.25	270.87	269.45	264.29	261.30	259.54	258.49
40000	371.34	368.33	361.16	359.26	352.39	348.40	346.05	344.65
50000	464.17	460.41	451.44	449.08	440.49	435.50	432.56	430.81
60000	557.00	552.49	541.73	538.89	528.58	522.59	519.07	516.98
70000	649.84	644.57	632.02	628.70	616.68	609.69	605.58	603.14
80000	742.67	736.65	722.31	718.52	704.78	696.79	692.09	689.30
90000	835.50	828.74	812.59	808.33	792.87	783.89	778.60	775.46
100000	928.33	920.82	902.88	898.15	880.97	870.99	865.11	861.62
110000	1021.17	1012.90	993.17	987.96	969.07	958.08	951.62	947.78
120000	1114.00	1104.98	1083.46	1077.77	1057.16	1045.18	1038.13	1033.95
130000	1206.83	1197.06	1173.74	1167.59	1145.26	1132.28	1124.64	1120.11
140000	1299.67	1289.14	1264.03	1257.40	1233.36	1219.38	1211.15	1206.27
150000	1392.50	1381.22	1354.32	1347.22	1321.45	1306.48	1297.66	1292.43
160000	1485.33	1473.30	1444.61	1437.03	1409.55	1393.57	1384.17	1378.59
170000	1578.17	1565.39	1534.89	1526.84	1497.65	1480.67	1470.68	1464.75
180000	1671.00	1657.47	1625.18	1616.66	1585.74	1567.77	1557.19	1550.92
190000	1763.83	1749.55	1715.44	1706.47	1673.84	1654.87	1643.70	1637.08
200000	1856.66	1841.63	1805.76	1796.29	1761.94	1741.97	1730.21	1723.24
210000	1949.50	1933.71	1896.04	1886.10	1850.03	1829.06	1816.72	1809.40
220000	2042.33	2025.79	1986.33	1975.91	1938.13	1916.16	1903.23	1895.56
230000	2135.16	2117.87	2076.62	2065.73	2026.23	2003.26	1989.74	1981.72
240000	2228.00	2209.95	2166.91	2155.54	2114.32	2090.36	2076.25	2067.89
250000	2320.83	2302.04	2257.19	2245.36	2202.42	2177.46	2162.76	2154.05
260000	2413.66	2394.12	2347.48	2335.17	2290.51	2264.55	2249.27	2240.21
270000	2506.50	2486.20	2437.77	2424.98	2378.61	2351.65	2335.78	2326.37
280000	2599.33	2578.28	2528.06	2514.80	2466.71	2438.75	2422.29	2412.53
290000	2692.16	2670.36	2618.35	2604.61	2554.80	2525.85	2508.80	2498.69
300000	2784.99	2762.44	2708.63	2694.43	2642.90	2612.95	2595.31	2584.86
310000	2877.83	2854.52	2798.92	2784.24	2731.00	2700.05	2681.82	2671.02
320000	2970.66	2946.60	2889.21	2874.05	2819.09	2787.14	2768.33	2757.18
330000	3063.49	3038.69	2979.50	2963.87	2907.19	2874.24	2854.84	2843.34
340000	3156.33	3130.77	3069.78	3053.68	2995.29	2961.34	2941.35	2929.50
350000	3249.16	3222.85	3160.07	3143.50	3083.38	3048.44	3027.86	3015.66
360000	3341.99	3314.93	3250.36	3233.31	3171.48	3135.54	3114.37	3101.83
370000	3434.82	3407.01	3340.65	3323.12	3259.58	3222.63	3200.89	3187.99
380000	3527.66	3499.09	3430.93	3412.94	3347.67	3309.73	3287.40	3274.15
390000	3620.49	3591.17	3521.22	3502.75	3435.77	3396.83	3373.91	3360.31
400000	3713.32	3683.25	3611.51	3592.57	3523.87	3483.93	3460.42	3446.47

BLENDED MONTHLY PAYMENTS 10¾%
AMORTIZATION IN YEARS

Amount	1	2	3	4	5	6	7	8
25	2.21	1.16	.82	.65	.54	.47	.43	.39
50	4.41	2.32	1.63	1.29	1.08	.94	.85	.78
100	8.82	4.64	3.26	2.57	2.16	1.88	1.69	1.55
200	17.64	9.28	6.51	5.13	4.31	3.76	3.38	3.09
300	26.45	13.92	9.76	7.69	6.46	5.64	5.07	4.64
400	35.27	18.56	13.01	10.25	8.61	7.52	6.75	6.18
500	44.08	23.20	16.26	12.81	10.76	9.40	8.44	7.73
600	52.90	27.84	19.51	15.37	12.91	11.28	10.13	9.27
700	61.71	32.47	22.76	17.93	15.06	13.16	11.81	10.82
800	70.53	37.11	26.01	20.49	17.21	15.04	13.50	12.36
900	79.35	41.75	29.26	23.06	19.36	16.91	15.19	13.91
1000	88.16	46.39	32.52	25.62	21.51	18.79	16.87	15.45
2000	176.32	92.77	65.03	51.23	43.01	37.58	33.74	30.90
3000	264.47	139.16	97.54	76.84	64.51	56.37	50.61	46.35
4000	352.63	185.54	130.05	102.45	86.01	75.16	67.48	61.80
5000	440.79	231.92	162.56	128.06	107.52	93.94	84.35	77.25
6000	528.94	278.31	195.07	153.67	129.02	112.73	101.22	92.70
7000	617.10	324.69	227.58	179.29	150.52	131.52	118.09	108.15
8000	705.26	371.08	260.09	204.90	172.02	150.31	134.96	123.60
9000	793.41	417.46	292.60	230.51	193.53	169.09	151.83	139.05
10000	881.57	463.84	325.11	256.12	215.03	187.88	168.70	154.50
20000	1763.13	927.68	650.21	512.24	430.05	375.76	337.39	308.99
30000	2644.70	1391.52	975.32	768.35	645.07	563.63	506.09	463.48
40000	3526.26	1855.36	1300.42	1024.47	860.10	751.51	674.78	617.97
50000	4407.83	2319.20	1625.52	1280.58	1075.12	939.38	843.48	772.46
60000	5289.39	2783.04	1950.63	1536.70	1290.14	1127.26	1012.17	926.95
70000	6170.96	3246.87	2275.73	1792.81	1505.16	1315.13	1180.87	1081.44
80000	7052.52	3710.71	2600.84	2048.93	1720.19	1503.01	1349.56	1235.93
90000	7934.09	4174.55	2925.94	2305.04	1935.21	1690.88	1518.26	1390.42
100000	8815.65	4638.39	3251.04	2561.16	2150.23	1878.76	1686.95	1544.91
110000	9697.22	5102.23	3576.15	2817.27	2365.25	2066.63	1855.65	1699.40
120000	10578.78	5566.07	3901.25	3073.39	2580.28	2254.51	2024.34	1853.89
130000	11460.34	6029.91	4226.36	3329.50	2795.30	2442.39	2193.04	2008.38
140000	12341.91	6493.74	4551.46	3585.62	3010.32	2630.26	2361.73	2162.87
150000	13223.47	6957.58	4876.56	3841.73	3225.34	2818.14	2530.42	2317.36
160000	14105.04	7421.42	5201.67	4097.85	3440.37	3006.01	2699.12	2471.85
170000	14986.60	7885.26	5526.77	4353.96	3655.39	3193.89	2867.81	2626.34
180000	15868.17	8349.10	5851.88	4610.08	3870.41	3381.76	3036.51	2780.83
190000	16749.73	8812.94	6176.98	4866.19	4085.43	3569.64	3205.20	2935.32
200000	17631.30	9276.77	6502.08	5122.31	4300.46	3757.51	3373.90	3089.81
210000	18512.86	9740.61	6827.19	5378.43	4515.48	3945.39	3542.59	3244.30
220000	19394.43	10204.45	7152.29	5634.54	4730.50	4133.26	3711.29	3398.79
230000	20275.99	10668.29	7477.40	5890.66	4945.52	4321.14	3879.98	3553.28
240000	21157.55	11132.13	7802.50	6146.77	5160.55	4509.02	4048.68	3707.77
250000	22039.12	11595.97	8127.60	6402.89	5375.57	4696.89	4217.37	3862.26
260000	22920.68	12059.81	8452.71	6659.00	5590.59	4884.77	4386.07	4016.75
270000	23802.25	12523.64	8777.81	6915.12	5805.61	5072.64	4554.76	4171.24
280000	24683.81	12987.48	9102.92	7171.23	6020.64	5260.52	4723.46	4325.73
290000	25565.38	13451.32	9428.02	7427.35	6235.66	5448.39	4892.15	4480.22
300000	26446.94	13915.16	9753.12	7683.46	6450.68	5636.27	5060.84	4634.71
310000	27328.51	14379.00	10078.23	7939.58	6665.70	5824.14	5229.54	4789.20
320000	28210.07	14842.84	10403.33	8195.69	6880.73	6012.02	5398.23	4943.69
330000	29091.64	15306.67	10728.44	8451.81	7095.75	6199.89	5566.93	5098.18
340000	29973.20	15770.51	11053.54	8707.92	7310.77	6387.77	5735.62	5252.67
350000	30854.77	16234.35	11378.64	8964.04	7525.79	6575.64	5904.32	5407.16
360000	31736.33	16698.19	11703.75	9220.15	7740.82	6763.52	6073.01	5561.65
370000	32617.89	17162.03	12028.85	9476.27	7955.84	6951.40	6241.71	5716.15
380000	33499.46	17625.87	12353.96	9732.38	8170.86	7139.27	6410.40	5870.64
390000	34381.02	18089.71	12679.06	9988.50	8385.88	7327.15	6579.10	6025.13
400000	35262.59	18553.54	13004.16	10244.61	8600.91	7515.02	6747.79	6179.62

10¾% BLENDED MONTHLY PAYMENTS
AMORTIZATION IN YEARS

Amount	9	10	11	12	13	14	15	16
25	.36	.34	.33	.31	.30	.29	.28	.27
50	.72	.68	.65	.62	.59	.57	.56	.54
100	1.44	1.36	1.29	1.23	1.18	1.14	1.11	1.08
200	2.88	2.71	2.57	2.46	2.36	2.28	2.22	2.16
300	4.31	4.06	3.85	3.68	3.54	3.42	3.32	3.24
400	5.75	5.41	5.13	4.91	4.72	4.56	4.43	4.32
500	7.19	6.76	6.41	6.13	5.90	5.70	5.54	5.40
600	8.62	8.11	7.69	7.36	7.08	6.84	6.64	6.47
700	10.06	9.46	8.97	8.58	8.25	7.98	7.75	7.55
800	11.49	10.81	10.26	9.81	9.43	9.12	8.86	8.63
900	12.93	12.16	11.54	11.03	10.61	10.26	9.96	9.71
1000	14.37	13.51	12.82	12.26	11.79	11.40	11.07	10.79
2000	28.73	27.01	25.63	24.51	23.58	22.79	22.13	21.57
3000	43.09	40.51	38.45	36.76	35.36	34.19	33.20	32.35
4000	57.45	54.02	51.26	49.01	47.15	45.58	44.26	43.14
5000	71.81	67.52	64.08	61.26	58.93	56.98	55.33	53.92
6000	86.17	81.02	76.89	73.51	70.72	68.37	66.39	64.70
7000	100.53	94.53	89.70	85.76	82.50	79.77	77.46	75.49
8000	114.89	108.03	102.52	98.02	94.29	91.16	88.52	86.27
9000	129.25	121.53	115.33	110.27	106.07	102.56	99.59	97.05
10000	143.61	135.03	128.15	122.52	117.86	113.95	110.65	107.84
20000	287.21	270.06	256.29	245.03	235.71	227.90	221.29	215.67
30000	430.81	405.09	384.43	367.54	353.56	341.84	331.94	323.50
40000	574.41	540.12	512.57	490.06	471.41	455.79	442.58	431.33
50000	718.01	675.15	640.71	612.57	589.26	569.74	553.23	539.16
60000	861.61	810.18	768.85	735.08	707.11	683.68	663.87	646.99
70000	1005.21	945.21	896.99	857.59	824.96	797.63	774.52	754.82
80000	1148.81	1080.24	1025.13	980.11	942.81	911.57	885.16	862.65
90000	1292.41	1215.27	1153.28	1102.62	1060.66	1025.52	995.81	970.48
100000	1436.01	1350.30	1281.42	1225.13	1178.51	1139.47	1106.45	1078.31
110000	1579.61	1485.33	1409.56	1347.64	1296.36	1253.41	1217.09	1186.14
120000	1723.22	1620.36	1537.70	1470.16	1414.22	1367.36	1327.74	1293.97
130000	1866.82	1755.39	1665.84	1592.67	1532.07	1481.30	1438.38	1401.80
140000	2010.42	1890.42	1793.98	1715.18	1649.92	1595.25	1549.03	1509.63
150000	2154.02	2025.45	1922.12	1837.70	1767.77	1709.20	1659.67	1617.47
160000	2297.62	2160.48	2050.26	1960.21	1885.62	1823.14	1770.32	1725.30
170000	2441.22	2295.51	2178.40	2082.72	2003.47	1937.09	1880.96	1833.13
180000	2584.82	2430.53	2306.55	2205.23	2121.32	2051.03	1991.61	1940.96
190000	2728.42	2565.56	2434.69	2327.75	2239.17	2164.98	2102.25	2048.79
200000	2872.02	2700.59	2562.83	2450.26	2357.02	2278.93	2212.89	2156.62
210000	3015.62	2835.62	2690.97	2572.77	2474.87	2392.87	2323.54	2264.45
220000	3159.22	2970.65	2819.11	2695.28	2592.72	2506.82	2434.18	2372.28
230000	3302.83	3105.68	2947.25	2817.80	2710.57	2620.76	2544.83	2480.11
240000	3446.43	3240.71	3075.39	2940.31	2828.43	2734.71	2655.47	2587.94
250000	3590.03	3375.74	3203.53	3062.82	2946.28	2848.66	2766.12	2695.77
260000	3733.63	3510.77	3331.68	3185.34	3064.13	2962.60	2876.76	2803.60
270000	3877.23	3645.80	3459.82	3307.85	3181.98	3076.55	2987.41	2911.43
280000	4020.83	3780.83	3587.96	3430.36	3299.83	3190.49	3098.05	3019.26
290000	4164.43	3915.86	3716.10	3552.87	3417.68	3304.44	3208.69	3127.09
300000	4308.03	4050.89	3844.24	3675.39	3535.53	3418.39	3319.34	3234.93
310000	4451.63	4185.92	3972.38	3797.90	3653.38	3532.33	3429.98	3342.76
320000	4595.23	4320.95	4100.52	3920.41	3771.23	3646.28	3540.63	3450.59
330000	4738.83	4455.98	4228.66	4042.92	3889.08	3760.22	3651.27	3558.42
340000	4882.44	4591.01	4356.80	4165.44	4006.93	3874.17	3761.92	3666.25
350000	5026.04	4726.04	4484.95	4287.95	4124.79	3988.12	3872.56	3774.08
360000	5169.64	4861.06	4613.09	4410.46	4242.64	4102.06	3983.21	3881.91
370000	5313.24	4996.09	4741.23	4532.98	4360.49	4216.01	4093.85	3989.74
380000	5456.84	5131.12	4869.37	4655.49	4478.34	4329.95	4204.49	4097.57
390000	5600.44	5266.15	4997.51	4778.00	4596.19	4443.90	4315.14	4205.40
400000	5744.04	5401.18	5125.65	4900.51	4714.04	4557.85	4425.78	4313.23

BLENDED MONTHLY PAYMENTS $10\frac{3}{4}\%$

AMORTIZATION IN YEARS

Amount	17	18	19	20	21	22	23	24
25	.27	.26	.26	.25	.25	.25	.25	.24
50	.53	.52	.51	.50	.50	.49	.49	.48
100	1.06	1.04	1.02	1.00	.99	.98	.97	.96
200	2.11	2.07	2.04	2.00	1.98	1.95	1.93	1.91
300	3.17	3.10	3.05	3.00	2.96	2.93	2.89	2.87
400	4.22	4.14	4.07	4.00	3.95	3.90	3.86	3.82
500	5.28	5.17	5.08	5.00	4.93	4.87	4.82	4.77
600	6.33	6.20	6.10	6.00	5.92	5.85	5.78	5.73
700	7.38	7.24	7.11	7.00	6.91	6.82	6.75	6.68
800	8.44	8.27	8.13	8.00	7.89	7.79	7.71	7.63
900	9.49	9.30	9.14	9.00	8.88	8.77	8.67	8.59
1000	10.55	10.34	10.16	10.00	9.86	9.74	9.64	9.54
2000	21.09	20.67	20.31	20.00	19.72	19.48	19.27	19.08
3000	31.63	31.00	30.46	29.99	29.58	29.22	28.90	28.62
4000	42.17	41.34	40.62	39.99	39.43	38.95	38.53	38.15
5000	52.71	51.67	50.77	49.98	49.29	48.69	48.16	47.69
6000	63.25	62.00	60.92	59.98	59.15	58.43	57.79	57.23
7000	73.80	72.34	71.07	69.97	69.01	68.16	67.42	66.76
8000	84.34	82.67	81.23	79.97	78.86	77.90	77.05	76.30
9000	94.88	93.00	91.38	89.96	88.72	87.64	86.68	85.84
10000	105.42	103.34	101.53	99.96	98.58	97.37	96.31	95.37
20000	210.84	206.67	203.06	199.91	197.15	194.74	192.61	190.74
30000	316.25	310.00	304.58	299.86	295.73	292.11	288.92	286.11
40000	421.67	413.34	406.11	399.81	394.30	389.47	385.22	381.47
50000	527.09	516.67	507.63	499.76	492.88	486.84	481.53	476.84
60000	632.50	620.00	609.16	599.71	591.45	584.21	577.83	572.21
70000	737.92	723.33	710.68	699.66	690.03	681.57	674.14	667.58
80000	843.34	826.67	812.21	799.62	788.60	778.94	770.44	762.94
90000	948.75	930.00	913.74	899.57	887.18	876.31	866.75	858.31
100000	1054.17	1033.33	1015.26	999.52	985.75	973.68	963.05	953.68
110000	1159.59	1136.67	1116.79	1099.47	1084.33	1071.04	1059.35	1049.04
120000	1265.00	1240.00	1218.31	1199.42	1182.90	1168.41	1155.66	1144.41
130000	1370.42	1343.33	1319.84	1299.37	1281.48	1265.78	1251.96	1239.78
140000	1475.83	1446.66	1421.36	1399.32	1380.05	1363.14	1348.27	1335.15
150000	1581.25	1550.00	1522.89	1499.27	1478.63	1460.51	1444.57	1430.51
160000	1686.67	1653.33	1624.41	1599.23	1577.20	1557.88	1540.88	1525.88
170000	1792.08	1756.66	1725.94	1699.18	1675.78	1655.25	1637.18	1621.25
180000	1897.50	1859.99	1827.47	1799.13	1774.35	1752.61	1733.49	1716.62
190000	2002.92	1963.33	1928.99	1899.08	1872.92	1849.98	1829.79	1811.98
200000	2108.33	2066.66	2030.52	1999.03	1971.50	1947.35	1926.10	1907.35
210000	2213.75	2169.99	2132.04	2098.98	2070.07	2044.71	2022.40	2002.72
220000	2319.17	2273.33	2233.57	2198.93	2168.65	2142.08	2118.70	2098.08
230000	2424.58	2376.66	2335.09	2298.88	2267.22	2239.45	2215.01	2193.45
240000	2530.00	2479.99	2436.62	2398.84	2365.80	2336.81	2311.31	2288.82
250000	2635.41	2583.32	2538.14	2498.79	2464.37	2434.18	2407.62	2384.19
260000	2740.83	2686.66	2639.67	2598.74	2562.95	2531.55	2503.92	2479.55
270000	2846.25	2789.99	2741.20	2698.69	2661.52	2628.92	2600.23	2574.92
280000	2951.66	2893.32	2842.72	2798.64	2760.10	2726.28	2696.53	2670.29
290000	3057.08	2996.66	2944.25	2898.59	2858.67	2823.65	2792.84	2765.66
300000	3162.50	3099.99	3045.77	2998.54	2957.25	2921.02	2889.14	2861.02
310000	3267.91	3203.32	3147.30	3098.50	3055.82	3018.38	2985.44	2956.39
320000	3373.33	3306.65	3248.82	3198.45	3154.40	3115.75	3081.75	3051.76
330000	3478.75	3409.99	3350.35	3298.40	3252.97	3213.12	3178.05	3147.12
340000	3584.16	3513.32	3451.87	3398.35	3351.55	3310.49	3274.36	3242.49
350000	3689.58	3616.65	3553.40	3498.30	3450.12	3407.85	3370.66	3337.86
360000	3794.99	3719.98	3654.93	3598.25	3548.70	3505.22	3466.97	3433.23
370000	3900.41	3823.32	3756.45	3698.20	3647.27	3602.59	3563.27	3528.59
380000	4005.83	3926.65	3857.98	3798.15	3745.84	3699.95	3659.58	3623.96
390000	4111.24	4029.98	3959.50	3898.11	3844.42	3797.32	3755.88	3719.33
400000	4216.66	4133.32	4061.03	3998.06	3942.99	3894.69	3852.19	3814.69

10¾% BLENDED MONTHLY PAYMENTS
AMORTIZATION IN YEARS

Amount	25	26	29	30	35	40	45	50
25	.24	.24	.24	.23	.23	.23	.23	.23
50	.48	.47	.47	.46	.45	.45	.45	.45
100	.95	.94	.93	.92	.90	.89	.89	.89
200	1.90	1.88	1.85	1.84	1.80	1.78	1.77	1.77
300	2.84	2.82	2.77	2.75	2.70	2.67	2.66	2.65
400	3.79	3.76	3.69	3.67	3.60	3.56	3.54	3.53
500	4.73	4.70	4.61	4.59	4.50	4.45	4.43	4.41
600	5.68	5.63	5.53	5.50	5.40	5.34	5.31	5.29
700	6.62	6.57	6.45	6.42	6.30	6.23	6.20	6.17
800	7.57	7.51	7.37	7.33	7.20	7.12	7.08	7.05
900	8.51	8.45	8.29	8.25	8.10	8.01	7.96	7.93
1000	9.46	9.39	9.21	9.17	9.00	8.90	8.85	8.82
2000	18.91	18.77	18.42	18.33	17.99	17.80	17.69	17.63
3000	28.37	28.15	27.62	27.49	26.99	26.70	26.54	26.44
4000	37.82	37.53	36.83	36.65	35.98	35.60	35.38	35.25
5000	47.27	46.91	46.03	45.81	44.98	44.50	44.22	44.06
6000	56.73	56.29	55.24	54.97	53.97	53.40	53.07	52.87
7000	66.18	65.67	64.45	64.13	62.97	62.30	61.91	61.68
8000	75.64	75.05	73.65	73.29	71.96	71.20	70.75	70.49
9000	85.09	84.43	82.86	82.45	80.95	80.10	79.60	79.30
10000	94.54	93.81	92.06	91.61	89.95	89.00	88.44	88.11
20000	189.08	187.61	184.12	183.21	179.89	177.99	176.88	176.22
30000	283.62	281.42	276.18	274.81	269.84	266.98	265.31	264.33
40000	378.16	375.22	368.24	366.41	359.78	355.97	353.75	352.44
50000	472.70	469.03	460.30	458.01	449.72	444.96	442.18	440.55
60000	567.24	562.83	552.36	549.61	539.67	533.95	530.62	528.66
70000	661.78	656.64	644.42	641.21	629.61	622.94	619.05	616.77
80000	756.31	750.44	736.48	732.81	719.56	711.93	707.49	704.88
90000	850.85	844.25	828.54	824.41	809.50	800.92	795.92	792.99
100000	945.39	938.05	920.60	916.01	899.44	889.91	884.36	881.10
110000	1039.93	1031.86	1012.66	1007.61	989.39	978.90	972.79	969.21
120000	1134.47	1125.66	1104.71	1099.21	1079.33	1067.89	1061.23	1057.32
130000	1229.01	1219.47	1196.77	1190.81	1169.27	1156.88	1149.66	1145.43
140000	1323.55	1313.27	1288.83	1282.41	1259.22	1245.87	1238.10	1233.54
150000	1418.08	1407.07	1380.89	1374.01	1349.16	1334.86	1326.53	1321.65
160000	1512.62	1500.88	1472.95	1465.61	1439.11	1423.85	1414.97	1409.76
170000	1607.16	1594.68	1565.01	1557.21	1529.05	1512.84	1503.41	1497.87
180000	1701.70	1688.49	1657.07	1648.81	1618.99	1601.83	1591.84	1585.98
190000	1796.24	1782.29	1749.13	1740.41	1708.94	1690.83	1680.28	1674.09
200000	1890.78	1876.10	1841.19	1832.01	1798.88	1779.82	1768.71	1762.20
210000	1985.32	1969.90	1933.25	1923.61	1888.82	1868.81	1857.15	1850.31
220000	2079.86	2063.71	2025.31	2015.21	1978.77	1957.80	1945.58	1938.42
230000	2174.39	2157.51	2117.37	2106.81	2068.71	2046.79	2034.02	2026.53
240000	2268.93	2251.32	2209.42	2198.41	2158.66	2135.78	2122.45	2114.64
250000	2363.47	2345.12	2301.48	2290.01	2248.60	2224.77	2210.89	2202.75
260000	2458.01	2438.93	2393.54	2381.61	2338.54	2313.76	2299.32	2290.86
270000	2552.55	2532.73	2485.60	2473.21	2428.49	2402.75	2387.76	2378.97
280000	2647.09	2626.53	2577.66	2564.81	2518.43	2491.74	2476.19	2467.07
290000	2741.63	2720.34	2669.72	2656.45	2608.37	2580.73	2564.63	2555.18
300000	2836.16	2814.14	2761.78	2748.01	2698.32	2669.72	2653.06	2643.29
310000	2930.70	2907.95	2853.84	2839.61	2788.26	2758.71	2741.50	2731.40
320000	3025.24	3001.75	2945.90	2931.21	2878.21	2847.70	2829.93	2819.51
330000	3119.78	3095.56	3037.96	3022.81	2968.15	2936.69	2918.37	2907.62
340000	3214.32	3189.36	3130.02	3114.41	3058.09	3025.68	3006.81	2995.73
350000	3308.86	3283.17	3222.08	3206.01	3148.04	3114.67	3095.24	3083.84
360000	3403.40	3376.97	3314.13	3297.61	3237.98	3203.66	3183.68	3171.95
370000	3497.93	3470.78	3406.19	3389.21	3327.92	3292.66	3272.11	3260.06
380000	3592.47	3564.58	3498.25	3480.81	3417.87	3381.65	3360.55	3348.17
390000	3687.01	3658.39	3590.31	3572.41	3507.81	3470.64	3448.98	3436.28
400000	3781.55	3752.19	3682.37	3664.01	3597.76	3559.63	3537.42	3524.39

132

BLENDED MONTHLY PAYMENTS

AMORTIZATION IN YEARS — **11%**

Amount	1	2	3	4	5	6	7	8
25	2.21	1.17	.82	.65	.55	.48	.43	.39
50	4.42	2.33	1.64	1.29	1.09	.95	.85	.78
100	8.83	4.65	3.27	2.58	2.17	1.90	1.70	1.56
200	17.66	9.30	6.53	5.15	4.33	3.79	3.40	3.12
300	26.49	13.95	9.79	7.72	6.49	5.68	5.10	4.68
400	35.31	18.60	13.05	10.30	8.65	7.57	6.80	6.24
500	44.14	23.25	16.32	12.87	10.82	9.46	8.50	7.79
600	52.97	27.90	19.58	15.44	12.98	11.35	10.20	9.35
700	61.79	32.55	22.84	18.01	15.14	13.24	11.90	10.91
800	70.62	37.20	26.10	20.59	17.30	15.13	13.60	12.47
900	79.45	41.85	29.37	23.16	19.46	17.02	15.30	14.02
1000	88.27	46.50	32.63	25.73	21.63	18.91	17.00	15.58
2000	176.54	92.99	65.25	51.46	43.25	37.82	33.99	31.16
3000	264.81	139.49	97.87	77.19	64.87	56.73	50.99	46.74
4000	353.08	185.98	130.50	102.91	86.49	75.64	67.98	62.31
5000	441.34	232.48	163.12	128.64	108.11	94.55	84.98	77.89
6000	529.61	278.97	195.74	154.37	129.73	113.46	101.97	93.47
7000	617.88	325.47	228.37	180.10	151.35	132.37	118.97	109.05
8000	706.15	371.96	260.99	205.82	172.97	151.28	135.96	124.62
9000	794.42	418.46	293.61	231.55	194.59	170.19	152.96	140.20
10000	882.68	464.95	326.24	257.28	216.21	189.10	169.95	155.78
20000	1765.36	929.90	652.47	514.55	432.42	378.19	339.89	311.55
30000	2648.04	1394.85	978.70	771.82	648.63	567.29	509.84	467.32
40000	3530.72	1859.79	1304.94	1029.09	864.84	756.38	679.78	623.09
50000	4413.40	2324.74	1631.17	1286.37	1081.05	945.47	849.73	778.86
60000	5296.08	2789.69	1957.40	1543.64	1297.26	1134.57	1019.67	934.63
70000	6178.76	3254.63	2283.64	1800.91	1513.47	1323.66	1189.62	1090.41
80000	7061.44	3719.58	2609.87	2058.18	1729.68	1512.76	1359.56	1246.18
90000	7944.12	4184.53	2936.10	2315.46	1945.89	1701.85	1529.51	1401.95
100000	8826.80	4649.47	3262.34	2572.73	2162.10	1890.94	1699.45	1557.72
110000	9709.48	5114.42	3588.57	2830.00	2378.31	2080.04	1869.39	1713.49
120000	10592.16	5579.37	3914.80	3087.27	2594.52	2269.13	2039.34	1869.26
130000	11474.83	6044.31	4241.04	3344.54	2810.73	2458.22	2209.28	2025.04
140000	12357.51	6509.26	4567.27	3601.82	3026.94	2647.32	2379.23	2180.81
150000	13240.19	6974.21	4893.50	3859.09	3243.15	2836.41	2549.17	2336.58
160000	14122.87	7439.15	5219.74	4116.36	3459.36	3025.51	2719.12	2492.35
170000	15005.55	7904.10	5545.97	4373.63	3675.57	3214.60	2889.06	2648.12
180000	15888.23	8369.05	5872.20	4630.91	3891.78	3403.69	3059.01	2803.89
190000	16770.91	8833.99	6198.44	4888.18	4107.99	3592.79	3228.95	2959.67
200000	17653.59	9298.94	6524.67	5145.45	4324.20	3781.88	3398.90	3115.44
210000	18536.27	9763.89	6850.90	5402.72	4540.41	3970.97	3568.84	3271.21
220000	19418.95	10228.83	7177.14	5659.99	4756.62	4160.07	3738.78	3426.98
230000	20301.63	10693.78	7503.37	5917.27	4972.83	4349.16	3908.73	3582.75
240000	21184.31	11158.73	7829.60	6174.54	5189.04	4538.26	4078.67	3738.52
250000	22066.98	11623.67	8155.84	6431.81	5405.25	4727.35	4248.62	3894.30
260000	22949.66	12088.62	8482.07	6689.08	5621.46	4916.44	4418.56	4050.07
270000	23832.34	12553.57	8808.30	6946.36	5837.67	5105.54	4588.51	4205.84
280000	24715.02	13018.51	9134.54	7203.63	6053.88	5294.63	4758.45	4361.61
290000	25597.70	13483.46	9460.77	7460.90	6270.09	5483.72	4928.40	4517.38
300000	26480.38	13948.41	9787.00	7718.17	6486.30	5672.82	5098.34	4673.15
310000	27363.06	14413.35	10113.24	7975.44	6702.51	5861.91	5268.28	4828.93
320000	28245.74	14878.30	10439.47	8232.72	6918.72	6051.01	5438.23	4984.70
330000	29128.42	15343.25	10765.70	8489.99	7134.93	6240.10	5608.17	5140.47
340000	30011.10	15808.19	11091.93	8747.26	7351.14	6429.19	5778.12	5296.24
350000	30893.78	16273.14	11418.17	9004.53	7567.35	6618.29	5948.06	5452.01
360000	31776.46	16738.09	11744.40	9261.81	7783.55	6807.38	6118.01	5607.78
370000	32659.13	17203.03	12070.63	9519.08	7999.76	6996.47	6287.95	5763.56
380000	33541.81	17667.98	12396.87	9776.35	8215.97	7185.57	6457.90	5919.33
390000	34424.49	18132.93	12723.10	10033.62	8432.18	7374.66	6627.84	6075.10
400000	35307.17	18597.87	13049.33	10290.89	8648.39	7563.76	6797.79	6230.87

133

Amount	9	10	11	12	13	14	15	16
25	.37	.35	.33	.31	.30	.29	.29	.28
50	.73	.69	.65	.62	.60	.58	.57	.55
100	1.45	1.37	1.30	1.24	1.20	1.16	1.13	1.10
200	2.90	2.73	2.60	2.48	2.39	2.31	2.25	2.19
300	4.35	4.10	3.89	3.72	3.58	3.47	3.37	3.29
400	5.80	5.46	5.19	4.96	4.78	4.62	4.49	4.38
500	7.25	6.82	6.48	6.20	5.97	5.78	5.61	5.47
600	8.70	8.19	7.78	7.44	7.16	6.93	6.73	6.57
700	10.15	9.55	9.07	8.68	8.35	8.08	7.85	7.66
800	11.60	10.91	10.37	9.92	9.55	9.24	8.98	8.75
900	13.05	12.28	11.66	11.16	10.74	10.39	10.10	9.85
1000	14.50	13.64	12.96	12.40	11.93	11.55	11.22	10.94
2000	28.99	27.28	25.91	24.79	23.86	23.09	22.43	21.87
3000	43.48	40.92	38.86	37.18	35.79	34.63	33.64	32.81
4000	57.97	54.55	51.81	49.57	47.72	46.17	44.86	43.74
5000	72.46	68.19	64.76	61.96	59.65	57.71	56.07	54.68
6000	86.95	81.83	77.71	74.35	71.57	69.25	67.28	65.61
7000	101.44	95.47	90.67	86.75	83.50	80.79	78.50	76.55
8000	115.94	109.10	103.62	99.14	95.43	92.33	89.71	87.48
9000	130.43	122.74	116.57	111.53	107.36	103.87	100.92	98.42
10000	144.92	136.38	129.52	123.92	119.29	115.41	112.14	109.35
20000	289.83	272.75	259.03	247.84	238.57	230.82	224.27	218.70
30000	434.75	409.12	388.55	371.75	357.85	346.23	336.40	328.04
40000	579.66	545.50	518.06	495.67	477.14	461.63	448.54	437.39
50000	724.57	681.87	647.58	619.59	596.42	577.04	560.67	546.73
60000	869.49	818.24	777.09	743.50	715.70	692.45	672.80	656.08
70000	1014.40	954.62	906.61	867.42	834.99	807.85	784.93	765.42
80000	1159.31	1090.99	1036.12	991.33	954.27	923.26	897.07	874.77
90000	1304.23	1227.36	1165.64	1115.25	1073.55	1038.67	1009.20	984.12
100000	1449.14	1363.73	1295.15	1239.17	1192.84	1154.07	1121.33	1093.46
110000	1594.05	1500.11	1424.67	1363.08	1312.12	1269.48	1233.46	1202.81
120000	1738.97	1636.48	1554.18	1487.00	1431.40	1384.89	1345.60	1312.15
130000	1883.88	1772.85	1683.70	1610.92	1550.69	1500.29	1457.73	1421.50
140000	2028.79	1909.23	1813.21	1734.83	1669.97	1615.70	1569.86	1530.84
150000	2173.71	2045.60	1942.73	1858.75	1789.25	1731.11	1682.00	1640.19
160000	2318.62	2181.97	2072.24	1982.66	1908.54	1846.51	1794.13	1749.53
170000	2463.53	2318.34	2201.76	2106.58	2027.82	1961.92	1906.26	1858.88
180000	2608.45	2454.72	2331.27	2230.50	2147.10	2077.33	2018.39	1968.23
190000	2753.36	2591.09	2460.79	2354.41	2266.39	2192.73	2130.53	2077.57
200000	2898.27	2727.46	2590.30	2478.33	2385.67	2308.14	2242.66	2186.92
210000	3043.19	2863.84	2719.82	2602.24	2504.95	2423.55	2354.79	2296.26
220000	3188.10	3000.21	2849.33	2726.16	2624.24	2538.95	2466.92	2405.61
230000	3333.02	3136.58	2978.85	2850.08	2743.52	2654.36	2579.06	2514.95
240000	3477.93	3272.95	3108.36	2973.99	2862.80	2769.77	2691.19	2624.30
250000	3622.84	3409.33	3237.88	3097.91	2982.09	2885.17	2803.32	2733.64
260000	3767.76	3545.70	3367.39	3221.83	3101.37	3000.58	2915.46	2842.99
270000	3912.67	3682.07	3496.91	3345.74	3220.65	3115.99	3027.59	2952.34
280000	4057.58	3818.45	3626.42	3469.66	3339.94	3231.40	3139.72	3061.68
290000	4202.50	3954.82	3755.94	3593.57	3459.22	3346.80	3251.85	3171.03
300000	4347.41	4091.19	3885.45	3717.49	3578.50	3462.21	3363.99	3280.37
310000	4492.32	4227.56	4014.97	3841.41	3697.79	3577.62	3476.12	3389.72
320000	4637.24	4363.94	4144.48	3965.32	3817.07	3693.02	3588.25	3499.06
330000	4782.15	4500.31	4274.00	4089.24	3936.35	3808.43	3700.38	3608.41
340000	4927.06	4636.68	4403.51	4213.15	4055.64	3923.84	3812.52	3717.75
350000	5071.98	4773.06	4533.03	4337.07	4174.92	4039.24	3924.65	3827.10
360000	5216.89	4909.43	4662.54	4460.99	4294.20	4154.65	4036.78	3936.45
370000	5361.80	5045.80	4792.06	4584.90	4413.49	4270.06	4148.91	4045.79
380000	5506.72	5182.17	4921.57	4708.82	4532.77	4385.46	4261.05	4155.14
390000	5651.63	5318.55	5051.09	4832.74	4652.05	4500.87	4373.18	4264.48
400000	5796.54	5454.92	5180.60	4956.65	4771.34	4616.28	4485.31	4373.83

BLENDED MONTHLY PAYMENTS 11%
AMORTIZATION IN YEARS

Amount	17	18	19	20	21	22	23	24
25	.27	.27	.26	.26	.26	.25	.25	.25
50	.54	.53	.52	.51	.51	.50	.49	.49
100	1.07	1.05	1.04	1.02	1.01	1.00	.98	.98
200	2.14	2.10	2.07	2.04	2.01	1.99	1.96	1.95
300	3.21	3.15	3.10	3.05	3.01	2.98	2.94	2.92
400	4.28	4.20	4.13	4.07	4.01	3.97	3.92	3.89
500	5.35	5.25	5.16	5.08	5.02	4.96	4.90	4.86
600	6.42	6.30	6.19	6.10	6.02	5.95	5.88	5.83
700	7.49	7.35	7.22	7.11	7.02	6.94	6.86	6.80
800	8.56	8.40	8.25	8.13	8.02	7.93	7.84	7.77
900	9.63	9.45	9.29	9.15	9.02	8.92	8.82	8.74
1000	10.70	10.49	10.32	10.16	10.03	9.91	9.80	9.71
2000	21.40	20.98	20.63	20.32	20.05	19.81	19.60	19.42
3000	32.09	31.47	30.94	30.47	30.07	29.71	29.40	29.12
4000	42.79	41.96	41.25	40.63	40.09	39.61	39.20	38.83
5000	53.48	52.45	51.56	50.79	50.11	49.52	49.00	48.54
6000	64.18	62.94	61.87	60.94	60.13	59.42	58.79	58.24
7000	74.87	73.43	72.19	71.10	70.15	69.32	68.59	67.95
8000	85.57	83.92	82.50	81.26	80.17	79.22	78.39	77.66
9000	96.27	94.41	92.81	91.41	90.19	89.13	88.19	87.36
10000	106.96	104.90	103.12	101.57	100.21	99.03	97.99	97.07
20000	213.92	209.80	206.24	203.13	200.42	198.05	195.97	194.13
30000	320.88	314.70	309.35	304.70	300.63	297.07	293.95	291.19
40000	427.83	419.60	412.47	406.26	400.84	396.10	391.93	388.26
50000	534.79	524.50	515.58	507.82	501.05	495.12	489.91	485.32
60000	641.75	629.40	618.70	609.39	601.26	594.14	587.89	582.38
70000	748.70	734.29	721.81	710.95	701.47	693.17	685.87	679.45
80000	855.66	839.19	824.93	812.52	801.68	792.19	783.85	776.51
90000	962.62	944.09	928.04	914.08	901.89	891.21	881.83	873.57
100000	1069.58	1048.99	1031.16	1015.64	1002.10	990.24	979.81	970.64
110000	1176.53	1153.89	1134.27	1117.21	1102.31	1089.26	1077.79	1067.70
120000	1283.49	1258.79	1237.39	1218.77	1202.52	1188.28	1175.78	1164.76
130000	1390.45	1363.68	1340.50	1320.34	1302.73	1287.31	1273.76	1261.82
140000	1497.40	1468.58	1443.62	1421.90	1402.94	1386.33	1371.74	1358.89
150000	1604.36	1573.48	1546.73	1523.46	1503.15	1485.35	1469.72	1455.95
160000	1711.32	1678.38	1649.85	1625.03	1603.36	1584.38	1567.70	1553.01
170000	1818.27	1783.28	1752.96	1726.59	1703.57	1683.40	1665.68	1650.08
180000	1925.23	1888.18	1856.08	1828.16	1803.78	1782.42	1763.66	1747.14
190000	2032.19	1993.07	1959.19	1929.72	1903.99	1881.44	1861.64	1844.20
200000	2139.15	2097.97	2062.31	2031.28	2004.20	1980.47	1959.62	1941.27
210000	2246.10	2202.87	2165.42	2132.85	2104.41	2079.49	2057.60	2038.33
220000	2353.06	2307.77	2268.54	2234.41	2204.62	2178.51	2155.58	2135.39
230000	2460.02	2412.67	2371.65	2335.98	2304.82	2277.54	2253.57	2232.45
240000	2566.97	2517.57	2474.77	2437.54	2405.03	2376.56	2351.55	2329.52
250000	2673.93	2622.46	2577.88	2539.10	2505.24	2475.58	2449.53	2426.58
260000	2780.89	2727.36	2681.00	2640.67	2605.45	2574.61	2547.51	2523.64
270000	2887.85	2832.26	2784.11	2742.23	2705.66	2673.63	2645.49	2620.71
280000	2994.80	2937.16	2887.23	2843.80	2805.87	2772.65	2743.47	2717.77
290000	3101.76	3042.06	2990.34	2945.36	2906.08	2871.68	2841.45	2814.83
300000	3208.72	3146.96	3093.46	3046.92	3006.29	2970.70	2939.43	2911.90
310000	3315.67	3251.85	3196.57	3148.49	3106.50	3069.72	3037.41	3008.96
320000	3422.63	3356.75	3299.69	3250.05	3206.71	3168.75	3135.39	3106.02
330000	3529.59	3461.65	3402.81	3351.62	3306.92	3267.77	3233.37	3203.09
340000	3636.54	3566.55	3505.92	3453.18	3407.13	3366.79	3331.36	3300.15
350000	3743.50	3671.45	3609.04	3554.74	3507.34	3465.81	3429.34	3397.21
360000	3850.46	3776.35	3712.15	3656.31	3607.55	3564.84	3527.32	3494.27
370000	3957.42	3881.24	3815.27	3757.87	3707.76	3663.86	3625.30	3591.34
380000	4064.37	3986.14	3918.38	3859.44	3807.97	3762.88	3723.28	3688.40
390000	4171.33	4091.04	4021.50	3961.00	3908.18	3861.91	3821.26	3785.46
400000	4278.29	4195.94	4124.61	4062.56	4008.39	3960.93	3919.24	3882.53

135

11% BLENDED MONTHLY PAYMENTS
AMORTIZATION IN YEARS

Amount	25	26	29	30	35	40	45	50
25	.25	.24	.24	.24	.23	.23	.23	.23
50	.49	.48	.47	.47	.46	.46	.46	.46
100	.97	.96	.94	.94	.92	.91	.91	.91
200	1.93	1.92	1.88	1.87	1.84	1.82	1.81	1.81
300	2.89	2.87	2.82	2.81	2.76	2.73	2.72	2.71
400	3.86	3.83	3.76	3.74	3.68	3.64	3.62	3.61
500	4.82	4.78	4.70	4.67	4.59	4.55	4.52	4.51
600	5.78	5.74	5.64	5.61	5.51	5.46	5.43	5.41
700	6.74	6.69	6.57	6.54	6.43	6.37	6.33	6.31
800	7.71	7.65	7.51	7.48	7.35	7.28	7.23	7.21
900	8.67	8.60	8.45	8.41	8.27	8.18	8.14	8.11
1000	9.63	9.56	9.39	9.34	9.18	9.09	9.04	9.01
2000	19.26	19.11	18.77	18.68	18.36	18.18	18.08	18.02
3000	28.88	28.67	28.16	28.02	27.54	27.27	27.11	27.02
4000	38.51	38.22	37.54	37.36	36.72	36.36	36.15	36.03
5000	48.13	47.77	46.92	46.70	45.90	45.45	45.19	45.03
6000	57.76	57.33	56.31	56.04	55.08	54.54	54.22	54.04
7000	67.38	66.88	65.69	65.38	64.26	63.63	63.26	63.05
8000	77.01	76.43	75.08	74.72	73.44	72.72	72.30	72.05
9000	86.63	85.99	84.46	84.06	82.62	81.80	81.33	81.06
10000	96.26	95.54	93.84	93.40	91.80	90.89	90.37	90.06
20000	192.51	191.08	187.68	186.79	183.60	181.78	180.73	180.12
30000	288.76	286.61	281.52	280.19	275.40	272.67	271.10	270.18
40000	385.02	382.15	375.36	373.58	367.19	363.56	361.46	360.24
50000	481.27	477.69	469.20	466.97	458.99	454.44	451.82	450.30
60000	577.52	573.22	563.04	560.37	550.79	545.33	542.19	540.36
70000	673.78	668.76	656.88	653.76	642.59	636.22	632.55	630.42
80000	770.00	764.30	750.71	747.16	734.38	727.11	722.92	720.48
90000	866.28	859.83	844.55	840.55	826.18	818.00	813.28	810.54
100000	962.53	955.37	938.39	933.94	917.98	908.88	903.64	900.60
110000	1058.79	1050.91	1032.23	1027.34	1009.78	999.77	994.01	990.66
120000	1155.04	1146.44	1126.07	1120.73	1101.57	1090.66	1084.37	1080.72
130000	1251.29	1241.98	1219.91	1214.12	1193.37	1181.55	1174.74	1170.78
140000	1347.55	1337.52	1313.75	1307.52	1285.17	1272.44	1265.10	1260.84
150000	1443.80	1433.05	1407.59	1400.91	1376.97	1363.32	1355.46	1350.90
160000	1540.05	1528.59	1501.42	1494.31	1468.76	1454.21	1445.83	1440.96
170000	1636.30	1624.13	1595.26	1587.70	1560.56	1545.10	1536.19	1531.02
180000	1732.56	1719.66	1689.10	1681.09	1652.36	1635.99	1626.55	1621.08
190000	1828.81	1815.20	1782.94	1774.49	1744.16	1726.88	1716.92	1711.14
200000	1925.06	1910.74	1876.78	1867.88	1835.95	1817.76	1807.28	1801.20
210000	2021.32	2006.27	1970.62	1961.27	1927.75	1908.65	1897.65	1891.26
220000	2117.57	2101.81	2064.46	2054.67	2019.55	1999.54	1988.01	1981.32
230000	2213.82	2197.34	2158.29	2148.06	2111.35	2090.43	2078.37	2071.38
240000	2310.08	2292.88	2252.13	2241.46	2203.14	2181.32	2168.74	2161.44
250000	2406.33	2388.42	2345.97	2334.85	2294.94	2272.20	2259.10	2251.50
260000	2502.58	2483.95	2439.81	2428.24	2386.74	2363.09	2349.47	2341.56
270000	2598.83	2579.49	2533.65	2521.64	2478.54	2453.98	2439.83	2431.62
280000	2695.09	2675.03	2627.49	2615.03	2570.33	2544.87	2530.19	2521.68
290000	2791.34	2770.56	2721.33	2708.42	2662.13	2635.76	2620.56	2611.74
300000	2887.59	2866.10	2815.17	2801.82	2753.93	2726.64	2710.92	2701.80
310000	2983.85	2961.64	2909.00	2895.21	2845.73	2817.53	2801.28	2791.86
320000	3080.10	3057.17	3002.84	2988.61	2937.52	2908.42	2891.65	2881.92
330000	3176.35	3152.71	3096.68	3082.00	3029.32	2999.31	2982.01	2971.98
340000	3272.60	3248.25	3190.52	3175.39	3121.12	3090.20	3072.38	3062.04
350000	3368.86	3343.78	3284.36	3268.79	3212.92	3181.08	3162.74	3152.10
360000	3465.11	3439.32	3378.20	3362.18	3304.71	3271.97	3253.10	3242.16
370000	3561.36	3534.86	3472.04	3455.58	3396.51	3362.86	3343.47	3332.22
380000	3657.62	3630.39	3565.87	3548.97	3488.31	3453.75	3433.83	3422.28
390000	3753.87	3725.93	3659.71	3642.36	3580.11	3544.64	3524.20	3512.34
400000	3850.12	3821.47	3753.55	3735.76	3671.90	3635.52	3614.56	3602.40

Amount	1	2	3	4	5	6	7	8
25	2.22	1.18	.83	.66	.56	.49	.44	.41
50	4.44	2.35	1.66	1.31	1.11	.97	.88	.81
100	8.88	4.70	3.31	2.62	2.21	1.94	1.75	1.61
200	17.75	9.39	6.62	5.24	4.42	3.88	3.50	3.22
300	26.62	14.09	9.93	7.86	6.63	5.82	5.25	4.83
400	35.49	18.78	13.24	10.48	8.84	7.76	7.00	6.44
500	44.36	23.47	16.54	13.10	11.05	9.70	8.75	8.05
600	53.23	28.17	19.85	15.72	13.26	11.64	10.50	9.66
700	62.10	32.86	23.16	18.34	15.47	13.58	12.25	11.27
800	70.98	37.56	26.47	20.96	17.68	15.52	14.00	12.88
900	79.85	42.25	29.77	23.58	19.89	17.46	15.75	14.49
1000	88.72	46.94	33.08	26.20	22.10	19.40	17.50	16.10
2000	177.43	93.88	66.16	52.39	44.20	38.80	35.00	32.19
3000	266.15	140.82	99.23	78.58	66.30	58.20	52.50	48.29
4000	354.86	187.76	132.31	104.77	88.40	77.60	70.00	64.38
5000	443.57	234.70	165.39	130.96	110.50	97.00	87.50	80.48
6000	532.29	281.64	198.46	157.16	132.60	116.40	104.99	96.57
7000	621.00	328.57	231.54	183.35	154.69	135.80	122.49	112.66
8000	709.71	375.51	264.61	209.54	176.79	155.20	139.99	128.76
9000	798.43	422.45	297.69	235.73	198.89	174.60	157.49	144.85
10000	887.14	469.39	330.77	261.92	220.99	194.00	174.99	160.95
20000	1774.27	938.77	661.53	523.84	441.97	388.00	349.97	321.89
30000	2661.41	1408.16	992.29	785.76	662.96	582.00	524.95	482.83
40000	3548.54	1877.54	1323.05	1047.68	883.94	776.00	699.94	643.77
50000	4435.68	2346.93	1653.82	1309.60	1104.93	970.00	874.92	804.72
60000	5322.81	2816.31	1984.58	1571.52	1325.91	1164.00	1049.90	965.66
70000	6209.95	3285.69	2315.34	1833.44	1546.90	1358.00	1224.89	1126.60
80000	7097.08	3755.08	2646.10	2095.36	1767.88	1552.00	1399.87	1287.54
90000	7984.21	4224.46	2976.87	2357.28	1988.87	1746.00	1574.85	1448.49
100000	8871.35	4693.85	3307.63	2619.20	2209.85	1940.00	1749.84	1609.43
110000	9758.48	5163.23	3638.39	2881.12	2430.84	2134.00	1924.82	1770.37
120000	10645.62	5632.61	3969.15	3143.04	2651.82	2328.00	2099.80	1931.31
130000	11532.75	6102.00	4299.92	3404.96	2872.80	2522.00	2274.79	2092.25
140000	12419.89	6571.38	4630.68	3666.88	3093.79	2716.00	2449.77	2253.20
150000	13307.02	7040.77	4961.44	3928.80	3314.77	2910.00	2624.75	2414.14
160000	14194.16	7510.15	5292.20	4190.72	3535.76	3104.00	2799.74	2575.08
170000	15081.29	7979.54	5622.96	4452.64	3756.74	3298.00	2974.72	2736.02
180000	15968.42	8448.92	5953.73	4714.55	3977.73	3492.00	3149.70	2896.97
190000	16855.56	8918.30	6284.49	4976.47	4198.71	3686.00	3324.69	3057.91
200000	17742.69	9387.69	6615.25	5238.39	4419.70	3880.00	3499.67	3218.85
210000	18629.83	9857.07	6946.01	5500.31	4640.68	4074.00	3674.65	3379.79
220000	19516.96	10326.46	7276.78	5762.23	4861.67	4268.00	3849.63	3540.73
230000	20404.10	10795.84	7607.54	6024.15	5082.65	4462.00	4024.62	3701.68
240000	21291.23	11265.22	7938.30	6286.07	5303.63	4656.00	4199.60	3862.62
250000	22178.36	11734.61	8269.06	6547.99	5524.62	4850.00	4374.58	4023.56
260000	23065.50	12203.99	8599.83	6809.91	5745.60	5044.00	4549.57	4184.50
270000	23952.63	12673.38	8930.59	7071.83	5966.59	5238.00	4724.55	4345.45
280000	24839.77	13142.76	9261.35	7333.75	6187.57	5432.00	4899.53	4506.39
290000	25726.90	13612.15	9592.11	7595.67	6408.56	5626.00	5074.52	4667.33
300000	26614.04	14081.53	9922.88	7857.59	6629.54	5820.00	5249.50	4828.27
310000	27501.17	14550.91	10253.64	8119.51	6850.53	6014.00	5424.48	4989.22
320000	28388.31	15020.30	10584.40	8381.43	7071.51	6208.00	5599.47	5150.16
330000	29275.44	15489.68	10915.16	8643.35	7292.50	6402.00	5774.45	5311.10
340000	30162.57	15959.07	11245.92	8905.27	7513.48	6596.00	5949.43	5472.04
350000	31049.71	16428.45	11576.69	9167.19	7734.47	6790.00	6124.42	5632.98
360000	31936.84	16897.83	11907.45	9429.10	7955.45	6984.00	6299.40	5793.93
370000	32823.98	17367.22	12238.21	9691.02	8176.43	7178.00	6474.38	5954.87
380000	33711.11	17836.60	12568.97	9952.94	8397.42	7372.00	6649.37	6115.81
390000	34598.25	18305.99	12899.74	10214.86	8618.40	7566.00	6824.35	6276.75
400000	35485.38	18775.37	13230.50	10476.78	8839.39	7760.00	6999.33	6437.70

12% BLENDED MONTHLY PAYMENTS
AMORTIZATION IN YEARS

Amount	9	10	11	12	13	14	15	16
25	.38	.36	.34	.33	.32	.31	.30	.29
50	.76	.71	.68	.65	.63	.61	.60	.58
100	1.51	1.42	1.36	1.30	1.26	1.22	1.19	1.16
200	3.01	2.84	2.71	2.60	2.51	2.43	2.37	2.31
300	4.51	4.26	4.06	3.89	3.76	3.64	3.55	3.47
400	6.01	5.68	5.41	5.19	5.01	4.86	4.73	4.62
500	7.52	7.10	6.76	6.48	6.26	6.07	5.91	5.78
600	9.02	8.51	8.11	7.78	7.51	7.28	7.09	6.93
700	10.52	9.93	9.46	9.08	8.76	8.50	8.28	8.09
800	12.02	11.35	10.81	10.37	10.01	9.71	9.46	9.24
900	13.52	12.77	12.16	11.67	11.26	10.92	10.64	10.40
1000	15.03	14.19	13.51	12.96	12.51	12.14	11.82	11.55
2000	30.05	28.37	27.02	25.92	25.02	24.27	23.64	23.10
3000	45.07	42.55	40.53	38.88	37.53	36.40	35.45	34.65
4000	60.09	56.73	54.03	51.84	50.04	48.53	47.27	46.20
5000	75.11	70.91	67.54	64.80	62.55	60.67	59.09	57.75
6000	90.13	85.09	81.05	77.76	75.05	72.80	70.90	69.29
7000	105.16	99.27	94.55	90.72	87.56	84.93	82.72	80.84
8000	120.18	113.45	108.06	103.68	100.07	97.06	94.53	92.39
9000	135.20	127.63	121.57	116.64	112.58	109.20	106.35	103.94
10000	150.22	141.81	135.08	129.60	125.09	121.33	118.17	115.49
20000	300.43	283.61	270.15	259.20	250.17	242.65	236.33	230.97
30000	450.65	425.41	405.22	388.79	375.25	363.97	354.49	346.45
40000	600.86	567.22	540.29	518.39	500.33	485.29	472.65	461.94
50000	751.08	709.02	675.36	647.98	625.42	606.62	590.81	577.42
60000	901.29	850.82	810.43	777.58	750.50	727.94	708.97	692.90
70000	1051.51	992.62	945.50	907.17	875.58	849.26	827.13	808.39
80000	1201.72	1134.43	1080.57	1036.77	1000.66	970.58	945.29	923.87
90000	1351.94	1276.23	1215.64	1166.36	1125.75	1091.91	1063.45	1039.35
100000	1502.15	1418.03	1350.71	1295.96	1250.83	1213.23	1181.61	1154.83
110000	1652.37	1559.83	1485.78	1425.55	1375.91	1334.55	1299.78	1270.32
120000	1802.58	1701.64	1620.85	1555.15	1500.99	1455.87	1417.94	1385.80
130000	1952.80	1843.44	1755.92	1684.74	1626.07	1577.19	1536.10	1501.28
140000	2103.01	1985.24	1891.00	1814.34	1751.16	1698.52	1654.26	1616.77
150000	2253.23	2127.05	2026.07	1943.93	1876.24	1819.84	1772.42	1732.25
160000	2403.44	2268.85	2161.14	2073.53	2001.32	1941.16	1890.58	1847.73
170000	2553.66	2410.65	2296.21	2203.12	2126.40	2062.48	2008.74	1963.21
180000	2703.87	2552.45	2431.28	2332.72	2251.49	2183.81	2126.90	2078.70
190000	2854.09	2694.26	2566.35	2462.31	2376.57	2305.13	2245.06	2194.18
200000	3004.30	2836.06	2701.42	2591.91	2501.65	2426.45	2363.22	2309.66
210000	3154.51	2977.86	2836.49	2721.50	2626.73	2547.77	2481.39	2425.15
220000	3304.73	3119.66	2971.56	2851.10	2751.82	2669.09	2599.55	2540.63
230000	3454.94	3261.47	3106.63	2980.69	2876.90	2790.42	2717.71	2656.11
240000	3605.16	3403.27	3241.70	3110.29	3001.98	2911.74	2835.87	2771.59
250000	3755.37	3545.07	3376.77	3239.88	3127.06	3033.06	2954.03	2887.08
260000	3905.59	3686.87	3511.84	3369.48	3252.14	3154.38	3072.19	3002.56
270000	4055.80	3828.68	3646.92	3499.07	3377.23	3275.71	3190.35	3118.04
280000	4206.02	3970.48	3781.99	3628.67	3502.31	3397.03	3308.51	3233.53
290000	4356.23	4112.28	3917.06	3758.26	3627.39	3518.35	3426.67	3349.01
300000	4506.45	4254.09	4052.13	3887.86	3752.47	3639.67	3544.83	3464.49
310000	4656.66	4395.89	4187.20	4017.46	3877.56	3760.99	3662.99	3579.97
320000	4806.88	4537.69	4322.27	4147.05	4002.64	3882.32	3781.16	3695.46
330000	4957.09	4679.49	4457.34	4276.65	4127.72	4003.64	3899.32	3810.94
340000	5107.31	4821.30	4592.41	4406.24	4252.80	4124.96	4017.48	3926.42
350000	5257.52	4963.10	4727.48	4535.84	4377.88	4246.28	4135.64	4041.91
360000	5407.74	5104.90	4862.55	4665.43	4502.97	4367.61	4253.80	4157.39
370000	5557.95	5246.70	4997.62	4795.03	4628.05	4488.93	4371.96	4272.87
380000	5708.17	5388.51	5132.69	4924.62	4753.13	4610.25	4490.12	4388.35
390000	5858.38	5530.31	5267.76	5054.22	4878.21	4731.57	4608.28	4503.84
400000	6008.59	5672.11	5402.84	5183.81	5003.30	4852.89	4726.44	4619.32

BLENDED MONTHLY PAYMENTS 12%
AMORTIZATION IN YEARS

Amount	17	18	19	20	21	22	23	24
25	.29	.28	.28	.28	.27	.27	.27	.26
50	.57	.56	.55	.55	.54	.53	.53	.52
100	1.14	1.12	1.10	1.09	1.07	1.06	1.05	1.04
200	2.27	2.23	2.20	2.17	2.14	2.12	2.10	2.08
300	3.40	3.34	3.29	3.25	3.21	3.18	3.15	3.12
400	4.53	4.45	4.39	4.33	4.28	4.23	4.20	4.16
500	5.66	5.57	5.48	5.41	5.35	5.29	5.24	5.20
600	6.80	6.68	6.58	6.49	6.41	6.35	6.29	6.24
700	7.93	7.79	7.67	7.57	7.48	7.41	7.34	7.28
800	9.06	8.90	8.77	8.65	8.55	8.46	8.39	8.32
900	10.19	10.02	9.87	9.73	9.62	9.52	9.43	9.36
1000	11.32	11.13	10.96	10.81	10.69	10.58	10.48	10.40
2000	22.64	22.25	21.92	21.62	21.37	21.15	20.96	20.79
3000	33.96	33.38	32.87	32.43	32.05	31.72	31.44	31.18
4000	45.28	44.50	43.83	43.24	42.74	42.30	41.91	41.58
5000	56.60	55.63	54.78	54.05	53.42	52.87	52.39	51.97
6000	67.92	66.75	65.74	64.86	64.10	63.44	62.87	62.36
7000	79.24	77.87	76.69	75.67	74.79	74.02	73.34	72.75
8000	90.56	89.00	87.65	86.48	85.47	84.59	83.82	83.15
9000	101.88	100.12	98.61	97.29	96.15	95.16	94.30	93.54
10000	113.20	111.25	109.56	108.10	106.84	105.74	104.77	103.93
20000	226.40	222.49	219.12	216.20	213.67	211.47	209.54	207.86
30000	339.60	333.73	328.67	324.30	320.50	317.20	314.31	311.79
40000	452.80	444.97	438.23	432.39	427.33	422.93	419.08	415.71
50000	566.00	556.21	547.78	540.49	534.16	528.66	523.85	519.64
60000	679.20	667.46	657.34	648.59	641.00	634.39	628.62	623.57
70000	792.40	778.70	766.89	756.69	747.83	740.12	733.38	727.50
80000	905.60	889.94	876.45	864.78	854.66	845.85	838.15	831.42
90000	1018.80	1001.18	986.01	972.88	961.49	951.58	942.92	935.35
100000	1132.00	1112.42	1095.56	1080.98	1068.32	1057.31	1047.69	1039.28
110000	1245.20	1223.67	1205.12	1189.08	1175.16	1163.04	1152.46	1143.21
120000	1358.40	1334.91	1314.67	1297.17	1281.99	1268.77	1257.23	1247.13
130000	1471.60	1446.15	1424.23	1405.27	1388.82	1374.50	1362.00	1351.06
140000	1584.80	1557.39	1533.78	1513.37	1495.65	1480.23	1466.76	1454.99
150000	1698.00	1668.63	1643.34	1621.47	1602.48	1585.96	1571.53	1558.92
160000	1811.20	1779.87	1752.90	1729.56	1709.31	1691.69	1676.30	1662.84
170000	1924.40	1891.12	1862.45	1837.66	1816.15	1797.42	1781.07	1766.77
180000	2037.60	2002.36	1972.01	1945.76	1922.98	1903.15	1885.84	1870.70
190000	2150.79	2113.60	2081.56	2053.86	2029.81	2008.88	1990.61	1974.62
200000	2263.99	2224.84	2191.12	2161.95	2136.64	2114.61	2095.38	2078.55
210000	2377.19	2336.08	2300.67	2270.05	2243.47	2220.34	2200.14	2182.48
220000	2490.39	2447.33	2410.23	2378.15	2350.31	2326.07	2304.91	2286.41
230000	2603.59	2558.57	2519.79	2486.25	2457.14	2431.80	2409.68	2390.33
240000	2716.79	2669.81	2629.34	2594.34	2563.97	2537.53	2514.45	2494.26
250000	2829.99	2781.05	2738.90	2702.44	2670.80	2643.26	2619.22	2598.19
260000	2943.19	2892.29	2848.45	2810.54	2777.63	2748.99	2723.99	2702.12
270000	3056.39	3003.54	2958.01	2918.64	2884.46	2854.72	2828.76	2806.04
280000	3169.59	3114.78	3067.56	3026.73	2991.30	2960.45	2933.52	2909.97
290000	3282.79	3226.02	3177.12	3134.83	3098.13	3066.18	3038.29	3013.90
300000	3395.99	3337.26	3286.68	3242.93	3204.96	3171.91	3143.06	3117.83
310000	3509.19	3448.50	3396.23	3351.02	3311.79	3277.64	3247.83	3221.75
320000	3622.39	3559.74	3505.79	3459.12	3418.62	3383.37	3352.60	3325.68
330000	3735.59	3670.99	3615.34	3567.22	3525.46	3489.10	3457.37	3429.61
340000	3848.79	3782.23	3724.90	3675.32	3632.29	3594.83	3562.14	3533.53
350000	3961.99	3893.47	3834.45	3783.41	3739.12	3700.56	3666.90	3637.46
360000	4075.19	4004.71	3944.01	3891.51	3845.95	3806.29	3771.67	3741.39
370000	4188.38	4115.95	4053.57	3999.61	3952.78	3912.02	3876.44	3845.32
380000	4301.58	4227.20	4163.12	4107.71	4059.61	4017.75	3981.21	3949.24
390000	4414.78	4338.44	4272.68	4215.80	4166.45	4123.48	4085.98	4053.17
400000	4527.98	4449.68	4382.23	4323.90	4273.28	4229.21	4190.75	4157.10

139

12% BLENDED MONTHLY PAYMENTS
AMORTIZATION IN YEARS

Amount	25	26	29	30	35	40	45	50
25	.26	.26	.26	.26	.25	.25	.25	.25
50	.52	.52	.51	.51	.50	.50	.50	.49
100	1.04	1.03	1.02	1.01	1.00	.99	.99	.98
200	2.07	2.06	2.03	2.02	1.99	1.98	1.97	1.96
300	3.10	3.08	3.04	3.02	2.98	2.96	2.95	2.94
400	4.13	4.11	4.05	4.03	3.98	3.95	3.93	3.92
500	5.16	5.13	5.06	5.04	4.97	4.93	4.91	4.90
600	6.20	6.16	6.07	6.04	5.96	5.92	5.89	5.88
700	7.23	7.18	7.08	7.05	6.95	6.90	6.87	6.86
800	8.26	8.21	8.09	8.06	7.95	7.89	7.85	7.84
900	9.29	9.23	9.10	9.06	8.94	8.87	8.83	8.81
1000	10.32	10.26	10.11	10.07	9.93	9.86	9.82	9.79
2000	20.64	20.51	20.21	20.13	19.86	19.71	19.63	19.58
3000	30.96	30.77	30.31	30.20	29.79	29.56	29.44	29.37
4000	41.28	41.02	40.42	40.26	39.71	39.41	39.25	39.16
5000	51.60	51.28	50.52	50.32	49.64	49.26	49.06	48.94
6000	61.92	61.53	60.62	60.39	59.57	59.12	58.87	58.73
7000	72.24	71.78	70.73	70.45	69.49	68.97	68.68	68.52
8000	82.56	82.04	80.83	80.52	79.42	78.82	78.49	78.31
9000	92.88	92.29	90.93	90.58	89.35	88.67	88.30	88.09
10000	103.19	102.55	101.03	100.64	99.27	98.52	98.11	97.88
20000	206.38	205.09	202.06	201.28	198.54	197.04	196.22	195.76
30000	309.57	307.63	303.09	301.92	297.81	295.56	294.32	293.63
40000	412.76	410.17	404.12	402.56	397.08	394.08	392.43	391.51
50000	515.95	512.72	505.15	503.20	496.35	492.60	490.53	489.39
60000	619.14	615.26	606.18	603.84	595.61	591.12	588.64	587.26
70000	722.33	717.80	707.21	704.48	694.88	689.64	686.75	685.14
80000	825.52	820.34	808.24	805.11	794.15	788.16	784.85	783.02
90000	928.71	922.89	909.27	905.75	893.42	886.68	882.96	880.89
100000	1031.90	1025.43	1010.30	1006.39	992.69	985.20	981.06	978.77
110000	1135.09	1127.97	1111.33	1107.03	1091.96	1083.72	1079.17	1076.65
120000	1238.28	1230.51	1212.35	1207.67	1191.22	1182.23	1177.27	1174.52
130000	1341.47	1333.06	1313.38	1308.31	1290.49	1280.75	1275.38	1272.40
140000	1444.66	1435.60	1414.41	1408.95	1389.76	1379.27	1373.49	1370.27
150000	1547.85	1538.14	1515.44	1509.59	1489.03	1477.79	1471.59	1468.15
160000	1651.04	1640.68	1616.47	1610.22	1588.30	1576.31	1569.70	1566.03
170000	1754.23	1743.23	1717.50	1710.86	1687.57	1674.83	1667.80	1663.90
180000	1857.42	1845.77	1818.53	1811.50	1786.83	1773.35	1765.91	1761.78
190000	1960.61	1948.31	1919.56	1912.14	1886.10	1871.87	1864.01	1859.66
200000	2063.80	2050.85	2020.59	2012.78	1985.37	1970.39	1962.12	1957.53
210000	2166.99	2153.40	2121.62	2113.42	2084.64	2068.91	2060.23	2055.41
220000	2270.18	2255.94	2222.65	2214.06	2183.91	2167.43	2158.33	2153.29
230000	2373.37	2358.48	2323.67	2314.70	2283.18	2265.95	2256.44	2251.16
240000	2476.56	2461.02	2424.70	2415.33	2382.44	2364.46	2354.54	2349.04
250000	2579.75	2563.57	2525.73	2515.97	2481.71	2462.98	2452.65	2446.92
260000	2682.94	2666.11	2626.76	2616.61	2580.98	2561.50	2550.75	2544.79
270000	2786.13	2768.65	2727.79	2717.25	2680.25	2660.02	2648.86	2642.67
280000	2889.32	2871.19	2828.82	2817.89	2779.52	2758.54	2746.97	2740.54
290000	2992.51	2973.74	2929.85	2918.53	2878.79	2857.06	2845.07	2838.42
300000	3095.70	3076.28	3030.88	3019.17	2978.05	2955.58	2943.18	2936.30
310000	3198.89	3178.82	3131.91	3119.81	3077.32	3054.10	3041.28	3034.17
320000	3302.08	3281.36	3232.94	3220.44	3176.59	3152.62	3139.39	3132.05
330000	3405.27	3383.91	3333.97	3321.08	3275.86	3251.14	3237.49	3229.93
340000	3508.46	3486.45	3434.99	3421.72	3375.13	3349.66	3335.60	3327.80
350000	3611.65	3588.99	3536.02	3522.36	3474.40	3448.18	3433.71	3425.68
360000	3714.84	3691.53	3637.05	3623.00	3573.66	3546.69	3531.81	3523.56
370000	3818.03	3794.07	3738.08	3723.64	3672.93	3645.21	3629.92	3621.43
380000	3921.22	3896.62	3839.11	3824.28	3772.20	3743.73	3728.02	3719.31
390000	4024.41	3999.16	3940.14	3924.92	3871.47	3842.25	3826.13	3817.18
400000	4127.60	4101.70	4041.17	4025.55	3970.74	3940.77	3924.23	3915.06

AMORTIZATION IN YEARS

Amount	1	2	3	4	5	6	7	8
25	2.23	1.19	.84	.67	.57	.50	.46	.42
50	4.46	2.37	1.68	1.34	1.13	1.00	.91	.84
100	8.92	4.74	3.36	2.67	2.26	1.99	1.81	1.67
200	17.84	9.48	6.71	5.34	4.52	3.98	3.61	3.33
300	26.75	14.22	10.06	8.00	6.78	5.97	5.41	4.99
400	35.67	18.96	13.42	10.67	9.04	7.96	7.21	6.65
500	44.58	23.70	16.77	13.33	11.30	9.95	9.01	8.31
600	53.50	28.43	20.12	16.00	13.55	11.94	10.81	9.98
700	62.42	33.17	23.48	18.67	15.81	13.93	12.61	11.64
800	71.33	37.91	26.83	21.33	18.07	15.92	14.41	13.30
900	80.25	42.65	30.18	24.00	20.33	17.91	16.21	14.96
1000	89.16	47.39	33.54	26.66	22.59	19.90	18.01	16.62
2000	178.32	94.77	67.07	53.32	45.17	39.80	36.02	33.24
3000	267.48	142.15	100.60	79.98	67.75	59.69	54.03	49.86
4000	356.64	189.54	134.13	106.64	90.33	79.59	72.04	66.48
5000	445.80	236.92	167.66	133.30	112.91	99.48	90.05	83.10
6000	534.96	284.30	201.19	159.96	135.49	119.38	108.05	99.72
7000	624.11	331.69	234.72	186.62	158.07	139.28	126.06	116.33
8000	713.27	379.07	268.25	213.28	180.65	159.17	144.07	132.95
9000	802.43	426.45	301.78	239.94	203.23	179.07	162.08	149.57
10000	891.59	473.83	335.32	266.60	225.81	198.96	180.09	166.19
20000	1783.17	947.66	670.63	533.20	451.61	397.92	360.17	332.37
30000	2674.76	1421.49	1005.94	799.80	677.41	596.88	540.25	498.56
40000	3566.34	1895.32	1341.25	1066.39	903.21	795.84	720.34	664.74
50000	4457.93	2369.15	1676.56	1332.99	1129.01	994.79	900.42	830.92
60000	5349.51	2842.98	2011.87	1599.59	1354.81	1193.75	1080.50	997.11
70000	6241.10	3316.81	2347.18	1866.18	1580.61	1392.71	1260.59	1163.29
80000	7132.68	3790.64	2682.49	2132.78	1806.41	1591.67	1440.67	1329.47
90000	8024.26	4264.46	3017.80	2399.38	2032.21	1790.63	1620.75	1495.66
100000	8915.85	4738.29	3353.11	2665.97	2258.01	1989.58	1800.84	1661.84
110000	9807.43	5212.12	3688.42	2932.57	2483.81	2188.54	1980.92	1828.02
120000	10699.02	5685.95	4023.73	3199.17	2709.61	2387.50	2161.00	1994.21
130000	11590.60	6159.78	4359.04	3465.76	2935.41	2586.46	2341.09	2160.39
140000	12482.19	6633.61	4694.35	3732.36	3161.21	2785.41	2521.17	2326.58
150000	13373.77	7107.44	5029.66	3998.96	3387.01	2984.37	2701.25	2492.76
160000	14265.36	7581.27	5364.97	4265.56	3612.81	3183.33	2881.34	2658.94
170000	15156.94	8055.10	5700.28	4532.15	3838.62	3382.29	3061.42	2825.13
180000	16048.52	8528.92	6035.59	4798.75	4064.42	3581.25	3241.50	2991.31
190000	16940.11	9002.75	6370.90	5065.35	4290.22	3780.20	3421.59	3157.49
200000	17831.69	9476.58	6706.21	5331.94	4516.02	3979.16	3601.67	3323.68
210000	18723.28	9950.41	7041.52	5598.54	4741.82	4178.12	3781.75	3489.86
220000	19614.86	10424.24	7376.83	5865.14	4967.62	4377.08	3961.84	3656.04
230000	20506.45	10898.07	7712.14	6131.73	5193.42	4576.03	4141.92	3822.23
240000	21398.03	11371.90	8047.45	6398.33	5419.22	4774.99	4322.00	3988.41
250000	22289.62	11845.73	8382.76	6664.93	5645.02	4973.95	4502.09	4154.59
260000	23181.20	12319.55	8718.08	6931.52	5870.82	5172.91	4682.17	4320.78
270000	24072.78	12793.38	9053.39	7198.12	6096.62	5371.87	4862.25	4486.96
280000	24964.37	13267.21	9388.70	7464.72	6322.42	5570.82	5042.34	4653.15
290000	25855.95	13741.04	9724.01	7731.32	6548.22	5769.78	5222.42	4819.33
300000	26747.54	14214.87	10059.32	7997.91	6774.02	5968.74	5402.50	4985.51
310000	27639.12	14688.70	10394.63	8264.51	6999.82	6167.70	5582.59	5151.70
320000	28530.71	15162.53	10729.94	8531.11	7225.62	6366.66	5762.67	5317.88
330000	29422.29	15636.36	11065.25	8797.70	7451.42	6565.61	5942.75	5484.06
340000	30313.88	16110.19	11400.56	9064.30	7677.23	6764.57	6122.84	5650.25
350000	31205.46	16584.01	11735.87	9330.90	7903.03	6963.53	6302.92	5816.43
360000	32097.04	17057.84	12071.18	9597.49	8128.83	7162.49	6483.00	5982.61
370000	32988.63	17531.67	12406.49	9864.09	8354.63	7361.44	6663.09	6148.80
380000	33880.21	18005.50	12741.80	10130.69	8580.43	7560.40	6843.17	6314.98
390000	34771.80	18479.33	13077.11	10397.28	8806.23	7759.36	7023.25	6481.17
400000	35663.38	18953.16	13412.42	10663.88	9032.03	7958.32	7203.34	6647.35

13% BLENDED MONTHLY PAYMENTS
AMORTIZATION IN YEARS

Amount	9	10	11	12	13	14	15	16
25	.39	.37	.36	.34	.33	.32	.32	.31
50	.78	.74	.71	.68	.66	.64	.63	.61
100	1.56	1.48	1.41	1.36	1.31	1.28	1.25	1.22
200	3.12	2.95	2.82	2.71	2.62	2.55	2.49	2.44
300	4.67	4.42	4.23	4.07	3.93	3.83	3.73	3.66
400	6.23	5.90	5.63	5.42	5.24	5.10	4.98	4.87
500	7.78	7.37	7.04	6.77	6.55	6.37	6.22	6.09
600	9.34	8.84	8.45	8.13	7.86	7.65	7.46	7.31
700	10.90	10.32	9.86	9.48	9.17	8.92	8.71	8.53
800	12.45	11.79	11.26	10.83	10.48	10.19	9.95	9.74
900	14.01	13.26	12.67	12.19	11.79	11.47	11.19	10.96
1000	15.56	14.74	14.08	13.54	13.10	12.74	12.44	12.18
2000	31.12	29.47	28.15	27.08	26.20	25.47	24.87	24.35
3000	46.68	44.20	42.22	40.62	39.30	38.21	37.30	36.53
4000	62.24	58.93	56.29	54.15	52.40	50.94	49.73	48.70
5000	77.80	73.66	70.37	67.69	65.50	63.68	62.16	60.87
6000	93.36	88.40	84.44	81.23	78.60	76.41	74.59	73.05
7000	108.92	103.13	98.51	94.77	91.70	89.15	87.02	85.22
8000	124.48	117.86	112.58	108.30	104.79	101.88	99.45	97.40
9000	140.04	132.59	126.65	121.84	117.89	114.62	111.88	109.57
10000	155.60	147.32	140.73	135.38	130.99	127.35	124.31	121.74
20000	311.20	294.64	281.45	270.75	261.98	254.70	248.61	243.48
30000	466.79	441.96	422.17	406.13	392.97	382.05	372.92	365.22
40000	622.39	589.28	562.89	541.50	523.95	509.40	497.22	486.96
50000	777.98	736.60	703.61	676.88	654.94	636.75	621.52	608.69
60000	933.58	883.92	844.33	812.25	785.93	764.09	745.83	730.43
70000	1089.17	1031.24	985.05	947.63	916.92	891.44	870.13	852.17
80000	1244.77	1178.56	1125.77	1083.00	1047.90	1018.79	994.43	973.91
90000	1400.36	1325.88	1266.49	1218.38	1178.89	1146.14	1118.74	1095.64
100000	1555.96	1473.20	1407.21	1353.75	1309.88	1273.49	1243.04	1217.38
110000	1711.55	1620.52	1547.93	1489.13	1440.86	1400.84	1367.35	1339.12
120000	1867.15	1767.84	1688.65	1624.50	1571.85	1528.18	1491.65	1460.86
130000	2022.74	1915.16	1829.38	1759.88	1702.84	1655.53	1615.95	1582.60
140000	2178.34	2062.48	1970.10	1895.25	1833.83	1782.88	1740.26	1704.33
150000	2333.93	2209.80	2110.82	2030.62	1964.81	1910.23	1864.56	1826.07
160000	2489.53	2357.12	2251.54	2166.00	2095.80	2037.58	1988.86	1947.81
170000	2645.12	2504.44	2392.26	2301.37	2226.79	2164.93	2113.17	2069.55
180000	2800.72	2651.76	2532.98	2436.75	2357.77	2292.27	2237.47	2191.28
190000	2956.31	2799.08	2673.70	2572.12	2488.76	2419.62	2361.78	2313.02
200000	3111.91	2946.40	2814.42	2707.50	2619.75	2546.97	2486.08	2434.76
210000	3267.51	3093.72	2955.14	2842.87	2750.74	2674.32	2610.38	2556.50
220000	3423.10	3241.04	3095.86	2978.25	2881.72	2801.67	2734.69	2678.23
230000	3578.70	3388.36	3236.58	3113.62	3012.71	2929.02	2858.99	2799.97
240000	3734.29	3535.68	3377.30	3249.00	3143.70	3056.36	2983.29	2921.71
250000	3889.89	3683.00	3518.03	3384.37	3274.68	3183.71	3107.60	3043.45
260000	4045.48	3830.31	3658.75	3519.75	3405.67	3311.06	3231.90	3165.19
270000	4201.08	3977.63	3799.47	3655.12	3536.66	3438.41	3356.21	3286.92
280000	4356.67	4124.95	3940.19	3790.50	3667.65	3565.76	3480.51	3408.66
290000	4512.27	4272.27	4080.91	3925.87	3798.63	3693.11	3604.81	3530.40
300000	4667.86	4419.59	4221.63	4061.24	3929.62	3820.45	3729.12	3652.14
310000	4823.46	4566.91	4362.35	4196.62	4060.61	3947.80	3853.42	3773.87
320000	4979.05	4714.23	4503.07	4331.99	4191.60	4075.15	3977.72	3895.61
330000	5134.65	4861.55	4643.79	4467.37	4322.58	4202.50	4102.03	4017.35
340000	5290.24	5008.87	4784.51	4602.74	4453.57	4329.85	4226.33	4139.09
350000	5445.84	5156.19	4925.23	4738.12	4584.56	4457.20	4350.64	4260.83
360000	5601.43	5303.51	5065.95	4873.49	4715.54	4584.54	4474.94	4382.56
370000	5757.03	5450.83	5206.68	5008.87	4846.53	4711.89	4599.24	4504.30
380000	5912.62	5598.15	5347.40	5144.24	4977.52	4839.24	4723.55	4626.04
390000	6068.22	5745.47	5488.12	5279.62	5108.51	4966.59	4847.85	4747.78
400000	6223.81	5892.79	5628.84	5414.99	5239.49	5093.94	4972.15	4869.51

142

BLENDED MONTHLY PAYMENTS 13%
AMORTIZATION IN YEARS

Amount	17	18	19	20	21	22	23	24
25	.30	.30	.30	.29	.29	.29	.28	.28
50	.60	.59	.59	.58	.57	.57	.56	.56
100	1.20	1.18	1.17	1.15	1.14	1.13	1.12	1.11
200	2.40	2.36	2.33	2.30	2.28	2.26	2.24	2.22
300	3.59	3.54	3.49	3.45	3.41	3.38	3.36	3.33
400	4.79	4.71	4.65	4.60	4.55	4.51	4.47	4.44
500	5.98	5.89	5.81	5.74	5.68	5.63	5.59	5.55
600	7.18	7.07	6.97	6.89	6.82	6.76	6.71	6.66
700	8.37	8.24	8.13	8.04	7.96	7.88	7.82	7.77
800	9.57	9.42	9.29	9.19	9.09	9.01	8.94	8.88
900	10.77	10.60	10.46	10.33	10.23	10.14	10.06	9.99
1000	11.96	11.78	11.62	11.48	11.36	11.26	11.17	11.10
2000	23.92	23.55	23.23	22.96	22.72	22.52	22.34	22.19
3000	35.87	35.32	34.84	34.43	34.08	33.77	33.51	33.28
4000	47.83	47.09	46.45	45.91	45.44	45.03	44.67	44.37
5000	59.79	58.86	58.06	57.38	56.79	56.28	55.84	55.46
6000	71.74	70.63	69.68	68.86	68.15	67.54	67.01	66.55
7000	83.70	82.40	81.29	80.33	79.51	78.80	78.18	77.64
8000	95.65	94.17	92.90	91.81	90.87	90.05	89.34	88.73
9000	107.61	105.94	104.51	103.28	102.22	101.31	100.51	99.82
10000	119.57	117.71	116.12	114.76	113.58	112.56	111.68	110.91
20000	239.13	235.42	232.24	229.51	227.16	225.12	223.35	221.82
30000	358.69	353.13	348.36	344.26	340.73	337.68	335.03	332.73
40000	478.25	470.83	464.48	459.02	454.31	450.24	446.70	443.64
50000	597.81	588.54	580.60	573.77	567.88	562.79	558.38	554.55
60000	717.38	706.25	696.71	688.52	681.46	675.35	670.05	665.45
70000	836.94	823.95	812.83	803.28	795.03	787.91	781.73	776.36
80000	956.50	941.66	928.95	918.03	908.61	900.47	893.40	887.27
90000	1076.06	1059.37	1045.07	1032.78	1022.19	1013.02	1005.08	998.18
100000	1195.62	1177.07	1161.19	1147.54	1135.76	1125.58	1116.75	1109.09
110000	1315.18	1294.78	1277.31	1262.29	1249.34	1238.14	1228.43	1219.99
120000	1434.75	1412.49	1393.42	1377.04	1362.91	1350.70	1340.10	1330.90
130000	1554.31	1530.19	1509.54	1491.79	1476.49	1463.25	1451.78	1441.81
140000	1673.87	1647.90	1625.66	1606.55	1590.06	1575.81	1563.45	1552.72
150000	1793.43	1765.61	1741.78	1721.30	1703.64	1688.37	1675.13	1663.63
160000	1912.99	1883.31	1857.90	1836.05	1817.22	1800.93	1786.80	1774.53
170000	2032.55	2001.02	1974.02	1950.81	1930.79	1913.48	1898.48	1885.44
180000	2152.12	2118.73	2090.13	2065.56	2044.37	2026.04	2010.15	1996.35
190000	2271.68	2236.43	2206.25	2180.31	2157.94	2138.60	2121.83	2107.26
200000	2391.24	2354.14	2322.37	2295.07	2271.52	2251.16	2233.50	2218.17
210000	2510.80	2471.85	2438.49	2409.82	2385.09	2363.71	2345.18	2329.08
220000	2630.36	2589.55	2554.61	2524.57	2498.67	2476.27	2456.85	2439.98
230000	2749.92	2707.26	2670.73	2639.32	2612.25	2588.83	2568.53	2550.89
240000	2869.49	2824.97	2786.84	2754.08	2725.82	2701.39	2680.20	2661.80
250000	2989.05	2942.67	2902.96	2868.83	2839.40	2813.94	2791.88	2772.71
260000	3108.61	3060.38	3019.08	2983.58	2952.97	2926.50	2903.55	2883.62
270000	3228.17	3178.09	3135.20	3098.34	3066.55	3039.06	3015.23	2994.52
280000	3347.73	3295.79	3251.32	3213.09	3180.12	3151.62	3126.90	3105.43
290000	3467.29	3413.50	3367.44	3327.84	3293.70	3264.17	3238.58	3216.34
300000	3586.86	3531.21	3483.55	3442.60	3407.28	3376.73	3350.25	3327.25
310000	3706.42	3648.91	3599.67	3557.35	3520.85	3489.29	3461.93	3438.16
320000	3825.98	3766.62	3715.79	3672.10	3634.43	3601.85	3573.60	3549.06
330000	3945.54	3884.33	3831.91	3786.86	3748.00	3714.40	3685.28	3659.97
340000	4065.10	4002.03	3948.03	3901.61	3861.58	3826.96	3796.95	3770.88
350000	4184.66	4119.74	4064.15	4016.36	3975.15	3939.52	3908.63	3881.79
360000	4304.23	4237.45	4180.26	4131.11	4088.73	4052.08	4020.30	3992.70
370000	4423.79	4355.15	4296.38	4245.87	4202.31	4164.63	4131.98	4103.61
380000	4543.35	4472.86	4412.50	4360.62	4315.88	4277.19	4243.65	4214.51
390000	4662.91	4590.57	4528.62	4475.37	4429.46	4389.75	4355.33	4325.42
400000	4782.47	4708.27	4644.74	4590.13	4543.03	4502.31	4467.00	4436.33

13% BLENDED MONTHLY PAYMENTS
AMORTIZATION IN YEARS

Amount	25	26	29	30	35	40	45	50
25	.28	.28	.28	.27	.27	.27	.27	.27
50	.56	.55	.55	.54	.54	.54	.53	.53
100	1.11	1.10	1.09	1.08	1.07	1.07	1.06	1.06
200	2.21	2.20	2.17	2.16	2.14	2.13	2.12	2.12
300	3.31	3.29	3.25	3.24	3.21	3.19	3.18	3.18
400	4.41	4.39	4.34	4.32	4.28	4.25	4.24	4.23
500	5.52	5.49	5.42	5.40	5.35	5.31	5.30	5.29
600	6.62	6.58	6.50	6.48	6.41	6.38	6.36	6.35
700	7.72	7.68	7.59	7.56	7.48	7.44	7.42	7.40
800	8.82	8.78	8.67	8.64	8.55	8.50	8.48	8.46
900	9.93	9.87	9.75	9.72	9.62	9.56	9.53	9.52
1000	11.03	10.97	10.84	10.80	10.69	10.62	10.59	10.58
2000	22.05	21.94	21.67	21.60	21.37	21.24	21.18	21.15
3000	33.08	32.90	32.50	32.40	32.05	31.86	31.77	31.72
4000	44.10	43.87	43.33	43.20	42.73	42.48	42.36	42.29
5000	55.13	54.83	54.16	53.99	53.41	53.10	52.94	52.86
6000	66.15	65.80	65.00	64.79	64.09	63.72	63.53	63.43
7000	77.17	76.77	75.83	75.59	74.77	74.34	74.12	74.00
8000	88.20	87.73	86.66	86.39	85.45	84.96	84.71	84.57
9000	99.22	98.70	97.49	97.19	96.14	95.58	95.29	95.14
10000	110.25	109.66	108.32	107.98	106.82	106.20	105.88	105.71
20000	220.49	219.32	216.64	215.96	213.63	212.40	211.76	211.42
30000	330.73	328.98	324.96	323.94	320.44	318.60	317.63	317.12
40000	440.97	438.64	433.28	431.92	427.25	424.80	423.51	422.83
50000	551.21	548.30	541.60	539.90	534.06	531.00	529.39	528.53
60000	661.45	657.96	649.92	647.88	640.87	637.20	635.26	634.24
70000	771.69	767.62	758.24	755.86	747.68	743.40	741.14	739.94
80000	881.93	877.28	866.56	863.84	854.50	849.60	847.02	845.65
90000	992.17	986.94	974.88	971.81	961.31	955.80	952.89	951.35
100000	1102.41	1096.59	1083.19	1079.79	1068.12	1062.00	1058.77	1057.06
110000	1212.65	1206.25	1191.51	1187.77	1174.93	1168.20	1164.65	1162.76
120000	1322.89	1315.91	1299.83	1295.75	1281.74	1274.40	1270.52	1268.47
130000	1433.13	1425.57	1408.15	1403.73	1388.55	1380.60	1376.40	1374.17
140000	1543.38	1535.23	1516.47	1511.71	1495.36	1486.80	1482.28	1479.88
150000	1653.62	1644.89	1624.79	1619.69	1602.18	1593.00	1588.15	1585.59
160000	1763.86	1754.55	1733.11	1727.67	1708.99	1699.20	1694.03	1691.29
170000	1874.10	1864.21	1841.43	1835.65	1815.80	1805.40	1799.91	1797.00
180000	1984.34	1973.87	1949.75	1943.62	1922.61	1911.60	1905.78	1902.70
190000	2094.58	2083.53	2058.06	2051.60	2029.42	2017.80	2011.66	2008.41
200000	2204.82	2193.18	2166.38	2159.58	2136.23	2124.00	2117.54	2114.11
210000	2315.06	2302.84	2274.70	2267.56	2243.04	2230.20	2223.41	2219.82
220000	2425.30	2412.50	2383.02	2375.54	2349.85	2336.40	2329.29	2325.52
230000	2535.54	2522.16	2491.34	2483.52	2456.67	2442.60	2435.17	2431.23
240000	2645.78	2631.82	2599.66	2591.50	2563.48	2548.80	2541.04	2536.93
250000	2756.02	2741.48	2707.98	2699.48	2670.29	2655.00	2646.92	2642.64
260000	2866.26	2851.14	2816.30	2807.45	2777.10	2761.20	2752.80	2748.34
270000	2976.51	2960.80	2924.62	2915.43	2883.91	2867.40	2858.67	2854.05
280000	3086.75	3070.46	3032.94	3023.41	2990.72	2973.59	2964.55	2959.75
290000	3196.99	3180.12	3141.25	3131.39	3097.53	3079.79	3070.43	3065.46
300000	3307.23	3289.77	3249.57	3239.37	3204.35	3185.99	3176.30	3171.17
310000	3417.47	3399.43	3357.89	3347.35	3311.16	3292.19	3282.18	3276.87
320000	3527.71	3509.09	3466.21	3455.33	3417.97	3398.39	3388.06	3382.58
330000	3637.95	3618.75	3574.53	3563.31	3524.78	3504.59	3493.93	3488.28
340000	3748.19	3728.41	3682.85	3671.29	3631.59	3610.79	3599.81	3593.99
350000	3858.43	3838.07	3791.17	3779.26	3738.40	3716.99	3705.69	3699.69
360000	3968.67	3947.73	3899.49	3887.24	3845.21	3823.19	3811.56	3805.40
370000	4078.91	4057.39	4007.81	3995.22	3952.02	3929.39	3917.44	3911.10
380000	4189.15	4167.05	4116.12	4103.20	4058.84	4035.59	4023.32	4016.81
390000	4299.39	4276.71	4224.44	4211.18	4165.65	4141.79	4129.19	4122.51
400000	4409.63	4386.36	4332.76	4319.16	4272.46	4247.99	4235.07	4228.22

BLENDED MONTHLY PAYMENTS 14%
AMORTIZATION IN YEARS

Amount	1	2	3	4	5	6	7	8
25	2.25	1.20	.85	.68	.58	.51	.47	.43
50	4.49	2.40	1.70	1.36	1.16	1.02	.93	.86
100	8.97	4.79	3.40	2.72	2.31	2.04	1.86	1.72
200	17.93	9.57	6.80	5.43	4.62	4.08	3.71	3.43
300	26.89	14.35	10.20	8.14	6.92	6.12	5.56	5.15
400	35.85	19.14	13.60	10.86	9.23	8.16	7.41	6.86
500	44.81	23.92	17.00	13.57	11.54	10.20	9.27	8.58
600	53.77	28.70	20.40	16.28	13.84	12.24	11.12	10.29
700	62.73	33.48	23.80	19.00	16.15	14.28	12.97	12.01
800	71.69	38.27	27.20	21.71	18.46	16.32	14.82	13.72
900	80.65	43.05	30.59	24.42	20.76	18.36	16.68	15.44
1000	89.61	47.83	33.99	27.14	23.07	20.40	18.53	17.15
2000	179.21	95.66	67.98	54.27	46.14	40.80	37.05	34.30
3000	268.81	143.49	101.97	81.40	69.20	61.19	55.58	51.45
4000	358.42	191.32	135.96	108.53	92.27	81.59	74.10	68.60
5000	448.02	239.15	169.94	135.66	115.33	101.99	92.63	85.75
6000	537.62	286.97	203.93	162.79	138.40	122.38	111.15	102.90
7000	627.23	334.80	237.92	189.92	161.46	142.78	129.68	120.05
8000	716.83	382.63	271.91	217.05	184.53	163.18	148.20	137.20
9000	806.43	430.46	305.89	244.18	207.60	183.57	166.72	154.35
10000	896.03	478.29	339.88	271.31	230.66	203.97	185.25	171.50
20000	1792.06	956.57	679.76	542.61	461.32	407.94	370.49	342.99
30000	2688.09	1434.85	1019.64	813.92	691.98	611.90	555.73	514.48
40000	3584.12	1913.13	1359.51	1085.22	922.63	815.87	740.98	685.98
50000	4480.15	2391.41	1699.39	1356.52	1153.29	1019.83	926.22	857.47
60000	5376.18	2869.69	2039.27	1627.83	1383.95	1223.80	1111.46	1028.96
70000	6272.21	3347.97	2379.14	1899.13	1614.60	1427.77	1296.71	1200.46
80000	7168.24	3826.25	2719.02	2170.44	1845.26	1631.73	1481.95	1371.95
90000	8064.27	4304.53	3058.90	2441.74	2075.92	1835.70	1667.19	1543.44
100000	8960.30	4782.81	3398.77	2713.04	2306.57	2039.66	1852.44	1714.94
110000	9856.33	5261.09	3738.65	2984.35	2537.23	2243.63	2037.68	1886.43
120000	10752.36	5739.37	4078.53	3255.65	2767.89	2447.60	2222.92	2057.92
130000	11648.39	6217.65	4418.41	3526.96	2998.54	2651.56	2408.16	2229.42
140000	12544.41	6695.93	4758.28	3798.26	3229.20	2855.53	2593.41	2400.91
150000	13440.44	7174.21	5098.16	4069.56	3459.86	3059.49	2778.65	2572.40
160000	14336.47	7652.49	5438.04	4340.87	3690.51	3263.46	2963.89	2743.90
170000	15232.50	8130.77	5777.91	4612.17	3921.17	3467.43	3149.14	2915.39
180000	16128.53	8609.05	6117.79	4883.48	4151.83	3671.39	3334.38	3086.88
190000	17024.56	9087.33	6457.67	5154.78	4382.49	3875.36	3519.62	3258.38
200000	17920.59	9565.62	6797.54	5426.08	4613.14	4079.32	3704.87	3429.87
210000	18816.62	10043.90	7137.42	5697.39	4843.80	4283.29	3890.11	3601.36
220000	19712.65	10522.18	7477.30	5968.69	5074.46	4487.25	4075.35	3772.86
230000	20608.68	11000.46	7817.18	6240.00	5305.11	4691.22	4260.60	3944.35
240000	21504.71	11478.74	8157.05	6511.30	5535.77	4895.19	4445.84	4115.84
250000	22400.74	11957.02	8496.93	6782.60	5766.43	5099.15	4631.08	4287.34
260000	23296.77	12435.30	8836.81	7053.91	5997.08	5303.12	4816.32	4458.83
270000	24192.79	12913.58	9176.68	7325.21	6227.74	5507.08	5001.57	4630.32
280000	25088.82	13391.86	9516.56	7596.52	6458.40	5711.05	5186.81	4801.82
290000	25984.85	13870.14	9856.44	7867.82	6689.05	5915.02	5372.05	4973.31
300000	26880.88	14348.42	10196.31	8139.12	6919.71	6118.98	5557.30	5144.80
310000	27776.91	14826.70	10536.19	8410.43	7150.37	6322.95	5742.54	5316.30
320000	28672.94	15304.98	10876.07	8681.73	7381.02	6526.91	5927.78	5487.79
330000	29568.97	15783.26	11215.95	8953.04	7611.68	6730.88	6113.03	5659.28
340000	30465.00	16261.54	11555.82	9224.34	7842.34	6934.85	6298.27	5830.78
350000	31361.03	16739.82	11895.70	9495.64	8072.99	7138.81	6483.51	6002.27
360000	32257.06	17218.10	12235.58	9766.95	8303.65	7342.78	6668.75	6173.76
370000	33153.09	17696.38	12575.45	10038.25	8534.31	7546.74	6854.00	6345.26
380000	34049.12	18174.66	12915.33	10309.56	8764.97	7750.71	7039.24	6516.75
390000	34945.15	18652.95	13255.21	10580.86	8995.62	7954.68	7224.48	6688.24
400000	35841.17	19131.23	13595.08	10852.16	9226.28	8158.64	7409.73	6859.74

14% BLENDED MONTHLY PAYMENTS
AMORTIZATION IN YEARS

Amount	9	10	11	12	13	14	15	16
25	.41	.39	.37	.36	.35	.34	.33	.33
50	.81	.77	.74	.71	.69	.67	.66	.65
100	1.62	1.53	1.47	1.42	1.37	1.34	1.31	1.29
200	3.23	3.06	2.93	2.83	2.74	2.67	2.62	2.57
300	4.84	4.59	4.40	4.24	4.11	4.01	3.92	3.85
400	6.45	6.12	5.86	5.65	5.48	5.34	5.23	5.13
500	8.06	7.65	7.33	7.07	6.85	6.68	6.53	6.41
600	9.67	9.18	8.79	8.48	8.22	8.01	7.84	7.69
700	11.28	10.71	10.26	9.89	9.59	9.35	9.14	8.97
800	12.89	12.24	11.72	11.30	10.96	10.68	10.45	10.25
900	14.50	13.77	13.19	12.72	12.33	12.02	11.75	11.53
1000	16.11	15.30	14.65	14.13	13.70	13.35	13.06	12.82
2000	32.22	30.59	29.30	28.25	27.40	26.70	26.12	25.63
3000	48.32	45.88	43.94	42.38	41.10	40.05	39.17	38.44
4000	64.43	61.17	58.59	56.50	54.80	53.40	52.23	51.25
5000	80.53	76.47	73.24	70.63	68.50	66.74	65.28	64.06
6000	96.64	91.76	87.88	84.75	82.20	80.09	78.34	76.87
7000	112.74	107.05	102.53	98.88	95.90	93.44	91.39	89.68
8000	128.85	122.34	117.17	113.00	109.60	106.79	104.45	102.49
9000	144.95	137.63	131.82	127.13	123.30	120.14	117.50	115.30
10000	161.06	152.93	146.47	141.25	137.00	133.48	130.56	128.11
20000	322.11	305.85	292.93	282.50	273.99	266.96	261.11	256.21
30000	483.16	458.77	439.39	423.75	410.98	400.44	391.66	384.31
40000	644.21	611.69	585.85	565.00	547.97	533.92	522.22	512.41
50000	805.27	764.61	732.31	706.25	684.97	667.39	652.77	640.51
60000	966.32	917.53	878.77	847.50	821.96	800.87	783.32	768.61
70000	1127.37	1070.45	1025.23	988.75	958.95	934.35	913.88	896.71
80000	1288.42	1223.37	1171.69	1130.00	1095.94	1067.83	1044.43	1024.81
90000	1449.47	1376.29	1318.15	1271.25	1232.93	1201.31	1174.98	1152.91
100000	1610.53	1529.21	1464.61	1412.50	1369.93	1334.78	1305.53	1281.02
110000	1771.58	1682.13	1611.07	1553.75	1506.92	1468.26	1436.09	1409.12
120000	1932.63	1835.05	1757.53	1695.00	1643.91	1601.74	1566.64	1537.22
130000	2093.68	1987.97	1903.99	1836.25	1780.90	1735.22	1697.19	1665.32
140000	2254.73	2140.89	2050.45	1977.50	1917.89	1868.70	1827.75	1793.42
150000	2415.79	2293.81	2196.92	2118.75	2054.89	2002.17	1958.30	1921.52
160000	2576.84	2446.73	2343.38	2260.00	2191.88	2135.65	2088.85	2049.62
170000	2737.89	2599.65	2489.84	2401.25	2328.87	2269.13	2219.41	2177.72
180000	2898.94	2752.57	2636.30	2542.50	2465.86	2402.61	2349.96	2305.82
190000	3060.00	2905.49	2782.76	2683.74	2602.85	2536.09	2480.51	2433.93
200000	3221.05	3058.41	2929.22	2824.99	2739.85	2669.56	2611.06	2562.03
210000	3382.10	3211.33	3075.68	2966.24	2876.84	2803.04	2741.62	2690.13
220000	3543.15	3364.25	3222.14	3107.49	3013.83	2936.52	2872.17	2818.23
230000	3704.20	3517.17	3368.60	3248.74	3150.82	3070.00	3002.72	2946.33
240000	3865.26	3670.09	3515.06	3389.99	3287.81	3203.48	3133.28	3074.43
250000	4026.31	3823.01	3661.52	3531.24	3424.81	3336.95	3263.83	3202.53
260000	4187.36	3975.93	3807.98	3672.49	3561.80	3470.43	3394.38	3330.63
270000	4348.41	4128.85	3954.44	3813.74	3698.79	3603.91	3524.94	3458.73
280000	4509.46	4281.77	4100.90	3954.99	3835.78	3737.39	3655.49	3586.83
290000	4670.52	4434.69	4247.37	4096.24	3972.77	3870.87	3786.04	3714.94
300000	4831.57	4587.61	4393.83	4237.49	4109.77	4004.34	3916.59	3843.04
310000	4992.62	4740.53	4540.29	4378.74	4246.76	4137.82	4047.15	3971.14
320000	5153.67	4893.45	4686.75	4519.99	4383.75	4271.30	4177.70	4099.24
330000	5314.72	5046.37	4833.21	4661.24	4520.74	4404.78	4308.25	4227.34
340000	5475.78	5199.29	4979.67	4802.49	4657.73	4538.26	4438.81	4355.44
350000	5636.83	5352.21	5126.13	4943.74	4794.73	4671.73	4569.36	4483.54
360000	5797.88	5505.13	5272.59	5084.99	4931.72	4805.21	4699.91	4611.64
370000	5958.93	5658.05	5419.05	5226.23	5068.71	4938.69	4830.46	4739.74
380000	6119.99	5810.97	5565.51	5367.48	5205.70	5072.17	4961.02	4867.85
390000	6281.04	5963.89	5711.97	5508.73	5342.69	5205.65	5091.57	4995.95
400000	6442.09	6116.81	5858.43	5649.98	5479.69	5339.12	5222.12	5124.05

BLENDED MONTHLY PAYMENTS 14%
AMORTIZATION IN YEARS

Amount	17	18	19	20	21	22	23	24
25	.32	.32	.31	.31	.31	.30	.30	.30
50	.64	.63	.62	.61	.61	.60	.60	.59
100	1.27	1.25	1.23	1.22	1.21	1.20	1.19	1.18
200	2.53	2.49	2.46	2.44	2.41	2.39	2.38	2.36
300	3.79	3.73	3.69	3.65	3.62	3.59	3.57	3.54
400	5.05	4.98	4.92	4.87	4.82	4.78	4.75	4.72
500	6.31	6.22	6.14	6.08	6.03	5.98	5.94	5.90
600	7.57	7.46	7.37	7.30	7.23	7.17	7.13	7.08
700	8.83	8.70	8.60	8.51	8.43	8.37	8.31	8.26
800	10.09	9.95	9.83	9.73	9.64	9.56	9.50	9.44
900	11.35	11.19	11.06	10.94	10.84	10.76	10.69	10.62
1000	12.61	12.43	12.28	12.16	12.05	11.95	11.87	11.80
2000	25.21	24.86	24.56	24.31	24.09	23.90	23.74	23.60
3000	37.82	37.29	36.84	36.46	36.13	35.85	35.61	35.40
4000	50.42	49.72	49.12	48.61	48.18	47.80	47.48	47.20
5000	63.02	62.15	61.40	60.76	60.22	59.75	59.35	59.00
6000	75.63	74.57	73.68	72.92	72.26	71.70	71.22	70.80
7000	88.23	87.00	85.96	85.07	84.30	83.65	83.08	82.60
8000	100.83	99.43	98.24	97.22	96.35	95.60	94.95	94.40
9000	113.44	111.86	110.52	109.37	108.39	107.55	106.82	106.19
10000	126.04	124.29	122.80	121.52	120.43	119.50	118.69	117.99
20000	252.07	248.57	245.59	243.04	240.86	238.99	237.37	235.98
30000	378.11	372.85	368.38	364.56	361.29	358.48	356.06	353.97
40000	504.14	497.13	491.17	486.08	481.71	477.97	474.74	471.96
50000	630.17	621.41	613.96	607.59	602.14	597.46	593.42	589.95
60000	756.21	745.69	736.75	729.11	722.57	716.95	712.11	707.94
70000	882.24	869.98	859.54	850.63	842.99	836.44	830.79	825.92
80000	1008.27	994.26	982.33	972.15	963.42	955.93	949.48	943.91
90000	1134.31	1118.54	1105.12	1093.66	1083.85	1075.42	1068.16	1061.90
100000	1260.34	1242.82	1227.91	1215.18	1204.27	1194.91	1186.84	1179.89
110000	1386.37	1367.10	1350.70	1336.70	1324.70	1314.40	1305.53	1297.88
120000	1512.41	1491.38	1473.49	1458.22	1445.13	1433.89	1424.21	1415.87
130000	1638.44	1615.67	1596.29	1579.73	1565.56	1553.38	1542.90	1533.85
140000	1764.48	1739.95	1719.08	1701.25	1685.98	1672.87	1661.58	1651.84
150000	1890.51	1864.23	1841.87	1822.77	1806.41	1792.36	1780.26	1769.83
160000	2016.54	1988.51	1964.66	1944.29	1926.84	1911.85	1898.95	1887.82
170000	2142.58	2112.79	2087.45	2065.80	2047.26	2031.34	2017.63	2005.81
180000	2268.61	2237.07	2210.24	2187.32	2167.69	2150.83	2136.31	2123.80
190000	2394.64	2361.36	2333.03	2308.84	2288.12	2270.32	2255.00	2241.79
200000	2520.68	2485.64	2455.82	2430.36	2408.54	2389.81	2373.68	2359.77
210000	2646.71	2609.92	2578.61	2551.87	2528.97	2509.30	2492.37	2477.76
220000	2772.74	2734.20	2701.40	2673.39	2649.40	2628.79	2611.05	2595.75
230000	2898.78	2858.48	2824.19	2794.91	2769.82	2748.28	2729.73	2713.74
240000	3024.81	2982.76	2946.98	2916.43	2890.25	2867.77	2848.42	2831.73
250000	3150.85	3107.05	3069.78	3037.94	3010.68	2987.26	2967.10	2949.72
260000	3276.88	3231.33	3192.57	3159.46	3131.11	3106.75	3085.79	3067.70
270000	3402.91	3355.61	3315.36	3280.98	3251.53	3226.24	3204.47	3185.69
280000	3528.95	3479.89	3438.15	3402.50	3371.96	3345.73	3323.15	3303.68
290000	3654.98	3604.17	3560.94	3524.02	3492.39	3465.22	3441.84	3421.67
300000	3781.01	3728.45	3683.73	3645.53	3612.81	3584.71	3560.52	3539.66
310000	3907.05	3852.74	3806.52	3767.05	3733.24	3704.20	3679.20	3657.65
320000	4033.08	3977.02	3929.31	3888.57	3853.67	3823.69	3797.89	3775.63
330000	4159.11	4101.30	4052.10	4010.09	3974.09	3943.18	3916.57	3893.62
340000	4285.15	4225.58	4174.89	4131.60	4094.52	4062.67	4035.26	4011.61
350000	4411.18	4349.86	4297.68	4253.12	4214.95	4182.16	4153.94	4129.60
360000	4537.21	4474.14	4420.47	4374.64	4335.37	4301.65	4272.62	4247.59
370000	4663.25	4598.43	4543.26	4496.16	4455.80	4421.14	4391.31	4365.58
380000	4789.28	4722.71	4666.06	4617.67	4576.23	4540.63	4509.99	4483.57
390000	4915.32	4846.99	4788.85	4739.19	4696.66	4660.12	4628.68	4601.55
400000	5041.35	4971.27	4911.64	4860.71	4817.08	4779.61	4747.36	4719.54

14% BLENDED MONTHLY PAYMENTS
AMORTIZATION IN YEARS

Amount	25	26	29	30	35	40	45	50
25	.30	.30	.29	.29	.29	.29	.29	.29
50	.59	.59	.58	.58	.58	.57	.57	.57
100	1.18	1.17	1.16	1.16	1.15	1.14	1.14	1.14
200	2.35	2.34	2.32	2.31	2.29	2.28	2.28	2.28
300	3.53	3.51	3.48	3.47	3.44	3.42	3.41	3.41
400	4.70	4.68	4.63	4.62	4.58	4.56	4.55	4.55
500	5.87	5.85	5.79	5.77	5.73	5.70	5.69	5.68
600	7.05	7.02	6.95	6.93	6.87	6.84	6.82	6.82
700	8.22	8.19	8.10	8.08	8.01	7.98	7.96	7.95
800	9.40	9.35	9.26	9.24	9.16	9.12	9.10	9.09
900	10.57	10.52	10.42	10.39	10.30	10.26	10.23	10.22
1000	11.74	11.69	11.57	11.54	11.45	11.40	11.37	11.36
2000	23.48	23.38	23.14	23.08	22.89	22.79	22.74	22.71
3000	35.22	35.07	34.71	34.62	34.33	34.18	34.10	34.07
4000	46.96	46.75	46.28	46.16	45.77	45.57	45.47	45.42
5000	58.70	58.44	57.85	57.70	57.21	56.96	56.84	56.77
6000	70.44	70.13	69.42	69.24	68.65	68.35	68.20	68.13
7000	82.18	81.81	80.99	80.78	80.09	79.74	79.57	79.48
8000	93.92	93.50	92.56	92.32	91.53	91.13	90.93	90.83
9000	105.65	105.19	104.12	103.86	102.97	102.52	102.30	102.19
10000	117.39	116.87	115.69	115.40	114.41	113.92	113.67	113.54
20000	234.78	233.74	231.38	230.79	228.82	227.83	227.33	227.07
30000	352.17	350.61	347.07	346.19	343.22	341.74	340.99	340.61
40000	469.56	467.48	462.76	461.58	457.63	455.65	454.65	454.14
50000	586.94	584.34	578.45	576.97	572.04	569.56	568.31	567.67
60000	704.33	701.21	694.14	692.37	686.44	683.47	681.97	681.21
70000	821.72	818.08	809.82	807.76	800.85	797.38	795.63	794.74
80000	939.11	934.95	925.51	923.16	915.26	911.29	909.29	908.27
90000	1056.49	1051.82	1041.20	1038.55	1029.66	1025.20	1022.95	1021.81
100000	1173.88	1168.68	1156.89	1153.94	1144.07	1139.11	1136.61	1135.34
110000	1291.27	1285.55	1272.58	1269.34	1258.47	1253.02	1250.27	1248.87
120000	1408.66	1402.42	1388.27	1384.73	1372.88	1366.93	1363.93	1362.41
130000	1526.04	1519.29	1503.95	1500.13	1487.29	1480.84	1477.59	1475.94
140000	1643.43	1636.16	1619.64	1615.52	1601.69	1594.75	1591.25	1589.47
150000	1760.82	1753.02	1735.33	1730.91	1716.10	1708.66	1704.91	1703.01
160000	1878.21	1869.89	1851.02	1846.31	1830.51	1822.57	1818.57	1816.54
170000	1995.60	1986.76	1966.71	1961.70	1944.91	1936.49	1932.23	1930.07
180000	2112.98	2103.63	2082.40	2077.10	2059.32	2050.40	2045.89	2043.61
190000	2230.37	2220.49	2198.08	2192.49	2173.72	2164.31	2159.55	2157.14
200000	2347.76	2337.36	2313.77	2307.88	2288.13	2278.22	2273.21	2270.67
210000	2465.15	2454.23	2429.46	2423.28	2402.54	2392.13	2386.87	2384.21
220000	2582.53	2571.10	2545.15	2538.67	2516.94	2506.04	2500.53	2497.74
230000	2699.92	2687.97	2660.84	2654.07	2631.35	2619.95	2614.19	2611.27
240000	2817.31	2804.83	2776.53	2769.46	2745.76	2733.86	2727.85	2724.81
250000	2934.70	2921.70	2892.21	2884.85	2860.16	2847.77	2841.51	2838.34
260000	3052.08	3038.57	3007.90	3000.25	2974.57	2961.68	2955.17	2951.87
270000	3169.47	3155.44	3123.59	3115.64	3088.97	3075.59	3068.83	3065.41
280000	3286.86	3272.31	3239.28	3231.04	3203.38	3189.50	3182.49	3178.94
290000	3404.25	3389.17	3354.97	3346.43	3317.79	3303.41	3296.15	3292.47
300000	3521.63	3506.04	3470.66	3461.82	3432.19	3417.32	3409.81	3406.01
310000	3639.02	3622.91	3586.34	3577.22	3546.60	3531.23	3523.47	3519.54
320000	3756.41	3739.78	3702.03	3692.61	3661.01	3645.14	3637.13	3633.08
330000	3873.80	3856.65	3817.72	3808.01	3775.41	3759.05	3750.79	3746.61
340000	3991.19	3973.51	3933.41	3923.40	3889.82	3872.97	3864.45	3860.14
350000	4108.57	4090.38	4049.10	4038.79	4004.22	3986.88	3978.11	3973.68
360000	4225.96	4207.25	4164.79	4154.19	4118.63	4100.79	4091.77	4087.21
370000	4343.35	4324.12	4280.47	4269.58	4233.04	4214.70	4205.43	4200.74
380000	4460.74	4440.98	4396.16	4384.98	4347.44	4328.61	4319.10	4314.28
390000	4578.12	4557.85	4511.85	4500.37	4461.85	4442.52	4432.76	4427.81
400000	4695.51	4674.72	4627.54	4615.76	4576.26	4556.43	4546.42	4541.34

BLENDED MONTHLY PAYMENTS 15%

AMORTIZATION IN YEARS

Amount	1	2	3	4	5	6	7	8
25	2.26	1.21	.87	.70	.59	.53	.48	.45
50	4.51	2.42	1.73	1.39	1.18	1.05	.96	.89
100	9.01	4.83	3.45	2.77	2.36	2.10	1.91	1.77
200	18.01	9.66	6.89	5.53	4.72	4.19	3.81	3.54
300	27.02	14.49	10.34	8.29	7.07	6.28	5.72	5.31
400	36.02	19.31	13.78	11.05	9.43	8.37	7.62	7.08
500	45.03	24.14	17.23	13.81	11.78	10.46	9.53	8.85
600	54.03	28.97	20.67	16.57	14.14	12.55	11.43	10.62
700	63.04	33.80	24.12	19.33	16.49	14.64	13.34	12.39
800	72.04	38.62	27.56	22.09	18.85	16.73	15.24	14.15
900	81.05	43.45	31.01	24.85	21.20	18.82	17.15	15.92
1000	90.05	48.28	34.45	27.61	23.56	20.91	19.05	17.69
2000	180.10	96.55	68.90	55.21	47.12	41.81	38.10	35.38
3000	270.15	144.83	103.34	82.82	70.67	62.71	57.14	53.07
4000	360.19	193.10	137.79	110.42	94.23	83.61	76.19	70.75
5000	450.24	241.37	172.24	138.03	117.78	104.52	95.24	88.44
6000	540.29	289.65	206.68	165.63	141.34	125.42	114.28	106.13
7000	630.33	337.92	241.13	193.23	164.89	146.32	133.33	123.81
8000	720.38	386.20	275.57	220.84	188.45	167.22	152.37	141.50
9000	810.43	434.47	310.02	248.44	212.00	188.13	171.42	159.19
10000	900.47	482.74	344.47	276.05	235.56	209.03	190.47	176.87
20000	1800.94	965.48	688.93	552.09	471.11	418.05	380.93	353.74
30000	2701.41	1448.22	1033.39	828.13	706.66	627.07	571.39	530.61
40000	3601.88	1930.96	1377.85	1104.17	942.21	836.10	761.85	707.48
50000	4502.35	2413.70	1722.31	1380.21	1177.77	1045.12	952.31	884.35
60000	5402.82	2896.44	2066.78	1656.25	1413.32	1254.14	1142.77	1061.22
70000	6303.29	3379.18	2411.24	1932.29	1648.87	1463.17	1333.23	1238.09
80000	7203.76	3861.92	2755.70	2208.33	1884.42	1672.19	1523.69	1414.96
90000	8104.22	4344.66	3100.16	2484.37	2119.98	1881.21	1714.15	1591.83
100000	9004.69	4827.40	3444.62	2760.41	2355.53	2090.23	1904.61	1768.70
110000	9905.16	5310.13	3789.08	3036.45	2591.08	2299.26	2095.07	1945.57
120000	10805.63	5792.87	4133.55	3312.49	2826.63	2508.28	2285.53	2122.43
130000	11706.10	6275.61	4478.01	3588.53	3062.19	2717.30	2475.99	2299.30
140000	12606.57	6758.35	4822.47	3864.57	3297.74	2926.33	2666.46	2476.17
150000	13507.04	7241.09	5166.93	4140.61	3533.29	3135.35	2856.92	2653.04
160000	14407.51	7723.83	5511.39	4416.65	3768.84	3344.37	3047.38	2829.91
170000	15307.98	8206.57	5855.85	4692.69	4004.40	3553.39	3237.84	3006.78
180000	16208.44	8689.31	6200.32	4968.73	4239.95	3762.42	3428.30	3183.65
190000	17108.91	9172.05	6544.78	5244.77	4475.50	3971.44	3618.76	3360.52
200000	18009.38	9654.79	6889.24	5520.81	4711.05	4180.46	3809.22	3537.39
210000	18909.85	10137.52	7233.70	5796.85	4946.60	4389.49	3999.68	3714.26
220000	19810.32	10620.26	7578.16	6072.89	5182.16	4598.51	4190.14	3891.13
230000	20710.79	11103.00	7922.63	6348.93	5417.71	4807.53	4380.60	4068.00
240000	21611.26	11585.74	8267.09	6624.97	5653.26	5016.56	4571.06	4244.86
250000	22511.73	12068.48	8611.55	6901.01	5888.81	5225.58	4761.52	4421.73
260000	23412.20	12551.22	8956.01	7177.05	6124.37	5434.60	4951.98	4598.60
270000	24312.66	13033.96	9300.47	7453.09	6359.92	5643.62	5142.45	4775.47
280000	25213.13	13516.70	9644.93	7729.13	6595.47	5852.65	5332.91	4952.34
290000	26113.60	13999.44	9989.40	8005.17	6831.02	6061.67	5523.37	5129.21
300000	27014.07	14482.18	10333.86	8281.21	7066.58	6270.69	5713.83	5306.08
310000	27914.54	14964.92	10678.32	8557.25	7302.13	6479.72	5904.29	5482.95
320000	28815.01	15447.65	11022.78	8833.29	7537.68	6688.74	6094.75	5659.82
330000	29715.48	15930.39	11367.24	9109.33	7773.23	6897.76	6285.21	5836.69
340000	30615.95	16413.13	11711.70	9385.37	8008.79	7106.78	6475.67	6013.56
350000	31516.42	16895.87	12056.17	9661.41	8244.34	7315.81	6666.13	6190.43
360000	32416.88	17378.61	12400.63	9937.45	8479.89	7524.83	6856.59	6367.29
370000	33317.35	17861.35	12745.09	10213.49	8715.44	7733.85	7047.05	6544.16
380000	34217.82	18344.09	13089.55	10489.53	8951.00	7942.88	7237.51	6721.03
390000	35118.29	18826.83	13434.01	10765.57	9186.55	8151.90	7427.97	6897.90
400000	36018.76	19309.57	13778.47	11041.61	9422.10	8360.92	7618.43	7074.77

15% BLENDED MONTHLY PAYMENTS
AMORTIZATION IN YEARS

Amount	9	10	11	12	13	14	15	16
25	.42	.40	.39	.37	.36	.35	.35	.34
50	.84	.80	.77	.74	.72	.70	.69	.68
100	1.67	1.59	1.53	1.48	1.44	1.40	1.37	1.35
200	3.34	3.18	3.05	2.95	2.87	2.80	2.74	2.70
300	5.00	4.76	4.57	4.42	4.30	4.20	4.11	4.04
400	6.67	6.35	6.10	5.89	5.73	5.59	5.48	5.39
500	8.33	7.94	7.62	7.37	7.16	6.99	6.85	6.73
600	10.00	9.52	9.14	8.84	8.59	8.39	8.22	8.08
700	11.67	11.11	10.67	10.31	10.02	9.78	9.59	9.42
800	13.33	12.69	12.19	11.78	11.45	11.18	10.96	10.77
900	15.00	14.28	13.71	13.25	12.88	12.58	12.33	12.12
1000	16.66	15.87	15.23	14.73	14.31	13.98	13.70	13.46
2000	33.32	31.73	30.46	29.45	28.62	27.95	27.39	26.92
3000	49.98	47.59	45.69	44.17	42.93	41.92	41.08	40.37
4000	66.64	63.45	60.92	58.89	57.24	55.89	54.77	53.83
5000	83.30	79.31	76.15	73.61	71.55	69.86	68.46	67.29
6000	99.95	95.17	91.38	88.33	85.86	83.83	82.15	80.74
7000	116.61	111.03	106.61	103.06	100.17	97.80	95.84	94.20
8000	133.27	126.89	121.83	117.78	114.48	111.77	109.53	107.66
9000	149.93	142.75	137.06	132.50	128.79	125.74	123.22	121.11
10000	166.59	158.61	152.29	147.22	143.10	139.71	136.91	134.57
20000	333.17	317.21	304.58	294.43	286.19	279.41	273.81	269.13
30000	499.75	475.81	456.86	441.65	429.28	419.12	410.71	403.70
40000	666.33	634.41	609.15	588.86	572.37	558.82	547.61	538.26
50000	832.92	793.01	761.44	736.08	715.46	698.53	684.51	672.82
60000	999.50	951.61	913.72	883.29	858.55	838.23	821.41	807.39
70000	1166.08	1110.21	1066.01	1030.51	1001.64	977.94	958.31	941.95
80000	1332.66	1268.81	1218.29	1177.72	1144.73	1117.64	1095.21	1076.52
90000	1499.25	1427.41	1370.58	1324.93	1287.82	1257.34	1232.11	1211.08
100000	1665.83	1586.01	1522.87	1472.15	1430.91	1397.05	1369.01	1345.64
110000	1832.41	1744.61	1675.15	1619.36	1574.00	1536.75	1505.91	1480.21
120000	1998.99	1903.21	1827.44	1766.58	1717.09	1676.46	1642.81	1614.77
130000	2165.58	2061.81	1979.72	1913.79	1860.18	1816.16	1779.71	1749.34
140000	2332.16	2220.41	2132.01	2061.01	2003.27	1955.87	1916.62	1883.90
150000	2498.74	2379.01	2284.30	2208.22	2146.36	2095.57	2053.52	2018.46
160000	2665.32	2537.61	2436.58	2355.43	2289.46	2235.27	2190.42	2153.03
170000	2831.91	2696.21	2588.87	2502.65	2432.55	2374.98	2327.32	2287.59
180000	2998.49	2854.81	2741.15	2649.86	2575.64	2514.68	2464.22	2422.16
190000	3165.07	3013.41	2893.44	2797.08	2718.73	2654.39	2601.12	2556.72
200000	3331.65	3172.01	3045.73	2944.29	2861.82	2794.09	2738.02	2691.28
210000	3498.24	3330.61	3198.01	3091.51	3004.91	2933.80	2874.92	2825.85
220000	3664.82	3489.21	3350.30	3238.72	3148.00	3073.50	3011.82	2960.41
230000	3831.40	3647.81	3502.59	3385.94	3291.09	3213.20	3148.72	3094.98
240000	3997.98	3806.41	3654.87	3533.15	3434.18	3352.91	3285.62	3229.54
250000	4164.57	3965.02	3807.16	3680.36	3577.27	3492.61	3422.52	3364.10
260000	4331.15	4123.62	3959.44	3827.58	3720.36	3632.32	3559.42	3498.67
270000	4497.73	4282.22	4111.73	3974.79	3863.45	3772.02	3696.32	3633.23
280000	4664.31	4440.82	4264.02	4122.01	4006.54	3911.73	3833.23	3767.80
290000	4830.90	4599.42	4416.30	4269.22	4149.63	4051.43	3970.13	3902.36
300000	4997.48	4758.02	4568.59	4416.44	4292.72	4191.13	4107.03	4036.92
310000	5164.06	4916.62	4720.87	4563.65	4435.82	4330.84	4243.93	4171.49
320000	5330.64	5075.22	4873.16	4710.86	4578.91	4470.54	4380.83	4306.05
330000	5497.23	5233.82	5025.45	4858.08	4722.00	4610.25	4517.73	4440.62
340000	5663.81	5392.42	5177.73	5005.29	4865.09	4749.95	4654.63	4575.18
350000	5830.39	5551.02	5330.02	5152.51	5008.18	4889.66	4791.53	4709.74
360000	5996.97	5709.62	5482.30	5299.72	5151.27	5029.36	4928.43	4844.31
370000	6163.55	5868.22	5634.59	5446.94	5294.36	5169.06	5065.33	4978.87
380000	6330.14	6026.82	5786.88	5594.15	5437.45	5308.77	5202.23	5113.44
390000	6496.72	6185.42	5939.16	5741.37	5580.54	5448.47	5339.13	5248.00
400000	6663.30	6344.02	6091.45	5888.58	5723.63	5588.18	5476.03	5382.56

BLENDED MONTHLY PAYMENTS 15%
AMORTIZATION IN YEARS

Amount	17	18	19	20	21	22	23	24
25	.34	.33	.33	.33	.32	.32	.32	.32
50	.67	.66	.65	.65	.64	.64	.63	.63
100	1.33	1.31	1.30	1.29	1.28	1.27	1.26	1.26
200	2.66	2.62	2.60	2.57	2.55	2.54	2.52	2.51
300	3.98	3.93	3.89	3.86	3.83	3.80	3.78	3.76
400	5.31	5.24	5.19	5.14	5.10	5.07	5.04	5.01
500	6.64	6.55	6.48	6.42	6.37	6.33	6.29	6.26
600	7.96	7.86	7.78	7.71	7.65	7.60	7.55	7.51
700	9.29	9.17	9.07	8.99	8.92	8.86	8.81	8.77
800	10.61	10.48	10.37	10.28	10.19	10.13	10.07	10.02
900	11.94	11.79	11.67	11.56	11.47	11.39	11.33	11.27
1000	13.27	13.10	12.96	12.84	12.74	12.66	12.58	12.52
2000	26.53	26.20	25.92	25.68	25.48	25.31	25.16	25.04
3000	39.79	39.29	38.87	38.52	38.22	37.96	37.74	37.55
4000	53.05	52.39	51.83	51.36	50.95	50.61	50.32	50.07
5000	66.31	65.48	64.79	64.19	63.69	63.26	62.90	62.58
6000	79.57	78.58	77.74	77.03	76.43	75.91	75.47	75.10
7000	92.83	91.67	90.70	89.87	89.17	88.56	88.05	87.61
8000	106.09	104.77	103.65	102.71	101.90	101.22	100.63	100.13
9000	119.35	117.87	116.61	115.55	114.64	113.87	113.21	112.64
10000	132.61	130.96	129.57	128.38	127.38	126.52	125.79	125.16
20000	265.22	261.92	259.13	256.76	254.75	253.03	251.57	250.31
30000	397.82	392.87	388.69	385.14	382.12	379.55	377.35	375.46
40000	530.43	523.83	518.25	513.52	509.49	506.06	503.13	500.62
50000	663.03	654.78	647.81	641.90	636.87	632.57	628.91	625.77
60000	795.64	785.74	777.37	770.28	764.24	759.09	754.69	750.92
70000	928.24	916.70	906.93	898.65	891.61	885.60	880.47	876.07
80000	1060.85	1047.65	1036.50	1027.03	1018.98	1012.12	1006.25	1001.23
90000	1193.45	1178.61	1166.06	1155.41	1146.35	1138.63	1132.03	1126.38
100000	1326.06	1309.56	1295.62	1283.79	1273.73	1265.14	1257.81	1251.53
110000	1458.66	1440.52	1425.18	1412.17	1401.10	1391.66	1383.59	1376.69
120000	1591.27	1571.48	1554.74	1540.55	1528.47	1518.17	1509.37	1501.84
130000	1723.87	1702.43	1684.30	1668.92	1655.84	1644.69	1635.15	1626.99
140000	1856.48	1833.39	1813.86	1797.30	1783.21	1771.20	1760.93	1752.14
150000	1989.09	1964.34	1943.43	1925.68	1910.59	1897.71	1886.71	1877.30
160000	2121.69	2095.30	2072.99	2054.06	2037.96	2024.23	2012.49	2002.45
170000	2254.30	2226.26	2202.55	2182.44	2165.33	2150.74	2138.27	2127.60
180000	2386.90	2357.21	2332.11	2310.82	2292.70	2277.25	2264.05	2252.75
190000	2519.51	2488.17	2461.67	2439.20	2420.07	2403.77	2389.83	2377.91
200000	2652.11	2619.12	2591.23	2567.57	2547.45	2530.28	2515.62	2503.06
210000	2784.72	2750.08	2720.79	2695.95	2674.82	2656.80	2641.40	2628.21
220000	2917.32	2881.04	2850.36	2824.33	2802.19	2783.31	2767.18	2753.37
230000	3049.93	3011.99	2979.92	2952.71	2929.56	2909.82	2892.96	2878.52
240000	3182.53	3142.95	3109.48	3081.09	3056.93	3036.34	3018.74	3003.67
250000	3315.14	3273.90	3239.04	3209.47	3184.31	3162.85	3144.52	3128.82
260000	3447.74	3404.86	3368.60	3337.84	3311.68	3289.37	3270.30	3253.98
270000	3580.35	3535.82	3498.16	3466.22	3439.05	3415.88	3396.08	3379.13
280000	3712.96	3666.77	3627.72	3594.60	3566.42	3542.39	3521.86	3504.28
290000	3845.56	3797.73	3757.29	3722.98	3693.79	3668.91	3647.64	3629.43
300000	3978.17	3928.68	3886.85	3851.36	3821.17	3795.42	3773.42	3754.59
310000	4110.77	4059.64	4016.41	3979.74	3948.54	3921.93	3899.20	3879.74
320000	4243.38	4190.60	4145.97	4108.12	4075.91	4048.45	4024.98	4004.89
330000	4375.98	4321.55	4275.53	4236.49	4203.28	4174.96	4150.76	4130.05
340000	4508.59	4452.51	4405.09	4364.87	4330.66	4301.48	4276.54	4255.20
350000	4641.19	4583.46	4534.65	4493.25	4458.03	4427.99	4402.32	4380.35
360000	4773.80	4714.42	4664.22	4621.63	4585.40	4554.50	4528.10	4505.50
370000	4906.40	4845.38	4793.78	4750.01	4712.77	4681.02	4653.88	4630.66
380000	5039.01	4976.33	4923.34	4878.39	4840.14	4807.53	4779.66	4755.81
390000	5171.61	5107.29	5052.90	5006.76	4967.52	4934.05	4905.45	4880.96
400000	5304.22	5238.24	5182.46	5135.14	5094.89	5060.56	5031.23	5006.12

151

15% BLENDED MONTHLY PAYMENTS
AMORTIZATION IN YEARS

Amount	25	26	29	30	35	40	45	50
25	.32	.32	.31	.31	.31	.31	.31	.31
50	.63	.63	.62	.62	.62	.61	.61	.61
100	1.25	1.25	1.24	1.23	1.23	1.22	1.22	1.22
200	2.50	2.49	2.47	2.46	2.45	2.44	2.43	2.43
300	3.74	3.73	3.70	3.69	3.67	3.65	3.65	3.65
400	4.99	4.97	4.93	4.92	4.89	4.87	4.86	4.86
500	6.24	6.21	6.16	6.15	6.11	6.09	6.08	6.07
600	7.48	7.45	7.39	7.38	7.33	7.30	7.29	7.29
700	8.73	8.70	8.62	8.61	8.55	8.52	8.51	8.50
800	9.97	9.94	9.85	9.83	9.77	9.74	9.72	9.71
900	11.22	11.18	11.09	11.06	10.99	10.95	10.94	10.93
1000	12.47	12.42	12.32	12.29	12.21	12.17	12.15	12.14
2000	24.93	24.84	24.63	24.58	24.41	24.33	24.29	24.28
3000	37.39	37.25	36.94	36.87	36.62	36.50	36.44	36.41
4000	49.85	49.67	49.25	49.15	48.82	48.66	48.58	48.55
5000	62.31	62.08	61.57	61.44	61.02	60.82	60.73	60.68
6000	74.77	74.50	73.88	73.73	73.23	72.99	72.87	72.82
7000	87.24	86.91	86.19	86.01	85.43	85.15	85.02	84.95
8000	99.70	99.33	98.50	98.30	97.63	97.31	97.16	97.09
9000	112.16	111.74	110.81	110.59	109.84	109.48	109.31	109.22
10000	124.62	124.16	123.13	122.87	122.04	121.64	121.45	121.36
20000	249.23	248.31	246.25	245.74	244.08	243.28	242.89	242.71
30000	373.85	372.46	369.37	368.61	366.11	364.92	364.34	364.06
40000	498.46	496.62	492.49	491.47	488.15	486.55	485.78	485.41
50000	623.08	620.77	615.61	614.34	610.19	608.19	607.23	606.76
60000	747.69	744.92	738.73	737.21	732.22	729.83	728.67	728.11
70000	872.31	869.07	861.85	860.07	854.26	851.47	850.12	849.47
80000	996.92	993.23	984.97	982.94	976.30	973.10	971.56	970.82
90000	1121.54	1117.38	1108.09	1105.81	1098.33	1094.74	1093.01	1092.17
100000	1246.15	1241.53	1231.21	1228.67	1220.37	1216.38	1214.45	1213.52
110000	1370.77	1365.68	1354.33	1351.54	1342.40	1338.02	1335.90	1334.87
120000	1495.38	1489.84	1477.45	1474.41	1464.44	1459.65	1457.34	1456.22
130000	1619.99	1613.99	1600.57	1597.27	1586.48	1581.29	1578.79	1577.57
140000	1744.61	1738.14	1723.69	1720.14	1708.51	1702.93	1700.23	1698.93
150000	1869.22	1862.29	1846.81	1843.01	1830.55	1824.57	1821.68	1820.28
160000	1993.84	1986.45	1969.93	1965.87	1952.59	1946.20	1943.12	1941.63
170000	2118.45	2110.60	2093.05	2088.74	2074.62	2067.84	2064.57	2062.98
180000	2243.07	2234.75	2216.17	2211.61	2196.66	2189.48	2186.01	2184.33
190000	2367.68	2358.90	2339.29	2334.47	2318.69	2311.12	2307.46	2305.68
200000	2492.30	2483.06	2462.41	2457.34	2440.73	2432.75	2428.90	2427.04
210000	2616.91	2607.21	2585.53	2580.21	2562.77	2554.39	2550.35	2548.39
220000	2741.53	2731.36	2708.65	2703.07	2684.80	2676.03	2671.79	2669.74
230000	2866.14	2855.51	2831.77	2825.94	2806.84	2797.66	2793.23	2791.09
240000	2990.75	2979.67	2954.89	2948.81	2928.88	2919.30	2914.68	2912.44
250000	3115.37	3103.82	3078.01	3071.67	3050.91	3040.94	3036.12	3033.79
260000	3239.98	3227.97	3201.13	3194.54	3172.95	3162.58	3157.57	3155.14
270000	3364.60	3352.12	3324.25	3317.41	3294.98	3284.21	3279.01	3276.50
280000	3489.21	3476.28	3447.37	3440.27	3417.02	3405.85	3400.46	3397.85
290000	3613.83	3600.43	3570.49	3563.14	3539.06	3527.49	3521.90	3519.20
300000	3738.44	3724.58	3693.61	3686.01	3661.09	3649.13	3643.35	3640.55
310000	3863.06	3848.73	3816.73	3808.87	3783.13	3770.76	3764.79	3761.90
320000	3987.67	3972.89	3939.85	3931.74	3905.17	3892.40	3886.24	3883.25
330000	4112.29	4097.04	4062.97	4054.61	4027.20	4014.04	4007.68	4004.61
340000	4236.90	4221.19	4186.09	4177.48	4149.24	4135.68	4129.13	4125.96
350000	4361.51	4345.35	4309.21	4300.34	4271.28	4257.31	4250.57	4247.31
360000	4486.13	4469.50	4432.33	4423.21	4393.31	4378.95	4372.02	4368.66
370000	4610.74	4593.65	4555.45	4546.08	4515.35	4500.59	4493.46	4490.01
380000	4735.36	4717.80	4678.57	4668.94	4637.38	4622.23	4614.91	4611.36
390000	4859.97	4841.96	4801.69	4791.81	4759.42	4743.86	4736.35	4732.71
400000	4984.59	4966.11	4924.81	4914.68	4881.46	4865.50	4857.80	4854.07

BLENDED MONTHLY PAYMENTS 16%
AMORTIZATION IN YEARS

Amount	1	2	3	4	5	6	7	8
25	2.27	1.22	.88	.71	.61	.54	.49	.46
50	4.53	2.44	1.75	1.41	1.21	1.08	.98	.92
100	9.05	4.88	3.50	2.81	2.41	2.15	1.96	1.83
200	18.10	9.75	6.99	5.62	4.81	4.29	3.92	3.65
300	27.15	14.62	10.48	8.43	7.22	6.43	5.88	5.47
400	36.20	19.49	13.97	11.24	9.62	8.57	7.83	7.30
500	45.25	24.37	17.46	14.05	12.03	10.71	9.79	9.12
600	54.30	29.24	20.95	16.85	14.43	12.85	11.75	10.94
700	63.35	34.11	24.44	19.66	16.84	14.99	13.71	12.77
800	72.40	38.98	27.93	22.47	19.24	17.14	15.66	14.59
900	81.45	43.85	31.42	25.28	21.65	19.28	17.62	16.41
1000	90.50	48.73	34.91	28.09	24.05	21.42	19.58	18.24
2000	180.99	97.45	69.82	56.17	48.10	42.83	39.15	36.47
3000	271.48	146.17	104.72	84.25	72.15	64.24	58.73	54.70
4000	361.97	194.89	139.63	112.33	96.20	85.66	78.30	72.93
5000	452.46	243.61	174.54	140.41	120.25	107.07	97.87	91.16
6000	542.95	292.33	209.44	168.49	144.30	128.48	117.45	109.39
7000	633.44	341.05	244.35	196.57	168.35	149.89	137.02	127.62
8000	723.93	389.77	279.26	224.65	192.39	171.31	156.59	145.85
9000	814.42	438.49	314.16	252.73	216.44	192.72	176.17	164.08
10000	904.91	487.21	349.07	280.81	240.49	214.13	195.74	182.31
20000	1809.81	974.41	698.13	561.61	480.98	428.26	391.47	364.62
30000	2714.71	1461.62	1047.20	842.42	721.46	642.39	587.21	546.93
40000	3619.62	1948.82	1396.26	1123.22	961.95	856.52	782.94	729.24
50000	4524.52	2436.03	1745.33	1404.03	1202.44	1070.64	978.68	911.55
60000	5429.42	2923.23	2094.39	1684.83	1442.92	1284.77	1174.41	1093.86
70000	6334.33	3410.43	2443.45	1965.64	1683.41	1498.90	1370.15	1276.17
80000	7239.23	3897.64	2792.52	2246.44	1923.89	1713.03	1565.88	1458.48
90000	8144.13	4384.84	3141.58	2527.25	2164.38	1927.15	1761.62	1640.78
100000	9049.04	4872.05	3490.65	2808.05	2404.87	2141.28	1957.35	1823.09
110000	9953.94	5359.25	3839.71	3088.85	2645.35	2355.41	2153.09	2005.40
120000	10858.84	5846.46	4188.78	3369.66	2885.84	2569.54	2348.82	2187.71
130000	11763.75	6333.66	4537.84	3650.46	3126.33	2783.66	2544.55	2370.02
140000	12668.65	6820.86	4886.90	3931.27	3366.81	2997.79	2740.29	2552.33
150000	13573.55	7308.07	5235.97	4212.07	3607.30	3211.92	2936.02	2734.64
160000	14478.46	7795.27	5585.03	4492.88	3847.78	3426.05	3131.76	2916.95
170000	15383.36	8282.48	5934.10	4773.68	4088.27	3640.17	3327.49	3099.25
180000	16288.26	8769.68	6283.16	5054.49	4328.76	3854.30	3523.23	3281.56
190000	17193.17	9256.88	6632.23	5335.29	4569.24	4068.43	3718.96	3463.87
200000	18098.07	9744.09	6981.29	5616.10	4809.73	4282.56	3914.70	3646.18
210000	19002.97	10231.29	7330.35	5896.90	5050.22	4496.68	4110.43	3828.49
220000	19907.88	10718.50	7679.42	6177.70	5290.70	4710.81	4306.17	4010.80
230000	20812.78	11205.70	8028.48	6458.51	5531.19	4924.94	4501.90	4193.11
240000	21717.68	11692.91	8377.55	6739.31	5771.67	5139.07	4697.63	4375.42
250000	22622.59	12180.11	8726.61	7020.12	6012.16	5353.19	4893.37	4557.72
260000	23527.49	12667.31	9075.68	7300.92	6252.65	5567.32	5089.10	4740.03
270000	24432.39	13154.52	9424.74	7581.73	6493.13	5781.45	5284.84	4922.34
280000	25337.30	13641.72	9773.80	7862.53	6733.62	5995.58	5480.57	5104.65
290000	26242.20	14128.93	10122.87	8143.34	6974.11	6209.70	5676.31	5286.96
300000	27147.10	14616.13	10471.93	8424.14	7214.59	6423.83	5872.04	5469.27
310000	28052.01	15103.34	10821.00	8704.94	7455.08	6637.96	6067.78	5651.58
320000	28956.91	15590.54	11170.06	8985.75	7695.56	6852.09	6263.51	5833.89
330000	29861.81	16077.74	11519.13	9266.55	7936.05	7066.22	6459.25	6016.19
340000	30766.72	16564.95	11868.19	9547.36	8176.54	7280.34	6654.98	6198.50
350000	31671.62	17052.15	12217.25	9828.16	8417.02	7494.47	6850.71	6380.81
360000	32576.52	17539.36	12566.32	10108.97	8657.51	7708.60	7046.45	6563.12
370000	33481.43	18026.56	12915.38	10389.77	8898.00	7922.73	7242.18	6745.43
380000	34386.33	18513.76	13264.45	10670.58	9138.48	8136.85	7437.92	6927.74
390000	35291.23	19000.97	13613.51	10951.38	9378.97	8350.98	7633.65	7110.05
400000	36196.14	19488.17	13962.58	11232.19	9619.45	8565.11	7829.39	7292.36

16% BLENDED MONTHLY PAYMENTS
AMORTIZATION IN YEARS

Amount	9	10	11	12	13	14	15	16
25	.44	.42	.40	.39	.38	.37	.36	.36
50	.87	.83	.80	.77	.75	.74	.72	.71
100	1.73	1.65	1.59	1.54	1.50	1.47	1.44	1.42
200	3.45	3.29	3.17	3.07	2.99	2.93	2.87	2.83
300	5.17	4.94	4.75	4.60	4.48	4.39	4.31	4.24
400	6.89	6.58	6.33	6.14	5.98	5.85	5.74	5.65
500	8.61	8.22	7.91	7.67	7.47	7.31	7.17	7.06
600	10.34	9.87	9.50	9.20	8.96	8.77	8.61	8.47
700	12.06	11.51	11.08	10.73	10.45	10.23	10.04	9.88
800	13.78	13.15	12.66	12.27	11.95	11.69	11.47	11.29
900	15.50	14.80	14.24	13.80	13.44	13.15	12.91	12.71
1000	17.22	16.44	15.82	15.33	14.93	14.61	14.34	14.12
2000	34.44	32.88	31.64	30.66	29.86	29.21	28.67	28.23
3000	51.66	49.31	47.46	45.98	44.79	43.81	43.01	42.34
4000	68.88	65.75	63.28	61.31	59.72	58.41	57.34	56.45
5000	86.10	82.18	79.10	76.64	74.64	73.02	71.67	70.56
6000	103.31	98.62	94.92	91.96	89.57	87.62	86.01	84.68
7000	120.53	115.05	110.74	107.29	104.50	102.22	100.34	98.79
8000	137.75	131.49	126.56	122.62	119.43	116.82	114.68	112.90
9000	154.97	147.93	142.38	137.94	134.35	131.42	129.01	127.01
10000	172.19	164.36	158.20	153.27	149.28	146.03	143.34	141.12
20000	344.37	328.72	316.39	306.53	298.56	292.05	286.68	282.24
30000	516.55	493.08	474.58	459.80	447.84	438.07	430.02	423.36
40000	688.74	657.43	632.78	613.06	597.11	584.09	573.36	564.48
50000	860.92	821.79	790.97	766.33	746.39	730.11	716.70	705.59
60000	1033.10	986.15	949.16	919.59	895.67	876.13	860.04	846.71
70000	1205.29	1150.50	1107.35	1072.85	1044.94	1022.15	1003.38	987.83
80000	1377.47	1314.86	1265.55	1226.12	1194.22	1168.17	1146.72	1128.95
90000	1549.65	1479.22	1423.74	1379.38	1343.50	1314.19	1290.06	1270.07
100000	1721.84	1643.58	1581.93	1532.65	1492.78	1460.21	1433.40	1411.18
110000	1894.02	1807.93	1740.12	1685.91	1642.05	1606.23	1576.74	1552.30
120000	2066.20	1972.29	1898.32	1839.18	1791.33	1752.25	1720.08	1693.42
130000	2238.39	2136.65	2056.51	1992.44	1940.61	1898.27	1863.42	1834.54
140000	2410.57	2301.00	2214.70	2145.70	2089.88	2044.29	2006.75	1975.65
150000	2582.75	2465.36	2372.89	2298.97	2239.16	2190.31	2150.09	2116.77
160000	2754.94	2629.72	2531.09	2452.23	2388.44	2336.33	2293.43	2257.89
170000	2927.12	2794.08	2689.28	2605.50	2537.72	2482.35	2436.77	2399.01
180000	3099.30	2958.43	2847.47	2758.76	2686.99	2628.37	2580.11	2540.13
190000	3271.49	3122.79	3005.66	2912.03	2836.27	2774.39	2723.45	2681.24
200000	3443.67	3287.15	3163.86	3065.29	2985.55	2920.41	2866.79	2822.36
210000	3615.85	3451.50	3322.05	3218.55	3134.82	3066.43	3010.13	2963.48
220000	3788.04	3615.86	3480.24	3371.82	3284.10	3212.45	3153.47	3104.60
230000	3960.22	3780.22	3638.43	3525.08	3433.38	3358.47	3296.81	3245.71
240000	4132.40	3944.58	3796.63	3678.35	3582.66	3504.49	3440.15	3386.83
250000	4304.59	4108.93	3954.82	3831.61	3731.93	3650.51	3583.49	3527.95
260000	4476.77	4273.29	4113.01	3984.88	3881.21	3796.53	3726.83	3669.07
270000	4648.95	4437.65	4271.21	4138.14	4030.49	3942.55	3870.16	3810.19
280000	4821.14	4602.00	4429.40	4291.40	4179.76	4088.57	4013.50	3951.30
290000	4993.32	4766.36	4587.59	4444.67	4329.04	4234.59	4156.84	4092.42
300000	5165.50	4930.72	4745.78	4597.93	4478.32	4380.61	4300.18	4233.54
310000	5337.69	5095.07	4903.98	4751.20	4627.59	4526.64	4443.52	4374.66
320000	5509.87	5259.43	5062.17	4904.46	4776.87	4672.66	4586.86	4515.78
330000	5682.05	5423.79	5220.36	5057.72	4926.15	4818.68	4730.20	4656.89
340000	5854.24	5588.15	5378.55	5210.99	5075.43	4964.70	4873.54	4798.01
350000	6026.42	5752.50	5536.75	5364.25	5224.70	5110.72	5016.88	4939.13
360000	6198.60	5916.86	5694.94	5517.52	5373.98	5256.74	5160.22	5080.25
370000	6370.79	6081.22	5853.13	5670.78	5523.26	5402.76	5303.56	5221.36
380000	6542.97	6245.57	6011.32	5824.05	5672.53	5548.78	5446.90	5362.48
390000	6715.15	6409.93	6169.52	5977.31	5821.81	5694.80	5590.24	5503.60
400000	6887.34	6574.29	6327.71	6130.57	5971.09	5840.82	5733.57	5644.72

BLENDED MONTHLY PAYMENTS 16%
AMORTIZATION IN YEARS

Amount	17	18	19	20	21	22	23	24
25	.35	.35	.35	.34	.34	.34	.34	.34
50	.70	.69	.69	.68	.68	.67	.67	.67
100	1.40	1.38	1.37	1.36	1.35	1.34	1.33	1.33
200	2.79	2.76	2.73	2.71	2.69	2.68	2.66	2.65
300	4.18	4.14	4.10	4.06	4.04	4.01	3.99	3.98
400	5.58	5.51	5.46	5.42	5.38	5.35	5.32	5.30
500	6.97	6.89	6.83	6.77	6.72	6.69	6.65	6.62
600	8.36	8.27	8.19	8.12	8.07	8.02	7.98	7.95
700	9.75	9.65	9.55	9.48	9.41	9.36	9.31	9.27
800	11.15	11.02	10.92	10.83	10.76	10.69	10.64	10.60
900	12.54	12.40	12.28	12.18	12.10	12.03	11.97	11.92
1000	13.93	13.78	13.65	13.54	13.44	13.37	13.30	13.24
2000	27.86	27.55	27.29	27.07	26.88	26.73	26.60	26.48
3000	41.79	41.32	40.93	40.60	40.32	40.09	39.89	39.72
4000	55.71	55.09	54.57	54.13	53.76	53.45	53.19	52.96
5000	69.64	68.86	68.21	67.67	67.20	66.81	66.48	66.20
6000	83.57	82.64	81.86	81.20	80.64	80.17	79.78	79.44
7000	97.49	96.41	95.50	94.73	94.08	93.54	93.07	92.68
8000	111.42	110.18	109.14	108.26	107.52	106.90	106.37	105.91
9000	125.35	123.95	122.78	121.80	120.96	120.26	119.66	119.15
10000	139.27	137.72	136.42	135.33	134.40	133.62	132.96	132.39
20000	278.54	275.44	272.84	270.65	268.80	267.24	265.91	264.78
30000	417.81	413.16	409.26	405.98	403.20	400.85	398.86	397.17
40000	557.07	550.88	545.68	541.30	537.60	534.47	531.81	529.55
50000	696.34	688.60	682.10	676.62	672.00	668.08	664.76	661.94
60000	835.61	826.32	818.52	811.95	806.40	801.70	797.71	794.33
70000	974.88	964.04	954.94	947.27	940.79	935.31	930.66	926.71
80000	1114.14	1101.76	1091.36	1082.59	1075.19	1068.93	1063.61	1059.10
90000	1253.41	1239.48	1227.78	1217.92	1209.59	1202.54	1196.57	1191.49
100000	1392.68	1377.20	1364.19	1353.24	1343.99	1336.16	1329.52	1323.87
110000	1531.95	1514.92	1500.61	1488.57	1478.39	1469.77	1462.47	1456.26
120000	1671.21	1652.64	1637.03	1623.89	1612.79	1603.39	1595.42	1588.65
130000	1810.48	1790.35	1773.45	1759.21	1747.19	1737.00	1728.37	1721.03
140000	1949.75	1928.07	1909.87	1894.54	1881.58	1870.62	1861.32	1853.42
150000	2089.02	2065.79	2046.29	2029.86	2015.98	2004.23	1994.27	1985.81
160000	2228.28	2203.51	2182.71	2165.18	2150.38	2137.85	2127.22	2118.20
170000	2367.55	2341.23	2319.13	2300.51	2284.78	2271.47	2260.17	2250.58
180000	2506.82	2478.95	2455.55	2435.83	2419.18	2405.08	2393.13	2382.97
190000	2646.09	2616.67	2591.97	2571.15	2553.58	2538.70	2526.08	2515.36
200000	2785.35	2754.39	2728.38	2706.48	2687.97	2672.31	2659.03	2647.74
210000	2924.62	2892.11	2864.80	2841.80	2822.37	2805.93	2791.98	2780.13
220000	3063.89	3029.83	3001.22	2977.13	2956.77	2939.54	2924.93	2912.52
230000	3203.16	3167.55	3137.64	3112.45	3091.17	3073.16	3057.88	3044.90
240000	3342.42	3305.27	3274.06	3247.77	3225.57	3206.77	3190.83	3177.29
250000	3481.69	3442.98	3410.48	3383.10	3359.97	3340.39	3323.78	3309.68
260000	3620.96	3580.70	3546.90	3518.42	3494.37	3474.00	3456.73	3442.06
270000	3760.22	3718.42	3683.32	3653.74	3628.76	3607.62	3589.69	3574.45
280000	3899.49	3856.14	3819.74	3789.07	3763.16	3741.23	3722.64	3706.84
290000	4038.76	3993.86	3956.16	3924.39	3897.56	3874.85	3855.59	3839.23
300000	4178.03	4131.58	4092.57	4059.71	4031.96	4008.46	3988.54	3971.61
310000	4317.29	4269.30	4228.99	4195.04	4166.36	4142.08	4121.49	4104.00
320000	4456.56	4407.02	4365.41	4330.36	4300.76	4275.70	4254.44	4236.39
330000	4595.83	4544.74	4501.83	4465.69	4435.16	4409.31	4387.39	4368.77
340000	4735.10	4682.46	4638.25	4601.01	4569.55	4542.93	4520.34	4501.16
350000	4874.36	4820.18	4774.67	4736.33	4703.95	4676.54	4653.29	4633.55
360000	5013.63	4957.90	4911.09	4871.66	4838.35	4810.16	4786.25	4765.93
370000	5152.90	5095.61	5047.51	5006.98	4972.75	4943.77	4919.20	4898.32
380000	5292.17	5233.33	5183.93	5142.30	5107.15	5077.39	5052.15	5030.71
390000	5431.43	5371.05	5320.34	5277.63	5241.55	5211.00	5185.10	5163.09
400000	5570.70	5508.77	5456.76	5412.95	5375.94	5344.62	5318.05	5295.48

155

16% BLENDED MONTHLY PAYMENTS
AMORTIZATION IN YEARS

Amount	25	26	29	30	35	40	45	50
25	.33	.33	.33	.33	.33	.33	.33	.33
50	.66	.66	.66	.66	.65	.65	.65	.65
100	1.32	1.32	1.31	1.31	1.30	1.30	1.30	1.30
200	2.64	2.63	2.62	2.61	2.60	2.59	2.59	2.59
300	3.96	3.95	3.92	3.92	3.90	3.89	3.88	3.88
400	5.28	5.26	5.23	5.22	5.19	5.18	5.17	5.17
500	6.60	6.58	6.53	6.52	6.49	6.47	6.47	6.46
600	7.92	7.89	7.84	7.83	7.79	7.77	7.76	7.75
700	9.24	9.21	9.15	9.13	9.08	9.06	9.05	9.05
800	10.56	10.52	10.45	10.44	10.38	10.35	10.34	10.34
900	11.88	11.84	11.76	11.74	11.68	11.65	11.63	11.63
1000	13.20	13.15	13.06	13.04	12.97	12.94	12.93	12.92
2000	26.39	26.30	26.12	26.08	25.94	25.88	25.85	25.84
3000	39.58	39.45	39.18	39.12	38.91	38.82	38.77	38.75
4000	52.77	52.60	52.24	52.16	51.88	51.75	51.69	51.67
5000	65.96	65.75	65.30	65.20	64.85	64.69	64.62	64.58
6000	79.15	78.90	78.36	78.23	77.82	77.63	77.54	77.50
7000	92.34	92.05	91.42	91.27	90.79	90.56	90.46	90.41
8000	105.53	105.20	104.48	104.31	103.76	103.50	103.38	103.33
9000	118.72	118.35	117.54	117.35	116.72	116.44	116.30	116.24
10000	131.91	131.50	130.60	130.39	129.69	129.37	129.23	129.16
20000	263.82	263.00	261.20	260.77	259.38	258.74	258.45	258.31
30000	395.73	394.50	391.80	391.15	389.07	388.11	387.67	387.46
40000	527.63	526.00	522.40	521.53	518.76	517.48	516.89	516.62
50000	659.54	657.50	653.00	651.92	648.44	646.85	646.11	645.77
60000	791.45	788.99	783.60	782.30	778.13	776.22	775.33	774.92
70000	923.35	920.49	914.20	912.68	907.82	905.59	904.55	904.08
80000	1055.26	1051.99	1044.80	1043.06	1037.51	1034.95	1033.78	1033.23
90000	1187.17	1183.49	1175.40	1173.44	1167.20	1164.32	1163.00	1162.38
100000	1319.07	1314.99	1305.99	1303.83	1296.88	1293.69	1292.22	1291.54
110000	1450.98	1446.49	1436.59	1434.21	1426.57	1423.06	1421.44	1420.69
120000	1582.89	1577.98	1567.19	1564.59	1556.26	1552.43	1550.66	1549.84
130000	1714.80	1709.48	1697.79	1694.97	1685.95	1681.80	1679.88	1679.00
140000	1846.70	1840.98	1828.39	1825.36	1815.63	1811.17	1809.10	1808.15
150000	1978.61	1972.48	1958.99	1955.74	1945.32	1940.54	1938.33	1937.30
160000	2110.52	2103.98	2089.59	2086.12	2075.01	2069.90	2067.55	2066.46
170000	2242.42	2235.48	2220.19	2216.50	2204.70	2199.27	2196.77	2195.61
180000	2374.33	2366.97	2350.79	2346.88	2334.39	2328.64	2325.99	2324.76
190000	2506.24	2498.47	2481.39	2477.27	2464.07	2458.01	2455.21	2453.92
200000	2638.14	2629.97	2611.98	2607.65	2593.76	2587.38	2584.43	2583.07
210000	2770.05	2761.47	2742.58	2738.03	2723.45	2716.75	2713.65	2712.22
220000	2901.96	2892.97	2873.18	2868.41	2853.14	2846.12	2842.88	2841.38
230000	3033.87	3024.47	3003.78	2998.80	2982.82	2975.48	2972.10	2970.53
240000	3165.77	3155.96	3134.38	3129.18	3112.51	3104.85	3101.32	3099.68
250000	3297.68	3287.46	3264.98	3259.56	3242.20	3234.22	3230.54	3228.84
260000	3429.59	3418.96	3395.58	3389.94	3371.89	3363.59	3359.76	3357.99
270000	3561.49	3550.46	3526.18	3520.32	3501.58	3492.96	3488.98	3487.14
280000	3693.40	3681.96	3656.78	3650.71	3631.26	3622.33	3618.20	3616.30
290000	3825.31	3813.46	3787.37	3781.09	3760.95	3751.70	3747.43	3745.45
300000	3957.21	3944.95	3917.97	3911.47	3890.64	3881.07	3876.65	3874.60
310000	4089.12	4076.45	4048.57	4041.85	4020.33	4010.43	4005.87	4003.76
320000	4221.03	4207.95	4179.17	4172.24	4150.02	4139.80	4135.09	4132.91
330000	4352.94	4339.45	4309.77	4302.62	4279.70	4269.17	4264.31	4262.06
340000	4484.84	4470.95	4440.37	4433.00	4409.39	4398.54	4393.53	4391.22
350000	4616.75	4602.45	4570.97	4563.38	4539.08	4527.91	4522.75	4520.37
360000	4748.66	4733.94	4701.57	4693.76	4668.77	4657.28	4651.98	4649.52
370000	4880.56	4865.44	4832.17	4824.15	4798.45	4786.65	4781.20	4778.68
380000	5012.47	4996.94	4962.77	4954.53	4928.14	4916.01	4910.42	4907.83
390000	5144.38	5128.44	5093.36	5084.91	5057.83	5045.38	5039.64	5036.98
400000	5276.28	5259.94	5223.96	5215.29	5187.52	5174.75	5168.86	5166.14

156

BLENDED MONTHLY PAYMENTS 17%
AMORTIZATION IN YEARS

Amount	1	2	3	4	5	6	7	8
25	2.28	1.23	.89	.72	.62	.55	.51	.47
50	4.55	2.46	1.77	1.43	1.23	1.10	1.01	.94
100	9.10	4.92	3.54	2.86	2.46	2.20	2.02	1.88
200	18.19	9.84	7.08	5.72	4.91	4.39	4.03	3.76
300	27.28	14.76	10.62	8.57	7.37	6.58	6.04	5.64
400	36.38	19.67	14.15	11.43	9.82	8.78	8.05	7.52
500	45.47	24.59	17.69	14.28	12.28	10.97	10.06	9.40
600	54.56	29.51	21.23	17.14	14.73	13.16	12.07	11.27
700	63.66	34.42	24.76	20.00	17.19	15.35	14.08	13.15
800	72.75	39.34	28.30	22.85	19.64	17.55	16.09	15.03
900	81.84	44.26	31.84	25.71	22.10	19.74	18.10	16.91
1000	90.94	49.17	35.37	28.56	24.55	21.93	20.11	18.79
2000	181.87	98.34	70.74	57.12	49.10	43.86	40.22	37.57
3000	272.80	147.51	106.11	85.68	73.64	65.79	60.32	56.35
4000	363.74	196.68	141.48	114.24	98.19	87.72	80.43	75.13
5000	454.67	245.84	176.85	142.80	122.73	109.64	100.54	93.91
6000	545.60	295.01	212.22	171.36	147.28	131.57	120.64	112.69
7000	636.54	344.18	247.58	199.92	171.83	153.50	140.75	131.47
8000	727.47	393.35	282.95	228.48	196.37	175.43	160.86	150.25
9000	818.40	442.51	318.32	257.04	220.92	197.36	180.96	169.03
10000	909.34	491.68	353.69	285.60	245.46	219.28	201.07	187.81
20000	1818.67	983.36	707.37	571.20	490.92	438.56	402.13	375.62
30000	2728.00	1475.03	1061.06	856.79	736.38	657.84	603.19	563.43
40000	3637.33	1966.71	1414.74	1142.39	981.83	877.12	804.26	751.24
50000	4546.67	2458.38	1768.43	1427.99	1227.29	1096.40	1005.32	939.05
60000	5456.00	2950.06	2122.11	1713.58	1472.75	1315.68	1206.38	1126.86
70000	6365.33	3441.74	2475.79	1999.18	1718.21	1534.95	1407.44	1314.67
80000	7274.66	3933.41	2829.48	2284.78	1963.66	1754.23	1608.51	1502.48
90000	8184.00	4425.09	3183.16	2570.37	2209.12	1973.51	1809.57	1690.29
100000	9093.33	4916.76	3536.85	2855.97	2454.58	2192.79	2010.63	1878.10
110000	10002.66	5408.44	3890.53	3141.57	2700.04	2412.07	2211.69	2065.91
120000	10911.99	5900.11	4244.22	3427.16	2945.49	2631.35	2412.76	2253.72
130000	11821.33	6391.79	4597.90	3712.76	3190.95	2850.63	2613.82	2441.53
140000	12730.66	6883.47	4951.58	3998.36	3436.41	3069.90	2814.88	2629.34
150000	13639.99	7375.14	5305.27	4283.95	3681.87	3289.18	3015.95	2817.15
160000	14549.32	7866.82	5658.95	4569.55	3927.32	3508.46	3217.01	3004.96
170000	15458.66	8358.49	6012.64	4855.15	4172.78	3727.74	3418.07	3192.77
180000	16367.99	8850.17	6366.32	5140.74	4418.24	3947.02	3619.13	3380.58
190000	17277.32	9341.85	6720.00	5426.34	4663.70	4166.30	3820.20	3568.39
200000	18186.65	9833.52	7073.69	5711.94	4909.15	4385.57	4021.26	3756.20
210000	19095.99	10325.20	7427.37	5997.53	5154.61	4604.85	4222.32	3944.01
220000	20005.32	10816.87	7781.06	6283.13	5400.07	4824.13	4423.38	4131.82
230000	20914.65	11308.55	8134.74	6568.73	5645.53	5043.41	4624.45	4319.63
240000	21823.98	11800.22	8488.43	6854.32	5890.98	5262.69	4825.51	4507.44
250000	22733.32	12291.90	8842.11	7139.92	6136.44	5481.97	5026.57	4695.25
260000	23642.65	12783.58	9195.79	7425.52	6381.90	5701.25	5227.64	4883.06
270000	24551.98	13275.25	9549.48	7711.11	6627.36	5920.52	5428.70	5070.87
280000	25461.31	13766.93	9903.16	7996.71	6872.81	6139.80	5629.76	5258.68
290000	26370.65	14258.60	10256.85	8282.31	7118.27	6359.08	5830.82	5446.49
300000	27279.98	14750.28	10610.53	8567.90	7363.73	6578.36	6031.89	5634.30
310000	28189.31	15241.96	10964.21	8853.50	7609.19	6797.64	6232.95	5822.11
320000	29098.64	15733.63	11317.90	9139.10	7854.64	7016.92	6434.01	6009.92
330000	30007.98	16225.31	11671.58	9424.69	8100.10	7236.20	6635.07	6197.73
340000	30917.31	16716.98	12025.27	9710.29	8345.56	7455.47	6836.14	6385.54
350000	31826.64	17208.66	12378.95	9995.89	8591.02	7674.75	7037.20	6573.35
360000	32735.97	17700.33	12732.64	10281.48	8836.47	7894.03	7238.26	6761.16
370000	33645.31	18192.01	13086.32	10567.08	9081.93	8113.31	7439.33	6948.97
380000	34554.64	18683.69	13440.00	10852.68	9327.39	8332.59	7640.39	7136.78
390000	35463.97	19175.36	13793.69	11138.27	9572.85	8551.87	7841.45	7324.59
400000	36373.30	19667.04	14147.37	11423.87	9818.30	8771.14	8042.51	7512.40

BLENDED MONTHLY PAYMENTS
AMORTIZATION IN YEARS

Amount	9	10	11	12	13	14	15	16
25	.45	.43	.42	.40	.39	.39	.38	.37
50	.89	.86	.83	.80	.78	.77	.75	.74
100	1.78	1.71	1.65	1.60	1.56	1.53	1.50	1.48
200	3.56	3.41	3.29	3.19	3.12	3.05	3.00	2.96
300	5.34	5.11	4.93	4.79	4.67	4.58	4.50	4.44
400	7.12	6.81	6.57	6.38	6.23	6.10	6.00	5.92
500	8.90	8.51	8.21	7.97	7.78	7.63	7.50	7.39
600	10.68	10.22	9.86	9.57	9.34	9.15	9.00	8.87
700	12.45	11.92	11.50	11.16	10.89	10.67	10.50	10.35
800	14.23	13.62	13.14	12.76	12.45	12.20	11.99	11.83
900	16.01	15.32	14.78	14.35	14.00	13.72	13.49	13.30
1000	17.79	17.02	16.42	15.94	15.56	15.25	14.99	14.78
2000	35.58	34.04	32.84	31.88	31.11	30.49	29.98	29.56
3000	53.36	51.06	49.26	47.82	46.67	45.73	44.96	44.33
4000	71.15	68.08	65.68	63.76	62.22	60.97	59.95	59.11
5000	88.93	85.10	82.09	79.70	77.78	76.21	74.94	73.88
6000	106.72	102.12	98.51	95.64	93.33	91.46	89.92	88.66
7000	124.50	119.14	114.93	111.58	108.89	106.70	104.91	103.43
8000	142.29	136.15	131.35	127.52	124.44	121.94	119.89	118.21
9000	160.07	153.17	147.76	143.46	140.00	137.18	134.88	132.98
10000	177.86	170.19	164.18	159.40	155.55	152.42	149.87	147.76
20000	355.71	340.38	328.36	318.79	311.10	304.84	299.73	295.51
30000	533.56	510.56	492.53	478.19	466.64	457.26	449.59	443.27
40000	711.41	680.75	656.71	637.58	622.19	609.68	599.45	591.02
50000	889.26	850.94	820.88	796.97	777.73	762.10	749.31	738.78
60000	1067.12	1021.12	985.06	956.37	933.28	914.52	899.17	886.53
70000	1244.97	1191.31	1149.24	1115.76	1088.82	1066.94	1049.03	1034.28
80000	1422.82	1361.50	1313.41	1275.16	1244.37	1219.36	1198.89	1182.04
90000	1600.67	1531.68	1477.59	1434.55	1399.91	1371.78	1348.75	1329.79
100000	1778.52	1701.87	1641.76	1593.94	1555.46	1524.20	1498.61	1477.55
110000	1956.37	1872.06	1805.94	1753.34	1711.00	1676.62	1648.47	1625.30
120000	2134.23	2042.24	1970.12	1912.73	1866.55	1829.04	1798.34	1773.05
130000	2312.08	2212.43	2134.29	2072.13	2022.10	1981.46	1948.20	1920.81
140000	2489.93	2382.62	2298.47	2231.52	2177.64	2133.88	2098.06	2068.56
150000	2667.78	2552.80	2462.64	2390.91	2333.19	2286.29	2247.92	2216.32
160000	2845.63	2722.99	2626.82	2550.31	2488.73	2438.71	2397.78	2364.07
170000	3023.48	2893.17	2790.99	2709.70	2644.28	2591.13	2547.64	2511.83
180000	3201.34	3063.36	2955.17	2869.10	2799.82	2743.55	2697.50	2659.58
190000	3379.19	3233.55	3119.35	3028.49	2955.37	2895.97	2847.36	2807.33
200000	3557.04	3403.73	3283.52	3187.88	3110.91	3048.39	2997.22	2955.09
210000	3734.89	3573.92	3447.70	3347.28	3266.46	3200.81	3147.08	3102.84
220000	3912.74	3744.11	3611.87	3506.67	3422.00	3353.23	3296.94	3250.60
230000	4090.59	3914.29	3776.05	3666.07	3577.55	3505.65	3446.81	3398.35
240000	4268.45	4084.48	3940.23	3825.46	3733.10	3658.07	3596.67	3546.10
250000	4446.30	4254.67	4104.40	3984.85	3888.64	3810.49	3746.53	3693.86
260000	4624.15	4424.85	4268.58	4144.25	4044.19	3962.91	3896.39	3841.61
270000	4802.00	4595.04	4432.75	4303.64	4199.73	4115.33	4046.25	3989.37
280000	4979.85	4765.23	4596.93	4463.03	4355.28	4267.75	4196.11	4137.12
290000	5157.70	4935.41	4761.11	4622.43	4510.82	4420.17	4345.97	4284.88
300000	5335.56	5105.60	4925.28	4781.82	4666.37	4572.58	4495.83	4432.63
310000	5513.41	5275.79	5089.46	4941.22	4821.91	4725.00	4645.69	4580.38
320000	5691.26	5445.97	5253.63	5100.61	4977.46	4877.42	4795.55	4728.14
330000	5869.11	5616.16	5417.81	5260.00	5133.00	5029.84	4945.41	4875.89
340000	6046.96	5786.34	5581.98	5419.40	5288.55	5182.26	5095.28	5023.65
350000	6224.81	5956.53	5746.16	5578.79	5444.09	5334.68	5245.14	5171.40
360000	6402.67	6126.72	5910.34	5738.19	5599.64	5487.10	5395.00	5319.15
370000	6580.52	6296.90	6074.51	5897.58	5755.19	5639.52	5544.86	5466.91
380000	6758.37	6467.09	6238.69	6056.97	5910.73	5791.94	5694.72	5614.66
390000	6936.22	6637.28	6402.86	6216.37	6066.28	5944.36	5844.58	5762.42
400000	7114.07	6807.46	6567.04	6375.76	6221.82	6096.78	5994.44	5910.17

BLENDED MONTHLY PAYMENTS 17%
AMORTIZATION IN YEARS

Amount	17	18	19	20	21	22	23	24
25	.37	.37	.36	.36	.36	.36	.36	.35
50	.74	.73	.72	.72	.71	.71	.71	.70
100	1.47	1.45	1.44	1.43	1.42	1.41	1.41	1.40
200	2.93	2.90	2.87	2.85	2.83	2.82	2.81	2.80
300	4.39	4.34	4.31	4.28	4.25	4.23	4.21	4.20
400	5.85	5.79	5.74	5.70	5.66	5.64	5.61	5.59
500	7.31	7.23	7.17	7.12	7.08	7.04	7.01	6.99
600	8.77	8.68	8.61	8.55	8.49	8.45	8.42	8.39
700	10.23	10.12	10.04	9.97	9.91	9.86	9.82	9.78
800	11.69	11.57	11.47	11.39	11.32	11.27	11.22	11.18
900	13.15	13.02	12.91	12.82	12.74	12.68	12.62	12.58
1000	14.61	14.46	14.34	14.24	14.15	14.08	14.02	13.97
2000	29.21	28.92	28.68	28.47	28.30	28.16	28.04	27.94
3000	43.81	43.37	43.01	42.71	42.45	42.24	42.06	41.91
4000	58.41	57.83	57.35	56.94	56.60	56.32	56.08	55.88
5000	73.01	72.29	71.68	71.18	70.75	70.40	70.10	69.84
6000	87.61	86.74	86.02	85.41	84.90	84.47	84.11	83.81
7000	102.21	101.20	100.35	99.64	99.05	98.55	98.13	97.78
8000	116.81	115.65	114.69	113.88	113.20	112.63	112.15	111.75
9000	131.41	130.11	129.02	128.11	127.35	126.71	126.17	125.72
10000	146.02	144.57	143.36	142.35	141.50	140.79	140.19	139.68
20000	292.03	289.13	286.71	284.69	282.99	281.57	280.37	279.36
30000	438.04	433.69	430.06	427.03	424.49	422.35	420.55	419.04
40000	584.05	578.25	573.42	569.37	565.98	563.13	560.74	558.72
50000	730.06	722.81	716.77	711.72	707.48	703.92	700.92	698.40
60000	876.07	867.37	860.12	854.06	848.97	844.70	841.10	838.07
70000	1022.08	1011.93	1003.48	996.40	990.47	985.48	981.29	977.75
80000	1168.09	1156.50	1146.83	1138.74	1131.96	1126.26	1121.47	1117.43
90000	1314.10	1301.06	1290.18	1281.08	1273.46	1267.05	1261.65	1257.11
100000	1460.11	1445.62	1433.53	1423.43	1414.95	1407.83	1401.84	1396.79
110000	1606.12	1590.18	1576.89	1565.77	1556.44	1548.61	1542.02	1536.46
120000	1752.13	1734.74	1720.24	1708.11	1697.94	1689.39	1682.20	1676.14
130000	1898.14	1879.30	1863.59	1850.45	1839.43	1830.18	1822.39	1815.82
140000	2044.15	2023.86	2006.95	1992.79	1980.93	1970.96	1962.57	1955.50
150000	2190.16	2168.43	2150.30	2135.14	2122.42	2111.74	2102.75	2095.18
160000	2336.17	2312.99	2293.65	2277.48	2263.92	2252.52	2242.94	2234.85
170000	2482.18	2457.55	2437.00	2419.82	2405.41	2393.31	2383.12	2374.53
180000	2628.19	2602.11	2580.36	2562.16	2546.91	2534.09	2523.30	2514.21
190000	2774.21	2746.67	2723.71	2704.50	2688.40	2674.87	2663.49	2653.89
200000	2920.22	2891.23	2867.06	2846.85	2829.89	2815.65	2803.67	2793.57
210000	3066.23	3035.79	3010.42	2989.19	2971.39	2956.44	2943.85	2933.25
220000	3212.24	3180.36	3153.77	3131.53	3112.88	3097.22	3084.03	3072.92
230000	3358.25	3324.92	3297.12	3273.87	3254.38	3238.00	3224.22	3212.60
240000	3504.26	3469.48	3440.47	3416.21	3395.87	3378.78	3364.40	3352.28
250000	3650.27	3614.04	3583.83	3558.56	3537.37	3519.57	3504.58	3491.96
260000	3796.28	3758.60	3727.18	3700.90	3678.86	3660.35	3644.77	3631.64
270000	3942.29	3903.16	3870.53	3843.24	3820.36	3801.13	3784.95	3771.31
280000	4088.30	4047.72	4013.89	3985.58	3961.85	3941.91	3925.13	3910.99
290000	4234.31	4192.29	4157.24	4127.92	4103.34	4082.70	4065.32	4050.67
300000	4380.32	4336.85	4300.59	4270.27	4244.84	4223.48	4205.50	4190.35
310000	4526.33	4481.41	4443.94	4412.61	4386.33	4364.26	4345.68	4330.03
320000	4672.34	4625.97	4587.30	4554.95	4527.83	4505.04	4485.87	4469.70
330000	4818.35	4770.53	4730.65	4697.29	4669.32	4645.82	4626.05	4609.38
340000	4964.36	4915.09	4874.00	4839.63	4810.82	4786.61	4766.23	4749.06
350000	5110.37	5059.65	5017.36	4981.98	4952.31	4927.39	4906.42	4888.74
360000	5256.38	5204.22	5160.71	5124.32	5093.81	5068.17	5046.60	5028.42
370000	5402.39	5348.78	5304.06	5266.66	5235.30	5208.95	5186.78	5168.10
380000	5548.41	5493.34	5447.41	5409.00	5376.80	5349.74	5326.97	5307.77
390000	5694.42	5637.90	5590.77	5551.34	5518.29	5490.52	5467.15	5447.45
400000	5840.43	5782.46	5734.12	5693.69	5659.78	5631.30	5607.33	5587.13

17% BLENDED MONTHLY PAYMENTS
AMORTIZATION IN YEARS

Amount	25	26	29	30	35	40	45	50
25	.35	.35	.35	.35	.35	.35	.35	.35
50	.70	.70	.70	.69	.69	.69	.69	.69
100	1.40	1.39	1.39	1.38	1.38	1.38	1.37	1.37
200	2.79	2.78	2.77	2.76	2.75	2.75	2.74	2.74
300	4.18	4.17	4.15	4.14	4.13	4.12	4.11	4.11
400	5.58	5.56	5.53	5.52	5.50	5.49	5.48	5.48
500	6.97	6.95	6.91	6.90	6.87	6.86	6.85	6.85
600	8.36	8.34	8.29	8.28	8.25	8.23	8.22	8.22
700	9.75	9.73	9.67	9.66	9.62	9.60	9.59	9.59
800	11.15	11.12	11.05	11.04	10.99	10.97	10.96	10.96
900	12.54	12.51	12.44	12.42	12.37	12.34	12.33	12.33
1000	13.93	13.89	13.82	13.80	13.74	13.71	13.70	13.70
2000	27.86	27.78	27.63	27.59	27.47	27.42	27.40	27.39
3000	41.78	41.67	41.44	41.38	41.21	41.13	41.10	41.09
4000	55.71	55.56	55.25	55.18	54.94	54.84	54.80	54.78
5000	69.63	69.45	69.06	68.97	68.68	68.55	68.50	68.47
6000	83.56	83.34	82.87	82.76	82.41	82.26	82.20	82.17
7000	97.48	97.23	96.68	96.55	96.15	95.97	95.89	95.86
8000	111.41	111.12	110.49	110.35	109.88	109.68	109.59	109.55
9000	125.33	125.01	124.31	124.14	123.62	123.39	123.29	123.25
10000	139.26	138.90	138.12	137.93	137.35	137.10	136.99	136.94
20000	278.51	277.79	276.23	275.86	274.70	274.20	273.97	273.87
30000	417.76	416.68	414.34	413.79	412.05	411.29	410.96	410.81
40000	557.01	555.57	552.45	551.72	549.40	548.39	547.94	547.74
50000	696.26	694.46	690.57	689.64	686.75	685.48	684.92	684.68
60000	835.52	833.36	828.68	827.57	824.10	822.58	821.91	821.61
70000	974.77	972.25	966.79	965.50	961.45	959.68	958.89	958.55
80000	1114.02	1111.14	1104.90	1103.43	1098.80	1096.77	1095.88	1095.48
90000	1253.27	1250.03	1243.02	1241.35	1236.15	1233.87	1232.86	1232.41
100000	1392.52	1388.92	1381.13	1379.28	1373.50	1370.96	1369.84	1369.35
110000	1531.78	1527.82	1519.24	1517.21	1510.85	1508.06	1506.83	1506.28
120000	1671.03	1666.71	1657.35	1655.14	1648.20	1645.16	1643.81	1643.22
130000	1810.28	1805.60	1795.46	1793.06	1785.55	1782.25	1780.80	1780.15
140000	1949.53	1944.49	1933.58	1930.99	1922.90	1919.35	1917.78	1917.09
150000	2088.78	2083.38	2071.69	2068.92	2060.25	2056.44	2054.76	2054.02
160000	2228.04	2222.28	2209.80	2206.85	2197.60	2193.54	2191.75	2190.96
170000	2367.29	2361.17	2347.91	2344.77	2334.95	2330.64	2328.73	2327.89
180000	2506.54	2500.06	2486.03	2482.70	2472.30	2467.73	2465.72	2464.82
190000	2645.79	2638.95	2624.14	2620.63	2609.65	2604.83	2602.70	2601.76
200000	2785.04	2777.84	2762.25	2758.56	2747.00	2741.92	2739.68	2738.69
210000	2924.30	2916.74	2900.36	2896.49	2884.35	2879.02	2876.67	2875.63
220000	3063.55	3055.63	3038.47	3034.41	3021.70	3016.12	3013.65	3012.56
230000	3202.80	3194.52	3176.59	3172.34	3159.05	3153.21	3150.63	3149.50
240000	3342.05	3333.41	3314.70	3310.27	3296.40	3290.31	3287.62	3286.43
250000	3481.30	3472.30	3452.81	3448.20	3433.75	3427.40	3424.60	3423.37
260000	3620.56	3611.20	3590.92	3586.12	3571.10	3564.50	3561.59	3560.30
270000	3759.81	3750.09	3729.04	3724.05	3708.45	3701.60	3698.57	3697.23
280000	3899.06	3888.98	3867.15	3861.98	3845.80	3838.69	3835.55	3834.17
290000	4038.31	4027.87	4005.26	3999.91	3983.15	3975.79	3972.54	3971.10
300000	4177.56	4166.76	4143.37	4137.83	4120.50	4112.88	4109.52	4108.04
310000	4316.82	4305.66	4281.48	4275.76	4257.85	4249.98	4246.51	4244.97
320000	4456.07	4444.55	4419.60	4413.69	4395.20	4387.08	4383.49	4381.91
330000	4595.32	4583.44	4557.71	4551.62	4532.55	4524.17	4520.47	4518.84
340000	4734.57	4722.33	4695.82	4689.54	4669.90	4661.27	4657.46	4655.78
350000	4873.82	4861.22	4833.93	4827.47	4807.25	4798.36	4794.44	4792.71
360000	5013.08	5000.12	4972.05	4965.40	4944.60	4935.46	4931.43	4929.64
370000	5152.33	5139.01	5110.16	5103.33	5081.95	5072.55	5068.41	5066.58
380000	5291.58	5277.90	5248.27	5241.26	5219.30	5209.65	5205.39	5203.51
390000	5430.83	5416.79	5386.38	5379.18	5356.65	5346.75	5342.38	5340.45
400000	5570.08	5555.68	5524.49	5517.11	5494.00	5483.84	5479.36	5477.38

160

BLENDED MONTHLY PAYMENTS 18%
AMORTIZATION IN YEARS

Amount	1	2	3	4	5	6	7	8
25	2.29	1.25	.90	.73	.63	.57	.52	.49
50	4.57	2.49	1.80	1.46	1.26	1.13	1.04	.97
100	9.14	4.97	3.59	2.91	2.51	2.25	2.07	1.94
200	18.28	9.93	7.17	5.81	5.01	4.49	4.13	3.87
300	27.42	14.89	10.75	8.72	7.52	6.74	6.20	5.81
400	36.56	19.85	14.34	11.62	10.02	8.98	8.26	7.74
500	45.69	24.81	17.92	14.53	12.53	11.23	10.33	9.67
600	54.83	29.77	21.50	17.43	15.03	13.47	12.39	11.61
700	63.97	34.74	25.09	20.33	17.54	15.72	14.46	13.54
800	73.11	39.70	28.67	23.24	20.04	17.96	16.52	15.47
900	82.24	44.66	32.25	26.14	22.55	20.21	18.58	17.41
1000	91.38	49.62	35.84	29.05	25.05	22.45	20.65	19.34
2000	182.76	99.24	71.67	58.09	50.10	44.90	41.29	38.68
3000	274.13	148.85	107.50	87.13	75.14	67.35	61.94	58.02
4000	365.51	198.47	143.33	116.17	100.19	89.79	82.58	77.35
5000	456.88	248.08	179.17	145.21	125.24	112.24	103.23	96.69
6000	548.26	297.70	215.00	174.25	150.28	134.69	123.87	116.03
7000	639.63	347.31	250.83	203.30	175.33	157.14	144.52	135.36
8000	731.01	396.93	286.66	232.34	200.38	179.58	165.16	154.70
9000	822.39	446.54	322.49	261.38	225.42	202.03	185.80	174.04
10000	913.76	496.16	358.33	290.42	250.47	224.48	206.45	193.37
20000	1827.52	992.31	716.65	580.84	500.94	448.95	412.89	386.74
30000	2741.27	1488.47	1074.97	871.25	751.40	673.43	619.34	580.11
40000	3655.03	1984.62	1433.29	1161.67	1001.87	897.90	825.78	773.48
50000	4568.79	2480.77	1791.61	1452.08	1252.33	1122.38	1032.22	966.85
60000	5482.54	2976.93	2149.93	1742.50	1502.80	1346.85	1238.67	1160.22
70000	6396.30	3473.08	2508.25	2032.92	1753.26	1571.33	1445.11	1353.59
80000	7310.06	3969.23	2866.57	2323.33	2003.73	1795.80	1651.55	1546.96
90000	8223.81	4465.39	3224.89	2613.75	2254.19	2020.27	1858.00	1740.33
100000	9137.57	4961.54	3583.22	2904.16	2504.66	2244.75	2064.44	1933.70
110000	10051.33	5457.70	3941.54	3194.58	2755.12	2469.22	2270.88	2127.07
120000	10965.08	5953.85	4299.86	3485.00	3005.59	2693.70	2477.33	2320.44
130000	11878.84	6450.00	4658.18	3775.41	3256.05	2918.17	2683.77	2513.81
140000	12792.59	6946.16	5016.50	4065.83	3506.52	3142.65	2890.21	2707.18
150000	13706.35	7442.31	5374.82	4356.24	3756.98	3367.12	3096.66	2900.55
160000	14620.11	7938.46	5733.14	4646.66	4007.45	3591.59	3303.10	3093.92
170000	15533.86	8434.62	6091.46	4937.07	4257.91	3816.07	3509.54	3287.29
180000	16447.62	8930.77	6449.78	5227.49	4508.38	4040.54	3715.99	3480.66
190000	17361.38	9426.93	6808.11	5517.91	4758.84	4265.02	3922.43	3674.03
200000	18275.13	9923.08	7166.43	5808.32	5009.31	4489.49	4128.87	3867.40
210000	19188.89	10419.23	7524.75	6098.74	5259.77	4713.97	4335.32	4060.77
220000	20102.65	10915.39	7883.07	6389.15	5510.24	4938.44	4541.76	4254.14
230000	21016.40	11411.54	8241.39	6679.57	5760.70	5162.91	4748.20	4447.51
240000	21930.16	11907.69	8599.71	6969.99	6011.17	5387.39	4954.65	4640.88
250000	22843.92	12403.85	8958.03	7260.40	6261.63	5611.86	5161.09	4834.25
260000	23757.67	12900.00	9316.35	7550.82	6512.10	5836.34	5367.53	5027.62
270000	24671.43	13396.16	9674.67	7841.23	6762.56	6060.81	5573.98	5220.99
280000	25585.18	13892.31	10032.99	8131.65	7013.03	6285.29	5780.42	5414.36
290000	26498.94	14388.46	10391.32	8422.06	7263.49	6509.76	5986.86	5607.73
300000	27412.70	14884.62	10749.64	8712.48	7513.96	6734.24	6193.31	5801.10
310000	28326.45	15380.77	11107.96	9002.90	7764.42	6958.71	6399.75	5994.47
320000	29240.21	15876.92	11466.28	9293.31	8014.89	7183.18	6606.19	6187.84
330000	30153.97	16373.08	11824.60	9583.73	8265.35	7407.66	6812.64	6381.21
340000	31067.72	16869.23	12182.92	9874.14	8515.82	7632.13	7019.08	6574.58
350000	31981.48	17365.39	12541.24	10164.56	8766.28	7856.61	7225.52	6767.95
360000	32895.24	17861.54	12899.56	10454.98	9016.75	8081.08	7431.97	6961.32
370000	33808.99	18357.69	13257.88	10745.39	9267.21	8305.56	7638.41	7154.69
380000	34722.75	18853.85	13616.21	11035.81	9517.68	8530.03	7844.85	7348.06
390000	35636.51	19350.00	13974.53	11326.22	9768.14	8754.50	8051.30	7541.43
400000	36550.26	19846.15	14332.85	11616.64	10018.61	8978.98	8257.74	7734.80

161

18% BLENDED MONTHLY PAYMENTS
AMORTIZATION IN YEARS

Amount	9	10	11	12	13	14	15	16
25	.46	.45	.43	.42	.41	.40	.40	.39
50	.92	.89	.86	.83	.81	.80	.79	.78
100	1.84	1.77	1.71	1.66	1.62	1.59	1.57	1.55
200	3.68	3.53	3.41	3.32	3.24	3.18	3.13	3.09
300	5.51	5.29	5.11	4.97	4.86	4.77	4.70	4.64
400	7.35	7.05	6.81	6.63	6.48	6.36	6.26	6.18
500	9.18	8.81	8.52	8.28	8.10	7.95	7.83	7.73
600	11.02	10.57	10.22	9.94	9.72	9.54	9.39	9.27
700	12.86	12.33	11.92	11.60	11.34	11.13	10.96	10.82
800	14.69	14.09	13.62	13.25	12.96	12.72	12.52	12.36
900	16.53	15.85	15.33	14.91	14.58	14.31	14.09	13.91
1000	18.36	17.61	17.03	16.56	16.19	15.89	15.65	15.45
2000	36.72	35.22	34.05	33.12	32.38	31.78	31.30	30.90
3000	55.08	52.83	51.07	49.68	48.57	47.67	46.94	46.34
4000	73.44	70.44	68.10	66.24	64.76	63.56	62.59	61.79
5000	91.80	88.05	85.12	82.80	80.95	79.45	78.23	77.24
6000	110.16	105.66	102.14	99.36	97.14	95.34	93.88	92.68
7000	128.51	123.26	119.17	115.92	113.33	111.23	109.53	108.13
8000	146.87	140.87	136.19	132.48	129.52	127.12	125.17	123.58
9000	165.23	158.48	153.21	149.04	145.71	143.01	140.82	139.02
10000	183.59	176.09	170.24	165.60	161.89	158.90	156.46	154.47
20000	367.17	352.17	340.47	331.20	323.78	317.79	312.92	308.93
30000	550.76	528.26	510.70	496.80	485.67	476.69	469.38	463.40
40000	734.34	704.34	680.93	662.40	647.56	635.58	625.84	617.86
50000	917.93	880.43	851.16	828.00	809.45	794.48	782.30	772.33
60000	1101.51	1056.51	1021.39	993.60	971.34	953.37	938.76	926.79
70000	1285.10	1232.60	1191.63	1159.19	1133.23	1112.27	1095.21	1081.26
80000	1468.68	1408.68	1361.86	1324.79	1295.12	1271.16	1251.67	1235.72
90000	1652.27	1584.77	1532.09	1490.39	1457.01	1430.06	1408.13	1390.19
100000	1835.85	1760.85	1702.32	1655.99	1618.90	1588.95	1564.59	1544.65
110000	2019.44	1936.94	1872.55	1821.59	1780.79	1747.85	1721.05	1699.12
120000	2203.02	2113.02	2042.78	1987.19	1942.68	1906.74	1877.51	1853.58
130000	2386.61	2289.11	2213.02	2152.78	2104.57	2065.64	2033.96	2008.05
140000	2570.19	2465.19	2383.25	2318.38	2266.46	2224.53	2190.42	2162.51
150000	2753.78	2641.28	2553.48	2483.98	2428.35	2383.43	2346.88	2316.98
160000	2937.36	2817.36	2723.71	2649.58	2590.24	2542.32	2503.34	2471.44
170000	3120.95	2993.45	2893.94	2815.18	2752.13	2701.21	2659.80	2625.91
180000	3304.53	3169.53	3064.17	2980.78	2914.02	2860.11	2816.26	2780.37
190000	3488.11	3345.62	3234.41	3146.37	3075.91	3019.00	2972.71	2934.84
200000	3671.70	3521.70	3404.64	3311.97	3237.80	3177.90	3129.17	3089.30
210000	3855.28	3697.79	3574.87	3477.57	3399.69	3336.79	3285.63	3243.77
220000	4038.87	3873.87	3745.10	3643.17	3561.58	3495.69	3442.09	3398.23
230000	4222.45	4049.96	3915.33	3808.77	3723.47	3654.58	3598.55	3552.70
240000	4406.04	4226.04	4085.56	3974.37	3885.36	3813.48	3755.01	3707.16
250000	4589.62	4402.13	4255.79	4139.96	4047.25	3972.37	3911.46	3861.63
260000	4773.21	4578.21	4426.03	4305.56	4209.14	4131.27	4067.92	4016.09
270000	4956.79	4754.30	4596.26	4471.16	4371.03	4290.16	4224.38	4170.56
280000	5140.38	4930.38	4766.49	4636.76	4532.92	4449.06	4380.84	4325.02
290000	5323.96	5106.47	4936.72	4802.36	4694.81	4607.95	4537.30	4479.49
300000	5507.55	5282.55	5106.95	4967.96	4856.70	4766.85	4693.76	4633.95
310000	5691.13	5458.64	5277.18	5133.55	5018.59	4925.74	4850.21	4788.42
320000	5874.72	5634.72	5447.42	5299.15	5180.48	5084.64	5006.67	4942.88
330000	6058.30	5810.81	5617.65	5464.75	5342.37	5243.53	5163.13	5097.35
340000	6241.89	5986.89	5787.88	5630.35	5504.26	5402.42	5319.59	5251.81
350000	6425.47	6162.98	5958.11	5795.95	5666.15	5561.32	5476.05	5406.28
360000	6609.06	6339.06	6128.34	5961.55	5828.04	5720.21	5632.51	5560.74
370000	6792.64	6515.15	6298.57	6127.14	5989.93	5879.11	5788.96	5715.21
380000	6976.22	6691.23	6468.81	6292.74	6151.82	6038.00	5945.42	5869.67
390000	7159.81	6867.32	6639.04	6458.34	6313.71	6196.90	6101.88	6024.14
400000	7343.39	7043.40	6809.27	6623.94	6475.60	6355.79	6258.34	6178.60

162

BLENDED MONTHLY PAYMENTS 18%
AMORTIZATION IN YEARS

Amount	17	18	19	20	21	22	23	24
25	.39	.38	.38	.38	.38	.38	.37	.37
50	.77	.76	.76	.75	.75	.75	.74	.74
100	1.53	1.52	1.51	1.50	1.49	1.49	1.48	1.48
200	3.06	3.03	3.01	2.99	2.98	2.97	2.95	2.95
300	4.59	4.55	4.52	4.49	4.46	4.45	4.43	4.42
400	6.12	6.06	6.02	5.98	5.95	5.93	5.90	5.89
500	7.65	7.58	7.52	7.48	7.44	7.41	7.38	7.36
600	9.17	9.09	9.03	8.97	8.92	8.89	8.85	8.83
700	10.70	10.61	10.53	10.46	10.41	10.37	10.33	10.30
800	12.23	12.12	12.03	11.96	11.90	11.85	11.80	11.77
900	13.76	13.64	13.54	13.45	13.38	13.33	13.28	13.24
1000	15.29	15.15	15.04	14.95	14.87	14.81	14.75	14.71
2000	30.57	30.30	30.08	29.89	29.73	29.61	29.50	29.41
3000	45.85	45.45	45.11	44.83	44.60	44.41	44.24	44.11
4000	61.14	60.59	60.15	59.77	59.46	59.21	58.99	58.81
5000	76.42	75.74	75.18	74.72	74.33	74.01	73.74	73.51
6000	91.70	90.89	90.22	89.66	89.19	88.81	88.48	88.21
7000	106.98	106.04	105.25	104.60	104.06	103.61	103.23	102.92
8000	122.27	121.18	120.29	119.54	118.92	118.41	117.98	117.62
9000	137.55	136.33	135.32	134.49	133.79	133.21	132.72	132.32
10000	152.83	151.48	150.36	149.43	148.65	148.01	147.47	147.02
20000	305.66	302.95	300.71	298.85	297.30	296.01	294.94	294.03
30000	458.48	454.43	451.06	448.27	445.95	444.02	442.40	441.05
40000	611.31	605.90	601.42	597.70	594.60	592.02	589.87	588.06
50000	764.14	757.37	751.77	747.12	743.25	740.03	737.33	735.08
60000	916.96	908.85	902.12	896.54	891.90	888.03	884.80	882.09
70000	1069.79	1060.32	1052.48	1045.97	1040.55	1036.03	1032.26	1029.11
80000	1222.61	1211.79	1202.83	1195.39	1189.20	1184.04	1179.73	1176.12
90000	1375.44	1363.27	1353.18	1344.81	1337.85	1332.04	1327.19	1323.14
100000	1528.27	1514.74	1503.54	1494.24	1486.50	1480.05	1474.66	1470.15
110000	1681.09	1666.21	1653.89	1643.66	1635.15	1628.05	1622.12	1617.17
120000	1833.92	1817.69	1804.24	1793.08	1783.80	1776.05	1769.59	1764.18
130000	1986.74	1969.16	1954.60	1942.51	1932.45	1924.06	1917.05	1911.20
140000	2139.57	2120.63	2104.95	2091.93	2081.09	2072.06	2064.52	2058.21
150000	2292.40	2272.11	2255.30	2241.35	2229.74	2220.07	2211.99	2205.23
160000	2445.22	2423.58	2405.66	2390.78	2378.39	2368.07	2359.45	2352.24
170000	2598.05	2575.05	2556.01	2540.20	2527.04	2516.07	2506.92	2499.26
180000	2750.87	2726.53	2706.36	2689.62	2675.69	2664.08	2654.38	2646.27
190000	2903.70	2878.00	2856.72	2839.05	2824.34	2812.08	2801.85	2793.29
200000	3056.53	3029.47	3007.07	2988.47	2972.99	2960.09	2949.31	2940.30
210000	3209.35	3180.95	3157.42	3137.89	3121.64	3108.09	3096.78	3087.32
220000	3362.18	3332.42	3307.78	3287.32	3270.29	3256.09	3244.24	3234.33
230000	3515.00	3483.89	3458.13	3436.74	3418.94	3404.10	3391.71	3381.35
240000	3667.83	3635.37	3608.48	3586.16	3567.59	3552.10	3539.17	3528.36
250000	3820.66	3786.84	3758.84	3735.58	3716.24	3700.11	3686.64	3675.38
260000	3973.48	3938.31	3909.19	3885.01	3864.89	3848.11	3834.10	3822.39
270000	4126.31	4089.79	4059.54	4034.43	4013.54	3996.12	3981.57	3969.41
280000	4279.13	4241.26	4209.90	4183.85	4162.18	4144.12	4129.04	4116.42
290000	4431.96	4392.73	4360.25	4333.28	4310.83	4292.12	4276.50	4263.44
300000	4584.79	4544.21	4510.60	4482.70	4459.48	4440.13	4423.97	4410.45
310000	4737.61	4695.68	4660.95	4632.12	4608.13	4588.13	4571.43	4557.47
320000	4890.44	4847.15	4811.31	4781.55	4756.78	4736.14	4718.90	4704.48
330000	5043.26	4998.63	4961.66	4930.97	4905.43	4884.14	4866.36	4851.50
340000	5196.09	5150.10	5112.01	5080.39	5054.08	5032.14	5013.83	4998.51
350000	5348.92	5301.57	5262.37	5229.82	5202.73	5180.15	5161.29	5145.53
360000	5501.74	5453.05	5412.72	5379.24	5351.38	5328.15	5308.76	5292.54
370000	5654.57	5604.52	5563.07	5528.66	5500.03	5476.16	5456.22	5439.56
380000	5807.39	5755.99	5713.43	5678.09	5648.68	5624.16	5603.69	5586.57
390000	5960.22	5907.47	5863.78	5827.51	5797.33	5772.16	5751.15	5733.59
400000	6113.05	6058.94	6014.13	5976.93	5945.98	5920.17	5898.62	5880.60

163

18% BLENDED MONTHLY PAYMENTS
AMORTIZATION IN YEARS

Amount	25	26	29	30	35	40	45	50
25	.37	.37	.37	.37	.37	.37	.37	.37
50	.74	.74	.73	.73	.73	.73	.73	.73
100	1.47	1.47	1.46	1.46	1.46	1.45	1.45	1.45
200	2.94	2.93	2.92	2.91	2.91	2.90	2.90	2.90
300	4.40	4.39	4.37	4.37	4.36	4.35	4.35	4.35
400	5.87	5.86	5.83	5.82	5.81	5.80	5.79	5.79
500	7.34	7.32	7.29	7.28	7.26	7.25	7.24	7.24
600	8.80	8.78	8.74	8.73	8.71	8.69	8.69	8.69
700	10.27	10.25	10.20	10.19	10.16	10.14	10.14	10.13
800	11.74	11.71	11.66	11.64	11.61	11.59	11.58	11.58
900	13.20	13.17	13.11	13.10	13.06	13.04	13.03	13.03
1000	14.67	14.64	14.57	14.55	14.51	14.49	14.48	14.47
2000	29.33	29.27	29.13	29.10	29.01	28.97	28.95	28.94
3000	44.00	43.90	43.70	43.65	43.51	43.45	43.42	43.41
4000	58.66	58.53	58.26	58.20	58.01	57.93	57.90	57.88
5000	73.32	73.17	72.83	72.75	72.51	72.41	72.37	72.35
6000	87.99	87.80	87.39	87.30	87.01	86.89	86.84	86.82
7000	102.65	102.43	101.96	101.85	101.51	101.37	101.31	101.29
8000	117.32	117.06	116.52	116.40	116.02	115.86	115.79	115.76
9000	131.98	131.69	131.09	130.95	130.52	130.34	130.26	130.23
10000	146.64	146.33	145.65	145.50	145.02	144.82	144.73	144.70
20000	293.28	292.65	291.30	290.99	290.03	289.63	289.46	289.39
30000	439.92	438.97	436.95	436.48	435.05	434.44	434.19	434.08
40000	586.56	585.29	582.60	581.97	580.06	579.26	578.92	578.77
50000	733.19	731.62	728.25	727.47	725.07	724.07	723.64	723.47
60000	879.83	877.94	873.90	872.96	870.09	868.88	868.37	868.16
70000	1026.47	1024.26	1019.55	1018.45	1015.10	1013.69	1013.10	1012.85
80000	1173.11	1170.58	1165.20	1163.94	1160.12	1158.51	1157.83	1157.54
90000	1319.75	1316.90	1310.85	1309.44	1305.13	1303.32	1302.56	1302.23
100000	1466.38	1463.23	1456.49	1454.93	1450.14	1448.13	1447.28	1446.93
110000	1613.02	1609.55	1602.14	1600.42	1595.16	1592.94	1592.01	1591.62
120000	1759.66	1755.87	1747.79	1745.91	1740.17	1737.76	1736.74	1736.31
130000	1906.30	1902.19	1893.44	1891.41	1885.19	1882.57	1881.47	1881.00
140000	2052.94	2048.52	2039.09	2036.90	2030.20	2027.38	2026.20	2025.69
150000	2199.57	2194.84	2184.74	2182.39	2175.21	2172.20	2170.92	2170.39
160000	2346.21	2341.16	2330.39	2327.88	2320.23	2317.01	2315.65	2315.08
170000	2492.85	2487.48	2476.04	2473.38	2465.24	2461.82	2460.38	2459.77
180000	2639.49	2633.80	2621.69	2618.87	2610.26	2606.63	2605.11	2604.46
190000	2786.13	2780.13	2767.34	2764.36	2755.27	2751.45	2749.83	2749.15
200000	2932.76	2926.45	2912.98	2909.85	2900.28	2896.26	2894.56	2893.85
210000	3079.40	3072.77	3058.63	3055.35	3045.30	3041.07	3039.29	3038.54
220000	3226.04	3219.09	3204.28	3200.84	3190.31	3185.88	3184.02	3183.23
230000	3372.68	3365.42	3349.93	3346.33	3335.32	3330.70	3328.75	3327.92
240000	3519.32	3511.74	3495.58	3491.82	3480.34	3475.51	3473.47	3472.62
250000	3665.95	3658.06	3641.23	3637.32	3625.35	3620.32	3618.20	3617.31
260000	3812.59	3804.38	3786.88	3782.81	3770.37	3765.14	3762.93	3762.00
270000	3959.23	3950.70	3932.53	3928.30	3915.38	3909.95	3907.66	3906.69
280000	4105.87	4097.03	4078.18	4073.79	4060.39	4054.76	4052.39	4051.38
290000	4252.51	4243.35	4223.82	4219.29	4205.41	4199.57	4197.11	4196.08
300000	4399.14	4389.67	4369.47	4364.78	4350.42	4344.39	4341.84	4340.77
310000	4545.78	4535.99	4515.12	4510.27	4495.44	4489.20	4486.57	4485.46
320000	4692.42	4682.32	4660.77	4655.76	4640.45	4634.01	4631.30	4630.15
330000	4839.06	4828.64	4806.42	4801.26	4785.46	4778.82	4776.03	4774.84
340000	4985.70	4974.96	4952.07	4946.75	4930.48	4923.64	4920.75	4919.54
350000	5132.33	5121.28	5097.72	5092.24	5075.49	5068.45	5065.48	5064.23
360000	5278.97	5267.60	5243.37	5237.73	5220.51	5213.26	5210.21	5208.92
370000	5425.61	5413.93	5389.02	5383.23	5365.52	5358.08	5354.94	5353.61
380000	5572.25	5560.25	5534.67	5528.72	5510.53	5502.89	5499.66	5498.30
390000	5718.89	5706.57	5680.31	5674.21	5655.55	5647.70	5644.39	5643.00
400000	5865.52	5852.89	5825.96	5819.70	5800.56	5792.51	5789.12	5787.69

BLENDED MONTHLY PAYMENTS 19%
AMORTIZATION IN YEARS

Amount	1	2	3	4	5	6	7	8
25	2.30	1.26	.91	.74	.64	.58	.53	.50
50	4.60	2.51	1.82	1.48	1.28	1.15	1.06	1.00
100	9.19	5.01	3.63	2.96	2.56	2.30	2.12	1.99
200	18.37	10.02	7.26	5.91	5.12	4.60	4.24	3.98
300	27.55	15.02	10.89	8.86	7.67	6.90	6.36	5.97
400	36.73	20.03	14.52	11.82	10.23	9.19	8.48	7.96
500	45.91	25.04	18.15	14.77	12.78	11.49	10.60	9.95
600	55.10	30.04	21.78	17.72	15.34	13.79	12.72	11.94
700	64.28	35.05	25.41	20.67	17.89	16.08	14.84	13.93
800	73.46	40.06	29.04	23.63	20.45	18.38	16.95	15.92
900	82.64	45.06	32.67	26.58	23.00	20.68	19.07	17.91
1000	91.82	50.07	36.30	29.53	25.56	22.98	21.19	19.90
2000	183.64	100.13	72.60	59.06	51.11	45.95	42.38	39.80
3000	275.46	150.20	108.90	88.58	76.66	68.92	63.57	59.70
4000	367.28	200.26	145.19	118.11	102.21	91.89	84.75	79.60
5000	459.09	250.32	181.49	147.64	127.76	114.86	105.94	99.50
6000	550.91	300.39	217.79	177.16	153.31	137.83	127.13	119.40
7000	642.73	350.45	254.09	206.69	178.86	160.80	148.32	139.30
8000	734.55	400.52	290.38	236.21	204.41	183.78	169.50	159.19
9000	826.36	450.58	326.68	265.74	229.96	206.75	190.69	179.09
10000	918.18	500.64	362.98	295.27	255.51	229.72	211.88	198.99
20000	1836.36	1001.28	725.95	590.53	511.02	459.43	423.75	397.98
30000	2754.53	1501.92	1088.93	885.79	766.53	689.15	635.63	596.97
40000	3672.71	2002.56	1451.90	1181.05	1022.04	918.86	847.50	795.95
50000	4590.88	2503.19	1814.88	1476.31	1277.55	1148.57	1059.38	994.94
60000	5509.06	3003.83	2177.85	1771.57	1533.05	1378.29	1271.25	1193.93
70000	6427.23	3504.47	2540.83	2066.84	1788.56	1608.00	1483.13	1392.91
80000	7345.41	4005.11	2903.80	2362.10	2044.07	1837.72	1695.00	1591.90
90000	8263.58	4505.74	3266.78	2657.36	2299.58	2067.43	1906.88	1790.89
100000	9181.76	5006.38	3629.75	2952.62	2555.09	2297.14	2118.75	1989.87
110000	10099.93	5507.02	3992.73	3247.88	2810.59	2526.86	2330.63	2188.86
120000	11018.11	6007.66	4355.70	3543.14	3066.10	2756.57	2542.50	2387.85
130000	11936.28	6508.30	4718.68	3838.40	3321.61	2986.28	2754.38	2586.83
140000	12854.46	7008.93	5081.65	4133.67	3577.12	3216.00	2966.25	2785.82
150000	13772.63	7509.57	5444.62	4428.93	3832.63	3445.71	3178.13	2984.81
160000	14690.81	8010.21	5807.60	4724.19	4088.14	3675.43	3390.00	3183.80
170000	15608.98	8510.85	6170.57	5019.45	4343.64	3905.14	3601.88	3382.78
180000	16527.16	9011.48	6533.55	5314.71	4599.15	4134.85	3813.75	3581.77
190000	17445.33	9512.12	6896.52	5609.97	4854.66	4364.57	4025.63	3780.76
200000	18363.51	10012.76	7259.50	5905.23	5110.17	4594.28	4237.50	3979.74
210000	19281.68	10513.40	7622.47	6200.50	5365.68	4823.99	4449.37	4178.73
220000	20199.86	11014.04	7985.45	6495.76	5621.18	5053.71	4661.25	4377.72
230000	21118.03	11514.67	8348.42	6791.02	5876.69	5283.42	4873.12	4576.70
240000	22036.21	12015.31	8711.39	7086.28	6132.20	5513.14	5085.00	4775.69
250000	22954.38	12515.95	9074.37	7381.54	6387.71	5742.85	5296.87	4974.68
260000	23872.56	13016.59	9437.34	7676.80	6643.22	5972.56	5508.75	5173.66
270000	24790.73	13517.22	9800.32	7972.06	6898.73	6202.28	5720.62	5372.65
280000	25708.91	14017.86	10163.29	8267.33	7154.23	6431.99	5932.50	5571.64
290000	26627.08	14518.50	10526.27	8562.59	7409.74	6661.70	6144.37	5770.63
300000	27545.26	15019.14	10889.24	8857.85	7665.25	6891.42	6356.25	5969.61
310000	28463.43	15519.78	11252.22	9153.11	7920.76	7121.13	6568.12	6168.60
320000	29381.61	16020.41	11615.19	9448.37	8176.27	7350.85	6780.00	6367.59
330000	30299.78	16521.05	11978.17	9743.63	8431.77	7580.56	6991.87	6566.57
340000	31217.96	17021.69	12341.14	10038.89	8687.28	7810.27	7203.75	6765.56
350000	32136.13	17522.33	12704.11	10334.16	8942.79	8039.99	7415.62	6964.55
360000	33054.31	18022.96	13067.09	10629.42	9198.30	8269.70	7627.50	7163.53
370000	33972.48	18523.60	13430.06	10924.68	9453.81	8499.42	7839.37	7362.52
380000	34890.66	19024.24	13793.04	11219.94	9709.32	8729.13	8051.25	7561.51
390000	35808.83	19524.88	14156.01	11515.20	9964.82	8958.84	8263.12	7760.49
400000	36727.01	20025.51	14518.99	11810.46	10220.33	9188.56	8475.00	7959.48

19% BLENDED MONTHLY PAYMENTS
AMORTIZATION IN YEARS

Amount	9	10	11	12	13	14	15	16
25	.48	.46	.45	.43	.43	.42	.41	.41
50	.95	.92	.89	.86	.85	.83	.82	.81
100	1.90	1.83	1.77	1.72	1.69	1.66	1.64	1.62
200	3.79	3.65	3.53	3.44	3.37	3.31	3.27	3.23
300	5.69	5.47	5.30	5.16	5.05	4.97	4.90	4.84
400	7.58	7.29	7.06	6.88	6.74	6.62	6.53	6.45
500	9.47	9.11	8.82	8.60	8.42	8.28	8.16	8.07
600	11.37	10.93	10.59	10.32	10.10	9.93	9.79	9.68
700	13.26	12.75	12.35	12.04	11.79	11.59	11.42	11.29
800	15.16	14.57	14.11	13.75	13.47	13.24	13.05	12.90
900	17.05	16.39	15.88	15.47	15.15	14.89	14.69	14.52
1000	18.94	18.21	17.64	17.19	16.84	16.55	16.32	16.13
2000	37.88	36.41	35.28	34.38	33.67	33.09	32.63	32.25
3000	56.82	54.62	52.91	51.57	50.50	49.64	48.94	48.38
4000	75.76	72.82	70.55	68.75	67.33	66.18	65.25	64.50
5000	94.69	91.03	88.18	85.94	84.16	82.73	81.57	80.63
6000	113.63	109.23	105.82	103.13	100.99	99.27	97.88	96.75
7000	132.57	127.44	123.45	120.32	117.82	115.81	114.19	112.87
8000	151.51	145.64	141.09	137.50	134.65	132.36	130.50	129.00
9000	170.45	163.85	158.72	154.69	151.48	148.90	146.82	145.12
10000	189.38	182.05	176.36	171.88	168.31	165.45	163.13	161.25
20000	378.76	364.10	352.72	343.75	336.61	330.89	326.25	322.49
30000	568.14	546.15	529.07	515.62	504.92	496.33	489.38	483.73
40000	757.52	728.20	705.43	687.50	673.22	661.77	652.50	644.97
50000	946.90	910.25	881.78	859.37	841.53	827.21	815.63	806.22
60000	1136.28	1092.30	1058.14	1031.24	1009.83	992.65	978.75	967.46
70000	1325.66	1274.35	1234.49	1203.11	1178.14	1158.09	1141.88	1128.70
80000	1515.04	1456.40	1410.85	1374.99	1346.44	1323.53	1305.00	1289.94
90000	1704.42	1638.44	1587.20	1546.86	1514.75	1488.97	1468.13	1451.19
100000	1893.80	1820.49	1763.56	1718.73	1683.05	1654.41	1631.25	1612.43
110000	2083.18	2002.54	1939.92	1890.60	1851.35	1819.85	1794.38	1773.67
120000	2272.56	2184.59	2116.27	2062.48	2019.66	1985.29	1957.50	1934.91
130000	2461.94	2366.64	2292.63	2234.35	2187.96	2150.73	2120.62	2096.16
140000	2651.32	2548.69	2468.98	2406.22	2356.27	2316.17	2283.75	2257.40
150000	2840.70	2730.74	2645.34	2578.09	2524.57	2481.61	2446.87	2418.64
160000	3030.08	2912.79	2821.69	2749.97	2692.88	2647.05	2610.00	2579.88
170000	3219.46	3094.84	2998.05	2921.84	2861.18	2812.49	2773.12	2741.13
180000	3408.84	3276.88	3174.40	3093.71	3029.49	2977.93	2936.25	2902.37
190000	3598.22	3458.93	3350.76	3265.58	3197.79	3143.37	3099.37	3063.61
200000	3787.59	3640.98	3527.12	3437.46	3366.09	3308.81	3262.50	3224.85
210000	3976.97	3823.03	3703.47	3609.33	3534.40	3474.25	3425.62	3386.10
220000	4166.35	4005.08	3879.83	3781.20	3702.70	3639.69	3588.75	3547.34
230000	4355.73	4187.13	4056.18	3953.07	3871.01	3805.13	3751.87	3708.58
240000	4545.11	4369.18	4232.54	4124.95	4039.31	3970.57	3914.99	3869.82
250000	4734.49	4551.23	4408.89	4296.82	4207.62	4136.01	4078.12	4031.07
260000	4923.87	4733.28	4585.25	4468.69	4375.92	4301.45	4241.24	4192.31
270000	5113.25	4915.32	4761.60	4640.57	4544.23	4466.89	4404.37	4353.55
280000	5302.63	5097.37	4937.96	4812.44	4712.53	4632.33	4567.49	4514.79
290000	5492.01	5279.42	5114.31	4984.31	4880.84	4797.77	4730.62	4676.04
300000	5681.39	5461.47	5290.67	5156.18	5049.14	4963.21	4893.74	4837.28
310000	5870.77	5643.52	5467.03	5328.06	5217.44	5128.65	5056.87	4998.52
320000	6060.15	5825.57	5643.38	5499.93	5385.75	5294.09	5219.99	5159.76
330000	6249.53	6007.62	5819.74	5671.80	5554.05	5459.53	5383.12	5321.01
340000	6438.91	6189.67	5996.09	5843.67	5722.36	5624.97	5546.24	5482.25
350000	6628.29	6371.72	6172.45	6015.55	5890.66	5790.41	5709.36	5643.49
360000	6817.67	6553.76	6348.80	6187.42	6058.97	5955.85	5872.49	5804.73
370000	7007.05	6735.81	6525.16	6359.29	6227.27	6121.29	6035.61	5965.97
380000	7196.43	6917.86	6701.51	6531.16	6395.58	6286.73	6198.74	6127.22
390000	7385.81	7099.91	6877.87	6703.04	6563.88	6452.17	6361.86	6288.46
400000	7575.18	7281.96	7054.23	6874.91	6732.18	6617.61	6524.99	6449.70

Amount	17	18	19	20	21	22	23	24
25	.40	.40	.40	.40	.39	.39	.39	.39
50	.80	.80	.79	.79	.78	.78	.78	.78
100	1.60	1.59	1.58	1.57	1.56	1.56	1.55	1.55
200	3.20	3.17	3.15	3.14	3.12	3.11	3.10	3.09
300	4.80	4.76	4.73	4.70	4.68	4.66	4.65	4.64
400	6.39	6.34	6.30	6.27	6.24	6.22	6.20	6.18
500	7.99	7.93	7.88	7.83	7.80	7.77	7.74	7.72
600	9.59	9.51	9.45	9.40	9.36	9.32	9.29	9.27
700	11.18	11.10	11.02	10.96	10.91	10.87	10.84	10.81
800	12.78	12.68	12.60	12.53	12.47	12.43	12.39	12.36
900	14.38	14.27	14.17	14.10	14.03	13.98	13.94	13.90
1000	15.98	15.85	15.75	15.66	15.59	15.53	15.48	15.44
2000	31.95	31.69	31.49	31.32	31.18	31.06	30.96	30.88
3000	47.92	47.54	47.23	46.97	46.76	46.59	46.44	46.32
4000	63.89	63.38	62.97	62.63	62.35	62.11	61.92	61.76
5000	79.86	79.23	78.71	78.28	77.93	77.64	77.40	77.20
6000	95.83	95.07	94.45	93.94	93.52	93.17	92.88	92.64
7000	111.80	110.92	110.19	109.60	109.10	108.69	108.36	108.08
8000	127.77	126.76	125.93	125.25	124.69	124.22	123.84	123.51
9000	143.74	142.61	141.67	140.91	140.27	139.75	139.31	138.95
10000	159.71	158.45	157.42	156.56	155.86	155.28	154.79	154.39
20000	319.42	316.90	314.83	313.12	311.71	310.55	309.58	308.78
30000	479.12	475.34	472.24	469.68	467.56	465.82	464.37	463.17
40000	638.83	633.79	629.65	626.24	623.42	621.09	619.16	617.55
50000	798.53	792.24	787.06	782.79	779.27	776.36	773.94	771.94
60000	958.24	950.68	944.47	939.35	935.12	931.63	928.73	926.33
70000	1117.94	1109.13	1101.88	1095.91	1090.98	1086.90	1083.52	1080.72
80000	1277.65	1267.57	1259.29	1252.47	1246.83	1242.17	1238.31	1235.10
90000	1437.36	1426.02	1416.70	1409.02	1402.68	1397.44	1393.09	1389.49
100000	1597.06	1584.47	1574.11	1565.58	1558.54	1552.71	1547.88	1543.88
110000	1756.77	1742.91	1731.52	1722.14	1714.39	1707.98	1702.67	1698.27
120000	1916.47	1901.36	1888.93	1878.70	1870.24	1863.25	1857.46	1852.65
130000	2076.18	2059.80	2046.35	2035.25	2026.09	2018.52	2012.24	2007.04
140000	2235.88	2218.25	2203.76	2191.81	2181.95	2173.79	2167.03	2161.43
150000	2395.59	2376.70	2361.17	2348.37	2337.80	2329.06	2321.82	2315.81
160000	2555.29	2535.14	2518.58	2504.93	2493.65	2484.33	2476.61	2470.20
170000	2715.00	2693.59	2675.99	2661.48	2649.51	2639.60	2631.39	2624.59
180000	2874.71	2852.04	2833.40	2818.04	2805.36	2794.87	2786.18	2778.98
190000	3034.41	3010.48	2990.81	2974.60	2961.21	2950.14	2940.97	2933.36
200000	3194.12	3168.93	3148.22	3131.16	3117.07	3105.41	3095.76	3087.75
210000	3353.82	3327.37	3305.63	3287.71	3272.92	3260.68	3250.54	3242.14
220000	3513.53	3485.82	3463.04	3444.27	3428.77	3415.95	3405.33	3396.53
230000	3673.23	3644.27	3620.45	3600.83	3584.63	3571.22	3560.12	3550.91
240000	3832.94	3802.71	3777.86	3757.39	3740.48	3726.49	3714.91	3705.30
250000	3992.65	3961.16	3935.27	3913.94	3896.33	3881.76	3869.70	3859.69
260000	4152.35	4119.60	4092.69	4070.50	4052.18	4037.03	4024.48	4014.08
270000	4312.06	4278.05	4250.10	4227.06	4208.04	4192.30	4179.27	4168.46
280000	4471.76	4436.50	4407.51	4383.62	4363.89	4347.57	4334.06	4322.85
290000	4631.47	4594.94	4564.92	4540.17	4519.74	4502.84	4488.85	4477.24
300000	4791.17	4753.39	4722.33	4696.73	4675.60	4658.11	4643.63	4631.62
310000	4950.88	4911.83	4879.74	4853.29	4831.45	4813.38	4798.42	4786.01
320000	5110.58	5070.28	5037.15	5009.85	4987.30	4968.65	4953.21	4940.40
330000	5270.29	5228.73	5194.56	5166.41	5143.16	5123.92	5108.00	5094.79
340000	5430.00	5387.17	5351.97	5322.96	5299.01	5279.20	5262.78	5249.17
350000	5589.70	5545.62	5509.38	5479.52	5454.86	5434.47	5417.57	5403.56
360000	5749.41	5704.07	5666.79	5636.08	5610.72	5589.74	5572.36	5557.95
370000	5909.11	5862.51	5824.20	5792.64	5766.57	5745.01	5727.15	5712.34
380000	6068.82	6020.96	5981.61	5949.19	5922.42	5900.28	5881.93	5866.72
390000	6228.52	6179.40	6139.03	6105.75	6078.27	6055.55	6036.72	6021.11
400000	6388.23	6337.85	6296.44	6262.31	6234.13	6210.82	6191.51	6175.50

19% BLENDED MONTHLY PAYMENTS
AMORTIZATION IN YEARS

Amount	25	26	29	30	35	40	45	50
25	.39	.39	.39	.39	.39	.39	.39	.39
50	.78	.77	.77	.77	.77	.77	.77	.77
100	1.55	1.54	1.54	1.54	1.53	1.53	1.53	1.53
200	3.09	3.08	3.07	3.07	3.06	3.06	3.05	3.05
300	4.63	4.62	4.60	4.60	4.59	4.58	4.58	4.58
400	6.17	6.16	6.13	6.13	6.11	6.11	6.10	6.10
500	7.71	7.69	7.66	7.66	7.64	7.63	7.63	7.63
600	9.25	9.23	9.20	9.19	9.17	9.16	9.15	9.15
700	10.79	10.77	10.73	10.72	10.69	10.68	10.68	10.67
800	12.33	12.31	12.26	12.25	12.22	12.21	12.20	12.20
900	13.87	13.85	13.79	13.78	13.75	13.73	13.73	13.72
1000	15.41	15.38	15.32	15.31	15.27	15.26	15.25	15.25
2000	30.82	30.76	30.64	30.62	30.54	30.51	30.50	30.49
3000	46.22	46.14	45.96	45.93	45.81	45.76	45.74	45.73
4000	61.63	61.52	61.28	61.23	61.07	61.01	60.99	60.97
5000	77.03	76.89	76.60	76.54	76.34	76.26	76.23	76.22
6000	92.44	92.27	91.92	91.85	91.61	91.51	91.48	91.46
7000	107.84	107.65	107.24	107.15	106.88	106.76	106.72	106.70
8000	123.25	123.03	122.56	122.46	122.14	122.02	121.97	121.94
9000	138.65	138.41	137.88	137.77	137.41	137.27	137.21	137.19
10000	154.06	153.78	153.20	153.07	152.68	152.52	152.46	152.43
20000	308.12	307.56	306.40	306.14	305.35	305.03	304.91	304.85
30000	462.17	461.34	459.60	459.21	458.02	457.55	457.36	457.28
40000	616.23	615.12	612.80	612.28	610.70	610.06	609.81	609.70
50000	770.28	768.90	766.00	765.34	763.37	762.58	762.26	762.13
60000	924.34	922.68	919.20	918.41	916.04	915.09	914.71	914.55
70000	1078.39	1076.46	1072.40	1071.48	1068.72	1067.60	1067.16	1066.98
80000	1232.45	1230.24	1225.60	1224.55	1221.39	1220.12	1219.61	1219.40
90000	1386.50	1384.02	1378.80	1377.61	1374.06	1372.63	1372.06	1371.82
100000	1540.56	1537.80	1532.00	1530.68	1526.73	1525.15	1524.51	1524.25
110000	1694.61	1691.57	1685.20	1683.75	1679.41	1677.66	1676.96	1676.67
120000	1848.67	1845.35	1838.40	1836.82	1832.08	1830.18	1829.41	1829.10
130000	2002.72	1999.13	1991.60	1989.89	1984.75	1982.69	1981.86	1981.52
140000	2156.78	2152.91	2144.80	2142.95	2137.43	2135.20	2134.31	2133.95
150000	2310.83	2306.69	2298.00	2296.02	2290.10	2287.72	2286.76	2286.37
160000	2464.89	2460.47	2451.20	2449.09	2442.77	2440.23	2439.21	2438.80
170000	2618.94	2614.25	2604.40	2602.16	2595.44	2592.75	2591.66	2591.22
180000	2773.00	2768.03	2757.60	2755.22	2748.12	2745.26	2744.11	2743.64
190000	2927.05	2921.81	2910.80	2908.29	2900.79	2897.77	2896.56	2896.07
200000	3081.11	3075.59	3064.00	3061.36	3053.46	3050.29	3049.01	3048.49
210000	3235.16	3229.36	3217.20	3214.43	3206.14	3202.80	3201.46	3200.92
220000	3389.22	3383.14	3370.40	3367.50	3358.81	3355.32	3353.91	3353.34
230000	3543.27	3536.92	3523.60	3520.56	3511.48	3507.83	3506.36	3505.77
240000	3697.33	3690.70	3676.80	3673.63	3664.16	3660.35	3658.81	3658.19
250000	3851.38	3844.48	3830.00	3826.70	3816.83	3812.86	3811.26	3810.62
260000	4005.44	3998.26	3983.20	3979.77	3969.50	3965.37	3963.71	3963.04
270000	4159.49	4152.04	4136.40	4132.83	4122.17	4117.89	4116.16	4115.46
280000	4313.55	4305.82	4289.60	4285.90	4274.85	4270.40	4268.61	4267.89
290000	4467.60	4459.60	4442.80	4438.97	4427.52	4422.92	4421.06	4420.31
300000	4621.66	4613.38	4596.00	4592.04	4580.19	4575.43	4573.51	4572.74
310000	4775.71	4767.15	4749.20	4745.11	4732.87	4727.95	4725.96	4725.16
320000	4929.77	4920.93	4902.40	4898.17	4885.54	4880.46	4878.41	4877.59
330000	5083.82	5074.71	5055.60	5051.24	5038.21	5032.97	5030.86	5030.01
340000	5237.88	5228.49	5208.80	5204.31	5190.88	5185.49	5183.31	5182.44
350000	5391.93	5382.27	5362.00	5357.38	5343.56	5338.00	5335.76	5334.86
360000	5545.99	5536.05	5515.20	5510.44	5496.23	5490.52	5488.21	5487.28
370000	5700.04	5689.83	5668.40	5663.51	5648.90	5643.03	5640.66	5639.71
380000	5854.10	5843.61	5821.60	5816.58	5801.58	5795.54	5793.11	5792.13
390000	6008.15	5997.39	5974.80	5969.65	5954.25	5948.06	5945.56	5944.56
400000	6162.21	6151.17	6128.00	6122.71	6106.92	6100.57	6098.01	6096.98

AMORTIZATION IN YEARS

Amount	1	2	3	4	5	6	7	8
25	2.31	1.27	.92	.76	.66	.59	.55	.52
50	4.62	2.53	1.84	1.51	1.31	1.18	1.09	1.03
100	9.23	5.06	3.68	3.01	2.61	2.35	2.18	2.05
200	18.46	10.11	7.36	6.01	5.22	4.70	4.35	4.10
300	27.68	15.16	11.03	9.01	7.82	7.05	6.53	6.14
400	36.91	20.21	14.71	12.01	10.43	9.40	8.70	8.19
500	46.13	25.26	18.39	15.01	13.03	11.75	10.87	10.24
600	55.36	30.31	22.06	18.01	15.64	14.10	13.05	12.28
700	64.59	35.36	25.74	21.01	18.25	16.45	15.22	14.33
800	73.81	40.42	29.42	24.02	20.85	18.80	17.39	16.38
900	83.04	45.47	33.09	27.02	23.46	21.15	19.57	18.42
1000	92.26	50.52	36.77	30.02	26.06	23.50	21.74	20.47
2000	184.52	101.03	73.53	60.03	52.12	47.00	43.48	40.94
3000	276.78	151.54	110.30	90.04	78.18	70.50	65.21	61.40
4000	369.04	202.06	147.06	120.06	104.24	94.00	86.95	81.87
5000	461.30	252.57	183.83	150.07	130.30	117.50	108.68	102.33
6000	553.56	303.08	220.59	180.08	156.36	141.00	130.42	122.80
7000	645.82	353.59	257.36	210.10	182.42	164.50	152.15	143.27
8000	738.08	404.11	294.12	240.11	208.47	188.00	173.89	163.73
9000	830.33	454.62	330.88	270.12	234.53	211.50	195.62	184.20
10000	922.59	505.13	367.65	300.14	260.59	235.00	217.36	204.66
20000	1845.18	1010.26	735.29	600.27	521.18	470.00	434.72	409.32
30000	2767.77	1515.39	1102.94	900.40	781.76	704.99	652.07	613.98
40000	3690.36	2020.52	1470.58	1200.54	1042.35	939.99	869.43	818.64
50000	4612.95	2525.64	1838.23	1500.67	1302.93	1174.98	1086.78	1023.30
60000	5535.54	3030.77	2205.87	1800.80	1563.52	1409.98	1304.14	1227.95
70000	6458.13	3535.90	2573.52	2100.94	1824.11	1644.97	1521.49	1432.61
80000	7380.71	4041.03	2941.16	2401.07	2084.69	1879.97	1738.85	1637.27
90000	8303.30	4546.15	3308.80	2701.20	2345.28	2114.96	1956.20	1841.93
100000	9225.89	5051.28	3676.45	3001.33	2605.86	2349.96	2173.56	2046.59
110000	10148.48	5556.41	4044.09	3301.47	2866.45	2584.96	2390.91	2251.25
120000	11071.07	6061.54	4411.74	3601.60	3127.03	2819.95	2608.27	2455.90
130000	11993.66	6566.66	4779.38	3901.73	3387.62	3054.95	2825.62	2660.56
140000	12916.25	7071.79	5147.03	4201.87	3648.21	3289.94	3042.98	2865.22
150000	13838.83	7576.92	5514.67	4502.00	3908.79	3524.94	3260.33	3069.88
160000	14761.42	8082.05	5882.31	4802.13	4169.38	3759.93	3477.69	3274.54
170000	15684.01	8587.18	6249.96	5102.26	4429.96	3994.93	3695.04	3479.20
180000	16606.60	9092.30	6617.60	5402.40	4690.55	4229.92	3912.40	3683.85
190000	17529.19	9597.43	6985.25	5702.53	4951.13	4464.92	4129.75	3888.51
200000	18451.78	10102.56	7352.89	6002.66	5211.72	4699.91	4347.11	4093.17
210000	19374.37	10607.69	7720.54	6302.80	5472.31	4934.91	4564.46	4297.83
220000	20296.95	11112.81	8088.18	6602.93	5732.89	5169.91	4781.82	4502.49
230000	21219.54	11617.94	8455.82	6903.06	5993.48	5404.90	4999.17	4707.15
240000	22142.13	12123.07	8823.47	7203.19	6254.06	5639.90	5216.53	4911.80
250000	23064.72	12628.20	9191.11	7503.33	6514.65	5874.89	5433.88	5116.46
260000	23987.31	13133.32	9558.76	7803.46	6775.24	6109.89	5651.24	5321.12
270000	24909.90	13638.45	9926.40	8103.59	7035.82	6344.88	5868.59	5525.78
280000	25832.49	14143.58	10294.05	8403.73	7296.41	6579.88	6085.95	5730.44
290000	26755.07	14648.71	10661.69	8703.86	7556.99	6814.87	6303.30	5935.10
300000	27677.66	15153.84	11029.33	9003.99	7817.58	7049.87	6520.66	6139.75
310000	28600.25	15658.96	11396.98	9304.12	8078.16	7284.86	6738.01	6344.41
320000	29522.84	16164.09	11764.62	9604.26	8338.75	7519.86	6955.37	6549.07
330000	30445.43	16669.22	12132.27	9904.39	8599.34	7754.86	7172.72	6753.73
340000	31368.02	17174.35	12499.91	10204.52	8859.92	7989.85	7390.08	6958.39
350000	32290.61	17679.47	12867.56	10504.66	9120.51	8224.85	7607.43	7163.04
360000	33213.19	18184.60	13235.20	10804.79	9381.09	8459.84	7824.79	7367.70
370000	34135.78	18689.73	13602.84	11104.92	9641.68	8694.84	8042.14	7572.36
380000	35058.37	19194.86	13970.49	11405.05	9902.26	8929.83	8259.50	7777.02
390000	35980.96	19699.98	14338.13	11705.19	10162.85	9164.83	8476.85	7981.68
400000	36903.55	20205.11	14705.78	12005.32	10423.44	9399.82	8694.21	8186.34

20% BLENDED MONTHLY PAYMENTS

AMORTIZATION IN YEARS

Amount	9	10	11	12	13	14	15	16
25	.49	.48	.46	.45	.44	.44	.43	.43
50	.98	.95	.92	.90	.88	.87	.85	.85
100	1.96	1.89	1.83	1.79	1.75	1.73	1.70	1.69
200	3.91	3.77	3.66	3.57	3.50	3.45	3.40	3.37
300	5.86	5.65	5.48	5.35	5.25	5.17	5.10	5.05
400	7.81	7.53	7.31	7.13	7.00	6.89	6.80	6.73
500	9.77	9.41	9.13	8.92	8.74	8.61	8.50	8.41
600	11.72	11.29	10.96	10.70	10.49	10.33	10.20	10.09
700	13.67	13.17	12.78	12.48	12.24	12.05	11.89	11.77
800	15.62	15.05	14.61	14.26	13.99	13.77	13.59	13.45
900	17.58	16.93	16.43	16.04	15.74	15.49	15.29	15.13
1000	19.53	18.81	18.26	17.83	17.48	17.21	16.99	16.81
2000	39.05	37.62	36.51	35.65	34.96	34.41	33.98	33.62
3000	58.57	56.43	54.77	53.47	52.44	51.62	50.96	50.43
4000	78.10	75.23	73.02	71.29	69.92	68.82	67.95	67.24
5000	97.62	94.04	91.28	89.11	87.40	86.03	84.93	84.04
6000	117.14	112.85	109.53	106.93	104.88	103.23	101.92	100.85
7000	136.67	131.66	127.79	124.75	122.35	120.44	118.90	117.66
8000	156.19	150.46	146.04	142.57	139.83	137.64	135.89	134.47
9000	175.71	169.27	164.29	160.40	157.31	154.85	152.87	151.28
10000	195.24	188.08	182.55	178.22	174.79	172.05	169.86	168.08
20000	390.47	376.15	365.09	356.43	349.57	344.10	339.71	336.16
30000	585.70	564.23	547.64	534.64	524.36	516.15	509.56	504.24
40000	780.94	752.30	730.18	712.85	699.14	688.20	679.42	672.32
50000	976.17	940.38	912.72	891.06	873.93	860.25	849.27	840.40
60000	1171.40	1128.45	1095.27	1069.28	1048.71	1032.30	1019.12	1008.48
70000	1366.64	1316.53	1277.81	1247.49	1223.49	1204.35	1188.97	1176.56
80000	1561.87	1504.60	1460.35	1425.70	1398.28	1376.40	1358.83	1344.64
90000	1757.10	1692.68	1642.90	1603.91	1573.06	1548.45	1528.68	1512.72
100000	1952.34	1880.75	1825.44	1782.12	1747.85	1720.50	1698.53	1680.80
110000	2147.57	2068.83	2007.98	1960.33	1922.63	1892.55	1868.38	1848.88
120000	2342.80	2256.90	2190.53	2138.55	2097.41	2064.59	2038.24	2016.96
130000	2538.03	2444.98	2373.07	2316.76	2272.20	2236.64	2208.09	2185.04
140000	2733.27	2633.05	2555.61	2494.97	2446.98	2408.69	2377.94	2353.12
150000	2928.50	2821.13	2738.16	2673.18	2621.77	2580.74	2547.80	2521.19
160000	3123.73	3009.20	2920.70	2851.39	2796.55	2752.79	2717.65	2689.27
170000	3318.97	3197.28	3103.24	3029.60	2971.33	2924.84	2887.50	2857.35
180000	3514.20	3385.35	3285.79	3207.82	3146.12	3096.89	3057.35	3025.43
190000	3709.43	3573.43	3468.33	3386.03	3320.90	3268.94	3227.21	3193.51
200000	3904.67	3761.50	3650.87	3564.24	3495.69	3440.99	3397.06	3361.59
210000	4099.90	3949.58	3833.42	3742.45	3670.47	3613.04	3566.91	3529.67
220000	4295.13	4137.65	4015.96	3920.66	3845.25	3785.09	3736.76	3697.75
230000	4490.37	4325.73	4198.50	4098.87	4020.04	3957.14	3906.62	3865.83
240000	4685.60	4513.80	4381.05	4277.09	4194.82	4129.18	4076.47	4033.91
250000	4880.83	4701.87	4563.59	4455.30	4369.61	4301.23	4246.32	4201.99
260000	5076.06	4889.95	4746.13	4633.51	4544.39	4473.28	4416.17	4370.07
270000	5271.30	5078.02	4928.68	4811.72	4719.17	4645.33	4586.03	4538.15
280000	5466.53	5266.10	5111.22	4989.93	4893.96	4817.38	4755.88	4706.23
290000	5661.76	5454.17	5293.76	5168.15	5068.74	4989.43	4925.73	4874.31
300000	5857.00	5642.25	5476.31	5346.36	5243.53	5161.48	5095.59	5042.38
310000	6052.23	5830.32	5658.85	5524.57	5418.31	5333.53	5265.44	5210.46
320000	6247.46	6018.40	5841.39	5702.78	5593.09	5505.58	5435.29	5378.54
330000	6442.70	6206.47	6023.94	5880.99	5767.88	5677.63	5605.14	5546.62
340000	6637.93	6394.55	6206.48	6059.20	5942.66	5849.68	5775.00	5714.70
350000	6833.16	6582.62	6389.02	6237.42	6117.45	6021.72	5944.85	5882.78
360000	7028.40	6770.70	6571.57	6415.63	6292.23	6193.77	6114.70	6050.86
370000	7223.63	6958.77	6754.11	6593.84	6467.01	6365.82	6284.55	6218.94
380000	7418.86	7146.85	6936.65	6772.05	6641.80	6537.87	6454.41	6387.02
390000	7614.09	7334.92	7119.20	6950.26	6816.58	6709.92	6624.26	6555.10
400000	7809.33	7523.00	7301.74	7128.47	6991.37	6881.97	6794.11	6723.18

170

BLENDED MONTHLY PAYMENTS 20%
AMORTIZATION IN YEARS

Amount	17	18	19	20	21	22	23	24
25	.42	.42	.42	.41	.41	.41	.41	.41
50	.84	.83	.83	.82	.82	.82	.82	.81
100	1.67	1.66	1.65	1.64	1.64	1.63	1.63	1.62
200	3.34	3.31	3.30	3.28	3.27	3.26	3.25	3.24
300	5.00	4.97	4.94	4.92	4.90	4.88	4.87	4.86
400	6.67	6.62	6.59	6.55	6.53	6.51	6.49	6.48
500	8.34	8.28	8.23	8.19	8.16	8.13	8.11	8.09
600	10.00	9.93	9.88	9.83	9.79	9.76	9.73	9.71
700	11.67	11.59	11.52	11.47	11.42	11.39	11.35	11.33
800	13.34	13.24	13.17	13.10	13.05	13.01	12.98	12.95
900	15.00	14.90	14.81	14.74	14.68	14.64	14.60	14.57
1000	16.67	16.55	16.46	16.38	16.31	16.26	16.22	16.18
2000	33.33	33.10	32.91	32.75	32.62	32.52	32.43	32.36
3000	50.00	49.65	49.36	49.13	48.93	48.78	48.65	48.54
4000	66.66	66.19	65.81	65.50	65.24	65.03	64.86	64.72
5000	83.33	82.74	82.26	81.87	81.55	81.29	81.08	80.90
6000	99.99	99.29	98.72	98.25	97.86	97.55	97.29	97.08
7000	116.65	115.84	115.17	114.62	114.17	113.81	113.50	113.26
8000	133.32	132.38	131.62	130.99	130.48	130.06	129.72	129.43
9000	149.98	148.93	148.07	147.37	146.79	146.32	145.93	145.61
10000	166.65	165.48	164.52	163.74	163.10	162.58	162.15	161.79
20000	333.29	330.95	329.04	327.48	326.20	325.15	324.29	323.58
30000	499.93	496.42	493.56	491.21	489.30	487.72	486.43	485.36
40000	666.57	661.89	658.07	654.95	652.39	650.29	648.57	647.15
50000	833.21	827.36	822.59	818.69	815.49	812.87	810.71	808.94
60000	999.85	992.83	987.11	982.42	978.59	975.44	972.85	970.72
70000	1166.50	1158.31	1151.62	1146.16	1141.68	1138.01	1134.99	1132.51
80000	1333.14	1323.78	1316.14	1309.90	1304.78	1300.58	1297.13	1294.30
90000	1499.78	1489.25	1480.66	1473.63	1467.88	1463.15	1459.27	1456.08
100000	1666.42	1654.72	1645.18	1637.37	1630.97	1625.73	1621.41	1617.87
110000	1833.06	1820.19	1809.69	1801.11	1794.07	1788.30	1783.55	1779.65
120000	1999.70	1985.66	1974.21	1964.84	1957.17	1950.87	1945.70	1941.44
130000	2166.34	2151.14	2138.73	2128.58	2120.26	2113.44	2107.84	2103.23
140000	2332.99	2316.61	2303.24	2292.31	2283.36	2276.01	2269.98	2265.01
150000	2499.63	2482.08	2467.76	2456.05	2446.46	2438.59	2432.12	2426.80
160000	2666.27	2647.55	2632.28	2619.79	2609.55	2601.16	2594.26	2588.59
170000	2832.91	2813.02	2796.79	2783.52	2772.65	2763.73	2756.40	2750.37
180000	2999.55	2978.49	2961.31	2947.26	2935.75	2926.30	2918.54	2912.16
190000	3166.19	3143.96	3125.83	3111.00	3098.85	3088.87	3080.68	3073.94
200000	3332.83	3309.44	3290.35	3274.73	3261.94	3251.45	3242.82	3235.73
210000	3499.48	3474.91	3454.86	3438.47	3425.04	3414.02	3404.96	3397.52
220000	3666.12	3640.38	3619.38	3602.21	3588.14	3576.59	3567.10	3559.30
230000	3832.76	3805.85	3783.90	3765.94	3751.23	3739.16	3729.25	3721.09
240000	3999.40	3971.32	3948.41	3929.68	3914.33	3901.73	3891.39	3882.88
250000	4166.05	4136.79	4112.93	4093.42	4077.43	4064.31	4053.53	4044.66
260000	4332.68	4302.27	4277.45	4257.15	4240.52	4226.88	4215.67	4206.45
270000	4499.32	4467.74	4441.96	4420.89	4403.62	4389.45	4377.81	4368.23
280000	4665.97	4633.21	4606.48	4584.62	4566.72	4552.02	4539.95	4530.02
290000	4832.61	4798.68	4771.00	4748.36	4729.81	4714.60	4702.09	4691.81
300000	4999.25	4964.15	4935.52	4912.10	4892.91	4877.17	4864.23	4853.59
310000	5165.89	5129.62	5100.03	5075.83	5056.01	5039.74	5026.37	5015.38
320000	5332.53	5295.09	5264.55	5239.57	5219.10	5202.31	5188.51	5177.17
330000	5499.17	5460.57	5429.07	5403.31	5382.20	5364.88	5350.65	5338.95
340000	5665.81	5626.04	5593.58	5567.04	5545.30	5527.46	5512.80	5500.74
350000	5832.46	5791.51	5758.10	5730.78	5708.40	5690.03	5674.94	5662.52
360000	5999.10	5956.98	5922.62	5894.52	5871.49	5852.60	5837.08	5824.31
370000	6165.74	6122.45	6087.13	6058.25	6034.59	6015.17	5999.22	5986.10
380000	6332.38	6287.92	6251.65	6221.99	6197.69	6177.74	6161.36	6147.88
390000	6499.02	6453.40	6416.17	6385.73	6360.78	6340.32	6323.50	6309.67
400000	6665.66	6618.87	6580.69	6549.46	6523.88	6502.89	6485.64	6471.46

171

20% BLENDED MONTHLY PAYMENTS
AMORTIZATION IN YEARS

Amount	25	26	29	30	35	40	45	50
25	.41	.41	.41	.41	.41	.41	.41	.41
50	.81	.81	.81	.81	.81	.81	.81	.81
100	1.62	1.62	1.61	1.61	1.61	1.61	1.61	1.61
200	3.23	3.23	3.22	3.22	3.21	3.21	3.21	3.21
300	4.85	4.84	4.83	4.82	4.81	4.81	4.81	4.81
400	6.46	6.46	6.44	6.43	6.42	6.41	6.41	6.41
500	8.08	8.07	8.04	8.04	8.02	8.01	8.01	8.01
600	9.69	9.68	9.65	9.64	9.62	9.62	9.61	9.61
700	11.31	11.29	11.26	11.25	11.23	11.22	11.22	11.21
800	12.92	12.91	12.87	12.86	12.83	12.82	12.82	12.82
900	14.54	14.52	14.47	14.46	14.43	14.42	14.42	14.42
1000	16.15	16.13	16.08	16.07	16.04	16.02	16.02	16.02
2000	32.30	32.26	32.16	32.13	32.07	32.04	32.03	32.03
3000	48.45	48.38	48.23	48.20	48.10	48.06	48.05	48.04
4000	64.60	64.51	64.31	64.26	64.13	64.08	64.06	64.06
5000	80.75	80.63	80.38	80.33	80.17	80.10	80.08	80.07
6000	96.90	96.76	96.46	96.39	96.20	96.12	96.09	96.08
7000	113.05	112.88	112.54	112.46	112.23	112.14	112.11	112.10
8000	129.20	129.01	128.61	128.52	128.26	128.16	128.12	128.11
9000	145.35	145.13	144.69	144.59	144.29	144.18	144.14	144.12
10000	161.50	161.26	160.76	160.65	160.33	160.20	160.15	160.14
20000	322.99	322.51	321.52	321.30	320.65	320.40	320.30	320.27
30000	484.49	483.77	482.28	481.94	480.97	480.60	480.45	480.40
40000	645.98	645.02	643.04	642.59	641.29	640.79	640.60	640.53
50000	807.48	806.27	803.79	803.24	801.61	800.99	800.75	800.66
60000	968.97	967.53	964.55	963.88	961.94	961.19	960.90	960.79
70000	1130.47	1128.78	1125.31	1124.53	1122.26	1121.38	1121.05	1120.92
80000	1291.96	1290.04	1286.07	1285.18	1282.58	1281.58	1281.20	1281.05
90000	1453.45	1451.29	1446.82	1445.82	1442.90	1441.78	1441.34	1441.18
100000	1614.95	1612.54	1607.58	1606.47	1603.22	1601.97	1601.49	1601.31
110000	1776.44	1773.80	1768.34	1767.11	1763.54	1762.17	1761.64	1761.44
120000	1937.94	1935.05	1929.10	1927.76	1923.87	1922.37	1921.79	1921.57
130000	2099.43	2096.31	2089.85	2088.41	2084.19	2082.56	2081.94	2081.70
140000	2260.93	2257.56	2250.61	2249.05	2244.51	2242.76	2242.09	2241.83
150000	2422.42	2418.81	2411.37	2409.70	2404.83	2402.96	2402.24	2401.96
160000	2583.92	2580.07	2572.13	2570.35	2565.15	2563.16	2562.39	2562.09
170000	2745.41	2741.32	2732.88	2730.99	2725.47	2723.35	2722.53	2722.22
180000	2906.90	2902.58	2893.64	2891.64	2885.80	2883.55	2882.68	2882.35
190000	3068.40	3063.83	3054.40	3052.28	3046.12	3043.75	3042.83	3042.48
200000	3229.89	3225.08	3215.16	3212.93	3206.44	3203.94	3202.98	3202.61
210000	3391.39	3386.34	3375.91	3373.58	3366.76	3364.14	3363.13	3362.74
220000	3552.88	3547.59	3536.67	3534.22	3527.08	3524.34	3523.28	3522.87
230000	3714.38	3708.85	3697.43	3694.87	3687.40	3684.53	3683.43	3683.00
240000	3875.87	3870.10	3858.19	3855.52	3847.73	3844.73	3843.58	3843.13
250000	4037.36	4031.35	4018.94	4016.16	4008.05	4004.93	4003.73	4003.26
260000	4198.86	4192.61	4179.70	4176.81	4168.37	4165.12	4163.87	4163.39
270000	4360.35	4353.86	4340.46	4337.45	4328.69	4325.32	4324.02	4323.52
280000	4521.85	4515.11	4501.22	4498.10	4489.01	4485.52	4484.17	4483.65
290000	4683.34	4676.37	4661.97	4658.75	4649.33	4645.71	4644.32	4643.78
300000	4844.84	4837.62	4822.73	4819.39	4809.66	4805.91	4804.47	4803.91
310000	5006.33	4998.88	4983.49	4980.04	4969.98	4966.11	4964.62	4964.04
320000	5167.83	5160.13	5144.25	5140.69	5130.30	5126.31	5124.77	5124.17
330000	5329.32	5321.38	5305.00	5301.33	5290.62	5286.50	5284.92	5284.30
340000	5490.81	5482.64	5465.76	5461.98	5450.94	5446.70	5445.06	5444.44
350000	5652.31	5643.89	5626.52	5622.62	5611.26	5606.90	5605.21	5604.57
360000	5813.80	5805.15	5787.28	5783.27	5771.59	5767.09	5765.36	5764.70
370000	5975.30	5966.40	5948.03	5943.92	5931.91	5927.29	5925.51	5924.83
380000	6136.79	6127.65	6108.79	6104.56	6092.23	6087.49	6085.66	6084.96
390000	6298.29	6288.91	6269.55	6265.21	6252.55	6247.68	6245.81	6245.09
400000	6459.78	6450.16	6430.31	6425.86	6412.87	6407.88	6405.96	6405.22

Amount	1	2	3	4	5	6	7	8
25	2.32	1.28	.94	.77	.67	.61	.56	.53
50	4.64	2.55	1.87	1.53	1.33	1.21	1.12	1.06
100	9.27	5.10	3.73	3.06	2.66	2.41	2.23	2.11
200	18.54	10.20	7.45	6.11	5.32	4.81	4.46	4.21
300	27.81	15.29	11.17	9.16	7.98	7.21	6.69	6.32
400	37.08	20.39	14.90	12.21	10.63	9.62	8.92	8.42
500	46.35	25.49	18.62	15.26	13.29	12.02	11.15	10.52
600	55.62	30.58	22.34	18.31	15.95	14.42	13.38	12.63
700	64.89	35.68	26.07	21.36	18.60	16.83	15.61	14.73
800	74.16	40.77	29.79	24.41	21.26	19.23	17.84	16.84
900	83.43	45.87	33.51	27.46	23.92	21.63	20.06	18.94
1000	92.70	50.97	37.24	30.51	26.57	24.04	22.29	21.04
2000	185.40	101.93	74.47	61.01	53.14	48.07	44.58	42.08
3000	278.10	152.89	111.70	91.51	79.71	72.10	66.87	63.12
4000	370.80	203.85	148.94	122.02	106.28	96.13	89.16	84.16
5000	463.50	254.82	186.17	152.52	132.85	120.16	111.45	105.20
6000	556.20	305.78	223.40	183.02	159.42	144.20	133.73	126.23
7000	648.90	356.74	260.64	213.53	185.99	168.23	156.02	147.27
8000	741.60	407.70	297.87	244.03	212.56	192.26	178.31	168.31
9000	834.30	458.67	335.10	274.53	239.13	216.29	200.60	189.35
10000	927.00	509.63	372.33	305.03	265.70	240.32	222.89	210.39
20000	1854.00	1019.25	744.66	610.06	531.40	480.64	445.77	420.77
30000	2781.00	1528.88	1116.99	915.09	797.10	720.96	668.65	631.15
40000	3707.99	2038.50	1489.32	1220.12	1062.79	961.28	891.53	841.53
50000	4634.99	2548.12	1861.65	1525.15	1328.49	1201.60	1114.42	1051.91
60000	5561.99	3057.75	2233.98	1830.18	1594.19	1441.91	1337.30	1262.30
70000	6488.98	3567.37	2606.31	2135.21	1859.88	1682.23	1560.18	1472.68
80000	7415.98	4076.99	2978.64	2440.24	2125.58	1922.55	1783.06	1683.06
90000	8342.98	4586.62	3350.97	2745.27	2391.28	2162.87	2005.95	1893.44
100000	9269.97	5096.24	3723.30	3050.30	2656.97	2403.19	2228.83	2103.82
110000	10196.97	5605.86	4095.63	3355.33	2922.67	2643.50	2451.71	2314.20
120000	11123.97	6115.49	4467.96	3660.36	3188.37	2883.82	2674.59	2524.59
130000	12050.96	6625.11	4840.29	3965.39	3454.07	3124.14	2897.48	2734.97
140000	12977.96	7134.73	5212.62	4270.42	3719.76	3364.46	3120.36	2945.35
150000	13904.96	7644.36	5584.95	4575.45	3985.46	3604.78	3343.24	3155.73
160000	14831.95	8153.98	5957.28	4880.48	4251.16	3845.09	3566.12	3366.11
170000	15758.95	8663.60	6329.61	5185.51	4516.85	4085.41	3789.01	3576.50
180000	16685.95	9173.23	6701.94	5490.54	4782.55	4325.73	4011.89	3786.88
190000	17612.94	9682.85	7074.27	5795.56	5048.25	4566.05	4234.77	3997.26
200000	18539.94	10192.47	7446.60	6100.59	5313.94	4806.37	4457.65	4207.64
210000	19466.94	10702.10	7818.93	6405.62	5579.64	5046.68	4680.54	4418.02
220000	20393.93	11211.72	8191.26	6710.65	5845.34	5287.00	4903.42	4628.40
230000	21320.93	11721.34	8563.59	7015.68	6111.03	5527.32	5126.30	4838.79
240000	22247.93	12230.97	8935.92	7320.71	6376.73	5767.64	5349.18	5049.17
250000	23174.92	12740.59	9308.25	7625.74	6642.43	6007.96	5572.07	5259.55
260000	24101.92	13250.21	9680.58	7930.77	6908.13	6248.28	5794.95	5469.93
270000	25028.92	13759.84	10052.91	8235.80	7173.82	6488.59	6017.83	5680.31
280000	25955.91	14269.46	10425.24	8540.83	7439.52	6728.91	6240.71	5890.70
290000	26882.91	14779.08	10797.57	8845.86	7705.22	6969.23	6463.60	6101.08
300000	27809.91	15288.71	11169.90	9150.89	7970.91	7209.55	6686.48	6311.46
310000	28736.90	15798.33	11542.23	9455.92	8236.61	7449.87	6909.36	6521.84
320000	29663.90	16307.95	11914.56	9760.95	8502.31	7690.18	7132.24	6732.22
330000	30590.90	16817.58	12286.89	10065.98	8768.00	7930.50	7355.13	6942.60
340000	31517.90	17327.20	12659.22	10371.01	9033.70	8170.82	7578.01	7152.99
350000	32444.89	17836.82	13031.55	10676.04	9299.40	8411.14	7800.89	7363.37
360000	33371.89	18346.45	13403.88	10981.07	9565.09	8651.46	8023.77	7573.75
370000	34298.89	18856.07	13776.21	11286.10	9830.79	8891.77	8246.66	7784.13
380000	35225.88	19365.69	14148.54	11591.12	10096.49	9132.09	8469.54	7994.51
390000	36152.88	19875.32	14520.87	11896.15	10362.19	9372.41	8692.42	8204.89
400000	37079.88	20384.94	14893.20	12201.18	10627.88	9612.73	8915.30	8415.28

21% BLENDED MONTHLY PAYMENTS
AMORTIZATION IN YEARS

Amount	9	10	11	12	13	14	15	16
25	.51	.49	.48	.47	.46	.45	.45	.44
50	1.01	.98	.95	.93	.91	.90	.89	.88
100	2.02	1.95	1.89	1.85	1.82	1.79	1.77	1.75
200	4.03	3.89	3.78	3.70	3.63	3.58	3.54	3.50
300	6.04	5.83	5.67	5.54	5.44	5.37	5.30	5.25
400	8.05	7.77	7.56	7.39	7.26	7.15	7.07	7.00
500	10.06	9.71	9.44	9.24	9.07	8.94	8.84	8.75
600	12.07	11.65	11.33	11.08	10.88	10.73	10.60	10.50
700	14.08	13.60	13.22	12.93	12.70	12.52	12.37	12.25
800	16.10	15.54	15.11	14.77	14.51	14.30	14.14	14.00
900	18.11	17.48	17.00	16.62	16.32	16.09	15.90	15.75
1000	20.12	19.42	18.88	18.47	18.14	17.88	17.67	17.50
2000	40.23	38.84	37.76	36.93	36.27	35.75	35.33	35.00
3000	60.35	58.25	56.64	55.39	54.40	53.62	53.00	52.50
4000	80.46	77.67	75.52	73.85	72.53	71.49	70.66	69.99
5000	100.58	97.08	94.40	92.31	90.67	89.36	88.32	87.49
6000	120.69	116.50	113.28	110.77	108.80	107.23	105.99	104.99
7000	140.80	135.92	132.16	129.23	126.93	125.11	123.65	122.48
8000	160.92	155.33	151.04	147.69	145.06	142.98	141.31	139.98
9000	181.03	174.75	169.92	166.15	163.20	160.85	158.98	157.48
10000	201.15	194.16	188.80	184.62	181.33	178.72	176.64	174.97
20000	402.29	388.32	377.59	369.23	362.65	357.44	353.28	349.94
30000	603.43	582.48	566.38	553.84	543.97	536.15	529.91	524.91
40000	804.58	776.64	755.17	738.45	725.30	714.87	706.55	699.88
50000	1005.72	970.80	943.96	923.06	906.62	893.59	883.19	874.85
60000	1206.86	1164.96	1132.75	1107.67	1087.94	1072.30	1059.82	1049.82
70000	1408.00	1359.12	1321.54	1292.28	1269.27	1251.02	1236.46	1224.79
80000	1609.15	1553.28	1510.33	1476.89	1450.59	1429.73	1413.10	1399.75
90000	1810.29	1747.44	1699.13	1661.50	1631.91	1608.45	1589.73	1574.72
100000	2011.43	1941.60	1887.92	1846.12	1813.23	1787.17	1766.37	1749.69
110000	2212.57	2135.76	2076.71	2030.73	1994.56	1965.88	1943.00	1924.66
120000	2413.72	2329.92	2265.50	2215.34	2175.88	2144.60	2119.64	2099.63
130000	2614.86	2524.07	2454.29	2399.95	2357.20	2323.31	2296.28	2274.60
140000	2816.00	2718.23	2643.08	2584.56	2538.53	2502.03	2472.91	2449.57
150000	3017.14	2912.39	2831.87	2769.17	2719.85	2680.75	2649.55	2624.54
160000	3218.29	3106.55	3020.66	2953.78	2901.17	2859.46	2826.19	2799.50
170000	3419.43	3300.71	3209.45	3138.39	3082.50	3038.18	3002.82	2974.47
180000	3620.57	3494.87	3398.25	3323.00	3263.82	3216.89	3179.46	3149.44
190000	3821.71	3689.03	3587.04	3507.61	3445.14	3395.61	3356.09	3324.41
200000	4022.86	3883.19	3775.83	3692.23	3626.46	3574.33	3532.73	3499.38
210000	4224.00	4077.35	3964.62	3876.84	3807.79	3753.04	3709.37	3674.35
220000	4425.14	4271.51	4153.41	4061.45	3989.11	3931.76	3886.00	3849.32
230000	4626.28	4465.67	4342.20	4246.06	4170.43	4110.48	4062.64	4024.29
240000	4827.43	4659.83	4530.99	4430.67	4351.76	4289.19	4239.28	4199.25
250000	5028.57	4853.98	4719.78	4615.28	4533.08	4467.91	4415.91	4374.22
260000	5229.71	5048.14	4908.58	4799.89	4714.40	4646.62	4592.55	4549.19
270000	5430.85	5242.30	5097.37	4984.50	4895.73	4825.34	4769.19	4724.16
280000	5632.00	5436.46	5286.16	5169.11	5077.05	5004.06	4945.82	4899.13
290000	5833.14	5630.62	5474.95	5353.72	5258.37	5182.77	5122.46	5074.10
300000	6034.28	5824.78	5663.74	5538.34	5439.69	5361.49	5299.09	5249.07
310000	6235.42	6018.94	5852.53	5722.95	5621.02	5540.20	5475.73	5424.03
320000	6436.57	6213.10	6041.32	5907.56	5802.34	5718.92	5652.37	5599.00
330000	6637.71	6407.26	6230.11	6092.17	5983.66	5897.64	5829.00	5773.97
340000	6838.85	6601.42	6418.90	6276.78	6164.99	6076.35	6005.64	5948.94
350000	7039.99	6795.58	6607.70	6461.39	6346.31	6255.07	6182.28	6123.91
360000	7241.14	6989.74	6796.49	6646.00	6527.63	6433.78	6358.91	6298.88
370000	7442.28	7183.90	6985.28	6830.61	6708.95	6612.50	6535.55	6473.85
380000	7643.42	7378.05	7174.07	7015.22	6890.28	6791.22	6712.18	6648.82
390000	7844.56	7572.21	7362.86	7199.83	7071.60	6969.93	6888.82	6823.78
400000	8045.71	7766.37	7551.65	7384.45	7252.92	7148.65	7065.46	6998.75

BLENDED MONTHLY PAYMENTS 21%

AMORTIZATION IN YEARS

Amount	17	18	19	20	21	22	23	24
25	.44	.44	.43	.43	.43	.43	.43	.43
50	.87	.87	.86	.86	.86	.85	.85	.85
100	1.74	1.73	1.72	1.71	1.71	1.70	1.70	1.70
200	3.48	3.46	3.44	3.42	3.41	3.40	3.40	3.39
300	5.21	5.18	5.15	5.13	5.12	5.10	5.09	5.08
400	6.95	6.91	6.87	6.84	6.82	6.80	6.79	6.77
500	8.69	8.63	8.59	8.55	8.52	8.50	8.48	8.47
600	10.42	10.36	10.30	10.26	10.23	10.20	10.18	10.16
700	12.16	12.08	12.02	11.97	11.93	11.90	11.87	11.85
800	13.90	13.81	13.74	13.68	13.63	13.60	13.57	13.54
900	15.63	15.53	15.45	15.39	15.34	15.30	15.26	15.23
1000	17.37	17.26	17.17	17.10	17.04	17.00	16.96	16.93
2000	34.73	34.51	34.34	34.20	34.08	33.99	33.91	33.85
3000	52.09	51.77	51.50	51.29	51.12	50.98	50.86	50.77
4000	69.46	69.02	68.67	68.39	68.15	67.97	67.81	67.69
5000	86.82	86.28	85.84	85.48	85.19	84.96	84.76	84.61
6000	104.18	103.53	103.00	102.58	102.23	101.95	101.72	101.53
7000	121.54	120.78	120.17	119.67	119.27	118.94	118.67	118.45
8000	138.91	138.04	137.34	136.77	136.30	135.93	135.62	135.37
9000	156.27	155.29	154.50	153.86	153.34	152.92	152.57	152.29
10000	173.63	172.55	171.67	170.96	170.38	169.91	169.52	169.21
20000	347.26	345.09	343.33	341.91	340.75	339.81	339.04	338.41
30000	520.88	517.63	515.00	512.86	511.12	509.71	508.56	507.62
40000	694.51	690.17	686.66	683.81	681.50	679.61	678.07	676.82
50000	868.14	862.72	858.33	854.76	851.87	849.51	847.59	846.03
60000	1041.76	1035.26	1029.99	1025.72	1022.24	1019.41	1017.11	1015.23
70000	1215.39	1207.80	1201.65	1196.67	1192.61	1189.31	1186.63	1184.43
80000	1389.01	1380.34	1373.32	1367.62	1362.99	1359.22	1356.14	1353.64
90000	1562.64	1552.88	1544.98	1538.57	1533.36	1529.12	1525.66	1522.84
100000	1736.27	1725.43	1716.65	1709.52	1703.73	1699.02	1695.18	1692.05
110000	1909.89	1897.97	1888.31	1880.47	1874.10	1868.92	1864.70	1861.25
120000	2083.52	2070.51	2059.97	2051.43	2044.48	2038.82	2034.21	2030.45
130000	2257.15	2243.05	2231.64	2222.38	2214.85	2208.72	2203.73	2199.66
140000	2430.77	2415.59	2403.30	2393.33	2385.22	2378.62	2373.25	2368.86
150000	2604.40	2588.14	2574.97	2564.28	2555.60	2548.53	2542.76	2538.07
160000	2778.02	2760.68	2746.63	2735.23	2725.97	2718.43	2712.28	2707.27
170000	2951.65	2933.22	2918.29	2906.18	2896.34	2888.33	2881.80	2876.47
180000	3125.28	3105.76	3089.96	3077.14	3066.71	3058.23	3051.32	3045.68
190000	3298.90	3278.30	3261.62	3248.09	3237.09	3228.13	3220.83	3214.88
200000	3472.53	3450.85	3433.29	3419.04	3407.46	3398.03	3390.35	3384.09
210000	3646.16	3623.39	3604.95	3589.99	3577.83	3567.93	3559.87	3553.29
220000	3819.78	3795.93	3776.62	3760.94	3748.20	3737.84	3729.39	3722.49
230000	3993.41	3968.47	3948.28	3931.89	3918.58	3907.74	3898.90	3891.70
240000	4167.03	4141.01	4119.94	4102.85	4088.95	4077.64	4068.42	4060.90
250000	4340.66	4313.56	4291.61	4273.80	4259.32	4247.54	4237.94	4230.11
260000	4514.29	4486.10	4463.27	4444.75	4429.69	4417.44	4407.46	4399.31
270000	4687.91	4658.64	4634.94	4615.70	4600.07	4587.34	4576.97	4568.52
280000	4861.54	4831.18	4806.60	4786.65	4770.44	4757.24	4746.49	4737.72
290000	5035.17	5003.72	4978.26	4957.60	4940.81	4927.15	4916.01	4906.92
300000	5208.79	5176.27	5149.93	5128.56	5111.19	5097.05	5085.52	5076.13
310000	5382.42	5348.81	5321.59	5299.51	5281.56	5266.95	5255.04	5245.33
320000	5556.04	5521.35	5493.26	5470.46	5451.93	5436.85	5424.56	5414.54
330000	5729.67	5693.89	5664.92	5641.41	5622.30	5606.75	5594.08	5583.74
340000	5903.30	5866.43	5836.58	5812.36	5792.68	5776.65	5763.59	5752.94
350000	6076.92	6038.98	6008.25	5983.32	5963.05	5946.55	5933.11	5922.15
360000	6250.55	6211.52	6179.91	6154.27	6133.42	6116.45	6102.63	6091.35
370000	6424.18	6384.06	6351.58	6325.22	6303.79	6286.36	6272.15	6260.56
380000	6597.80	6556.60	6523.24	6496.17	6474.17	6456.26	6441.66	6429.76
390000	6771.43	6729.14	6694.90	6667.12	6644.54	6626.16	6611.18	6598.96
400000	6945.05	6901.69	6866.57	6838.07	6814.91	6796.06	6780.70	6768.17

21% BLENDED MONTHLY PAYMENTS
AMORTIZATION IN YEARS

Amount	25	26	29	30	35	40	45	50
25	.43	.43	.43	.43	.42	.42	.42	.42
50	.85	.85	.85	.85	.84	.84	.84	.84
100	1.69	1.69	1.69	1.69	1.68	1.68	1.68	1.68
200	3.38	3.38	3.37	3.37	3.36	3.36	3.36	3.36
300	5.07	5.07	5.05	5.05	5.04	5.04	5.04	5.04
400	6.76	6.75	6.74	6.73	6.72	6.72	6.72	6.72
500	8.45	8.44	8.42	8.42	8.40	8.40	8.40	8.40
600	10.14	10.13	10.10	10.10	10.08	10.08	10.07	10.07
700	11.83	11.82	11.79	11.78	11.76	11.76	11.75	11.75
800	13.52	13.50	13.47	13.46	13.44	13.43	13.43	13.43
900	15.21	15.19	15.15	15.14	15.12	15.11	15.11	15.11
1000	16.90	16.88	16.84	16.83	16.80	16.79	16.79	16.79
2000	33.79	33.75	33.67	33.65	33.60	33.58	33.57	33.57
3000	50.69	50.63	50.50	50.47	50.39	50.36	50.35	50.35
4000	67.58	67.50	67.33	67.29	67.19	67.15	67.13	67.13
5000	84.48	84.37	84.16	84.12	83.98	83.93	83.92	83.91
6000	101.37	101.25	100.99	100.94	100.78	100.72	100.70	100.69
7000	118.27	118.12	117.83	117.76	117.57	117.51	117.48	117.47
8000	135.16	135.00	134.66	134.58	134.37	134.29	134.26	134.25
9000	152.06	151.87	151.49	151.40	151.17	151.08	151.04	151.03
10000	168.95	168.74	168.32	168.23	167.96	167.86	167.83	167.81
20000	337.90	337.48	336.64	336.45	335.92	335.72	335.65	335.62
30000	506.85	506.22	504.95	504.67	503.87	503.58	503.47	503.43
40000	675.80	674.96	673.27	672.89	671.83	671.44	671.29	671.24
50000	844.75	843.70	841.58	841.12	839.79	839.30	839.12	839.05
60000	1013.70	1012.44	1009.90	1009.34	1007.74	1007.15	1006.94	1006.86
70000	1182.64	1181.18	1178.21	1177.56	1175.70	1175.01	1174.76	1174.67
80000	1351.59	1349.92	1346.53	1345.78	1343.65	1342.87	1342.58	1342.48
90000	1520.54	1518.66	1514.84	1514.00	1511.61	1510.73	1510.40	1510.29
100000	1689.49	1687.40	1683.16	1682.23	1679.57	1678.59	1678.23	1678.09
110000	1858.44	1856.14	1851.47	1850.45	1847.52	1846.45	1846.05	1845.90
120000	2027.39	2024.88	2019.79	2018.67	2015.48	2014.30	2013.87	2013.71
130000	2196.33	2193.62	2188.10	2186.89	2183.43	2182.16	2181.69	2181.52
140000	2365.28	2362.36	2356.42	2355.11	2351.39	2350.02	2349.52	2349.33
150000	2534.23	2531.10	2524.74	2523.34	2519.35	2517.88	2517.34	2517.14
160000	2703.18	2699.84	2693.05	2691.56	2687.30	2685.74	2685.16	2684.95
170000	2872.13	2868.58	2861.37	2859.78	2855.26	2853.59	2852.98	2852.76
180000	3041.08	3037.32	3029.68	3028.00	3023.21	3021.45	3020.80	3020.57
190000	3210.02	3206.06	3198.00	3196.22	3191.17	3189.31	3188.63	3188.37
200000	3378.97	3374.80	3366.31	3364.45	3359.13	3357.17	3356.45	3356.18
210000	3547.92	3543.54	3534.63	3532.67	3527.08	3525.03	3524.27	3523.99
220000	3716.87	3712.28	3702.94	3700.89	3695.04	3692.89	3692.09	3691.80
230000	3885.82	3881.02	3871.26	3869.11	3862.99	3860.74	3859.92	3859.61
240000	4054.77	4049.75	4039.57	4037.33	4030.95	4028.60	4027.74	4027.42
250000	4223.72	4218.49	4207.89	4205.56	4198.91	4196.46	4195.56	4195.23
260000	4392.66	4387.23	4376.20	4373.78	4366.86	4364.32	4363.38	4363.04
270000	4561.61	4555.97	4544.52	4542.00	4534.82	4532.18	4531.20	4530.85
280000	4730.56	4724.71	4712.84	4710.22	4702.77	4700.03	4699.03	4698.66
290000	4899.51	4893.45	4881.15	4878.44	4870.73	4867.89	4866.85	4866.46
300000	5068.46	5062.19	5049.47	5046.67	5038.69	5035.75	5034.67	5034.27
310000	5237.41	5230.93	5217.78	5214.89	5206.64	5203.61	5202.49	5202.08
320000	5406.35	5399.67	5386.10	5383.11	5374.60	5371.47	5370.32	5369.89
330000	5575.30	5568.41	5554.41	5551.33	5542.55	5539.33	5538.14	5537.70
340000	5744.25	5737.15	5722.73	5719.56	5710.51	5707.18	5705.96	5705.51
350000	5913.20	5905.89	5891.04	5887.78	5878.47	5875.04	5873.78	5873.32
360000	6082.15	6074.63	6059.36	6056.00	6046.42	6042.90	6041.60	6041.13
370000	6251.10	6243.37	6227.67	6224.22	6214.38	6210.76	6209.43	6208.94
380000	6420.04	6412.11	6395.99	6392.44	6382.33	6378.62	6377.25	6376.74
390000	6588.99	6580.85	6564.30	6560.67	6550.29	6546.48	6545.07	6544.55
400000	6757.94	6749.59	6732.62	6728.89	6718.25	6714.33	6712.89	6712.36